CONTRIBUTIONS
TO THE ETHNOLOGY OF THE KWAKIUTL

COLUMBIA UNIVERSITY CONTRIBUTIONS TO
ANTHROPOLOGY

Edited by FRANZ BOAS

VOLUME III

CONTRIBUTIONS TO THE ETHNOLOGY OF THE KWAKIUTL

BY

FRANZ BOAS

AMS PRESS
NEW YORK

Reprinted with the permission of
Columbia University Press
From the edition of 1925, New York
First AMS EDITION published 1969
Manufactured in the United States of America

Library of Congress Catalogue Card Number: 77-82353

AMS PRESS, INC.
New York, N. Y.   10003

CONTENTS.

—◦—◇—◦—

INTRODUCTION.

The following Kwakiutl texts deal with dreams and with information relating to the social organization of the tribe. Since the expense of composition has risen enormously during the last few years, the publication of this material has been possible only by the employment of a photostatic process.

The material was obtained from Mr. George Hunt of Fort Rupert, British Columbia, a half-blood Indian who speaks Kwakiutl as his native language, and whom I have trained in phonetic writing. The material, therefore, continues the series of texts in the publication "Kwakiutl Ethnology" (Thirty-Fifth Annual Report of the Bureau of American Ethnology) which was collected in the same manner.

As stated in the report referred to the phonetic rendering of Kwakiutl by Mr. Hunt is not absolutely reliable. He is particularly uncertain in regard to the character of vowels, and when words are unknown to me I cannot decide whether u or wa, E or a are meant. On the whole, howewer, I believe the number of words of this kind is not very great.

I do not give a vocabulary accompanying the present texts because a fairly full vocabulary has been published in the Thirty-fifth Annual Report of the Bureau of American Ethnology, and the additions to the vocabulary are not very numerous.

The following list contains previous publications on Kwakiutl ethnology in text:

1. The Social Organization and the Secret Societies of the Kwakiutl Indians. Report of the U. S. National Museum for 1895, pp. 311-738. Washington, Government Printing Press, 1897. (The songs contained in this publication were reprinted in revised form in No. 2 in this list.)
2. Kwakiutl Texts. Publications of the Jesup North Pacific Expedition, Vol. III, pp. 1-532. Leiden, E. J. Brill, 1902-1905.
3. Kwakiutl Texts - Second Series. Publications of the Jesup North Pacific Expedition, Vol. X, pp. 1-269. Leiden, E. J. Brill, 1906.
4. Ethnology of the Kwakiutl. 35 th Annual Report of the Bureau of American Ethnology. Parts I and II, pp. 41-1437, Washington, Government Printing Office. 1921.
5. The Rival Chiefs, a Kwakiutl Story, by George Hunt. Boas Anniversary Volume, pp. 108-136. New-York, G. E. Stechert and Co., 1906.

6. Kwakiutl Tales. Columbia University Contributions to Anthropology, Vol. II, pp. 1-495. New-York, Columbia University Press. 1910.
7. Kwakiutl, An Illustrative Sketch in the Handbook of American Languages, Part 1. pp. 423-557. Bulletin 40 of the Bureau of American Ethnology. Washington, Government Printing Office, 1911.
8. A Revised List of Kwakiutl Suffixes. International Journal of American Linguistics, Vol. III, pp. 117-131. New-York, Columbia University, 1924.

The following alphabet has been used:

E

i e, î, ê, a, ô, o u

ī ē, ë, ä, ā, â, ō ū
u

E	obscure e, as in flower.
i e	are probably the same sound, intermediate between the continental values of i and e.
î	i in hill.
ê	e in fell.
a	has its continental value.
ô	German o in voll.
o u	are probably the same sound, intermediate between the continental values of o and u.
ë	a somewhat doubtful sound, varying greatly in its pronunciation among different individuals between ē and êī.
ä	German ä in Bär.
â	aw in law.
u	indicates that the preceding consonant is pronounced with u position of the mouth.

	Sonans.	Surd.	Fortis.	Spirans.	Nasal.
Velar	g̣	q	q!	x	
Palatal	g(w)	k(w)	k!(w)	x̣(w)	
Anterior palatal	g·	k·	k·!	x·	
Alveolar	d (dz)	t (ts)	t! (ts!)	s	n
Labial	b	p	p!		m
Lateral	Ḷ	L	L!	ʟ̷	l
Glottal Stop	ε				
	h, y, w				

D R E A M S

1. Mēxēs Wēgwaᵋnākŭla.

Laɛng·ēk· dōqwaxɛn k!wǟʟᴀᵋyâxa mɛtsa ʟ̣ōᵋɛng·ēda xumdē.
Wǟ, lǟɛng·ɛn hē g·îl dōqwasɛᵋwŭn xwǟxumt!ayo. Wǟ, laɛng·ɛn dō-
xᵋwaʟɛlaqēxs qɛk!ŭsaē. Wǟ, laɛng·ɛn dōxᵋwaʟɛlaxa dzaᵋwŭn ǟxts!-
5 âq. Wǟ, laᵋmɛn ts!ɛx·ᵋĪda.

2. Mēxēs TsɛxᵋwĪdē.

Mēxɛlēk· g·ǟxᵋɛng·ɛ ʟēᵋlǟlasōᵋsa ᵋxᵋɛng·ä bɛgwǟnɛma qaɛ-
ng·ɛnuᵋx̣ᵘ lä hanǟʟ!aɛng·ɛ ʟɛᵋwē laɛng·ɛxwa ǟʟ!ēx. Wǟ, laɛng·a-
ᵋmēsɛn läg·ēq. Wǟ, k·!ēsᵋɛng·aᵋmēsɛnuᵋx̣ᵘ ǟʟ̣ɛgîlaxs laɛng·aē
10 dōxᵋwaʟɛlaxa gēwas. Laɛng·ē wǟx· hänɫᵋĪdɛq. Wǟ, laɛng·ē yîm-
ɫᵋĪdē hänʟɛmx·dä. Wǟ, laᵋmɛn ts!ɛx·ᵋĪda laxēq.

3. Mēxēs K!wǟk!wabǟlasɛmē.

Laɛng·ēk· tewĪx·axa ᵋmɛlxʟō laɛng·ɛx Dzǟwadē. Wǟ, laɛng·-
ɛn dōxᵋwaʟɛlaxa maᵋɫē ᵋmɛlxʟō. Wǟ, laɛng·ɛn hänɫᵋĪdɛq. Wǟ,
laɛng·ɛn ᵋwīla q!âpaq. Wǟ, laɛng·ɛn yîmɫᵋĪdɛq qɛn ǟxâlēx yî-
15 x̣ᵘsɛmaᵋyas qɛn g·îg·aalēdalēxa yîx̣ᵘsɛmaᵋyē. Wǟ, laɛng·ɛn wŭʟɛ-
laxa qaᵋyǟlä laɛng·ɛxɛn ᵋnǟlaᵋyē. Wǟ, laɛng·ɛn dōxᵋwĪdɛq.
Laɛng·ɛn dōxᵋwaʟɛlaɛng·ɛxa maᵋɫē g·îᵋla ʟōma nɛx̱wǟɫa g·ǟxᵋɛng·-
ɛn. Wǟ, laɛng·ɛn hēɫomǟla dǟx·ᵋĪdxɛn dɛnwēsɛlaɛng·ä qɛn hēɫᵋĪ-
dēxa ᵋnɛmē. Wǟ, laɛng·aᵋmē ɫɛᵋla. Wǟ, laɛng·ɛn hänɫᵋĪdxa ᵋnɛ-
20 mēx·däs. Wǟ, lǟxʟ̣ēᵋmē ōdzɛg·aaʟɛlē hänʟaᵋyas. Wǟ, g·ǟxᵋɛng·aᵋ-
mē dǟx·ᵋĪd g·ǟxᵋɛng·ɛn. Wǟ, laᵋmɛn ts!ɛx·ᵋĪd lǟxēq.

D R E A M S

1. Dream of Wēgwaᶜnākŭla.

I went to look after my mink and otter traps. Then the otter trap was looked after by me first. Then I saw that it had fallen. Then I saw that a silver salmon was in it. Then I awoke.

2. Dream of Tsɛxᶜwĭd.

I dreamed that I was asked by a handsome man to go hunting with him in the woods. I followed him and we had not gone far into the woods when I saw a deer. I was about to shoot it when my gun burst. Then I awoke.

3. Dream of K!wāk!wabālasɛmē.

I dreamed I was going mountain goat hunting in Knight Inlet. Then I saw two mountain goats. Then I shot them. I hit both and I butchered them. I took out the kidney fat and put the kidney fat down on the rock. Then I heard the noise of walking up the river from me. Then I looked there and then I saw two grizzlybears quite near to me. Then I just had time to take up my gun and I hit the one. Then it was dead. Then I shot the other one. Unfortunately my shot missed it. Then it took hold of me. After that I awoke.

4. Mēxēs Ōmx·ídē.

Laɛng·ēg·a lāxaxa x·Iqayalaɛng·ä lālaaɛng·ɛ lāxa Awīk·!ē-
noxᵘ. Wä, laɛng·ɛn lāg·aa lāx G·íp!a. Wä, laɛng·ɛn ts!âsōᵉsa
k·āk·agɛdzɛwayo. Wä, hēx·ᵉídaɛng·aᵉmēsɛn laɛng·ɛ k·ēʟa. Wä,
5 laɛng·ē q!ēdzâlaɛng·ɛn k·ēʟɛmaxa mɛ̀ɛk·ē. Wä, laɛng·aᵉmē ēk·ɛn
nâqaᵉyasɛn laɛng·aēnaᵉyē hēx·ᵉídaɛm q!ɛyōʟaxa mɛ̀ɛk·ᵉɛng·ä. Wä,
laɛng·ɛn ēt!ēd ts!ɛxᵉstɛndaɛng·ɛxɛn k·ēʟɛmē. Wä, g·ílᵉɛng·aᵉ-
mēsē ᵉwīᵉlaᵉstaɛng·a laɛng·a äxaasē ɓɛm kŭsx·ālaɛng·ēda mɛ̀ɛk·ē
laɛng·ɛ ladzōdxɛn k·ēʟɛmē. Wä, laɛng·ɛn k!ŭlsᵉīdxa mɛ̀ɛk·ē la-
10 ɛng·ɛxɛn k·ēʟɛmē. Wä, k·!ēsᵉɛng·aᵉmēsɛn nɛgōyodɛx ᵉwāsgɛmasᵉɛn-
g·asɛn k·ēʟɛmaxs laɛng·aasa gwɛᵉyīm lādzɛdɛq. Wä, laɛng·ē ma-
x·ᵉídēda gwɛᵉyīmᵉɛng·ä. Wä, laɛng·ɛn k·!ēs hēɛōmalaɛng·ɛ ts!ɛ-
xᵉstɛndxa äpsɛx·sᵉäsa k·ēʟɛm g·āxᵉɛng·ɛ g·ēxsāla laɛng·ɛxɛn k·ē-
ʟats!ē bâta. Wä, laɛng·aᵉmē qɛp!aʟaᵉya bâtē. Wä, laɛng·aᵉma
15 gwɛᵉyīm ᵉwīᵉlaɛng·ɛ nēxᵉwŭɛtōdxa k·ēʟɛmē. Wä, laᵉmɛn ts!ɛx·ᵉīd
lāxēq.

5. Mēxēs ʟ!âʟ!ɛɛɛwēdzɛmga.

Mēxɛlēg·asa q!ēnɛmᵉɛng·ä dzāxŭn laɛng·ɛx Dzāwadē. Wä, la-
ɛng·anuᵉxᵘ xōtasa xōdayoɛng·ä lāq wīᵉlaqɛng·adzânuᵉxᵘ gēg·íɛtsI-
20 la xōtaxs laɛng·aē qōt!anuᵉxᵘ xōdats!ä xwāk!ŭnäxa dzāxŭn. Laɛn-
g·ɛnuᵉxᵘ nāᵉnakwa. Wä, g·ílᵉɛng·aᵉmēsɛnuᵉxᵘ lāg·aa laɛng·ɛxɛnu-
ᵉxᵘ k·!āx·ᵉīdxa dzāxŭn qaɛng·ɛnuᵉxᵘ k·!āg·aɛlsɛlaq. Wä, laɛng·-
aᵉmē qōt!ēda ᵉnɛmsgɛmē ᵉlāp!ɛs. Wä, laɛng·ɛᵉmē x·ísᵉɛlsa dzāxŭn
lāxēqxa äxts!ɓɛng·ē lāxa ᵉlāp!ɛsᵉɛng·ä. Wä, laᵉmɛn ts!ɛx·ᵉīda.

25 #### 6. Mēxēs Gwāgwadaxɛla.

Wa, laɛng·ɛn hâmsaxa q!ēnɛma q!ɛndzɛkᵘ laɛng·ɛxwa āʟ!ōx ʟɛᵉwa q!ēnɛmᵉɛng·ä gwādɛma. Wä, laɛng·ɛn q!ɛyōʟa. Wä, g·āxᵉɛng·ɛn
hēᵉlaxa mōkwa bēbɛgwānɛm qa g·āxᵉɛng·ē ōxʟōɛt!âlaq. Wä, laɛng·a-
ᵉmɛn k!wēlats laɛng·ɛxwa mōsgɛmakwē Kwāg·uɛa. Wä, laɛng·ɛn ēt!ē-
30 da hâmsaxa q!ɛmdzɛkᵘ. Wä, laɛng·ɛn yílkwa. Wä, laᵉmɛn ts!ɛx·ᵉīd
lāxēq.

4. Dream of Omx·îd.

I dreamed that I went aboard a steamer and I went to Rivers
Inlet. Then I arrived at G·îp!a. Then I was given a drift net.
Immediately I went fishing. Oh, there were many sockeye salmon
in my net. Then my heart was glad because I had at once caught
many sockeye salmon. Then I threw my net back into the water.
Then as soon as it was in the water I dreamed that the sockeye
salmon were splashing and they went into my net. Then I took the
salmon out of my net. I had not reached the middle of the extent
of my net when a whale went into it. Then the whale swam away.
I had no time to throw into the water the other half of the net
which was in my boat that contained the net. Then the boat capsized and the whale pulled out the whole net. I awoke after this.

5.   Dream of ʟ!āʟ!ɛx̣ewēdzɛmga.

I dreamed that there were many olachen in Knight Inlet. We
caught them in bag nets. We had not been fishing with bag nets
for a long time before the canoe containing the bag net was full
of olachen. Then we went home. As soon as we arrived we carried
up the olachen and put them on the ground. Then the hole in the
ground was full. Then the olachen which had been in the hole disappeared. Then I awoke.[1]

6. Dream of Gwāgwadaxɛla.

I dreamed I went to pick many salmon berries in the woods
and also many blueberries. I obtained many. Then I asked four
men to help me carrying them out of the woods. That was the time
when I gave a feast to the four Kwag·uʟ tribes. Then I went a-
gain to pick salmon berries and I hurt myself. After that I awoke.

---

[1]This dream signifies that there were many olachen in the
river but that the water was so high that the fisherman could not
use their bag nets.

7. Aᴇ̆k·aɛng·ɛ mē̆xē̆s Haē̆ᴌaᵋlas.

Mē̆xᴇlē̆ g·āx ganö̆ᴌasa ĕx·sokwa ts!ᴇdāqᵋᴇng·ɛ g·āx ᴌē̆ᵋlālaɛng·ɛ
g·āxᴇn qaɛng·aɛnuᵋx̣ᵘ lē̆ hămsaxa gwādᴇmᴇng·ä. Wä, laɛng·aᵋmē̆sᴇnuᵋx̣ᵘ
laɛng·ᴇxox āᴌ!äxs Tsāxis. Ā laɛng·ᴇg·anuᵋx̣ᵘ dōxᵋwaᴌᴇlaɛng·ᴇxa q!ē̆-
5°   nᴇmᵋᴇng·ä gwādᴇm ᴌoᵋᴇng·ē̆da âᵋᴇng·aᵋma la gᴇtgᴇt!ᴇsa ᵋnōx̣ᵘmᴇsasē̆s
äwâxaxᴌâlasᵋᴇng·äxa ᵋnō̆xwa. Wä, laɛng·aᵋmē̆sᴇnuᵋx̣ᵘ k·!ı̂ᴌts!ōts la-
ɛng·ᴇxᴇnuᵋx̣ᵘ hămᵋyats!ē̆ laɛlxäᴇng·a. Wä āᴌᵋᴇng·aᵋwisē̆ qōqü̆t!aᴇn-
g·anuᵋx̣ᵘ hămᵋyats!ē̆ laɛlxäᴇng·a. Wä, laᵋmᴇn ts!ᴇx·ᵋı̂d lāxē̆q.

Wä, laᴇm q!ālē̆ Haē̆ᴌaᵋlasaxs lag·aē̆ᴌē̆ q!uᵋlāᴌ lāxa gwât!ᴇnxē̆
10   lāxē̆q.

8. Mē̆xē̆s Wäʟ̣idē̆.

Mē̆xᴇlē̆k· la hămsaxa qᴇk·!aālē̆ᴇng·ä lāxwa āᴌ!ē̆x ᴌo̥ᵋᴇng·ōx Mā-
witsax. Wä, laɛng·aᵋmē̆sᴇnuᵋx̣ᵘ āᴌōlsᴇlaᴇng·a läg·a dōxᵋwaᴌᴇlaᴇn-
g·ᴇxa sē̆ᴌᴇm. Wä, laɛng·anuᵋx̣ᵘ k·ı̂ᴌᵋı̂ts. Wä, laᵋmᴇn ts!ᴇx·ᵋı̂da.
15   9. Mē̆xē̆s ᴌ!āᴌᴇmē̆g·iᵋlakᵘ.

Mē̆xᴇlᴇg·aᴇng·ɛ hămsaxa q!ē̆nᴇmᵋᴇng·ä nᴇk!ü̆ᴌa laɛng·ᴇx G·iō̆x.
Wä, laɛng·ᴇn dōqü̆laxa q!ē̆nᴇmᵋᴇng·ä hăᵋnon xwē̆lawa laɛng·ᴇx wäs
G·iō̆x. Wä, laɛng·ᴇn kwē̆xasᴇn sᴇk·!aganoᴇng·ä lāxa hăᵋnonē̆. Wä,
laɛng·ᴇnq!eyō̆ᴌxa nᴇk!ü̆ᴌē̆. Wä, g·āxᵋᴇng·aᵋmᴇn näᵋnakwa. Wä, lᴇn
20   wē̆g·aa lāxᴇn g·ōkwaxg·ı̂n läk· ts!ᴇx·ᵋı̂da.

10. Mē̆xē̆s ᴌ!āʟ!aᴌawı̆dzᴇmga.

Mē̆xᴇlē̆k· laɛng·ɛ dzē̆k·axa g·āwē̆q!ānᴇmᵋᴇng·ä laɛng·ᴇxwa ᴌ!ᴇmā-
isᵋᴇng·ᴇx. Wä, laɛng·ᴇn dzē̆k·a. Wä, k·!ē̆sᵋᴇng·aᵋmē̆sᴇn gē̆g·ı̂lē̆s
dzē̆k·aᵋᴇng·a laasᴇn k·!ı̂lakwē̆ äxᵋaᴌᴇlaᴇng·ɛ lāxa tᴇlqwa. Wä, g·ā-
25   xᵋᴇng·ē̆ nē̆ᴌᵋı̂dē̆da ᵋwālasᵋᴇng·ä tᴇq!waxa dzᴇmsgᴇmlisē̆. Wä, laᵋmᴇn
ts!ᴇx·ᵋı̂da qaxg·ı̂n âlē̆k· k·ı̂ᴌᵋı̂dē̆s.

11. Mē̆xē̆s Qāsᴇlas

Mē̆xᴇlē̆k· laɛng·a ʟ̣āx̣ᵋwüt!alaᴇng·ᴇx Q!ᴇmsᴇxᴌä̆. Wä, laɛng·ᴇn
dzē̆x·ᵋı̂da. Wä laɛng·ē̆ q!ē̆nᴇma g·āwē̆q!ānᴇmᵋᴇng·äᴇn dzē̆g·anᴇmᴇng·a.
Wä, laɛng·aᵋmē̆sᴇn gwāᴌ dzē̆k·a. Laᴇng·ᴇn wāx· lāxsd äxᵋē̆dxᴇn dzē̆-
g·ats!ē̆ lᴇxaᵋya hănxsᵋᴇng·ɛ lāxa ʟ̣āwats!ē̆ xwāxwagü̆m. Wä, laɛng·a-

7. Good dream of HaêLaᵋlas.

I dreamed last night of a pretty woman who came to call me to
pick cranberries. We went inland. Then we saw many cranberries
and blueberry bushes which were hanging down with many blueberries
hanging from the points (of the branches) and so we shook them into our berry picking baskets. Then our berry picking baskets were
full. I awoke after that.

Then Ha̧êLaᵋlas knew that she was going to keep alive until
the season of cranberry picking.

8. Dream of Wäʟid.

I dreamed I was going to pick dogwood berries inland, together
with Māwitsa. Then we went inland and I saw a snake. Then we were
afraid of it and I awoke.

9. Dream of ʟ!āɫɛmēg·iᵋlakᵘ.

I dreamed that I went to pick many salal berries at G·iōx.
Then I saw many hump-backed salmon spawning in the river of G·iōx.
Then I struck the salmon with my cane. Then I got many salal ber-
ries. Then I went home. Before I arrived at home I woke up.[1]

10. Dream of ʟ!āʟ!aɫawïdzɛmga.

I dreamed that I was going to dig clams on the beach here.
Then I was digging. I had not been digging long before my digging
stick struck something soft. Then there came out and showed itself
a large squid which had buried itself on the beach. Then I awoke because I was very much afraid of it.

11. Dream of Qāsɛlas.

I dreamed I was going seawards to Shell Island. Then I was
digging. I had obtained many clams by digging. Then I stopped digging. Then I intended to go to my canoe to get the clam basket

---

[1] This dream signifies that the woman who dreams will live until
the salal berries are ripe but that she will be sick before that time.

ᵉmɛn dōxᶜwaʟɛlaɛng·ɛxɛn ʟ̣āwats!ē xwāx̣wagŭmxs laē ts!aqâla lax gwa-
ᶜn̑̆ᶜyas Q!ɛmsɛxʟ̣ä. Wä, laɛng·aᶜmē g·îx̂ . Wä, hᵉᶜmēsɛn wŭl̇ᶜɛm
lɛlāxsɛᶜyasᶜɛng·ē. Wä, hᵉᶜmas lāg·il̇asɛn l̇āᶜwŭnɛmēx gwēx·ᶜîd g·ā-
xɛn. Wä, laᶜmɛn ts!ɛx·ᶜîda. Âla hāsɛla tɛkŭlaxɛn mɛk!ŭbâᶜyaqɛn.

5   12. ᶜyäk·aɛng·ɛ mēxēs Lɛgŭᶜlas.

Q!ēnɛmᶜɛng·aēda wasîläxa aɛntē wānaᶜyaɛng·a mēxēx lax·däs
ɛlāq ᶜnāx⸱ᶜîdɛx gaālax·dē. Wä, laɛng·ē q!ēnɛma aɛntᶜɛng·äsɛms
g·ōkulōta Kwāg·ul̇ē ᶜnēk·ē Lɛgŭᶜlasaxs laē māl̇mēxts!a qaɛn.

Wä, hᵉᶜɛm gwɛᶜyōsa g·ālē bāk!um g·āx ts!ɛk·!āl̇ɛlēda hayal̇îᶜ-
10 lagasaxs ᶜyāx·sɛᶜmaēda ts!ɛx·q!ōlɛmʟa g·āxʟ qaēda aɛntaxs hᵉᶜmaē
ts!ɛx·q!ōlɛmē yîxs mēxayaē lāg·il̇as k·!ēts!ēnoxᵘ ɛnt!ata ts!ɛx·-
q!äxa aɛntē qaxs aɛmsaē lāx ɛnt!atsɛᶜwa aɛntē qaxs g·îlᶜmaē ɛnt!-
ata ts!ɛx·q!äxa aɛntē laē hᵉx·ᶜîdaɛm xɛnl̇ᶜîdēda ts!ɛx·q!ā. Wä,
hᵉᶜmis lāg·il̇as k·îlɛm haᶜmāᶜya aɛntasa ts!ɛx·q!äsa bāk!umē.

15

13. Mēxēs Wāl̇ɛwîdē.

Mēxɛlēk· tēxᶜstaɛng·ɛxg·anuᶜx̣ᵘ sɛᶜyoᶜnākŭlaɛng·ēk· lāxa ōx̣ᵘ-
sidzaᶜyasa hāᶜyîmᶜstaɛng·ä. Wä, laɛng·ɛn âla k·îl̇ᶜîda hᵉᶜmēsɛn
la ts!ɛx·ᶜîdaasē.

14. Mēxēs Mɛlēdē.

20   Mēxɛlēk· t!āt!alax·daᶜnɛmsa ʟ̣âsᶜɛng·ä laɛng·ɛxwa āʟ!ēx. Wä,
laɛng·ɛn q!āʟɛlaɛmxg·axs ᶜnāx̣waɛng·aᶜmaēx q!wēl̇ᶜîdaɛng·ɛn xāqēx.
Wä, laɛng·ɛn ᶜlāp!qēqoyosɛn g·ōkŭlōta Kwāg·ul̇. Wä, wēg·aalē la-
ɛng·ɛxɛn gōkwaxg·în läk· ts!ɛx·ᶜîda.

15. Mēxēs Gwāgwạdāxɛla.

25   Mēxɛlēg·aɛng·ɛ sēx̣ᶜwîd ʟ̣ɛᶜwŭn mōkwēx sāsɛm. Wä, laɛng·ēl̇g·a-
nuᶜx̣ᵘ laɛng·ɛx Xumdasbē. Wä, laɛng·ɛnuᶜx̣ᵘ lāg·aaɛng·ɛ lāx nɛgɛ-
t!äs P!ɛlɛms laɛng·aasē p!ɛlxɛlax·ᶜîdaxa âlaɛng·ä gɛnk·a. Wä, la-

which was in the little clam digging canoe. Then I saw that my
clam digging canoe was drifting about north of Shell Island. It
was drifting away. Then I shouted in vain. That was the reason
why my husband called ma and I awoke. My heart was beating vio-
lently.

12. Dream of Lɛgŭ^ɛlas.

Much herring-spawn spawned the herrings. This was my dream
in the morning when day was almost breaking. There was much herring-spawn for our tribe, the Kwāg·uɬ, said Lɛgŭ^ɛlas when he told
me his dream.

This was explained by the ancient Indians as meaning that the
spirits would come and that a bad epidemic would break out at the
herring spawning, for the spawn is an epidemic when one dreams of
it. Therefore no sick person is allowed to eat herring-spawn, for
it has an evil effect when herring-spawn is eaten, for when a sick
person eats herring spawn his sickness will increase. Therefore
is the eating of herring-spawn a cause of fear for the sick ones
among the Indians.

13. Dream of Wāɬɛwid.

I dreamed I fell into the water while we were paddling at the
foot of the mountain in deep water. I was frightened very much,
and that was the moment when I awoke.

14. Dream of Mɛɬēd.

I dreamed I fell from a tree here (behind the houses) inland.
Then I knew that I had broken all my bones. Then I was dug up by
my tribe, the Kwāg·uɬ. Then had not yet reached my house when I
awoke.

15. Dream of Gwāgwadāxɛla.

I dreamed I was out paddling with my four children. Then we
were going to Xumdasbē. When we were opposite P!ɛlɛms it became
very thick and foggy. Then we were lost in the fog. I was just

ɛng·aᵋmɛnuᵋx̣ᵘ p!ɛlxp!ɛlxɛʟāyanɛma. Wä, âɛng·aᵋmēsɛn k!wāg·aaɫɛxs
laɛng·ɛnuᵋx̣ᵘ yāyats!ä xwāk!ūna. Wä, laɛng·aᵋmɛn gwāɫ sēxwa. Wä,
âɛng·aᵋmēsɛnuᵋx̣ᵘ la ts!ɛts!āxsäɛng·a. Wä, laɛng·ē gānoɫᵋɪda. Wä,
laɛng·ɛn mēxᵋɪda. Wä, laɛng·ɛn ts!ɛk·!ɛxsdɛndxɛnuᵋx̣ᵘ yāyats!ē
5 xwāk!ūnäxs laē qwaɫᵋɛlyo laɛng·ɛxa ăᵋwĪnak!wa. Wä, la p!ɛlxɛla-
x·säma. Wä, laɛng·ɛn k·!ēs maɫt!älaxa ăᵋwĪnak!wa. Wä, laɛng·ē
lōsᵋɪda. Wä, laɛng·ɛn maɫt!ēg·aaʟɛlaɛng·ɛqēxs häē Yūʟ!ē. Wä, laᵋmɛn ts!ɛx·ᵋɪ̇û lāxēq.

16. Mēxēs ʟ!āqwadzē.

10 Mēxɛlēg·asa ɫāk·aɛng·ä x·Īqaᵋyala laɛng·ɛxōx ʟɛᵋladēx. La-
ɛng·ē q!ēx·sēda bēbɛgwānɛm ʟɛᵋwa ts!ēdāxᵋɛng·ä ɫēɫɛᵋlaxɛn laɛng·ä
q!āsōxs pɛx̆ūmēᵋstalaē. Wä, laɛng·ɛn hēɫaqasōᵋsa māmaɫa qaɛng·ēda
ᵋnāɫᵋnɛmōkwē bɛgwānɛmɛn q!āsɛᵋwasa nɛqāsgɛmē dāla. Wä, laɛng·a-
xaa q!ēnɛma gwĪɫgwälaɛng·äɛn q!āsɛᵋwa. Wä, laɛng·ē ʟōma ŏk·ɛn
15 nâqaᵋyasɛn q!ɛyōʟ!ēnaᵋyē lāq. Wä, laᵋmɛn ts!ɛx·ᵋɪd lāxēq.

17. Mēxēs G·Īʟa.

Mēxɛlēk· laɛng·ɛ sēxwa ʟ̣ōᵋɛng·ɛn gɛnɛmē lālaaɛng·ɛ lāxa AwĪ-
k·!ēnoxᵘ k·āk·ēḷēsa. Wä, laɛng·anuᵋx̣ᵘ lāg·aa laɛng·ɛx Ōgwiwa
laɛng·aasē mɛʟɛg·Īlisa. Wä, laɛng·ɛn wĪsogūʟɛmēɛng·ɛt!ɛn lats!â
20 laɛng·ɛx Gwāɫgwaʟ!alālis. Wä, laɛng·ɛn wāx· laloʟ!a qɛn laɛng·ē
lāx Gɛyaxstaᵋyē. Lādzēk·asᵋɛng·aᵋmē äbēqwa mɛɫasa. Wä, laɛng·-
aᵋmɛn gɛnɛmē wāx· tsāɫa. Wä, laɛng·aᵋmē wĪts!ēg·ēxa dɛmsx·äxs
qŭɫᵋaɫɛxɛlayâᵋē laɛng·ɛxɛn sāk·Īlisē. Wä, laɛng·aᵋmɛnuᵋx̣ᵘ q!wā-
q!wasâla ʟ̣ōᵋɛng·ɛn gɛnɛmē. Wä, laᵋmɛn ts!ɛx·ᵋɪd laxēq.

25 ## 18. Mēxēs Ēwanux̣ᵘdzē.

Mēxɛlēg·as ʟɛᵋlɛndzɛwēk·a laxsᵋɛng·ɛxēs ōmpē X·āx·ɛlq!ayo-
gwiᵋlakwaxs yāyasɛlaaxēs g·asɛlinē bâta. Wä, laɛng·ɛn yāyasɛ-
laxɛn xwāxwagūmᵋɛng·ä. Wä, laɛng·ē k·atālēda g·Īlt!aɛng·ä q!ē-
xāɫa. Wä, hēɛng·aᵋmēsɛn la hānbɛndaɛng·ē. Wä, laɛng·ē X·āx·ɛl-
30 q!ayogwiᵋlakwē hänx·ᵋɪd lāx äpsbēɛng·äsa q!ēxaɫē. Wä, laɛng·ē
ʟɛᵋlɛndzɛwēk·ē lāk·!ɛndxa ōbaᵋyasa q!ēxaɫē qaᵋs g·āxᵋɛng·ē qādzɛ-

sitting still in our travelling canoe. Then I stopped paddling.
In my dream we were drifting about on the water. Then it became
night and I went to sleep. When I awoke our travelling canoe was
being rolled against the rocks. It was still foggy. I did not
know the rocks. Then it cleared up and I knew that this was Yūʟ!ē.
Then I awoke.

16. Dream of ʟ!āqwadzē.

I dreamed that a steamer had been wrecked here at ʟɛᶜlad,
and that many men and women had perished and that they were found
drifting about. Then I was paid by the whites ten dollars for
every man found by me. Many pieces of clothing were found by me.
Then I was very glad on account of the large amount that I received. Then I woke up.

17. Dream of G·îʟa.

I dreamed that I was paddling with my wife to Rivers Inlet
to go fishing. When we reached Cape Caution a southeasterly gale
began to blow, but we were unable to enter Gwā̆ɫḡwaʟ!alālis. Then
I tried to reach Gɛyaxstaᶜyē. Then the sea was boiling on account
of the southeasterly gale. My wife tried to bail out the canoe
but she could not cope with the sea.water which was thrown into
my boat. Then we cried, I and my wife. Then I awoke.

18. Dream of Ēwanuxᵘdzē.

I dreamed of ʟɛᶜlɛndzōᶜ, that she was going in the boat of
her father X·ā̱x·ɛlq!ayogwiᶜlakᵘ, and that she was travelling in
his gasoline launch. Then I went out in my little canoe. A long
log was drifting on the water and so I was on one end of the
drifting log in my canoe, and X·ā̱x·ɛlq!ayogwiᶜlakᵘ was in his
launch on the other end. Then ʟɛᶜlɛndzō̆ᶜ stepped on the end of

Ȼɛnēq g·āg·axaɛng·ɛ g·āxᶜɛng·ɛ. Wa̓, wēg·aaɛng·ɛt!ēxs laɛng·aē tē-
xsta. Wä, laɛng·ɛ häyînsɛla. Wä, laɛng·ɛn dɛxᵘsta qɛn dāsᶜida-
ɛng·ē wüȻɛm āläqē laɛng·ɛxa baᶜnē. Wä, laɛng·ɛn k·!ēs q!āq. Wä,
g·āxᶜɛng·ɛn q!āxᶜwida, laɛng·ɛn dōxᶜwaʟɛlax G̱ûyōsdēdzasaxs laɛng·-
5 aē q!ɛȻwɛsdēsɛlaɛng·ɛx Ƚɛᶜlɛndzewēk·axs laɛng·aē Ȼɛᶜla. Wä, laᶜmɛn ts!ɛx·ᶜîd lāxēq.

19. Mēxēs ᶜyäk·âyugwa.

Mēxɛlēg·aqē x̱ûmtanuᶜx̱ᵘ g·ōx̱ᵘᶜɛng·ä laɛng·ɛx G·iōx. Wä, la-
ɛng·aᶜmē ᶜnāx̱wa q!ûlx·ᶜîdaɛng·ɛnuᶜx̱ᵘ dēdamalax·dä. Wä, laɛng·aᶜ-
10 mɛnuᶜx̱ᵘ âlak·!āla wîwasilag·a. Wä, laᶜmɛn ts!ɛx·ᶜîd lāxēq.

20. Mēxēs Q!wālax·flayugwa.

G·āxᶜɛng·aēda ᶜnāx̱wa lēlqwalaʟaᶜya p!ēkᵘ laɛng·ɛx Awaxɛlag·-
flis. Wä, laɛng·ē ʟālîᶜlalē Awaxɛlag·flisaq qa laɛng·ēs ʟ!ɛx̱wa
laɛng·ɛx g·ōkwas. Wä, laɛng·ē qātap!ɛx·ᶜîdē ʟābidē ʟōᶜ Nɛg·äxa
15 g·îgɛmaᶜyasa Mamalēleqala. Wä, laɛng·aᶜmē k!ûnxstowē ʟābidē. Wä,
laɛng·ē Nɛg·ä q!ɛlt!ōdxa ʟ!āqwa gaᶜs yäxᶜwîdēsa q!ɛldɛkwē ʟ!āqwa
laɛng·ɛx ʟābidē. Wä, laɛng·ē ʟābidē ōgwaqa q!ɛlt!ōdxa ʟ!āqwa
qaᶜs yäxᶜwidaɛng·ēs laɛng·ɛx Nɛg·ä. Wä̱, laɛng·aᶜmē xōmaȻɛlaɛng·-
ēda Mamalēleqala ʟɛᶜwa Kwāg·uȻē. Wä, laɛng·ɛn âla k·fȻᶜîda. Wä,
20 hēɛmxanawēsɛn lāg·iȻa ts!ɛx'ᶜîdē.

21. Mēxēs G̱ûyōsdēdzas.

Laɛng·ēk· sēxᶜwida qɛn lä laɛng·ɛxa Mamalēleqala laqēxs g·ō-
kûlaɛng·aē lāx Nōx̱ᵘdɛma. Wä, laɛng·ɛn lāg·aa. Wä, hēx·ᶜidaᶜɛng·a-
ᶜmēsɛn gwēg̱ûguᶜnaxɛn g·îg·äȻaakwē qaɛng·ɛn k·flᶜwēnēᶜʟax K·înts!ē-
25 gumēxa q!ɛy̱âx ʟ!āqwa. Wä, laɛng·aᶜmē gûᶜnasa q!ēnɛmᶜɛng·ä dāla-
ɛng·ɛ g·āxᶜɛng·ɛn. Wä, laɛng·aᶜmɛn ēk·!ēqala qaēda sɛk·!āp!ɛnx·ᶜ-
îdē lōxsɛmx·ᶜîd dāla gûᶜnēsa Mamalēleqala g·āxᶜɛng·ɛn. Wä, laɛng·-
g·ɛnᴋ·flxᶜwîts laɛng·ɛx K·înts!ēgum. Wä, laɛng·aᶜmɛn ʟ!āg̱wats
lāxēq. Wä, laᶜmɛn ts!ɛx·ᶜîd lāxēq.

the log and walked across it towards me. Before she reached me
she fell into the water and sank. Then I jumped into the water
and looked in vain for her down below. I did not find her.
Then I came up and saw Gŭyōsdĕdzas carrying Lɛᵋlɛndzōᵋ in his
arms. She was dead. Then I awoke.

19. Dream of ᵋyāk·âyugwa.

I dreamed our house in G·ᵼōx was on fire. Then all our property burned up and we were very poor and I woke up.

20. Dream of Q!wālax·ᵼlayugwa.

In my dream all the tribe came invited by Âwaxɛlag·ᵼlis.
Then Awaxɛlag·ᵼlis invited the people to a feast, and they were
to eat in his house after their journey. Then Lābid and Nɛg·ā,
chief of the Mamalēleqala quarrelled. Then Lābid promised to
give a potlatch and then Nɛg·ä broke a copper and gave the pieces
to Lābid. Then Lābid broke a copper and gave the pieces to Nɛg·ä.
Then the Mamalēleqala and the Kwāg·uᵼ quarrelled and I was really
afraid. That must have been the reason why I awoke.

21. Dream of Gŭyōsdedzas.

In my dream I paddled to the Mamalēleqala who weredliving
in Nōxᵘdɛm. Then I arrived there. Then I asked at once payment
for that which they had received from me, for I was intanding to
buy the expensive copper K·ᵼnts!ēgum. Then they paid me many
dollars and I was glad on account of the five thousand dollars
which the Mamalēleqala had paid me. Then I bought the copper
K·ᵼnts!ēgum with it. Then I was the owner of the copper. After
that I awoke.

22. Mēxēs Yāqōl̥as.

Mēxɛlēg·asa q!ēnɛmᶜɛng·ä lēlqwǎlaʟēᶜɛng·ɛ g·äx ʟēƚɛlānɛmᶜɛn-
g·ɛs Nɛqâp!ɛnk·ɛmōƚ. Laɛng·ē xwāsaɛng·ēda g·ɪgǎmaᶜyōƚē laɛng·ɛ-
xēs nōƚɛmaƚaēnaᶜyē. Wä,laɛng·ē q!ɛltaxa ʟ!āqwaɛng·ä qaᶜs yāxᶜwi-
5 dēsa q!ɛldɛxᵘᶜɛng·ä lāx Ḁgwiᶜla. Wä, laɛng·ē Ḁgwiᶜlōƚē ōgwaqa
q!ɛlt!ēdxēs ʟ!āqwaɛng·ä qaᶜs yāxᶜwidēsa q!ɛldɛkwē lāx Nɛqâp!ɛnk·-
ɛmōƚ. Wä, laᶜmɛn ts!ɛx·ᶜɪd lāxēq.

23. Mēxēs Nōƚbē.

Mēxɛlēk· laɛng·ɛ p!ēkᵘ laɛng·ɛxa Dzāwadɛēnoxwē. Wä, laɛng·-
10 ɛn dōqǔlaxa g·ɪg·ɛgǎmaᶜyas q!ɛltap!xa ʟ!āʟ!ɛqwa. Wä, laɛng·ɛn
yāxᶜwitsōᶜsa q!ɛldɛkwē yɪ̄ɛng·ɛs Sēsaxâlas. Wä, laɛng·ɛn q!ɛlt!ē-
dɛx G·ɪ̄lg·atō Māxᶜēnoxᵘxa q!ɛyōxwē ʟ!āqwa qɛn yāxᶜwidaɛng·ēx Sēsaxâlas. Wä, laɛng·aᶜmē ᶜyāk·ḁɛng·ɛ g·āxɛn. Wä, laᶜmɛn ts!ɛx·-
ᶜɪd lāxēq.

15 ### 24. Mēxēa Ts!āg·ōƚ.

Yɪ̄kwɪ̄ƚᶜɛng·ēk· ʟɛᶜwē gɛnɛmᶜōƚē Kǔnxǔlayugwäx gānoʟē. Wä,
laɛng·ē bɛxᵘk·!ōdɛqalaɛng·ēda ts!ɛdāx. Wä, laɛng·ɛᶜmox yāya-
kwɪ̄ƚtsɪ̄laɛng·ōxda Kwāg·uƚɛx. Wä, laɛng·ɛn gomēkᵘ ʟɛᶜwǔn gɛnɛm-
ᶜōƚ. Wä, laɛng·ē ts!ɛlk·ɛlakwa yɪ̄kwɪ̄lɛmᶜɛng·ä g·ɪ̄ng·ɪ̄nānɛmasa
20 ts!ɛlts!ɛlk·asa k·amäsa ts!ēk!wa. Wä, laɛng·aᶜmɛnuᶜxᵘ läsaᶜlayō
laɛngɛxa mōsgɛms g·ɪg·ōxᵘᶜɛng·a. Wä, g·ɪ̄lᶜmēsɛnuᶜxᵘ ᶜwɪᶜla ʟō-
ᶜɛng·ēda Kwāg·uƚ laɛng·ɛ gwāƚ läsalaxa mōsgɛmsē g·ig·ōkwa. La-
ɛng·ēg·anuᶜxᵘ ᶜwɪᶜla hōgwɪ̄ʟ lāx g·ōxᵘᶜɛng·äɛn. Wä, laᶜmɛn ts!ɛ-
x·ᶜɪda.

25 ### 25. Mēxēs K·!ēdēƚɛm.

Mēxɛlēg·ax gānoʟasa mōsmosa g·āxᶜɛng·ɛ qâqaᶜya g·axᶜɛng·ɛn.
Laɛng·ē hēƚts!axʟä g·āxᶜɛng·ɛn. Wä, laɛng·ē dāx·dasaɛng·ɛ g·āxɛn.
Wä, hēᶜmēsɛn la ts!ɛx·ᶜɪdaasē lāxɛn mēᶜxenaᶜyē.

26. Ēk·aɛng·ɛ qaēda hǎnʟ!ēnoxᵘ.

Mēxɛlēk· bāk·ōɛng·ɛ ʟōᶜɛng·ɛn ʟ̥âlax gânoʟē. Wä laɛng·aᶜmɛn
ᶜnɛxwālaɛng·ɛ ʟɛᶜwēlaɛng·ɛxwa āʟanḁᶜyaxsa g·ōkǔlaxa ḁla x·ɪ̄sa.
Lɛn ts!ɛx·ᶜɪda.

22. Dream of Yāqōᴌas.

I..dreamed that many tribes came invited by the late Nɛqāp!-
ɛnk·ɛm. Then the late chief became ecstatic in his quality of
fool dancer. Then he broke a copper and gave the pieces to the
late Âgwiᵋla. Then the late Âgwiᵋla broke a copper and gave
the pieces to the late Nɛqāp!ɛnk·ɛm. Then I awoke.

23. Dream of Nōᴌbē.

I dreamed that I had been invited by the Dzāwadɛēnoxᵘ.
Then I saw how the chiefs broke coppers against one another.
Then Sēsaxâlas gave a piece to me. Then I broke The Long Killer-
whale, an expensive copper, and gave it to Sēsaxâlas. Thus he
was vanquished by me. Then I awoke.

24. Dream of Ts!āg·ōᴌ.

I dreamed I had twins last night with my late wife Kŭnxa-
layugwa. One was a boy, the other a girl. Then the Kwāg·uᴌ
followed the twin customs. I and my late wife painted our faces
with ochre. The twins each wore wing feathers of gulls. Then
we were led around four houses, and when we and the Kwag·uᴌ finished walking around four houses we want into my house. Then I
awoke.

25. Dream of K·!ēdēᴌɛm.

I dreamed last night that a bull followed me. Then he over-
took me and overpowered me. At that time I awoke from my sleep.

26. Good Dream of a Hunter.

I dreamed that I met my sweetheart last night and I lay
with her behind the village, and it seemed true. Then I woke up.

27. Aik·aɛng·ɛ mɛ̄xɛ̄sa hănʟ.ᵉnoxwax Ōmx·Ïd.

Xwānałɛlaɛng·ĕk· qɛn laɛng·ŏ laᶜsta lāxwa wāx qaɛn laĕnĕʟĕ
hānaʟ.ał. Wä, laɛng·ɛn aʟōłɛlaɛng·a qɛn lä laɛng·ɛx ᶜnɛldzäsa
wāx. K·!ĕsᶜɛng·aᶜmĕsɛn lāg·aa laɛng·ɛxɛn hĕmɛnałaᶜma laᶜstaasa
5 laɛng·ĕg·a dōxᶜwaʟɛlaxɛn ʟâläxs ts.ᵉlxɛlgayaaxa łɛnɛmx·dĕ. Wä,
laɛng·ɛn qāsᶜïd qɛn läɛng·ĕ lāq. Wä, hĕx·ᶜïdaɛng·aᶜmĕsɛnuᶜxᵘ
nɛxwālax·ᶜïda. Wä, g·ïlᶜɛng·aᶜmĕsɛnuᶜxᵘ gwāła laɛng·ĕg·anuᶜxᵘ
laᶜstɛx·ᶜïda ʟɛᶜwün ʟâla. Wä, g·ïlᶜɛng·aᶜmĕsɛnuᶜxᵘ gwāł laᶜsta
ʟɛᶜwĕ laɛng·aĕ hĕ g·ïl laɛng·ɛ nä̆ᶜnakwa. Wä, laᶜmɛn ts.ᵉɛx·ᶜï-
10 daxa âla x·ïsaɛn mɛ̄xaᶜya.

28. Mɛ̄xɛ̄s K·!āmaxālas.

Sāłaɛng·ĕg·a ʟōᶜɛng·ĕda q.ᵉɛ̄nɛma ts.ᵉɛ̄daqa laɛng·ɛxɛnuᶜxᵘ
g·ōkwɛ̄x. Wä, g·ïlᶜɛng·aᶜmĕsɛnuᶜxᵘ gĕg·ïlïł sālaɛng·a g·āxᶜɛng·-
aasɛn łä̆ᶜwünɛmᶜɛng·ä g·āxɛʟ laɛng·ɛxɛnuᶜxᵘ g·ōkwa qaᶜs k·!ĕla-
15 x·ᶜïdĕ g·āxᶜɛng·ɛn. Wä, laᶜmɛn ts.ᵉɛx·ᶜïdĕ lāxĕq.

29. Mɛ̄xɛ̄s Abāyaa.

Mɛ̄xɛlĕk· laɛng·ɛ hămsaxa q.ᵉɛ̄nɛmᶜɛng·ä tsɛlxwa laɛng·ɛxa
tsɛlxᵘmadzɛkülaɛng·ä ĕg·ɛmĕngwisa. Wä, laɛng·ɛn mā̆ʟt.ᵉĕg·aaʟɛ-
laɛng·ɛqĕxs hĕᶜmĕk· hämsaxa tsɛlxwĕ Dzāwadĕ. Wä, laɛng·ɛn dōxᶜ-
20 waʟɛlaɛng·ɛxa mᵚwa g·ïg·ïla. Wä, laɛng·ɛn hĕłtsâsĕ wāx·a qaxs
g·āxᶜɛng·aᶜmaĕ qāqaᶜyaɛng·ĕda ᶜnɛma g·âla g·āxᶜɛng·ɛn. Wä, la-
ɛng·ŏ dāx·ᶜïd g·āxᶜɛng·ɛn. Wä, laɛng·ɛn dōxᶜwïdɛq ᶜmāsʟĕs yâᶜx
Tᵚanisĕx. Wä, laɛng·aᶜmōx ᶜnĕx· qaᶜs dāx·dasĕ g·āxᶜɛng·ɛn. Wä,
laɛng·ɛnuᶜxᵘ dādɛgâlaɛng·a. Wä, laɛng·aᶜmɛn ᶜyāk·â laɛng·ɛq.
25 Wä, laɛng·aᶜmĕ ᶜnɛxwālax·ᶜïd g·āxᶜɛng·ɛn. Wä, laɛng·ɛn wāx· näᶜnakwa. Wä, laɛng·ɛn q.ᵉwadzɛtâya. Wä, laᶜmɛn ts.ᵉɛx·ᶜïda lāxĕq.

30. Mɛ̄xɛ̄s Tsɛxwäsɛlasōᶜ.

G·āxᶜɛng·aɛn sāsɛmᶜōła ʟĕᶜlāla g·āxᶜɛng·ɛn qɛn lä lāx gwɛᶜ-
yâsĕ ĕx·ᶜɛng·ɛ ä̆ᶜwïnagwisa yïx lä ᶜwïᶜlāłaatsɛns lä k·!ĕk·!ᵉyowa.

27. Good Dream of the Hunter Ōmx·ı̄d.

I dreamed that I made ready to bathe in the river here for
I intended to go hunting. Then I went inland to the upper part
of the river. Before I came ιo the place where I am accustomed
to bathe I saw my sweetheart coming through the salal bushes.
I went to her and immediately we lay down. After that we went
bathing, I and my sweetheart. After we had finished, I and she,
she went home first. Then I awoke from this dream which seemed
as if it had really happened. [1]

28. Dream of K·!āmaxālas.

In my dream I and many women were singing love songs in our
house. After we had been singing for a long time my husband came
into my house and beat me. Then I awoke.

29. Dream of Abāyaa.

I dreamed I was going to pick crabapples in a patch of crab-
apple trees which were growing on a pretty level place. Then I
recognized that it was Knight Inlet where I was picking crabapples.
Then I saw four grizzly bears. I tried to run away for one of the
bears pursued me. It took hold of me. I looked at it, and what
should it be but this man Tsānis here. Then he said he would over-
power me. Then we took hold of each other and I succumbed and he
embraced me. Then I wanted to go home. On the way I was weeping.
Then I awoke.[2]

30. Dream of Tsɛxwäsɛlasōᵋ.

In my dream my late child came to invite me to go from here to

---

[1] This dream corresponds to the procedure of the hunter who tries
to secure good fortune.

, [2] This dream means that Abāyaa will be with child.

Wä, hёx·ᵋidaɛng·aᵋmēsɛn xwānaɫᵋida. Wä, lɛn ts!ɛx·ᵋītsa hādzɛx-
stälä.

31. ᵋyäk·aɛng·ɛ mēxēs ᵋnɛmōkŭyalis.

Hёᵋmaaxg·în laɛng·ēq ɭōᵋɛng·în gɛnɛmē laɛng·ɛxa ᵋwālasᵋɛng·ä
5 dzōyagɛkᵘ g·ōkwa. Wä, laɛng·anuᵋx̣ᵘ ăxk·!ālasōᵋsa bɛgwānɛmᵋɛng·ä
qɛnuᵋx̣ᵘ lä k!ŭsᵋālĭɫ laɛng·ɛxa hёɫk·!ōdɛnēgwĭɫasa ōxɫālĭɫasa g·ō-
kwē. Wä, laɛng·aᵋmēsɛnuᵋx̣ᵘ k!ŭsᵋālĭɫa. Wä, laɛng·ɛn dōxᵋwaɭɛla-
qēxs ᵋnāxwaᵋmaē laɛng·ɛ ɫēɫɛᵋla q!ēnɛmᵋɛng·ä bēbɛgwānɛmaxa ᵋnāxwa-
ɛng·aᵋma g·ayōɫᵋɛng·ɛ lāx g·īg·ɛgɛmaᵋyōɫasa Mamalēleqala yîɛng·ɛx
10 Gŭyōɫɛlasᵋwŭɫē ɭōᵋɛng·ē Nɛg·ɛōɫē, wä hёɛng·aɛm k!ŭdzēɫ laɛng·ɛxa
ōgwiwaᵋlĭɫᵋɛng·äsa g·ōkwē ɭōᵋɛng·ēda q!ēnɛma q!ŭlsq!ŭlᵋyax bēbɛgwā-
nɛmᵋɛng·ä. Wä, laɛng·ē k·!āgĭg·aɫtᵋᵋya saōx̣ᵘᵋɛng·ä lāxa t!ёx·îla-
ɛng·äsa g·ōkwē. Wä, hёɛng·aᵋmēsē k!ŭdzɛdzᵋᵋyō T!ēqwapᵋwŭɫē ɭōᵋ-
ɛng·ēs ᵋnēᵋnɛmōkᵘᵋwŭɫa. Wä, laɛng·ē Gŭyōɫɛlasē yāq!ɛg·aᵋɫa. Wä,
15 laɛng·ē T!ēqwapē dāsdaɫas wāɫdɛmᵋɛng·äs Gŭyōɫɛlas. Wä, hёɛng·aᵋ-
mēs laɛng·ɛ k·!ēlax·ᵋidaasɛx T!ēqwapdē. Wä, laɛng·aᵋmē ɫɛᵋlē T!ē-
qwapdē. Wä, hёɛng·aᵋmēs g·āᵋxats X·îlxᵋītōɫ ăxk·!ālaɛng·ɛ g·āxɛn
ɭōᵋɛng·ɛn gɛnɛmē qɛnuᵋx̣ᵘ lä hōqawɛlsa lāxa g·ōx̣ᵘᵋɛng·äsa lēslâlēnoxwē. Wä, laɛng·aᵋmēsɛnuᵋx̣ᵘ lāxa t!ёx·îla q!āq!alak·!ɛnux̣ᵘs X·î-
20 lxᵋītē. Wä, laɛng·aᵋmē ᵋnēk·a qaᵋsō k·!ēs la hōqawɛls lāxwa g·ō-
kᵘqɛnuᵋx̣ᵘ laᵋmēts xɛk·!ax·daᵋxᵘɭōl, ᵋnēk·ē. Wä, g·āxᵋɛng·aᵋmēsɛn-
uᵋx̣ᵘ näᵋnakwa yîxs laɛng·aē xōmāɫɛlēda lēslâlēnoxwē.

Wä, hёɛm ᵋwālas ᵋyax·sɛm mēxaᵋya. Wä, laɛm ts!ɛk·!āɫɛlaqēxs
ᵋyāx·sɛᵋmaēda ts!ɛx·q!ōlɛmɭaxa q!ēx·saasɭasa bāk!umē ɫēɫɛᵋlɫ.

25 ### 32. Mēxēs ɭ!āqwag·ilayugwa.

Mēxɛlēg·asɛn ɭâlōɫa g·āxᵋɛng·ɛ ɭēᵋlāla g·āxᵋɛng·ɛn qɛnuᵋx̣ᵘ
laɛng·ē sēx·wīd ɭōᵋɛng·ē. Laɛng·ɛn mɛlqwālaɛmqēxs gɛᵋyoɫaōɫa
ɫɛᵋla. Wä, laɛng·ɛn ᵋnēx·qɛxg·în q!ɛmsēk·. Wä, laɛng·ē ᵋyäk·îlĭ-
ɫa qaᵋs dādɛx·sᵋɛlĭɫaɛng·ē g·āxᵋɛng·ɛn. Wä, laᵋmɛn gwēgwaɫtsäɛng·a.
Wä, laᵋmɛn ts!ɛx·ᵋīda.

the place which they call the beautiful Country, the place where
all those go who are no more. I got ready at once. Then I was
awakened by a noise.

31. Bad Dream of ᵋnɛmōkūyalis.

It was this way, that I and my wife were in a large house with
many platforms. Then we were asked by a man to sit down in the
house in the rear corner at the right hand side, and so we sat down
in the house. Then I saw all those who were dead, many men, some
of the late chiefs of the Mamaléleqala, that is, the late G̣ūyōᶄɛ-
las, and the late Nɛg·ē, who were sitting in the rear of the house,
and also many old men. And on a platform made of boards placed
over the door of the house, the late T!ēqwap was sitting with his
late friends. Then G̣ūyōᶄɛlas spoke and T!ēqwap ridiculed the
speech of G̣ūyōᶄɛlas. Then he killed T!ēqwap, and T!ēqwap was dead.
That was the moment that the late X·îlxᵋît asked me and my wife to
leave the house of the ghosts. We went to the door led by X·îl-
xᵋît. Then he said, "If you do not go out of this house immediately you will stay here forever." Then we went home while the ghosts
were fighting.

This is a great bad dream. It announces that a bad epidemic
is going to come and that many Indians will die.

32. Dream of ʟ!āqwag·ilayugwa.

I dreamed of my late lover who came to call me to go paddling with him, and then it occurred to me that he had been dead
for a long time. I said to him that I did not care to go. Then
he became angry and took hold of me. Then I cried out. Then I
awoke.

33. Mᴇ̄xᴇ̄s Kᐧ!ämaxalas.

Mᴇ̄xᴇlēg·a łᴇᶜlᶜᴇng·ᴇx gānołē laᴇng·ᴇn layōsᴇn kᐧ!ēsᶜᴇng·ä
małt!ēł ᵉx·ᶜᴇng·ᴇ ts!ᴇdāq laᴇng·ᴇxa ᵉg·ᴇmēngwisᶜᴇng·a aᶜwĭnagwi-
saxa g·ōkŭlasasa ts!ēdaxsᴇmᶜᴇng·axa kᐧ!eâsaᴇng·ä ᶜnᴇmōx̱ᵘ bᴇgwā-
5 nᴇm bᴇk!ŭgēs. Wä, laᴇng·ēda ᶜnᴇmōx̱ᵘᶜᴇng·ä wŭła g·āx̱ᶜᴇng·ᴇn·
wĭx·sōxda aᶜwĭnagwixēx lāxōs nâqaᶜyēx, ᶜnex·ᶜᴇng·ē g·āx̱ᶜᴇng·ᴇn.
Wä, laᴇng·ᴇn x̱ŭlx̱ŭlts!ēqalaᴇng·ᴇ lāq. Wä, laᴇng·aᶜmēsᴇn nēła-
ᴇng·ᴇq. Wä, laᴇng·ē k·āya g·āx̱ᶜᴇng·ᴇn. Wä, laᶜmᴇn ts!ᴇx·ᶜĬd lā-
x̱ēq.

10   34.Mᴇ̄xᴇ̄s ʟ!āłᴇmēg·iᶜlakᵘ.

G·āx̱ᶜᴇng·aᴇn ōmpᶜwŭła dōqwa g·āx̱ᶜᴇng·ᴇn lāxᴇn g·ōkwēx.
Wä, laᴇng·aᶜmēsē ʟēᶜlālaᴇng·ᴇ g·āx̱ᶜᴇng·ᴇn qᴇn lāᴇn lāx g·okŭlas.
Wä, laᴇng·aᶜmēsᴇn xwānałᶜĭda qᴇn lä läg·ēq. Laᴇng·ēg·a mᴇlx̱ᶜwa-
ʟᴇlaqēxs gᴇyōłaōła łᴇᶜlᴇn ōmpᶜwŭła. Wä, laᴇng·ᴇn âla ts!ᴇṉx̱ᵘ-
15 sēxs g·āxaē ʟēᶜlālaᴇng·ᴇ g·āx̱ᶜᴇng·ᴇn qaēda lēslâlēnoxwē. Wä, laᶜmᴇn ts!ᴇx·ᶜĭda.

35. Mᴇ̄xᴇ̄s ʟ!āqwåł.

Laᴇng·ēk· dzēg·ᴇt!axa g·āwēq!ānᴇm laᴇng·ᴇx Āʟanōdzaᶜyē. Wä,
laᴇng·aᶜmēsᴇn ᵉx·ᶜag·alis laᴇng·ᴇxa g·āwēgadē. Laᴇng·ēk· dōx-
20 ᶜwaʟᴇlaxa q!ēnᴇmē ts!ēdaqa k!ŭtsēᶜstālaxa lᴇgwisē. Wä, laᴇng·ᴇ
äbāsᶜwŭłē ʟᴇᶜwis ᶜnᴇmōx̱ᵘᶜwŭłē ʟ!āqwałłᶜwŭłē ʟᴇᶜwōxda lāx xᴇnʟᴇla
ts!ᴇx·q!ōx Gaäxstālasēx k!wāgelisxa haäyałilagas yĭxᴇns gwᴇᶜyō
lēslâlēnoxwa. Wä, laᴇng·aᶜmē ts!ēsaxa g·āwēq!ānᴇm qaᶜs ts!ēkwēq.
Wä, laᴇng·ē äbāsᶜwŭłē ʟēᶜlāla g·āx̱ᶜᴇng·ᴇn qᴇn laᴇng·ē ts!āts!ē-
25 k!wālaq. Wä, laᴇng·ᴇn āʟēᶜsta qᴇn laᴇng·ē k!wāg·ĭlisē. Wä, la-
ᴇng·ᴇn k·!ēs małt!ālaxa waōkᵘ ts!ēdaqaxa gᴇyōłᶜwŭłaxᴇnt łēłᴇᶜla.
Wä, laᴇng·ē ʟ!āqwałłᶜwŭłē ᶜnēx· qᴇn ts!āts!ēk!walēxa ts!ēdzᴇkwē
g·āwēq!ānᴇma. Wä, laᴇng·ē äbāsᶜwŭłē k·!ēsᶜᴇng·ᴇ hēłq!ālᴇn ts!ē-
ts!ēk!wālaq " qaxg·ĭn k·!ēsēk· ᶜnēx· qa g·āxēsōx g·āxᴇns qa hē·
30 x·säᶜmēsōx q!äp!äłōtᴇn x̱ŭnōkwaē łāᶜwŭnᴇmasōx," ᶜnēx·ᶜᴇng·ē. Wä,
laᴇng·aᶜmē äbāsᶜwŭłē ᶜyālaqaᴇng·ᴇ g·āxᴇn qᴇn g·āxē näᶜnakwa. Wä,

33. Dream of K·!ämaxalas.

I dreamed last night that I was dead ánd I was taken away by
a pretty woman who was unknown to me to a nice beach to a village
in which there were only women, not a single man among them. Then
one of them asked me, "How do you like this beach?" she said to
me. I felt depressed there and I told her so. Then she chased me
away. Then I awoke.

34. Dream of ʟ!āʟɛmēg·iᵋlakᵘ.

In my dream my late father came to see me in my house here.
Then he invited me to go to his village, and so I made ready to
follow him. Then it occurred to me that my late father had died
long ago. I became very angry because he had come on behalf of
the ghosts to invite me. Then I awoke.

35. Dream of ʟ!āqwäʟ.

I dreamed that I was going digging clams on (the island)
 Åʟanōdzaᵋyē. And so I approached the beach where there are clams.
I saw many women sitting around a fire on the beach. There were
your late mother and her late friend ʟ!āqwaʟ, and the sick Gaāx-
stālas was sitting with the spirits, for that is the way we call
the ghosts. They were roasting clams and eating them. Then your
mother called me to eat clams with them. I went ashore and sat
down. I did not know the other women, but they probably died long
ago. Then ʟ!āqwaʟ wanted that I should eat roasted clams with
them. Your mother did not permit me to eat clams with them, " for
I do not wish her to come to us. She shall remain with my son,
her husband," thus she said. Then your late mother sent me away
home. Then I left them and went aboard my little travelling canoe.
Then I awoke.

g·äx^εɛng·ɛn bâsē qɛn lāxs^εɛng·ē lāxɛn yâ^εyats!ä sɛk·ɛlisa. Wä,
la^εmɛn ts!ɛx·^εɪd lāxēq.

36. Mēxēs Gwŭyosdēdzas.

Mēxɛlēk· laɛng·ɛ sēx^εwidayosɛn gagɛmp^εwŭɫa. Laɛng·ɛn āɫ^εɛm
5 q!âɫ^εaɫ̣ɛlaɛng·ɛqēxs gɛyōɫaōɫa ɫɛ^εlaxg·anu^εx^u laɛng·ēg·a qwēsg·ila-
ɛng·a. Wä, laɛng·ē āɫē^εsta laɛng·ɛx Ë̆g·isbalis. Wä, hē̆ɛng·a^εmēsɛn
la bâɛng·ɛs qɛn g·āx^εɛng·ē qasaēsɛlaɛng·axg·ɪn g·âxēk· nä^εnakwa.
Wä, g·āx^εɛng·ɛn lāx G·iōx. Wä, laɛng·ɛn k·!eâs gwäwē^εlas^εɛng·ɛ lāxa wäs G·iōx. Wä, laɛng·ɛn wāx· gɛlx·^εida. Wä, laɛng·ɛn ɛlāq wē-
10 x·^εɛna. Wä, hē̆^εmēsɛn la ts!ɛx·^εɪdaasē.

37. Mēxēs Yäqawɪdē.

Laɛng·ēg·a sēxwa lälaaɛng·ɛ lāx Gwadzē^εyaxa ganuɫ^εɛng·ä. Wä,
g·ɪl^εɛng·a^εmēsɛn lāg·aa laɛng·ɛx Q!ɛmsɛxlä läɛng·ēk· wŭɫ̣āx^εaɫ̣ɛla-
ɛng·ɛxa q!ēk·!älä hä^εyäɫa sä^εlälaxa ^εnēx·^εɛng·aē qä^εyasas:
15   Lɛn yayaēx^εalisak·as ^εnähɛnk·!ɛmlisaɫxahanhan g·ɪya^εya;
         ha ha yi^εya ha ha.
         ^εya ōgŭxsâlēhēsɫɛhahahan q!wahahats!ēn̄ē^εʟa qahahahan
         g·ɪya^εya; ha ha yi^εya ha ha.
Wä, mā^εɫtsɛmk·!ɛnälaɛng·a^εmɛn q!āsɛ^εwē laɛng·ɛx qä^εyas^εɛng·äsa sā-
20 lɛmas hä^εyäɫaɛng·äsa lēslâlēnox^u. Wä, laɛng·ɛnhē̆nakŭla laɛng·ɛx
Gwadzē^εyē. Wä, laɛng·ɛn lāg·aaxa laɛng·ē nä^εnakŭla. Wä, la^εmɛn
ts!ɛx·^εɪd lāxēq.

38. Mēxēs Tsɛx^εwɪdē.

G·āx^εɛng·ēk· ʟē^εlalasō^εsɛn ōmp^εwŭɫa qɛn laɛng·ē lāx gwɛ^εyas
25 ēk· a^εwɪnagwisa. Wä, laɛng·a^εmēsɛn lāg·ēq. Wä, laɛng·anu^εx^u lā-
g·aa lāx g·ōx^{uε}ɛng·ä^εs. Wä, laɛng·anu^εx^u hōgwiʟa laɛng·äx g·ōkwas.
Wä, laɛng·ē äxk·!äla qɛn k!wäg·aliɫē. Wä, laɛng·a^εmē nēɫaxs ʟō^ε-
maē wɪwosilaga lāxēs äxāsē: Dōx^εwidasxɛn ku^εlēlasēx. La^εmɛn
k·!eâs māma, lāxaɛn k·!eâs hē̆ɫila^εya, ^εnēx·^εɛng·ē g·āx^εɛng·ɛn.
30 Wä, âɛng·a^εmēsɛn ʟāx^εŭlɪɫa qɛn g·āx^εɛng·ē nä^εnakwa. Wä, la^εmɛn
ts!ɛx·^εɪda.

36. Bad dream of Gwŭyosdēdzas.

I dreamed that I was being paddled about by my late grandfather. I only recollected that he had died long ago after we were far away. Then we landed on a sandy point. I left him and went along the beach and came home. I came to G·iōx. Then I could not get across the river of G·iōx. I began to swim and I was almost drowned. At that moment I awoke.

37. Dream of Yäqawĭd.

In my dream I was paddling to Gwadzēᵉat night. As soon as I arrived at Shell Island I heard the voices of many young men who were singing love songs and they said these words:

I give it up to win my love in this world; ha ha yiᵋya

ha ha.

Oh, in another way will go down my crying on account

of my love; ha ha yiᵋya ha ha.

I learned two lines of the words of the love song of the young men of the ghosts. Then I went right on to Gwadzēᵋ and I arrived there when the day broke. Then I awoke.

38. Dream of Tsɛxᵋwĭd.

In my dream I was called by my late father to a place which he called the Nice Country. Then I followed him. We came to his house. I entered his house. Then he asked me to sit down on the floor. Then he told me it was a very poor place where he was: (he said), "Look at my bed. I have no cover, nothing to maintain myself." Thus he said to me. Then I arose and went home. Then I awoke.[1]

---

[1]After this dream Tsɛxᵋwĭd burned two pairs of blankets and food for the soul of his late father.

39. Mēxēs Hɛx·hak!waēdzɛmga.

(Koskimo)

Mēxaëg·înʟax nēg·ɛxᵘ yîk·atsē q!ēnɛmx·st!aaxwa lāk·as ɫɛᶜɫaa
ts!ēts!ādaxst!aaxwa yîk·ast!aax̭ûx Ak·ilayugwaōɫ ʟōᶜkwast!aaxwē Ā-
5 dahōɫk·ast!aaxwē ʟōᶜkwast!aaxwē ʟ!āqwag·ilayugwaōɫk·ast!aaxwē ʟōᶜkwast!aaxwē ʟ!āʟ!aqwaōɫwŭɫēk·ast!aaxwē. Wä, hëk·asᶜɛmxat! lak·as
geōɫ lāk·as ᶜwîᶜlak·as ɫēᶜɫaa. Wä, lāk·ast!aaxwē lāxst!aaxᵘ g·ā-
xᶜalisk·adzōɫ lāk·ast!aax̭ûx Xŭtēs. Wä, lāk·ast!aaxwē Ak·ilayugwa
ʟēɫᶜaɫɛxsak·ast!aax̭ûx Hɛx·hāk!waēdzɛmga ʟōᶜx·st!aaxwē ʟ!aqwaga.
10 Wä, lāx·st!aaxwē hōxᶜwaɫɛxst!aaxᵘ lāk·ast!aax̭ûx yāᶜyats!äsē k·!ē-
sk·asē la aōmsk·asa. Wä lax·st!aaxwē ʟɛxɛlēsa. Wä, lax·st!aaxwē
gagäɫak·ast!aaxᵘ ʟēxᶜēdayox·st!aaxwa. G·āxk·asɛn dōxᶜwaʟɛlak·asx·-
st!aaxᵘsxē q!ēnɛmk·asē mēᶜmä ɛk·ax·st!aaxᵘ lak·asx·st!aaxᵘxē ʟ!ā-
sagwisk·atsē gōkwax·st!aaxᵘ lāk·asɛx Xŭtēs. Wä, lax·st!aaxwē t!ā-
15 t!aqwasōᶜkwatsē t!ēt!aq!wēnoxᵘk·asasē Gōsg·imoxᵘk·asē. Wä, lāk·-
ast!aaxwē qōqŭt!ak·asē t!āt!aq!waats!ēx·st!aaxwas memanagoɫk·asa.
Wä, lāk·asᶜɛmxaɛn ts!ɛx·ᶜîd lāk·asxēq.

Wä, yîx gwēbaɫaasasa g·ālabaᶜyasa mēxaᶜyē qa Hɛx·hak!waē-
dzɛmga ʟōᶜ ʟ!āqwaga yîxs hēᶜmaē āɫēs q!wēq!ŭᶜlē. Wä, lä lāxsē
20 bɛxᶜŭnāᶜyasēx yāᶜyats!äsa bēbɛxᶜŭnāᶜyasa la gäɫa ɫēɫɛᶜla. Wä,
laɛm q!alēda mēxɛläxs lɛᶜmaē ɛlāq ɫēɫɛᶜla maᶜlōkwē. Wä, lä ɛlx-
ʟaᶜya mēxaᶜyas q!ēnɛm k·!ōtɛla, wä laɛm q!ālaxs lāg·aēʟē q!ŭᶜ-
lāɫ lāxa k·!ōt!ɛnxē.

40. Mēxēs Ts!ālaliɫiᶜlakᵘ.

25 Mēx·ɛlēk· laɛng·ɛ ʟēᶜlānɛmsɛn ōmpᶜwŭɫa laɛng·ɛx Ts!ädē. Wä,
laɛng·ɛn ʟ!ɛlēwēqēxs gɛyōɫaōɫa ɫɛᶜla. Laɛng·aᶜmēsɛn lāx g·ōxᵘᶜ-
ɛng·äsē qɛn laɛng·ē k!waîɫ laɛng·ɛx g·ōkwas. Wä, laɛng·ē yāq!ɛg·-
aᶜɫa, laɛng·ē ᶜnēk·a: Gēlak·as la q!āgwid, ēsaēʟɛn ɛ̂ɛm ᶜnēx· qɛn
g·āxē hēɫiᶜlälaxēs gwēx·sdɛmōs qɛn damōdālēxwa ts!ēts!ɛx·q!ōlɛma-
30 qōs ɫālaxwîlaᶜyā̂ qaxg·în dōqŭlaᶜmēg·axs hēmɛnāɫaᶜmaaqōs ts!ɛx·q!a,
ᶜnēx·ᶜɛng·ē ōmpᶜwŭɫɛn. Wä, laɛng·ē ʟɛxomāxōtsēs ᶜwāx·sōɫts!ānaᶜyē

39. Dream of Hɛx·hak!waēdzɛmga.

(Koskimo)

At night I dreamed of many dead women, of the late Ak·ila-
yugwa, the late Ada, the late ᴌ!āqwag·ilayugwa and the late ᴌ!ā-
ᴌ!aqwaōł. They had all been dead a long time. They came a-
shore at Xŭtēs. Then Ak·ilayugwa called Hɛx·hak!waēdzɛmga and
ᴌ!āqwaga to come aboard the canoe. They went aboard the canoe
of the supernatural ones. They steered away from shore. After
they had been under way for some time I saw many salmon jumping
on the beach seaward from the village Xŭtēs. They were speared
by the spearsmen of the Koskimo, and the spearsmen's canoes were
full. After this I awoke.

This is the meaning of the beginning of the dream for Hɛx·-
hak!waēdzɛmga and ᴌ!āqwaga -- for they were still alive -- whose
souls went aboard the canoe of the souls of those who had died
long ago. Then the dreamer knew that these two were almost dead.
At the end of the dream about the many salmon, she knew that she
would live until the salmon run.

40. Dream of Ts!âlaliłiᶜlakᵘ.

I dreamed I was invited by my late father to Ts!ädē. I
had forgotten that he was dead long ago. I entered his house and
sat on the floor of his house. Then he spoke and said, "I wish to
cure you of your ways and to remove those sicknesses which cause
you pain, for I see you are always ill." Thus said my late father.
Then with both his hands he squeezed both sides of my head down-
wards to the lower end of my back. Then he closed both hands and

laɛng·ɛxg·în ᵋwāx·sanôʟɛmēk· häxalaɛng·ɛ lāxg·în ôdzoxsdēk·. Wä,
hḛɛng·aᵋmēs la ʟɛlqoxᵋwîdaats ēᵋeᵋyasâs qaᵋs mɛqôstôdēsa ts!ɛx·q!ô-
lɛmē. Wä, laɛng·ē môp!ɛna hḛ gwēx·ᵋidē. Wä, g·flᵋmēsē gwāɫᵋɛng·a
laē ᵋyālaqaɛng·ɛ g·āxɛn qɛn g·āxē näᵋnakwa. Wä, laᵋmɛn ts!ɛx·ᵋîd
5 lāxēq.

41. Mēxēs Q!ēq!ɛx·ʟāla.

Mēxɛlēk· laɛng·ɛ hānaʟ!a laɛng·ɛxa mēgwatē laɛng·ɛx Māp!ɛgɛm.
Wä, laɛng·ɛn q!ɛyôʟxa mēgwatē. Wä, g·āxᵋɛng·ɛn näᵋnakwa laɛng·ɛxôx
Tsāxisēx. Wä, hēx·ᵋidaɛng·ɛᵋmēsɛn ts!ɛx·ᵋîdxa mēgwatᵋɛng·ä. Wä,
10 g·flᵋɛng·aᵋmēsɛn gwāɫ ts!ɛx·aqēxs laɛng·ēg·a yîmɫᵋîdɛq. Wä, la-
ɛng·ɛn q!āxa xwēᵋlaɛng·ä g·îts!āxa pôxûnsasa ᵋwālasē mēgwata. Wä,
laɛng·aᵋmɛn ʟ̠ôgwalaq. Âɛng·aᵋmēsɛn la q!wālaɫîdɛq laɛng·ɛxa āʟ!ē.
Wä, laɛng·ɛn k!wēlasᵋîtsa mēgwatē laɛng·ɛxwa Kwākwag·uɫēx. Wä,
g·flᵋɛng·aᵋmēsɛn gwāɫ k!wēlasa. Laɛng·ēk· t!ēx·ᵋalîɫa. Wä, la-
15 ɛng·ɛn mēxᵋēda. G·āxᵋɛng·ēda bɛgwānɛma k!wāg·alîɫ laɛng·ɛxɛn ʟ!ā-
salîɫē. Wä, laɛng·ē ᵋnēk·a, " Wḛg·a k·!ēs kuᵋlîɫʟɛ ʟɛᵋwis gɛnɛ-
maôsaxa môxᵋûnxʟa ts!āwûnxa āʟas amēɫālax qaēs ʟ̠ôgwaᵋyaôsa xwēᵉla
g·āxɛn," ᵋnēx·ᵋɛng·ēda bɛgwānɛm g·āxᵋɛng·ɛn. Wä, laᵋmɛn ts!ɛx·-
ᵋîd lāxēq.
20   ### 42. Mēxēs Alak·ilayugwa.

Mēxɛlēg·a laɛng·ɛ lawîɫ yāᵋyasɛlaɛng·ɛxa xwāxwagûma. Wä,
k·!ēsᵋɛng·aᵋmēsɛn nɛqâlēxs laɛng·aē ts!āq!wag·flisa. Wä, laɛng·-
ɛn ʟāɫax Nɛxāgadē. Wä, laɛng·ᵋmē qâp!îdaɛng·ɛn yaᵋyats!ä xwāxwaguma. Wä, laɛng·ɛn lāsgɛmdxa xwāxwagumaxs laē qɛpâlaɛng·a.
25 Wä, laɛng·ɛn hāxsɛmēʟēq. Wä, g·āxᵋɛng·ēda ts!ēk!wa p!ɛʟɛᵋnakûla
qaᵋs g·āxᵋɛng·ē k!wāsgɛmdxa âg·iwaᵋyasa qɛpâla xwāxwaguma. Wä,
laɛng·ē dāx·ᵋîdɛxg·în aᵋyasôkᵘ. Wä, laɛng·ē äxk·!āla qɛnuᵋxᵘ qā-
qasamak·a. Wä, laɛng·aᵋmɛnuᵋxᵘ lāg·aa lāx Baas. Wä, laɛng·aᵋmē ʟ̠ē-
xsᵋāla g·āxᵋɛng·ɛn qɛn gwayiᵋlālas qaēda ᵋwālasʟa ts!ɛx·qôlɛmɫxwa
30 hḛɛnxʟɛx ᵋnēx·ᵋɛng·ēxs laɛng·aē hôxᵋwîtsa xwēᵋlaɛng·a. Wä,laɛng·ē
äxᵋaʟɛlôtsa xwēᵋlē lāxg·în bɛnbāg·asg·în ʟ!ɛmak!ûbânokᵘ qaᵋs ʟɛx-

drew up the disease. Four times he did so. After he did so he
sent me home. Then I awoke.

41. Dream of Q!ēq!ɛx·ʟāla.

I dreamed I was going sealing near Māp!ɛgɛm. There I got
many seals. I came home here to Fort Rupert. Immediately I
singed the seals. After I was through singeing I butchered them.
Then I found a quartz crystal in the stomach of a large seal.
Then I had a treasure. Then I hid it in the woods. Then I gave
a feast to the Kwāg·uɫ tribes with the seals. After I had given
the feast I lay down. Then I dreamed that I was asleep. A man
came and sat down by my side, towards the middle of the house.
Then he said, "You must not lie down with your wife for four years
else you will be unlucky, for you have received your treasure, the
quartz crystal, from me." Thus the man spoke to me. Then I awoke.

42. Dream of Alak·ilayugwa.

I dreamed I travelled across the water in a small canoe. I
was not half way across when a northwesterly gale began to blow.
I steered towards Nɛxāgad, Then my small travelling canoe capsized. I climbed out of the small canoe that was drifting upside
down on the water. I lay on it with my chest down. Then a gull
came flying and alighted on the bow of the small canoe that was
drifting on the water. It took my hand and told me to walk on
top of the water. Thus I arrived at Blunden Harbor. Then he
taught me what to do when a great epidemic should come in summer.
He said so, and spit out a quartz crystal. Then he put the quartz
crystal into my body at the lower end of my sternum and pressed it

ḅɛtɛndēq. Wä, laɛng·ŏ̄ ᵉnēk·a. Wä, laɛms nānaxts!ɛᵉwa g·axɛn qaᵉs
yadɛnᴸōs qaxs lɛᵉmaaqōs ᵉwālasᴸ pä̆xalaᴸōᴸ, ᵉnɛx·ᵉɛng·ēda ts!ēk!wa.
Wä, lāᴸɛs ᴸē̆gadɛᴸts Q!ŭᵉlɛnts!ēsɛmē̆ga lāxēq, ᵉnēx·ᵉɛng·ēda ts!ē̄-
kwa. Wä, laᵉmɛn ts!ɛx·ᵉīd lāxēq.

5   43. Mē̄xēs Qɛldō̆dzɛm.

Hě̆ᵉmēxs laē q!ēx·sēda g·īg·ɛgä̆maᵉyasa ᵉnäxwa lŏ̆ʞqwälaᴸaᵉya
g·aᵉyala lāxa ᵉwālasē̆ ts!ɛx·q!ōlɛma flu. Wä, laᵉmē̄sɛnuᵉxᵘ ᵉnäxwa
dŏ̆qŭlax Q̌ᵃᵉlädē̆ yīxs ā̆laᵉmaē̆ laɛm xɛnᴸɛla ts!ɛx·q!a qaxs laē̆ hä̆-
yō̆lēsᵉɛm la lɛxōk!wäla. Wä, lāxaē̆ hē̆mɛnwälēda ᴸɛnxstō̆ ᴸɛndɛqᵘ
10 lāx·x·īndzasas. Wä, la ts!ɛk!waläs hāsaᵉyē̆. Wä, laᵉmē̄ k·ēs la
hē̆ᴸats!ā̆la qāsa. Wä, laᵉmē̆ ts!ɛk·!ā̆ᴸɛlasōxs lɛᵉmaē̆ q!ɛyōkwē̆ lä
wē̆k·!īx·ᵉīda. Wä, laᵉmē̆ ā̆ᴸɛbō̆p!ɛmxwaᵉs qɛlgwīᴸa yīx Q!ŭᵉlädē̆.
Wä, la' yāwasᵉīd mēxᵉida. Wä, lāᵉlaē̆ mēxɛlasa ā̆ᴸaᵉmɛn g·āx g·āxē̆-
ᴸa lāx g·ō̆kwas. Wä, lāᵉlaē̆ ᵉnēk·a ā̆ᴸanɛmaq: Gwāᴸdzā̆s ḥě̆ gwē̆g·īlē̆
15 Q!ŭᵉläd, qā̆st, qaᵉs laōs lā̆ᵉsta lāxwa wāx gaā̆laᴸa ᴸɛᵉwa dzāqwa. Mō̆-
p!ɛnxwaᵉsᴸē̆ ᵉnālaᴸēs hē̆x·dɛmᴸaōs gwē̆g·ilaᴸē̆ qaᵉsō̆ ŏ̆x·ᵉē̆dᴸō̆ laɛms
k·!ō̆qŭlaᴸɛx m̥agats!ē̆ᴸa qaᵉs tsē̆x·ᵉīdaōsas lāxwa wāx qaᵉsō̆ lā̆ᴸ k̥!wa-
ᵉstalisᴸō̆ᴸ. Wä, lāᴸɛs gŭqaᴸts!a ᵉwābɛts!ā̆sa nāgats!ē̆ lāxōs ēwanu-
ᴸxawaᵉyaqōs. Wä, mā̆ᴸɛxᴸa ᵉwābɛts!ā̆la nāgats!ēs gŭxᵉīdayōs lāxō̆s
20 hē̆ᴸk·!ō̆dɛnuᴸxawaᵉyaqōs; wä mā̆ᴸɛxᴸaɛmxaāwis lāxs gɛmxanuᴸxawaᵉyē̆x,
ᵉnēx·ᵉɛng·ɛᵉlaēda ā̆ᴸanɛmᵉɛng·äx Q!ŭᵉlädē̆. Wä, laᵉmɛn bā̆wēda ā̆ᴸa-
ᵉnɛmē̆.

     Wä, hē̆x·ᵉidaᵉmēsē̆ Q!ŭᵉlädē̆ äxᵉēdxa n̄āgats!ē̆ qaᵉs lä g·īlᵉnā̆-
kŭla qaᵉs lä k!waᵉsta lāxa wa qaᵉs tsē̆x·ᵉīdēsa nāgats!ē̆ lāxa ᵉwāpē̆
25 qaᵉs gŭxᵉīdēs lāxēs hē̆ᴸk·!ō̆dɛnuᴸxawaᵉyē̆. Wä, lä mā̆ᴸp!ɛna hē̆ gwēx·-
ᵉidō̆. Wä, lāxaē̆ hē̆ɛm gwēx·ᵉīdxēs gɛmxanuᴸxawaᵉyē̆. Wä, lä gwā̆ᴸɛxs
laē̆ gɛlᵉnakŭlaxs laē̆ laēᴸ lāxēs g·ō̆kwēxa laɛm gä̆ᴸak·as ᵉnāla qaxs
q!ēnɛmaēda bē̆bɛgwānɛm dō̆qŭlaqēxs laē̆ k!waᵉstālis lāxa wa wax·dzā̆la
lɛxā̆xs k!wastalisaē̆; ɛsx·axat!. Wä, mō̆p!ɛnxwaᵉsᵉmēs ᵉnālä hē̆ gwē̆-
30 g·ilaxs laē̆ ᴸak!wē̆masᵉida. Wä, lä äxk·!ālaxa ᵉnäxwa bē̆bɛgwānɛmxa
ts!ɛx·q!äsa flu qa ō̆gwaqēs laᵉsta lāxa wa. Wä, hě̆ᵉmis ᵉnäxwa ŏ̆x·-

in. Then he said, "Now make a rattle in my form (imitate me).
Then you will be a great shaman," thus said the gull. "Now you
shall have the name Q!ŭᵋlɛnts!ᵋᵉsɛmēga from now on." Then I awoke.[1]

43. Dream of Qɛldēdzɛm.[2]

It was at the time that many chiefs of all the tribes died
of the great epidemic, influenza. Then we all saw that Q!ŭᵋläd
was really sick, for he was coughing all the time and yellow fluid
was running all the time from his nose. His breath was short and
he was not able to walk. Then he was informed of the death of
many people. For seven days he was in bed, I mean Q!ŭᵋläd. Then
he slept for a short time. Then it is said he had a dream of a
wolf which came into his house. Then it is said the wolf spoke
to him and said, "Do not act like this, Q!ŭᵋläd, good friend, but
go into the water of this river morning and evening. For four
days do this if you want to get well, and take a bucket and dip
water out of this river while you are sitting in the water, and
pour the water in the bucket over both sides of your neck. Two
buckets full of water in the bucket pour over the right side of
your neck, and in the same way two buckets full over the left side
of your neck." Thus said the wolf in the dream of Q!ŭᵋläd. Then
the wolf left.

Immediately Q!ŭᵋläd took a bucket and crawled away to sit
down in the water of the river. He took up water with his bucket
and poured it over the right side of his neck. Twice he did so.
Then he also poured it over the left side of his neck. When he
had finished doing so he crawled back into his house a long time
after day had come; and many men saw him sitting in the water of

---

[1] This dream is typical for the initiation of a shaman. The
novice dreams in this way of dying persons, of the War-spirit
(Winālag·flis) or of other supernatural beings (hayaẍilagas).

[2] As a shaman this man had the name Q!ŭᵋläd.

ᵋꟾdēda hₐ̆ gwēx·ᵋidē wāɫdɛmas. ᵋnɛmōxᵘᵋmē Awālasɛlaɫ ɫɛᵋlasa pēpɛ-
xālaxa laᵋsta lāxa wŭdaᵋsta wa. Hₐ̆dɛnuᵋxᷟ lāg·iɫa xɛnyasasēxs
ts!ɛlqwaē ₐ̆x· k·!āɫɛlēs ōk!winaᵋyasēs ts!ɛlqwäxa gaāläxs laē laᵋsta lāxa wŭdaᵋsta wa. Wä, nōgwaᵋmēs dōqŭlaq ʮōᵋ Mɛlēdē ʮōᵋ Âgwi-

5 lagɛmaᵋyē ʮōᵋ K!wāk!wabalasɛmaᵋyē ʮɛᵋwa q!ēnɛmē ōgŭla bēbɛgwanɛma
wꟾtnᷠstsg·ꟾn wāɫdɛmk· qa Q!ŭᵋlädē. Lаɛm lāba.

10

44. Mēxēs Tōgŭmālis.

Wä, hₐ̆ɛmxaāwisē gwäla mēxaᵋyas Tōgŭmālisxa päxᵋla, yꟾxs mēxɛ-
laē. G·āxᵋɛng·ēda tämꟾnasē äxk·!ālaq qa läs laᵋsta laɛng·ɛxa

15 q!ɛwēg·alasasa g·ōkŭla laɛng·ɛxg·a Tsāxisɛk·, yꟾxs laē xɛnʮɛlasa
ᵋwālas ts!ɛx·q!ōlɛma flu. Wä, laɛng·aɛmxaɛn äxk·!ālasōᵋ qɛn lä
k!waᵋsta lāqēxa gaāläxs g·ālaē ᵋnāᵋnakŭla qɛn xōsitēsa wŭdaᵋsta
ᵋwāpa ʮɛᵋwa la dzaxq!āla. Wä, hēx·ᵋidaɛng·aᵋmēsɛn laɛng·a läg·-
ēxa tämꟾnasē. Wä, laɛng·aᵋmē ts!āts!ɛmx·sꟾla qɛn gwēg·ilasg·ꟾn.

20 Laɛng·ēk· laᵋsta. Wä, hēᵋmēsɛn lāg·iɫa hₐ̆ gwēg·ilēxg·ꟾn lēk· lɛ-
xōxᵋwida qɛn hēx·ᵋidaᵋmē laᵋsta lāxwa q!ɛwēg·alasaxsɛns g·ōkwēx.
Wä, hēᵋmēsɛn lāg·iɫa k·!ēs la ts!ɛx·q!aēnoxwē. Wä, hēᵋm päxāla-
masa tämꟾnasax Tōgŭmālis. Wä, hēᵋmis päxälāmasa āʮaᵋnɛmax Q!ŭᵋ-
lädē.

25 ## 45. Mēxēs Gwāgwadaxɛla.

Mēxɛlēg·asɛn äbɛmpᵋwŭɫa g·āxᵋɛng·ɛ äxk·!āla qɛn hēmɛnāɫaᵋmē
la q!wāxētasa q!waxē laɛng·ɛxa waɛng·ä lāxwa aʮēg·aᵋyaxsɛns g·ō-
kŭlasēxa gēgaāla ʮɛᵋwa dzādzɛqwa. Wä, qaᵋsō hₐ̆ɫ gwēg·ilaʮē laᵋmēts k·!ēs ts!ɛx·q!aēnoxᵘʮōʮ ᵋnēx·ᵋɛng·aɛn äbɛmpᵋwŭɫē g·axᵋ-

30 ɛng·ɛn. Wä, hēx·ᵋidaᵋmēsɛn la laᵋsta laxēq.

the river coughing all the time while he was sitting there and also sneezing. After he had sone so for four days he became strong. Then he asked the people who were suffering from influenza to go into the water of the river. All those who acted according to his words recovered. Only Awālasɛlaⱬ died, the only one among the shamans who went into the water of the cold river. And this is the reason why we were surprised that the bodies of those who were sick of the fever were steaming in the morning when they went into the cold river. I myself say him, and Mɛlēd and Agwilagɛmēu and K!wā-k!wabalasɛmēᶜ and many other men were witnesses of what I say about Q!ū́ᶜläd. Now that is the end.

44. Dream of Tōgŭmālis.

This was also the dream of the shaman Tōgŭmālis as he was dreaming: " A squirrel came here and asked me to go into the water of the pond behind the village of Fort Rupert," for he was very sick of the influenza. " Then I was asked to sit down in the water early in the morning when day broke, and to spray myself with cold water also late in the evening. And I obeyed the squirrel. Then it showed to me what I was to do, and I went into the water. Therefore I do this when I begin to cough. Then I go immediately into the water in this pond behind our house. Therefore I am never sick." It was a squirrel that made Tōgŭmālis a shaman and it was a wolf that made Q!ū́ᶜläd a shaman.

45. Dream of Gwāgwadaxɛla.

I dreamed of my late mother who asked me to rub my body always with branches of hemlock trees[1] in the river behind our village in the morning and in the evening, " and if you do this you will never be sick," thus said my late mother to me. After that I went immediately into the water.

---

[1] This is the usual method of ceremonial purification.

46. Mē̆xēs ᵋmā̱x̣ŭlag·flis.

Mē̆xɛlēg·asą q!ēnɛmᵋɛng·ä bebɛgwanɛm k!ŭdzīⱡ lāxą g·ōx̣ᵘᵋ-
ɛng·äɛn lä laēⱢasᵋɛng·a. Wä, laɛng·ɛn ᵋÿäg·1ᵋ1ɛmᵋɛng·ɛsa g·ī̆gɛ-
maᵋyasxa ā̆laɛng·ä ⱡā̆wisᵋɛng·ɛ g·āxᵋɛng·ɛn. Wä, laɛng·aᵋmē̆ k·ayɛ-
5 wŭlsa g·āxᵋɛng·ɛn. Wä, laɛng·ɛn nēⱡasōᵋɛng·ɛsa ōgŭᵋlaᵋma bɛgwā-
nɛmɛng·a. Wä, laɛng·ē ᵋnēk·ᵋɛng·a g·āxᵋɛng·ɛn: Nōgwaᵋmɛnuᵋx̣ᵘ
ts!ēts!ax·q!ōlɛma lāxɛnuᵋx̣ᵘ ᵋnāⱡᵋnɛmōk!wēnaᵋyē̆ bɛgwānɛma. Laᵋmē̆-
sɛnuᵋx̣ᵘ k!wāla gwāgwēx·sᵋālа lāxɛnuᵋx̣ᵘ läläsⱢāxwa hē̆ɛnxⱢēx. Wä,
hāg·a lāwŭlsɛx, ᵋnēx·ᵋɛng·ēda bɛgwānɛmᵋɛng·ā̆ g·āxᵋɛng·ɛn. Wä, la-
10 ɛng·ɛn wāx· lāwŭls lāxa t!ē̱x·flaɛng·äsa ᵋwālasᵋɛng·a g·ōkwa g·ā-
xᵋɛng·aasa g·flx·dē yāyaq!ɛntaᵋma bɛgwānɛma g·āxᵋɛng·īn qaᵋs
q!wēsᵋidēsēs hēⱡk·!ōⱡts!ānaᵋyēeng·ä laɛng·ɛxg·īn hēⱡk·!ōdɛnōdzē.
Wä, laɛng·ē ᵋnēk·a: Yŭɛms g·aᵋyālasⱢōda ts!ɛx·q!ōlɛmē̆ la äxᵋā-
Ɫɛla lōⱢ, ᵋnēx·ᵋɛng·ē g·āxɛn. Wä, laɛm ts!ɛx·ᵋīd lāxēq.

47. ᵋyäk·aɛnk· mē̆xēs Lɛk·âsa.

15
Mē̆xɛlēg·as Lāg·ɛyōsᵋwŭⱡ g·āxᵋɛng·ɛ k!wāᵋs laɛng·ɛx Ɫ!āsanā̆-
ᵋyasɛn g·ōx̣ᵘᵋɛng·ä. Wä, laɛng·ē äxk·!āla qa ᵋwī̆ᵋlēsōx lāᵋstɛn
g·ōkŭlōtᵋɛng·ä lāxa waɛng·äɛn k·!ēs māⱡt!ēⱡa qaēda ᵋwālasⱢa ts!ɛ-
x·q!ōlɛmxwa hē̆ɛnxⱢɛx ᵋnēx·ᵋɛng·ē g·āxɛn qaxs hē̆ᵋmaē̆ k·!ēs k!ŭt!a-
20 Ɫɛlatsa ts!ɛx·q!ōlɛma lāⱢa laᵋstaⱡ lāxa wa ᵋnēx·ᵋɛng·ē g·āxɛn.
Wä, laᵋmɛn ts!ɛx·ᵋīd lāxēq qɛn lä laᵋsta lāxwa wāx.

48. Aɛnk·aɛnk· mē̆xēs K·!ēdēⱡɛm.

Mē̆xɛlēg·asa g·āxᵋɛng·ä dōqwa g·āxᵋɛng·ɛnⱢɛn ōmpᵋwŭⱡa. La-
ɛng·ē Ɫē̱xsᵋāla g·āxᵋɛng·ɛn qɛn k·!ēsē̆ xɛnⱢɛla nōⱡaⱡts!ɛm qaɛng·ēda
25 hē̆ⱡēeng·ä g·āxᵋɛng·ɛn qaᵋs dādaalē̆ g·āxᵋɛng·ɛn qaᵋs ē̆qaɛng·ē g·ā-
xᵋɛng·ɛn qaɛng·ɛn ⱡɛᵋlē̆. Wä, hē̆ɛng·aᵋmēs wā̆ᵋlē̆ wā̆ⱡdɛmᵋɛng·äsē̆
g·āxᵋɛng·ɛnⱢaxg·īn. Läk· ts!ɛx·ᵋīda.

49. Mē̆xēs ᵋmā̱x̣walag·flis.

Hē̆ɛng·ēk· q!ɛlsalē̆ äxās Dals. Wä, laɛng·ē q!ēnɛma ā̆ⱡogŭᵋla
30 sēsak·ɛlēs hānamā̆la laɛng·ɛxɛn ᵋwāx·sēⱢaᵋyēxɛn k·!ēsa maⱡt!ēⱡᵋ-
ɛng·a. Wä, laɛng·ɛn maⱡt!ēg·aaⱢɛlaɛng·ɛx ᵋnɛmōgwisxa Nāk!wax·-

46. Dream of ᵋmāxŭlag·îlis.

I dreamed of many men who were sitting in a house. I entered
but I was not welcome to the chief who was very angry against me.
Then I was addressed by another man who said to me: "We are the
diseases, every one of us men who are assembled here, and we are
discussing where we shall go next summer. Now go out!" said the man
to me. When I was about to go out of the door of the large house
the man who had talked to me came and pinched me with his right
hand in my right side, saying, "You are going to die of the sickness which has taken hold of you now." And then I awoke.

47. Bad Dream of Lɛk·âsa.

I dreamed that the late Lāg·ɛyŏs came and ʒat down on the floor
of my house and he asked my whole tribe to go into the water of a
river which I did not know, on account of a great epidemic which
was to come this summer. Thus he said to me, and those would not be
infected in the epidemic who would go into the river. Thus he said
to me. Then I awoke. Then I went into the water of this river.

48. Good dream of K·!ēdēꞎɛm.

I dreamed I saw my late father who advised me not to be care-
less and to behave well and that he was going to " take something"[1]
on account of witchcraft practised against me in order to kill me.
That was the end of his speech to me and I awoke.

49. Dream of ᵋmāxwalag·îlis.

In my dream I was at anchor at Dals. There were many canoes

---

[1]When a person is bewitched by bringing into contact some ex-
cretion of his body with some part of a human skeleton, the witchcraft my be counteracted by " taking" some analogous material and
repeating the action of witchcraft.

daᵉxᵘ. Hёɛng·aɛm mak·āⁱē sak·ɛlisas laɛng·ɛxɛn hānwälasē. Wä,

laɛng·axaē maⁱt!ēg·aaʟɛla g·āxᵉɛng·ɛn. Wä, la'ɛng·ō ᵉnēk·a: ᵉya,

nɛgŭmp, wäg·iⁱla yāʟ!ᑱʟɛx qaōxda hängēʟēsɛᵉwaqɛns. Yŭɛm hayaⁱi-

lagasʟōx yōx gwɛᵉyâsa q!ŭlsq!ŭlyaxᵘdäɛns Wīnalag·ⁱlisa, ᵉnēxᵉɛn-

5   g·ɛxs laē dɛnx·ᵉīdaᵉɛng·ɛxēs q!ɛltsɛmē. Wä, wīsomālaɛng·ɛt!ē wī-

xɛlisē q!ɛltsɛmasēxs laē ts!āx·ᵉīdaɛng·ēda dɛmɵx·ē. Wä, laɛng·a-

ᵉmē q!ɛkwaɛng·ēda äwᑱsgɛmē gɛlaᵉya. Wä, laɛng·aᵉmɛn ʟ̣ōᵉ ᵉnɛmō-

gwisē āʟēᵉsta qɛnuᵉxᵘ lē lāxa g·ōkwē laɛng·ɛx Dals. Wä, āⁱᵉɛng·-

aᵉmēsa hayaⁱilagas g·āxᵉɛng·ɛ sēxᵉwīd qaᵉs g·āxē mɛxāʟē laɛng·ɛxɛ-

10   nuᵉxᵘ ʟ!āsaᵉyaxg·anuᵉxᵘ läk· ᵉwīᵉlōⁱtᑱ laɛng·ɛxɛnuᵉxᵘ yaᵉyats!ē

sēsak·ɛlisa. Wä, laᵉmɛn ts!ɛx·ᵉīd lāxēq.

Lɛn ōtstō mēxᵉida, g·āxᵉɛng·aasa bɛgwanɛm g·āxᵉɛng·ɛn. Wä,

laɛng·ē nᵉēk·a: Laɛms hēⁱaxaxs laēx hālabala āʟēᵉsta qaxs lɛᵉmaē

xwānaⁱɛlēda hayaⁱilagas qaᵉs dāg·ⁱlayōdē lax·daᵉxōʟ, ᵉnēx·ᵉɛng·ē

15   g·āxᵉɛng·ɛn. Wä, laᵉmɛn ts!ɛx·ᵉīd lāxēq.

50. Mēxēs Lɛk·âsa.

Mēxɛlēg·a laɛng·ɛ hānaʟ!axa mēgwatē laɛng·ɛx X̱wēgats!ē. Wä,

laɛng·ɛn lāg·aāla lāxōx āⁱanᑱᵉyaxs laɛng·ɛn lᑱⁱtᑱ laɛng·ɛxɛn yāᵉ-

yats!ē xwᑱx̱wagŭma qɛn mōgwanōdēq. Wä, laɛng·ɛn qāsᵉida qɛn laɛng·ē

20   lāxa ʟ!āsanᑱᵉyas X̱wēgats!ē. Wä, laɛng·ɛn dōxᵉwaʟɛlaxa maᵉⁱtsɛmē

äwᑱ mēgwat g·ɛᵉyaɛng·ɛ lāxa k!wäsē. Wä, laɛng·ɛn hānaʟ!aq. Wä,

lɛn dōxᵉwaʟɛlaɛng·ɛqēxs sēsɛᵉyats!âxa g·ⁱlsg·ⁱlt!a sɛᵉya laɛng·ɛx

x·ix·ōmsas. Wä, laɛng·ē bēbɛgwänɛmgɛmē g̱ōgŭmaᵉyas. Wä, laɛng·a-

ᵉmɛn q!âⁱᵉaʟɛlaɛng·ɛqēxs hēᵉmaē ʟ̣ēgadɛs bɛgwīs. Wä, laɛng·ɛn k·î-

25   ⁱɛla hänⁱᵉīdɛq. Wä,g·āxᵉɛng·ɛn bᑱs, qäɛng·ɛnʟaxg·în k·ⁱⁱᵉīdē-

g·as. Wä, lɛn wēg·aa laɛng·ɛxɛn xwᑱx̱wagŭmaxg·în läk· ts!ɛx·ᵉīda.

51. Mēxēs Ōmx·idē.

Mēxɛlēg·a laɛng·ɛ qāsa ʟ̣ōᵉɛng·ɛn ᵉnɛmōkwē Y̱āxʟɛn. Wä, la-

ɛng·ɛnuᵉxᵘ lāx·sᑱ lāxa t!ɛx·sᑱlaxa wädzō k·!ōk!ŭsxa k·!ēsē dōgŭ-

30   ⁱas ōgwäxtᑱᵉyē laɛng·ɛxa ёk·!ē. Wä, g·ⁱlᵉɛng·aᵉmēsɛnuᵉxᵘ lāx·sᑱ-

xg·anuᵉxᵘ laɛng·ēk· dōxᵉwaʟɛlax ᵉgɛnɛmᵉōⁱas Y̱āxʟɛn,yîɛng·ɛx ʟ!ā-

on both sides on the water and they were not known to me. Then I
discovered in his canoe close to me at the place where I was at
anchor ᵉnɛmōgwis, the Nāk!wax·daᵉxᵘ. He said, " Oh, son-in-law,
take care, for these who are at anchor here are the spirits who are
referred to by the people of ancient times as War-spirits," thus
he said to me and hauled in his anchor. Before he had pulled up
his anchor a strong tide began to run. Big waves were breaking.
Then I and ᵉnɛmōgwis went ashore and to the house in Dals. Then
the spirits came along paddling and stopped on the water near the
place where we had gotten out of our canoes. After that I awoke.

Then I went to sleep again and a man came and said, "You did
well to go ashore quickly for the spirits were ready to take you,"
thus he said to me. Then I awoke.

5o. Dream of Lɛk·âsa.

I dreamed I had gone sealing on X̣wēgats!ē. I arrived at the
point lying towards the mouth and stepped out of my small travelling canoe in order to place the anchor line on shore. Then I went
to the sea side of X̣wēgats!ē. There I saw two large seals lying
on a seal-rock and I was about to shoot them. Then I saw that
their heads had long hair and they had human faces. I discovered
that they were what is called Sea-men. Then I was afraid to shoot
them. I went away from them. Now I was afraid of them. I had
not arrived at my small travelling canoe when I awoke.

51. Dream of Ōmx·ïd.

I dreamed I was taking a walk with my friend Yāxɛn. We were
passing through a door in a wide wall which was standing on the
ground. Its upper end was invisible. As soon as we had passed
through I saw the late wife of Yāxɛn, ʟ!ālēx̣ïlayugwa. Then I saw

3*

lêɫꞮlayugwôɫē. Wä, laɛng·anuᴇxᵘ dôxᶜwaʟɛlaɛng·ᴇqēxs hᵛᶜmaaxōʟ
g·ōxᵘᶜɛng·ᴇsa lēslâlēnoxwē. Wä, laɛng·ē ʟ!âlēɫꞮlayugwôɫ ʟēᶜlâ-
laxēs ɫâᶜwûnᴇmē Yāxʟᴇn qa läs lāqēxs kŭᶜlꞮlasᶜᴇng·ē. Wä, laɛng·-
aᶜmēsᴇn ᶜnᴇmōkwē Yāxʟᴇn qaᶜs laɛng·ē kŭlg·aᶜlꞮɫ lāq. Wä, âɛng·a-

5 ᶜmēsᴇn la ʟaᶜwꞮɫa x·Ɪts!ax·fꞮlaɛng·ᴇqēxs laē amaɫâlaɛng·a. Wä, la-
ɛng·ē ʟ!âlēɫꞮlayugwa äxk·!âlaɛng·ᴇ g·āxᴇn qᴇn g·āxē näᶜnakwa qaxs
laᶜmēk· xᴇk·!ag·în ɫâᶜwûnᴇmk·, ᶜnēx·ᶜᴇng·ē. Wä, laᶜmᴇn ts!ᴇx·ᶜꞮda.

52. Mēxēs Tsōp!alē.

Laɛng·ēk· qāsa laɛng·ᴇxwa āʟ!äsa k·!ēsᶜᴇng·äᴇn maɫt!ēɫ äᶜwꞮ-

10 nagwisa. Wä, laɛng·ᴇn dôxᶜwaʟɛlaxa g·ōkŭlä lāx ōxᵘsidzaᶜyasa nᴇ-
g·äɛng·ä. Wä, laɛng·ᴇn laēʟ laɛng·ᴇxa g·ōkwē. Wä, laɛng·ē k·!eâs
k!waꞮɫ lāq. Wä, laɛng·ᴇn dôdᴇqwalꞮɫɛla lāx äᶜwꞮᶜstalꞮɫas. Wä,
laɛng·ᴇn dōqŭlaxa xāɫxᴇqasa bᴇgwānᴇmē q!ēnᴇm äxᴇmts!âxa xēxᴇtsᴇmē.
Wä, laɛng·ᴇn âlak·!âla la ts!ᴇndᴇk·asē. Wä, laᶜmᴇn ts!ᴇx·ᶜꞮd lā-

15 xēq.

53. Mēxēs K·!ēdēɫᴇmaᶜyē.

G·āxᶜᴇng·aēda hayaɫꞮlagasᶜᴇng·ä q!ēnᴇm dāɛng·ᴇxwa g·Ɪgᴇma-
ᶜyōx ᶜmâxwax. Wä, laɛng·ōx q!ᴇmsa lā lāq. Wä, âᶜmēsōx laɛng·ᴇ
boyâ. Wä, laɛng·aᶜmē dāg·flxʟalēda hayaɫꞮlagasaxa bābagŭmaxs laa

20 bâɛng·a. Wä, laɛng·aᶜmᴇns g·kŭlōtēx q!äk·aɛng·ᴇxa hayaɫꞮlagasaxs
laa dāg·flxʟâlaɛng·ᴇxa bābagŭma. Wä, laɛng·ē k·!ēs q!āsᴇᶜwa. Wä,
laᶜmᴇn ts!ᴇx·ᶜꞮd lāxēq.

54. Mēxēs Wâk·as.

(Koskimo)

25   Mēxaēk· lāx·st!aaxᵘ lak·ast!aaxᵘ g·Ɪg·flisᴇla lāk·asᴇx Mādē.
Lāx·st!aaxᵘᶜwŭn dôxᶜwaʟak·ast!aaxᵘxē q!emâlax·st!aaxwa bēbᴇkumâla
ʟōᶜk·asē ts!ēts!ᴇdaxx·st!aaxwa laōstaalax·st!aaxᵘk·as lak·asᴇx
was Mādē. Lāk·ast!aaxwa aʟʟēx·st!aaxᵘ dôxwaʟak·ast!aaxᵘ g·āxk·a-
sᴇn. Wä, lāx·st!aaxwē dōt!ᴇg·aᶜɫk·ast!aaxᵘ g·āxk·asᴇn. Wä, la-

30 x·st!aaxwē ᶜnēx·a: Gwak·asla g·āx g·ēqᴇlsa lak·asxō t!ᴇx·äxs Ha-
yaɫilagas. Hēk·asᶜᴇmxat! HayaɫꞮlagaskꞏasa lak·as laōstala lak·as-

that this was the house of the ghosts. ʟ!ālēⱡīlayugwa called her
husband Yāxʟɛn to come to her and to lie down. Then my friend
Yāxʟɛn went and lay down with her. I was left standing and saw
how they were playing together. Then ʟ!ālēⱡīlayugwa asked me to
go home, "for my husband is going to stay away,"thus she said.
Then I awoke.

52. Dream of Tsōp!alē.

In my dream I went inland to a place which I did not know.
I saw a house at the foot of a mountain. I entered the house. I
did not sit down on the floor. I looked about in the house. Then
I saw human bones, many in boxes. I was frightened. Then I a-

53. Dream of K·!ēdēⱡɛm.

In my dream many spirits came to get chief ᵋmāxwa. He, however, did not want to go along. Then he was left by them. When
the spirits went away they took along a boy. Then our tribe discovered that the spirits had taken along a boy. He was not found.
Then I awoke.

54. Dream of Wāk·as.
(Koskimo)

I dreamed I was walking along the river of Mādē. There I
saw many men walking about and also women. They were going up the
river of Mādē. The last one (of these people) saw me and spoke
to me. He said, "Do not walk on the ground that belongs to these
spirits who are walking along this river, and they intend to bathe
in this river." Thus the man spoke to me. Then I awoke.

xē·wa lak·asʟaxaȫx g·ĭg·fⱡtālak·asʟa lak·asxō wak·asēx, ᵋnēx·-
st!aaxwa bɛkumālax·staaxwē g·āxk·asɛn. Wä, lak·asmɛn ts!ak·!ɛ-
xᵋĭda.

55. Mēxēs Ǥayōʟɛlas.

5 ʟōᵋmɛn k·fⱡᵋĭdaɛng·ɛsɛn mēxaᵋyax ǥānoʟē, yîxg·în mēxɛlēk· sē-
xᵋwidaɛng·a ʟāsgɛmēx X̱wēgats!ē. Wä, laɛng·ɛn ɛlāq lāg·aala. La-
ɛng·aasa dɛmsx·ē ts!äᵋlälaɛng·a. Wä, laɛng·ɛn âlax·it sēxᵋwida.
K·!ēts!ɛmᵋɛng·aᵋmēsɛn lālax·ʟālaxa ts!āla. Wä, laɛng·aᵋmɛn ʟāsgɛmēx X̱wēgats!ē. Wä, âx·st!aakᵘᵋɛng·aᵋmē X̱wēgats!ē la ʟāgŭt!āⱡa
10 g·āxɛn. Wä, laɛng·aᵋmē g·āx q!ēnɛma ts!ēk!wē. Wä, laɛng·ɛn q!â-
ⱡᵋaʟɛlaqēxs qwāx̱ŭʟaᵋyaēda ᵋyāg·îmas X̱wēgats!ē. Wä, laɛng·ɛn âla
k·fⱡᵋĭtsē. Wä, laᵋmɛn gwēx·ᵋĭtsōᵋsɛn gɛnɛmē lāxēq.

56. Mēxēs K!wāmaxālas.

Laɛng·ēk· dzādzōts!axa dzâlē laɛng·ɛxwa ʟ!ɛmāisēx. Wä, la-
15 ɛng·ɛn lāg·aa lāxa Dzōdzadē. Wä, laɛng·aᵋmēsɛn dzādzōts!ɛx·ᵋĭda.
Wä, hēɛng·aᵋmēs āⱡɛs mōsgɛmᵋɛng·ɛn dzādzōts!ānɛmaxs laɛng·aē p!ɛ-
lxᵋĭdaxa âlä gɛnk·aɛng·a. Wä, laɛng·ē g·āxa âlä ëx·sōkᵘ bɛgwā-
nɛmᵋɛng·a. Wä, laɛng·ē yāq!ɛg·aᵋⱡa. Wä, laɛng·ē ᵋnēk·a: Ǥēla
K!wāmaxālas qɛns lä lāxa q!ēq!ädäxa dzâlē, ᵋnēx·ᵋɛng·ē g·āxɛn.
20 Wä, hēx·ᵋĭdaɛng·aᵋmēsɛn laɛng·ɛ lāsgɛmēq. Wä, laɛng·ɛn k!ēs maⱡt!älaxa bɛgwānɛmᵋɛng·ä. Wä, laɛng·ɛn k!ēs dōqŭlaxɛnuᵋxᵘ lālaä
qaxs âlaɛng·aē la gɛnk·aɛng·ēda p!ɛlxɛla. Wä, laɛng·anuᵋxᵘ hō-
gwĬʟ laɛng·ɛxa ᵋwālasᵋɛng·ä g·ōkwa. Wä, laɛng·ē ᵋnēk·ēda bɛgwā-
nɛmᵋɛng·ä: Yūᵋmɛn g·ōkwōx. Nōgwaɛm ʟ!āgwag·ila ʟɛwŭlgāmēs Q!ōmo-
25 gwē. Wä, laᵋmēsɛn gɛg·adʟōs K!wāmaxālas qa lālag·iⱡtsa k·!ēx·-
k·!adzɛkwaxs ʟēʟām lāx âsa, ᵋnēx·ᵋɛng·ē ʟ!āqwag·ila g·āxᵋɛng·în.
Wä, laɛng·aᵋmēsɛn ëx·ak·ᵋɛng·ɛx wāⱡdɛmas. Wä, laɛng·ɛn ⱡāᵋwadɛs
ʟ!āqwag·ila. Wä, laɛng·aᵋmē ʟōma aëk·ila g·āxᵋɛng·ɛn. Wä, lä
ᵋnēx·ᵋɛng·ē ʟ!āqwag·ila g·āxᵋɛng·ɛn: Wäg·iⱡla ᵋyāʟ!âʟɛx qaxs lɛ-
30 ᵋmaēx xɛk·!āⱡ g·āxɛn. Wä,hēᵋmēsɛn ts!ɛx·ᵋĭdg·iⱡē.

55. Dream of Gayōlɛlas

In my dream I was much afraid last night when I dreamed I was out paddling and steered towards X̣wēgats!ē. I had almost arrived there when a strong tide began to run. Then I paddlẹd hard but I could not make any headway against the tide. I was steering towards X̣wēgats!ē, but it was as though X̣wēgats!ē was pushing me away. Then many gulls came. Now I knew that the sea monster of X̣wēgats!ē was about to come up. Then I was very much afraid. Then I was awakened by my wife.[1]

56. Dream of K!wāmaxālas.

In my dream I was walking along the beach to get cockles. Then I came to Dzōdzad looking for cockles. When I had found four cockles a thick fog came up. Then a very beautiful man came. He spoke and said, " Come, K!wāmaxalas, let us go where there are many cockles," thus he said to me. I followed him at once. I did not know the man, and I did not see where we were going, because the fog was very thick. Then we entered a large house, and the man said, " This is my house. I am ʟ!āqwag·ila, the prince of Q!ōmogwa. Now I shall have you for my wife, K!wāmaxālas, and these carved posts I shall give to your father," thus said ʟ!ā-qwag·ila to me. I agreed to his words and I had ʟ!āqwag·ila for my husband. He was very kind to me. ʟ!āgwag·ila said to me, "Now take care. You are going to stay with me all the time." And so I awoke.

---

[1]This dream signifies that a relative of the dreamer is going to drown.

57. Mᴇ̄xē.

Mᴇ̄xɛlēg·a qāqᴇsuls ʟᴇᶜwa ᶜwālasᶜᴇng·ä g·îla lāx Dzāwadē. Hë-
ᴇng·ēg·a g·ōкǔlē. Wä, laᴇng·aᶜmēsᴇn hanāʟ!aq laᴇng·aasē ʟạ̄xᶜwᴇl-
saᴇng·a qaᶜs yāq!ᴇg·aᶜɫē g·äxᶜᴇng·ᴇn. Laᴇng·ē ᶜnēk·a: Gwala xǔ-
5   nōkᵘ. Nōğwaᴇms ōmpᶜwǔɫōs g·ayala lāxg·în lāx· gwēx·sdᴇma. Hāg·a
lāxg·ada ᶜnᴇldzēg·asa wax qaᶜs häōs hänɫᶜîdaasg·a g·îlag·as, ᶜnēx·-
ᶜᴇng·ēda ᶜwālas g·îla. Wä, laᴇng·ᴇn qās ᶜida; laᴇng·ᴇn dōxᶜwaʟᴇla-
ᴇng·ᴇxa q!ēnᴇmᶜᴇng·ä g·îla. Wä, laᴇng·ᴇn k·îɫᶜîts. Wä, laᴇng-
·aᶜmᴇn hëɫts!âsē. Wä, laᴇng·ᴇn dᴁlxǔla wāx·a laᴇng·ᴇxg·în laᶜ-
10   mēk· lāɫ näᶜnaxᵘᶜᴇng·ᴇ lāxᴇn g·ōxᵘᶜᴇng·ä. Wä, k·!ēsᶜᴇng·at!ᴇn
qwēsg·ilaᴇng·ᴇxg·în läg·a ēt!ēdaᴇng·ᴇ dōxᶜwaʟᴇlaxa q!ēmâläᴇng·ä
g·îla. Wä lāxᴇntᴇn âla k·îɫᶜîdaᴇng·ᴇs läg·iɫa ts!ᴇx·ᶜîdē.

58. Mᴇ̄xēs Häyosdēsᴇlasxa ʟ!āʟ!ayadzaᶜyē.

Hēᶜmaaxg·în kǔᶜlēɫēk· lāxᴇnuᶜxᵘ g·ōkwē lāx Dzāwadē ʟᴇᶜwǔn ɫā-
15   ᶜwǔnᴇmē Wäʟēdē, ᶜnēk·ē Häyosdēsᴇlas. Wä, laᴇm māɫmēxts!asēs mēxaᶜyē g·äxᴇn yîxs ʟ!āʟ!ayadzayaē Häyosdēsᴇlasē. Wä, lāxaē ʟ!āʟ!a-
yadzaᶜyē ɫāᶜwǔnᴇmasē Wäʟēdē. Wä, lä ᶜnēk·a:

Hēᶜmaaxg·ᴇnuᶜxᵘ k!ǔts!ᴇsᶜᴇng·ēk· lāx ʟ!āsanâᶜyaᴇng·äsᴇnuᶜxᵘ
gōkwaxa gaālaᴇng·ä ɩoᶜᴇng·ōx Wäʟēdēxxa dzādzᴇxwēlaᴇnxē. Wä, laᴇn-
20   g·anuᶜxᵘ wǔʟāx āʟᴇlaxa dᴇnxk·!âlaᴇng·ä lāxa ōxᶜsîwaᶜyas wäs Dzāwadē
g·äxᶜǔstālaᴇng·a. Wä gwāɫᴇlaᴇng·aᶜmēsēnuᶜxᵘ q!äg·ēx qayāsᶜᴇng·äsa
q!ᴇmdᴇmē dᴇnxᶜālaᶜyoᴇng·ᴇsa dᴇnxk·!āla. Wä, g·aᶜmēs qāyatsa q!ᴇm-
dᴇmasē g·ada yîx wǔʟᴇɫas Häyosdēsᴇlas ɩoᶜᴇng·ēs ɫāᶜwǔnᴇmē:

G·āg·axᶜa nōgwa laōʟaê̈ ɩōgwalaë̈s mēmᴇyōxwanaê̈ yōʟ ɩō-
25   gwalaë̈yahë̈k·asᶜo, haᶜyo, haᶜyo, haᶜyo.

G·āg·axᶜalë̈tk·asᶜohos ɩōgwalaë̈s mēmᴇyōxwanaë̈sg·aho
mämᴇnɫᴇyēs ɩōgwalaë̈s mēmᴇyoxwanaê̈.

Wä laᴇng·ē q!wēɫᶜēdēda dᴇnxᴇᶜlālaᴇng·ᴇx ʟ!āsamâᶜyas g·ōkwas
Häyosdēsᴇlas, laᴇng·aas Häyosdēsᴇlasē dōxᶜwaʟᴇlaxa ämäsgᴇmala ts!-
30   ᴇdāxᶜᴇng·a g·äx g·äx·ᶜîdaᴇng·ᴇ lāx dᴇnxk·!âlasdäsa dᴇnxᴇla q!ᴇ-
ɫᴇlaxa hëᴇng·ä gwēx·s āɫᶜᴇm mäyoʟᴇm g·înänᴇm qaᶜs laᴇng·ē q!ᴇɫk·!-

57. A Dream.

I dreamed I had gone out and met a large grizzly bear in
Knight Inlet. That is where I live. And so I shot at it, and it
stood up and spoke to me and said, "Do not do that, child. I am
your late father. I was killed by that which looks the way I
look now. Go up the river, and there is a place where you are
going to see grizzly bears." Thus said the large grizzly bear.
Then I went and in my dream I saw many grizzly bears. Then I was
afraid. I ran away from them intending to run home. I had not
gone very far when I saw many more grizzly bears walking about.
I woke up , evidently because I was very much afraid.

58. Dream of One of Twins.

"I was lying in our house in Knight Inlet with my husband,
Wäౖēd," said Häyosdēsɛlas. And then she told me her dream, for
Häyosdēsɛlas was one of twins, and her husband, Wäౖēd, was also
one of twins. She said:

"I dreamed that we were sitting on the floor of our house, I
and Wäౖēd, in the morning at the time when the olachen were running.
We heard the sound of a song at the mouth of the river of
Knight Inlet. It was coming up the river. Then we began to understand
the words of the song which was being sung." And these
are the words of the song heard by Häyosdēsɛlas and her husband:

> The treasure of the salmon is coming to you, the
> great treasure. Haᶜyo, haᶜyo, haᶜyo.
> Beautifully he is coming, the treasure of the salmon,
> this Mämɛnɬaᶜya of the salmon.

Then the singing in front of the house of Häyosdēsɛlas
stopped and in her dream Häyosdēsɛlas saw a small woman coming
from the place where the sound of the singing had been. In her
arms she carried something that was like a new born child, and

ɛlgɛntsa g·înānɛmē laɛng·ɛx Hǟyosdēsɛlas. Wä, laɛng·ē x·îsᵋîdē

da g·înānɛmē laɛng·ɛx tɛk·!äs Hǟyosdēsɛlas. Wä, laɛng·ɛ ᵋnēk·ē

Mɛyōxwaxsɛm laɛng·ɛx Hǟyosdēsɛlas: Laɛms ʟēxᵋēdʟɛs Māmɛnⱡaᵋyē

lāxōs ʟōgwaᵋyēx g·āxɛn, ᵋnēk·ēxs laē x·îsᵋîda. Wä, hëᵋmis la

5 g·äg·îʟɛlatsɛn gɛnɛmē la bɛwēxᵋwîtsōx wîsax, ᵋnēk·ē Wäʟēdē yîxs

laē māⱡmēxts!a qaɛn. Wä, laɛm lāba laxēq.

Wä, g·îlᵋmēsē hēⱡogwîla bɛwēkwē Hǟyosdēsɛlasē laē mayoⱡᵋîtsa

bābagumē. Wä, g·îlᵋmēsē ganuⱡᵋîda laē ēt!ēd mēxɛlasa ämäsgɛmala

Mɛyōxwaxsɛm·g·āxᵋɛng·ɛ k!wāg·alîⱡ lāxg·în hēⱡk·!ōdɛnōdzēlîⱡᵋɛng·-

10 äɛn. Wä, laɛng·ē q!ɛⱡɛlîⱡaxōx wîsax laɛng·ɛxōx Māmɛnⱡaᵋyēx. Wä,

laɛng·ē yāq!eg·aᵋⱡa. Wä, laɛng·ē ᵋnēk· g·āxᵋɛng·în: Laɛms ᵋyā-

ʟ!âʟōʟ qâst qag·as ʟōgwēx·dōxg·ōs ʟɛᵋwōs ⱡāᵋwŭnɛmēx. Wēg·a hēmɛ-

naⱡaɛm gōmsasa gŭgumᵋyîmē ʟɛᵋwōs ⱡāᵋwŭnɛmē, wä, g·aᵋmēsg·a Māmɛn-

ⱡaᵋyēk·. Wä, hēᵋmis qaᵋs ᵋnāxwaᵋmaōs ʟâʟanâᵋlōs x·ix·ōmsaxa ma-

15 ēmaⱡts!aqē ts!ɛlts!ɛlk·sa k·aᵋmäsa ts!ēg·inaga. Wä, lāʟē gwäᵋyîmē

k·!ātsɛmēʟas xaāp!aʟasōx. Wä, hēᵋmaa qasō k·!ēs nānagēg·ēʟxɛn wäⱡ-

dɛmē lōʟ lāxa ᵋnɛmx·ᵋîdāⱡa laᵋmēsɛn g·āx ētoxwaⱡxwa g·înānɛmēx,

ᵋnēx·ᵋɛng·ē g·āxɛn, ᵋnēk·ē Hǟyosdēsɛlax g·āxɛn laē māⱡmēxts!a.

Wä, laᵋmē xaapēlasēᵋwa qɛxɛyowē gwēx·sɛmala xaāp!a. Wä, lā-

20 xaē äxᵋētsēᵋwa ts!ɛlts!ɛlk·asa ts!ēg·inaga qa ʟâʟanɛwēs x·ix·ōmsas

Hǟyosdēsɛlasē ʟɛᵋwis ⱡāᵋwŭnɛmē Wäʟēdē. Wä, lä k·!eâs gwɛᵋyōʟasɛx

gŭgŭmᵋyîma. Wä, hēt!a la mōsgɛmēk·îlaxa ᵋmɛkŭlē xŭnōkwas Hǟyosdē-

sɛlasaxs g·āxaē Wäʟēdē yîx ⱡāᵋwŭnɛmas Hǟyosdēsɛlas lāxg·în g·ō-

kŭk·, wä, lä ᵋnēk·a: ᵋya qâst, yäk·aɛng·ɛnʟax ganōʟē qaōx wîsax.

25 Wä, laᵋmē māⱡmēxts!a qaɛn. Wä, lä ᵋnēk·a: G·āxᵋɛng·aa ᵋwîlx·wil-

g·ɛʟaᵋya mēmaᵋya mɛxamālis laɛng·ɛxōx Tsāxisax laɛng·aas ɛlāq ᵋnā-

x·ᵋîdɛx gaālax·dē. Wä, g·āxᵋɛng·ē gwɛᵋyâsɛn gɛnɛmē Mɛyōxwaxsɛm,

g·āxᵋɛng·ɛ g·āxēʟa laɛng·ɛxɛnuᵋxᵘ g·ōkwēx. Wä, laɛng·ē âlak·!āla

ⱡāwis g·āxɛnuᵋxᵘ ʟōᵋɛng·ɛn gɛnɛmōx Hǟyosdēsɛlasēx. Wä, laɛng·ē

30 ᵋnēk·a: G·āx·mɛnuᵋxᵘ dāxōx Māmɛnⱡayaᵋyēxlāxɛn wäⱡdɛmx·ᵋîdäōʟ Hǟ-

yosdēsɛlas qaᵋsō k·ʲ!ēs ᵋwîᵋla nānagēg·ēxɛn ʟēxsᵋalayu qaᵋs äxsɛᵋ-

she placed the child in the lap of Häyosdēsɛlas. Then the child disappeared in the body of Häyosdēsɛlas. Then the salmon woman said to Häyosdēsɛlas, "You will call this treasure which you received from me Māmɛnłaɛya," thus she said and disappeared. "From that time on my wife was pregnant with this child," said Wäꞁēd when he was telling me this dream. Now that is the end of this.

When Häyosdēsɛlas had been pregnant the right length of time she gave birth to a boy. As soon as night came she dreamed again. of the little salmon woman. "She came and sat down on the floor of the house at my right side. She was carrying this little child Māmɛnłaɛya in her arms and she spoke. She said to me, 'Now be careful, friend, of this your treasure, you and your husband. Always paint yourself with ochre, you and your husband, and also this Māmɛnłaɛya. And also put on the sides of the head two feathers of a gull, and the painting on the cradle shall be a whale. And furthermore, if you do not obey what I tell you, I am going to come and take back this child.' Thus she said to me in my dream," said Häyosdēsɛlas to me as she was telling me her dream.

Then a cradle with a notched head piece was made and gull feathers were placed on each side of the head of Häyosdēsɛlas and her husband Wäꞁēd. They were not able to get any ochre. Now the child of Häyosdēsɛlas was four months old. Then Wäꞁēd, the husband of Häyosdēsɛlas came into my house and said, "Oh friend, last night I had an evil dream relating to this child." And so he told me his dream. He said, "All kinds of salmon came to me in canoes here to Fort Rupert in the morning when day was dawning. Then she of whom my wife spoke, the salmon woman, came into my house. She was very angry with us, particularly with my wife Häyosdēsɛlas. She said, "We have come to take away Māmɛnłaɛya, according to what I told Häyosdēsɛlas, namely, if you did not follow all my instructions relating to the dress which Māmɛnłaɛya should wear (which I gave you

wōs qa q!wālax·ᴸtsōx MāmɛnⱢayaᵋyēx lāxōs, g·āxᵋēnaᵋyē lāx·daᵋxōʟ,
ᵋnēx·ᵋɛng·ē Mɛyōxwaxsɛmaxs laɛng·aē q!ɛⱢɛlỊⱢaxa g·înānɛmaxs laē lā-
wɛls lāxa t!ɛx·îla. Wä, laɛng·aᵋmē lāxsē Mɛyōxwaxsɛm lāxa āʟɛnxē-
ɛng·ä xwāk!üna. Wä, laɛng·ē ᵋwỊ� la sɛbɛʟaᵋya q!ēnɛmᵋɛng·ä xwāxwak!ü-
5 nasa mēmɛyōxwana.

Wä, hëx·ᵋidaᵋmēsɛn ts!āk·!îxᵋIda qɛn dōxᵋwỊdēx MāmɛnⱢayaᵋyē.
Wä, lɛn dōqŭlaqēxs kuᵋlēⱢᵋmaē. Wä, lɛn gwēx·ᵋidɛx Hāyosdēsɛlasē.
Wä, laᵋmēsɛn māⱢmexts!asɛn mēxaᵋyē. Wä, g·îlᵋmēsɛn ᵋwỊᵋla nēⱢasɛn
mēxaᵋyē lāq laas yāq!ɛg·aᵋⱢē Hāyosdēsɛlasē. Wä, lä ᵋnēk·a: GwāⱢɛ-
10 laᵋmēg·în k·îⱢāla qaxs gwāⱢɛlaᵋmaē ᵋnēk·a g·āxē taōtsōx MāmɛnⱢayaᵋyēx g·āxɛns yîxs ᵋnēk·aē Mɛyōxwaxsɛm g·āxɛn qaᵋsō k·!ēs ᵋwỊᵋla äxᵋ-
ēdɛⱢxɛn la ʟēʟɛqalasōᵋ qaᵋs äxsɛᵋwōs qa q!wāq!ülax·ʟɛnsōx MāmɛnⱢayaᵋyēx g·āxʟɛn xwēlaqaⱢ dāʟɛq ᵋnēk·aē. Wä, hēɛmxanawis ᵋnēᵋnak·ỊⱢts
Mɛyōxwaxsɛmē qaxg·îns hewäxēk· lāʟɛx gŭgŭmᵋyîma qaōx, ᵋnēk·ē.
15 Wä, yŭduxᵋp!ɛnxwaᵋsᵋmēs ᵋnālässa g·înānɛmaxs laē wỊk·!îxᵋēda.
Wä, g·āxᵋmēsɛn äxēlaxg·ada qɛxɛyōkᵘ gwēx·sɛmāla xaāp!a. Wä, laɛm
lāba laxēq.

59. Mēxēs Gaaxstālas.

Mēxɛlē g·āx gānoʟasa ᵋwỊᵋwŭlsgɛmakwa lēlqwälaⱢaᵋya g·āxᵋɛng·ɛ
20 ʟēⱢāᵋlamɛmᵋɛng·ɛsa g·îgāmēyōⱢaē Nɛg·ädzēyōⱢa. Wä, laɛng·ē yäwix·î-
laxa âlaɛng·a ëk·!ēqala ᵋnāxwaɛng·ēda bēbɛgwānɛmᵋɛng·ä ʟɛᵋwa ts!ē-
dāxᵋɛng·ä. Wä, laɛng·ɛn äxsōᵋ qɛn x·îsᵋIdē. Wä, laɛng·aᵋmēsɛn x·î-
sᵋIda. Wä, laɛng·ɛn dōqŭlaɛng·ɛxa ts!äqag·ilä naualakwa, yîxs laɛn-
g·aa p!ɛⱢᵋIda qaᵋs lä taōdaɛng·ɛn lāx g·ōkwasa ts!äqag·ilä naualakwa.
25 Wä, laɛng·aᵋmē q!aq!ōʟ!āmatsa tōxᵋwỊdē g·āxᵋɛng·ɛn ᵋnāxwä gwaᵋyîᵋ-
lälatsa tōxᵋwidē. Wä, laɛng·aᵋmē qɛx·ᵋId g·āxᵋɛng·ɛn qaᵋs lä läᵋ-
stalỊⱢɛlaɛng·ɛsg·în x·ōmsɛk· laɛng·ɛxa lɛqāwalỊⱢᵋɛng·äsa ᵋwālasᵋ-
ɛng·ä g·ōkwa. Wä, g·āxᵋɛng·ē xwēlaqa äxᵋāʟɛlōdaɛng·ɛsg·în x·ōm-
sɛk·. Wä, laᵋmɛn ts!ɛx·ᵋIda.

30

at the time) when he came to you.' Thus said the salmon woman, and
she took the child in her arms and went out of the door. Then the
salmon woman went aboard the canoe from the side of the canoe which
was towards the shore. Then the many canoes of the salmon went away.

"As soon as I awoke I looked at Māmɛnⱡaᶜya. I saw he was lying
in the house. Then I called Hāyosdēsɛlas and told her my dream. As
soon as I had told my dream to her Hāyosdēsɛlas spoke and said,
'Right from the beginning I was afraid on account of what she said
in the beginning when she brought Māmɛnⱡaᶜya to us. For the salmon
woman said "If you do not do everything I tell you, if any of these
is not taken for the dress of Māmɛnⱡaᶜya, I shall come back and
take him," as she said this. Now it seems the salmon woman means
that we never got ochre for him.'"

Three days after this the child died. I have got the notched
cradle with the painting of the whale. That is all.

59. Dream of Ḡaaxstālas.

I dreamed last night about all the tribes that had been invited
by the late chief Nɛg·ädzē. He gave a winter ceremonial and all the
men and women were very happy. Then I was taken and I was to disappear, and so I disappeared. Then I saw the supernatural beings,
the Givers of the Winter Ceremonial. They flew and took me to the
house of the magical powers, the Givers of the Winter Ceremonial.
That was the place where I was taught the war dance, all the ways
of the war dance. Then my head was cut off and I walked with my
head around the fire in the middle of a large house. Then my head
was put back. After that I awoke.

60. Mēxēs Q̣!walɛnts!ēsxa päxala.

Mēxɛlēg·a laɛng·ɛ lāxa ëk·!adzēlisasɛns ᵋnālax. Laɛng·ɛn qā̃-
saɛng·a. Wä, laɛng·ɛn dōxᵋwaʟɛlaxa g·ōkwa. Wä, laɛng·ɛn gwäᵋsta
laɛng·ɛxa g·ōkwē. Wä, k·!ēsᵋɛng·aᵋmēsɛn ëx·ᵋag·aaʟɛlaɛng·ɛ lāqēxs
5   g·āxᵋɛng·aēda âlä ëx·sōkᵘ ts!ɛdāxᵋɛng·a qaᵋs g·āxᵋɛng·ē qāqaᵋyāla-
ɛng·ɛ g·āxɛn. Wä, hëɛng·aᵋmēs g·îlᵋɛng·ɛ yāq!ɛg·aᵋɫa ts!ɛdāqē
g·āxᵋɛng·ɛn. Wä, laɛng·ē ᵋnēk·a: Gēlak·asᵋla ādä. Sōᵋmɛn gwe-
ᵋyō qɛn ɫāᵋwŭnɛms. Gēlag·a qɛns lä hōgwîʟa lāxg·a gō̃xᵘg·asg·în
ōmpa, ᵋnēx·ᵋɛng·ēda ts!ɛdāqē g·āxᵋɛng·în. Wä, laɛng·aᵋmēsɛnuᵋx̣ᵘ
10 hōgwîʟ laɛng·ɛxa âlä laɛng·ɛ ëx· g·ōkwa. Wä, laɛng·ēda ts!ɛdāqē
nēɫaxēs ōmpᵋɛng·äxs lɛᵋmaē ɫāᵋwadɛn. Wä, laɛng·ē âla ts!ɛnkwa la-
q!ŭlyox̣ᵋŭn bɛgwānɛms wāɫdɛmasēs xŭnōkwē. Wä, laɛng·aɛm k·!ēs
hēɫq!alēda bɛgwānɛmɛn gɛg·adɛs xŭnōkwas. Wä, laɛng·ɛᵋma bɛgwānɛmē ᵋnēx·ᵋɛng·ɛ qaᵋs k·!ēlax·ᵋîdē g·āxᵋɛng·ɛn. Wä, laɛng·ɛn âla
15 k·îɫᵋîtsē. Wä, hëɛmxanawēsɛn lāg·iɫa ts!ɛx·ᵋîdē.

Wä, lɛn ētstō mēxᵋida qaxa k·!ēsᵋmaē ëx·aɫa qaᵋs ᵋnāx·ᵋîdē.
Wä, g·āxxɛn mēxɛlasa ts!ɛdāqē ēt!ēda. Laɛng·ē ᵋnēk·a: Hāg·a laᵋsta lāxa wa qaᵋs hēɫaxēʟōsaxwa hëɛnxʟēx qaxs hëᵋmaē ax·iᵋlälaxɛns
ᵋnālāqɛn ōmpē, ᵋnēx·ᵋɛng·ēda ts!ɛdāqē g·āxᵋɛng·ɛn. Wä, hëx·ᵋida-
20 ɛng·aᵋmēsɛn la laᵋstaɛng·ɛ lāxa wä ōgŭᵋla lāxōx wäxs Tsāxis. Wä,
hëɛng·aᵋmēsɛn āɫē gwāɫ laᵋstaɛng·ɛ lāxa wäxg·în lēx· ts!ɛx·ᵋîda.

Wä, g·îlᵋmēsɛn ts!āk·!ɛxᵋîdɛxg·în läk· ḷāx̣ᵋŭlîɫ qɛn lä laᵋsta
lāxwa wäxs Tsāxis.

61. Mēxēs Lɛk·âsa.

25 Mēxɛlēg·a g·āxᵋɛng·ɛ ʟēᵋlālasōᵋsa bɛgwānɛma qɛnuᵋx̣ᵘ laɛng·ē
laɛng·ɛxa ëk·!adzēlisasɛns ᵋnāla. Wä, laɛng·ē dāx·ᵋidaɛng·ɛxg·în
hēɫk·!ōɫts!ānē aᵋyasō. Wä, laɛng·ē wîg·îlsa dāɫax·säxɛn aᵋyasōxs
läg·anuᵋx̣ᵘ nɛqostâla ëk·!ōɫela. Wä, laɛng·anuᵋx̣ᵘ lāx·sâ lāxa
t!ēx·îlä laɛng·ɛx nɛgɛdzâᵋyōs ëk·!adzēlisasɛns ᵋnālax. Wä, laɛn-
30 g·ēda bɛgwānɛmē ts!āts!ɛmx·silasa ᵋnāxwa äxäxîɫ ˈ⸌ ᵌɛxa g·ōkwa.
Wä, laɛng·ē ᵋnēx· qɛnuᵋx̣ᵘ lä qāsᵋida.Wä, laɛng·ɛnuᵋx̣ᵘ qāsᵋida.

60. Dream of the shaman Q!walɛnts!ēs.

I dreamed I had gone to the other side of our world the sky
I went up and saw a house. Then I approached the house. Before
I was close to it a very beautiful woman came up to me. Then the
woman spoke first to me. She said, "Thank you, lord. You are the
one to whom I refer as my husband. Come, let us go into into the
house of this,my father," thus the woman said to me. Then we
entered the beautiful house. Then the woman told her father that
she had me for her husband. He became very angry, the one who was
a very old man, on account of the speech of his daughter. The man
would not permit me to have his child as my wife. Then the man
said he was going to knock me down. Then I was very much afraid
of him. This was evidently the cause why I awoke.

Then I went to sleep again, for it was not yet near morning.
Then the dream about the woman came again. She said," Go into
the water in the river so that you may be successful this summer.
My father is the one who takes care of the world," thus she said
to me. Immediately I went into the water of the river, into this
river of Fort Rupert. After I finished bathing I woke up.

As soon as I began to be awake, I went into the water of this
river of Fort Rupert.

61. Dream of Lɛk·âs.

I dreamed I had been called by a man to go with him to the
upper side of our world the sky . He took my right hand.
Then he went up holding my hand while we were going straight up.
Then we passed through the door in the middle of the upper side of
our world. The man showed me everything that was in the house
there. Then he said to me that we should go on. We went along.
Then we came to the hole in the edge of the world. Then he said,

Wä, laᴇng·ᵋmē ᵋnēx· qaᵋs lä ts!äts!ᴇmx·silas kwax̣ūnxelisasᴇns ᵋnālax g·äxᵋᴇng·ᴇn. Wä, laᴇng·ᴇnuᵋx̣ᵘ lāg·aa laᴇng·ᴇxa kwax̣ūnxᴇlisasᴇns ᵋnālax laᴇng·aas ᵋnēk·a: Yūᴇm lālax·sâlatsa g·îng·înānᴇmaxs laē bᴇwēx̣ᵘᵋwidayōsēs abᴇmpʟē g·äx·îd lāx ĕk·!adzēlisasa ᵋnālax. Wä, hāg·a lāx·sōx qaᵋs laōs näᵋnakwa. Âᴇmʟᴇn g·iwalaʟōʟ qaᵋs k·!ēsaōs ƛāx̣ūmala lāxēs qats!ēnēᵋʟaōs, ᵋnēx·ᵋᴇng·ēda bᴇgwānᴇm g·äxᵋᴇng·ᴇn. Wä, g·äxᵋᴇng·ᴇn qāsᵋida. Wä, wēg·aat!ᴇnʟaxg·în läk· ts!ᴇx·ᵋîda.

62. Mēxēs ᵋmāx̣ūlag·îlis.

Laᴇng·ēk· p!āʟiᵋläla laᴇng·ᴇxa ĕk·!ē. Hĕᴇng·ᴇ g̣wēx·s lāladzolits!a ăxāsasa t!ōt!ō yîxs nēƛāƛaᴇng·aᵋmaēda t!ōt!oxa ᵋnāla. Wä, laᴇng·ᴇn ᵋnāx̣wa dōqūlaxōx ăᵋwîᵋstaᴇng·äxsᴇns ᵋnālax. Wä, laᴇng·ᴇn wāx· ᵋnēx· qᴇn g·äxᵋᴇng·ē banēᵋsta. Wä, laᴇng·ᴇn k·!eâs g̣wēx·ᵋidaasᵋᴇng·a. Wä, laᴇng·ᴇn âlak·!āla k·îƛᵋîda. Wä, laᵋmᴇn ts!ᴇx·ᵋîd laxēq.

63. Mēxēs ᵋnāx·nag·ᴇm.

Mēxᴇlēg·a laᴇng·ᴇ lāxa g·ōkwasa mäēsila laᴇng·ᴇx ʟ!äsōdēsasens ᵋnālax. Wä, laᴇng·ᴇn k·!ēs q!âʟᴇlaxᴇn lāg·iƛᵋᴇng·ä lāq. Wä, laᴇng·ᴇn dōqūlaᴇng·ᴇxᴇn ōmpᵋwūƛa lāq. Wä, laᴇng·ē ᵋyāk·!āla g·äxᵋᴇng·ᴇnʟaxg·în läk· lāx ăxāsᵋᴇng·äᵋs. Wä, laᴇng·ē ăxk·!āla g·äxᵋᴇngᴇn qᴇn g·äxē näᵋnakwa. Wä, laᴇng·ᴇn mᴇlx̣ᵋwaʟᴇlaqēxs g̣ᴇyōƛaōƛa ƛᴇᵋlᴇn ōmpᵋwūƛa. Wä, g·äxᵋᴇng·ᴇn näᵋnakwa. Wä, laᵋmᴇn ts!ᴇx·ᵋîda lāxēq.

64. Mēxēs Gwāgwadaxᴇla.

Mēxᴇlēg·a layōᴇng·ᴇ lāxa qwēsalä ăᵋwînagwisa yîᴇng·asa bᴇgwānᴇmaᴇn k·!ēsᵋᴇng·ᴇ maƛt!ēƛa. Wä, laᴇng·aᵋmᴇnuᵋx̣ᵘ yāyasᴇlaxa ōgūqāƛä x̣wāk!ūna. Wä, laᴇng·ᴇn ᵋnēnk·!ēxᵋîd qᴇn wūʟäxa bᴇgwānᴇmᵋᴇng·ä lāx g·ayoᵋlasᵋᴇng·äs. Wä, laᴇng·ē yāq!ᴇg·aᵋƛa. Wä, laᴇng·ē ᵋnēk·a: Q!âʟᴇlaᵋmᴇnʟaxs ᵋnēnk·!ēgaᵋyaq!ōs yîxs ᵋnēk·aaqōs wūʟaōs lāxᴇn g·ayōᵋlasa. Wä, laᵋmēsᴇn nēƛaʟōʟ. Nōgwaᴇm māƛp!ᴇnatosaxa ᵋwālasē t!ōt!ōxēs dōg̣ūƛōᵋsaxa dzāqwa, ᵋnēx·ᵋᴇng·ēda bᴇgwānᴇmē. Wä, laᴇng·ᴇn âla k·îƛᵋîts wāƛdᴇmas. Wä, laᵋmᴇn ts!ᴇx·ᵋîda lᴇn ētstō mēxᵋîda.

"Through this (hole) pass the children when they are born, when they come from the upper side of the world. Now pass through it and go home. I am going to help you that it may not be hard for you to pass through." Then I went on, but before I arrived I awoke.

62. Dream of ᵋmāx̣ūlag·īlis.

In my dream I flew upwards. It was as though I was going to the place where the stars are, for the stars were showing in the daytime. I saw all around our world. Then I wished in vain to go down again. I was not able to do so. I was very much afraid. Then I awoke.

63. Dream of ᵋnāx·nag·ᴇm.

I dreamed I was going to the house of the Master of the Salmon on the sea side of our world. I do not know why I was going there. There I saw my late father. Then he scolded me because I had gone to the place where he was. He asked me to·go back home. Then I remembered that my late father had died long ago. Then I went home. Then I awoke.

64. Dream of Gwāgwadaxᴇla.

I dreamed I had been taken by a man unknown to me to a distant place. We were travelling in a strange looking canoe. I thought I would ask the man where he came from. Then he spoke to me and said, "I know your thoughts. You wish to ask me where I come from. I will tell you. I am the great star which goes down twice and which you see in the evening," said the man. Then I was afraid on account of his speech. I awoke and I went to sleep again.

65. ᵋyäk·aɛng·ɛ mēxēs G̱aaxstālas.

Laɛng·a laɛng·ɛxwa āʟ!ēx sɛnqaxa dɛᵋnas ʟ̣ōᵋɛng·ɛn ɫāᵋwŭnɛmōɫ-
ɫē ʟɛlēlɛwēk·ᵋwŭɫē. Wä, g·îlᵋɛng·aᵋmēsɛnuᵋx̣u āʟɛg·ila laɛng·aɛn
ɫāᵋwŭnɛmōɫē ʟɛlēlɛwēk·ᵋwŭɫē äxk·!ālaɛng·ɛ g·āxᵋɛng·ɛn qɛnuᵋx̣u
5 k!ŭsᵋɛlsē. Wä, laɛng·anuᵋx̣u k!ŭsᵋɛlsa. Wä, laɛng·aᵋmɛn mɛlxᵋwa-
ʟɛlaqēxs g̱ɛyōɫaōɫ ɫɛᵋla. Wä, laɛng·ē ᵋnēk·a: ᵋya, adä, ʟōmaᵋ-
mɛn q!ayaqɛlōs. Wä, lɛn âlak·!āla ɫɛng·as qaᵋs, q!āgwidä. Wä,
lâg·anɛms k·!ēs âʟat!a g·îg·aēxᵋēdaēnoxu g·āxɛnʟaxs laēx ɫāᵋwadɛ-
sōx Nōɫbaᵋyax. Wä, laᵋmēsɛn lāɫ lats!âɫ lāxs bâts!âq!ōs qɛn âba-
10 yadaōs, ᵋnēk·ēxs laē x·îsᵋida. Wä, laɛng·ɛn qâsᵋida qɛn lāɛng·ē
lāxa wîg·ɛxɛkŭla qɛn sɛnxᵋēdē laɛng·ɛxa ēx·p!ēqala dzɛsɛqwa. Wä,
laɛng·ē q!ēnɛmᵋɛng·ɛn sɛngānɛmē dɛᵋnasa. Wä, laɛng·ɛn yîɫtsɛmdɛq
qɛn ōxʟɛx·ᵋîdēq. Wä, g·āxᵋɛng·ɛn nä̈ᵋnakwa laɛng·ɛxɛnuᵋx̣u g·ōkwēx.
Wä, hēx·ᵋidaɛng·aᵋmēsɛn ts!ɛk·!âɫɛlaɛng·ɛxɛn ɫāᵋwŭnɛmēx. Wä, laɛn-
15 g·aᵋmē bābalɛn ɫāᵋwŭnɛmaxa g̱ɛyōɫᵋwŭɫa ɫɛᵋla. Wä, laɛng·aᵋmē ᵋnēk-
k·ɛn ɫāᵋwŭnɛmē qaᵋs k·!ēlax·ᵋîdē g·āxᵋɛng·ɛn. Wä, laɛng·ɛn âlax·-
ᵋîd k·îɫᵋîts lāg·iɫa ts!ɛx·ᵋîdē lāxēq.

66. Mēxēs K·!āsōgwiᵋlakᵘ.

Mēxɛlēg·aqē g·āxᵋɛng·ōxda ᵋmɛkŭlax laɛng·ɛxwa baᵋnēx ä̈ᵋwîna-
20 gwisa. Wä, g·îlᵋɛng·aᵋmēsē g·āxᵋɛlsᵋɛng·a g·āxaasa bɛgwānɛma g·ā-
xɛwŭlsᵋɛng·a lāx t!ɛnâᵋyasa ᵋmɛkŭla. Wä, laɛng·ē ʟɛxsᵋālaxwa
Kwāg·uɫēx qa k·!ēsēsōx ʟ!ēʟ!ɛsap!a ʟ̣ōᵋ qa k·!ēsēsōx g·ālōʟap!ax
dādɛk·asasēs bɛx̣ŭtē ʟ̣ōᵋ qa k·!ēsēsōx ɫēmɛmax g̱ɛnɛmasēs bɛx̣ŭtē.
Hēᵋmis qa hēmɛnaɫaᵋmēsōx ts!ɛlwaqaxa bɛkwēlēnokwaɛns qa wāxēsē
25 g·îwala lax·daᵋxōʟ, ᵋnēx·ᵋɛng·ēda bɛgwānɛmaṣa ᵋmɛkŭla. Wä, laᵋmɛn ts!ɛx·ᵋîda.

67. Mēxēs Mɛlēdē.

Mēxɛlēk· laɛng·ɛ lāxa ēk·!â ä̈ᵋwînagwisaxa âlaɛng·ä̈ ēk·a.
Laɛng·ɛn dōqŭlaxa q!ēnɛmᵋɛng·äxa ᵋnāxwax·st!aaxuᵋma ts!ēdāq.
Wä, g·āxᵋɛng·ēda ᵋnɛmōkwē lāq qaᵋs yāyaq!ɛntēᵋmē g·āxᵋɛng·ɛn.
Wä, laɛng·aᵋmē ʟɛxsᵋāla g·āxᵋɛng·ɛn qɛn gwāɫlag·i ʟɛlk!wāla qax-

65. Bad Dream of Ġaaxstālas.

In my dream I went into the woods to peel cedar bark, together with my late husband Lɛlēlɛwēk·. We were going inland. Then my late husband asked me to lie down with him. Then we lay down. Then it occurred to me that he had died long ago. Then he said, "Oh mistress, I am in great trouble for your sake. I long for you very much, mistress. You do not think of me at all since you have Nōⱡbēᵋ for your husband. So I am going to enter your womb that you may become my mother," thus he said and disappeared. Then in my dream I went to a cedar grove and peeled a good many cedar trees. I had a great deal of cedar bark which I had peeled. Then I tied it up and put it on my back. In my dream I came to my house and in my dream I told my husband. Then my husband became jealous on account of the one who had died long ago. In my dream my husband said he would beat me. Then I was afraid and therefore I awoke.[1]

66. Dream of K·ꞏⱡāsōgwiᵋlakᵘ.

I dreamed that the Moon came down to our world. As soon as she reached the ground a man stepped out of the side door of the Moon. Then he told the Kwāg·uⱡ not to hate one another and not to steal the property of their fellow men and not to seduce the wives of their fellow men and also this, that they should pray to the Creator of man, "that he may pity you and help you," said the moon man. Then I awoke.

67. Dream of Mɛlēd.

I dreamed I was going to the upper world, which was very beautiful. Then I saw many people and all of them seemed to be women. One of them came to me and spoke to me and advised me never to

---

[1]This dream means that the dreamer will have a son, but also that her husband will die shortly after the birth of the child.

g·ɛnuᵋx̣ᵘ q!âʟɛlaᵋmē g·āxs hᵉmɛnāx̣aᵋmaaqōs ʟēlk!wālaxs yāq!ɛnt!ā-

laaqōs lāxa k!wēx̣ē lāxēs g·ōkwaōs lāxa baᵋnē ᵋᵋwĭnagwisa. Wä,

qasō hēx·sä gwēk·!ālaʟē laᵋmēts x̣ālawax̣ɛlaʟōx̣ lāxwa g·ĭgɛmaq!ɛnuᵋx̣ᵘ

qasō dādɛlĭt!asōx̣tsōx. Wä, hēᵋmis qaᵋs k·!ēsaōs g·ĭlōʟax dādɛk·a-

5 sas ᵋnɛmwiyōtē. Wä, hēᵋmis qaᵋs k·!ēsaōs ʟ!ēsilaxēs bɛx̣ᵋwŭtōs.

Wä, hēᵋmaa qasō nānagēg·ē ᵋwĭᵋlaxɛn wāx̣dɛmiᵋläla lâʟ lāʟɛs k·!eâs

k·ĭᵋlɛmʟōx̣, ᵋnēx·ᵋɛng·ē g·āxᵋɛng·ɛn. Wä, laɛng·aᵋmē äxk·!āla qɛn

g·āxē näᵋnakwa. Wä, laɛng·ē äxstōdaxa t!ēx·ĭläsa āʟanâᵋyasa ᵋwā-

lasᵋɛng·ä g·ōkwa. Wä, laɛng·ɛn lāwɛlsa. Wä, âɛng·aᵋmēsɛn hᵉp!-

10 ax̣to dōx̣ᵗwaʟɛlaxɛn g·ōx̣ᵘᵋɛng·ä. Wä, laᵋmɛn ts!ɛx·ᵋĭd laxēq.

68. Mēxēs ᵋmāx̣ŭlag·ĭlis.

Mēxɛlēg·ĭnʟas **Mr. Hall** g̣ānoʟē ᵋnēk·ē ᵋmāx̣ŭlag·ĭlis g·āxɛn-

ʟaxa lāxɛntē maᵋx̣ɛnxē ts!äwŭnxas ᵋnēx·dɛmas g·āxɛn. Wä, la ᵋnēk·a:

K!waēx̣ᵋɛng·ēk· lāxa ᵋēsᵋɛng·ä nōs g·ōkwa laɛng·ɛn nanâqēx·-

15 silaɛng·ɛxɛn nâqaᵋyē sɛnaɛng·ɛx g·ōgwadäsa ᵋēsᵋɛng·ä ᵉx· g·ōx̣ᵘᵋ-

ɛng·ɛn lä k!waēᵋlasᵋɛng·a. Wä, laɛng·ē yāq!eg·aᵋx̣ᵋɛng·ōda bɛgwā-

nɛma laɛng·ɛxɛn aᵋwāp!ēlĭx̣ē. Wä laɛng·ē ᵋnēx·ᵋɛng·a: Wä, ᵋnɛ-

mwɛyōt, ᵋmāx̣ŭlag·ĭlis, ᵋmāsōs äxsɛwēx lāxwa g·ōkwēx ᵋnēx·ᵋɛng·ē.

Wa laɛng·ɛn mɛlsᵋĭda qaɛng·ɛn dōx̣ᵋwĭdēq. Wä, laɛng·ɛn max̣t!ēg·a-

20 aʟɛlaqēxs hēɛng·aē **Mr. A. J. Hall** xa lāᵋlɛladōx̣as ᵋyĭlisē. Wä,

laɛng·aᵋmē g·ĭlt!a ts!ōlɛmᵋɛng·ē q!ōx̣ᵘts!âᵋyas dādatɛ!awakwa. Wä,

laɛng·ē ts!ōlɛmᵋɛng·ē ʟɛtɛmx̣ᵋɛng·äs hâbɛtsɛma. Wä, laɛng·ē aᵋmō-

tsēᵋstaax̣ᵘsa k·âlēda ʟɛtɛmx̣ᵋɛng·äs. Wä, laɛng·ē lɛqēᵋwālaxa k·â-

lē hēɛng·ē gwēx·sa ʟ!ēsɛla. Wä, laɛng·ē qɛnxâlaxa gɛlg·ɛx·âla

25 k·âlk·!ɛnᵋɛng·a. Wä, laɛng·ɛn ʟâxᵋŭlĭx̣ᵋɛng·a qɛn sāx̣aɛng·ēsɛn

hēx̣k·!ōts!ānaᵋyē, laɛng·aᵋmɛn wāx· ᵋnēk·ᵋɛng·a qɛn dābax̣ts!anēq.

Wä, laɛng·ē ᵋnēk·a k·!ē k·!ē qaxg·ĭn laᵋmē ōgŭxᵋĭda, qaxg·ĭn g·a-

ᵋmēk· ʟēxsᵋālayox̣ōʟ lāx Tsāxisē, yĭxg·ĭn lâk· q!wālax·ʟɛna qaxg·ĭn

laᵋmēk· lāxa ᵉk·a äᵋwĭnagwisa. Hēᵋmēsɛn lāg·ix̣a k·!ēs dābax̣ts!ā-

30 nɛndōʟ qaxs k·!ēsaaqōs ᵋnɛmx·ᵋĭdaloʟ lāxɛn ʟᵉxsᵋālayox̣aōʟ ᵋnēx·ᵋ-

ɛng·ēxs laɛng·aē x·ĭsᵋĭda. Wä, laɛm lābēda mēxaᵋyas ᵋmāx̣ŭlag·ĭ-

speak a lie," for I know that you always lie when you talk about
the feasts that you give to your tribe in the country down below.
If you go on talking this way you will fare ill with our chief
here when he judges you. And you shall not steal your brother's
property and you shall not hate your fellow men. If you obey
what I tell you will have no reason to fear,' thus she said to me.
Then she asked me to go home. She opened the rear door of the
house and I went out, and when I looked up I saw my house. Then
I awoke.

68. Dream of ᵉmáx̣ŭlag·flis.[1]

"I dreamed this night of Mr. Hall," said ᵉmáx̣ŭlag·flis to
me. It may be two years since he told me this dream. He said:—

I dreamed I was sitting in a house, not mine, and I thought
in my mind who might be the owner of the bad house in which I was
sitting. Then a man behind me spoke and said, "Oh brother, ᵉmá-
x̣ŭlag·flis, what are you doing in this house?" I turned around
and looked at him and recognized Mr. Hall, the former missionary
at Alert Bay. He wore a long black coat and a black cap covered
his head. His black cap was embroidered all around with gold.
On his forehead he wore gold which shone like the sun. Then I
arose and stretched out my hand, intending to take his hand. Then
he said, " Oh, no! I am now different; for as I used to preach to
you at Fort Rupert I am dressed thus because I am now in the world
above. I cannot take your hand because you did not obey what I
preached to you," thus he said and he disappeared. That was the end
of the dream of ᵉmáx̣ŭlag·flis on the twenty-eighth of February.

---

[1] This man is known as a dreamer. He belongs to the Sēnʟ!ɛm.

lîsaxa hä^εmā^εɫgūnāɫεxsagâla ^εnāla lāxa February.

Wä, lä ɛlāq lābēda ^εmɛkŭlasa April g·āxaa k·ꞏādɛkwē g·äx·ît lāx England tsꞏεk·ꞏāɫɛlas Mr. Hallaxs wēk·ꞏîx^εēdaaxa āιɛbōxsagâla ^εnālasa ^εmɛgwabâsa qꞏēxɛlaxa February. Wä, lēx·a^εmēsεn lā-

5 g·îɫa ōqꞏŭsεx mēxa^εyas ^εmāx̱ŭlag·îlisē yîxs hṏx·^εidə^εmaē g·āx māɫmēxtsꞏasēs mēxa^εyaxa gaālāsēs mēxɛlax·dɛmas Mr. Hallē qꞏwālεn-kwa.

Wä, hêεm gwɛ^εyōsa bākꞏumē âlak·ꞏāla mēxtsꞏasa ιōε aēk·aεng·ε.

When the month of April was almost gone a letter came from England telling of Mr. Hall's death on the twenty-seventh day of the month of February. The only point that makes me believe the dream of ᵋmāx̣ūlag·ᶦlis is that he came at once and told me about his dream in the morning he had dreamed about Mr. Hall dressed up in this way.

That is what is called by the Indians a true dreamer and a good dream.

RANK PROPERTY AND INHERITANCE

Gɛlp!ēnoxᵘ ʟɛᵋwa t!ăgwig·ē.

Wä, hěᵋmaēxs k!wēlasaēda bɛgwānɛmaxa q!ēsgɛmakwē lēlqwălaʟa-
ᵋya; wä, g·îlᵋmēsē ʟ!ōpa t!ɛxᵘsōsxa ᵋnāxwa hěᵋmaōmasa; wä, lä äxts!ōyowa haᵋmäʟasa k!wēƚē lāxa ƚōɛlq!wē; wä, g·îlᵋmēsē la ᵋwῑᵋla
5 äxts!ɛᵋwakwa ƚōɛlq!wäsa hěᵋmaōmasē laas ʟaxᵋūlῑƚa ɛlkwäsa g·Igɛ-
maᵋyēxa k!wēlasē.   Wä, lä yāq!ɛg·aᵋƚēda ɛlkwa. Wä, lä ᵋnēk·a:
Qäʟ qäʟas hěᵋmaēx gwēk·!älasē, ēx·laxaēʟɛn qɛnʟō ɛ̂ɛm lāx ʟäqax·sa-
x·ᵃῙdlaxō qaōx Mɛ̂ᵋnakūläxwa k·!ēsᵋōnokwax·sa gɛlpa ça äwɛ̂xaᵋlatsa
k!wēƚē lāxa ᵋnäƚᵋnɛmēxʟa ƚōq!wa. Wä, sōᵋmēts Yäqoʟ!ēqɛlas laɛms
10 g·āxʟ t!ägwig·exg·ada gɛlp!ēnoxūk· yῑxg·a Mɛ̂ᵋnakūlak· yūʟax k·!ē-
k·!ɛsᵋōnokwaaqōsasa hě gwēg·ilē ᵋnēk·ē yῑxs g·ayōƚaē Mɛ̂ᵋnakūla
lāx ᵋnɛᵋmēmotasa Sēnʟ!ɛmē. Wä, lä g·ayōƚē Yäqoʟ!ēqɛlasē lāx ᵋnɛᵋmēmotasa kŭkwāk!ūmasa Gwētɛʟa. Wä, hēx·ᵋidaᵋmēsē Mɛ̂ᵋnakūla ʟōᵋ
Yäqoʟ!ēqɛlas g·āx lax ᵋmɛxēlasasa ƚōɛlq!wē qaᵋs hōsᵋῙdēq. Hěmē
15 Mɛ̂ᵋnakūla hōsaq lāqēxs ʟ!ɛnqaasa g·îlt!a ts!ēsʟāla daaxᵘs lāxa
ƚōɛlq!wē. Wä, g·îlᵋmēsē nɛqäxʟēda ƚōɛlq!wa hōsēᵋs laē ᵋņēk·ē Mɛ̂-
ᵋnakūla nɛqäxʟaᵋai. Wä, la Yäqoʟ!ēqɛlas t!äxᵋwῑdxa ᵋnɛmē lāxēs
qōmäsēs hěƚk·!ōts!ānaᵋyē lāqēxs ɛ̂ᵋmaē ɛlxʟaᵋya t!ägwig·aᵋyē Yäqo-
ʟ!ēqɛlas yîs Mɛ̂ᵋnakūlaxa gɛlp!ēnoxwē. Wä, g·îlᵋmēsē mäƚtsɛmg·u-
20 stɛ̂wa ƚōɛlq!wē hōsēs Mɛ̂ᵋnakūla laē ᵋnēk·a maᵋƚtsɛmg·astɛ̂ai. Wä,
la Yäqoʟ!ēqɛlasē t!äxᵋwῑdxēs ts!ɛmälax·ts!ānaᵋyē. Wä, hēx·säᵋmēsē
gwēg·ilē. Wä, g·îlᵋmēsē yūduxᵘsɛmg·ustɛ̂wēxʟēda ƚōɛlq!wa laē la

RANK, PROPERTY AND INHERITANCE

Counter and Tally Keeper.

When a man gives a feast to different tribes/and when the clover
roots or all kinds of food are done,/the food that is to be eaten by
the guests is put into the dishes.   As soon as all(5)the food has
been put into the dishes, the speaker of the chief,/the host, stands
up, and the speaker speaks and says:/"Yes, indeed this is the way to
speak.   However, would it be good, if I should just ask anyone to
call out the names?/ For here is Mâᶜnakŭla, whose hereditary privilege
it is to count the number of/guests to each dish. And you, Yäqoʟ!ēqɛ-
las, you(10)will come and count with Mâᶜnakŭla, for you have this/
hereditary privilige of doing so," said he, for Mâᶜnakŭla belongs to
the/numaym Sēnʟ!ɛm and Yäqoʟēqɛlas belongs to the/numaym Kŭkwāk!ŭm
of the Northerners.   And immediately Mâᶜnakŭla and/Yäqoʟ!ēqɛlas come
to the dishes that are on the floor, and begin to count.   It is(15)
Mâᶜnakŭla who counts them pushing with the long tongs which he is carry-
ing/the dishes, and after he has counted ten dishes, then Mânakŭla says/
"Ten dishes," and Yäqoʟ!ēqɛlas folds under/the thumb of his right hand,
for Yäqoʟ!ēqɛlas is the tally keeper/of Mâᶜnakŭla, who is the counter.
And as soon as twenty(20)dishes have been counted by Mâᶜnakŭla, he
says, "Twenty dishes," and/then Yäqoʟ!ēqɛlas folds down his first finger, and he continues/doing so, and as soon as there are thirty dishes,

yŭduxᵘp!ɛna ᵋnēk·ēda g·ɛlp!ēnoxwē nɛqäxʟa. Wä, läda t!ägwig·aᵋyē
yîx Yãqoʟ!ēqɛlas t!äxᵋwîdxēs ᵋnōlax·ts!ānaᵋyē. Wä, g·îlᵋmēsē
gwäⱬ hōsaxa ⱬōɛlq!wē laē Mäᵋnakŭla ʟōᵋ Yãqoʟ!ēqɛlas qãsᵋida qaᵋs
lä ʟaxᵋwalîⱬdaᵋxᵘ läx ʟ!ãsalîⱬasa k!wēⱬē. Wä, la Mäᵋnakŭla ᵋnēx·-
5   xēs t!ägwig·aᵋyē Yãqoʟ!ēqɛlas: Q!ēq!aʟ!alaʟox läxa ᵋnɛmēxʟa ⱬō-
q!wa, ᵋnēk·ēxs laē hōsᵋidxa bɛgwānɛmē. Wēg·a t!ägwig·ēʟɛx.
ᵋnɛmōkᵘ, maᵋlōkᵘ, yŭdukᵘ, mōkᵘ, sɛk·!ōkᵘ, q!ɛʟ!ōkᵘ, ᵋnɛmēxʟa ⱬō-
q!wa. ᵋnɛmōkᵘ, maᵋlōkᵘ, yŭdukᵘ, mōkᵘ, sɛk·!ōkᵘ, q!ɛʟ!ōkᵘ, maⱬɛx-
ʟa ⱬōɛlq!wa. ᵋnɛmōkᵘ, maᵋlōkᵘ, yŭdukᵘ, mōkᵘ, sɛk·!ōkᵘ, q!ɛʟ!ōkᵘ,
10 yŭduxᵘxʟa ⱬōɛlq!wa. Wä, hēᵋmis la t!ägwig·ēsōᵋs Yãqoʟ!ēqɛlas.
Wä, hēɛm k·!ēk·!ɛsᵋonokwē Mäᵋnakŭla ʟōᵋ Yãqoʟ!ēqɛlatsēs gwigwäla-
g·îlîlasē g·äg·îʟɛla läxa nŭx̣ᵘneᵋmisē läx Qãlogwis. Wä, laɛm
k·!eâs gwēx·ᵋidaas las läxēs ts!ɛdāqē x̣ŭnōkwa yîxs k·!eâsaē bɛgwānɛms sãsɛmas, wä, hēᵋmisēs hēnax·ᵋidaats las läxa bɛgwānɛmē
15 x̣ŭnōx̣ᵘsēs ts!āᵋya ᵋnax̣wa yîx Mäᵋnakŭla ʟōᵋ Yãq!oʟ!ēqɛlas. Wä,
la k·!ēs q!ŭnāla hēdēda ᵋnōlast!ɛgɛmaᵋyē bɛgwānɛm x̣ŭnōx̣ᵘsa gɛlp-
p!ēnoxᵘ lāats gɛlp!ēnoxᵘᵋᵋenaᵋyasēs ōmpē yîxs häē q!ŭnāla lāatsa
gɛlp!ēnoxwa ämāᵋyînxaᵋyas sãsɛmas. Wä, hēɛmxaäwisē gwēg·ilēda
t!ägwig·ēᵋ läx wäⱬdɛmasa bāk!ŭm yîxs ᵋnēk·aaq nɛnōlowa ᵋnōlast!-
20 ɛgɛmaᵋyē sãsɛma. Wä, la ᵋnēk·ɛq nēnâgadēda ämāᵋyînxaᵋyas sãsɛmas. Wä, laɛm lāba.

K!wäk!waxsdalaxa q!äp!äēnoxᵘ.

Wä, hēᵋmaē K!wäk!waxsdalaxa q!äp!äēnoxwasa ᵋnɛᵋmēmotasa
Kŭkwäk!ŭmasa Gwētɛla. Wä, laɛm ᵋnɛmōxᵋŭm q!ap!äxa äʟɛbōxgɛma-
25 k·!ɛs ᵋnäⱬᵋnɛᵋmēmatsa Gwētɛla. Wä, hēɛm âlak·!äla g·äg·îʟɛlē
K!wäk!waxsdala läxa ts!ɛts!âqâ läx Qãlogwisxa nŭx̣ᵘnēᵋmisē. Wä,
hēɛm ʟ̣ēgɛmsē läxēs Q!äp!äēnoxwaē Pɛxɛmaᵋya, yîxs laē yãqwasa ʟ!ä-
gɛkwē ʟɛᵋwa yãsɛkwē ʟɛᵋwa ts!ōⱬna ʟɛᵋwa qɛmx̣wa läxa ᵋnax̣wa bēbɛgwānɛma ʟɛᵋwa ᵋnax̣wa ts!ēdaqa ʟɛᵋwa ᵋnax̣wa g·îng·înānɛma. Wä,
30 lä ʟ̣ēgadɛs K·!âdē läxa bāx̣ŭs. Wä, lä ʟ̣ēgadɛs T!ēqwap yîxs laē
ᵋwālas k!wēlatsa ʟ!ēᵋna läx Dzāwadē, yîxs gɛgadaēda g·aläs K·!â-

then(1)the counter says, "Three times ten dishes," and the tally
keeper,/Yäqoʟ!ᴇqɛlas, then folds under his middle finger, and after/
they finish counting the dishes, Mâᶜnakŭla and Yäqoʟ!ᴇqɛlas go and/
stand at the outer end of the guests and Mâᶜnakŭla says(5)to his
tally keeper, Yäqoʟ!ᴇqɛlas, "There will be six men to each dish,"/
thus he says while he is counting the men," Now keep the tally. One
man, two men, three men, four men, five men, six men. One dish!/ One
man two men, three men, four men, five men, six men./ Two dishes!
One man, two men, three men, four men, five men, six men.(10) Three
dishes!" Now Yäqoʟ!ᴇqɛlas keeps tally./ This is the hereditary
office of Mâᶜnakŭla and Yäqoʟ!ᴇqɛlas that they are doing/beginning
from the myth people at Crooked Beach. They/cannot give this to their
daughters if they have no/sons, and they must give it to the son(15)
of their younger brothers, both Mâᶜnakŭla and Yäqoʟ!ᴇqɛlas./ Often
it is not the oldest son who is a counter. If the father is a counter,
then generally/the youngest one of the children will be the counter,
and this is also in the same way with/the tally keeper, according to
the words of the Indians; for they say that the oldest children are
foolish(20)and they say that the youngest children are clever./ That
is the end.

K!wāk!waxsdala, the Assembler.

And now about K!wāk!waxsdala, the Assembler of the numaym/of the
Kŭkwāk!ŭmasa of the Gwētɛla. Hé is the only one who assembles the
seven(25)numayms of the Gwētɛla. And K!wāk!waxsdala really began/from
the Winter Ceremonial at Crooked Beach of the Myth People./ And his
name is Assembler-Chief-Shaman, namely when he distributes/red cedar
bark and tallow and charcoal and eagle down to all the/men and all the
women and all the children(30). And his name is K·!âdē in the secular
seawon, and his name is T!ēqwap when/he gives a great grease feast in

däs k·!ēdēɫas Wanukwa, yîx Ts!ɛts!âɫaɫē. Hēɛm bâx̱ŭs ʟēg̱ɛms ʟɛm-
k·!alē Wanuk^u. Wä, lā^ɛlaē x̱ŭngwadɛx·^ɛÎdē K·!âdē lāxēs g̱ɛnɛmasa
bābagŭmē. Wä, la Wanukwē ʟēg̱ɛmg·îlxʟālax Hayaɫk·înē qa ʟēg̱ɛmsēs
ts!ōx̱^uʟɛma. Wä, la^ɛmē ʟēg̱adēda g·înānɛmas Hayaɫk·înē. Wä, lā^ɛlaē
5 ēt!ēd x̱ŭngwadɛx·^ɛÎdɛsa bābagŭmē. Wä, lā^ɛlaē Wanukwē ʟēg̱ɛmg·îlxʟā-
lax Hä^ɛmasi^ɛlakwē qa ʟēg̱ɛmsēs ts!ōx̱^uʟɛma. Wä, la^ɛmē ʟēg̱adēda bābagŭmas Hä^ɛmasi^ɛlak^u. Wä, laɛm g·ayōɫē Wanuk^u lāx ^ɛnɛ^ɛmēmotasa
Wawŭlibâ^ɛyē. Wä, lä g·ayōɫē g̱ɛnɛmas yîx Wäʟēdē lāxa ^ɛnɛ^ɛmēmotasa
Wîwomasg̱ɛmasa Mamalēleqala yîxs k·!ēdēɫaē Wäʟēdäs Sēsaxâlas. Wä,
10 g·îl^ɛmēsē q!ŭlsq!ŭlyax^ɛwÎdē Hayaɫk·în ʟɛ^ɛwēs ts!ā^ɛyē Hä^ɛmasi^ɛlakwē
la hēɛm la ʟ!āyowē Hayaɫk·înaxēs ōmp K·!âdē. Wä, lāxaē äx^ɛēdxa
q!äp!ä lāxa ts!ēts!ēqa. Wä, hë^ɛmis ts!ɛx·^ɛāʟɛla lāx nâqa^ɛyas ts!ā-
^ɛyäsē Hä^ɛmasi^ɛlakwē qaxs wäx·aē äx^ɛēxsd qa^ɛs hëäx^ɛēdxa q!äp!ēkwē
lax k·!ēs^ɛâsēs ōmpē. Wä, lä yäx·sto^ɛsē Hayaɫk·înas lāxēs ts!ā^ɛya.
15 Wä, hë^ɛmis lāg·iɫas Hä^ɛmasi^ɛlakwē la bâsēs ōmpē qa^ɛs lä lāxēs äbās-
k·!ōtē. Wä, la^ɛmē äx^ɛēdxa q!äp!äēnox^u qa^ɛs lä q!äp!äēnox^usa Wäwŭ-
libâ^ɛyē ^ɛnɛ^ɛmēmota. Wä, laɛm q!äp!äēnox^usa ^ɛwālas Kwäg·uɫa lāxēq.
Wä, lä hë^ɛmē Hä^ɛmasi^ɛlakwē äx^ɛēdxa äʟɛbōg̱ŭg·iyowē bēbɛgwanɛm qa
aaxsîlaxa ^ɛnāx̱wa dōg̱ŭɫts lāxēs ōmpē K·!âdē ʟɛ^ɛwa aaxsîlaxa k·âdzɛ-
20 kwē dēdɛg̱ɛmyâ ʟɛ^ɛwa yäsɛk^u ʟɛ^ɛwa ts!ōɫna ʟɛ^ɛwa ʟ!āg̱ɛkwē ʟɛ^ɛwa qäm-
x̱wa. Wä, laɛm ʟēg̱adē Hä^ɛmasi^ɛlakwas ʟɛmk·!äla lāxa ts!ēts!ēqa
lāxēq. Wä, la^ɛmē g̱ɛg·adɛx·^ɛÎdē Hä^ɛmasi^ɛlakwas Gwâgwadaxɛla yîx
k·!ēdēɫas Yāxʟɛnxag·ayōɫē lāx ^ɛnɛ^ɛmēmotasa Haänʟēnâ. Wä, laɛm
x̱ŭngwadɛx·^ɛÎdē Hä^ɛmasi^ɛlak^u ʟɛ^ɛwis g̱ɛnɛmē Gwâgwadaxɛläsa bābagŭmē.
25 Wä, la Yāxʟɛn ʟēg̱ɛmg·îlxʟālax Hɛx·hak!wa^ɛsag̱ɛmē qa ʟēg̱ɛmsēs ts!ō-
x̱^uʟɛma. Wä, lä ēt!ēd x̱ŭngwadɛx·^ɛÎdɛsa bābagŭmē. Wä, lāxaē Yāxʟɛn
ʟēg̱ɛmg·îlxʟālax Tsɛx^ɛwÎdē qa ʟēg̱ɛmsēs ts!ōx̱^uʟɛma. Wä, hë^ɛmisē
Tsɛx^ɛwÎdē la ʟēg̱adɛs Nŭx̱^unē^ɛmis lāxēs q!äp!äēnoxwaē, yîxs laē bâsēs ōmpē qa^ɛs lä lāxēs äbask·!ōtē. Wä, laɛmx̱aē äx^ɛēdxa q!äp!ä
30 qa^ɛs ʟēg̱adɛs Q!äp!äēnox^u Pɛxɛma^ɛya. Wä,lä ʟēg̱adɛs Nŭx̱^unē^ɛmis yîxs
laē ^ɛnɛmōx^ɛŭm la q!ŭ^ɛla yîxs laē wÎk·!ɛx^ɛÎdē K!wâk!waxsdalax·dē.

Knight Inlet. At first K!ǎdē(1) had for his wife a princess of Wanuku,
namely Ts!ɛts!ǎlaɫ, and the secular name/of ʟɛmk·!ala is Wanuku. Then
K·!ǎdē had a child from his wife,/a boy, and then Wanuku gave the name
Hayaɫk·ĭn as a marriage name to his/ grandson, and now the child had
the name Hayaɫk·ĭn. Then(5)he had another child, a boy, and Wanuku
gave the marriage name/Hǟᵋmasiᵋlaku as a name to his grandson, and then
the boy had the name/Hǟᵋmasiᵋlaku. Now Wanuku belonged to the nu-
maym/Wǎwŭlabǎᵋyē and his wife Wǎḙēd belonged to the numaym of/Wīwomas-
gɛm of the Mamalēlᵉqala, and Wǎḙēd was the princess of Sēsaxǎlas.(10)
Now as soon as Hayaɫk·ĭn and his younger brother Hǟᵋmasiᵋlaku were
grown up/Hayaɫk·ĭn took the place of his father K·!ǎdē and he also
took the/office of Assembler in the Winter Ceremonial, and so his
younger brother/Hǟᵋmasiᵋlaku became sick at heart for he wished in
vain to take the office of Assembler/from the privileges of his father.
Then Hayaɫk·ĭn did not want to give it up to his younger brother,(15)
and therefore Hǟᵋmasiᵋlaku left his father and went to his mother's
side,/and he took the office of Assembler, and was Assembler of the numaym Wǎwŭlibǎᵋyē. Then he was Assembler of the Great Kwāg·uɫ./ And
then Hǟᵋmasiᵋlaku took seventeen men to/take care of everything seen
by him at (the house of) his father K·!ǎdē. And he took care of the
soft cedar bark(20)for wiping the face, and the tallow and the charcoal and the red cedar bark and the down./ And then Hǟᵋmasiᵋlaku
had the name ʟɛmk·!ala in the Winter Ceremonial./ Then Hǟᵋmasiᵋlaku
had for his wife Gwāgwadaxɛla, the/princess of Yāxʟɛn, who came from
the numaym Haǎnaḙēno. Then/Hǟᵋmasiᵋlaku had a child with his wife,
Gwāgwadaxɛla, a boy,(25)and then Yāxʟɛn gave the marriage name Hɛx·hǎ-
k!waēsagɛmēᵋ to be the name of his/grandson. Then he had another child,
a boy, and Yāxʟɛn/gave the marriage name Tsɛxᵋwīd to be the name of his
grandson. And so/Tsɛxᵋwīd had the name Nŭxᵘnēᵋmis as Assembler, for
he went and left/his father and went to his mother's side, and he also
took the office of Assembler,(30) and had the name Assembler-Head-Sha-
man. And now he had the name Nŭxᵘnēᵋmis, for he/was the only one that

Wä, la kᐧ!eâs sāsɛm q!ŭᶜlas, wä, la kᐧ!eâs mãgᐧiⱡ ⱡḗⱡɛⱡâlas. Wä,

hēᶜmis lāgᐧiⱡas âɛm xᐧîsᶜîdē ⱡōgɛmas K!wãk!waxsdalaxᐧdē. Wä, lā-

xaē hēᶜm gwēxᐧᶜîdē ʟɛmkᐧ!ãᶜlōⱡē. Laɛmxaē ᶜwîᶜla ⱡēⱡɛᶜla lāgᐧiⱡas

kᐧ!eâs la q!ãp!aēnoxᵘsa ᶜwālas Kwãgᐧuⱡ. Wä, la ᶜnɛmōx̱ᵘᶜmē Nŭx̱ᵘnēᶜ-

5   misē gagäⱡa q!ŭᶜla. Wä, lä ᶜnɛmōx̱ᶜŭm la q!ãp!aēnoxᵘsa Gwētɛla ⱡɛ-

ᶜwa Q!ōmoyâᶜyē ⱡɛᶜwa ᶜwālas Kwãgᐧuⱡa. Wä, lä wēkᐧ!îxᶜēda yîx Nŭ-

x̱ᵘnēᶜmisdē. Wä, laᶜmēsē bɛgwānɛm x̱ŭnōx̱ᵘs Hɛxᐧhãk!waēsagɛmaxa ⱡē-

gadäs Häᶜmasiᶜlakᵘ yîxs x̱ŭnōkwaē Häᶜmasiᶜlakwas Hɛxᐧhãk!waēsagɛmē

ⱡɛᶜwis gɛnɛmē Hɛxᐧhãk!waēdzɛmga yîx ts!ɛdāqē x̱ŭnōx̱ᵘs Y̱āqaⱡᶜɛnlisxa

10   gᐧayoⱡē lāx ᶜnɛᶜmēmotasa Gᐧēxsɛmasa Nɛqɛmgᐧîlisɛla. Wä, hēᶜmēsē

Häᶜmasiᶜlakᵘ la ʟ!āyoxēs q!ŭᶜlēyoⱡē Nŭx̱ᵘnēᶜmiswoⱡē. Wä, laɛm q!ãp-

!aēnoxwē Häᶜmasiᶜlakwē. Laɛm ⱡēgadɛs Nŭx̱ᵘnēᶜmisē lāxa ts!ēts!ēqa.

Wä, lä ⱡēgadɛs Omxᐧᶜîdē lāxa bāx̱ŭsē. Wä, laɛm ts!āᶜyē Häᶜmasiᶜlakw-

as sāsɛmas Hɛxᐧhãk!waēsagɛmē yîxs ts!ɛdāqaē Kᐧ!äsogwiᶜlax̱ᵘxa ᶜnōlas-

15   t!ɛgɛmaᶜyas sāsɛmas. Wä, lä kᐧ!eâs gwēxᐧᶜîdaas äxᶜēdxa q!ãp!ä qaxs

ts!ɛdāqaē. Wä, lāⱡa hēɛm la äxᶜēdɛx k!waᶜyas Hɛxᐧhãk!waēsagɛmēxᐧdē

yîxs laē wîkᐧ!ɛxᶜēda yîxs wāxᐧᶜmaē ts!ɛdāqa yîx Kᐧ!äsogwiᶜlakᵘ. Wä,

laᶜmēsʟa wŭq!wäsē Häᶜmasiᶜlakᵘ yîx ts!āᶜyäs Kᐧ!äsogwiᶜlakwē äxᶜēdɛx

k!waᶜyas Tsɛxᶜwîdēxa la ⱡēgadɛs Ōmxᐧᶜîdē qaxs kᐧ!eâsaē x̱ŭnōx̱ᵘs Ōm-

20   xᐧᶜîdōⱡē, yîxs ts!āᶜyaē Tsɛxᶜwîdäs Hɛxᐧhãk!waēsagɛmaᶜyēxa maᶜlōkwē

bēbɛgwānɛm sāsɛms Y̱āxʟɛnōⱡē ⱡɛᶜwis gɛnɛmōⱡē Aōmōⱡᶜwŭⱡēxa ts!ɛdāqē

x̱ŭnōx̱ᵘs Wadzeyōⱡɛxa gᐧayōⱡē lāxa ᶜnɛᶜmēmotasa Q!ɛmq!ɛmtalaⱡasa Dɛ-

naxᐧdaᶜx̱ᵘ. Wä, lä ᶜnēxᐧsōᶜxs hēᶜmaē lāgᐧiⱡas Wadzē la q!ãp!aēnoxᵘsa

ᶜnɛᶜmēmotasa Q!ɛmq!ɛmtalaⱡaxs laē Aōmōⱡ ts!ɛkᐧ!āⱡelasa q!ãp!aēnox-

25   wēs ⱡāᶜwadaasē qaxs kᐧ!eâsaē q!ãp!äᶜnoxᵘsa Dɛnaxᐧdaᶜxwē gᐧālagwis

Aōmōⱡaxs laē ⱡāᶜwadɛs Y̱āxʟɛnē. Wä, lāxaē hēɛm gwäⱡa wāⱡdɛmasa gᐧā-

lē Kwākŭgᐧuⱡ qaēda ᶜnɛᶜmēmotasa Wîwomasgɛmasa Mamalēleqala qa Wä-

ⱡēdäxs gᐧäxaē ⱡāᶜwadɛs Wanukwēxa qâp!aēnoxwasa Wāwŭlibâᶜyē. Wä,

laɛmᶜlaē q!ãp!äᶜnoxwē Sēsax̱âlasasa ᶜnɛmēmotasa Wîwōmasgɛm gᐧägᐧî-

30   ʟɛlaxs laē ⱡāᶜwadɛs kᐧ!ēdēⱡas Wanukwē qaxs kᐧ!eâsaē q!ãp!äᶜnoxᵘsa

Mamalēleqala gᐧālagawis Wäⱡēdäxs laē ⱡāᶜwadɛs Wanukwē. Wä, hēɛm

was still alive, for now K!wāk!waxsdala died and(1)he had no child
living, and he had no near relatives./ Therefore the name K!wāk!wax-
sdala just disappeared. And/the same happened to ʟɛmk·!ala. They
also were all dead, and therefore/there is no Assembler among the
Great Kwag·uł. Only Nūx̣ᵘneᵋmis(5)was still living, and he is now the
only Assembler of the Gwētɛla and/the Q!ōmoyâᵋyē and of the Great
Kwag·iuł. Then Nūx̣ᵘnēᵋmis died/ Now the son of Hɛx·hăk!waēsagɛmēᵋ/
who had the name/Häᵋmasiᵋlakᵘ, that is, the child Häᵋ masiᵋlakᵘ was
the son of Hɛx·hăk!waēsagēmēᵋ/and his wife Hɛx·hăk!waēdzɛmga, the
daughter of Yāqołᵋɛnlis(10)who came from the numaym G·ēxsɛm of the
Nāqɛmg·ꞁlisɛla. And/Häᵋmasiᵋlakᵘ changed places with his late uncle Nūx̣ᵘnēᵋmis. Then/Häᵋmasiᵋlakᵘ was Assembler and had the name
Nūx̣ᵘnēᵋmis in the Winter Ceremonial,/and his name was Ōmx·ᵋꞮd in the
secular season. Now Häᵋmasiᵋlakᵘ was the younger/son among the children of Hɛx·hăk!waēsagɛmēᵃ, for a woman was K·!äsogwiᵋlakᵘ,/the oldest
(15) one among his children. She could not in any way take the office
of Assembler because she was/a woman, but she took the seat of the
late Hɛx·hăk!waēsagɛmēᵋ/when he died, although she was a woman, namely K·!äsogwiᵋlakᵘ. Now/her brother, Häᵋmasiᵋlakᵘ, that is, the
younger brother of K·!äsogwiᵋlakᵘ,took/the seat of TsɛxᵋwꞮd, and he
took the name Ōmx·ᵋꞮd, for the late Ōmx·ᵋꞮd had no child.(20) For
TsɛxᵋwꞮd was the younger brother of Hɛx·hăk!waēsagɛmēᵋ among the two/
sons of the late Yāxʟɛn and his late wife Aōmōł, the daughter/of
Wadzē who came from the numaym Q!ɛmq!ɛmtalał of the/Dɛnax·daᵋxᵘ.
And it is said that this is the reason why Wadzē became the Assem-
bler/of the numaym Q!ɛmq!ɛmtalał, that Aēmōł told about the Assembler
(25)for the Dɛnax·daᵋxᵘ had no assembler before/Aōmōł had for her husband Yāxʟɛn, and also this is the saying of the former/Kwag·uł about
the numaym WꞮwomasgɛm of the Mamalēleqala, that/WäꞬēd came and had for
her husband Wanukᵘ, the Assembler of the Wāwŭlibâᵋyē./ Then Sēsaxâlas
of the numaym WꞮwomasgɛm was Assembler, beginning(30)at the time when
the princess of Wanukᵘ took a husband,for there was no Assembler of/the
Mamalēleqala before WäꞬēd took for her husband Wanukᵘ. This/a disgrace

qǃamäsa Dᴇnax·daᵋxᵘ ʟᴇᵋwa Mamalēleqala lāxg·ada Kwākũg·uⱡē qaxs
âᵋmaē ᵋnᴇmāx· îs ʟ̣ōᵋ g· îlōʟ̣ānᴇmaxēs qǃâpǃaēnoxwē. Wä, laᴇm lāba.

Succession.

Hë̆ᵋmaēs wũlāsᴇᵋwōs lāxa bᴇgwānᴇmaxs qǃēqǃapaē lāxēs sāsᴇmē
5 ʟᴇᵋwis gᴇnᴇmē lāx gwäⱡaasas ʟǃāⱡäyĭg· flisxa la yāwasᵋîd ʟ̣ēgadᴇs
Hawīlkũlaⱡ lāxēs ōmpēxa g·ayoⱡē lāx ᵋnᴇᵋmēmotasa Kũkwākǃũmasa Qǃō-
mayâᵋyē. Wä, lä xŭnōkwë äbᴇmpas ʟǃāⱡäyĭg·flisas Tᴇlēg·alēdzᴇmga-
xa tsǃᴇdāqē xŭnōxᵘs Wanukwēxa g·ayoⱡē lāx ᵋnᴇᵋmēmotasa Wäwŭlibâᵋye.
Wä, la hëx·säᴇm alaⱡaats ʟǃāⱡäyĭg·flisēda ᵋnᴇᵋmēmotasēs ōmpa Kũkwā-
10 kǃŭm. Wä, laᴇm Kũkwakǃŭmaxsᴇmē ʟǃāⱡäyĭg·flisē lāxēq. Wä, lä k·ǃēs
alaⱡa lāxa ᵋnᴇᵋmēmotas Wanukᵘᵋwũⱡasa Wäwŭlibâᵋyē yîxs âyadaē Tᴇlē-
g·alēdzᴇmgä Wanukᵘᵋwũⱡē. Wä, la ʟǃāⱡäyĭg·flisē äbāyadᴇs Tᴇlēg·al-
ēdzᴇmga. Wä, hë̆ᵋmis lāg·iⱡas ʟǃāⱡäyĭg·flisē Wäwalipk'ǃōtǃᴇnaxsᴇmē.
Wä, lä k·ǃēs ᴇlg·flgē lāxa ᵋnᴇᵋmēmotasēs äbäsk·ǃōta Wäwalibâᵋyē
15 qaxs häē âlak·ǃāla ᴇlg·flgayaasa ᵋnᴇᵋmēmōtasa Kũkwākǃumasa Qǃōmoya-
ᵋyē lāx ᵋnᴇᵋmēmotas ōmpᵋwũⱡas ʟǃāⱡäyĭg·flisē yîxs âᵋyadaas Hawīlkũlaⱡᵋwũⱡē. Wä, hë̆ᵋmis lāg·iⱡas âlak·ǃāla la Kũkwākǃũmaxsᴇmē̦ ʟǃāⱡä-
yĭg·flisē lāxēq. Wä, lä xŭngwadᴇx·ᵋîdᴇs Ādag·iᵋlakwē. Wä, la Ādag·
g·iᵋlakwē äxᵋēdᴇx kǃwaᵋyas Häwīlkũlaⱡ lāxa ᵋnᴇᵋmēmotasa Kũkwākǃũma-
20 sa Qǃōmoyâᵋyē qäʟ̣axs ᵋnōlastǃᴇgᴇmaᵋyē Ādag·iᵋlakwas sāsᴇmas ʟǃāⱡä-
yĭg·flisē. Wä, lä wēk·ǃîxᵋîdē Hämasaqa yîx wũqǃa ᵋnōlas Tᴇlēg·alē-
dzᴇmgaxa xŭngwadäs ʟǃāⱡäyĭg·flisē. Wä, hë̆ᵋmis lāg·iⱡas äpsōtǃᴇnaᵋ-
yas Ādag·iᵋlakwē äxᵋēdᴇx kǃwaᵋyas Hämasaqoⱡē qaxs ᵋnōlawäᵋlîⱡaē Hämasaqoⱡē. Wä, lāxaē ᵋnōlawäᵋlîⱡē Hawīlkũlaⱡᵋwũⱡē. Wä, lāxaē Ādag·i-
25 ᵋlakwē ᵋnōlawäᵋlîⱡ lāxēs äbᴇmpē ʟǃāⱡäyĭg·flisē. Wä, lāxaē äbᴇmpasēe
Tᴇlēg·alēdzᴇmga ᵋnōlawäᵋlîⱡ lāxēs äbᴇmpē Wäʟ̣idē lāx lāg·iⱡas mamalē-
lexk·ǃōtᴇmē ʟǃāⱡäyĭg·flisē. Wä, hë̆ᵋmaa qō xŭngwadē Hämasaqäs ᵋnᴇmō-
kwa g·înānᴇma lālaxsdē k·ǃeâs gwēx·ᵋidaas äxᵋēdē Ādag·iᵋlakwax kǃwaᵋyas Hämasaqoⱡē qaxs hë̆ᵋmēlaxē xŭnōxᵘlaxas wāx·ᵋᴇm tsǃātsǃadagᴇma
30 lālaxē äxᵋēdᴇx kǃwaᵋyas. Wä, lä hewäxaᴇm xŭngwadᴇx·ᵋîdē Hämasaqoⱡē.
Wä, hë̆ᵋmis lāg·iⱡas lāyowa kǃwaᵋyas lāx Ādag·iᵋlakwē yîxs mäᵋⱡᴇnxaē

for the Dɛnax·da^ɛx^u and the Mamalēleqala among the Kwag·uⱡ tribes,
for/it is just as if they had stolen the office of Assembler. That
is the end.

Succession.

This was asked by you about a man who has many children (5)
with his wife in the way (it was) with ʟ!āⱡāyīg·flis who for a while
had the name/Hawīlkŭlaⱡ from her father who came from the numaym Kŭkwāk!ŭm of the/Q!ōmoyâ^ɛyē. She was the daughter, the mother of ʟ!ā-
ⱡāyīg·flis, Tɛlēg·alīdzɛmga,/the daughter of Wanuk^u who came from the
numaym Wāwŭlibâ^ɛyē./ And really ʟ!āⱡāyīg·flis belonged to the numaym
of her father, the Kŭkwāk!ŭm,(10) and ʟ!āⱡāyīg·flis was a Kŭkwāk!ŭm
woman after this She did not/really belong to the numaym of the late
Wanuk^u, the Wāwŭlibâ^ɛyē, for Tɛlēg·alīdzɛmga had for her father/ the
late Wanuk^u, and ʟ!āⱡāyīg·flis had for her mother Tɛlēg·alīdzɛmga./
Therefore, ʟ!āⱡāyīg·flis was on one side a Wāwŭlibâ^ɛyē./ And she did
not stay with the numaym of her mother's side, the Wāwŭlibâ^ɛyē, (15)
for she really stayed with the numaym Kŭkwāk!ŭm of the Q!ōmoyâ^ɛyē,/
the numaym of the late father of ʟ!āⱡāyīg·flis, for she had as her
father the late Hawīlkŭlaⱡ./Therefore, ʟ!āⱡāyīg·flis was really a Kŭ-
kwāk!ŭm woman/after this. Then she had a child, Ādag·i^ɛlak^u, and Āda·
g·i^ɛlak^u/took the seat of Hawīlkŭlaⱡ in the numaym Kŭkwāk!ŭm (20) of
the Q!ōmoyâ^ɛyē, for indeed Ādag·i^ɛlak^u was the eldest son among the
children of/ʟ!āⱡāyīg·flis. Then Hāmasaqa died, the elder brother of
Tɛlēg·alīdzɛmga,/who had for her daughter ʟ!āⱡāyīg·flis., and there-
fore, on one side/Ādag·i^ɛlak^u took the seat of the late Hāmasaqa, for
the late Hāmasaqa belonged to the eldest line of the house. And the
late Hawīlkŭlaⱡ also belonged to the eldest line of the house, and Ā-
dag·i^ɛlak^u (25) also belonged to the eldest line of the house through
his mother ʟ!āⱡāyīg·flis, and also her mother/Tɛlēg·alīdzɛmga belonge·
to the eldest line of the house through her mother, Wäʟid. And there·
fore/ʟ!āⱡāyīg·flis was on one side Mamalēleqala. Now if Hāmasaqa had
had one/child, there would have been no way for Ādag·i^ɛlak^u to take

ts!äwŭnxē äxēlē ʟ!āłäyīg·flisaxa k!waᵋyasēs ōmpᵋwŭłē Hawīlkŭlałᵋwŭłē ʟᴇᵋwa k!waᵋyasēs q!ŭlēᵋyołē Hämasaqołē. Wä, g·flᵋmēsē nᴇxʟa-
äx·ᵋīd la bᴇgwānᴇmē Ādag·iᵋlakᵘ yīx ᵋnōlast!ᴇgᴇmaᵋyas sāsᴇmas ʟ!ā-
łäyīg·flisaxs laē lāsasa māᵋłē k!wä ʟᴇᵋwa māᵋłē ʟēʟᴇgᴇm lāxēs xŭ-
5 nōkwē Ādag·iᵋlakwē. Wä, lāxaē lāsas k!waᵋyas ʟᴇk·āsa lāxa ts!ᴇdāqē
xŭnōxᵘsxa ʟēgadäs Wäʟidē. Wä, laᴇm gwāgwaaqas lāxa Mamalēleqala.
Wä, lēx·aᵋmēs la axēᵋlakᵘ las ʟ!āłäyīg·flisē k!waᵋyas ʟ!āqoʟasᵋwŭł-
łē ʟōᵋ k·!ēk·!ᴇsᵋâs. Wä, laᴇm lābawīsʟa.

_____

Wä, hёᵋmaē ʟ!āłäyīg·flis yīx k·!ēdēłas Hawīlkŭlałᵋwŭłēxa wā-
10 x·ᵋᴇm ts!ᴇdāqa lä äxᵋēdᴇx k!waᵋyasēs q!ŭlēᵋyē Hämasaqa ʟᴇᵋwa dāgᴇmaᵋyē ʟōᵋ ᵋnāxwē k·!ēk·!ᴇsᵋâs. Wä, g·flᵋmēsē łᴇᵋlē Hämasaqołē laē
ʟēgadē ʟ!āłäyīg·flisas Wak·adzē lāxa bāxŭsē. Wä, lä ʟēgadᴇs ʟᴇm-
k·!āla lāxa ts!ēts!ēqa. Wä, lāxaē ʟēgadᴇs Māxᵋēnox lāxa gŭmᵋyasaxa
hēłᵋaxʟäyo. Wä, lä ʟēgadᴇs Kwax·sēᵋstāladzē yīxs laē k!wēłē ʟ!āłä-
15 yīg·flisxa la ʟēgadᴇs Wāk·adzēxs laē łᴇᵋlēs q!ŭlēᵋyołē Hämasaqołē
Wä, lāxaē gᴇg·adē äpsōt!ᴇmaᵋyas Wāk·adzäsa ʟēgᴇmasēs änēsᵋwŭłe
Ts!ᴇts!āłałᵋwŭłē lāxa bāxŭsē. Wä, lä ʟēgadᴇs Q!ēgᴇmāla lāxa ts!ē-
ts!ēqa. Wä, lä ʟēgadᴇs Kŭskŭs lāxa gŭmᵋyasap!aēda haᵋyāłᵋa. Wä,
lä ʟēgadᴇs Tsᴇxŭla lāxa ts!ēdaqaxs hёē gŭmaᵋyasap!ē. Wä, maᵋłgŭ-
20 nałtsᴇmē ʟēʟᴇgᴇmas ōgŭᵋla lāxēs ts!ᴇdāgᴇxʟäyuwē ʟ!āłäyīg·flis qaxs
ōgŭᵋlaᵋmaē yāqwasᴇᵋwaxs laē łaᵋwadesēs łāᵋwŭnᴇmē K!wāk!wabalasᴇma-
ᵋyēxᴇn xŭnōkwē yīnʟaxg·în _George Hunt_. Wä, hёᵋmēsᴇn lāg·iła ālak-
k·!āla q!āʟᴇlax gwaᵋyiᵋlälasas ᵋnāᵋnᴇmsgᴇmagowē ʟēʟᴇgᴇmas ʟ!āłäyī-
g·flisē lāxēq.

25   Wä, lä łᴇᵋlē ōmpas ʟ!āłäyīg·flisēxa la ʟēgadᴇs Wāk·adzē yīx
ōmpasē Hawīlkŭlałᵋwŭłē. Wä, laᵋmēda la ʟēgadᴇs Wāk·adzē äxᵋēdᴇx
k!waᵋyasēs ōmpdē ʟᴇᵋwa hōqwastāla g·ōkwą. Wä, hёᵋmis mᴇᵋwēxʟa łē-
łōqŭliła; wä, hёᵋmis ʟēʟᴇgᴇmasē Hawīlkŭlałxa ʟēłᴇᵋlayuxʟäᵋyasēxa
hamałela lēᵋlqŭlaʟaᵋya; hёᵋmis k!wēladzᴇxʟäyāsē Kwāküx·âlas; hёᵋ-
30 misē t!ᴇnsēlax·läyâs Yāqoʟadzē; wä, hёᵋmisē hēłᵋax·läyâsē ᵋwābidoᵋ;
wä, hёᵋmisē nōłᴇmāłax·läyâsē G·āg·iqoʟ!alag·flis lāxa ts!ēts!eqa.

the/seat of the late Hāmasaqa., for it would belong to his child; even if she had been a girl (30) she would have taken his seat. But the late Hāmasaqa never had a child/and therefore his seat went to Ādag·iᵋlakᵘ. Then for two years (1) ᴸ!āx̌āyīg·flis kept the seat of her late father, the late Hawīlkūlax̌,/and the seat of her late uncle, the late Hāmasaqa. And when he grew up/to be a man, Ādag·iᵋlakᵘ, the eldest one among the children of ᴸ!āx̌āyag·flis,/she gave over to him the two seats and the two names tö her son,(5) Ādag·iᵋlakᵘ. And she also gave the seat of Lɛk·âs to her daughter/who had the name Wäʟid. Then she went over to the Mamalēḷeqala/and it is only kept by ᴸ!āx̌ā-yīg·flis the seat of the late ᴸ!āqoʟas/and his privileges. And so this is the end.

And now ᴸ!āx̌āyag·flis, that is the princess of the late Hawīlkū-lax̌,(10) although she is a woman, took the seat of her uncle Hämasaqa, and the office of. giving away property/and all his privileges. And when Hämasaqa died/ᴸ!āx̌āyīg·flis had the name Wāk·adzē in the secular season; and she had the name/Lɛᴍk·!ála in the winter ceremonial; and she had the name Māxᵋēnoxᵘ for the giving away ceremonial/of the young men; and she had the name Kwax·sēᵋstāladzē when she went to a feast; she, ᴸ!āx̌āyīg·flis‚ (15) who had the name Wāk·adzō when her uncle, Hämasaqa, died./ Now Wāk·adzē had as a wife "of the other side" the name of her late aunt,/Ts!ɛts!âlax̌, in the secular season; and she had the name Q!ēgɛmāla in the winter ceremonial;/and she had the name Küs-küs in the giving away ceremonial of the young men; and/she had the name Tsɛxüla when the women gave away property to one another. And(20) she had all eight names in addition to her woman's name ᴸ!āx̌āyīg·flis. And/it is also given to her besides now that she is married to K!wā-k!wabālasɛmēᵋ,/my son, and I am George Hunt. And that is how I really know/all about the nine different names of/ᴸ!āx̌āyīg·flis.

(25) And now died the father of ᴸ!āx̌āyīg·flis, whose name was now Wāk·adzē, that is/her father, the late Hawīlkūlax̌. And now she, whose name was Wāk·adzē took the/seat of her late father and the Vom-

Wä, lāxaē gɛg·adō āpsōt!ɛnaᶜyas yîxaasēs ānēsᶜwüłɛxa ḷēgadä ᶜmāx·mɛ-
wēdzɛmga. Wä, lä ḷēgadɛs Mɛnłōsɛlas lāxa gwēgŭdza. Wä, lāxaē ḷēgadɛs K!wēkwēs lāxa ts!ēdaqaxs gŭmᶜyasap!aē. Wä, hēᶜmēsa dāgɛmaᶜyē
lā lāxa āłē Hawīlkŭlała. Wä, g·îlᶜmēsē ɛlāq nɛxi̯aāx·ᶜîd bɛgwānɛmē

5   Ādag·iᶜlakwaxa laēda āłē Hawīlkŭlał yîx ʟ!āłäyÎg·îlisē lâsa ᶜwIᶜlasɛn
la ḷēḷɛqaᶜlayox ʟ!āłäyig·îlisē lāxēs ᶜnōlast!ɛgɛmaᶜyē xŭnōkwē Ādag·i-
ᶜlakwē; wä, hēᶜmisē k!waᶜyas Wāk·adzē ᶜwIᶜla lā lax Ādag·iᶜlakwē ᶜwI-
ᶜlēda ḷēḷɛgɛmē ḷɛᶜwa ts!ēdagɛxʟäᶜyo ḷēḷɛgɛma; wä, hēᶜmēsa māᶜłēdāła
dāgɛmaᶜya. Wä, laᶜmē la maᶜłē k!waᶜyas Ādag·iᶜlaxᵘxa la ḷēgadɛs Wā-

10 k·adzē ḷōᶜ Hawīlkŭlał. Wä, laɛmxaē lāba lāxēq.

      Wä, hēᶜmaē ʟ!āłäyÎg·îlisē yîxs ts!āts!adagɛmaēda māk·îläx Āda-
g·iᶜlakwēxa la ḷēgadɛs Wāk·adzē ḷōᶜ Hawīlkŭlałxa ḷēgadɛs Wäḷidē. Wä,
lāxaē ʟ!āłäyÎg·îlisē lâsasēs ḷēgɛmē Lɛk·âsa lāxēs ts!ɛdāqē xŭnōkwē
Wäḷidē. Wä, laɛm la ḷâgaᶜyē Wäḷidē lāxa ᶜnɛᶜmēmotasa Mamalēleq!äm

15 lāxēq ḷōᶜ ᶜwIᶜlē ḷēḷɛgɛmas ḷɛᶜwa g·ōkwē. Wä, laᶜmē ʟ!āłäyÎg·îlisē
lās Wäḷidēxa la ḷēgadɛs Lɛk·âsa lāxēs äbāsk·!ōtē lāxa Mamalēleqala
lax k!waᶜyas Lɛk·âsᶜōłē. Wä, hēᶜmis la gɛnɛms Wäḷidēxa la ḷēgadɛs Lɛ-
k·âsaxēs äbɛmpē ʟ!āłäyÎg·îlisē. Wä, lä lēx·aɛm äxēlaxᵘs ʟ!āłäyig·î-
lisa ḷēgɛmē L!āqoḷas lāg·iłas bābagŭxa lāxa Mamalēleqala yîx ʟ!āła-

20 yÎg·îlisē. Wä, âᶜmisē ʟ!āłäyÎg·îlisē la nōmadzÎłtsēs xŭnōkwē Hawīlkŭlał.   Wä, laɛm ᶜnɛmāx·îs ḷōᶜ nâqēg·îlē ʟ!āłäyÎg·îlisē qaēs xŭnōkwē Hawīlkŭlał lāxēs ᶜnɛᶜmēmota Kŭkwāk!ŭmasa Q!ōmoyâᶜyē. Wä, lāxaē
hēᶜm gwäła lāxa ᶜnɛᶜmēmotasa Wāwŭlibâᶜyē qaēs xŭnōkwē. Wä, laɛm lāba laxēq.

iting Beam house and also the four feasting dishes/and also the different names of Hawīlkǔlał, the name for inviting (30) the different tribes; and his feast giving name, Kwākǔx·âlas; and also/his giving away name Yāqoᴌadzē; and also his young man's name, ᵋwābidōᵋ; and also/his fool dancer name G·āg·iqoᴌ!ālag·flis in the winter ceremonial. (1) And now she had as her wife "of the other side" the body of her late aunt whose name was ᵋmāx·ꬵᴇwēdzᴇꬱga;/and she had the name Mᴇnᴚōsᴇlas in the gwēgǔdza; and she also had the name/K!wēkwēs in the giving away of the young women. And also the office of giving away property/went to the new Hawīlkǔlał. And when Ādag·iᵋlakᵘ was nearly a full grown man,(5) then the new Hawīlkǔlał, that is ᴌ!āᴚāyīg·flis, she, ᴌ!āᴚāyīg·flis, gave over all/that I have mentioned to her eldest child, Ādag·iᵋlakᵘ./ And also the seats of Wāk·adzē all went to Ādag·iᵋlakᵘ, and all/his different names and the different women's names and also the two/offices of giving away property. And now Ādag·iᵋlakᵘ had two seats, he whose name is now Wāk·adzē (10) and Hawīlkǔlał. Now this is the end of this.

And now about ᴌ!āᴚāyīg·flis and her little girl, the next child to Ādag·iᵋlakᵘ/whose name is now Wāk·adzē and Hawīlkǔlał; and her name is Wäᴌid. Now/ᴌ!āᴚāyīg·flis gave the name Lᴇk·âs to her daughter/ Wäᴌid. Then Wäᴌid had her place in the numaym Mamalēleq!am (15) and all her different names and her house. And now ᴌ!āᴚāyīg·flis/gave to Wäᴌid whose name is now Lᴇk·âs on her mother's side among the Mamalēleqala,/the seat of the late Lᴇk·âs. And now the wife of Wäᴌid,whose name is now Lᴇk·âs, is/her mother. And ᴌ!āᴚāyīg·flis only kept/the name ᴌ!āqoᴌas, and that is why L!āᴚāyīg·flis is a man among the Mamalēleqala.(20)And ᴌ!āᴚāyīg·flis is only the old man of her child Hawīlkǔlał./ ᴌ!āᴚāyīg·flis is like the counsellor of her child/Hawīlkǔlał in the numaym Kǔkwak!um of the.Q!ōmoyâᵋyē. And it is the same in the numaym Wāwǔlibâᵋyē of her child. Now that is the end.

A Family History

Wä, laᵋmɛn ōt!ēdeł gwāgwēx·sᵋālał lāxēs k·!ātaᵋyōs lāxa aᴌɛ-
bōxsᵋagâla ᵋnāla lāxa ᵋmɛgwābâᵋyasa ts!ātap!ēxa December:

Wä, hēᵋmaē ᵋmāx̱ᵘmɛwēsagɛmaᵋyēxa g·ĭgɛmaᵋyasa ᵋnɛᵋmēmotāsa

5 Dzɛndzɛnx·q!ayo. Wä, lä gɛg·adɛs ᴌɛlɛndzɛᵋwēk· lāxa wŭq!äs Lā-
lak·ots!axa g·āyołē lāx ᵋnɛᵋmēmotasa Mamalēleq!äm yĭxs gɛg·adaē
Lālak·ots!a yĭs Hamdzidēxa ts!ɛdāqē xŭnōx̱ᵘs Yāqałᵋänlidzēxa g·ā-
yołē lāx ᵋnɛᵋmēmotasa Nāx·naxŭᵋlasa Qwēqᵘsōt!ēnoxᵘ. Wä, laᵋmē
k·!eâs xŭnōx̱ᵘs Lālak·ots!a ᴌɛᵋwis gɛnɛmē Hamdzidē. Wä, la wŭq!wä-

10 sē ᴌɛlɛndzɛᵋwēk· ᴌɛᵋwis łāᵋwŭnɛmē ᵋmāx̱ᵘmɛwēsagɛmaᵋyē xŭngwadɛx·ᵊĭ-
tsa bābagŭmē lāxg·a Tsāxisɛk·. Wä, g·ĭlᵋmēsē q!ālēda âlak·!āla
g·ĭgɛmaᵋyē Lālak·ots!axēs wŭq!wa ᴌɛlɛndzɛᵋwēk·axs lɛᵋmaē māᵋyołᵋĭ-
tsa bābagŭmē, wä, la aðk·ĭnē nâqaᵋyas Lālak·ots!a qaxs laē q!āla-
qēxs bɛgwānɛmaē māᵗyoᴌɛmasēs wŭq!wa. Lāg·iłas mōxsasa ᵋnāxwa hēᵋ-

15 maōmas lāxa ᵋwālasē xwāk·!ūna. Wä, g·āxē wāwałqālas lāxēs q!ŭlēsē
ᵋmāx̱ᵘmɛwēsagɛmaᵋyē. Wä, lä ᴌēgɛmg·ĭlxᴌālax ᵋmāxŭlag·ĭlis qa ᴌē-
gɛmsēs ᴌōlēᵋyē. Wä, laᵋmē Lālak·ots!a nēłaxēs q!ŭlēsē ᵋmāx̱ᵘmɛwē-
sagɛmaᵋyē yĭxs lɛᵋmaē äxᵋēdełxa g·ĭnānɛmēxēs ᴌōlēᵋyē qaᵋs lālag·-
g·ĭłts gwāłɛlaɛm äxᵋēdᴌɛx k!waᵋyas Lālak·ots!a lāxēs ᵋnɛᵋmēmota

20 Mamalēleq!äm ᵋnēk·ē. Wä, âᵋmisē ᵋnāxwa ēx·ᵋak·a ᵋnɛmēmotasa Dzɛn-
dzɛnx·q!ayo lāx wāłɛmas Lālak·ots!a. Wä, laɛm âɛm lāł q!wā-
q!waxaᴌɛx ᵋmāxŭlag·ĭlisēxēs ᴌōlēᵋyē. Wä, laᵋmē ōt!ēd la xŭngwa-
dɛx·ᵋĭdē ᴌɛlɛndzɛᵋwēk·asa ts!āts!adagɛmē. Wä, lä hēᵋmē ᵋmāx̱ᵘmɛ-
wēsagɛmaᵋyē ᴌēxᵋēts ᵋwālasᴌāla. Wä, maᵋlōkwē sāsɛmas ᴌɛlɛndzɛᵋ-

25 wēk· ᴌɛᵋwis łāᵋwŭnɛmē ᵋmāx̱ᵘmɛwēsagɛmaᵋyē. Wä, g·ĭlᵋmēsē nɛxlaâ-
x·ᵋĭd la bɛgwānɛmē ᵋmāxŭlag·ĭlisē lāas wēk!ĭx·ᵋĭdē ompdäsē yĭx
ᵋmāx̱ᵘmɛwēsɛgɛmēx·dē. Wä, laᵋmē ᵋmāxŭlag·ĭlisē ᴌaxstōdxēs ōmpdē.
Wä, laɛm ᴌēgadē ᵋmāxŭlag·ĭlisēsas māx̱ᵘmɛwēsagɛmaᵋyē lāxēq.

Wä, k·ēst!a gäłaxs g·āxaēda ᵋwālas xwāk!ūna g·āx·alis q!ä-

30 laxa bēbɛgwānɛmē. Wä, hēstaɛm ᵋnɛᵋmēmōtsa Mamalēleq!ämxa k!ŭdzɛ-
xsāla lāx ᵋwālas xwāk!ūnä. Wä, hēᵋmis lāg·alisē ᴌ!ɛmaisas g·ō-

A Family History

Now I will again talk about your letter of the/twenty-
seventh of the Split Moon, that is December:/

It was ᵋmāx·mɛwēsagɛmēᵋ who was chief of the numaym(5)
Dzɛndzɛnx·q!ayo. He had for his wife Łɛlɛndzɛᵋwēk·, the sister
of/Lālak·ots!a who came from the numaym Mamalēleq!ăm, for Lala-
k·ots!a had for his wife/Hamdzid, the daughter of Yāqałᵋănlidzē/
who came from the numaym Nāx·naxūᵋla of the Qwēqᵘsot!ēnoxᵘ. Now/
Lālak·ots!a and his wife Hamdzid had no children. And his sister
(10) Łɛlɛndzɛᵋwēk· and her husband ᵋmāx·mɛwēsagɛmēᵂ had a/son
here at Fort Rupert. And as soon as the great/chief Lālak·ots!a
learned that his sister Łɛlɛndzɛᵋwēk· had given birth to a/boy,
the heart of Lālak·ots!a was very glad, for he had found out/
that the newborn child of his sister was a boy. Therefore he
loaded with all kinds of(15)food a large canoe and came to give
a marriage gift to his brother-in-law/ᵋmāxᵘmɛwēsagɛmēᵋ. And he
gave the marriage name ᵋmāxūlag·flis as a/name to his nephew.
Then Lālak·ots!a told his brother-in-law ᵋmāx·mɛwēsagɛmēᵋ/that
he was going to take the child, his nephew, and that he should/
be ready to take the seat of Lālak·ots!a in his numaym(20)Mama-
lēleq!ăm. Thus he said, and the whole numaym Dzɛndzɛnx·q!ayo
agreed to/what Lālak·ots!a said. Now he was just waiting for/
ᵋmāxūlag·flis, his nephew, to grow up. Now Łɛlɛndzɛᵋwēk· had
another child, a girl, and it was ᵋmāx·mɛwēsagɛmēᵋ/who gave her
the name ᵋwālasʟala. Now they had two children, Łɛlɛndzɛᵋwēk·(25)
and her husband ᵋmāx·mɛwēsagɛmēᵋ. As soon as/ᵋmāxūlag·flis was
a full grown man his father,/ᵋmāx·mɛwēsagɛmēᵋ, died, and now
ᵋmāxūlag·flis took the place of his late father./Then ᵋmāxūlag·flis
had the name ᵋmāx·mɛwēsagɛmēᵋ after this./

It was not long before a large canoe came to the beach with
many(30)men, and they belonged to the numaym Mamalēleq!ăm, those
who were sitting in/the large canoe. And it was there that they
came ashore at the beach of the house of(1)him whose name was

kwasa la ʟē̆gadɛs ᵋmāx̣ᵘmɛwē̆sagɛmaᵋyē̆. Wä, g·āx̄ē̆ ᵋwīᵋla hōx̄ᵋwŭs-
dē̆sa lāxa ʟ!ɛmaisē̆ qaᵋs lä hō̆gwiʟ lāx g·ō̆kwas ᵋmāx̣ᵘmɛwē̆sagɛmaᵋyē̆
qaᵋs ᵋwīᵋlē̆ k!ŭs̄ᵋālīx̱ lāx ä̆ᵋwīʟɛlä̆sa t!ɛx·x̱lä̆sa g·ō̆kwē̆. Wä, laᵋ-
mē̆sɛnuᵋx̣ᵘ ᵋwīᵋla la hō̆gwiʟ ō̆gwaqa qɛnuᵋx̣ᵘ hō̆ʟē̆lē̆x lāg·ix̱as x̱ɛn-
5 ʟɛla x̱ŭlsa lāxē̆s g·āx̄ᵋalē̆sɛlaē̆. Wä, lä ʟₐ̆x̄ᵋwalīx̱a ᵋnɛmō̆kwē̆ lā̆q xa
ʟē̆gadä̆s K!waē̆lask·ɛn yī̆xs hē̆ᵋmaē̆ ɛlkwasa g·īgɛmaᵋyē̆ Lālak·ots!a
yī̆x q!ŭlē̆ᵋyas ᵋmāx̣ᵘmɛwē̆sagɛmaᵋyē̆. Wä, la yā̆q!ɛg·aᵋx̱ē̆ K!waē̆lask·ɛn.
Wä, lä ᵋnē̆k·a, G·āx̄ᵋmɛn Kwakŭg·ux̱, g·āx̄ᵋmɛn ᵋyā̆lagɛma ᵋyā̆lagɛmsa
ᵋwā̆lasa g·īgɛmaᵋyaxa ᵋwā̆lasa g·īgɛmaᵋyaɛnsaxg·ins haᵋmā̆x̱ɛlē̆k· lē̆l-
10 qwā̆laʟaᵋyaxē̆s mā̆x̱t!ē̆x̱aō̆s Kwakŭg·ux̱xa q!ä̆nā̆lä̆ ʟē̆x̱ɛla lā̆ʟaxs haᵋmā̆x̱ɛ-
laē̆x lē̆lqwā̆laʟaᵋya,yī̆xa lä mā̆mē̆xᵋaᵋx̱alīx̱a yī̆xa ᵋwā̆lasa g·īgāmaᵋyē̆
Lālak·ots!a. Wä, hē̆ᵋmis lāg·ix̱asē̆ ᵋyā̆laqanuᵋx̣ᵘ qɛnuᵋx̣ᵘ g·āx̄ē̆ dā̆ʟ
g·īgāmē̆ ᵋmāx̣ᵘmɛwē̆sagɛmē̆ qaᵋs laō̆s k!wastō̆lē̆x̱axᵘ k!wä̆x·dä̆s, qaxs
k·!e̊ₐsaē̆ hē̆x̱ō̆ äx̄ᵋē̆dɛx k!wä̆x·dä̆s ō̆gŭᵋla lā̆ʟ g·īgāmē̆ᵋ. Wä, x̱wē̆laqɛ-
15 lē̆sᵋɛmāx·īns qɛns hē̆x̱ts!ē̆qē̆xs k·!ē̆sᵋmaa wŭyī̆msᵋalīx̱a, ᵋnē̆k·ē̆.

Wä, hë̆x·ᵋidaᵋmē̆sē̆ x̱ɛlɛndzɛᵋwē̆k·ē̆ yī̆x ä̆bɛmpasa āx̱ ᵋmāx̣ᵘmɛwē̆-
sagɛmaᵋya yā̆q!ɛg·aᵋx̱a. Wä, lä ᵋnē̆k·a,qa ᵋmā̆sē̆wē̆tsē̆s wā̆x̱dɛmʟaō̆s,
yō̆ʟaxs ᵋnɛᵋmē̆motaaxsg·īn x̱ŭnō̆kŭk· qaxs hë̆x·sä̆ᵋmaē̆x gwä̆x̱ɛxa wā̆x̱-
dɛmasɛn g·īgɛmaᵋya wŭq!wē̆ Lālak·ots!a yī̆x ᵋwā̆lasa Kwāx·x̱lanō̆kŭ-
20 maᵋya yī̆xs gwā̆x̱ɛlaᵋmaa ᵋnē̆k· qa yŭᵋmē̆sɛn x̱ŭnō̆kwē̆x ʟ!ā̆yō̆s. Wä,
wag·ax·īns haᵋliᵋlä̆la ᵋmō̆xsa qɛns lā̆lag·i haᵋyax̱ts!aaqē̆ ᵋnē̆k·ē̆ x̱ɛ-
lɛndzɛᵋwē̆k·ē̆.

Wä, hë̆x·ᵋidaᵋmē̆sē̆ ᵋmō̆xsasē̆s ᵋmɛmᵋwā̆la lāxa x̱wā̆k!ŭna. Wä,
g·īlᵋmē̆sē̆ ᵋwī̆lxsa laē̆ ʟₑx̄ᵋīda. Wä, lä lāg·aa lāx Mē̆mk·ŭmlisaxa
25 la ɛlā̆q ᵋnāx·ᵋida. Wä, hë̆x·ᵋidaᵋmē̆sē̆ x̱ɛlɛndzɛᵋwē̆k· ʟₑᵋwis x̱ŭnō̆-
kwē̆ ᵋmāx̣ᵘmɛwē̆sagɛmaᵋyē̆ la hō̆x̄ᵋwŭsdē̆s qaᵋs lä hō̆gwiʟ lāx g·ō̆kwasa
wāwē̆k·!ɛq!ē̆ Lālak·ots!a. Wä, hē̆ᵋmis k!wā̆g·alīx̱ē̆ ᵋmāx̣ᵘmɛwē̆sagɛma-
ᵋya mak·ä̆x̱a lāx hō̆x̱k·!ō̆dɛnō̆ʟɛmalīx̱asē̆s q!ŭlē̆ᵋyē̆ Lālak·ots!a. Wä,
laɛm ʟₐ̆ā̆p!ē̆līx̱ē̆da q!ɛyō̆xwē̆ ʟ!ā̆qwa, yī̆x Lē̆ta lāxa wāwē̆k·!ɛq!a g·ī-
30 gāmaᵋya. Wä, lä ʟₐ̆nō̆ʟɛmalīx̱a ᵋnɛmsgɛmē̆ q!ɛyō̆x ʟ!ā̆qwaqxa ʟē̆gadä̆s
Qolō̆ma yī̆x k·ilk·x̱lwänɛmas Lālak·ots!a. Wä, g·īlᵋmē̆sē̆ g·äx ᵋwīᵋ-

now ᵋmāx·mɛwēsagɛmēᵋ. And they all came and walked up/the beach
and went into the house of ᵋmāx·mɛwēsagɛmēᵋ/and they all sat
down inside by the door of the house. We all/of us went also
into the house to listen why(5)those who came to the beach were
very downhearted. Then arose one of them/whose name was Kwḷa-
ēlask·ɛn, for he was the speaker of chief Lālak·otsḷa/the uncle
of ᵋmāx·mɛwēsagɛmēᵋ. Now Kḷwaēlask·ɛn spoke/and said:" I come,
Kwag·uⱡ, I come sent by, sent by the/great chief, our great
chief, that(10)it may be known to you, strange tribes, Kwag·uⱡ,
that he who always invited you, strange/tribes, that he is going
to sleep in the house, the great chief/Lālak·otsḷa. Therefore,
he sent us that we should come and get/you, great chief ᵋmāx·mɛ-
wēsagɛmēᵋ, that you may go and sit down in his former seat, for
there is/no one who is the right one to take the seat, other than
you, chief. Now let us go back(15)that we may reach there before he dies," said he.

Immediately Ɫɛlɛndzeᵋwēk·, the mother of the new ᵋmāxmɛwē-
sagɛmēᵋ/spoke and said: " What can you say/you numaym of my son
here? For always were this way the words of the/great chief, of
my brother, Lalak·otsḷa, that ᵋwālas Kwāx·ïlanōkūmēᵋ,(20)for he
has already said that my son here shall take his place. Now/
let us quickly load our canoes that we may reach him in time,"
thus said/Ɫɛlɛndzeᵋwēk·.

Immediately they loaded their cargo in the canoe and/when
the canoe was loaded they started. They arrived at Mēmk·ūmlia(25)
when it was nearly daylight, and immediately Ɫɛlɛndzeᵋwēk· and
her son,/ᵋmāx·mɛwēsagɛmēᵋ went up the beach and went into the
house of/the dying Lālak·otsḷa, and there ᵋmāx·mɛwēsagɛmēᵋ sat
down/near the right hand side of his uncle, Lālak·otsḷa./Behind
the head of the dying chief stood the expensive copper Lēta(30)
and at the side of his head stood another expensive copper named/
Beaver-Face, which had been bought by Lālak·otsḷa. As soon as the

laēɫē ᵋnɛᵋmēmotas Lălak·ots!a lāas yāq!ɛg·aᵋɫē ɛlkwäs Lālak·ots!a

yîx K!waēlask·ɛn. Wä, lä ᵋnēk·a: G·āxᵋmɛnuᵋxᵘ g·ĭgämēᵋ g·āxᵋmɛ-

nuᵋxᵘ hɛlä g·ĭgämēᶠ. G·āxᵋmōx ᵋmāxᵘmɛwēsagɛmaᵋyēx, g·āxᵋmōx g·ĭ-

gämēᶠ. Wä, hĕɛm laē walē wāɫdɛmas,lāalasē bɛlasōᵋs Hamdzidē yîx

5 gɛnɛmas Lālak·ots!a. Wä, lāᵋlaē ᵋnēk·ē Hamdzidäxs laē yāq!ɛg·aᶠ-

ɫa qaxs lɛᵋmaē ɫɛnēᵋstaēɫē Lālak·ots!a. Wa, g·ōkŭlōt. Wa, laᵋ-

mōx, laᵋmōx lādzēᵋmōx x·ōyoxwalisa ᵋwālasdēx g·ĭgämaᵋyaxɛn g·ĭ-

qēlasōᵋx·dēx ʟɛᵋwŭn ōmpēxōx Yāqaɫᵋänlidzēx. Wä, hāg·îɫla g·ĭgä-

mēᶠ Lālak·ots!a yōʟ ᵋwālas Kwāx·ĭlanōkŭmēᶠ,hāg·îɫla k·!eâsēg·în

10 māyadɛma qaxg·în âlēk· hēɫāxamas lāxɛn g·ĭqēlaēnoyōʟ g·ĭgämēᶠ,

ᵋnēx·ᵋlaēxs laē däx·ᵋidɛx Lētaxa ᵋwālasē ʟ!āqwa ʟɛᵋwa ᵋnɛmsgɛma-

sē yîx Qolōma. Wä, lāᵋlaē ᵋnēk·a: Wä, gēlag·a xŭnōkᵘ, gēla-

dzēla yūʟ ᵋmāxᵘmɛwēsagɛmē yūʟ ᵋwālas Kwāx·ĭlanōkŭmē qaxs ᵋnēxᵋ-

maōx q!ŭlēx·dēx qaᵋs hĕᵋmaōs g·îl ʟēgɛmē ᵋwālas Kwāx·ĭlanōkŭma-

15 ᵋyē. Wä, laɛmxaāwisē lāʟē k!wäx·däsōx lâʟ g·ĭgämēᶠ ʟōᵋ k·!ēk·!ɛ-

sᵋōxᵘdäsēx q!ŭlēx·dēx lâʟ, yūᵋmesa g·ōxᵘdäxs; wä, g·aᵋmēsēg·ada

ʟēʟɛgadɛk· ʟ!āʟ!ɛqwa laɛmk· lāɫ lâʟ, ᵋnēk·ēxs laē ts!âs lāx ᵋmā-

xᵘmɛwēsagɛmaᵋyē. Wä, laᵋmē k·!ēs q!āq!ēk·ɛlax Lālak·ots!axs lɛ-

ᵋmaaxōʟ wēk·!ɛxᵋida.

20   Wä, laɛmʟa ᵋmāxᵘmɛwēsagɛmaᵋyē äxᵋēdxa maᵋɫtsɛmē ʟ!āʟ!ɛqwa

qaᵋs g·ēxēq lāxa ōts!âlĭɫē. Wä, la ᵋmāxᵘmɛwēsagɛmaᵋyē äxk·!ālax

K!waēlask·ɛnxa ɛlkwē qa läs ʟēᵋlālaxa ɫawits!ēs ʟɛᵋwa Mādiɫbē

ʟɛᵋwa Dɛnax·daᵋxᵘ ʟɛᵋwa Aᵋwaĭʟɛla ʟɛᵋwa Dzāwadɛēnoxᵘ ʟɛᵋwa Gwa-

waēnoxᵘ ʟɛᵋwa Hāxwāmis ʟɛᵋwa Qwēqᵘsōt!ēnoxᵘ ʟɛwa ᵋnɛmgis ʟɛᵋwa

25 Gwētɛla ʟɛᵋwa Q!ōmoyâᵋyē ʟɛᵋwa ᵋwālas Kwāg·uɫ ʟɛᵋwa Q!ōmk·!ŭt!-

ɛs qa läs ᵋwĭᵋla wŭnɛmtaxa g·ĭgämex·dē Lālak·ots!ax·dē.

   Wä, laᵋmē ʟɛxᵋĭdēda mōts!aqē xwāxwak!ŭna qaᵋs lä ʟēᵋlālaxa

yŭduxᵘsɛᵋmagŭg·ɛyowē lēlqwälaʟaᵋya. Wä, g·îlᵋmisē ᵋwĭᵋla la ʟɛxᵋ-

ĭda lāsa waōkwē ämlēxᵘ Mamalēlēqala hōgŭxs laxa ōgŭᵋla xwāxŭxwā-

30 gŭm qaᵋs lä ēkwax äpsanâᵋyasa ämaᵋyē ʟâtsɛmāla ᵋmɛk·âla lāx ᵋnā-

lanōʟɛmaᵋyas ᵋmēmkŭmlis qa dɛk·aatsa g·ĭgämēx·dē. Wä, g·îlᵋmisē

(1) whole numaym of Lālak·ōts!a had come in, the speaker of Lālak·o=
ts!a,/Kwaēlask·ɛn, spoke and said, "We come, chief, we come/back,
chief. Now ᵋmāxᵘmɛwēsaɡɛmēᵋ has come, he came, chief."/ And
there stopped his speech, for Hamdzid, (5) the wife of Lālak·ots!a,
forbade him (to go on). Then Hamdzid said as she spoke that/Lā-
lak·ots!a was already unconscious: "Enough, o tribe, enough!/
Now the great one will have a rest, the great chief whom I made
a chief/together with my father, Yāqaɬᵋānlidzē, here. Now go a-
way, chief,/Lālak·ots!a, you, ᵋwālas Kwāx·flanōkūmēᵋ, go away.
There is nothing (10) for me to regret, for I have done well in
making you a chief, chief."/ Thus she said, and she took Lēta,
the great copper,and the other copper,/Beaver-Face,and she said:
"Now come, child, come,/you ᵋmāxᵘmɛwēsaɡɛmēᵋ, you ᵋwālas Kwax·f-
lanōkūmēᵋ, for/this your late uncle said that your first name is
ᵋwālas Kwax·flanōkūmēᵋ.(15) Now his former seat will also go to
you, chief, and the former privileges/of your uncle will go to you,
and his house, and also these/coppers which have names will go to
you", she said as she gave them to ᵋmāxᵘmɛwēsaɡɛmēᵋ./ She did not
know that Lālak·ots!a was/already dead.(20)

　　Then ᵋmāxᵘmɛwēsaɡɛmēᵋ took the two coppers/and put them into
the bedroom. Then ᵋmāxᵘmɛwēsaɡɛmēᵋ asked/K!waēlask·ɛn, the speaker, to invite the Ɬāwits!ēs and the Mādiɬbē/and the Dɛnax·daᵋxᵘ
and the AᵋwaĬlɛla and the DzāwadɛŌnoxᵘ and the Gwawaēnoxᵘ/and the
Hāxwāmis and the Qwēqᵘsōt!ēnoxᵘ and the ᵋnɛmɡis and the (25) Gwētɛla and the Q!ōmcyāᵋyē and the ᵋwālas Kwāɡ·uɬ and the Q!ōmk·!ū-
t!ɛs/that all should go to bury the late chief, Lālak·ots!ax·dē./

　　Then four canoes started and went to invite the/thirteen
tribes,and as soon as they all had started/the other Mamalēleqala
who were left behind went in other small canoes (30) to clear one
side of the island on the south side of/Mēmkūmlis, which is covered with small trees, for the burial place of the past chief. When

gwáł ēkwaxs laē g·ōkwēlaxa g·ōx̱ᵘbỉdawē. Hayałomalaa g̱wałamasqēxs
k·!ēsᶜmaē g·āxa lēlqwälaᴌaᶜyē g·āxts!ȃ lāx Mēmkŭmlỉs. Wä, laɛmᴌō̱-
da nēnȃgadē ᴌ!ēgŭmg·ỉla qa sāleg·ayayōxa g·ỉgāmēx·dē. Wä, laɛm
qāᶜyasᶜɛnts wāxap!ɛnasas ᴌēłɛlaxa lēlqwälaᴌaᶜyē ᴌō̱ᶜ wāxap!ɛnasas
5 k!wēlatsa ᴌ!ē̱ᶜna ᴌō̱xs máłp!ɛnaē yāg·ỉᴌɛlaxō̱da ᴌō̱xs ᶜnɛmp!ɛnaē sāk·-
axō̱tsa xwāx̱ŭk!ŭna ᴌō̱xs q!ēnɛmaē t!ɛnsēladzaᶜyas. Wä, lä ɛlxᴌaᶜyē
q!ɛt!ɛdzaᶜyasēxa ᴌ!āᴌ!ɛqwa hästaɛm la qāᶜyasᶜɛndaᶜyoxa ᴌ!ēgŭmasa
nēnȃgadē. Wä, lä nɛᶜwỉᶜlalē qāᶜya̱sasa ᶜnɛmsgɛmē ᴌ!ēgŭm āxäsa ᶜnɛmōkwē nȃgadä g·äg·ỉᴌɛla lāx g·ỉlg·alỉsasa g·ỉgāmēx·dē g·āxᶜaᴌɛla
10 laqēxs laē wēk·!ɛxᶜỉda.

ᴌ!äq!walayo qa Lālak·ots!a.

Hana, hana, hana. Laᶜmē k·oxsɛlēsē̱ qɛlqatawalēsdēs ᶜnāla.

Hana, hana, hana. Laᶜmē qɛltoᶜyak·ỉlisē qɛldɛmx·dēs ᶜnāla.

Hana, hana, hana. Laᶜmē x·ōyoxwalēsɛns g·ỉgāmēdzēx·dēa.

15 Hana, hana, hana. Laᶜmē lāx·staalēsɛns g·ỉgāmēdzēx·dēa,

Hana, hana, hana, xa hälag·ỉlēdzēx·dēa wâx·sbɛndālax·dēa
ᶜwāᶜwalasdɛmx·sỉlaxɛns g·ỉgāmēdzēx·dēa,

Hana, hana, hana, xa p!ēp!adzɛyōsdēa g·ỉgāmaᶜyaxa q!ŭlēxᴌɛᶜ-
yaᶜma Lālak·ots!adzēx·dēaxa ᶜwālasa g·ỉgāmēdzēx·dēa,

20 Hana, hana, hana, xa āmāx̱ŭlałdēa g·ỉgāmaˢyaxa q!ŭlēxᴌɛᶜyaᶜma
Amāx̱ŭlałdzēx·dēaxa ᶜwālasa g·ỉgāmēdzēx·dēa,

Hana, hana, hana, xa sāk·axō̱dalałdēa g·ỉgāmaᶜyaxa q!ŭlēxᴌɛᶜ-
yaᶜma Wỉxwˉ.qȃgāmēdzēx·dēaxa ᶜwālasa g·ỉgāmēdzēx·dēa,

Hana, hana, hana, xa k!wälasɛlałdzēx·dēa g·ỉgāmaᶜyaxa q!ŭlēx-
25 ᴌɛᶜyaᶜma ᶜwālas Kwāx·ỉlanōkŭmēdzēx·dēaxa ᶜwālasa
g·ỉgāmaēdzēx·dēa,

they (1) had cleared it they built a small house and they tried to
finish it as quickly as possible/before the tribes came in to Mĕm-
kŭmlis. Then/the song makers made a mourning song to sing for the
late chief. They/put words into it (saying) how many times he had
invited the tribes, and how many times (5) he had given grease
feasts, and how many times he had given away property, and the one
time he had given away/canoes, and how many times he had given potlatches to hiw own tribe, and last/how many times he had broken coppers. All these words were put into the mourning song by the/song
makers. And the words of another mourning song were the family history, the work of another/song maker, beginning with the first ancestors of the chief and coming down (10) to the time that he died.

Mourning Song for Lalak·ots!a.

Hana, hana, hana. It broke down, the post of the world./

Hana, hana, hana. It fell down to the ground, the post of the
    world./

Hana, hana, hana. Our great chief has taken a rest.(15)

Hana, hana, hana. Now our past chief has fallen down./

Hana, hana, hana, the great one who continually gave away proper-
    ty at each end of the year,/who made great potlatches, our
    great chief./

Hana, hana, hana, the one who made potlatches all the time, the
    chief whose own name was/Lālak·ots!a, the great chief. (20)

Hana, hana, hana, the great chief who danced the potlatch dance,
    whose own name was/Amāxŭlaȴ, the great chief. /

Hana, hana, hana, the one who gave the Giving-Away-Canoes dance,
    the chief whose own name was/Wᴉxᶜwŭqâgɛmê', the great chief./

Hana,hana, hana, the one who gave the Feast-Giving dance, the
    chief whose own name was (25) ᶜwālas Kwāx·ilanōkŭmê, the
    great chief.

Hana, hana, hana, xa lāx·sᶜɛnda'aᴸdzĕx·dĕaxa q!ɛq!ɛltalaᴸdĕa
g·îgămaᶜyaxa q!ülēxʟɛᶜyaᶜma Lāx·sᶜɛndalaᴸdzĕx·dĕaxa
ᶜwālasa g·îgămēdzēx·dĕa,

Hana, hana, hana, xa sapstɛndalaᴸdzēx·dĕa g·îgămaᶜyaxa q!ulēx-
5   ʟɛᶜyaᶜma Ɲenōlōx·dĕaɛns ᶜwālasa g·îgămēdzēxᴭdĕa lēlqwălaʟĕ,

Hana, hana, hana, xa ʟ!ɛmkwalaᴸdzēx·dĕa g·îgămaᶜyaxa q!ülēx-
ʟɛᶜyaᶜma Yāqaxɛlag·îlisdzēx·dĕaxa ᶜwālasa g·îgămē-
dzēx·dĕa,

10   Hana, hana, hana, xa k·!älak·ɛlaᴸdzēx·dĕaxɛns g·îgămaᶜyaxa
q!ülāxʟɛᶜyaᶜma K·îlɛmgilēdzēx·dĕaxa ᶜwālasa g·î-
gămēdzēx·dĕa,

Hana, hana, hana, xa qōtēx·alaᴸdzēx·dĕaxɛns g·îgămaᶜyaxa q!ü-
lēxʟɛᶜyaᶜma ᶜmāxŭyaᶜlisdzēxdĕaxa ᶜwālasa g·îgămē-
15   dzēx·dĕa,

Hana, hana, hana, xa k·!ēdadaēnoxwalaᴸdzēx·dĕaxɛns g·îgăma-
ᶜya x!ülēxʟɛᶜyaᶜma G·îgămēdzēx·dĕaxa ᶜwālasᶜaxālisa
g·îqaxālisdzēx·dĕa,

Hana, hana, hana, xa tsōkŭlaᴸdzēx·dĕaxɛns g·îgămaᶜyaxa q!ülē-
20   xʟɛᶜyaᶜma Yāqawîdalaᴸdzēx·dĕaxa ᶜwālasᶜaxālisa g·î-
qaxālisdzēx·dĕa,

Hana, hana, hana, xa ᶜyāg·îʟɛlaxōdalaᴸdzēx·dĕaxɛns g·îgămaᶜ-
yaxg·îns lēlqwălaʟĕxa q!ülēxʟɛᶜyaᶜma ʟāʟelîʟalaᴸa
Haᶜmāseᶜyasdzē Hāmdzidēadzēx·dĕaxa ᶜwālasᶜaxālisa
25   g·îqaxālisdzēx·dĕaxaɛns g·îgămaᶜya. Hāladzē lāg·a-
x·îns g·îgămēdzēx·dĕa, laᶜmē qɛlyax·ᶜālisa ᶜwālas-
ᶜaxalisa g·îgămaᶜyîns lēlqwălaʟĕ,

Hana, hana, hana, nâya. Hana nâ.

Wä, hĕᶜmis g·ālabaᶜya mōsgɛmakwē Kwākwag·uᴸaxs g·āxaē ᶜyîᶜyɛ-
30   pɛmāᴸēs ᶜyaēyats!äxs g·āxaē sɛltāᴸa ēaʟɛx·äla ᶜnāx̱waɛm dɛnxalasēs
g·îg·îldzɛᶜyāla ʟ!ēʟ!aq!wala 'ᴸāxēs ᶜnālᶜnɛmsgɛmakwē.   Wä, hĕɛm

Hana, hana, hana, the one who gave the Property-Destroying dance, the Copper-Breaking dance,/the chief whose own name was Lāx·-sᶜɛndalaɫ,/the great chief.

Hana, hana, hana, the one who gave the Throwing-into-the-Water dance, the chief whose own name was Nɛnōlo, the great chief of all the/tribes.(7)

Hana, hana, hana, the one who gave the Giving-Away-of-the-Roof-Boards dance, the great chief/whose own name was Yāqaxɛlag·í-lis, the/great chief.(10)

Hana, hana, hana, the one who gave Striking-to-Kill dance,the great chief/whose own name was Kîlɛmgilis, the great/chief./

Hana, hana, hana, the one who gave the Marriage-Debt-Paying dance, our great chief/whose own name was ᶜmax̣wayaᶜlis, the great/chief.(16)

Hana, hana, hana, he who gave the Paying-for-his Princess dance, our great chief/whose own name was G·îgāmēᶜ, the great chief/who came down from above./

Hana, hana, hana, the one who gave the Canoe-Breaking dance, the great chief whose/own name was Yäqawidalaɫ, the great chief who came/down from above.(22)

Hana, hana, hana, the one who gave the Giving-Away-Bad-Things dance, our chief,/tribes, whose own name was Lāʟēliʟalaɫ, Hamasēᶜya, Hāmdzid, the great chief who came down from above,/ our chief. Go now, great one, go great past chief. Now he is taking a rest/who was really a great chief, who came down from above, tribes.(28)

Hana, hana, hana, nâya. Hana nâ. /

The four tribes of the Kwag·uɫ were the first to come.(30) When their canoes came abreast they approached slowly singing their/ancestral songs for the dead. That is (1) what is re-

gwü^εyōsa g·ālē bāk!um g·ēx·gwa^εlāla ʟ!äq!walē. Wä, g·îl^εmisē

g·āx^εalisa Kwākwag·uƚē g·āxaasa ^εnɛmgisē mɛxāʟē lāx ʟ!āsēʟa^εyas.

Wä, g·āxēda Ƚāwits!ēs mɛxāʟē lāx ʟ!āsēʟa^εyasa ^εnɛmgîsē, g·a gwä-

ƚēg·a. Wä, g·îl^εmisē ^εwī^εla g·āx mɛxāʟa^ε-

5 ya yūduxᵘsέmagŭg·ɛyowē lēlqwälaʟa^εya laē

q!wäʟ^εîd ^εwī^εla ʟ!äq!wäla. Wä, hế^εmis ʟā-

x^εŭƚɛxs lāxēs ^εyā^εyats!ē Nɛqāp!ɛnk·ɛmōƚē.

Wä, la^εmē ts!ɛlqwaqax ^εmāxᵘmɛwēsagɛma^εyē.

Wä, laɛm ʟēgadɛs ^εwālas Kwāx·ilanōkŭmē yîx

10 ^εnɛmsgɛmē ʟēgɛms Lālak·ots!ax·dē.

Kwag·uƚ
^εnɛmgis
Ƚāwîts!ēs
Mādiƚbē
Dɛnax·da^ε xᵘ
A^εwaîʟɛla
Dzawadɛēnoxᵘ
Gwawaēnoxᵘ
Haxwāmis
Qwēqᵘsōt!ēnoxᵘ

Wä, g·îl^εmisē q!ŭlbē ts!ɛlwaq!ēna^εyas Nɛqāp!ɛnk·ɛmōƚē lāas

ʟax^εwŭƚɛxsa g·îgāma^εyē Hāwîlkŭlaƚwŭƚēxa xāmagɛma^εyē g·îgāmēsa

^εnɛ^εmēmotasa Kŭkwāk!ŭmasa Q!ōmoyā^εyē. Wä, lāxaē ts!ɛlwaqax ^εwā-

las Kwāx·îlanōkŭmē. Wä, g·îl^εmisē q!ŭlbē ts!ɛlwaq!ēna^εyas laē

15 ʟāx^εŭƚɛxʙa g·îgāma^εyē Hä^εmasaqoƚē qa^εs ts!ɛlwaqax ^εwālas Kwāx·î-

lanōkŭmē; yîx Hä^εmasaqōƚaxs g·āyoƚaē lāx ^εnɛ^εmēmotasa Wāwŭlîbā^ε-

yē. Wä, lä ^εnāxwa ^εnāƚ^εnɛmōkwē ts!ɛlwaqäsa âlak·!āla g·îg·ɛgā-

mēsa ^εnāƚ^εnɛmsgέmakwē lāxa lēɛlqwälaʟa^εya.

Hết! lāg·iƚas lēx·aɛm ts!ɛlwaqēda âlak·!āla g·îg·ɛgāmēxs wîk·!-

20 ɛx^εēdaēda âlak·!āla g·îgāma^εyē Lālak·ots!ax·dē. Wä, g·îl^εmisē

wîk·!ɛx^εîdēda k·!ēsâ nâxsâla bɛgwānɛma, wä, â^εmisa âlak·!āla

g·îgāmē q!wēʟāƚaxs laē ts!ɛlwaqēda k·!ēsē nâxsâla bɛgwānɛmx xŭnō-

xᵘdäsa la wîk·!ɛx^εîda.

Wä, g·îl^εmisē ^εwī^εla gwāƚ ts!ɛlwaqēda g·îg·ɛgɛma^εyasa lēɛl-

25 qwälaʟa^εyaxs laē ʟēƚwŭƚto^εyosa ɛlkwas ^εwālas Kwax·îlanōkŭmē yîx

K!waēlask·ɛn. Wä, la^εmē ^εwī^εla hōx^εwŭƚtâ^εwa bēbɛgwānɛm lāxēs

^εyaē'^εyats!ē. Wä, la^εmē lāƚ wŭnɛmtaƚxa g·îgāmēx·dē lāxa la gwā-

ƚa g·ōxᵘbido^ε qaē. Wä, la k·!ēs gäƚēda wŭnɛmtäxs g·āxaē aēdaa-

qa qaxs lɛ^εmaē dzāqwa gaxg·în la^εmēk· g·iwāla, yîn George Hunt,

30 lāxa wŭnɛmtäxa g·îgāmaōƚē. Wä, g·îl^εmisē g·āx ^εwī^εlēda bēbɛgwā-

nɛmaxs laē äxk·!ālasō^ε qa läs ^εwī^εla hōgwiʟ lāx g·ōkwasa la ʟē-

ferred to by the ancient Indians as the mourning song for a lost
chief. And when/the Kwag·uł had come to the beach, there arrived
the ᵋnɛmgis and stopped outside of them/ And then came the Ḻāwi-

ts!ēs and stopped outside the ᵋnɛmgis in

this manner./ And when they had all come

and stopped,(5) the thirteen tribes,then

they/stopped singing their mourning songs.

Then/Nɛqāp!ɛnk·ɛm arose in his canoe/and

comforted ᵋmāx̣ᵘmɛwēsagɛmēᵋ/ whose name was

Kwag·uł
ᵋnɛmgis
Ḻāwits!ēs
Mādiłbē
Dɛnax·daᵋxᵘ
AᵋwaⁱLɛla
Dzawadɛēnoxᵘ
Gwawaēnoxᵘ
Haxwāmis
Qwēqᵘsōt!ēnoxᵘ

ᵋwālas Kwāx·ilanōkūmēᵋ, the (10) other name of Ḻālak·ots!a.

As soon as Nɛqāp!ɛnk·ɛm ended his speech,/arose chief Hāwīl-
kūlał, the head chief of the/numaym Kūkwāk!ūm of the Q!ōmoyáᵋyē,
and he also comforted/ᵋwālas Kwāx·ilanōkūmēᵋ. And when his comforting was at an end (15) chief Hämasaqa arose and comforted
ᵋwālas Kwāx·ilanōkūmēᵋ;/Hämasaqa came from the numaym Wāwŭlibá-
ᵋya./ And each of the real chiefs/of every tribe spoke comforting words.

The reason why only real chiefs spoke comforting words was
that (20) Ḻālak·ots!a who died was a real chief. When/a man
dies who is not noble, then those who are real chiefs/are silent
and only men who are not noble speak comforting words/to the children of the deceased.

As soon as thé chiefs of the tribes had finished speaking
their words (25) they were called ashore by the speaker of ᵋwālas
Kwāx·ilanōkūmēᵋ, that is/K!waēlask·ɛn. Then all the men went a-
shore from their/canoes. They were going to bury the chief in the/
small house which was now ready for him. It was not long before
he was buried and they came/back for it was evening. And I, George
Hunt, (30) helped them burying the chief. When all the men came
back/they were told to go into the house of him (1) whose name was now

gadɛs ᵋwālas Kwax·îlanōkū́mē. Wä, laᵋmē ʟ!ɛxwīlag·iƛa haᵋmáƛɛla
lēɛlqwälaʟaᵋya. Wä, laᵋmē hēwäxa k!wēᵋlāla dɛnxᵋēda; wä läxaē
hēwäxa ʟ!äq!wāla qaxs aēk·ilaēda g·ālē bāk!um ʟ!äqwālaxa dzāqwa,
yîxs ᵋnēk·aēda g·ālē bāk!umqēxs ᵋnɛᵋmāƛilaaxa ʟ!äᵋyâxa la ƛɛᵋlaxs
5 ʟ!äq!wālaēda wŭnɛmdɛlɛla lēlqwälaʟaᵋyaxa la ɛlāq dzāqwa.

　　Wä, g·îlᵋmisē gwāƛ ʟ!ɛxwīda haᵋmaƛɛla lēɛlqwälaʟɛxs laē ᵋwîᵋla hōqawɛls läxa g·ōkwa. Wä, lēx·aᵋmis k·!ēs hōqawɛlsa q!äq!astâsa
haᵋmaƛɛla lēɛlqwälaʟaᵋya. Wä, laᵋmē gwēƛᵋalēlɛms K!waēlask·ɛn,
yîxa ɛlkwa. Wä, lä äxᵋēdxa k!waxʟāᵋwē ĕx·lax xâsɛᵋwē qaᵋs ts!awa-
10 naᵋqēs läxa q!äq!asto. Wä, lēda q!äq!asto xōxoxᵘsᵋalaxa k!waxʟāᵋ-
wē. Wä, g·îlᵋmisē k·ōtaq laɛm hēƛᵋalis xēxâᵋyaxs laē K!waēlask·ɛn
äxk·!älaxa q!ēq!äq!asto qa ᵋnɛmāg·îliƛēs k·atɛmlîƛelasa xōkwē
k!waxʟâ la ʟ̣ēʟ̣axwaᵋyasa aƛogŭq!ɛsē ᵋnāƛᵋnɛᵋmēmatsa yŭduxᵘsɛᵋmagu-
gɛyowē lēɛlqwälaʟaᵋya. Wä, hēɛmxaäwisē waxokwa q!ēq!aq!astowē yŭ-
15 dugŭg·ɛyâᵋē bēbɛgwānɛma. Wä, la k·!ēs gēg·îlîƛɛxs laē gwäƛa.

　　Wä, lēda ɛlkwē K!waēlask·ɛn nēƛax ᵋwālas Kwax·îlanōkūmēxs
lɛᵋmaē gwäƛa q!ēq!äq!asto. Wä, g·äxē ᵋwālas Kwax·îlanōkūmē k!wäg·
g·aᵋlîƛ qaᵋs waʟanɛqēxa q!ēq!aq!astowē läx âwäxagɛwasa ʟ̣äʟ̣ɛxwaᵋ-
yasa haᵋmaƛɛla lēɛlqwalaʟaᵋya. Wä, lä ʟ̣ɛxᵋîdɛx·daᵋxŭx aaʟ̣ɛbōp!-
20 ɛnyag·ala q!äq!aʟ!ɛsgɛmg·ustâla maᵋƛgŭnalokᵘ la haᵋwäsɛwakᵘ hēya-
gowa bēbɛgwänɛmē. Wä, laᵋmē äxᵋwŭƛt!älîƛasɛᵋwa maᵋƛp!ɛnx·ᵋîdē
lōxsɛmx·ᵋîd p!ɛlxɛlasgɛma qaᵋs g·äxē ᵋmōgwaᵋlîᵋlɛm läxa hēƛk·!ō-
tiwaliƛa lōxsɛmx·ᵋîdē; wä, lä äxᵋaᵋlîᵋlɛma lōxsɛmx·ᵋîdē läxa gɛm-
xōtewalîƛē. Wä, hēᵋmis la dānɛwēsōᵋsa q!ēq!aq!ästowē qaᵋs yäqo-
25 mēs läxēs g·ig·ōkŭlōtē.

　　Wä, g·îlᵋmisē ᵋwîlxtoᵋwa ᵋnäxwa k!wēk!wälasa haᵋmaƛɛla lēɛlqwälaʟaᵋya lä g·îl äxᵋēdɛx ᵋyāqŭlaʟaxa mäk·!ɛxsdaᵋyē ᵋyāqŭlaƛ p!ɛl-
xɛlasgɛma qa bɛnaēƛēs laē ᵋmōgwaᵋlîƛelas läxa nɛqēwaᵋlîƛasa g·ō-
kwē. Wä. lä, ĕk·!aᵋlîƛē p!ɛlxɛlasgɛmē ᵋyāqŭlaƛxa ᵋnālîʟɛlǟsa g·ālē
30 la äxᵋaᵋlîᵋlɛma. Wä, lä ĕk·!ɛnxaᵋya p!ɛlxɛlasgɛmē ᵋyāqŭlaƛxa Gwētɛla. Wä, lä bɛnaᵋyēäxʟasa Q!ōmoyâᵋyē; wä, lä bɛnaᵋyēäxʟasa ᵋwä-

ᵋwālas Kwāx·îlanōkŭmēˢ. Then they gave food to the different/
tribes. They never sang feasting songs and they/never sang
mourning songs, for the ancient Indians were careful not to sing
mourning songs in the evening/for the ancient Indians said it
would bring short life to the one who takes the place of the dead
one when(5) they sing mourning songs at the burying by the tribes
when it is near evening.

After the various tribes had eaten they all/went out of the
house, and the only ones who did not go out were the name-keepers
of the/various tribes. They were distributed in the house by K!waē-
lask·ɛn,/the speaker. Then he took ᵗcedarsticks which split readily
and distributed them (10) among the name-keepers. Then the name-
keepers split up the cedar sticks/and as soon as they thought they
had split enough K!waēlask·ɛn/told the name-keepers to put down at
the same time the split/cedar sticks for the seats of the various
numayms of the thirteen/tribes. That is also the number of the name-
keepers, who are thirteen (15) men. They did not take long doing this/

Then the speaker, K!waēlask·ɛn, told ᵋwālas Kwāx·îlanōkŭmēᵋ/that
the name-keepers had finished. Then ᵋwālas Kwāx·îlanōkŭmēᵋ came and
sat down/and asked each of the name-keepers how many seats/there
were in the various tribes, and they gave the names of (20) six
hundred fifty eight seats, counting/all the men. Then they took
two/thousand blankets and put them down, on the right hand side/
one thousand, and one thousand on the left hand side./And the name-
keepers took them from there and gave them (25) to their tribes.

When they are giving to all the seats of the different tribes,/
they first take the blankets which are to be given to the last one/
so that they are underneath when they put them down in the rear of
the house/and on top of them are the blankets which will be given
to those next before those that (30) had first been put down. And
the top pile of blankets will be given to the Gwētɛla/and under them
are those for the Q!ōmoyāᵋyē, and under them those for the (1)ᵋwālas

6*

las Kwag·uⱡē; wä, lä bɛnaᶜyēäxʟasa Q.ōmk·.ut.ɛsas ᶜwälas Kwāg·uⱡ;
wä, lä bɛnaᶜyēäxʟasa ᶜnɛmgis; wä, lä bɛnaᶜyēäxʟasa ⱡawits.ēs; wä,
lä bɛnaᶜyēäxʟasa Mādiⱡbē;wä, lä bɛnaᶜya p.ɛlxɛlasgɛmäxʟasa Dɛnax·-
daᶜxᵘ; wä lä bɛnaᶜyēäxʟasa AᶜwaIleʟa; wä, lä bɛnaᶜyēäxʟasa Qwōqᵘ-
5 sōt.ēnoxᵘ; wä, lä bɛnaᶜyēäxʟasa Dzawadɛēnoxᵘ; wä, lä bɛnaᶜyēäxʟasa
Häx̱wämis; wä, lä bɛnaᶜyēäxʟasa Gwawaēnoxᵘ. Wä, hĕɛm māg·iⱡ bɛna-
lIⱡa Gwawaēnoxᵘ qaxs lēx·aᶜmaē ɛlxʟē ᶜyäxᶜwitsōx laē ᶜwIlxtowa haᶜmaⱡɛla lēɛlqwälaʟaᶜya. Wä, g·Ilᶜmēse gwäⱡa q.ēq.aq.astōxs laē
yäwasᶜId mēxᶜIda qaxs gag·ustâwiʟē ᶜwIᶜlaʟa haᶜmaⱡɛla lēɛlqwälaʟa-
10 ᶜya.

Wä, g·Ilᶜmisē ᶜnäx·ᶜIdxa gaäla laē ᶜwIᶜla ts.ɛx·ᶜIdēda haᶜmaⱡɛla lēɛlqwaʟaᶜya. Wä, lä hĕɛm gaäxstalis g·Ig·aēʟɛlasē. Wä, g·I-
lᶜmisē gwäⱡ gaäxstalaxs g·äxaē ʟēᶜlälasōᶜ qaᶜs lälag·i hōgwēʟa
läx g·ōkwas ᶜwälas Kwäx·Ilanokűmē. Wä, läx·daᶜxwē ᶜwIᶜla hōgwiʟa.
15 Wä, g·Ilᶜmisē ᶜwIᶜlaēʟa laasē K.waēlask·ɛnxa ɛlkwax·däs Lälak·o-
ts.ax·dē yäq.ɛg·aᶜⱡa. Wä, laᶜmē mōᶜlasa haᶜmaⱡɛla lēɛlqwalaʟɛxs
laē ᶜwIᶜla hōgwIʟa. Wä, lä gwēgɛmx·ᶜId läxēs g·ōkűlōta Mamalēleqala yIxs häē k.űsᶜäⱡēda ōgwiwaᶜlIⱡasa g·ōkwē. Wä, lä ᶜnēk·a:
Wäg·Iⱡla g·ōkűlōt. Wäg·Iⱡla lädzaqwaʟɛx qaᶜs ʟ.äq.wälaōs yIsa
20 g·Ixgwalalaᶜyäōs g·ōkűlōt, ᶜnēk·ē. Wä, lä äxᶜētsɛᶜwa q.ēnɛmē
k·.ēs äwâ t.ēsema qaᶜs lä ts.äwanaēdzɛma maēmaᶜⱡtsɛm läxa ᶜnäⱡᶜ-
nɛmōkwē bēbɛgwänɛmsa Mamalēleqala. Wä, g·Ilᶜmisē ᶜwIlxtosa maēma-
ᶜⱡtsɛmē ḻasâlayo t.ēsɛmsa ʟ.äq.wäla laas dâqâlē Ts.ōxᵘts.aēsoⱡēxa
nâgadäsa Qwēqᵘsōt.ēnoxwē. Wä, laᶜmē ᶜnäx̱wa dɛnxᶜIdēda Mamalēleqa-
25 läsa nɛwēᶜlaläs g·Ilg·alisas Lälak·ots.ax·dē ʟ.äq.wäla. Wä, g·Ilᶜ-
misē q.űlbēda nɛwēᶜlalayo ʟ.äq.wäla wä, lä dâqâlē Tsätsoyalidēxa
nâgadäsa ᶜnɛᶜmēmotasa Mamalēleq.ämasa q.ayâläx wäxap.ɛnasas ʟēⱡɛlaxa ᶜnäx̱wa lēlqwälaʟaᶜya ḻōᶜ t.ɛnsēlaaxēs g·ōkűlōtē ḻōᶜ säk·.ɛ-
dzaᶜyasēsa xwäx̱űk.űna läxa ᶜnäx̱wa lēlqwälaʟaᶜya ḻōᶜ wäxap.ɛnasas
30 ʟ.ēᶜnag·ila k.wēlasa ḻōᶜ wäxap.ɛnasas q.ɛltaxa ʟ.äʟ.ɛqwa ḻōᶜ wäxa-
p.ɛnasas ʟ.ɛmkwas säläsēs g·ōkwē ḻōᶜ wäxap.ɛnasas yäwix·Ila qaēda

Kwāg·uⱡ, and under them those for the Q!ōmk·!ūt!ēs of the ᵋwālas
Kwāg·uⱡ,/and under them those for the ᵋnᴇmgis, and under them those
for the ⱡāwits!ēs, and/under them those for the Mādiⱡbē, and under
them those for the Dᴇnax·daᵋxᵘ,/and under them those for the AᵋwaI-
ʟᴇla, and under them those for the Qwēqᵘsōt!ēnoxᵘ,(5) and under them
those for the DzāwadᴇēnoxU, and under them those for the/Hāxwāmis,
and under them those for the Gwawaēnoxᵘ, and nearest to the floor
are those for the/Gwawaēnoxᵘ, for they are the last to whom it is
given when it is given to all the different/tribes. And when the
name-keepers are ready, they/sleep for a little while, for all of
the tribes are going to rise early in the morning.(10) —/

As soon as it becomes day in the morning, the various tribes
awake/and they eat their breakfast, and after/they have finished
taking their breakfast, they are called to go into/the house of ᵋwālas Kwāx·ĭlanōkŭmēᵋ, and they all go in.(15) And when they were all
in K!waēlask·ᴇn, the speaker of the late Lālak·ots!a,/spoke and
thanked the various tribes/that they all had come inside. Then he
turned his face to his tribe, the Mamalēleqala,/who were sitting
in the rear of the house, and he said,/"Now, my tribe, cry and sing
the mourning song of/(20) your lost chief, my tribe,"said he. Then
were taken many/stones that were not large, and two were given to
each/of the men of the Mamalēleqala, and as soon as each had two/
"time keeping stones for the mourning song", then Ts!oxᵘts!aēs,/
the song maker of the Qwēqᵘsōt!ēnoxᵘ, began a song and all the Mamalēleqala sang (25) the family history about the first Lālak·ots!a
as a mourning song. And when the/family history mourning song was
at an end, then Tsātsoᵋyalid/the song maker of the numaym Mamalēleq!-
ǎm, began a song counting the number of times he had invited/all the
tribes, and given away property to his own tribe, and given away/
canoes to all the tribes; and the number of times (30) he had given
grease feasts; and the number of times he had broken coppers; and
the number of times/he had given away the roof of his house; and

ᵉnᾱxwa lēlqwᾰlaʟaᵉya ʟ̣ōᵉ wᾱxap!ɛnasas t!ɛnsila yᾰwix·ꜰla; wᾰ, hēᵉ‑
mis wᾱxap!ɛnasas aⱡōsgɛma ʟēⱡɛlaxa ᵉnɛmsgɛᵉmakwē lᾱxa lēlqwᾰlaʟaᵉyē;
wᾰ, hēᵉmis wᾱxap!ɛnasas aⱡōsgɛma yᾰwix·ꜰla qaēda ᵉnɛmsgɛᵉmakwē lᾱxa
lēlqwᾰlaʟaᵉyē; wᾰ, hēᵉmisē wᾱxap!ɛnasas aⱡōsgɛma sᾱk·axōtsa xwᾱxū‑
5 k!ūna lᾱxa ᵉnɛmsgɛᵉmakwē lēlqwᾰlaʟaᵉya; wᾰ,hēᵉmisē wᾱxap!ɛnasas
aⱡōsgɛma ʟ!ēᵉnag·ila k!wēlas qaēda ᵉnɛmsgɛᵉmakwē lēlqwᾰlaʟaᵉyē;wᾰ,
hēᵉmisē wᾱxap!ɛnasas ʟ!ɛmkwax sᾰläsēs g·ōkwē qaēda ᵉnɛmsgɛᵉmakwē
lēlqwᾰlaʟaᵉya ʟɛᵉwis ʟ!ɛmk!ūdzaᵉyē qaēs g·ōkūlōt. Wᾰ, g·ꜰlᵉmisē
ᵉwīᵉla la qaᵉyatsa ʟ!ᾱq!wᾱla yīxg·ada lᾱk· k·!ᾱtaⱡa, laē ɛlxʟ̣ē qa‑
10 ᵉyasᵉɛndayuwē wᾱxap!ɛnasas qotēx·a ʟ̣ōᵉ ʟ̣ᾱk·ɛᵉyaᵉyas q!ēq!ɛyox ʟ!ᾱ‑
ʟ!ɛqwa ʟ̣ōᵉ wᾱxats!agasasa k!wᾱxsạlats!ē xwᾱxūk!ūna. Wᾰ, g·ꜰlᵉmisē
ᵉwīᵉlaxs laē ɑ̂ɛm la q!wēⱡᵉidēda dɛnxɛläsa ʟ!ᾱq!wᾱlaxa ɑ̂lä g·ꜰlsg·‑
ꜰlt!a ʟ!ēʟ!ᾱq!wᾱla.

Wᾰ, g·ꜰlᵉmisē q!ūlbēda maᵉⱡtsɛmē ʟēʟ!ᾱq!wᾱla laas ʟ̣ᾱxᵉwalꞮⱡē
15 K!waēlask·ɛnxa ɛlkwᾰs Lᾱlak·ots!ax·dē. Wᾰ, lä yᾰq!ɛg·aᵉⱡạ. Wᾰ,
lä ᵉnēk·a: ᵉya, haᵉmaⱡɛⱡ lēɛlqwᾰlaʟē, lɛᵉmas wūlɛlax gwᾰlag·ilꞮ‑
dzasasa ᵉwᾱlasdᾰ g·Ɪgɛmaᵉyē Lᾱlak·ots!ax·dᾰ yīx ᵉwalas Kwax·ꜰlanō‑
kūmaᵉya ᵉnēk·ēxs laē ʟēᵉlᾱlax ᵉmaxᵘmɛwēsagɛmaᵉyē, yīx ʟ̣ōlēx·dᾰs
Lᾱlak·ots!ax·dē. Wᾰ, hēx·ᵉidaᵉmisē ᵉmaxᵘmɛwēsagɛmaᵉyē la ʟạᵉwūno‑
20 dzɛlꞮⱡax K!waēlask·ɛn. Wᾰ, lä K!waēlask·ɛn ᵉnēk·a: Wēg·a dōxᵉwi‑
dɛx haᵉmaⱡɛl lēɛlqwᾰlaʟē, g·ᾱxᵉɛmk· g·ᾱxᵉɛng·Ɪn g·Ɪgᾱmēk· alōlxᵉ‑
wida. G·ᾱxᵉɛmg·a ᵉwᾱlasɛk· Kwax·ꜰlanōkūmaᵉya; ɑ̂ɛmk· alōmasᵉꞮd g·Ɪ‑
gᾱmaᵉya; ɑ̂ɛmk· la ēk·g·Ɪn nᾷqēk·, haᵉmaⱡɛl lēɛlqwᾰlaʟai. Laɛmḷɛns
wᾱx·sadzɛn ʟ̣ōᵉ Lᾱlak·ots!ä lᾱxēs lä laasa. Wᾰ, laᵉmēsɛn lᾱⱡ ᾱxᵉē‑
25 dɛⱡxa yᾰq!ɛntp!ēqasa g·Ɪgᾱmēx·dᾰ qᾱ lᾱlag·isē lᾱxg·a ᵉwᾱlasɛk·
Kwax·ꜰlanokūmaᵉya, ᵉnēk·ēxs laē lats!ᾱlꞮⱡ lᾱxa ōts!ᾱlꞮⱡē. Wᾰ,
k·!ēst!a gᾰⱡaxs g·ᾱxaē dᾱlaxa yᾰq!ɛntp!ēqē ʟ̣ōᵉ Qolōma ʟ̣ōᵉ Lēta qaᵉs
lä ts!ᾷs lᾱxa la ʟ̣ēgadɛs ᵉwᾱlas Kwax·ꜰlanokūmē, yīx ᵉmaxᵘmɛwēsage‑
maᵉyē. Wᾰ, la ᵉwᾱlas Kwax·ꜰlanokūmē dᾱx·ᵉꞮdxa maᵉⱡtsɛmē ʟ!ᾱʟ!ɛqwa
30 lɛᵉwa k·!ēg·edɛkwē yᾰq!ɛntp!ēqa, wᾰ, lä xᾱʟ!ɛx·ᵉꞮd yᾰq!ɛg·aᵉⱡa.
Wᾰ, lä ᵉnēk·a: ᵉya, lēlqwᾰlaʟai, wᾱʟ!ēmasʟaᵉwēsɛn qɛn ᵉnɛmx·ᵉida‑

the number of times he had given a winter dance to (1) all the
tribes; and the number of times he had given a winter dance to his
own tribe; and/the number of times he had invited each one of the
other tribes;/and the number of times he had given a winter dance
to each of the other/tribes; and the number of times he had given
canoes (5) to each of the other tribes; and the number of times/he
had given a grease feast for each of the other tribes;/and the number of times he had given away the roof of his house to each/of the
other tribes; and the number of times he had given away the roof of
his house to his own tribe. And/all of this was in the words of the
mourning song that is now written down here. Then the last (10)
words were the number of times he had paid the marriage debt, and
when he had put up an expensive copper as a mast/and when his princess had been sitting in the canoe. And when/all of this was done,
only then stopped the singing of the mourning songs. They are really
long/the mourning songs for the dead.

As soon as the two mourning songs were at an end/K!waēlask·ɛn,
the speaker of Lālak·ots!a, arose, and he spoke and (15) said: "Oh,
tribes, did you hear what was done/by the great chief, Lālak·ots!a,
that ᵋwālas Kwāx·flanōkūmēᵋ?"/said he as he called ᵋmāxᵘmɛwēsagɛmēᵋ,
the nephew of/Lālak·ots!a. Immediately ᵋmāxᵘmɛwēsagɛmēᵋ went and
stood alongside of (20) K!waēlask·ɛn. Then K!waēlask·ɛn said,"Look
at him/tribes, he came, he came, my new chief./ Now come, ᵋwālas
Kwāx·flanōkūmēᵋ, it is only a new chief./ Now my heart feels glad,
tribes. Now we are/parted on each side from Lālak·ots!a, from the
place where he has gone to. Now I shall go and take the (25) speaker's staff of the late chief that it may go to ᵋwālas/Kwāx·flanōkū-
mēᵋ! " Thus he said and went into the bedroom. It/was not long before he came out carrying the speaker's staff and the (coppers) Beaver and Lēta, and/gave them to him whose name was now ᵋwālas Kwāx·-
flanōkūmēᵋ, that is ᵋmāxᵘmɛwēsagɛmēᵋ./ Then ᵋwālas Kwāx·flanōkūmēᵋ
took the two coppers (30) and the carved speaker's staff and he spoke

ɫēsɛn lâᴸanɛmᴸa lāx gwälag·ꭰlidzasasɛn g·ꭲgämēx·dä q!ūlēᵋya, ᵋnēk·ē.
Wä, laᵋmē q!wēɫᵋid lāxēq. Wä, laᵋmē ᵋyaxᵋwiḑayowa p!ɛlxɛlasgɛmē
lāxēq lāxa haᵋmaɫɛla lēɛlqwälaᴸaᵋya. Wä, laᵋmēda ɛlkwa, yꭲx K!waē-
lask·ɛn la ɛlkwas ᵋwālas Kwax·ꭰlanokǔmaᵋyē, wä laᵋmē K!waēlas-

5   k·ɛn nēɫaxa g·ꭲg·ɛgämaᵋyasa haᵋmaɫɛla lēɛlqwälalaᴸēs wāɫdɛmxᴸäs Lā-
lak·ots!ax·dē, yꭲxs laē wāwēk·!ɛq!a qaēs kēk·!ɛsᵋōx·dēxa ᵋwꭲᵋlaɛm
gwǔᵋyōs qa lēs lāxa la ᴸēgadɛs ᵋwālas Kwax·ꭰlanōkǔmē lāxēs mag·iɫdē
ᴸōlēᵋya.

Wä, la wuᴸasōᵋs Nɛqāp!ɛnk·ɛmː ᵋmasē gwǔᵋyâsɛn ᵋnɛmōxᵘdē qa lēs

10 lāxōx ᵋmāx̌ᵘmɛwēsagɛmaᵋyēxwa lāx ᴸēgadɛs ᵋwālas Kwax·ꭰlanōkǔmē qaᵋs
ᵋnāx̌waᵋmaōs ᴸēᴸɛqɛlaq ᵋnēk·ē. Wä, hët! ᵋnēnak·its Nɛqāp!ɛnk·ɛmōɫē
yꭲx lāg·iɫas xɛnᴸɛla ts!âsāɫa lāxēs gwēk!älag·ꭰlꭲlas qaxs hēᵋmaē
q!ɛltap!ōts Nɛqāp!ɛnk·ɛmōɫē Lālak·ots!ōɫē lāg·iɫas ᵋnɛmālasē g·ꭲ-
q!ēnaᵋyas. Wä, laᵋmē K!waēlask·ɛnxa ɛlkwa ᵋnēx·xa aᵋlꭡɫɛlas wāɫdɛ-

15 mēᵋ läᵋläs Lālak·ots!ax·dē qa lēsa k·!ēk·!ɛsᵋâs lāx ᵋwālas Kwax·-
ꭰlanōkǔmē.Wä, la K!waēlask·ɛn yāq!ɛg·aᵋɫa.Wä,lä ᵋnēk·aː Hēɛm gwǔᵋyâsɛn g·ꭲgämēx·dä qa lēs lāxōx ᵋwālas Kwax·ꭰlanōkǔmaᵋya dāgɛmaᵋyē
ᴸɛᵋwa g·ōkwēx ᴸɛᵋwa ɫōɛlqwalꭡɫēxwa nānēx ɫōqwalꭡɫa, yūᵋmēsa sꭡsɛ-
yuᴸēx ɫōqwalꭡɫa, yūᵋmisa ts!awēx ɫōqwalꭡɫa,yūᵋmēsa dzōnoq!wax ɫōqwa-

20 lꭡɫa; wä, hēᵋmis k!waᵋyas; hēᵋmēsa g·āg·ꭲgɛlaqǔla dzōnoq!wāla; hēᵋmisa g·āg·ꭲgɛlaqǔla xāxalōlaqwala; hēᵋmisa yāq!änt!ālasa yāq!ɛntp-
!ēq; hēᵋmisa yālaxᴸɛnē lāxa bāx̌ǔsē; wä, hēᵋmisa q!ɛltɛlg·ꭡsxa ᴸ!ā-
qwasa g·ꭲg·ꭲgämaᵋyē; wä, hēᵋmisa q!ap!ēnoxᵘ lāxa ts!ēts!ēqa ᴸɛᵋwis
yiyälaxᴸɛnē; wä, yūdzēᵋmisōx Lētax ᴸɛᵋwōx Qōlomaxwa äwāᵋwēx ᴸ!ā-

25 ᴸ!ɛqwa, ᴸ!āqwaꭡɫᵋawēsɛn g·ꭲgämēx·dä, ᵋnēk·ē. Wä, laᵋmē ᵋwālas
Kwax·ꭰlanokǔmē hēɛm dāgɛmēxēs yāqwala p!ɛlxɛlasgɛma lāxa haᵋmaɫɛla
lēɛlqwaᴸaᵋya. Wä, laᵋmē yāxᵋwitsa p!ɛlxɛlasgɛmē lāxēs ᴸēgɛmē ᵋmā-
x̌ᵘmɛwēsagɛmaᵋyē lāxēs ᵋnɛmēmota Dzɛndzɛnx·q!ayo qaxs hēᵋmaē ᴸēgɛ-
mas dāɫax k!waᵋyas lāxēs ᵋnɛᵋmēmotē. Wä, g·ꭰlᵋmisē g·āx nä᷃ᵋnakᵘ

30 lāxg·a Tsāxisɛk· lāxaē dāgɛmēsēs ᵋnɛᵋmēmota Dzɛndzɛnx·q!ayâx yāqwa-
asa p!ɛlxɛlasgɛmē ᴸōxs k·ak·!ālaē yꭡsa ɫōq!wē lāxa ᵋwalas k!wēᵋla-

a few words./He said: "Oh tribes, I shall not be weak, that I may
equal (1) what was done by my chief, my uncle,' said he./After this
he stopped speaking. Then the blankets were given away/to the different tribes. Then Kwaēlask·ɛn,/the speaker of ᵋwālas Kwāx·ꟾlanōku-
mēᵋ,(5)told the chiefs of the various tribes the last words of Lā-
lak·ots!a/when he was dying, referring to the privileges and all/he
had wished to give to him whose name was now ᵋwālas Kw̄ax·ꟾlanōkumēᵋ,
the next one in his house,/his nephew.

Then he was asked by Nɛqāp!ɛnk·ɛm: "What did my past friend
refer to (10) that should go to ᵋmāx̣ᵘmɛwēsagɛmēᵋ here, he who is
now called ᵋwālas Kwāx·ꟾlanōkūmēᵋ, that/you all give him that name,"
said he. And this was what Nɛqāp!ɛnk·ɛm meant,/the reason ɩhy he
urged very strongly what he was speaking about was because/Nɛqāp!ɛ-
nk·ɛm was the rival in copper breaking of the late Lālak·ots!a.
Therefore their chief's rank was of equal value./ Now K!waēlask·ɛn,
the speaker, told them the various (15) wishes of Lālak·ots!a that
his privileges should go to ᵋwalas Kwāx·ꟾlanōkūmēᵋ./ Then K!waēlas-
k·ɛn spoke and said, "This was referred to/by my past chief, that
it should go to ᵋwālas Kwāx·ꟾlanōkūmēᵋ the office of giving away
property,/and this house and these house dishes, the Grizzly-Bear
house dish and also the Double-Headed-Serpent/house dish, and the
Beaver house dish and the Dzōnoq!wa dish (20) and also his seat,
and the Dzōnoq!wa cry and also/the cry of Driving-Away, and also
the speaking with the speaker's staff/and also the secret song of
the secular season, and also the copper breaking of the coppers/of
other chiefs, and the Gatherer of the winter ceremonial, and his/
secret songs, and also this great Lēta and Beaver, the great coppers (25) left behind by my past chief,"/said he. Now ᵋwālas Kwāx·-
ꟾlanōkūmēᵋ had the office of giving away property and the giving
away of blankets to the different/tribes. And he gave away blankets
to his own name ᵋmāx̣ᵘmɛwēsagɛmōᵋ/in the numaym Dzɛndzɛnx·q!ayo, that
is, his name/in which he holds the seat in his numaym. As soon as he

tsǃa ʟǃēᵋna. Hāsɛmxaēx ᵋmāx̣ᵘmɛwēsagɛmaᵋyē kˑǃēsᵋâ gˑägˑꜞʟɛlaxs
gˑālaē bɛkŭmgˑalisa nūx̣ᵘnemˑisē.

Wä, hēɛm kˑǃēs qǃŭnāla lā lāxa tsǃāᵋyaxa dāgɛmaᵋyē qaxs lēxˑ-
aᵋmaēda ᵋnōlastǃɛgɛmaᵋyē xŭnōx̣ᵘ äxᵋēdxa dāgɛmaᵋyasa ᵋnāᷣᵋnɛmēmasasa
5 ᵋnāx̣wa lēlꞯwälaʟaᵋya, wäxˑᵋɛm tsǃɛdāꞯa ᵋnōlastǃɛgɛmaᵋyas sāsɛmasa
dāgɛmaᵋyē, lē äxᵋēdaɛmꞯēxs wäxˑᵋmaē tsǃɛdāꞯa. Wä, lä qǃŭnāla wä-
xˑa bɛgwänɛmē tsǃāᵋyasa ᵋnōlastǃɛgɛmaᵋyē tsǃɛdāꞯ ᷣɛnɛmaēxsdxa dāgɛmaᵋyē lāxēs ᵋnōla. Wä, lä ᵋnāx̣waᵋma gˑꞮgˑɛgāmaᵋyē yäxˑstōts
qaxs kˑǃēsaē lāyo lāxa mäkˑꞏfläxa ᵋnōlastǃɛgɛmaᵋyē. Wä, lēxˑaᵋmis
10 lāxˑdɛmsa dāgɛmaᵋyē lāxa tsǃāᵋyäxs ᷣɛᵋlaēs ᵋnōlastǃɛgɛmaᵋyē. Wä,
laɛm kˑǃēs hēnaxˑᵋꞮdayo lāꞯ. Wä, hēɛm hēxˑdɛms gwēxˑᵋꞮdɛxs kˑǃēsaē hēᷣomāla xŭngwadɛxˑᵋꞮdē ᵋnōlastǃɛgɛmaᵋyasēxs laē ᷣɛᵋla. Wä,
gˑfꞯ lᵋmis hēwäxa xŭngwadɛxˑᵋꞮdēda dāgɛmaᵋyē laē âɛm xwāyɛnkǃwax
ᵋnōlastǃɛgɛmaᵋyas sāsɛmasēs mägˑiᷣē ꞯēꞯɛꞯâlaxa nâxsâla bɛgwänɛma.
15 Wä, laᵋmē la ᵋwꞮᵋlasēs kˑǃēkˑǃɛsᵋo lāꞯ ꞯɛᵋwa dāgɛmaᵋyē qäꞯaxs lɛᵋmaē xŭngwadɛs. Wä, la kˑǃeâs ᵋyaxˑsɛm waᷣdɛms tsǃātsǃaᵋyasa dāgɛ-
maᵋyē.lāxēq.
Wä, laᵋmē ᵋwālas Kwaxˑflanōkŭmaᵋyē haᵋnꞮᷣâlaxa ᵋwālasē gˑil-
das lāxēs gˑŏkwē lāx Mēmkŭmlis. Wä, gˑfꞯ lᵋmisē yāqwasōᵋsa pǃɛlxɛ-
20 lasgɛmasēs gˑōkŭlōtē la ꞯēꞯɛꞯâläs äxᵋēdxa yaqǃwēmäs pǃɛlxɛlasgɛm
qaᵋs lä äxtsǃōts lāxa ᵋwālasē gˑfldasa. Wä, lä qǃŭnāla hēᵋmē
ɛlkwäsē Kǃwaēlaskˑɛn äxᵋēdɛx yāqǃwēmäs ᵋwālas Kwaxˑflanōkŭmē qaᵋs
lē latsǃōts lāxa ᵋwālasē gˑfldasa qaxs hēᵋmaē gˑōkŭmtsǃâliᷣē
Kǃwaēlaskˑɛnē gˑōkwas ᵋwālas Kwaxˑflanōkŭmaᵋyē. Wä, hēɛm hēxˑ-
25 dɛms gwēgˑilatsēxs gˑäxaē ᵋwālas Kwaxˑflanōkŭmaᵋyē lāxgˑa Tsāxisɛkˑ. Wä, gˑfꞯ lᵋmisē gˑäx lāxgˑa Tsāxisɛkˑ, wä, lä yāqwanokwē
ᵋnɛᵋmēmotas ᵋwālas Kwaxˑflanōkŭmaᵋyasa pǃɛlxɛlasgɛmē lāx Mēmkŭmlis. Wä, lä hēᵋmē ɛlkwäs, yꞮx Kǃwaēlaskˑɛn dāgɛmēxa pǃɛlxɛlasgɛmē. Wä, laɛm mɛx̣ᵘstɛᵋwēs ᵋwālas Kwaxˑflanōkŭmaᵋyē.lāxēq. Wä,

comes home (30) here to Fort Rupert he has also the office of giving
away property to his numaym Dzɛndzɛnx·qǃayo when they give away /
blankets and when they give feasting dishes in a great grease feast
(1). It is also ᵋmāxᵘmɛwēsagɛmēᵋ's privilege coming from the/time
of the myth people./

This office of giving away property never goes to a younger brother; it is only/the eldest child that takes the office of giving a-
way property to all the different (5) tribes. Even if a girl is the
eldest one of the children/of the one whose office is to give away
property, she takes it although she is a woman. Often/the younger
brother of the eldest sister tries to take away/the office of giving
away property from his elder sister, but all the chiefs do not agree/
because it never goes to the next one to the eldest. The only time
(10) the office of giving away property is given to the younger brother is when the eldest one dies, then/it cannot be denied him. The
time when this is done is when/ the eldest one does not live long e-
nough to have a child before he dies./ When the one whose office is
this,to give away property, never had a child, he adopts the/eldest
one among the children of his nearest relative, a nobleman.(15) Then
all his privileges go to him and also the office of giving away property, for indeed he is/now his child. Then no bad word is said by
the younger brother of him whose office is this to give away property/
after this./

Now ᵋwālas Kwāx·flanōkūmēᵋ left a very large box/in his house
at Mēmkūmlis and when his tribe came to give him blankets(20) then
his relatives took the blankets that were given to him/and put them
into the large box, and often it is/the speaker Kǃwaēlask·ɛn who
takes what is given to ᵋwālas Kwāx·flanōkūmēᵋ and/puts it into the
large box, for/ Kǃwaēlask·ɛn lives in the house of ᵋwālas Kwāx·fla-
nōkūmēᵋ. The time he does (25) this is when ᵋwālas Kwāx·flanōkūmēᵋ
goes to Fort Rupert./ And when he comes here to Fort Rupert and one
of the/numaym of ᵋwālas Kwāx·flanōkūmēᵋ gives away blankets at Mēm-

lāxaē haᵋnīꟻa ᵋwālas g·ꟻldas lāx g·ōkwas lāxg·a Tsāxistk· qa äxts!âlats yaq!wēmās p!ɛlxɛlasgɛm lāxēs ᵋnɛmsgɛmē ꞈēgɛmē ᵋmāxᵘmɛwēsagɛmaᵋyē, lāxēs ᵋnɛᵋmēmota Dzɛndzɛnx·q!ayowē.

Wä, laᵋmɛn lâsʟ lāx ᵋwālas Kwax·ꟻlanōkümaᵋyaxs laē wīk!!ɛxᵋ-
5 ꟻdēda bɛgwānɛmq!ālamēxa ꞈēgadās Hawasɛlaꟼxa g·ayoꟼē lāx ᵋnɛᵋmēmotasa Wīwomasgɛmasa Mamalēleqala. Wä, la gɛg·adē Hawasɛlaꟼas Hä-
k!üg·ilaōgwaxa ts!ɛdāqē xünōxᵘs Ts!ɛxᵋwīdēxa g·ayoꟼē lāx ᵋnɛᵋmēmotasa Sīsɛnʟaᵋyasa Mamalēlaqala. Wä, la sāsɛmnokwē Häk!üg·ilaō-
gwasa yüdukwē eᵋëx·sokᵘ ts!ɛdāqa lāxēs g·ālē ꟼāᵋwünɛmē Gwaᵋwīnaxa
10 g·ayoꟼē lāx ᵋnɛᵋmēmotasa Mamalēleq!äm. Wä, laɛmxaē bɛgwānɛmq!ā-
lamē Gwaᵋwina. Wä, la wāꞈadē Hawāsɛlaꟼas Häk!üg·ilaōgwa. Wä, â͏ᵋ-
mis la k!watoxstē Hawasɛlaꟼē ꞈɛᵋwis ꞈâlē. Häk!üg·ilaōgwa. Wä, laᵋmē māwa Häk!üg·ilaōgwa ꞈɛᵋwis yüdukwē ts!ēdaq sāsɛm lāx g·ōkwas
Hawasɛlaꟼ lāx g·ōkwas ᵋwālas Kwax·ꟻlanōkümaᵋyē. Wä, laᵋmē Hawasɛ-
15 laꟼ k·!ēs p!ɛts!ēnoxwa k·!ēsxat! k!wēlats!ēnoxwa. Wä, hēᵋmis lā-
g·iꟼas ꞈēqálasōᵋs q!ülsɛm lāx gwēk·!alasaxa k·!ēs k!wēlats!ēnoxᵘ-
xēs g·ōkülōtō.Wä,ᵋnɛmp!ɛnaɛmᵋlaē p!ɛsaxēs g·ōkülotaxa Mamalēleqala;
lāg·iꟼas ꞈēgadɛs Hawasɛlaꟼ.. Wä, laᵋmē nâꞁeg·ilag·iꟼtsēs k!watoxs-
dotē Häk!üg·ilaōgwa. Wä, laᵋmē ᵋnēk·ē Häk!üg·ilaōgwa qaᵋs lālag·i
20 ᵋnɛlk·ila lāxa Ts!āmasē yꟻsēs yüdukwē eᵋëx·sōkᵘ ts!ēdaqa qa ꞁās
ʟ!ɛtasōᵋsa māmaꟼᵋa qaxs k·!eâsᵋmaē laɛm ꟼāᵋwadɛsa yüdukwē xünyꟻn-
g·ōs Hawasɛlaꟼē. Wä, laᵋmē lā lāxa Ts!āmas sɛk·!ālaxa xwēdɛkwē
xwāk!üna. Wä, laᵋmē lāg·aa lāxa Ts!āmas. Wä, laᵋmē ʟ!ēʟ!âsgasᵋ-
idēda yüdukwē eᵋëx·sōkᵘ ᵋnɛmēmagas ts!ēdaqa ꞈoᵋmis äbɛmpē Häk!ü-
25 g·ilaōgwa. Wä, ᵋnɛmxᵋɛnxē ts!āwünxas hēlēda Ts!āmasaxs g·āxaē näᵋnakwa. Wä, laᵋmē q!ɛyōʟē Hawasɛlaꟼaxa dāla. Wä, hëx·ᵋidaᵋmisē
k·ꟻlxwax Sēxᵋetg·ila Max·ts!ōlɛmxa q!ɛyōxwē ʟ!āqwa. Wä, laɛm k·ꟻ-
lxwē Häk!üg·ilaōgwa ꞈɛᵋwis yüdukwē ts!ēdaq sāsɛmxa ʟ!āqwa. Wä,
lä sɛp!ēts lāx Hawasɛlaꟼ. Wä, lä ts!ɛxq!ɛx·ᵋidēda āmaᵋyꟻnxaᵋyasa
30 yüdukwē ᵋnɛmēmagasa. Wä, lä k·!ēs gaēꟼ qɛlgwiꟼaxs laē wīk·!ɛxᵋIda.
Wä, lāxaē wīk·!ɛxᵋIdēda q!âyꟻwēx·däs sāsɛmas Häk!üg·ilaōgwa. Wä,

kůmlis,/then it is that the speaker K!waēlask·ɛn, performs the office of giving away property with the blankets./ He is the repres-
entative of ᵋwālas Kwāx·ílanōkǔmēᵋ in this way. And (1) he also has
a large box in his house here in Fort Rupert, to put into it/the
blánkets that are given to him in his other name ᵋmāxᵘmɛwēsagɛmēᵋ/
in the numaym Dzɛndxɛnx·q!ayo./

Now I will pass over from ᵋwālas Kwāx·ílanōkǔmēᵋ.(5) There died
a common man whose name was Hawasɛlaɬ, who belonged to the numaym/
WĪwomasgɛm of the Mamalēleqala. Hawasɛlaɬ had for his wife Hǟk!ǔ-
g·ilaōgwa/the daughter of Ts!ɛxᵋwĪd who came from the numaym/SĪsɛn-
ʟ!āᵋ of the Mamalēlaqala. Now Hǟk!ǔg·ilaōgwa had three pretty
girls as children from her first husband,GwaᵋwĪna, (10) who belonged
to the numaym Mamalēleq!ǟm, and Gwaᵋwina was also a common man./
Then Hawasɛlaɬ had Hǟk!ǔg·ilaōgwa as his sweetheart, and they just/
lived together, Hawasɛlaɬ and his sweetheart Hǟk!ǔg·ilaōgwa. Then/
Hǟk!ǔg·ilaōgwa moved with her three daughters to the house of/Hawa-
sɛlaɬ, in the house of ᵋwālas Kwāx·ílanōkǔmēᵋ. And Hawasɛlaɬ (15)
never gave a potlatch and never gave a feast, and therefore/he was
called 'clay-face", as they call those who never give a feast/to
their tribe. Only once he gave a potlatch to his tribe,the Mamalēleqala,/and therefore his name was Hawasɛlaɬ. Now he was instructed
by/Hǟk!ǔg·ilaōgwa with whom he lived,and Hǟk!ǔg·ilaōgwa said that
they should go (20) south to Victoria with her three pretty girls that
they should be/prostitutes among the whites, for none of them had a
husband, the three step-daughters/of Hawasɛlaɬ. Now they went to Victoria, five in a long-nosed/canoe Now they arrived in Victoria,and
they became prostitutes,/the three pretty sisters and their mother,
Hǟk!ǔg·ilaōgwa.(25) They stayed one winter in Victoria and then they
went home./ Now Hawasɛlaɬ obtained much money from this and immediately they/bought the expensive copper, 'Dry-Mouth-Maker-Cause-of-
Shame.' Then/Hǟk!ǔg·ilaōgwa and her three daughters bought the copper
and/gave it to Hawasɛlaɬ. Now the youngest of the (30) three daughters

lāxaēda ᵋnōlast!ᴇgᴇmēx·dē wīk·!ᴇxᵋīda. Wä, laᵋmē ᵋwīᵋla ⱡēⱡᴇᵋlēda
yŭduxᵘdē ts!ēdaq sāsems Häk!ŭg·ilaōgwa. Wä, la Häk!ŭg·ilaōgwa wᴇ-
q!wanᵢxᵘsa ˪ēgadäs T!ēqwap. Wä, laᵋmē T!ēqwap ᵋnēx·qēxs ēqasᴇᵋwa-
ēs ˪ōˌalēgasdē qaēs gwēx·ᵋidaasaxs laē k·flxwax Sēxᵋētg·ila Max·-
5 ts!ōlᴇma qa Hawasᴇlaⱡ qaxs âᵋmaē bᴇgwānᴇmq!ālᴇma qaxs k·!ēsaēda
âlak·!āla g·īg·ᴇgämē hēⱡq!ālaxa bᴇgwānᴇmq!ālᴇmē k·flxwaxa q.ēq!ᴇ-
yoxwē ˪!āˌ!ᴇqwa. Wä, hēᵋmis ᵋnēnak·iⱡts T!ēqwapaq ēgᴇkwēs ˪ōˌa-
lēgasdē. Wä, laᵋmē k·fⱡᵋīdē Hawasᴇlaⱡ lāxēq qaxs lᴇᵋmaē ts!ᴇx·-
q!ᴇx·ᵋīd ōgwaqa. Wä,laᵋmē ˪ēᵋlālaxēs ᵋnᴇᵋmēmōtaxa Wīwomasgᴇmē.
10 Wä, g·flᵋmisē g·āx ᵋwīᵋlaēˌa lāx g·ōkwas ᵋwālas Kwax·flanōkŭmaᵋyē,
wä lä yāqᴇg·aᵋⱡē Hawasᴇlaⱡ. Wä, la ᵋnēk·a: Ëx·ᵋma lāx k·!ēs gäⱡa
sᴇraxᴇn lāg·iⱡa ˪ēᵋlalōˌ ᵋnᴇᵋmēmot. Hēdᴇn lāg·iⱡa ˪ēᵋlālōˌ qaᵋs
g·āxaōs hōˌēlaxg·fn wāⱡdᴇmˌᴇk·, ᵋnēk·ēxs laē dāxᵋīdᴇx Sēxᵋētg·ila
Mäx·ts!ōlᴇmxēs āⱡᵋᴇm k·flwānᴇm ˪!āqwa. Wä, lä ᵋnēk·a: Dōqŭlaᵋ-
15 maaqōs g·āxᴇn yūˌ ᵋwālatsᴇm ᵋnᴇᵋmēmot, yūˌ Wīwomasgᴇmxg·fn k·!eâs-
ēk· xŭnōkwa qa äxᵋēdᴇxg·ada ᵋwalasᴇk· ˪ēgad ˪!āqwa. Wä, lēx·aᵋm-
isᴇn dōgŭⱡ ēx· laatsᴇk· lāxōx ᵋwālasēx Kwax·flanōkŭmaᵋya ˪ᴇᵋwŭn
˪āxwaᵋyē ˪ōᵋgŭn ˪ēgᴇmg·fn. Wä, gēlag·a xŭnōxᵘ yūˌ ᵋwālas Kwax·f-
lanōkŭmē dāx·ᵋīdg·as ˪!āqwag·ōs. Laᴇms ˪ēgadᴇⱡts Sexŭqâla lāx
20 ᵋnᴇᵋmēmotasa Wīwomasgᴇmē, ᵋnēk·ē. Wä, hēx·ᵋidaᵋmisē ᵋwālas Kwa-
x·flanōkŭmaᵋyē la dāx·ᵋīdxa ˪!āqwa qaᵋs mōlēs̄ wāⱡdᴇmas Hawasᴇlaⱡ-
xa laᴇm xᴇnˌᴇla ts!ᴇx·q!a. Wä, k·!ēst!a gäⱡaxs laē wīk·!ᴇxᵋīda.
Wä,g·flᵋmisē g·āx näᵋnakwa wŭnᴇmtäx Hawasᴇlaⱡdē laē ᵋwālas Kwax·f-
lanōkŭmaᵋyē p!ᴇsasa p!ᴇlxᴇlasgᴇmē lāxa Mamalēleqala. Wä, laᵋmē g·a-
25 ᵋyoqâ lāxēs āⱡē ᵋnᴇᵋmēmotaxa Wīwomasgᴇmē. Wä, laᵋmē ˪ēgadᴇs Sēxŭqâla lāxēq. Wä, la k·!ēs dāgᴇmaᵋyē Sēxŭqâla lāxēs yāqŭlaxa p!ᴇlxᴇlas-
gᴇma qaxs k·!ēsaē Hawasᴇlaⱡdē dāgᴇmēsēs ᵋnᴇᵋmēmotasa Wīwomasgᴇmē
qaxs âᵋmaē bᴇgwānᴇmq!ālᴇma, yfxs häē Nᴇg·ä dāgᴇmäsa ᵋnᴇᵋmēmotasa Wīwomasgᴇmē. Wä, laᵋmē yŭduxᵘsᴇmē ˪ēˌᴇgᴇmas, wä, lä yŭduxwē k!wēk!wa-
30 ᵋyasxᴇns gwŭᵋyō ˪ēˌaxwaᵋya lāxa yŭduxᵘsᴇᵋmak!ŭsē ᵋnāⱡᵋnᴇmēmasa.
Wä, la maᵋⱡa dāgᴇmaᵋyē la äaxsīlaxᵘa. Wä, lä mak·!ᴇxsdaᵋyē ˪āx-

became sick and she was not long sick in bed before she died./And
then the second of the children of Hāk!ŭg·ilaōgwa died, and (1)
then the eldest one also died. All died, the/three daughters of
Hāk!ŭg·ilaōgwa. Now Hāk!ŭg·ilaōgwa/had a brother whose name was
T!ēqwap. Now T!ēqwap said his nieces had been bewitched/on account
of what they had done in buying the copper, 'Dry-Mouth-Maker-Cause-
of-Shame" (5) for Hawasɛlaȴ, for he was only a common man and/the
real chiefs do not allow a common man to buy expensive/coppers. That
is what T!ēqwap meant when he said that his nieces had been bewitched./ Now Hawasɛlaȴ became afraid after this, for he became sick/also.
Then he called his numaym, the Wīwomasgɛm,(10) and as soon as they
were all in the house of ᵋwālas Kwāx·ilanōkŭmēᵋ,/Hawasɛlaȴ spoke and
said: "It is good that you do not long/guess the reason why I called
you,/that you may come to listen to what I say." Thus he said and
took 'Dry-Mouth-Maker-/Cause-of-Shame' , the copper he had just
bought, and he said, "Look at me,(15) you great numaym, you Wīwomasgɛm, that I have no/child to take this great copper which has a name.
Now I shall only/see that it will best go to this ᵋwālas Kwāx·ilanō-
kŭmēᵋ, and/also my seat and my name. Go child, you ᵋwālas Kwāx·ila-
nōkŭmēᵋ,/take hold of your copper. Now your name shall be Sēxŭqâla
in the (20) numaym Wīwomasgɛm." So he said, and immediately ᵋwālas
Kwāx·ilanokŭmēᵋ/took the copper and thanked for his speech Hawasɛlaȴ/
who was now very sick. He was not long in this way before he died./
And as soon as those came home who had buried Hawasɛlaȴ, then ᵋwālas
Kwāx·ilanōkŭmēᵋ/gave away blankets to the Mamalēleqala. He gave
these out (25) of his new numaym, Wīwomasgɛm. And now his name was
Sēxŭqâla/after this. Now Sēxŭqâla has not the office of giving a-
way property when he gives away blankets,/for Hāwasɛlaȴ had not the
office of giving away/property to his numaym, the Wīwomasgɛm,/for
he was only a common man, and it was Nɛg·ä who had the office of
giving away property in the numaym Wīwomasgɛm./ Now he had three
names and three seats,(30) that we call standing places, in the three

wgᵉyas lāxa ᶜnɛᶜmēmotasa Wᶦwomasgɛm, yᶦx ʟâxwaᶜyas Hawasɛlaⱡdē. Wä,
laɛm yawasᶜᶦd lāba.

Wä, laᶜmēsɛn gwāgwēx·sᶜalaⱡ lāx T!ēqwapxa g·āyoⱡē lāx ᶜnɛᶜmēmotasa Sᶦsɛnʟ!aᶜyasa Mamalēleqala yᶦx wɛq!wäs Häk!ūg·ilaōgwa yᶦx
5 k!watoxsdōtas Hawasɛlaⱡdē yᶦxs ts!āᶜyaē T!ēqwapas Häk!ūg·ilaōgwa.
Wä, lāx·daᶜxwē sāsɛmsa ʟēgadā Hayaⱡk·ɛnxa bɛgwānɛmq!ālɛmē g·ayoⱡ
lāx ᶜnɛᶜmēmotasa Sᶦsɛnʟ!ēᶜ. Wä, lä gɛg·adē Hayaⱡk·ɛnas Qwāqwanē-
dzɛmgaxa āᶜmaxat! ts!ɛdāqax·sāla. Wä, laᶜmē T!ēqwap nāgadēs bɛgwā-
nɛᶜmēnaᶜyē yᶦxs q!ēq!ädaaxa dādɛk·asē. Wä, lä hēwäxa gɛg·adaxēs
10 ᶜwāᶜwasdɛmē bɛgwānɛma g·āxᶜaʟɛlaqēxs laē ⱡɛᶜla. Wä, laᶜmisē T!ē-
qwapē hēmɛnāⱡaɛm p!ɛsa laxaē hēmɛnaⱡaɛm bābaxᵘsɛgoliⱡ k!wēlasxa lēlqwälaʟaᶜyē. Wä, lä ʟēgadɛs T!ēqwap lāxa k!wēlas. Wä, lä ʟēgadɛs
Wāmis lāxap!ɛsäsa p!ɛlxɛlasgɛmē. Wä, hēᶜmisɛn lāⱡ ʟēqɛlayuqē
Wāmisē lāxɛn k·!āt!ēnaᶜyas. Wä, laɛmxaē Wāmisē ʟ!ēdzɛⱡtsa g·ᶦg·ɛ-
15 gāmaᶜyasa Mamalēleqala qaxs g·ᶦlᶜmaē p!ɛsēda ᶜnɛmōkwē lāxa g·ᶦg·ɛ-
gāmaᶜyē laē Wāmis ōgwaqa p!ɛsasa p!ɛlxɛlasgɛmē, hē gwēx·s aɛmⱡaⱡa-
sēs g·ᶦg·ɛgɛmaᶜyē lāxēs gwēg·ilasē. Wä, lēx·aᶜmēs ʟēʟɛʟâlasa Wāmisē ᶜwālas Kwax·ᶦlanōkümaᶜyē. Wä, lä axᶦla Wāmisax K·!āᶜnaxa
q!ɛyōxwē ʟ!āqwa. Wä,lāᶜlaē k·fⱡᶜᶦdē Wāmisas g·ᶦg·ɛgāmaᶜyasēs g·ō-
20 külōtaxs hēmɛnaⱡaᶜmaē gɛnāⱡasōᶜ qa ⱡɛᶜlēs. Wä, hēᶜmis lāg·iⱡas ʟē-
ᶜlālē Wāmisaxa Mamalēleqāla qa läs ᶜwᶦᶜla hōgwiʟ lāx g·ōkwas. Wä,
g·ᶦlᶜmisē g·āx ᶜwᶦᶜlaᶜʟa laas hämg·ᶦlaq. Wä, g·ᶦlᶜmisē gwäⱡ haᶜmāpa k!wēⱡaxs laē yāq!ɛg·aᶜⱡē Wāmis. Wä, lä ᶜnēk·a: Wäɛntsōs hō-
ʟēlaxg·ᶦn wäⱡdɛmʟɛk· lāʟ, g·ōkülōt qa gwäⱡaasasēs nēnāqayōs qaɛn
25 yᶦxs wäⱡaqēlaaqōs qɛn k·!ēaxᵘᶜwide lāxwa ᶜnālax,yúʟaxa g·ᶦg·ɛgɛmaᶜ-
yaaqōs. Wä, la ēx·ᶜmis wäⱡagɛⱡōs, ᶜnēk·ēxs laē dāx·ᶜidxēs ʟ!āqwē
K·!āna. Wä, lä ᶜnēk·a: Gēla xūnōkᵘ, yōʟ ᶜwālas Kwax·ᶦlanōkümēᶠ
qɛns g·āxē q!waēⱡ lāxg·a, ᶜnēk·ē. Wä, hēx·ᶜidaᶜmisē ᶜwālas Kwax·ᶦ-
lanōkümaᶜyē la ʟaᶜwɛnōdzɛlᶦⱡax Wāmisē. Wä, la Wāmis ts!âsa ʟ!āqwa
30 lāx ᶜwālas Kwax·ᶦlanōkümaᶜyē. Wä, lä ᶜnēk·ē Wāmisax ᶜwālas Kwax·-
ᶦlanōkümaᶜyē: Wēg·a dāx·ᶜᶦdɛxg·as k·!ōtɛlag·ōs, g·ᶦgāmēᶜ lāxg·a

tribes,/and he had two offices of giving away property to take
care of, and his last(1)seat was in the numaym Wīwomasgɛm.   It
was the seat of Hawasɛlaɫ. Now/for a while this is ended./

Now I will talk about T!ḗqwap who belonged to the numaym/Sīsɛnɫ-
ɫ!ḗᴄ of the Mamalḗleqala, who was a brother of Häk!ūg·ilaṓgwa who
(5) lived together with Hawasɛlaɫ. Now T!ḗqwap was the younger brother of Häk!ūg·ilaṓgwa/and they were the children of one whose name
was Hayaɫk·ɛn, a common man of the/numaym Sīsɛnɫ!ḗᴄ. And Hayaɫk·ɛn
had for his wife Qwāqwanḗdzɛmga/who was also only a common woman.
Now T!ḗqwap was clever in his ways,/for he had much property. And he
never had a wife (10) in his lifetime, from the time when he became
a man until he died. And then/T!ḗqwap always gave potlatches and he
also gave feasts to the tribes, although he had no wife./ And he had
the name T!ḗqwap for the feasts and the name/Wāmis for the giving
away of blankets, and I shall call him hereafter/Wāmis in my writing
about him. Now Wāmis was also hated by the chiefs (15) of the Mamalḗleqala, for when one of the chiefs gave away property/then Wāmis
also gave away blankets, just as if he were making fun of/the chief
in doing so. The only friend of Wāmis/was ᴄwālas Kwāx·flanṓkūmḗᴄ.
Now Wāmis kept Crow,/the expensive copper. Then Wāmis-became afraid
of the chiefs of his tribe (20) for they kept on threatening to kill
him. Therefore,/Wāmis called the Mamalḗleqala to come all into his
house. And/when they were all inside he gave them to eat and after
the guests had eaten/Wāmis spoke and said: "Now listen/to what I say
to you,my tribe, on account of the way your hearts are all against
(25) me, for you wish me to disappear from the world, you chiefs./
Now your wish is good," said he and he took his copper/Crow and he
said: "Come, you child, you ᴄwālas Kwāx·flanṓkūmḗᴄ,/and let us stand
here,"said he. Immediately ᴄwālas Kwāx·flanṓkūmḗᴄ/stood by the side
of Wāmis. Then Wāmis gave the copper (30) to ᴄwālas Kwāx·flanṓkūmḗᴄ./
Then Wāmis said to ᴄwālas Kwāx·flanṓkūmḗᴄ: " Take hold of your salmon
chief, of this (1) Crow. Now you will go to my seat, which will be

K·ǃának·. Laᵋms lāɬ lāxɛn ʟāxwaᵋyē lāxēs lāʟōs ᵋnɛᵋmēmota Sǃsɛnʟǃa-
ᵋyē. Wä, lāʟɛs lāxōtɛɬxōx K·ǃánax qaᵋs pǃɛsaōsas k·ĭlwayoʟaqᵘ lāxēs
gwüᵋyōʟaōs qaᵋs pǃɛsasōᵋʟōs. Wä, lä gwēgɛmx·ᵋĭd lāxa Mamaʟēleqala.
Wä, g·ōkŭlōt, laᵋmɛn ɬᵋla lāxēs wāʟagɛɬōs , g·ōkŭlōt. Wä, laᵋmɛn
5 äxᵋēdɛxg·ada g·ĭgāmēk· lāxg·a Wāmisɛk· qa lēs lāxɛn kǃwäx·dē. Wä,
hëᵋmēq, ᵋnēk·ē. Wä, laᵋmē mōlē ᵋwālas Kwax·ĭlanokŭmaᵋyas wāʟdɛmas.
Wä, laɛm la k·ǃeâs ʟāxwēs Tǃēqwapē yĭxa ʟēgadx·dä Wamisē lāxēq qaxs
laē ᵋwĭᵋlasēs ʟǃāqwax·dē k·ǃāna ʟɛᵋwēs ʟāxwēx·dē lāx ᵋwālas Kwax·ĭ-
lanōkŭmaᵋyē. Wä, âᵋmisē tsǃäwŭnxᵋĭdɛxs laē wĭk·ǃɛxᵋĭdē Tǃēqwapdē.
10 Wñ, laᵋmē mōwē kǃwēkǃwaᵋyas ᵋwalas Kwax·ĭlanōkŭmaᵋyē lāxēq, yĭxs
k·ǃēsaē ʟēʟɛʟâlē ᵋwālas Kwax·ĭlanokŭmaᵋyē lāx Tǃēqapdē yĭxs lēx·aᵋmaē
lāg·iʟas hë gwēx·ᵋĭdē qaxs lēx·aᵋmaē ᵋwālas Kwax·ĭlanōkŭmaᵋyē k·ǃēs
mōmaᵋyālax Tǃēqwapdē. Wä, laɛmxaē yāwasᵋĭd lāba.

Wä, laᵋmē mōxᵋwidāʟa kǃwēkǃwaᵋyas ᵋwālas Kwax·ĭlanōkŭmē lāxēq.
15 Wä, lɛn k·ǃēs qǃâʟɛlax lāg·iʟas la ʟâgēx ᵋnɛᵋmēmotasa Lēlɛᵋwag·il-
asa Dzāwadɛēnoxᵘ yĭxs ʟēgadaē ᵋwālas Kwax·ĭlanokŭmaᵋyas Yāqâlasē
lāxēs ᵋnɛᵋmēmota Lēlɛᵋwag·ila. Wä, laɛmxaē dāgɛmēsa ᵋnɛᵋmēmotasa
Lēlɛᵋwag·ila. Hëᵋmēsɛn lāg·iʟa k·ōtaqē g·ĭgāmaᵋyē lä ʟāxstɛᵋwēsōs
lāx ᵋnɛᵋmēmotasa Lēlɛᵋwag·ila qaxs hëᵋmaē māmaʟtǃēk·ǃēsa bākǃŭma-
20 qēxs g·ĭgāmaēda dāgɛmaᶜyaxa ᵋnāxwa lēlqwālaʟaᵋya. Wä, laᵋmē sɛk·ǃ-
ax·ᵋĭdāʟa kǃwaᵋyas ᵋwālas Kwax·ĭlanōkŭmaᵋyē lāxēq. Wä, lä ᵋnāxwaɛm
häx·hanᵋēʟa äwaᵋwē g·ĭlg·ĭldas lāxa g·og·ōkwas lāxēs ᵋnēᵋnɛᵋmēmotē
qa äxtsǃâlasɛx yāqǃwēmās pǃɛlxɛlasgɛm ʟɛᵋwa qǃɛng·äxtâla ʟɛᵋwa dā-
lēg·a k·ǃōkwala. Hëᵋm ᵋwĭᵋla la äxtsǃâlayo lāxa g·ĭlg·ĭldas yixs
25 k·ǃēsaē nɛgēsē ᵋwālas Kwax·ĭlanōkŭmēᶜ lāx g·ōxᵘdɛmsasēs ᵋnāʟᵋnɛᵋmē-
masē qaxs hëᵋmaēda g·ĭlg·ĭldasē ʟɛᵋwa ʟēʟɛgɛmas dāʟax kǃwēkǃwaᵋyas
lāxa sɛk·ǃax·ᵋĭdāʟa kǃwēkǃwäs lāxa sɛk·ǃāsgɛᵋmakǃŭsē ᵋnāʟᵋnɛᵋmēmasa.

Wä, la gɛg·adē ᵋwālas Kwax·ĭlanōkŭmēs K·ōgwisilaogwa yĭx k·ǃē-
dēʟas G·ēxk·ɛnxa g·āyoʟē lāx ᵋnɛᵋmemotasa ʟǃāʟǃɛlāminasa ᵋnɛmgēs.
30 Wä, la xŭngwadɛx·ᵋĭtsa bābagŭmē. Wä, la G·ēxk·ɛn ʟēgɛmg·ĭlxʟâlax
Wāsaʟaas qa ʟōgɛmsēs tsǃōxᵘʟɛma. Wä, laᵋmē ʟēgɛmsa bābagŭmē Wāsa-

yours in the numaym SīsɛnⱠ!ḗᵋ;/and you will sell this Crow to give
away the price/to whomever you ʷish it to be given." And he turned
his face to the Mamalēleqala:/ "Now, tribe, now I am dead, according
to your wish, tribe. Now I (5) take this chief here, this Wāmis,to
go to my seat./ ' This is all,' said he. Then ᵋwālas Kwāx·īlanokǔmēᵋ
thanked him for what he had said./ Now T!ēqwap had no seat after
that, he whose name had been Wāmis, for he had given/everything,his
copper Crow and his seat to ᵋwālas Kwāx·īlanokǔmēᵋ./ When winter
came T!ēqwap died,(10) and now ᵋwālas Kwāx·īlanokǔmēᵋ had four seats
after this. But/ᵋwālas Kwāx·īlanokǔmēᵋ was no relative of T!ēqwap.
It was only/because ᵋwālas Kwāx·īlanokǔmēᵋ did not hurt with words
T!ēqwap. Now this is at an end for a while.

Now ᵋwālas Kwāx·īlanokǔme had four seats after this.(15) I do
not know why he stands among the numaym Lēlɛᵋwag·ila/of the Dzāwadɛēnoxᵘ, for ᵋwālas Kwāx·īlanokǔme has the name Yāqâlas/in the numaym Lēlɛᵋwag·ila, and he has also the office of giving away property in the/Lēlɛᵋwag·ila. Therefore I suppose that it was the chief
whose seat was given to him/in the numaym Lēlɛᵋwag·ila, for it is a
sign among the Indians (20) that he is a chief, the one who has the
office of giving away property among the tribes. Now/ᵋwālas Kwāx·ī-
lanokǔmēᵋ had five seats after this, and they/kept large boxes in
his houses in his numayms/and put into them the blankets that were
given to him and the button blankets and the silver/bracelets. All
these were put into the boxes when (25) ᵋwālas Kwāx·īlanokǔmēᵋ was
not present in the villages of the numayms,/for the boxes are for
the names of his different seats/in the five different numayms.

Now ᵋwālas Kwāx·īlanokǔmēᵋ had for his wife K·ōgwisilaogwa,
the princess/of G·ēxk·ɛn of the numaym Ⱡ!āⱠ!ɛlāmin of the ᵋnɛmgēs.
(30) Then they had a child, a boy, and G·ēxk·ɛn gave the marriage
name/Wāsaⱡaas for the name of his grandchild, and the name of the
boy was Wāsaⱡaas.(1) Then they had again a child, a girl, and ᵋwā-

laasē. Wä, lä ēt!ōd xŭngwadɛx·ᵋĪtsa ts!āts!adagɛmē. Wä, lä ᵋwālas
Kwax·ꜰlanōkŭmaᵋyē ʟēxᵋēts Yāsɛkwē lāq. Wä, lāʟa G·ēxk·ɛnē ʟēgɛm-
g·ꜰIxʟālax Mɛᵋlēdē qa ʟēgɛmsēs ts!ōxᵘʟɛmaǥasē. Wä, laᵋmē ʟēgɛmē
Mɛᵋlēdäsa ts!āts!adagɛmē. Wä ᴍaᵋlōkwē sāsɛmas ᵋwālas Kwax·ꜰlanō-

5 kŭmaᵋyē ʟɛᵋwis ǥɛnɛmē K·ōgwisilaogwa. Wä, g·ꜰlᵋɛmꜱwisē ꜱɛᵋlꜱē
ᵋwālas Kwax·ꜰlanōkŭmaᵋyē lāʟē Wasaꜱaasē ᵋwĪᵋla ax ᵋēdɛꜱxa sɛk·!ā-
x·ᵋidāꜱa k!wēk!wäsēs ōmpē ʟōᵋ ᵋnāxwa k·!ēk·!ɛsᵋōs. Wä, hēstaɛm
k·!eâs gwēx·ᵋidaats la k·!ēsᵋogŭlxʟēs ᵋwālas Kwax·ꜰlanōkŭmaᵋyēs
g·äg·ꜰʟɛla ʟēʟɛǥɛm lāxēs g·ꜰlg·alisē lāxēs nɛǥŭmpē ʟɛᵋwis g·ōkwē

10 ʟɛᵋwa ꜱōɛlqwälĪꜱē. Wä, lēx·aᵋmis la k·!ēsᵋogŭlxʟēsēda k·!ēsᵋōgŭ-
lxʟaᵋyasēs nɛǥŭmpē lāq.

Wä, hēᵋmaē ᵋwālas Kwax·ꜰlanōkŭmaᵋyē yĪxs häaɛl gwēᵋnakŭla g·äg-
g·ꜰʟɛlaxs g·ālaē bɛgwänɛmx·ᵋĪdē Dzɛnx·q!ayōwē lāx Tayagwoꜱē,yĪxs hē-
wäxaē k·!ēs xŭngwadɛx·ᵋĪdēda g·aläs ᵋmāxᵘmɛwēsagɛmēsa ᵋnɛmōkwē bāba-

15 gŭmē hēᵋmisa ᵋnɛmōkwē ts!āts!adagɛmē. Wä hēt!a q!ŭnālatsēxs ᵋnɛmōxᵘᵋ-
maēda bābagŭmē xŭnōxᵘs. Wä,g·ꜰlᵋmisē maᵋlōkwē sāsɛmas lä hēx·säᵋma
bābagŭmē ᵋnōla. Wä, lä ts!aᵋyēda ts!āts!adagɛmē qaxs k·!ēsᵋmaaɛl
ᵋnɛmp!ɛna maᵋlōkᵘ bɛgwänɛmx·sä sāsɛmas ᵋmāxᵘmɛwēsagɛmaᵋyē yĪxs âᵋmaē
bɛxᵘk·!ōdɛqɛlēda ts!ɛdāqē. Wä, hēᵋmis hēwaxag·iꜱts x·Ī̂sᵋĪdē ʟēgɛmas

20 qaxs hēꜱomālaē xŭngwadɛx·ᵋĪdɛxs k·!ēsᵋmaē ꜱɛᵋla.

Wä, laᵋmisɛn gwagwēx·s�‌alaꜱ lāx ᵋwalasʟāla, yĪx wŭq!wäs
ᵋmāxᵘmɛwēsagɛmaᵋyē, yĪxs laē ꜱāᵋwadɛs HäwĪlkŭlaꜱxa xamagɛmaᵋyē
g·Īgāmēsa ᵋnɛᵋmēmotasa Kŭkwāk!ŭmasa Qōmoyâᵋyē. Wä, lä xŭngwadɛ-
x·ᵋĪtsa bābagŭmē. Wä, lä HäwĪlkŭlaꜱ ʟēxᵋēts Ādag·iᵋlakᵘ lāxēs

25 xŭnōkwē. Wä, laɛm g·ꜰnꜱɛxʟālax Ādag·iᵋlakᵘ. Wä, la ᵋmāxᵘmɛwēsa-
ǥɛmaᵋyē, yĪx ᵋwālas Kwax·ꜰlanōkŭmaᵋyē ʟēgɛmg·ꜰIxʟālax Wābidoᵋ qa
ʟēgɛmsēs ʟōlēᵋyē, Wä, laᵋmē ᵋnɛmōxᵘᵋɛm xŭnōxᵋs HawĪlkŭlaꜱ ʟɛᵋwis
ǥɛnɛmē ᵋwālasʟāla. Wä, g·ꜰlᵋmisē ɛlāq nɛxʟaax·ᵋĪd bɛgwänɛmxs laē
HawĪlkŭlaꜱ ʟēxᵋĪts Häxŭyōsɛmaᵋyē lāx Ādag·iᵋlakᵘ. Wä, laɛm häsᵋɛm

30 HawĪlkŭlaꜱē ʟēxʟɛǥɛmiꜱa yĪx Häxŭyōsɛmaᵋyē. Wä, lä ts!ɛx·q!ɛx·ᵋĪdē
ᵋwālasʟāla. Wä, lä wĪk·!ɛxᵋĪda. Wä, lāxaē ts!ɛx·q!ɛx·ᵋĪdē Häxŭ-

las/Kwāx·īlanokŭmēᶜ called her Yāsɛkᵘ. But G·ēxk·ɛn gave the name/ Mɛᶜlēd as a name for his granddaughter. Then the name/of the girl was Mɛᶜlēd. Two children had ᶜwālas Kwāx·īlanokŭmēᶜ (5) and his wife, K·ōgwisilaogwa, and when he is dead/that is ᶜwālas Kwāx·īlanokŭmēᶜ, then Wāsaᴸaas will take all the five/seats of his father and all his privileges, but there is/no way for ᶜwālas Kwāx·īlanokŭmēᶜ to give these privileges in marriage to his son-in-law, the names which came down from his ancestors and his house (10) and the house dishes. The only privileges he can give away are the privileges given to him/by his father-in-law./

And thus it is about ᶜwālas Kwāx·īlanokŭmēᶜ, for it is said that it happened this way/from the beginning when first Dzɛnx·q!ayu became a man at Tayagwoᴸ, that/never once did ᶜmāx̣ᵘmɛwēsagɛmēᶜ have no child, but that he had one boy (15) and also one girl. But generally they had only one/son, and when there were two children, always/the elder one was a boy and the younger one a girl. For not once,/it is said, were both children of ᶜmāx̣ᵘmɛwēsagɛmēᶜ boys, but it was/a boy alongside of a girl. And therefore the name has never disappeared,(20) for they came to have children before they died./

Now I shall talk about ᶜwālasᴸāla, the sister of/ᶜmāx̣ᵘmɛwēsagɛmēᶜ, for she had as husband Hawīlkŭlaᴸ, the head chief/of the numaym Kŭkwāk!ŭm of the Q!ōmoyāᶜyē. They had a child,/a boy, and Hawīlkŭlaᴸ gave the name Ādag·iᶜlakᵘ to his (25) child. Now Adag·iᶜlakᵘ is his child's name. Then ᶜmāx̣ᵘmɛwēsagɛmēᶜ/that is, ᶜwālas Kwāx·īlanokŭmēᶜ,gave the marriage name Wābidōᶜ for/the name of his nephew. Now he was the only child of Hawīlkŭlaᴸ and his wife, ᶜwālasᴸāla. Now when he was nearly a grown man,/Hawīlkŭlaᴸ gave Ādag·iᶜlakᵘ the name Hȧxŭyosɛmēᶜ. This (30) Hȧxŭyosɛmēᶜ was Hawīkŭlaᴸ's family name. Then ᶜwālasᴸāla became sick/and she died. Then Hȧxŭyosɛmēᶜ became sick (1) and he also died. Then Hawīlkŭlaᴸ

yōsᴇmaᶜyē. Wä, lāxaē wīk·!ᴇxᶜīda‿ Wä, laᶜmē Hawīlkūlaⱬē gᴇg·adᴇ-
x·ᶜīts Tᴇlēg·alīdzᴇmga, yīx k·!ēdēⱬas Wanukᵘxa g·ayōⱬē lāx ᶜnᴇᶜmēmotasa Wawūᶅibâyēᶜ. Wä, la gᴇg·adē Wanukwas Wäᶅidēxa k·!ēdēⱬas
Lᴇk·âsaxa g·ayōⱬē lāx ᶜnᴇᶜmēmotasa Mamalēleq!äm. Wä, lä xŭngwadē

5 Wanukwas Hämasaqa lāxēs g·alōⱬa gᴇnᴇmē Ts!ᴇts!âlaⱬxa k·!ēdēⱬas Hē-
mōtᴇlasōᶜxa g·ayōⱬē lāx ᶜnᴇᶜmēmotasa Dzᴇndzᴇnx·q!ayo. Wä, la gᴇ-
g·adē Hämasaqäs Hânōsᴇnāgaxa ts!ᴇdāqē xŭnōxᵘs Lālaganōgwiᶜlakwēxa.
g·ayōⱬē lāx ᶜnᴇᶜmēmotasa Kūkwāk!ūmasa Q!ōmoyâᶜyē. Wä, laᶜmē hĕwäxa xŭngwadᴇx·ᶜīdē Hämasaqōⱬē ᶅᴇᶜwis gᴇnᴇmōⱬē Hânosᴇnāgōⱬē. Wä,

10 lāxaē hĕwäxa xŭngwadᴇx·ᶜīdē Lᴇk·âsōⱬē ᶅᴇᶜwis gᴇnᴇmōⱬē Xwēlagēᶅas-
wūⱬēxa ts!ᴇdāqē xŭnōxᵘs G·ayōsdäswūⱬēxa g·ayōⱬē lāx ᶜnᴇᶜmēmotasa
Wīwomasgᴇmasa Mamalēleqala. Wä, lāᶅa Hawīlkūlaⱬ ᶅᴇᶜwis gᴇnᴇmē Tᴇ-
lēg·alīdzᴇmga xŭngwadᴇx·ᶜītsa ts!āts!adagᴇmē. Wä, la Wanukwūⱬē
ᶅēgᴇmg·fīxᶅālax ᶅ!āⱬᴇyīg·fīlisē qa ᶅēgᴇmsēs ts!ōxᵘᶅᴇmagasē. Wä, la-

15 ᶜmē ᶅēgᴇmsa ts!āts!adagᴇmē ᶅ!āⱬᴇyīg·fīlisē lāxēq. Wä, laᶜmē ᶜnᴇmōx-
ᶜŭm xŭnōxᵘs Hawīlkūlaⱬē ᶅ!āⱬᴇyīg·fīlisē. Wä, laᶜmē wīk·!ᴇxᶜīdē Wa-
nuxᵘdē. Wä, lä Hamasaqōⱬ hēᴇm äxᶜēd ᶜwīᶜlax k·!ēk·!ᴇsᶜōxᵘdäsēs
ōmpdē ᶅōᶜ k!wäx·däs. Wä, lāxaē wīk·!ᴇxᶜīdē Lᴇk·âsax·dē lāx ᶜmēmkŭm-
līs. Wä, yīxs häē g·âlagawē wīk·!ᴇxᵘīdē.Wäᶅidäsēs ōmpdē Lᴇk·âsax·dē.

20 Wä, hēᶜmis lāg·iⱬas hēᶜmē Tᴇlēg·alīdzᴇmga ᶜwīᶜla äxᶜēdᴇx k·!ēk·!ᴇs-
ᶜâs ᶅᴇᶜwis k!waᶜyē. Wä, laᴇm ᶅēgadē Tᴇlēg·alīdzᴇmgäs Lᴇk·âsa lāxēq. Wä, la Hämasaqa ᶅēgadᴇs Wāk·adzē, yīx ᶜnᴇmsgᴇmx·dē ᶅēgᴇms Wa-
nuxᵘdē. Wä, lä wīk·!ᴇxᶜīdē Tᴇlēg·alīdzᴇmgax·dxa lāx·dē ᶅēgadᴇs Lᴇ-
k·âsa lāxēs ᶜnᴇᶜmēmotasa Mamalēleq!äm. Wä, la ᶅ!āⱬᴇyīg·fīlisē ᶅax-

25 stōdxēs äbᴇmpdē lāx Lᴇk·âsa lāxa ᶜnᴇᶜmēmotasa Mamalēleq!äm. Wä,
laᶜmē ᶅ!āⱬᴇyīg·fīlisē bᴇgŭxᶅälax Lᴇk·âsa. Wä, laᴇm ᶜwīᶜla äxᶜēdēda
äⱬē Lᴇk·âsax k·!ēk·!ᴇsᶜâs Lᴇk·âsōⱬē ᶅōᶜ ᶅēgᴇmas. Wä, lä wīk·!ᴇ-
xᶜīdē Wāk·adzē, yīx Hämasaqa, laas Lᴇk·âsa, yīx ᶅ!āⱬᴇyīg·fīlisē
ᶜwīᶜla äxᶜēdᴇx ᶅēgᴇmas Hämasaqa. yīxs ōgūᶜlaᶜmaē k!waᶜyas lāx k!wa-

30 ᶜyas Wanukwūⱬē lāxēs ᶜnᴇmēmotasa Wawūᶅibâᶜyē, yīxs g·fīᶜmaē wīk·!-
ᴇxᶜīdē Wanukwūⱬē laē Hämasaqa äxᶜēdᴇx k!waᶜyas ᶅōᶜ ᶜnᴇmsgᴇmē ᶅēgᴇms

took for his wife/Tɛlēg·alīdzɛmga, the princess of Wanuk^u who came
from the numaym/Wawŭlibâ^ɛyē. And Wanuk^u had for his wife Wäʟid,
the princess of/Lɛk·âs who came from the numaym Mamalēleq!ăm. Now
Wanuk^u had a child, (5) Hämasaqa, by his first wife, Ts!ɛts!âlaɫ,
the princess of/Hēmōtɛlasō^ɛ who cᴍe from the numaym Dzɛndzɛnx·q!ayo.
And/Hämasaqa had for his wife Hânosɛmāga, the daughter of Ƶālaganō-
gwi^ɛlak^u/from the numaym Kŭkwāk!ŭm of the Q!ōmoyâ^ɛyē. Now they nev-
er/had a child, Hämasaqa and his wife Hânosɛnāga, and (10) Lɛk·âs
also never had a child with his wife X̣wēlagêʟas,/the daughter of
G·ayōsdäs who came from the numaym/Wīwomasgɛm of the Mamalēleqala.
But Hawīlkŭlaɫ and his wife,Tɛlēg·alīdzɛmga,/had a child, a girl,
and Wanuk^u/gave the name ʟ!āɫɛyīg·flis as a name to his granddaughter. Now (15) the name of the girl was ʟ!āɫɛyīg·flis after this.
Now/ʟ!āɫɛyīg·flis was the only child of Hawīlkŭlaɫ. Then Wanuk^u
died/and Hämasaqa took all the privileges of his late/father and
his seat. Then Lɛk·âs died at ^ɛmēmkŭmlis,/and Wäʟid had died before her father, Lɛk·âs; (20) therefore, Tɛlēg·alīdzɛmga took his
privileges/and his seat, and now the name of Tɛlēg·alīdzɛmga was
Lɛk·âs after this./ Then Hämasaqa had the name Wāk·adzē, one of
the other names of Wanuk^u./ Then Tɛlēg·alīdzɛmga died, whose name
was now Lɛk·âs/in the numaym Mamalēleq!ăm. Then ʟ!āɫɛyīg·flis took
the place of her (25) mother, Lɛk·âs, in the numaym Mamalēleq!ăm.
Now/ʟ!āɫɛyīg·flis had the man's name Lɛk·âs. Now the new Lɛk·âs
took all/the privileges of the late Lɛk·âs and her name. Then died/
Wāk·adzē, namely Hämasaqa, and Lɛk·âs, namely ʟ!āɫɛyīg·flis,/took
all the names of Hämasaqa, for his seat was different from the seat
of (30) Wanuk^u in the numaym Wawŭlibâ^ɛyē, for when Wanuk^u died Hämasaqa took his seat and another name (1) of Wanuk^u, that is Wāk·a-

Wanukwüℓē Wāk·adzē ιō^ε ^εwī^εℓē k·ꞌēk·ꞌεs^εâs. Wä, la^εmē ma^εlōx^u la
bεgwānεmē Hämasaqa ιō^ε Wāk·adzē. Wä, g·îl^εmisē yāqwēda pꞌεsäsa
pꞌεlxεlasgεm laē yāx^εwītsε^εwē Wāk·adzē. Wä, lä ēt.ꞌēd yāx^εwītsε^εwē
Hämasaqa läx gwälεläs. Wä, la^εmē yūdux^us^εäℓa lä ιꞌäℓεyīg·îlis la^ε-
5 mē ιêgadεs Lεk·âsa läxa Mamalēleq.ꞌäm; wä, lä ιêgadεs Wāk·adzē ιō^ε
Hämasaqa läxēs ^εnε^εmēmotasa Wāwŭlibâ^εyē. Wä, lä wīk·ꞌεx^εīdē Hawīlkŭlaℓdē yîx ōmpdäs ιꞌäℓεyīg·îlisxa xamagεma^εyē g·īgämēsa Kükwāk.ꞌü-
masa Q.ꞌōmoyâ^εyē. Wä, la^εmē ιêgadē ιꞌäℓεyīg·îlisas Hawīlkŭlaℓ läxēq. Wä, la^εmē äx^εēdē ιꞌäℓεyīg·îlisaxa hōqustâla g·ōkwa ιε^εwa ^εnäx-
10 wa k·ꞌēk·ꞌεs^εo g·īx·g·aēℓεq ιε^εwa dāgεma^εyē. Wä,laεm ιäxoma^εya äℓē
Hawīlkŭlaℓtsa ^εmεkŭma^εyas ^εnäl^εnε^εmēmasasa Q.ꞌōmoyâ^εyēxa Kükwāk.ꞌü-
mē. Wä, laεm ts.ꞌεdāxstεwēιεlaxēs ōmpdē Hawīlkŭlaℓdē. Wä, laεm mōs-
gεmē ιêιεgεmas. Wä, hẽεmaxaāwisē ^εwāxa k.ꞌwēk.ꞌwa^εyas. Wä, la äx^εē-
daεmxaax dāgεma^εyas Wāk·adzēoℓē läxa ^εnε^εmēmotasa Wāwŭlibâ^εyē. Wä,
15 la mäℓē dāgεma^εyas ιō^ε dāgεma^εyasēs ōmpdē.

Wä, lä^εlaē Wäιidōℓē yîx gεnεmōℓas Wanukwüℓē ιō^εlēnux^us ιꞌäqoιas. Wä, hẽεm g·ōgwadεsa g·ōkwē ιêgadεs Q.ꞌaāts.ꞌē g·ōk^uxa g·ayōℓē
läxa ^εnε^εmēmotasa Wīwomasgεmasa Mamalēleqala, yîxs hẽ^εmaē ^εnε^εmē-
mōts ōmp^εwüℓas ιꞌäqoιasxa ιꞌäqoιasιa^εmaxat.ꞌ. Wä, hẽ^εlat.ꞌa äbεmpas
20 ιꞌäqoιas yîx Ōmaēℓī^εlak^u ts.ꞌä^εyas Wäιidē, yîx gεnεmas Wanukwüℓē,
wä, la k·ꞌeâs xünōx^us ιꞌäqoιasē ιε^εwis gεnεmē Ḡaaxstälas. Wä, lä
ts.ꞌεx·qꞌεx·^εīdē ιꞌäqoιasē. Wä, lä^εlaē ^εnēx· qa hẽ^εmisē ιꞌäℓεyīg·î-
lisē yîxa äℓē Hawīlkŭlaℓ ^εwī^εla äx^εēdεx ιêgεmas ιε^εwis k·ꞌēk·ꞌεs^εo
ιε^εwa ιêgadē g·ōkwa, yîx Q.ꞌaāts.ꞌē. Wä, la^εmē wīk·ꞌεx^εīda yîx ιꞌä-
25 qoιasdē. Wä, la^εmē Hawīlkŭlaℓ ^εwī^εla äx^εēdεx ιêgεmas ιō^ε k.ꞌwa^εyas
ιō^ε k·ꞌēk·ꞌεs^εäs ιε^εwa g·ōx^udäs. Wä, la^εmē sεk·ꞌäsgεmē ιêιεgεmas,
yîx Hämasaqa ιō^ε Wāk·adzē ιō^ε Hawīlkŭlaℓ läxg·a Tsäxisεk·. Wä, hẽ-
^εmis Lεk·âsa ιō^ε ιꞌäqōιas ιêιεgεms läxēs Mamalēlexk·ꞌōt.ꞌēna^εyē.
Wä, ᴀ^εmisιa ts.ꞌεdāgεx·ꞌälax ιꞌäℓεyīg·îlisē. Wä, la^εmē ^εnäxwaεm ha-
30 ^εnēℓa äwä^εwē g·îlg·îldas läx g·ig·ōkwas Hawīlkŭlaℓē qa lats.ꞌâlasεx
yaēq.ꞌwēmäs läxa pꞌεsäsa pꞌεlxεlasgεmē ιε^εwa qꞌεng·äxtâla ιε^εwa dä-

dze, and all of his privileges. Now he was two men/namely Hämasaqa and Wāk·adzē, and when they gave away/blankets they gave to Wā-
k·adzē and they also gave to/Hämasaqa as a second place. Now ᴌ!ā-
ᵶɛyĪg·flis had three places.(5) She had the name Lɛk·âs among the
Mamalēleq!ăm and she had the names Wāk·adzē and/Hämasaqa in the numaym Wawŭlibậᶜyē. Then HawĪlkŭlaᵶ died,/the father of ᴌ!āᵶɛyĪg·f-
lis, the head chief of the Kŭkwāk!ŭm/of the Q!ōmoyậᶜyē. Then ᴌ!ā-
ᵶɛyĪg·flis had the name HawĪlkŭlaᵶ after this./ Then ᴌ!āᵶɛyĪg·flis
took the Vomiting-Beam-House and all (10) the privileges belonging
to it, and the office of giving away property. Now/the new HawĪlkŭlaᵶ stood at the head of the first numaym of the Q!ōmoyậᶜyē. the
Kŭkwāk!ŭm./ (Although) she was a woman she stood in the place of her
late father, HawĪlkŭlaᵶ. Now she had four/names, and that also was
the number of her seats. And she also took/the office of giving a-
way property of Wāk·adzē in the numaym Wawŭlibậᶜyē. Then (15) she
had two offices, his office of giving away property and the office
of giving away property of her late father./

Now it is said that Wāᶫid, the wife of Wanukᵘ, had a nephew,
ᴌ!āqoᶫas./ He owned the house whose name was Q!aats!ē, the house
which belongs/to the numaym WĪwomasgɛm of the Mamalēleqala, for
that was the numaym/of the father of ᴌ!āqoᶫas who was also ᴌ!āqo-
ᶫas. And it is said that the mother of (20) ᴌ!āqoᶫas, ŌᶜmaēᵶĪᶜlakᵘ,
was the younger sister of Wāᶫid, the wife of Wanukᵘ./ They had no
children, ŌᶜmaēᵶĪᶜlakᵘ and her husband Ǥaaxstālas. Then/ᴌ!āqoᶫas
fell sick, and he wished that ᴌ!āᵶɛyĪg·flis,/the new HawĪlkŭlaᵶ,
should take his name and his privileges/and the house named Q!aa-
ts!ē. Now ᴌ!āqoᶫas died.(25) Then HawĪlkŭlaᵶ took all the names
and seats/and privileges and his house. Now she had five names,/
Hämasaqa and Wāk·adzē and HawĪlkŭlaᵶ at Fort Rupert, and/Lɛk·âs and
ᴌ!āqoᶫas on the side of the Mamalēleqala./But ᴌ!āᵶɛyĪg·flis was just
her woman's name. Now there were (30) large boxes in all the houses
of HawĪlkŭlaᵶ to put into them/what is given to her in the giving

lēg·a k·!ōkŭla qaxs k·!ēsaē ᵋnɛmp!ɛna ʟ!ɛlēwēsōᵋsa p!ēsäsa p!ɛlxɛ-
lasgɛmē. Wä, laɛm yāwasᵋîd lāba.

Wä, la Hawîlkŭlaɫ, yîx ʟ!āɫɛyîg·flisē la ɫāᵋwadɛs K!wāk!waba-
lasɛmaᵋyē, yîxg·în q!âyɛᵋwēk· xŭnōkwaxa ʟēgadäs <u>Jonathan</u> <u>Hunt</u> lāxa
5 māmaɫa. Wä, lä xŭngwadɛx·ᵋîtsa bābagŭmē. Wä, lä ʟ!āɫɛyîg·flisē
ʟēxᵋēts Adag·iᵋlakwē lāxēs xŭnōkwē qaxs hēᵋmaē g·îl g·înɫɛxʟäyosa
Hawîlkŭlaɫᵋnākŭlaxs g·ālaōɫēx ᵋnāg·flisɛns ᵋnālax. Wä, g·flᵋmisē
ts!äts!adagɛma ᵋnōlast!ɛgɛmaᵋyē laē ʟēxᵋētsōᵋs Adaga. Wä, lä ēt!-
ēd xŭngwadɛx·ᵋîtsa ts!äts!adagɛmē. Wä, hēɛmxaāwisē Hawîlkŭlaɫē
10 ʟēgɛmg·flxʟālax Wäʟidē qa ʟēgɛmsēs xŭnōkwē. Wä, ᵓaɛm äxᵋēd lāx
ʟēxʟɛgɛmēɫas lāxēs äbāsk·!ōtē qa k·!eâsaē gwēx·ᵋîdaas ʟēgɛmg·flx-
ʟālax Adag·iᵋlakᵘ qaxs g·ayōɫaē ʟēgɛm lāxa g·flg·alîsa Hawîlkŭlaɫ,
yîxs ʟēqēlayaē Adag·iᵋlakᵘ qaēda ᵋnōlast!ɛgɛmaᵋyē. Wä, la k·!ēs
lāyowa ʟēgɛm Adag·iᵋlakᵘ lāxa ts!āᵋya. Wä, laᵋmē maᵋlōkwē sāsɛmas
15 Hawîlkŭlaɫ ʟɛᵋwis ɫāᵋwunɛmē K!wāk!wabalasɛmaᵋyē lāx Adag·iᵋlakwē
ʟōᵋ Wäʟidē. Wä, lāxaē ēt!ēd xŭngwadɛx·ᵋîtsa ts!äts!adagɛmē. Wä,
la Hawîlkŭlaɫ ʟɛxᵋēts ᵋmāxᵘmɛwēdzɛmga lāxa ts!äts!adagɛmē lāx ʟēgɛmas wûq!äsa g·ālä Hawîlkŭlaɫa. Wä, lāxaē ēt!ēd xŭngwadɛx·ᵋîtsa
bābagŭmē. Wä, la Hawîlkŭlaɫ ʟɛxᵋēts Gaaxstālas lāxa bābagŭmē.
20 Wä, laᵋmē Hawîlkŭlaɫē äxᵋēdxa ʟēgɛmē lāx ʟēxʟɛgɛmēɫas Lɛk·âsa lāxa
Mamalēleqala qaxs ʟēgadaaᵋlaē äbɛmpᵋwŭɫas Lɛk·âsäs Gaaxstālasē.
Wä, la Hawîlkŭlaɫē ʟēxᵋēts Gaaxstālas lāxēs bābagŭmē xŭnōkwa. Wä,
lä ēt!ēd xŭngwadɛx·ᵋîtsa ts!äts!adāgɛmē. Wä, la Hawîlkŭlaɫē ʟēxᵋēts Lɛlāk·ɛnēdzɛmga lāxēs ts!äts!adagɛmē xŭnōkwa. Wä, laᵋmē äxᵋ-
25 ēdē Hawîlkŭlaɫaxa ʟēgɛmē lāx ʟēxʟɛgɛmîɫas Wanukᵋwŭɫē, yîxs Lɛlāk·-
ɛnēdzɛmgax·ʟaaᵋlaē äbɛmpas Wanukᵋwŭɫē. Wä, laᵋmē ʟēgɛmsa ts!äts!-
adagɛmē Lɛlāk·ɛnēdzɛmga laxēq.

Wä, sɛk·!ōk·ɛwē sāsɛmas Hawîlkŭlaɫē yîx ʟ!āɫɛyîg·flisē ʟɛᵋwis
ɫāᵋwŭnɛmē K!wāk!wabalasɛmaᵋyēxa g·ayōɫē lāx ᵋnɛᵋmēmotasa Haănaʟē-
30 nâsa Q!ōmoyâᵋyē.

of blankets and of button blankets and of silver (1) bracelets, for
she is never once forgotten in the giving away of blankets./ Now
this is the end for a while./

Then Hawĭlkŭlaɫ, namely, ʟ!āɫɛyĭg·flis, took for her husband
K!wāk!wabalasɛmēᵋ,/my middle son, whose name is Jonathan Hunt among
the (5) white people, and they had a boy. Then ʟ!āɫɛyĭg·flis/
named her child Ādag·iᵋlakᵘ,for that was the child's name of/Hawĭl-
kŭlaɫ in the beginning when the first light came into our world.
And when/the eldest child is a girl, she is called Ādaga. And then
again/she got a child, a girl, and Hawĭlkŭlaɫ gave/the marriage name
Wäꞁid for the name of her child. Then she took the (10) family name
from her mother's side, for she cannot give away in marriage/the
name Ādag·iᵋlakᵘ because the name belongs to the ancestors of Hawĭlkŭlaɫ,/for the name Ādag·iᵋlakᵘ is given to the eldest one, and
never/is the name Ādag·iᵋlakᵘ given to a younger brother. Now two
children had (15) Hawĭlkŭlaɫ and her husband, K!wāk!wabalasɛmēᵋ,
Ādag·iᵋlakᵘ/and Wäꞁid. Then she had another child, a girl./ Then
Hawĭlkŭlaɫ called the girl ᵋmāxᵘmɛwēdzɛmga, the name of/the sister
of the first Hawĭlkŭlaɫ. Then she had another child,/a boy, and
Hawĭlkŭlaɫ gave the name Ǥaaxstālas to the boy.(20) Now Hawĭlkŭlaɫ
took the family name of Lɛk·âs among the/Mamalēleqala, for it is
said the mother of Lɛk·âs had the name Ǥaaxstālas./ Now Hawĭlkŭlaɫ
named her son Ǥaaxstālas. Then/they had another child, a girl, and
Hawĭlkŭlaɫ named/her daughter Lɛlāk·ɛnēdzɛmga. Now (25) Hawĭlkŭlaɫ
took the name from the family name of Wanukᵘ, for Lɛlāk·ɛnēdzɛmga,/
it is said, was the name of the mother of Wanukᵘ. Now the name of
the girl/was Lɛlāk·ɛnēdzɛmga after this.

Now Hawĭlkŭlaɫ, that is ʟ!āɫɛyĭg·flisē, had five children with
her/husband, K!wāk!wabalasɛmēᵋ, who belonged to the numaym Haãnaꞁē-
no/of the Q!ōmayâᵋyē.

Wä, laᵋmēs Hawīlkūlaⱡ ᵋnēx· qa p!ᴇsēs Ādag·iᵋlakwaxa Gwētᴇla
ⱡᴇᵋwa Q!ōmoyâᵋyē qa wēg·is ⱡēgadᴇs ᵋmᴇmx·â Hämasaqa. Wä, laᵋmē
lāⱡa ᵋnᴇmsgᴇmē ⱡēgᴇms Hawīlkūlaⱡē lāxēs xūnōkwē Ādag·iᵋlakᵘ. Wä,
laᵋmē lâsa Hawīlkūlaⱡasa dāgᴇmaᵋyē lāxēs xūnōkwēda la ⱡēgadᴇs ᵋmᴇ-
5   mx·â Hämasaqa ⱡᴇᵋwa ᵋnāxwa k·!ēk·!ᴇsᵋâs Hämasaqōⱡē ⱡᴇᵋwa g·ōkwē
ᵋwīᵋla. Wä, laᵋmē dāgᴇmaᵋyē ᵋmᴇmx·â Hämasaqäsēs ᵋnᴇᵋmēmotasa Wä-
wūlibâᵋyē. Wä, lāxaē Hawīlkūlaⱡ, yīx ⱡ!āⱡᴇyīg·flisē ⱡēᵋlālaxēs
ᵋnᴇᵋmēmotaxa Kūkwāk!ūmasa Q!ōmoyâᵋyē qa lās ᵋwiᵋla hōgwīⱡ lāx g·ō-
kwasa g·ālē Hawīlkūlaⱡa. Wä, g·flᵋmisē g·āx ᵋwīᵋlaēⱡa laē häᵋm-
10   g·īlaxēs ᵋnᴇᵋmēmotē. Wä, g·flᵋmisē gwāⱡ haᵋmāpa k!wēⱡē laas yāq!-
ᴇg·aᵋⱡē Nōlisxa g·ayōⱡē lāx ᵋnᴇᵋmēmotas. Wä, lä ᵋnēk·a: Wäᴇntsōs
hōⱡēlax nōs ᵋnᴇᵋmēmot lāxg·a gwäⱡaasⱡᴇg·asg·ín wāⱡdᴇmⱡᴇk·. Qâⱡ,
qäⱡaxs hēⱡaxaq!amaē yīxg·a Hawīlkūlaⱡᴇk· yīxs läk· mayōⱡᵋīdᴇsg·as
ōmpᴇk·xg·ada hēlēmâsᴇk· lāxg·a ᵋmᴇmx·â Hämasaqak·. Wä, laᴇm läk·
15   lâsaⱡg·a Hawīlkūlaⱡg·asē ⱡēgᴇmē Hawīlkūlaⱡ lāx ᵋmᴇmx·â Hämasaqa
ⱡᴇᵋwa k!waᵋyas ⱡᴇᵋwa hōqustâlax g·ōkwa ⱡᴇᵋwōxda ᵋnāxwax k·!ēk·!ᴇ-
sᵋō g·ix·g·aēⱡ lāqᵘ, wä hēᵋmisa dāgᴇmaᵋyē. Wä, laᵋmē ᵋwīᵋla,
ᵋnēk·ē.

Wä, laᵋmᴇn gwāⱡ ⱡēqalas Hawīlkūlaⱡ lāx ⱡ!āⱡᴇyīg·flis qaxs lᴇ-
20   ᵋmaē ēt!ēd ts!ᴇdāxsēᵋstalīⱡa. Wä, lä äxᵋētsᴇᵋwa maᵋⱡp!ᴇnyag·i
p!ᴇlxᴇlasgᴇma qaᵋs g·āxē mōgwalēᵋlᴇm lāx ⱡaᵋwīᵋlasas Nōlisē. Wä,
la Nōlisē dāx·ᵋīdxa ᵋnᴇmxsa p!ᴇlxᴇlasgᴇma qaᵋs dālalīⱡēqēxs laē
ⱡēᵋlālaxa āⱡē Hawīlkūlaⱡa lāx Ādag·iᵋlakᵘ, yīxa la ⱡēgadᴇs ᵋmᴇmx·â
Hämasaqa. Wä, hēx·ᵋidaᵋmisa la ⱡēgadᴇs Hawīlkūlaⱡ la qaᵋs ⱡaᵋwū-
25   nōdzᴇlīⱡēx Nōlis. Wä, lä yāq!ᴇg·aᵋⱡē Nōlisē. Wä, lä ᵋnēk·a: ᵋwa,
ᵋnᴇᵋmēmot, wēg·a dōxᵋwidᴇx g·āxᵋᴇmk· g·āxᵋᴇmg·ada x·ōmsg·íns nōs
ᵋnᴇᵋmēmot lāxg·a Hawīlkūlaⱡᴇk·xg·ada läk· ⱡ!āyᴇwīᵋlälakwaxg·ada
alōmasᴇk· la g·īgāmaᵋyaxg·ada äxnōgwadg·asa nᴇqēwalēⱡasa g·ōkwē
qaxs k!waᵋya, ᵋnēk·ē. Wä, lä ⱡᴇp!ēdxa ᵋnᴇmxsa p!ᴇlxᴇlasgᴇma. Wä,
30   laᵋmē ᵋnēk·a: Laᴇm p!ᴇlxᴇlasgᴇm qaᵋs Gwētᴇl, laᴇm p!ᴇlxᴇlasgᴇm
qaᵋs ᵋwālas Kwāg·uⱡ; laᴇm p!ᴇlxᴇlasgᴇm qaᵋs Q!ōmk·!ūt!ᴇs. Laᴇms

Now Hawīlkūlaɫ wished Ädag·iᵋlakᵘ should give away property to
the Gwētela/and the Q!ōmoyäᵋyē in order to be called ᵋmɛmx·ä Hämasaqa. Now/one name of Hawīlkūlaɫ was to go to her child Ädag·iᵋlakᵘ
Then/Hawilkūlaɫ passed over the office of giving away property to
her child, whose name was now (5) ᵋmɛmx·ä Hämasaqa , and all the
privileges of Hämasaqa and the house./ Now ᵋmɛmx·ä Hämasaqa had the
office of giving away property to his numaym, Wawūlibäᵋyē./ Then
Hawīlkūlaɫ, that is ʟ!āɫɛyīg·flis, called her/numaym, the Kūkwāk!ūm
of the Q!ōmayäᵋyē, to come into the house/of the first Hawīlkūlaɫ.
And as soon as they were all in (10) she gave her numaym to eat.
After the guests had eaten,/Nōlis, who belongs to her numaym, spoke
and said: "Listen/to me, my numaym, to what I am going to tell you
here. Indeed/indeed, she has done right, this Hawīlkūlaɫ, for she
has given birth to this,/her father, a good man, this ᵋmɛmx·ä Hämasaqa. Now (15) Hawīlkūlaɫ will give over her name Hawīlkūlaɫ to
ᵋmɛmx·ä Hämasaqa,/and her seat and the Vomiting-Beam House, and all
the privileges/that are owned by her, and also the office of giving
away property. That is all,"/said he./

Now I will stop calling ʟ!āɫɛyīg·flis Hawīlkūlaɫ, for she is
(20) again only a woman. Now two hundred/blankets were taken and
put down at the place where Nōlis stood in the house. And/Nōlis
took up one pair of blankets and held it up as he/called the new
Hawīlkūlal, that is Ädag·iᵋlakᵘ, the one whose name was now ᵋmɛmx·ä/
Hämasaqa. Then immediately the one who had the name Hawīlkūlaɫ went
and stood by the side of (25) Nōlis. Then Nōlis spoke and said,
"Oh,/numaym, look at him. He came, he came, our head, our/numaym
to this Hāwīlkūlaɫ, who has been changed about/and is now a new
chief, who owns the rear of the house/as his seat," said he. Then
he unfolded one pair of blankets and (30) said, "Now this is a
blanket for you, Gwētɛla; this is a blanket/for you, ᵋwālas Kwāg·uɫ;
this is a blanket for you, Q!ōmk·!ūt!ɛs. Now (1) you will come and

g·āxʟ x·Īts!ax·ꟾlaʟɛx Wäʟidē xŭnōkwaˌ Hawĭlkŭlaⱡ lāxg·adɛxs maᶜⱡ-
p!ɛnyag·īg·ada p!ɛlxɛlasgɛmk·, ᶜnēk·ē. Wä, laᶜmēda āⱡē Hawĭlkŭlaⱡ
la xŭngwadɛsēs wŭq!wē Wäʟidē qaxs k·!ēsᶜmaē̓ xŭngwadɛēnoxwē Hawĭl-
kŭlaⱡē, yĭxs hē̓ē gwēg·ilēda g·ālē bāk!ŭma. Wä, g·ꟾlᶜmisē xŭngwada
5 laē hē̓ɛm äxᶜētsɛᶜwēs xŭnōkwē qaᶜs lē yĭxwa qa p!äȳâs p!ɛlxɛlasgɛma.
Wä, laᶜmē ᶜnɛmāx·ꟾsa maᶜⱡp!ɛnyag·i p!ɛlxⱶlasgɛm ʟōᶜ ɛlg·aaʟɛlōtsa
ʟēgɛmē Hawĭlkŭlaⱡ lāx Ādag·iᶜlakwē. (ᶜnɛmāx·ꟾs ʟɛᶜwa lɛbɛlädaxs
tsāsɛyōdaaxa g·Ɪng·Ɪnānɛmē qa ʟēgadēsēsēs ʟēgɛmē.) Wä, hē̓ᶜmis tsā-
sɛyōdaēnēᶜsa bāk!ŭmaxs p!ɛsaē yĭsa p!ɛlxɛlasgɛmē qa ɛlg·aaʟɛlēsa
10 ʟēgɛmē lāxa g·Ɪnānɛmē ʟōᶜma g·īg·ɛgāmaᶜyaxa g·ꟾlᶜmaē mɛnⱡᶜĪtsēs
g·Īgɛxʟäyo ʟēgɛma laē p!ɛsᶜĪtsa p!ɛlxɛlasgɛmē qa ɛlg·aaʟɛlēsēs gwŭ-
ᶜyō qaᶜs äⱡ ʟēgɛma, ᶜnɛmāx·ꟾs ʟōᶜ hāⱡaqēda lâⱡaxa alōmas ʟēgɛmaxa
ᶜnāxwa bēbɛgwānɛmasa p!ɛlxɛlasgɛmē qa ʟē̓qɛlēsēsa āⱡtsɛmē ʟēgɛm lāq
Wä, laᶜmē hē̓ᶜmēda āⱡē Hawĭlkŭlaⱡ dāgɛmēxa p!ɛlxɛlasgɛmaxs laē yā-
15 qwas lāxa Gwētɛla ʟɛᶜwa ᶜwālas Kwāg·uⱡ ʟɛᶜwa Q!ōmk·!ŭt!ɛsē. Wä,
laɛm yāwasᶜĪd lāba.

Wä, hē̓t!aʟɛn ēdzagŭmʟē ᶜwālas Kwax·ꟾlanōkŭmaᶜyē, yĭxs sɛk·!a-
x·ᶜĪdālaēs k!waᶜyē. Wä, hē̓ᶜmaēxs ʟēgadaas ᶜmāxᵘmɛwēsagɛmaᶜyē lāxa
ᶜwālas Kwāg·uⱡ. Wä, lä gɛg·adɛs Lɛlāk·ɛnēdzɛmgaxa �fiɛm ʟēgɛm ᶜnɛms-
gɛmsēs ābɛmpē lāxa bāxŭs. Wä, lä ʟēgadɛs X·Īts!ax·ꟾlasōgwiᶜlakᵘ
20 lāxa ts!ēts!ēqa. Wä, la ᶜmāxᵘmɛwēsagɛmaᶜyē ʟēgadɛs ʟäᶜlaᶜlakᵘ lāxa ts!ēts!ēqa. Wä, hē̓ɛm lāg·iⱡas gɛg·adɛsa ʟēgɛmaɛēs ābɛmpē yāqwap!aᶜmaaxaēda ts!ēdaqē lāxa bāxŭsē. Wä, lāxaē yāqwap!aɛmxaaxs
laē ts!ēts!ēqɛda Kwākwāg·uⱡē ʟōxs laē p!ēkᵘ lāxa aⱡōgŭxsɛᶜmakwē
lēlqwālaʟaᶜya.

25   Wä, la ᶜmāxᵘmɛwēsagɛmaᶜyē ʟēgadɛs ᶜwālas Kwax·ꟾlanōkŭmaᶜyē
lāxēs äbask·!ōta Mamalēleqala. Wä, lä ʟēgadɛs ᶜnɛmsgɛmk·!äla lāxa
ts!ēts!ēqa. Wä, lāxaē gɛg·adɛsa ʟēgɛmē Mɛᶜlēdēxa ʟēgɛmālas änēsᶜ-
wŭⱡas Lālak·ots!ōⱡē. Wä, la ʟēgadɛs Tɛⱡts!aas lāxa ts!ēts!ēqa.
Wä, lāxaē ᶜmāxᵘmɛwēsagɛmaᶜyē ʟēgadɛs Sēxŭqâla lāxa Mamalēleqala.
30 Wä, lä ʟēgadɛs ʟäx·sᶜāla lāxa ts!ēts!ēqa. Wä, lä gɛg·adɛsa ʟēgɛmē

see Wäḷid, the child of Hawīlkŭlaɫ, with/two hundred blankets,"
said he. Now the new Hawīlkŭlaɫ/had for his child his sister,
Wäḷid, for Hawīlkŭlaɫ was not yet old enough to have children./
For that is the way of the ancient Indians, when (a person) has a
child (5) that chilᾳ is taken to dance in the giving away of blankets./ The two hundred blankets are just like fastening/the name
Hawīlkŭlaɫ on Ādag·iᵋlakᵘ.(This is just like a priest/baptising the
children to have their names.) And it is the/baptising of the Indians; the giving away of blankets fastens (10) a name on a child.
And chiefs, when they are tired of/their chief's name, they give
away blankets to fasten on whatever/new name they want, just as
though in obtaining a new name with blankets/all the men were paid
to call him the new name./ Now the new Hawīlkŭlaɫ had the office
of giving away property and blankets in the giving away (15) to
the Gwɛtɛla and the ᵋwālas Kwāg·uɫ and the Q!ōmk·!ūt!ɛs . Now this
is ended for a while.

Now the subject of my talk will be again ᵋwālas Kwāx·ílanokŭmēᵋ
who had five/seats. Now his name was ᵋmāxᵘmɛwēsagɛmēᵋ among the/
ᵋwālas Kwāg·uɫ. And he had for his wife Lɛlāk·ɛnēdzɛmga; that is
just another name/of his mother in the secular season, and her name
was X·Its!ax·ílasōgwIᵋlakᵘ (20) in the winter ceremonial. And ᵋmāxᵘmɛwēsagɛmēᵋ had the name ᴌāᵋlāᵋlakᵘ in the/winter ceremonial, And the
reason why he had for his wife the name of his mother/is that the women give away property to one another in the secular season; and the
Kwag·uɫ also give away property to one another/during the winter ceremonial and when they are invited by other/tribes./

(25) And ᵋmāxᵘmɛwēsagɛmēᵋ had the name ᵋwālas Kwāx·ílanokŭmēᵋ/on
his mother's side among the Mamalēleqala. And he had the name ᵋnɛ-
msgɛmk·!āla in the/winter ceremonial; and he had for his wife the
name Mɛᵋlēd, the name of an aunt of/Lālak·ots!a, and her name is
Tɛɫts!aas in the winter ceremonial./ And ᵋmāxᵘmɛwēsagɛmēᵋ had the
name Sēxŭqâla among the Mamalēleqala;(30) and he had the name ᴌäx·-

ʟ!ăⱫʟ!aⱫɛlɪsĭlaŏgwa lāxa băx̯ŭs; wä, lä ʟ̣ĕgadɛs K·!ănawĕga lāxa
ts!ēts!ēqa. Wä, lāxaē ᵋmāxᵘmɛwĕsagɛmaᵋyə ʟ̣ĕgadɛs Wāmisē lāxa Ma-
malēleqaɪa. Wä, lä ʟ̣ĕgadɛs Wĭg·flis lāxa ꜰs!ēts!ēqa. Wä, lä gɛ-
g·adɛsa ʟ̣ĕgɛmē K·!äsogwiᵋlakᵘ lāxa băx̯ŭs; wä, lä ʟ̣ĕgadɛs MɛnⱫŏ-
5   sɛlas lāxa ts!ēts!ēqa. Wä, lāxaē ᵋmāxᵘmɛwĕsagɛmaᵋyē ʟ̣ĕgadɛs Yā-
qŏʟas lāxa ᵋnɛᵋmēmotasa Lŏlɛᵋwag·ĭläsa Dzāwadɛēnoxᵘ; wä, lä ʟ̣ĕga-
dɛs Dzax̯ᵘts!āla lāxa ts!ēts!ēqa. Wä, lä gɛg·adɛsa ʟ̣ĕgɛmē LɛᵋwaⱫ-
q!ānakᵘ lāxa băx̯ŭs; wä, lä ʟ̣ĕgadᵉs ᵋmɛk·ālɛls lāxa ts!ēts!ēqa. Wä,
laɛm lāba lāxēq.

10   Wä̱, hĕɛm gwɛᵋyâsa bāk!ŭmē gɛg·adɛsēs āpsŏt!ēnaᵋyē lāx gwäⱫa-
asas ᵋmāxᵘmɛwĕsagɛmaᵋyē. Wä, lä âlax·ᵋĭd la gɛg·adɛs K·ŏgwisila-
ŏgwa. Wä, g·flᵋmisē gɛg·ădɛx·ᵋĭdɛs K·ŏgwisilaŏgwa laē x·fsāʟɛlē
gɛnɛmbuⱫāsēxa âɛm ʟ̣ĕgɛmē Lɛlāk·ɛnēdzɛmga qaxs lɛᵋmaē âlax·ᵋĭd gɛ-
g·ada. Wä, lāʟ̣ē mŏsgɛma ʟ̣ĕʟ̣ɛgɛm gɛgɛnɛms.

15   Wä, lɛn k·!ēs q!âʟɛlax gwēgŭmᵋyadzɛxⱫäyâs ᵋmāx̯ᵘmɛwĕsagɛmaᵋyē
lāxēs ᵋwāxaasē ʟ̣ɛᵋwis gɛgɛnɛmē. Wä, laɛm lāba..

The Acquisition of Names.

1. The name of the newborn child.

Wä, hĕᵋmaaxs g·ālaē māᵋyuʟē ʟ!āx·ʟ!alĭdzɛmgäsa bābagŭmē, yĭxs
20   Ⱬāᵋwadaē ʟ!āx·ʟ!alĭdzɛmgäs ʟ!āqoʟasxa xamagɛmaᵋyē g·ĭgāmēsa ᵋnɛᵋmə-
mutasa Yaēx·agɛmaᵋyasa Q!ŏmoyâᵋyē lāx Tsaxis. Wä, hēx·ᵋidaᵋmis
ʟ̣ĕgadēda bābagŭmas Tsaxis.

sᵋāla in the winter ceremonial. And he had for his wife the name/
(1) ʟ!āʌ̣!aʌ̣ɛlīsīlaōgwa in the secular season, and she had the name
X̣·!ānawēga in the winter/ceremonial. And ᵋmāx̣ᵘmɛwēsagɛmēᵋ also had
the name Wāmis among the Mamalēleqala/and his name was Wīg·īlis in
the winter ceremonial. And he/had for his wife the name K·!äsog-
wiᵋlakᵘ in the secular season, and her name was Mɛnʌ̣ōsɛlas/ (5) in
the winter ceremonial. And ᵋmāx̣ᵘmɛwēsagɛmēᵋ also had the name Yā-
qōʟas/ in the numaym Lēlɛᵋwag·ila of the Dzāwadɛēnoxᵘ, and he had
the name Dzax̣ᵘts!âla/in the winter ceremonial. And he had for his
wife the name Lɛᵋwaīʌ̣q!ānakᵘ/in the secular season, and she had the
name ᵋmɛk·ālɛls in the winter ceremonial. Now/that is the end of
this. (10)

This is what is called by the Indians "to have for a wife the
other side," namely the way/ᵋmāx̣ᵘmɛwēsagɛmēᵋ (had names for wives).
Now he really had for his wife K·ōgwisilaōgwa./ And when he took
K·ōgwisilaōgwa for his wife the imaginary wives disappeared./ That
is, Lɛlāk·ɛnēdzɛmga was only a name, for now he really had a wife./
There were still four names as his wives. (15)

I do not know the ochre names of ᵋmāx̣ᵘmɛwēsagɛmēᵋ,/their
whole number, and those of his wives. This is the end.

The Acquisition of Names
1. The name of the newborn child.

When ʟ!ax·ʟ!alīdzɛmga first gave birth to a boy, for/(20) ʟ!a-
x·ʟ!alīdzɛmga had for her husband ʟ!āqoʟas, the head chief of the
numaym/ Yaēx·agɛmēᵋ of the Q!ōmoyâᵋyē at Fort Rupert, then at once/
the child had the name Fort Rupert.

2. The name of the ten moons old child.

Wä, laɛm nɛqasgɛmē ᵋmɛkúlʼasa bãbagúmē g·äg·ꜜlɛla lāx xāᵋyuɫdɛ-
mas ʟꜞäx·ʟꜞalᴉdzɛmgäs ʟ̣ogadɛs Tsaxis. Wä, g·ꜞlᵋmisē hᵉɫogwilaxs
laē ʟꜞáqoʟas, yᴉx ōmpas Tsaxis ʟēᵋlāla ᵋwᴉᵋlaxa Kwãkwä̆g̣uɫē qa läs
5 ᵋwᴉᵋla hōgwᴉʟ lāx g·ōkwasxa ᵋnēk·a qãsa maᵋlōkwa bēbɛgwãnɛm: G·ä-
xᵋmɛnuᵋxᵘ qãsaē qãns lē gwãgúmᵋyãla lāxwa hᵉɫogwilax, ᵋnēk·ē lāx
tꜞɛx·fläs g·ig·ōkwasa Kwãkwä̆g·uɫē. Wä, g·ꜞlᵋmisē g·äx ᵋwᴉᵋlaēʟa
ᵋnãxwa bēbɛgwãnɛm ʟɛᵋwa haᵋyäɫᵋa ʟoᵋma g·ꜞng·ꜞnãnɛmē, laas äxk·ꜞã-
lasɛᵋwēda tsꜞɛdãqē ʟēgadɛ Aōmōɫxa g·ayoɫē lāx ᵋnɛᵋmēmotasa Haãnaʟi-
10 nãsa Q̣ꜞōmoyä̆ᵋyē qa läs tsꜞɛx·sɛmdɛx sɛᵋyäs x·ōmsasa hᵉɫogwila bãbagúma, qaxs hᵉᵋmaē k·ꜞēsᵋōs Aōmōɫa tsꜞɛx·sɛmdäxa hᵉɫogwila g·ꜞng·ꜞnã-
nɛma. Wä,lä ʟēᵋlãlasɛᵋwa ōgü̆la tsꜞɛdãqxa gúmsaʟasa gúmsē lāxa
g·ꜞnãnɛmē. Wä, la ʟēᵋlãlasɛᵋwa maᵋlōkwē k·ꜞēsᵋonuxᵘsa kúnxwētäsa
kúnxwēdɛm. Wä, hᵉᵋm ʟēgadēda ᵋmaᵋlōkwē tsꜞēdaxs kwēkúnxwētꜞēnoxᵘ.
15 Wä, lä ʟēgadēda gúmsɛlg·ꜞsē tsꜞɛdãxs gúmsɛlg·ꜞsxa hᵉɫogwila. Wä,
la ʟēgadēda tsꜞɛx·sɛmdʟax sɛᵋyäs x·ōmsasa bãbagúmas tsꜞɛx·sɛmdɛl-
g·ꜞsxa hᵉɫogwila.

Wä, g·ꜞlᵋmisē la ᵋwᴉᵋla kꜞús̆ᵋālᴉɫa sɛk·ꜞãkwē tsꜞɛdãq lāxa
ōgwiwaᵋlᴉɫasa g·ōkwē lāx kꜞwaēlasas ʟꜞäx·ʟꜞalᴉdzɛmga, yᴉx abɛmpas
20 Tsaxisxa hᵉɫogwila bãbagúma, wä, lä Aōmōɫē äxᵋēdxēs ʟꜞɛmqꜞax·ä xagɛmē qaxs g·äxᵋmaē dãlaxa ʟꜞɛmqꜞax·ä xagɛma ʟɛᵋwa aēk·ꜞaakwē xōkᵘ
kꜞwaxʟä̆ᵋwa. Hᵉᵋm ʟēgadēda xōkwē kꜞwaxʟä̆ᵋwas tsēᵋnanoxa tsꜞɛx·sɛmdäx
sɛᵋyäsa hᵉɫogwila. Wä, lä Aōmōɫē äxk·ꜞãlax ʟꜞäx·ʟꜞalᴉdzɛmga qa ha-
qwäɫēsa g·ꜞnãnɛmē lāx ōkwäx·aᵋyas. Wä, la Aōmōɫē xaxᵋētsa ʟꜞɛmqꜞax·ä
25 xagɛm lāx sɛᵋyäs x·ōmsasa g·ꜞnãnɛmē qa ᵋnãxwēs qꜞwäx·ᵋᴉdēda sɛᵋya.
Wä, g·ꜞlᵋmisē ᵋnãxwa la qꜞwäɫēda sɛᵋya laē äxᵋēdxa xōkwē kꜞwaxʟä̆ᵋwa
qaᵋs mɛx·ʟɛndēs ōbaᵋyas lāxa lɛgwᴉɫē. Wä, g·ꜞlᵋmisē x·ᴉxᵋēdɛxs laē
dãx·ᵋitsēs gɛmxōɫtsꜞānaᵋyē lāxa ʟꜞɛmqꜞax·ä xagɛma qaᵋs makꜞꜞsalēs
ōxwäᵋyasa xagɛmē lāx ʟꜞēsas hᵉɫk·ꜞōdɛnōʟɛmaᵋyas x·ōmsasa g·ꜞnãnɛmē.
30 Wä, laɛm nēnɛlatãlē sɛᵋyäsa g·ꜞnãnɛmē lāx ēk·ꜞǫtx·äyasa xagɛmē. Wä,
hᵉᵋmis la tsꜞētsꜞɛx·atãsōᵋs Aōmōɫē. Wä, lä k·ꜞēs gēg·ꜞlᴉɫɛxs laē

2. The name of the ten moons old child.

For ten moons the boy, beginning from the time when he was
born by/ʟ!ax·ʟ!alîdzɛmga had the name **Fort Rupert**.   As soon as
he had the right age, (that is ten moons old)/ then ʟ!āqoʟas, the father of Fort Rupert called all the Kwāg·uⁿ tribes to go (5) into his
house, and the two men who invite said, "We come/to invite you to
help to paint this one who is ten moons old.' Thus they said at
the/door of the houses of the Kwāg·uⁿ tribes. And when all the men
had come in/and the young men and also the children, they asked/ a
woman whose name is Aōmōⁿ, who belongs to the numaym Haānaʟino (10)
of the Q!ōmoyâᶜyē, to scorch off the hair of the head of the ten
moons old boy,/for this is the privilege of Aōmōⁿ, to scorch off the
hair of the ten moons old child./ Then other women were called, the
one who was to paint the child with ochre/and the two were called
whose privilege it is to put on the leg/and arm-rings. And these two
women have the name The-Ones-to-Put-on-the-Leg-and-Arm-Rings,(15)
and/ the one who scorches the hair of the head of the boy has the
name Scorcher-of-the-/Ten-Moons-Old-Child.

As soon as the five women had sat down in the/rear of the
house, where sat ʟ!ax·ʟ!alîdzɛmga, the mother (20) of Fort Rupert,
the ten moons old boy, then Aōmōⁿ took her yew wood/comb, for she
came carrying her yew wood comb and well split/cedar wood. And
this is the name of the cedar wood, means of scorching off/the hair
of the ten moons old child. Then Aōmōⁿ asked ʟ!ax·ʟ!alîdzɛmga to
put on his stomach/the child on her knees. Then Aōmōⁿ combed with
the yew wood (25) comb the head of the child so that each hair stood
on end./ And when all the hair stood on end, then she too' the split
cedar wood/and lit it in the fire. And when it caught fire she/took
with her left hand the yew wood comb and put/the teeth of the comb
close to the skin of the right hand side of the head of the child
(30) and then the hair of the child showed on the upper side of the
comb. And/ then it was that Aōmōⁿ scorched off,and it was not long

8*

gwāɫa. Wä, g·îlᵋmisē gwāɫē Aōmōɫē ts!ɛx·sɛmda laē äxᵋēdxa hě gwēx·sa
ɫōq!wē qaᵋs gwaxts!ōdēsa wŭdaᵋsta ᵋwāpē lāxa kwädzats!ēʟaxa g·înānɛ-
mē. Wä, lä däx·ᵋîdxa ts!ēsʟāla qaᵋs k·!îp!îdēs lāxa k·!ēsē ᵋwālas
x·îxsɛmāla t!ēsɛma qaᵋs k·!îpstɛndēs lāxa ᵋwābɛts!âwasa kwädzats!ēʟa-
5 xa g·înānɛmē. Wä, mōꝫgɛma x·îx·îxsɛmāla t!ēsɛm hēᵋyagō k·!îpᵋstanoᵋ
lāxa ᵋwābats!âwasa kwädzats!ēʟaxa hěɫogwila g·înānɛma. Wä, g·îlᵋmisē
gwāɫa laē Aōmōɫē q!aɫᵋîdxa g·înānɛmē qaᵋs nɛɫk·ax·alîɫēqēxs laē mōp!-
ɛna äxᵋstɛndxēs hěɫk·!ōɫts!ānaᵋyē lāxa ts!ɛlxᵋstax·sōkŭla ᵋwāpa qaᵋs
mōp!ɛnē ʟoxsɛmtsēs k!ŭnkwaxts!ānaᵋyē lāx x·ōmsasa g·înānɛmē. Wä lā-
10 wisʟē kwäsᵋîdɛx x·ōmsas. Wä, g·îlᵋmisē gwāɫa laē ts!oxwit!ēdɛx ōk!wi-
naᵋyas. Wä, g·îlᵋmisē gwāɫa laē äxᵋēdē Aōmōɫaxa aěk·!aakwē q!uyaakᵘ
k·ādzɛkwa qaᵋs dēg·it!ēdēs lāxa g·înānɛmē. Wä, laɛm gwāɫē ēaᵋxēnaᵋ-
yas Aōmōɫē. Wä, hěɛm k·!ēsᵋos g·äg·îʟɛla lāxa nūyîmbalisas Aōmōɫē.

Wä, lēda maᵋlōkwē ts!ēdaq q!aɫaxʟaᵋyaxa g·înānɛmē lāx Aōmōɫē
15 qaᵋs k·ɛnxwit!ēdēsa k·ɛnxwidɛmasa g·înānɛmēxa ʟēgadäs Tsaxisē. Wä,
g·îlᵋmisē gwāɫa maᵋlokwē ts!ēdàq k·ɛnxwîtasa k·ɛnxwidɛmē lāxa g·î-
nānɛmē laaᵋa gŭmsɛlg·îsē ts!ēdaq q!aɫaxʟaᵋyaxa g·înānɛmē lāxa ts!ē-
daqē qaᵋs k!wāk·äx·alîɫēs. Wä, laᵋmē wäxēda ts!ɛdāqaxa ᵋnāxwa bēbɛgwānɛm ʟɛᵋwa haᵋyāɫᵋa ʟōᵋma ᵋnāxwa g·îng·înānɛm qa wäg·is ᵋnāxwa
20 gŭmsᵋîda, âᵋmē ᵋnēk·ɛxs laē gŭmsᵋîdxa x·ōmsasa g·înānɛmē ʟɛᵋwis
gōgŭmaᵋyē.

Wä, g·îlᵋmisē gwāɫa ʟɛᵋwa ᵋnāxwa bēbɛgwānɛm gŭmsa laaᵋa qɛx·-
atodɛlg·îlsē ts!ēdaq q!aɫaxʟaᵋyaxa g·înānɛmē lāxa gŭmsɛlg·îsē
ts!ēdaqa. Wä, hěɛm qɛx·atōtsa wäwadē yɛmɛlkᵘ lāx x·ōmsas Tsaxisaxs
25 g·ālaē māᵋyoʟɛmsēs abɛmpē ʟ!āx·ʟ!alîdzɛmga qa g·îltɛmēs Tsaxisē.
Wä, laɛm qɛx·atōtsa lālaxwiwaᵋyē lāxa g·înānɛmē.

Wä, g·îlᵋmisē gwāɫa laaᵋ ʟāx·walîɫē ʟ!āqoʟas, yîx ōmpas Tsaxisē.
Wä, lä yāq!ɛg·aᵋɫa. Wä, lä ᵋnēk·a: Wä, g·ōɫg·ŭkŭlōt, laᵋmē gwāɫalē-
ɫa yîx ēaᵋxēnaᵋyasa sɛk·!âkwēx ts!ēdaqaxwa k·!ēk·!esᵋonukwēx yîsōs
30 gwēgwälag·îlîᵋlasaxg·în xunōkŭk· lāxg·a Tsaxisɛk·. Wä, laɛmk·ʟ!ā-
yuxᵘʟäʟ. Laɛms gwāɫ ʟēqalaʟɛ́ Tsaxisē lāx g·în xunōkŭk·. Laɛms

before she (1) finished. And when Aōmō̱ɫ had finished scorching off
the hair, she took something like/a dish and she poured cold water
into it as a wash-basin for the child./ Then she took tongs and
picked up red-hot stones which were not large/and she put them into
the wash-basin for the (5) child. She put four red-hot stones/into
the water in the wash-basin for the ten moons old child. As soon
as/she had finished Aōmō̱ɫ took the child in her arms and laid it on
its back. And four times/she dipped her right hand into the luke-
warm water and/four times she pressed her wet hands on the head of
the child, and,finally,(10) she washed its head. When she had finished she washed its body,/and when she had finished Aōmō̱ɫ took the
well rubbed shredded/cedar bark and wiped off the child with it.
Now is finished the work of/Aōmō̱ɫ, and this is her privilege beginning from the family history of Aōmō̱ɫ./

Then the two women took the child from Aōmō̱ɫ (15) and they put
the straps on the child whose name was Fort Rupert. And/when the
two women had put the straps around the legs and arms of the child/
the painter woman took the child away from the women/and put it on
her knee. Then the woman said to all the men/and the young men and
all the children to go ahead and (20) to paint themselves with ochre
She just said so and painted the head of the child and its/face./

After she had finished and when all the men had painted themselves,/the woman who puts the kerchief around the head took the
child from the painter/woman. She is the one who put the split
kelp around the head of Fort Rupert when (25) he was first born by
his mother, ʟ!ax·ʟ!alīdzɛmga, so that Fort Rupert might have a long
head./ Then she put the kerchief around the head of the child.

When she had finished, arose ʟ!āqoʟas, the father of Fort
Rupert./ He spoke and said: " Oh, tribes, now is finished/ the
work of these five women, of those who have the privilege of doing
what (30) they have been doing to my child, Fort Rupert. Now/his

ᴌē̱qalaᴌɛs Wāwaᴌk·î̄nē̄ lā̱q̱ɛk·. Wä, laɛmk· g·î̄nᴌaxᴌälax Wāwaᴌk·î̄nē̄
qa ᴕ̂ē̄nē̄ᶜmaᴌas mā̄ᶜyoᴌaxᴌäyowē̄ Tsaxisē̄, ᶜnē̄k·ē̄. Wä, laᶜmē̄ yāx̱ᶜwî̄tsa
q!ē̄nɛmē̄ laalax̱wî̄wē̄ lāxa ᶜnāx̱wa bē̄bɛgwānɛm ᴌɛᶜwa g·î̄ng·î̄nānɛmē̄. Wä,
laɛm hē̄ᴌogwilaxᴌäyowē̄ Wāwaᴌk·î̄nē̄. Wä, laɛm gwāᴌ lāxa maᶜᴌtsɛmē̄
5 ᴌē̱ᴌɛ̱ɡ̱ɛma.

3. The name of the young man.

Wä, g·î̄lᶜmisē̄ mō̄xsa ᶜnäläsa k·ɛnx̱widɛma laas lawuyâ. Wä, la-
ᶜmē̄ ᴌē̄ᶜlälē̄ ʟ!ā̱q̱oᴌasaxa ᶜnāx̱wa haᶜyāᴌᶜa qa läs ᶜwî̄ᶜla hō̄g̱wî̄ᴌ lāx
g·ō̄kwas. Wä, laɛm k·!eᴕ̂s lāsa bē̄bɛgwānɛmē̄ qaxs hē̄ᶜmaē̄ ᴌē̱gadɛs haᶜ-
10 yaᴌᶜaē̄lkwē̄. Wä, g·î̄lᶜmisē̄ g·āx ᶜwî̄ᶜlaᶜᴌa haᶜyāᴌᶜäxs laē̄ äxk·!ā̄lē̄
ʟ!ā̱q̱ōᴌas qa yāq!änt!ā̄lē̄sa ᶜnɛmō̄kwē̄ hē̄ᴌᶜa g·ayō̄ᴌ lāx ᶜnɛᶜmē̄motasa
Yaē̄x·agɛmaᶜyē̄ qaxs hē̄ᶜmaē̄ ᶜnɛᶜmē̄mō̄ts ʟ!ā̱q̱oᴌasē̄. Wä, lä ᴌāx̱ᶜwalî̄ᴌa
qaᶜs nē̄ᴌē̄xa ᶜnāx̱wa haᶜyāᴌᶜaq̱ēxs lɛᶜmaē̄ lawuyowē̄da k·ɛnx̱wî̄dɛmas Wā-
waᴌk·î̄naᶜyē̄. Wä, laᶜmē̄sɛk· ᶜnɛmasg·ada lāalax̱wiwē̄k· lāᴌ ᶜnāx̱wa ha-
15 ᶜyāᴌᶜas Gwē̄tɛl ᴌō̄s haᶜyāᴌᶜas ᶜwālas Kwāg·uᴌ ᴌō̄ᶜs haᶜyāᴌᶜas Q!ō̄mk·!-
ūt!ɛs, wä, sō̄ᶜmē̄ts nō̄s g·ō̄kūlō̄t haᶜyāᴌᶜäq̱ō̄s Q!ō̄moyūwē̄, ᶜnē̄k·ē̄xs laē̄
ʟ!ā̱q̱oᴌas äxᶜē̄dxa lāwats!ē̄ g·î̄ldasa qāᶜs g·āxē̄ hāng·aᶜlî̄ᴌas lāx ʟ!ā-
salî̄ᴌasa hē̄ᴌᶜaxa yāq!änt!ā̄la. Wä, lä hē̄ᶜmē̄ ʟ!ā̱q̱ōᴌasē̄ dāᴌts!â̄laxa
lāālax̱wî̄waᶜyē̄ lāxa g·î̄ldasē̄ qāᶜs ts!ō̄x·ts!okwē̄s lāxa hē̄ᴌᶜaxa yāq!änt-
20 t!ā̄lɛlg·î̄sē̄. Wä, lä ᶜnē̄k·ɛxs laē̄ dzoxwāᴌasa ᶜnɛmē̄ lālax̱wiwaᶜya.
Laɛm ᶜnɛmyō̄s Wāwaᴌk·î̄nē̄ lāᴌ K!walayu. Wä, laɛm yaxᶜwî̄tsa lālax̱wi-
waᶜyē̄ lāx K!wālayu lāxē̄s wāᴌdɛmē̄ qaxs ᶜnāx̱wē̄da haᶜyāᴌᶜa la nē̄ᴌᶜî̄dē̄s
ᶜnɛmaxᴌäyu lāxē̄s laē̄naᶜyē̄ yaqwasē̄ᶜs Wāwaᴌk·î̄nē̄. Wä, g·î̄lᶜmisē̄ ᶜwî̄ᶜ-
la la yaxᶜwî̄dayuwa laalax̱wiwaᶜyē̄ lāxa haᶜyāᴌᶜäxs laas ᶜnē̄k·ē̄da ya-
25 q!änt!ā̄lɛlg·î̄sē̄ hē̄ᴌᶜa: Laɛms gwāᴌ ᴌē̱q̱älas Wāwaᴌk·î̄nē̄ lāxg·a Wāwaᴌ-
k·î̄nē̄k· qaxs laᶜmē̄k· ᶜnɛmx·ᴌälaᴌax Mē̄gwat, ᶜnē̄k·ē̄. Wä, laᶜmē̄ ᴌē̱ga-
dē̄ Wāwaᴌk·î̄naᶜyas Mē̄gwat lāxē̄q.

pert, now (1) his name will be Wāwaɫk·ín. Now his child's name will
be Wāwaɫk·ín,/for his birth name was Fort Rupert," thus he said. Then
he gave away/many kerchiefs to all the men and the children. Now/his
nine months name is Wāwaɫk·ín. Now it is finished about two (5)
names./

3. The name of the young man.

After he had the leg and arm-straps on for four days they were
taken off. Then/ʟ!āqoḷas invited all the young men to go into/his
house. Now there were none of the men, for this has the name (10)
"young men gathered in the house." As soon as all the young men
were in/ʟ!āqoḷas asked one young man who belonged to the numaym/Ya-
ēx·agɛmēᴱ, for that is the numaym of ʟ!āqoḷas, to make a speech.
And he arose/and told all the young men that now the leg and arm
straps of/Wāwaɫk·ín had been taken off. "Now he will give a kerchief
to you, young men of the (15) Gwētɛla and to you, young men of the
ᴱwālas Kwāg·uɫ, and also to you, young men of the Q!ōmk!ūt!ɛs/and you
young men of my tribe, Q!ōmoyāᴱyē," thus he said. And/ʟ!āqoḷas
took the box containing the kerchiefs and he put it down in front
of the/young man who was speaking. And then ʟ!āqoḷas took the/ker-
chiefs out of the box and gave them to the young man who spoke for
him.(20) Then he said as he was holding up one of the kerchiefs:/
" This is one given by Wāwaɫk·ín to K!walayu," and he gave the ker-
chief/to K!walayu as he said so, for all the young men now used/their
first names as they were given (kerchiefs) by Wāwaɫk·ín. When all/
the kerchiefs had been given to the young man, then said/ (25) the
young man, the speaker,"Now you finish calling Wāwaɫk·ín this name
Wāwaɫk·ín,/for now he has as his name hereafter Seal,"said he. Now
Wāwaɫk·ín had the name/Seal after this.

4. Q!ɛmdadē gŭmᵋyasa.

Wä, lāxɛntē mōxᵋŭnxē ts!aᵋwŭnxas ʟēgadɛs Mēgwat, wä, la ōmpas
yĭx ʟ!āqoʟas k·flx̣waxa q!ēnɛmē q!ēq!asᵋɛnaᵋya ʟɛᵋwa ᵋnāx̣wa qaᵋs
gwēx·sdɛm gwēɫgwäla lāxa k·f1ᵋwĬᵋlasē. Wä, lä ᵋmɛgwaᵋlĬƚas läxēs
5 g·ōkwē. Wä, lä ʟēᵋlālax ᵋnāx̣wa haᵋyaƚᵋasēs ᵋnɛmēmotasa Yaēx·agɛma-
ᵋyē qa läs ᵋwĬᵋla hōg̈wĬʟ läx g·ōkwas. Wä, g·f1ᵋmisē la ᵋwĬᵋlaēʟa
haᵋyāƚᵋäxs laē ʟ!āqoʟas nēƚaxa hāᵋyāƚᵋäxs laᵋmē ᵋnēx· qa gŭmᵋyasē
Mēgwataxa haᵋyāƚᵋäsa Gwētɛla ʟɛᵋwa ᵋwälas Kwāg·uƚ ʟɛᵋwa Q!ōmk·!ū-
t!ɛsē. Wä, laᵋmēsōx q!ɛmdadɛ≀ts gŭmᵋyayalaʟa q!ɛmdɛma. Wä, laᵋ-
10 mēsōx gŭmᵋyadzɛxʟ̣ālaʟɛx Sāts!ɛm. Wä laᵋmōx gwāƚ ʟēgadɛs Mēgwat
läxēq, ᵋnēk·ē. Wä, laᵋmē q!ämdĬƚēda haᵋyāƚᵋäsa aƚtsɛmē gɛmᵋyayala-
yu q!ɛmdɛm. Wä, lēda waōkwē haᵋyāƚᵋa doxᵋwɛlsaxa g·f1t!a dɛnɛm läx
ʟ!āsanāᵋyasa g·ōkwē qaᵋs lē gɛxᵋwŭndalasa q!ēq!āsanaᵋyē ʟɛᵋwa ᵋnāx̣-
wa āƚᵋogŭᵋqāƚa gwēɫgwäla lāq. Wä, la hē gwäƚēda ts!ōxwäxa gwēɫgwä-
15 laxs laē lɛmx̣wasōᵋs ts!ōxwäq. Wä, g·f1ᵋmisē gwäƚa laasa maᵋlōkwē
haᵋyāƚᵋa qāsaxa ᵋnēk·ē: Laᵋmɛnuᵋxᵘ qāsa qaēda gŭmᵋyasāʟē Sāts!ɛm
lā̂ʟ haᵋyāƚᵋā. Hālāg·flēʟɛsä ᵋnēk·ēda maᵋlōkwē haᵋyāƚᵋa läx aᵋwĬʟɛ-
läs t!ēt!ɛx·flāsa ᵋnāx̣wa g·ig·ōkwa. Wä, g·f1ᵋmisē g·āx aēdaaqēda
maᵋlōkᵘ qāsɛlg·fs haᵋyāƚᵋaxs laē ᵋwĬᵋla hōg̈ŭwɛlsa q!ämdēƚax·dē haᵋ-
20 yāƚᵋa qaᵋs lē k·!ūsɛls läx mäg·fxsēg·aᵋyasa tsaqɛmaᵋyasa g·ōkwē.
Wä, g·āxēda haᵋyāƚᵋäsa Gwētɛla ʟɛᵋwa ᵋwalas Kwāg·uƚ ʟɛᵋwa Q!ōmk·!ū-
t!ɛsē k!ūsɛls läxa ʟ!āsaᵋyas. Wä, g·f1ᵋmisē g·āx ᵋ~Ĭᵋlg·aɛlsa
laas ʟ̣āxŭlsēda ᵋnɛᵋmōkwē hēƚᵋaxa yāq!änt!āla qa Mēgwataxs laē ᵋnɛma.
Wä, lä yāq!ɛg·aᵋƚa. Wä, lä ᵋnēk·a: Wä, gēlag·a haᵋyāƚᵋōt, qaᵋs g·ā-
25 xaōs gŭmᵋyasasōᵋsg·ɛnuᵋxᵘ nāxsâlagēk· läxg·a Mēgwatɛk·xg·ada lāk·
ʟ!āyuxʟä. Laɛmk· gŭmᵋyadzaxʟ̣ālax Sāts!ɛm. Wä, laᵋmēts ʟēqalaʟɛs
Sātsɛm lāqɛk·, ᵋnēk·ēxs laē gwēgɛmx·ᵋĬd läx haᵋyāƚᵋäsēs ᵋnɛᵋmēmotē.
Wä, lä ᵋnēk·a: Wēg·a dɛnxᵋĬtsa gŭmᵋyaᵋyālä q!ɛmdɛmsg·fns nâxsâlagēk·,
ᵋnēk·ē. Wä, lä ᵋnāx̣wa q!wāg·flsa haᵋyāƚᵋäs ᵋnɛᵋmēmotas qaᵋs dɛnxᵋ-
30 Ĭdēsa āƚtsɛmē gŭmᵋyaᵋyaᵋlayu q!ɛmdɛmaxa ᵋnēk·a:

4. Painting with song.

Now for four years his name might be Seal. Then his father/
L!āqoᶫas bought many shirts and all kinds of/clothing in the store
and he piled it up in his (5) house. Then he called all the young
men of his numaym Yaēx·agɛmē⁶/to come into his house. When all the
young men were inside L!āqoᶫas told the young men that he wished/Seal
should have the paint-giving-away to the young men of the Gwētɛla
and the ⁶wālas Kwāg·uⱡ and the Q!ōmk·!ūt!ɛs,/and that he should have
the painting with song, and then (10) he would have the paint-name
Spring Salmon after this. "Then he will no longer have the name
Seal/after that," thus he said. Now the young men sang in the house
the new-paint-giving-away/-song.Then the other young men stretched
out a long rope/outside of the house and they hung the shirts and/
various other kinds of clothing on it in the same way as those who
wash clothing(15)do to dry it after washing.As soon as this was done
two/young men called saying,"Now we call for the paint-giving-away
of Spring Salmon/to you, young men. Come quickly," said the two
young men inside/the doors of all the houses. When the two young
men who had invited came back,/all those young men who had been singing inside went out (20) and sat down close to the front of the
house./ Then the young men of the Gwētɛla and ⁶wālas Kwāg·uⱡ and
Q!ōmk·!ūt!ɛs/sat down seawards from them. And when all had come
from inside/one young man arose, who had spoken for Seal when he
gave away for the first time./ He spoke and said,"Fellow young men,
you have come to the (25) giving-away of paint of our respected Seal
here, whose/name will now be changed. Now his paint-giving-away-
name will be Spring Salmon. Now you will call him/Spring Salmon,"
thus he said. Then he turned his face to the young men of his numaym/
and he said," Now sing the song of the paint-giving-away of our respected one,"/thus he said. Then all the young men of his numaym
stood up and sang(30)the new song of the paint-giving-away, which said

Wâ hâ ha yē ya hā hâ hâ ha.

Lādzēᵉyaɛmk· yāwix·ꞟlahēdzēg·a ᶜwālahädzägēlēdzēk· Sāts!ɛm-
dzēya.

Hâ, wâ hâ ha yē ya hā hâ hâ ha.

5   Ladzēᵉyaɛmk·ᶜwālahädzēyaᴸagŭm yāsᶜidēaᴸaha lahauᴸa g·ꞟn-
g·ꞟnahanɛms lēᴇlqwǎlahaᴸaëxg·ahada ᶜwālahädzägēlēdzēk·
Sāts!ɛmdzēya.

Hâ, wâ hâ ha yē ya hā hâ hâ ha.

Wähäg·adzē lahag·a mōhomasᶜidēahaᴸax wīhisawaᴸax Ts!ɛsqwa-
10   nahaowaxēs yahalasᴇᶜwahaqōs Sāts!ɛmdzēya.

Hâ, wâ hâ ha yē ya hā hâ hâ ha

Wuꞟ.

Wä, g·ꞟlᶜmisē q!ŭlbēda gŭmᶜyaᶜyāᶜlayu q!ɛmdɛma laēda äxaᶜyē
qaᶜs yāq!änt!ālē hëꞟᶜa dāx·ᶜīdxa ᶜnɛmē q!asɛnaᶜya qaᶜs ᴸēxᶜēdēs gŭm-
15   ᶜyadzaxᴸäᶜyâsa xŭnōkwasa kwēkwēxa ᴸēgadäs Kwäts!ē. Wä, lä ᶜnēk·äxs
laē yāxᶜwītsa q!asɛnaᶜyē lāq: Laɛms yāgwadɛsēqä Kwäts!aai,ᶜnɛm q!ā-
sɛnaᶜya, ᶜnēk·ē qaxs ᶜnāxwaᶜmaē la ᴸēᴸɛgadēda haᶜyāꞟᶜäsēs gwēgŭmᶜya-
dzaxᴸäyu ᴸēᴸɛgɛma. Wä, laɛm ōguxᶜīdē ᴸēᴸɛgɛmasa haᶜyāꞟᶜa lāxēs ᶜnē-
nɛmxᴸäyu ᴸēᴸɛgɛma. Wä, g·ꞟlᶜmisē ᶜwīlxtosa q!ēq!ɛsɛnaᶜyaxs laē ᶜwī-
20   ᶜla hōqŭwɛls lāxa g·ōkwē. Wä, laɛm k·!eâs lāsa la gēgɛg·ad bēbɛgwānɛm k!wägēlīꞟxa haᶜyāꞟᶜa.Wä, la mōsgɛmē ōgŭqiᶜläla ᴸēᴸɛgɛms Sāts!ɛmē.

5. ᴸɛpa.

Wä, lä q!äp!ēx·ᶜīdē ᴸ!äqoᴸasaxa q!ēnɛmē p!ɛlp!ɛlxɛᶜma laɛm k·ꞟl-
25   xwaq lāxēs g·ōkŭlōtē. Wä, laɛm lāxōdē ᴸ!äqoᴸasaxa lāk·!ɛndē alōmas
p!ɛlxɛlasgɛm qa k·ꞟlxwasɛᶜwēsēsa q!ɛᴸ!a p!ɛlp!ɛlxɛᶜma lāxa ᶜnāꞟᶜnɛ-
mxsa alōmas p!ɛlxɛlasgɛm.Wä,g·ꞟlᶜmisē ᶜwīᶜla k·ꞟlᶜwānɛma alōmasē
p!ɛlxɛlasgɛmsēs g·ōkŭlōtē,wä,la ᴸēᶜlālē ᴸ!äqoᴸasaxēs ᶜnɛᶜmēmotē qa
läs ᶜwīᶜla hōgwīᴸ lāx g·ōkwas. Wä, g·ꞟlᶜmisē g·äx ᶜwīᶜlaēᴸaxa âla-
30   k·!ꞟn bēbɛgwānɛma, wä, laɛm k·!eâs lāsa haᶜyāꞟᶜa lāq qaxs lɛᶜmaē

Wâ hâ ha yē ya hā hâ hâ ha.

    The great one will not move, the greatest one, the great

        Spring Salmon.

Hâ, wâ hâ ha yē ya hā hâ hâ ha.

    The greatest one will give away now to the children of the

        tribes, this greatest one, the great Spring Salmon.

Hâ, wâ hâ ha yē ya hā hâ hâ ha.

    Go on great one, hurt the young children, the humble spar-

        rows who are being teased by you, great Spring Salmon.

Hâ, wâ hâ ha yē ya hā hâ hâ ha.

    Wuî.

As soon as the song of the paint-giving-away was finished/
the young man whose work it was to speak took one shirt and named
the (15) paint-giving-away name of the Son of the Eagle, whose name
was Kwäts!ē. Then he said/as he gave away the shirt to him, "Now
this is given to you, Kwäts!ē, one shirt,"/said he, as he named the
.names of the young men with their paint-giving-away/names. Then the
young men also changed their names from the first giving-away/names.
As soon as each had received a shirt they all went (20) out of the
house. It was not given to the married men/who sat among the young
men. Now this is the fourth different name of/Spring Salmon.

5. Spreading Out.

Now, ᴌ!āqoʟas assembled many old blankets which he bought (25)
from his tribe. Now ᴌ!āqoʟas sold one hundred new/blankets; there
were six old blankets to be bought for one pair of/new blankets.
When the new blankets had been bought/by the tribe, ᴌ!āqoʟas called
his numaym to/come into his house. So all the (30) real men came in.
None of the young men went with them for now (1) Spring Salmon was to

Sāts!ɛm ᒪе̄gadɛⱢtsa ᒪе̄ĝɛmasa bɛgwānɛmē̄ lāxē̄s laē̄nē̄ᒪē̄ ᒪɛpasa p!ɛl-
p!ɛlxɛᶜmē̄ lāxē̄s g·ōkŭlōtē̄. Wä, g·flᶜmisē̄ g·āx ᶜwīᶜla k!ŭsᶜalīⱢa,
yîx ᶜnɛᶜmē̄motas ᒪ!āqoᒪas laē̄ nēⱢaxē̄s ᶜnɛᶜmē̄mōtaxs lɛᶜmaē̄ xŭnōkwas,
yîx Sāts!ɛmē̄ ᒪɛpaⱢⱢa Gwētɛla ᒪɛᶜwa ᶜwālas Kwāg·uⱢ ᒪɛᶜwa Q!ōmk·!ŭt-
5 t!ɛs. Wä, hē̄ᶜmisē̄xs lɛᶜmaē̄ bɛgwŭxᒪ̄ālaᒪē̄ Sāts!ɛmax G·Ixsē̄ᶜstalīs-
ɛmaᶜyē̄.Wä,wē̄g·a yäqŭmx·ᶜItsa p!ɛlp!ɛlxɛᶜmax lāxɛns g·ōⱢg·okŭlōtax,
ᶜnē̄k·ē̄. Wä, hē̄x·ᶜidaᶜmisa q!āq!asto bɛgwānɛm la k!wāg·aᶜlIⱢ lāxa
nɛqē̄waᶜlIⱢasa g·ōkwē̄. Wä, lē̄da ōgŭᶜlaᶜmē̄ bɛgwānɛm dāx·ᶜIdxa ᶜnɛ-
mē̄ p!ɛlxɛᶜma qaᶜs k·!axᶜāᶜlIⱢē̄s. Wä, lē̄da q!āq!asto bɛgwānɛm ᒪɛ̄xᶜ-
10 ē̄dɛx ᒪē̄ᒪɛĝɛmasa yaē̄gwadᒪas. Wä, g·flᶜmisē̄ ᶜwīᶜla yäqumakwa bē̄bɛ-
gwānɛmasa yŭduxᵘsɛᶜmakwē̄ Kwakwāg·uⱢa laasa maᶜlōkwē̄ bē̄bɛgwānɛm ᶜyä-
lagɛm qaᶜs lē̄ qāsa. Wä, lē̄ hōqŭwɛls lāxa g·ōkwas ᒪ!āqoᒪas qaᶜs lē̄
ᒪaxstōlsax t!ɛx·flās g·ōkwasa Gwētɛla. Wä, lä ᶜnē̄k·a ᶜnɛmōkwē̄
bɛgwānɛma: G·āxᶜmɛnuᶜxᶜ qāsai qa G·Ixsē̄ᶜstalīsɛmaᶜyē̄xwa bɛxᵘsē̄ᶜ-
15 stalIⱢaxōx Sāts!ɛmē̄x, ᶜnē̄k·ē̄. Wä, la ᶜnē̄k·a ᶜnɛmōkwas: Halag·flē̄-
ᒪɛsai, ᶜnē̄k·ē̄. Wä, la hē̄x·sä gwē̄k·!ālaxs laē̄ läᒪ!ɛsala lāxa ᶜnāxwa g·ig·ōkwa. Wä, laɛm ᶜnāxwa g·āxa bē̄bɛgwānɛm ᒪɛᶜwa bābabagwāxa
ts!ē̄daqa ᒪɛᶜwa lā ᒪɛpasa haᶜyāⱢᶜa. Wä, la k·!eās g·āxsa k·!ē̄sē̄
ᒪɛp!ē̄noxᵘsa haᶜyāⱢᶜa. Wä, g·flᶜmisē̄ g·āx ᶜwIᶜlaē̄ᒪ lāxa g·ōkwaxs
20 laē̄ ᒪ!āqoᒪas nēⱢaxa ᶜnāxwa bē̄bɛgwānɛmxs lɛᶜmaē̄s xŭnōkwē̄ Sāts!ɛm
ᒪ!āyuxᒪäxē̄s ᒪē̄ĝɛmē̄, yîxs lɛᶜmaē̄ bɛgŭxᒪälax G·Ixsē̄ᶜstalīsɛmaᶜyē̄.
Wä, lɛn nɛgɛⱢtawē̄x t!ɛx·ilaᶜyasɛn wīwōmpᶜwŭⱢa qɛn gwē̄ᶜnākŭlas qaɛn
ᒪawɛlgɛmaᶜyē̄x, ᶜnē̄k·ē̄. Wä, laᶜmē̄ yäxᶜwItsa ᶜnāⱢᶜnɛmē̄ p!ɛlxɛᶜma lāxa ᶜnāⱢᶜmɛmōkwē̄ bɛgwānɛma. Wä, g·flᶜmisē̄ ᶜwIᶜla yäxᶜwidayuwa p!ɛl-
25 p!ɛlxɛᶜma lāas ᒪaxŭlIⱢē̄ g·Igāmaᶜyasa G·ēxsɛmasa Gwētɛlaxa ᒪē̄gadäs
YäqawId. Wä, lä yāq!ɛg·aᶜⱢa. Wä, lē̄ ᶜnē̄k·a: ᶜwa, g·Igāmē̄ ᒪ!āqoᒪas,
lɛᶜmē̄ gwāⱢa., laᶜmē̄ gwāⱢē̄ wāⱢdɛmaōs qaōs ᒪawɛlgɛmaᶜyaq!ōsxōⱪ G·Ix-
sē̄ᶜstalīsɛmaᶜyē̄x. Laɛms nɛgɛⱢtewē̄x gwē̄g·ilasasɛns wīwōmpᶜwŭⱢa.
Wä, laᶜmē̄sɛn äxᶜē̄dɛⱢg·In k·!ē̄sᶜōg·In. Wä, laᶜmɛn ᒪē̄ᶜlalōᒪ Q!ōmo-
30 yāwē̄ ᒪōᶜs ᶜwālas Kwāg·uⱢ ᒪōᶜs Q!ōmk·!ŭt!ɛs qaᶜs lālag·iᒪōs k!wā-
k!wanōᒪamālIⱢxwa alōmasax g·Igāmaᶜyaxōx G·Ixsē̄ᶜstalīsɛmaᶜyax. La-

have the name of a man as he will now spread out the old blankets/
among his tribe. As soon as they came they all sat down,/the numaym of ᴸ!āqoʟas. Then he told his numaym that his son,/Spring
Salmon, would spread out for the Gwētɛla and the ᵋwālas Kwag·uⱫ
and the Q!ōmk·!ūt!ɛs, (5) and that Spring Salmon would now have
the man's name G·Ixsē̆ᵋstalIsɛmē̆ᵋ. "Now go on and give away the
old blankets to our tribes,"/he said. Immediately the name keeper
sat down in the/middle of the rear of the house, and the various
men took each one/old blanket and put it down. Then the name keeper called (10) out the name of the one to whom it was to be given.
Then they received blankets, all the men/of the three tribes of the
Kwag·uⱫ. Then two men were sent/to go back. These went out of the
house of ᴸ!āqoʟas and/stopped at the doors of the houses of the
Gwētɛla and then one man said,/"We come to invite on behalf of G·Ix-
sē̆ᵋstalIsɛmē̆ᵋ,/for he will now turn into a man (15) this Spring
Salmon,"said he. Then another one said, "Go quickly,"/said he, and
they kept on saying so as they went into each/house. Then all came,
the men and the women who have men's names,/and those of the young
men who had spread out, but none came of the/young men who had not
spread out. When they had all come into the house (20) ᴸ!āqoʟas
told all the men that the name of his child, Spring Salmon/would.
be changed, for now his man's name would be G·Ixsē̆ᵋstalIsɛmē̆ᵋ./
"I follow the road made by our forefathers, for I wish it thus on
behalf of my/prince," said he. Then he gave away one old blanket
to/each man. When all the old blankets had been given away (25)
then arose the chief of the G·ēxsɛm of the Gwētɛla, whose name was/
YāqawId and he spoke and said, "Chief ᴸ!āqoʟas,/now it is finished,
what you said on behalf of your prince, this G·Ixsē̆ᵋstalIsɛmē̆ᵋ./
Now he has followed the ways of our forefathers./ Now I wish to
make use of my privilege, Now I invite you Q!ōmoyâᵋyē (30) and
you, ᵋwālas Kwāg·uⱫ and you Q!ōmk·!ūt!ɛs to go/and sit down on

ɛms läⁱʟôʟ g·Ꮖgämē, ᶜnēk·ē.

Wä, g·flᶜmisē q!ûlba wäʟdɛmas Yäqawɪd laē ᶜwɪᶜla hôqûwɛlsa bēbɛgwänɛm läxa g·ōkwas ʟ!äqoʟas. Wä, laᶜmē ʟ!äqoʟas ts!ɛlgwaʟxēs
ᶜnɛᶜmēmotē ʟɛᶜwa q!äq!astowē bɛgwänɛm qa k·!ēsēs la ōgwaqa hôqû-
5 wɛls läx g·ōkwas. Wä, laᶜmē ʟ!äqoʟas äxᶜēdxa maᶜʟp!ɛnyag·axsa p!ɛl-
xɛlasgɛm qaᶜs g·äxē mɛgûlɪʟas läxa ōgwiwaᶜlɪʟasēs g·ōkwē. Wä, lä
yäq!ɛg·aᶜʟa. Wä, lä ᶜnēk·a: Wēg·a dōqwaʟaxg·ɪn gwēᶜnäkûlasɛk·,ᶜnɛ-
ᶜmēmot.Laɛmk· qädzuʟas G·ɪxsēᶜstalɪsɛmaᶜyē g·ada maᶜʟp!ɛnyag·axsɛk·
p!ɛlxɛlasgɛma qag·ō läʟ k!wēʟlō. Wä, hēᶜmēsɛns dɛnxᶜidayuʟa q!ɛm-
10 dɛmasa g·älä ʟ!äqoʟasxs g·älaôʟa bɛkûmg·alisɛns qwēsbalisa qɛns
gägasōdamēsɛns gägɛmpēx q!ɛmdɛma qaxō läʟ laēʟōx G·ɪxsēᶜstalɪsɛmaᶜ-
yēx, ᶜnēk·ē. Wä, g·flᶜmisē ᶜnäxwa gwäʟē wäʟdɛmas, laēda q!äq!asto
bɛgwänɛm yäqumx·ᶜɪtsa maᶜʟp!ɛnyag·axsa p!ɛlxɛlasgɛm läxa yûduxᵘsɛʟ
makwē Kwäkwag·uʟa. Wä, laᶜmē ʟäʟaxbaᶜya maᶜlōkwē bēbɛgwänɛmxa
15 ᶜnäʟᶜnɛmxsa p!ɛlxɛlasgɛma. Wä, g·flᶜmisē gwäʟa laē ᶜwɪᶜla hôqûwɛls läxa g·ōkwē.

Wä g·flᶜmisē ᶜnäx·ᶜɪdxa ʟɛnsē laas ʟēᶜlälē Yäqawɪdäxa ᶜnäxwa
bēbɛgwänɛmsa Q!ōmoyäᶜyē ʟɛᶜwa ᶜwälas Kwäg·uʟ ʟɛᶜwa Q!ōmk·!ût!ɛsē.
Wä, g·flᶜmisē g·äx ᶜwɪᶜlaēʟa laas ʟaxûwalɪʟē Yäqawɪdē qaᶜs yäq!ɛ-
20 g·aᶜʟē. Wä, lä ᶜnēk·a: Gēlag·a, Q!ōmoyawē, gēlag·a ᶜwälas Kwäg·uʟ
gēlag·a Q!ōmk·!ût!ɛs. Wēg·a hēʟᶜaᶜlɪʟ läxs k!wēk!waᶜyaqōs. Laᶜmō
hēʟᶜiläᶜlakwa, ᶜnēk·ēxs laē gwēgɛmx·ᶜɪd läxa t!ɛx·fläsēs g·ōkwē
qaxs hēᶜmaē ᶜwɪᶜla k!ûdziʟa Gwētɛla. Wä, lä ᶜnēk·a: Qäʟaxs ᶜnē-
x·ᶜmaɛns gaagɛmpᶜwûʟa, nōs g·ig·ɛgämē. Wä, k·!ēsᶜmɛns ᶜwɪᶜlaēʟa.
25 Wä, gēlag·a g·Ꮖgämē Awad ʟōs Ôdzēᶜstalis ʟōᶜs ʟ!äqwalaʟ ʟōᶜs Hämd-
dzid qaᶜs läx·daᶜxwaōs ētsēᶜstaxa alōmasa g·Ꮖgämaᶜyē G·ɪxsēᶜstalɪ-
sɛmaᶜya qa g·äxēgē k!wastōlɪʟaxg·as k!wäk·, ᶜnēk·ē. Wä, hēx·ᶜida-
ᶜmisa mōkwē g·Ꮖg·ɛgämē la hôqûwɛls läxa g·ōkwē. Wä,lē ʟ!äqoʟas ʟa-
xuwalɪʟ läxēs k!waēᶜlasa hēʟk·!ōtewaᶜlɪʟasa g·ōkwē qaᶜs äxk·!älēxa
30 haᶜyäʟᶜäsa Q!ōmoyäᶜyē qa läs läsgɛmēqɛxs laē läwɛlsa. Wä, g·flᶜ-
misē läg·aa läxēs g·ōkwē laē ʟ!äqoʟas k!wäg·aᶜlɪʟa. Wä, lēda ᶜnɛ-

each side of this new chief, G·IxsēᵋstalĪsɛmēᵋ. (1) Now go,chief," said he./

As soon as Yäqawīd had finished his speech all the men went out/ of the house of ʟ!āqoʟas. Then ʟ!āqoʟas requested/his numaym to stay and he also asked the name-keepers not to go out (5) of the house. Then ʟ!āqoʟas took the two hundred blankets/and put them down in the rear of his house. Then he/spoke and said, "Go on and see how I am going,/numaym, for this is the way of walking of G·Ix-sēᵋstalĪsɛmēʼ, these two hundred/blankets, if he should go to a feast. And then we will sing (10) the song of the first ʟ!āqoʟas, when first in the remote past our/grandfather became a man, that we may sing our grandfather s song when G·IxsēᵋstalĪsɛmēᵋ should go into the house,"/thus said he. When the speeches were finished the name keep-ers/ gave the names for the two hundred blankets among the three/Kwag·uⱡ tribes. Then two men stood (15) each at one end of one pair of blankets. As soon as this was done they all went/out of the house./

As soon as it was day next morning Yäqawīd called all/the men of the Q!ōmoyâᵋyē and the ᵋwālas Kwāg·uⱡ and the Q!ōmk·!ūt!ɛs,/and as soon as they all came in Yäqawīd arose and spoke.(20) He said, " Welcome, Q!ōmoyâᵋyē. Welcome ᵋwālas Kwāg·uⱡ./ Welcome Q!ōmk·!ūt!ɛs. Now sit well down in your seats which are/well arranged around here," thus said he, and turned his face to the door of his house/ for there all the Gwētɛla were sitting. Then he said," Yes, this was said/by our grandfathers, my chiefs. We are not yet all come in. (25) Now come,chief Awadē, and Ōdzēᵋstalis,and ʟ!āqwalaⱡ,and Hămdzid./ Go all of you and call again the new chief,G·IxsēᵋstalĪsɛmēᵋ,/to sit down in his seat here," said he. And immediately/the four chiefs went out of the house. And then ʟ!āqoʟas got up/from where he was sitting on the right hand side of the rear of the house and he asked (30) the young men of the Q!ōmoyâᵋyē to follow him as he went out and when/he arrived in his house ʟ!āqoʟas sat down. And then one (1)

ᵋmōkwē lāxa g·ᴵgāmaᵋyē yᴵx Λwadē yāq!ᴇg·aᵋɫa. Wä, lä ᵋnēk·a: G·āx-
xᵋmᴇnuᵋxᵘ ētsēᵋstōʟ g·ᴵgämē G·ᴵxsēᵋstalᴵsᴇmē qaᵋs laōs k!wastōᵋlᴵ-
ɫaxs k!waᵋyōs, ᵋnēk·ē. Wä, g·ᴵlᵋmisē q!ülbē wäɫdᴇmas laē ʟ!āqoʟas
äxēdxa māᵋɫᴇxsa p!ᴇlxᴇlasgᴇm qaᵋs ts!awēs lāx Λwadē. Wä, lāxaē
5 ts!âsa māᵋɫᴇxsa p!ᴇlxᴇlasgᴇm lāx Ōdzēᵋstālis, hēᵋmisa māᵋɫᴇxsa lāx
ʟ!āqwaɫaɫē, hēᵋmisa māᵋɫᴇxsa lāx Hämdzidē. Wä, hēᴇm ʟēgadēda maᵋ-
ɫgünäɫᴇxsa p!ᴇlxᴇlasgᴇmas ētsēᵋstānᴇmxa g·ālaqa k!wēɫa. Wä, g·ᴵ-
lᵋmisē gwäɫē ʟ!āqoʟas ts!awanaqasa p!ᴇlxᴇlasgᴇmē lāxa mōkwē ētsē-
ᵋstᴇlg·ᴵs g·ᴵg·ᴇgāmaᵋya laē hōqüwᴇls lāxa g·ōkwē qäqälax G·ᴵxsē -
10 ᵋstalᴵsᴇmaᵋyē. Wä, la ᴇlxʟaᵋyēda haᵋyāɫᵋa ᵋnāxwa k·!ēk·!ᴇxsaya-
p!ālaxa p!ēp!ᴇlxᴇlasgᴇmē ʟōᵋmē ʟ!āqoʟas. Wä, g·ᴵlᵋmisē lāg·aēda
mōkwē g·ᴵg·ᴇgämēᵋ lāx ʟ!āsanāᵋyas g·ōkwas Yāqawᴵdē laas Λwadē laēʟ
lāxa g·ōkwē. Wä, lä ʟaxᵋwaliɫ lāx aᵋwᴵʟᴇläsa t!ᴇx·fla. Wä, lä
ᵋnēk·a : G·āxᵋᴇmg·ada g·ᴵgāmēk· yᴵxg·a G·ᴵxsēᵋstalᴵsᴇmēk·, ᵋnēk·-
15 exs laē taōts G·ᴵxsēᵋstalᴵsᴇmē lāxa nᴇqoʟewaᵋlᴵɫasa g·ōkwē. Wä,
g·ᴵlᵋmisē gwayōɫᴇla lāxēs k!waᵋyē laas Yāqawᴵdē ᵋnēk·a: Qāsak·as
g·ᴵgāmē lāxōs k·!ēsᵋōᵋwᴵlasaqōs. Wä, g·ᴵlᵋmisē k!wag·alᴵɫa g·āxa-
ᴇs g·āxēʟē ʟ!āqoʟas ʟᴇᵋwa haᵋyāɫᵋa qaᵋs lē k·!ᴇxᵋaᵋlᴵɫasa p!ᴇlxᴇ-
lasgᴇm lāxa ōgwaᵋlᴵɫasa g·ōkwē. Wä, laᵋmē ʟ!āqoʟasē äxk·!ālaxa Q!ō-
20 moyāᵋyē qa gagāsōdēs dᴇnxᵋēda. Wä, hēx·ᵋidaᵋmisa nāgadē dāqālasa
gwᴇᵋyâs ʟ!āqoʟas qa dᴇnxᵋidayus yᴵxg·a:

G·ᴵgāmahayᴵn, g·ᴵgāmahag·ᴵn, g·ᴵgāmahag·ᴵnʟōs nᴇlahamistala
hâ yä hwâ yä hwâ yä hwâ yä hēyā hā.

Hēɫoanᴇn lahax gatasᴇᵋwahasa gag·adēnahamᴇᵋnēxwēhēxwa nᴇlaha-
25   mistala
hâ yä hwâ yä hwâ yä hwâ yä hēyā hā.

Hēɫoanᴇn lahax satahasᴇᵋwahasa sādᴇk!wahamᴇᵋnēxwēhēxwa nᴇlahamistala
hâ yä hwâ yä hwâ yä hwâ yä hēyā hā.

30   Hēɫoanᴇn lahax ʟ!ēsahasᴇᵋwahasa ʟ!ēsʟᴇnahamᴇᵋnēxwēdēxwa nᴇlahamistala
hâ yä hwâ yä hwâ yä hwâ yä hēya hā.

of the chiefs, Âwadē, spɔke and said,/ " We come now to call you
again, chief G·Ixsē^εstalIsɛmē, to go and sit/in your seat," he said.
And when he had finished his speech, then ʟ!āqoʟas/took two pairs of
blankets and he gave them to Âwadē. Then he also (5) gave two pairs
of blankets to Ōdzē^εstalis, and also two pairs to/ʟ!āqwalaɫ, and also two pairs to Hǎmdzid. And the name of the two pairs/of blankets
is "calling the first one to receive' again to the feast." And
when/ʟ!āqoʟas had finished giving the blankets to the four/chiefs
who went to call, then G·Ixsē^εstalIsɛmē went out of the house with
them. (10) Then the young men went after them, all carrying on their
shoulders/blankets, and also ʟ!āqoʟas (went with them). And when the/
four chiefs arrived outside the house of YǎqawId, then Âwadē went in-
to/ the house and stood inside the door. And then/he said: " He has
come, this G·Ixsē^εstalIsɛmē," said he. (15) And they led G·Ixsē^εstal-
Isɛmē to the middle of the rear of the house. And/as he was going
towards his seat YǎqawId said, " Walk on,/good chief, to the place to
which you are entitled in your house." And as he sat down/ʟ!āqoʟas
and the young men came and put down the blankets/in the rear of the
house. And then ʟ!āqoʟas told the Q!ōmoyâ^εyē (20) to sing the grandfathers' song, and immediately the song leaders began to sing/what
ʟ!āqoʟas had told them to sing, thus:

> I am a chief, I am a chief, I am your chief, who is flying about.
>> Hâ yä hwâ yä hwâ yä hwâ yä hēyä hā.
> I am too great to be bitten by those little flies that are fly-
> ing about.
>> Hâ yä hwâ yä hwâ yä hwâ yä hēyä hā.
> I am too great to be desired as food by those little horseflies
> that are flying about.
>> Hâ yä hwâ yä hwâ yä hwâ yä hēyä hā.
> I am too great to be bitten by those little mosquitoes that are
> flying about.
>> Hâ yä hwâ yä hwâ yä hwâ yä hēyä hā.

9

Wä, g·îlᵋmi̥ṣē q!ǔlbēda q!ᴇmdᴇm laas yāq!ᴇg·aᵋᴸē ʟ!āqoʟas. Wä,

lä ᵋnēk·a: Lᴇᵋmas wǔʟᴇlaa yōʟ g·Îg·ᴇgämē. Hēᵋmᴇn gwasx·äla q!ᴇmdᴇm

g·äg·îʟᴇla lāxᴇn g·îᶜlēnaᵋyē bᴇkwēlēs bᴇkwēlēnokwaᴇns ᵋnēk·ēxs laē

gwēgᴇmx·ᵋÎd lāxa k!wādzēlasasa g·Îg·ᴇgämaᵋyasa Q!ōmoyâᵋyē. Wä, lä

5 ʟēᵋlälax ᴧwadēxa g·Îgämaᵋyasa Kǔkwäk!ǔm, yÎxa ᵋnᴇᵋmēmotasa Q!ōmoyâ-

ᵋyē. Wä, lä Âwadē ʟāwanodzaᵋlÎ̱ᴸaq qaᵋs dāx·ᵋÎdēxa ᵋnᴇmxsa p!ᴇlxᴇ-

lasgᴇm. Wä, lä yāq!ᴇg·aᵋᴸa. Wä, lä ᵋnēk·a: ᴧlᴈsēs wā̱ᴸdᴇmâs g·Îgämēᵋ

ʟ!āqoʟas qaēda nǔyämbalis q!ᴇmdᴇma qa ᵋmāsēsᴇns wā̱ᴸdᴇma, nōs g·ōkǔ-

lōt, ᵋnēk·ē. Wä, lä dzōx̱ǔstōdxa ᵋnᴇmxsa p!ᴇlxᴇlasgᴇma. Wä, lä hä-

10 sᴇla ᵋnēk·a: Laᴇm qādzōsᴇn alōmasē g·Îgämaᵋyē G·ixsēᵋstalÎsᴇmaᵋyē

qaᵋs Gwētᴇl maᵋᴸp!ᴇnyag·ak· p!ᴇlxᴇlasgᴇma. Wä, lä ēt!ēd dzox̱ustōd-

xaaxa ᵋnᴇmxsa p!ᴇlxᴇlasgᴇma. Wä, lāxaē ᵋnēk·a: Laᴇm qādzosᴇn alō-

masē g·Îgämaᵋyē G·Îxsēᵋstalîsᴇmaᵋyē qaᵋs ᵋwālas Kwāg·uᴸ lāk·!ᴇndē

p!ᴇlxᴇlasgᴇma. Wä, lāxaē ēt!ēd dzux̱ustōdxa ᵋnᴇmxsa p!ᴇlxᴇlasgᴇma.

15 Wä, lāxaē ᵋnēk·a: Laᴇm qādzosᴇn alōmasē g·Îgämaᵋyē G·Îxsēᵋstalîsᴇ-

maᵋyē qaᵋs Q!ōmk·!ǔt!ᴇs lāk·!ᴇndē p!ᴇlxᴇlasgᴇma. Wä, laᵋmēsᴇn yāxᵋ-

wÎdʟasᴇk· lāx·daᵋxōʟ, ᵋnēk·ēxs laē hōsᵋaᵋlÎᴸaxa lāk·!ᴇndᴇxsa p!ᴇlxᴇ-

lasgᴇm qaēda Gwētᴇla. Wä, lä hōsᵋaᵋlÎᴸaxa sᴇk·!asogwasa p!ᴇlxᴇlasgᴇm

qaēda ᵋwālas Kwāg·uᴸ. Wä, hēᴇmxaäwisē ᵋwāxaxsa p!ᴇlxᴇlasgᴇm qaēda

20 Q!ōmk·!ǔt!ᴇsē. Wä, laᵋmē maēmaᵋlōkwa bēbᴇgwänᴇm lāxa ᵋnāᴸᵋnᴇmxsa

p!ᴇlxᴇlasgᴇm laē yāxᵋwidayâ. Wä, hēᴇm ʟēgadᴇs ʟāʟaxbaᵋya maᵋlōkwē

bēbᴇgwänᴇmxa ᵋnᴇmxsa p!ᴇlxᴇlasgᴇma. Wä, g·îlᵋmisē gwāᴸ yāqwasa qä-

dzō p!ᴇlxᴇlasgᴇma laē ᵋnēk·ē Âwadē: ᵋya, Kwākwäg·uᴸ, k·!ēsʟē ʟayux-

ʟäʟē G·Îxsēᵋstalîsᴇmaᵋyē. Hᴇ̈x·säᴇm ʟēg·ᴇmsg·a G·Îxsēᵋstalîsᴇmaᵋyē

.5 âᵋmōx ᴇlg·aaʟᴇlōdᴀyu lāqᴇk· ᵋnēk·ē. Wä, laᵋmē YāqawÎdē mōlas gwēx·-

ᵋÎdaasas. Wä, lāwisʟē hämg·Îlax·ᵋÎdxēs ʟōᵋlänᴇmē. Wä, g·îlᵋmisē

gwāᴸ haᵋmāpaxs laē ᵋwÎᵋla hōquwᴇls lāxa g·ōkwē. Wä laᴇm k·!eâs gwēx·-

ᵋÎdaasē G·Îxsēᵋstalîsᴇmaᵋyē k·!ēs la k!wēla. Wä, laᴇm yāwasᵋÎd läba.

As soon as the song was ended ᴸ!āqoꞁas spoke and/said: "Have you heard, chiefs? That is my song which/comes from the end, beginning/when I was first created by our creator." Thus he said as he/turned his face to the place where were sitting the chiefs of the Q!ōmoyâ⁶yē. Then (5) he called Âwadē, the chief of the Kŭkwāk!ŭm, a numaym of the Q!ōmoyâ⁶yē./ Then Âwadē stood at his side and took up one pair of blankets./ He spoke and said: "It is true what you say, chief/ᴸ!āqoꞁas about the song which comes from the most ancient myth, for what should we say, my tribe?"/said he, and ne held up the one pair of blankets and spoke loudly. (10) "This is the place for him to walk on, my new chief, G·Ixsē⁶stalIsᴇmē,/for you, Gwētᴇla, two hundred blankets." And again he held up/one pair of blankets. "This is for him to walk on, my new/chief, G·Ixsē⁶stalIsᴇmē, for you, ⁶wālas Kwāg·uꞋ,/one hundred blankets." And again he held up one pair of blankets (15) and he said again, "This is for him to walk on, my new chief, G·Ixsē⁶stalIsᴇmē,/for you, Q!ōmk·!ūt!ᴇs, one hundred blankets. Now I am going to give them away to/you," said he as he counted out one hundred blankets/for the Gwētᴇla. Then he counted out fifty pairs of blankets/for the ⁶wālas Kwāg·uꞋ and then also the same number of pairs of blankets for the (20) Q!ōmk·!ūt!ᴇs. Now there were two men for each pair of/blankets as they were given away. This is called "Two men standing at the ends/of one pair of blankets." Then after the blankets had been given away for/the place on which he was to walk Âwadē said: "Oh Kwāg·uꞋ, he will not change his name/G·Ixsē⁶stalIsᴇmē. He still has the name G·Ixsē⁶stalIsᴇmē, (25) only it has been fastened to him by this," said he, and now Yāqawid thanked him for what he had done./ Finally they gave food to the guests and after/they had eaten they all went out of the house. After this/G·Ixsē⁶stalIsᴇmē had to go to the feasts./ Now this will be ended for a while./

6.

Wä, lax·st!aakwē mōxŭnxē ts!awŭnxas ʟ!āqoʟas x·ōsäɫaxs laē sēxᵋ-
widē G·Ixsēᵋstalīsɛmaᵋyē lāxg·a Tsāxisɛk· Wä, g·āxᵋmisē näᵋnakwaxs
laē qɛpa yāᵋyats!äs lāxa k·!ēs ʟ!āsäɫa qaxg·ın dōqŭlaᵋmēg·aqēxs
5   laē qɛp!ēdēda x̱wāx̱wagŭmē. Wä, g·āxē G·ıxsēᵋstalīsɛmaᵋyē g·āxsᵋa.
Wä, lä lâsdēs lāxa ʟ!ɛmaisē qaᵋs lä laēʟ lāxēs g·ōkwē. Wä, g·flᵋ-
misē gwāɫ ʟ!āyuts!ōdxēs gwēɫgwälaxs laē ʟ!āqoʟas ᵋyālaqasa maᵋlōkwē
bēbɛgwānɛm qa läs ᵋwīᵋla lāʟ!äsala lāx g·ıg·ōkwasa Gwētɛla ʟɛᵋwa
ᵋwālas Kwāg·uɫ ʟɛᵋwa Q!ōmk·!ūt!ɛs qa ᵋnēk·ēs: Dēg·itaʟɛns Gwētɛl
10 lāxwa qɛpaxōx G·Ixsēᵋstalīsɛmaᵋyēx. Wä, la ᵋnēk· lāxa ᵋwālas Kwā-
g·uɫ:Dēg·itaʟɛns ᵋwālas Kwāg·uɫ lāxwa qɛpaxōx G·Ixsēᵋstalīsɛmaᵋyēx.
Wä, la ᵋnēk· lāxa Q!ōmk·!ūt!ɛs. Dēg·itaʟɛns Q!ōmk·!ūt!ɛs lāxwa qɛpaxōx G·Ixsēᵋstalīsɛmaᵋyēx. Hālag·flīɫʟɛsē, ᵋnēk·ē. Wä, lä hēx·ᵋ-
idaɛm la ᵋwīᵋla hōgwīʟa bēbɛgwānɛmasa yŭduxᵘsɛᵋmakwē Kwākwāg·uɫ lāx
15 g·ōkwas ʟ!āqoʟasē. Wä, g·flᵋmisē g·āx ᵋwīᵋlaēʟa laas ʟ!āqoʟas äxᵋ-
wŭɫts!âlīɫaxa sɛk·!ax·sokwē p!ɛlxɛlasgɛm lāxa ōts!âlīɫē qaᵋs g·āxē
gɛmxᵋalīɫas lāxa ōgwiwaᵋlīɫasēs g·ōkwē. Wä, lä yāq!ɛg·aᵋɫa. Wä,
lä ᵋnēk·a: ᵋwa, gēlag·a, Kwākwāg·uɫ lāxwa ʟēgadäxsēs ʟēgɛmēxwa mɛm-
x·ts!asɛla dēg·itaxg·ada qɛpag·ın ʟawɛlgɛmēk·. Laɛmk· wāx· hayaɫ-
20 k!ŭlasōs äxīᵋlälä g·āxɛns, ᵋnēk·ēxs laē dāx·ᵋīdxa ᵋnɛmxsa p!ɛlxɛ-
lasgɛma. Wä, lä ᵋnēk·a: Laᵋmɛn dēg·itsg·ada sɛk·!ax·sōkŭk· p!ɛlxɛ-
lasgɛm lāxa qɛpē G·Ixsēᵋstalīsɛmaᵋyē, ᵋnēk·ēxs laē ʟēᵋlālaxa q!aq!-
astowē qa läs ʟēgēg·ēx ʟēʟɛgɛmasa ᵋnāxwa bēbɛgwānɛma. Wä, g·flᵋ-
misē lä k!wāg·alīɫa q!āq!asto begwānɛm lāx ᵋmawīlasasa p!ɛlxɛlas-
25 gɛmē laas ᵋnēk·a q!āq!astowē bɛgwānɛma: Maᵋmōgwadzɛwēʟa bēbɛgwānɛm
lāxwa ᵋnäɫᵋnɛmxsax p!ɛlxɛlasgɛma ᵋnēk·ē. Wä, laᵋmēda q!āq!astowē
bɛgwānɛm ʟɛʟāqɛlax ʟēʟɛgɛmasa mōkwē bēbɛgwānɛm. Wä, lä ʟ!āqoʟas
hāsāla yāq!wālas lāqēxs ᵋnēk·aē ʟ!āqoʟasaxs laē yāqwasa p!ɛlxɛlas-
gɛmē. Laɛm dēg·idɛms G·Ixsēᵋstalīsɛmaᵋyē lāʟōʟ Ȧwaxɛlag·flisai.
30 Laɛm dēg·idɛms G·Ixsēᵋstalīsɛmaᵋyē lāʟōʟ K·ımk·aqawīdai. Laɛm dē-
g·idɛms G·Ixsēᵋstalīsɛmaᵋyē lāʟōʟ Dōqwaisai. Laɛm dēg·idɛms G·Ixsē-

6.

For about four years ʟ!áqoᵤas took a rest. Then/G·Ixsēᵉstal-
Isɛmē went paddling at Fort Rupert here, and when he came home/his
canoe capsized not far out, for I saw him when (5) the little canoe
capsized. Then G·Ixsēᵉstalisɛmē came ashore/and he went up the beach
and went into his house and after/he had changed his clothes ʟ!áqoᵤas
sent two/men to go into all the houses of the Gwētɛla and the/ᵉwālas
Kwāg·uⁱ and the Q!ōmk·ūt!ɛs and they were to say, "We are going to
wipe off, Gwētɛla,(10) the capsizing of G·Ixsēᵉstalisɛmē." And then
they said to the ᵉwālas Kwāg·uⁱ,/ "We are going to wipe off, ᵉwālas
Kwāg·uⁱ, the capsizing of G·Ixsēᵉstalisɛmē."/ And then they said to
the Q!ōmk·!ūt!ɛs, "We are going to wipe off, Q!ōmk·!ūt!ɛs, this/cap-
sizing of G·Ixsēᵉstalisɛmē. Go quickly," they said. Immediately/
all the men of the three Kwāg·uⁱ tribes went into the (15) house of
ʟ!áqoᵤas and as soon as they were all in ʟ!áqoᵤas/took fifty blankets
out of the bedroom, and he came and/put them down in the rear of his
house. Then he spoke and/said: "Now come, Kwāg·uⁱ, to this that is
called/wiping off the shame of this capsizing of my prince. In vain
(20) the one who made us tried to hurt him," he said as he took one
pair of blankets./ And he said, "Now I wipe his body with these fifty
blankets/on account of the capsizing of G·Ixsēᵉstalisɛmē," said he,
and called the name-keepers/to name the names of all the men. As
soon as/the name-keepers had gone and sat down at the place where
the blankets were piled up, (25) the name-keepers said, " There will
be four men/for each pair of blankets," said they. Then the name-
keepers/called the names of four men and ʟ!áqoᵤas/said loudly giving
them away,--when ʟ!áqoᵤas was saying that he was giving away the
blankets,/--" Now this is the means of wiping the body of G·Ixsēᵉstal-
Isɛmē for you , Áwaxɛlag· îlis. (30) Now this is the means of wiping
the body of G·Ixsēᵉstalisɛmē for you, K·îmk·aqawīd. Now this is the
means of wiping the body/of G·Ixsēᵉstalisɛmē for you, Dōqwais.
Now this is the means of wiping the body of G·Ixsēᵉstalisɛmē

ᵋstalῙsemaᶜyē laʟōʟ Nɛg·ädzē, ᶜnēk·ēxs laē ᶜnēk·a; Xwäkōx p!ɛlxɛ-
lasgɛm lâl g·Ῐg·ɛgämē, ᶜnēk·ēxs laē x·alaᶜlῙⱡasa ᶜnɛmxsa p!ɛlxɛ-
lasgɛma. Wä, lēda ts!ats!ᾶᶜmiⱡē hēⱡᶜa g·āyoⱡ lāx ᶜnɛᵐēmotas ʟ!ā-
qoʟas dāx·ᶜῙdxa ᶜnɛmxsa p!ɛlxɛlasgɛm qaᶜs lä ts!âs lāx Âwaxɛlag·-
5 flisē. Wä, lä Âwaxɛlag·flisē ts!awanaēsasa ᶜnāⱡᶜnɛmē p!ēp!ɛlxɛᶜ-
ma lāxēs waōgŭdzᾶᶜyaxa ᶜnɛmxsa p!ɛlxɛlasgɛma. Wä, la ᶜnāxwaɛm hē
g·wēx·ᶜidēda bēbɛgwānɛmē. Wä, laɛm g·wāⱡ lāxēq.

7. T!ɛnsῙla YäwῙx·ila.

Wä, laᶜmē t!ɛnsῙla yäwῙx·ilē ʟ!āqoʟaᶾ. Wä, laᶜmē g·ɛnɛmasē
10 ʟ!āx·ʟ!alῙdzɛmga g·ōkŭnē lāxēs ōmpē Lɛlak·Ῐnisxa xāmagɛmaᶜyē g·Ῑ-
gamēsa ᶜnɛᶜmēmotasa SῙsɛnʟ!aᶜyasa Ⱡāwits!ēs. Wä, laᶜmē x·ῙsᶜῙdē
G·ῙxsēᶜstalῙsɛmaᶜyē. Wä, g·āxē näᶜnakwē ʟ!ax·ʟ!alῙdzɛmga. Wä,
laɛm mōts!aqēda äwāᶜwē xwāxŭk!ūna qōqŭt!axa ᶜnāxwa hēmaōmas g·āx
wāwaⱡqälayus Lɛlak·Ῐnis ʟɛᶜwis g·ōkŭlota Ⱡāwits!ēs. Wä, laᶜmē ts!ē-
15 ts!eqēda Q!ōmoyᾶᶜyē. Wä, lä maᶜⱡtsɛmg·Ῑlaxa ᶜmɛkŭla x·Ῑsāⱡē G·Ῑx-
sēᶜstalῙsemaᶜyaxs laē k·Ῑmyasōᶜsa Gwētɛla ʟɛᶜwa ᶜwālas Kwāg·uⱡ ʟɛᶜwa Q!ōmk·!ŭt!ɛsē. Wä, laɛm hämshämts!ɛsē G·ῙxsēᶜstalῙsemaᶜyē. Wä,
laɛm ʟēgadɛs Yāqosɛlag·flis. Wä, lāʟa g·ālag·awē nān lāxēs q!ŭlēᶜ-
yē Yāqoʟ!ēqɛla. Wä, la ʟēgadɛs Hägämalag·flis. Wä, lä nŭⱡɛmaⱡa
20 lāxēs gagɛmpē Lɛlak·Ῐnisxa g·Ῑgämaᶜyasa Ⱡāwits!ēs. Wä, la ʟēgadɛs
Sāyak·!a. Wä, maᶜⱡtsɛmē q!ɛmq!ɛmdɛmas Yāqosɛlag·flis lāqēxs hämshämts!ɛsaē lāxēs ōmpē ʟ!āqoʟas. Wä, lä maᶜⱡᶜɛnxē ts!āwŭnxas hämshämts!ɛsa laē gwetsēᶜsta. Wä, laɛm yāwisᶜῙd lāba.

8. T!ɛnsῙla P!ɛsa.

25 Wä, laᶜmē ʟāʟawɛlxsῙla ʟ!āqoʟasasa aʟɛbōp!ɛnyag·ē p!ɛlxɛlas-
gɛm qa t!ɛnsῙlaᶜyōs G·ῙxsēᶜstalῙsemaᶜyē qaxs hēᶜmaē āⱡēs lastōdē
ᶜnāxwa la gwāⱡ gwaᶜyiᶜlälats ʟ!āqoʟasē qaēs xŭnōkwē G·ῙxsēᶜstalῙ-
semaᶜyē qaᶜs ʟēgadēs ʟawɛlgɛmaᶜyas ʟ!āqoʟas. Wä, laɛm ʟ!āyuxʟäⱡē
G·ῙxsēᶜstalῙsemaᶜyē qaxs lɛᶜmaē ʟawɛlgaxʟälax Yāqoʟasɛmaᶜyē qaxs
30 k·!ēsaē ʟawɛlgaxʟayuwē G·ῙxsēᶜstalῙsemaᶜyē. Wä, laᶜmēsen ʟēqɛl-

(1)for you,Nɛg·ä," said he. And he said, "This blanket is torn/
for you, chiefs," he said as he threw down one pair of blankets./
Then a young man gave out the blankets. He came from the numaym
of ʟ!āqoʟas./ He took up one pair of blankets and gave it to Âwax-
ɛlag·îlis (5) and Âwaxɛlag·îlis gave to each of his partners one old
blanket/for the one pair of blankets, and all/the men did the same.
That is the end of this./

7. Giving the Winter Dance to His Own Tribe.

Now ʟ!āqoʟas gave a winter dance to his own tribe, and his wife
(10)ʟ!ax·ʟ!alîdzɛmga went to visit the house of her father, Lɛlak·-
înis, the head chief/of the numaym Sîsɛnʟ!ēᵋ of the Ławits!ēs. Then/
G·Ixsēᵋstalîsɛmē disappeared and ʟ!ax·ʟ!alîdzɛmga came home. Then/
four large canoes were filled with all kinds of food and/were given
as a marriage gift by Lɛlak·înis and his tribe, the Łāwits!ēs. Now
the (15) Q!ōmoyâᵋye had a winter dance. For two moons G·Ixsēᵋstalî-
sɛmē stayed away,/and then was caught by the Gwētɛla and the ᵋwālas
Kwāg·uł and the/Q!ōmk·!ūt!ɛs. And now G·Ixsēᵋstalîsɛmē was Hămshămts!ɛs and/his name was Yāqosɛlag·îlis. But first he had been a grizzly bear through his uncle/Yāqoʟ!ēqɛla, and his name was Hägămalag·-
îlis, and he had been a fool dancer (20) through his grandfather Lɛ-
lak·înis, the chief of the Łāwits!ēs and his name was/Sāyak·!a. And
two were the songs of Yāqosɛlag·îlis as Hămshămts!ɛs/through his father, ʟ!āqoʟas. Then for two winters he was Hămshămts!ɛs,/and then
he became a member of the sparrow society. And now for a short time
this is ended./

8. Giving Away to his Own Tribe.

(25) Now ʟ!āqoʟas took care of his prince with seven hundred
blankets/to be given away by G·Ixsēᵋstalîsɛmē to his own tribe. For
he just repeated/everything that ʟ!āqoʟas had already done for his
son G·Ixsēᵋstalîsɛmē/that he might be called the prince of ʟ!āqoʟas.
Now/G·Ixsēᵋstalîsɛmē changed his name and now his prince's name is
Yāqoʟasɛmēᵋ, for (30) G·Ixsēᵋstalîsɛmē is not a prince's name. And

aʟɛs Yāqoʟasɛmaᵋyē lāq. Wä, laᵋmē ɬaladak!wālaxa sēsɛk·!axsa p!ɛ-
lxɛlasgɛm lāx g·ĭg·ɛgāmaᵋyasa Gwētɛla ʟɛᵋwa ᵋwālas Kwāg·uɬ ʟɛᵋwa
Q!ōmk·ūt!ɛs. Wä, la ᵋnāɬᵋnɛmxsa p!ɛlxɛlasgɛmē ɬaladak!wālanɛmē lāxa
bēbɛgwānɛmq!ālamē, yĭxa g·ĭg·ɛgāmaᵋyē ɬadɛkwasa sɛk·!axsa p!ɛlxɛlas-
5 gɛm lāx Yāqoʟasɛmaᵋyē. Wä, lāʟē Yāqoʟasɛmaᵋyē g·ĭnᵋwasa sɛk·!axsa
p!ɛlxɛlasgɛm lāx ɬadɛgwaᵋyâsa g·ĭgāmaᵋyē. Wä, la nɛnqaxsago ʟɛᵋwa
ɬadagwayâxs laē yāxᵋwidayu lāxa g·ĭgāmaᵋyē. Wä, lāxaē hēɛm gwēx·ᵋ-
ĭdxa ᵋnɛmxsa p!ɛlxɛlasgɛm ɬadagwayusa bɛgwānɛmq!ālɛmē. Laɛm maᵋɬɛ-
xsa p!ɛlxɛlasgɛmē yāxᵋwidayâq. Wä, g·ĭlᵋmisē k·!ēs ɬadɛkwēda g·ĭg-
10 āmaᵋyasa sɛk·!axsa p!ɛlxɛlasgɛma laē âɛm yūduxwaxsa p!ɛlxɛlasgɛmēda
yāxᵋwidayâq. Wä, g·ĭlᵋmisē k·!ēs ɬadakwēda bɛgwānɛmq!ālāsa ᵋnɛmxsa
p!ɛlxɛlasgɛma laē yāxᵋwitsōsa ōxᵘsaakwē p!ɛlxɛlasgɛma. Wä, gĭlᵋmisē
ᵋwĭᵋla ɬēɬadɛkwēda Gwētɛla ʟɛᵋwa ᵋwālas Kwag·uɬ ʟɛᵋwa Q!ōmk·!ūt!ɛsē
laas ʟ!āqoʟas äxk·!ālaxa nâgadē qa q!ɛmdēɬēs ʟɛᵋwa Q!ōmoyâᵋyēxa dzā-
15 qwa lāx āɬtsɛma baxŭᵋyāla q!ɛmdɛma. Wä, g·ĭlᵋmisē dzāqwaxs laēda
maᵋlōkwē haᵋyāɬᵋa q!ɛmdiᵋlālaxa Q!ōmoyâᵋyēxa ᵋnēk·ē lāx aᵋwĭʟɛläsa
t!ēt!ɛx·fläsa g·ĭg·ōkwasa Q!ōmoyâᵋyē: G·āxᵋmɛnuᵋxᵘ q!ɛmdiᵋlālōʟai
Q!ōmoyáᵋyai qa Yāqoʟasɛmaᵋyai ʟawɛlgɛmaᵋyas ʟ!āqoʟas ᵋnēk·ē.Wä,hēᵋmis
g·ĭl laēʟa nâgadēxa ʟēgadäs Laxsōdalasōᵋ qaᵋs dɛnxᵋĭdē qa hōʟēlēs
20 ʟ!āqoʟasaxa āɬtsɛmē äxēs q!ɛmdɛma. Wä, hēᵋmis la ᵋnēx·ᵋalĭɬaᵋlats
ʟ!āqoʟasasēs gwēᵋyō qa qāyatsa q!ɛmdɛmʟasēs ʟawɛlgɛmaᵋyē Yāqoʟasɛmaᵋyē. Wä, g·ĭlᵋmisē gwāɬa qāyasasa āɬtsɛmē q!ɛmdɛma laasa maᵋlōkwē haᵋyaɬᵋa qatsēᵋstaxa ᵋnāxwa bēbɛgwānɛmsa Q!ōmoyâᵋyē qa g·āxlag·ĭs
q!ɛmdēɬa. Wä, laᵋmēda k!wēk!wanōʟɛmaᵋyasa nâgadē la k!ŭsᵋalĭɬ lāx
25 wāx·sagawaᵋlĭɬasa nâgadē. Wä, laᵋmēda nâgadē k·!ēs hasɛlaxs laē dɛ-
nxᵋĭda. Wä, âᵋmisa k!wēk!wanōʟɛmaᵋyas q!wēʟāɬa qaxs q!āq!ōʟ!aax

now I will call him (1) Yāqoᶦasɛmē after this. Now he said he would
loan out five pairs of/blankets to the chiefs of the Gwētɛla and the
ᶜwālas Kwāg·uⱡ and the/Qǃōmk·ǃūtǃɛs, and he said he would loan outl
one pair og blankets to/each common man. The obligation of the
chiefs to Yāqoᶦasɛmē was five pairs of blankets. (5) Then Yāqoᶦasɛmē
added five pairs of/blankets to the obligation of the chiefs and now
the obligation was ten pairs/(of blankets) when these were given to
the chiefs. And he did the same/with the one pair of blankets as an
obligation to the common people. Now two pairs of/blankets were giv-
en to them. When the obligation of the chiefs is not(10)five pairs
of blankets, then only three pairs of blankets/are given to them and
when the common people are not obligated with one pair of/blankets
then they are given a single blanket. And when/they had all been
given, the Gwētɛla and the ᶜwālas Kwāg·uⱡ and the Qǃōmk·ǃūtes,/then
ᴸǃāqoᶦas told his song-maker to sing in the house with the Qǃōmoyāᶜyē
that evening (15) the new secular song. And when evening came/two
young men went to call the Qǃōmoyāᶜyē that they should sing in the
house. And they said at the/doors of the houses of the Qǃōmoyāᶜyē:
"We come to tell you to sing in the house,/Qǃōmoyāᶜyē, for Yāqoᶦasɛmē, the prince of ᴸǃāqoᶦas," said they. And the first/to go
in was the song-maker, whose name is Laxsōdalasōᶜ, and he sang for
(20) ᴸǃāqoᶦas to hear the new song which he had made. And that was
when he was told/by ᴸǃāqoᶦas what words he wished put into the song
for his prince, Yāqoᶦasɛmē./ And when he had finished the words of
the new song, then the two/young men went around to call all the men
of the Qǃōmoyāᶜyē to come and/sing in the house. Then those who sit
on each side of the song-leader went and sat down there (25) on each
side of the song-leader. The song-leader did not sing loud when he
sang/and those who sat on each side of the song-leader just kept quiet

---

[1] This means that the blankets are given out as a loan which had
to be accepted and which had to be returned with interest either to
the person who makes the loan or his successor.

q!ɛmtîla꜅yasa nâgadē. Wä, lä mōp!ɛna lɛlbɛndēda nâgadē ꜅nɛmōk!wāla
dɛnxɛla. Wä, g·îl꜅misē q!ûlbēda la ɛlxɩ̣ēsa mōp!ɛnōta, laēda nâgadē
꜅nēk·a. Wäg·îⱡlax·îns hasōstâɩ dɛnx꜅îda qaxs lɛ꜅maaqōs q!âⱡ꜅aɩɛlaxɛn
dɛnx꜅îdayux ꜅nēk·ēxs laē dâqâlasēs q!ɛmtîla꜅yē. Wä, la꜅mē ꜅nāxwa
5 hāsɛla dɛnxɛlēda bēbɛgwānɛmē. Wä, â꜅misa nâgadē ɩ!ēq!odalasa qāqa꜅-
yasasēs q!ɛmtîla꜅yē q!ɛmdɛma. Wä, g·a꜅mis q!ɛmdɛmsēg·a t!ɛnsila
q!ɛmdɛm.

Wâ hâ yä wâ hu wā ha ha
Ladzehɵmäɩâhâxs yawihëx·ilēdzēlɛns g·îgämähayēx yahawix·îl-
10 ēsɩa yäyahawinqalisɩ̣ähans g·îgämahayēx lēlqwälaɩai; ya
wâ hâ yä.
Lahamɛns yāha x·îts!ax·îlahaɩaxwaha gwälēhēdzēx g·îgämaha꜅ya-
xwa nûyɛmbalihesēx g·îgämahayaxwa ɩ̣ä꜅wɛlxsē꜅stālahadzēx g·î-
gämaha꜅yaxwa g·îxsē꜅stālahadzēx g·îgämaha꜅yēx lēlqwälahaɩai;
15 ya wâ hâ yä.
Wä, lahamɛns g·îgämaha꜅ya ɩ̣ēqa꜅yahahäⱡtsēs q!ûlēhēxɩa꜅yadzēɛmēk·
G·îxse꜅stahalîsɛma꜅yē ɩ̣ēgɛhamsɛn gāgahämpdzēyuⱡaxa q!ûlēhēx-
ɩa꜅yadzē ɩ!āqoɩadzēyuⱡa. Wä, lēhēda q!ûlēhēxɩa꜅yadzē ɩ!āso-
tiwahalidzēyuⱡa. Wä, lēhēda q!ûlēhēxɩa꜅yadzē ɩ!āqoɩahasɛmä-
20 dzēyuⱡa g·îgämaha꜅ya lēlqwälahaɩai; ya wâ, yūhûmɛn g·îqag·ēhē-
waha yux lēlqwälahaɩai, ya wâ hâ yä.
Lahamɛns ya hōlēlaⱡxɛns g·îgämahayēx lēlqwälahaɩai. Lahamōx nû-
sayahaⱡtsēs nûⱡahag·iwahayaxa q!ûlēhēxɩeyadɩē ɩ!āqoɩasa ɩ!ä-
ɩ!aqwaaladzēyuⱡa g·îgämahayaxs lahayuⱡa lax·s꜅ɛndēyahaxa ɩ̣ē-
25 gɛmnuxᵘdzēyuⱡa Nangɛmahaladzēyuⱡa ɩ̣ō꜅ ɩ̣ēgɛmnuxᵘdzēyuⱡa Mä-
wahak·!ahadxēyuⱡa ɩ̣ō꜅ ɩ̣ēgɛmnuxᵘdzēyuⱡa Lētahadzēyuⱡa ɩ̣ō꜅ ɩ̣ē-
gɛmnuxᵘdzēyuⱡa Ângwahaladzēyuⱡa yaēxɩɛnahasɛhan g·îgämahayēx
lēlqwälahaɩai, yûɛm ɩ!äɩ!aqwäsɛns g·îgämahayēx lēlqwälahaɩai;
ya wâ hâ yä.

for they were learning the (1) song made by the song-maker. Then
four times the song-maker went to the end of the song, singing a-
lone./ As soon as the last one of the four was at an end, the song-
maker/said: "Now we will sing it loud, for now you have learned
this that/I am singing," said he as he started the song he had made.
Now all the (5) men sang loud, and the song-maker just called out
the words of the/song he had made. And this is his song, the song
of/giving away property to his own tribe. /

    Wâ hâ yä wâ hu wā ha ha

        The great one will move, this chief. He will move,(10)
        move about our chief, tribes; ya/wâ hâ yä.

    Now we shall look on the great one who was already a chief/at
        the beginning of mythical times; this chief who is all over
        a great first-born prince/ who is all over a great chief,
        this chief, this chief, tribes; (15) ya wâ hâ yä./

    Now our chief will pronounce his own great name,/First-all-
        over-Chief, the name of my great late grandfather/whose own
        great name was the great Copper-Place; and also was his own
        name/Seaside-of-World, and also was his own name From-Whom-
        Coppers-are-Obtained, (20) this chief, tribes, ya wâ , my
        chief before me,/oh tribes! ya wâ hâ ya./

    We will listen to our chief, tribes' He will/tell the myth of
        his Fool of olden times, his own, whose name was Copper-
        Place,/the Great-One-from-whom-one-tries-to-get-Coppers,
        the chief, for he broke (25) (the copper) that has the
        great name Grizzly-Bear-Face, and the one that has the great
        name/Sea-Lion and the one that has the great name Searching
        and the one/that has the great name Cloudy, the property of
        my chief,/tribes. These are the coppers of my chief, tribes!/
        ya wâ hâ yä./

Wä, g·îlᵉmisê âlak·ǃäla ᵉnäxwa qǃälêda bêbɛgwänɛmasa Qǃômoyâᵉ_
yaxa âⱡtsɛmê qǃɛmdɛma laê ᵉwîᵉla hôqŭwɛls läx g·ôkwas ʟǃäqoʟas. Wä,
laᵉmê gänuⱡᵉîda. Wä, g·îlᵉmisê ᵉnäx·ᵉîdxa gaäläxs laê ᵉwîᵉla ʟäxᵉ_
wîdêda bêbɛgwänɛmasa Qǃômoyâᵉyê qaᵉs ᵉnäxwê halamaxstê gaaxstäla.

5 Wä, g·îlᵉmisê ʟǃäqoʟas k·ôtaq laɛm ᵉwîᵉla gwäl haᵉmäpa loê ᵉyälaqa-
sês qǃŭlyagwîⱡa ʟêgadäs X·îlqîlagɛmaᵉyê qa läs ʟaxᵉwɛls läx ʟǃäsaᵉ_
nâᵉyas g·ôkwas qa x·îtsǃaᵉnâᵉlesêxa Kwakŭĝ·ŭⱡê qa ʟêqɛlêsêx Qǃêx·ʟä-
laga wɛqǃwäs Yaqoʟasɛmaᵉyê. Wä, lêda qǃŭlyakwê X·îlqîlagɛmaᵉyê lä
lawɛls läxa tǃɛx·îläsa g·ôkwê qaᵉs ʟaxᵉwɛîsê. Wä, lä häsɛla ᵉnêka:

10 Laɛms x·îtsǃax·îlaʟôʟai Gwetɛlai läx Qǃêx·ʟälagai xŭnôkwas Yäqoʟasɛmaᵉyê. Laɛms x·îtsǃax·îlaʟôʟai ᵉwälas Kwäg·uⱡai läx, Qǃêx·ʟälagai
xŭnôkwas Yäqoʟasɛmaᵉyê. Laɛms x·îtsǃax·îlaʟôʟai Qǃômk·ǃŭtǃɛsai läx
Qǃêx·ʟälagai xŭnôkwas Yäqoʟasɛmaᵉyê. Halaxsʟasai ᵉnêk·ê. Wä, la
hᵉx·ᵉidaᵉma Gwêtɛla ʟɛᵉwa ᵉwälas Kwäg·uⱡ ʟɛᵉwa Qǃômk·ǃŭtǃɛs ᵉwîᵉla

15 lä läx g·ôkwas ʟǃäqôʟas qas lä ᵉwîᵉla kǃŭsᵉäliⱡ läx wäx·sanêgwîⱡasa
g·ôkwê qaxs haaʟaⱡ kǃŭdzîⱡa Qǃômoyâᵉya ôgwiwaᵉlîⱡasa g·ôkwê. Wä,
g·îlᵉmisê ᵉwîᵉla kǃŭsᵉäliⱡa g·äxaas ʟǃäqoʟas x·îlqɛlaxa maᵉⱡaxsa pǃɛlxɛlasgɛm qâᵉs ʟäxᵉwalîⱡê läx ʟǃäsɛx·dzamâᵉyasa Qǃômoyâᵉyê. Wä, lä
yäqǃɛg·aᵉⱡa. Wä, lä ᵉnêk·a: Wä, gêlag·a Gwêtɛl; wä, gêlag·a ᵉwälas

20 Kwäg·uⱡ, Qǃômk·ǃŭtǃɛs. Hêⱡᵉalîⱡ läxa g·ôkwaxsg·în ʟawɛlgämêk·läxg·a
Yäqoʟasɛmêk·, ᵉnêk·exs laê gwêgɛmx·ᵉîd läxa Qǃômoyâᵉyê. Wä, lä ᵉnê-
k·aʟaᵉmɛn tɛlqwasa maᵉⱡɛxsa pǃɛlxɛlasgɛm läxwa nâgadêx qaᵉs qǃɛmtîlaᵉyê, ᵉnêk·ê. Wä, hᵉx·ᵉidaᵉmisa nâgadê äxk·ǃälaxa ᵉnäxwa bêbɛgwänɛm-
sa Qǃômoyâᵉyê qa qǃwäg·alîⱡês qa ᵉnäxwês äʟagɛmäⱡa läxa ôgwiwaᵉlîⱡasa

25 g·ôkwê. Wä, lä hᵉx·ᵉidaᵉma nâgadê dâqâlasês qǃɛmtîlaᵉyê. Wä, laᵉmê
ᵉnäxwa dɛnxɛlêda Qǃômoyâᵉyê. Wä, g·äxᵉmê yîxwê Qǃêx·ʟälaga. Wä,g·axê
wŭqǃwäsê, yîx Yäqoʟasɛmaᵉyê ʟaxwêmîⱡa. Wä, g·îlᵉmisê gwäⱡa dɛnxɛla
laê ʟǃäqoʟas yäxᵉwîtsa pǃɛlxɛlasgɛm. Wä, g·îlᵉmisê ᵉwîᵉlxtôd yäxᵉwîtsa pǃɛlxɛlasgɛmê läxa yŭduxᵘsɛᵉmakwê Kwäkwäg·uⱡ laê ᵉwîᵉla hôquwɛls

30 läxa g·ôkwê. Wä, laɛmxaê yäwasᵉîd gwäⱡ läxêq.

(1) And when all the men of the Q!ŏmoyâᵋyē knew well/ the new song, they all went out of the house of ʟ!âqoʟas. Then/ night came. When day broke in the morning they all got up,/ the men of the Q!ŏ-moyâᵋyē and they all quickly ate their breakfast. (5) When ʟ!âqoʟas thought they had all finished eating he sent out the/ old man of his house, whose name was X·ĭlqĭlagɛmēᵋ to go and stand outside the/ house and to call as spectators the Kwāg·uⱡ tribes and to call the name of Q!ēx·ʟālaga/ the sister of Yāqoʟasɛmēᵋ. Then the old man X·ĭlqĭlagɛmēᵋ/ went out of the door of the house and he stood up and he said out loud: (10) " Now you will be spectators, you Gwētɛla, for Q!ēx·ʟālaga the child of Yāqoʟasɛmēᵋ./ Now you will be spectators, you ᵋwālas Kwāg·uⱡ, for Q!ēx·ʟālaga,/ the child of Yāqoʟasɛmēᵋ. Now you will be spectators, you Q!ŏmk·!ūt!ɛs, for/ Q!ēx·ʟālaga, the child of Yāqoʟasɛmēᵋ. You will quickly get into your canoes," he said. And/ immediately the Gwētɛla and the ᵋwālas Kwāg·uⱡ and the Q!ŏmk·!ūt!ɛs all (15) went to the house of ʟ!âqoʟas and they all sat down at each side of the/ house. And the Q!ŏmoyâᵋyē sat down at the rear of the house, and/ when they had all sat down ʟ!âqoʟas came in carrying in his hand two pairs of/ blankets and he stood at the outside of the Q!ŏmoyâᵋyē. Then/ he spoke and said: " Come now, Gwētɛla. Come now, (20) ᵋwālas Kwāg·uⱡ and Q!ŏ-mk·!ūt!ɛs. Be comfortable here in the house of my prince, this/ Yā-qoʟasɛmēᵋ," said he as he turned his face to the Q!ŏmoyâᵋyē. Then he said,/ " Now I will make a soft layer with these two pairs of blank-ets for the song-maker for the/ song which he has made," he said. Im-mediately the song-maker told all the men/ of the Q!ŏmoyâᵋyē to stand up and turn their faces to the rear of the (25) house. Then immediately the song-maker began to sing the song he had made. Now/ they all sang, the Q!ŏmoyâᵋyē. Then Q!ēx·ʟālaga came dancing and/ her brother Yāqo-ʟasɛmēᵋ came and stood close to her. When they had finished singing,/ ʟ!âqoʟas gave away blankets and as soon as he had given away all/ the blankets to the three tribes of the Kwāg·uⱡ they all went out of the (30) house. Now for a short time this is ended/

142

9. ᵋmāxwaxa Mamalēleqala ʟɛᵋwa ᶠnɛmɡis ʟɛᵋwa Ł̄awits!ēs.

Wä, laᵋmē ʟ!āqoʟas k·ˀiˡwānɛmax Wīnaxa ʟ!āqwa lāx Hămdzidxa

g·Igāmaᵋyasa Hĕłdzaᵋqᵘ. Wä, la ʟ!āqoʟas ts!âsa ʟ!āqwa Wīna lāxēs

ʟ̣awɛlɡɛmaᵋyē Yāqoʟasɛmaᵋyē. Wä, la Yāqoʟasɛmaᵋyē laxōdɛx Wīna.

5 Wä, la k·ˀiˡxwē g·Igāmaᵋyasa Ł̄awits!ēsax Wīna. Wä, laᵋmē K·!âdēxa

g·Igāmaᵋyasa Ł̄awits!ēs k·ˀiˡxwasa sɛk·!āp!ɛnyag·inâla p!ɛlxɛlasɡɛm

lāxa ʟ!āqwē Wīna. Wä,laᵋmēda Q!ōmoyâᵋyē ᵋwiᵋla la lāx Qālogwis k·ˀi-

lwālaxa ʟ!āqwē Wīna lāx K·!âdē. Wä, g·ˀiˡᵋmisē gwāł k·ˀiˡxwē K·!âdäx

Wīna g·āxaxs ᵋmâlēda yaᵋyats!äsa Q!ōmoyâᵋyaxa sɛk·!āp!ɛnyag·inâla

10 p!ɛlxɛlasɡɛma qaᵋs g·āxē lāx Tsāxis. Wä, g·ˀiˡᵋmisē g·āxᵋaʟɛla lāx

ʟ!ɛmâisas Tsāxis laas ʟ̣āxᵋwałaxsē ʟ!āqoʟas qaᵋs yāq!ɛg·aᵋłē. Wä,

lä ᵋnēk·a.

G·āxᵋmɛn, Gwētɛl, g·āxᵋmɛn ᵋwālas Kwāg·uł, Q!ōmk·!ūt!ɛs. Laᵋmē

lāxa Wīnax·dä. Laᵋmisɛns lāł lēʟɛlałxa lēlqwalaʟaᵋyax ētoxsaʟa ᵋnēk·ē.

15 Wä, lä ʟ̣axᵋwɛlsēda g·āgułē lāxa ᵋnɛᵋmēmotasa Kŭkwāk!ŭmasa Gwētɛla

qaᵋs yāq!ɛg·ᵍᵋłe nānaxᵋmēx wāłdɛmas ʟ!āqoʟas. Wä, lä ᵋnēk·a: Wä,

ɡēlag·a, g·Igāmēᵋ ʟ!āqoʟas. Wä, ɡēlag·a g·Igāmēᵋ Yāqoʟasɛmēᵋ. Ala-

ʟasēs wāłdɛmōsxa la lāg·aē Wīnä, ɡēlak·asᵋla. Wä, g·āxʟɛlag·axa lēl-

qwālaʟaᵋya lāxwa ᵋwālasēx äwiˡhagwisa, ᵋnēk·ēxs laē ᵋnēk·a: Lāᵋmɛn

20 ʟēᵋlalōʟai Q!ōmuyâᵋyai qag·in g·Igāmēk· lāxg·a Nɛqāp!ɛnk·ɛmk·. Laɛmɜ

g·āxʟa tɛłts!ał lāxg·a g·ōkᵘg·as, ᵋnēk·ē.

Wä, laᵋmē ᵋwiᵋla wāłdɛmas , laē hēx·ᵋidaɛm ᵋwiᵋla hōxᵋwŭłtâwe

Q!ōmoyâᵋyē lāxēs yaᵋyats!ē x̱wāx̱ŭk·!ŭna qaᵋs ᵋmōłtōdēsa p!ɛlxɛlasɡɛmē

qaᵋs lē ᵋmawiˡas lāx g·ōkwas ʟ!āqoʟas. Wä, g·ˀiˡᵋmisē ᵋwiᵋlōsdēsa

25 p!ɛlxɛlasɡɛmaxs laasa ētsēᵋstaxa haᵋyāłᵋäsa ᵋnɛᵋmēmotasa Kŭkwāk!ŭm-

asa Gwētɛla. Wä, g·ˀiˡᵋmisē g·āx ᵋwiᵋlaēʟa Q!ōmoyâᵋyē qaxs hēᵋmaē

âlak·!āla k!wēłē, wä, lä äxsɛᵋwa ᵋwālas Kwāg·uł ʟɛᵋwa Q!ōmk·!ūt!ɛs

qa g·āxēs ᵋwiᵋla k!wamēł̣a qa ᵋwiᵋlēs hōlēlax ts!ēts!ɛk·!āʟɛmas ʟ!ā-

qoʟasē ʟɛᵋwis gwēg·ilasʟa qō g·āxʟa lēlqwālaʟaᵋyē. Wä, g·ˀiˡᵋmisē

9. The giving away of property to the Mamalēleqăla and
the ᵋnɛmgis and the Łāwits!ēs.

Now ʟ!āqoʟas bought War, the copper, from Hămdzid,/the chief
of the Hᵉⱡdzaᵋqᵘ. Then ʟ!āqoʟas gave the copper War to his/prince,
Yāqoʟasɛmēᵋ, and Yāqoʟasɛmēᵋ put up War for sale. (5) Then the
chief of the Łāwits!ēs bought War. And now K·âdē,/the chief of
the Łāwits!ēs, bought with fifteen hundred blankets the/copper War,
and the Q!ōmoyâᵋyē all went to Qālogwis to sell the/copper War to
K·âdē. And when K·âdē had finished buying/War, they loaded the
travelling canoes of the Q!ōmoyâᵋyē with fifteen hundred (10) blankets and they brought them to Fort Rupert. And when they arrived
at the/beach of Fort Rupert ʟ!āqoʟas stood up in the canoe and
spoke and/he said:/

" I have come, Gwētɛla. I have come, ᵋwālas Kwāg·uⱡ and Q!ōm-
k·!ūt!ɛs. Now/War has gone down. Now we will invite all the tribes
three days from now," he said. (15) Then stood up one who belonged to the numaym of the Kŭkwāk!ŭm of the Gwētɛla,/and he spoke
answering the speech of ʟ!āqoʟas. He said:/ " Come, chief ʟ!āqo-
ʟas. Come, chief Yāqoʟasɛmēᵗ./ Your speech is true that War has
arrived. Let them all come,/all the tribes, to this great place,"
he said. Then he said: " Now (20) I invite you, Q!ōmoyâᵋyē, on
behalf of my chief here, this Nɛqāp!ɛnk·ɛm. Now/ you will come
and warm yourselves in his house." said he./

That is all he said. Then immediately the/Q!ōmoyâᵋyē all got
out of their travelling canoes and they unloaded the blankets/and
carried them into the house of ʟ!āqoʟas. When they had carried up
all the (25) blank ts they came back to call the young men of the
numaym of the Kŭkwāk!ŭm/of the Gwētɛla. When all the Q!ōmoyâᵋyē
came, for it is they who are the/ true feasters. Then the ᵋwālas
Kwāg·uⱡ and the Q!ōmk·!ūt!ɛs/were asked tö come and sit down by
their side and listen to the news which would be told by/ʟ!āqoʟas,
and what he was going to do when the tribes would come.

g·āx ɛwīɛlaēʟa laas hëx·ɛidaɛm·hämg·ʟ̣lasɛɛwa Q!ōmoyâɛyē. Wä, laɛm
k·!eâs wāɫdɛms wawax·saxʟawaɛliʎa Gwētɛla ʟɛɛwa Q!ōmoyâɛyē ōgüɛla
lāqə̄xs âɛmaē tētak!wālap!a. Wä, g·ɪ̂lɛmisē gwāɫ haɛmāpɛxs laē ʟ̣āxɛ-
walɪʎē ʟ̣!āqoʟasē qaɛs yāq!ɛg·aᶜʎē gwēgɛmāʎa lāxa Q!ōmoyâɛyē. Wä, lä
5 ɛnēk·a: Ēsɛmaēʟɛn wēg·ɪ̂ʟa, nōs g·Ɪ̂g·ɛgämēɛ;ēsɛmaēʟɛn nēʎaʎxɛns qwē-
sēg·aɛliʎē g·Ɪ̂g·ɛgämaɛya yɪ̂s laēnēɛmas halɪ̂ɛläla g·āxʟa lēlqwälaʟaɛyē lāxɛns ɛwālasēx aɛwɪnagwisa, ɛnēkɛɛxs laē gwēgɛmx·ɛɪd lāxa t!ɛ-
x·ɪ̂läsa g·ōkwē qaxs häē k!üdzɪʎa Gwētɛla ʟɛɛwa ɛwālas Kwāg·uʎ ʟɛɛwa
Q!ōmk·!üt!ɛsēxa ɛwīɛlaɛm k!waɛmēʎa. Wä, lä ɛnēk·a: ʎlaʟasēs nâqaɛ-
10 yaqōs, g·Ɪ̂g·ɛgämēɛ, ʎlaʟasēs laēnaɛyōs ɛnēx· qɛn g·āxē tɛʎts!a lāxōs
g·ōkwaqōs g·Ɪ̂gämēɛ Nɛqāp!ɛnk·ɛm. G·āxɛmɛn, g·āxɛmɛn ɛmálaxwa sɛk·!-
āp!ɛnyag·anâlax p!ɛlxɛlasgɛm k·ɪ̂lōmx Wɪnax·dä. Laɛmē lāxa. Laɛmēsɛn hēlōʟ Gwētɛl, ɛwālas Kwāg·uʎ, Q!ōmk·!üt!ɛs qɛns lē ʟēɛlālaxa Mamalēleqala ʟɛɛwa ɛnɛmgis ʟɛɛwa Ʌ̣āwits!ēsax ētoxsaʟa qō gwāʎʟɛn layō-
15 ʟēda k·!ɪ̂tɛla lāxg·ɪ̂n g·Ɪ̂qēlasōkᵘ lāxg·a ʟ̣!āsotiwalisɛk·, yɪ̂xg·ada lāk·
ʟ̣!āyuxʟäg·a Ỵiqoʟasɛmaɛyē. Wä, laɛms ʟ̣ēqalaʟɛs ʟ̣!āsotiwalis lāqɛk·.
Yüɛmoq g·Ɪ̂g·ɛgämēɛ. Wä, laɛmēsɛn hēlōʟ nēnâgad qaɛs dɛnxɛidaōsas
ʟ̣āʟawayuxᵘsɪla q!ɛmdɛma, ɛnēk·a. Wä, lä Nɛqāp!ɛnk·ɛmē mōɛlas wāɫdɛmas.

Wä, g·ɪ̂lɛmɪsē gwāʎē wāldɛmas laē hōqüwels ɛwīɛla lāxa g·ōkwē.
20 Wä, g·ɪ̂lɛmisē ɛnāx·ɛɪdxa gaalāxs laē ʟ̣!āqoʟas ɛyālaqasa mōkwē haɛyāʎ-
ɛâk·!ɪ̂n bēbɛgwānɛm qa lēs sēxɛwida äläx mōts!aqa g·ɪ̂lsg·ɪ̂lt!a dzāsɛ-
ɛqwa qa maɛʎp!ɛng·iʎbēs lāxɛns q!wâq!wax·ts!ānaɛyēx yɪ̂x wāg·idasas ō-
xʟaɛyas maɛʎts!aqa sēsɛk·!ap!ɛng·ag·ayuwas aɛwâsgɛmas. Wä, la maɛʎts!aqa ɛnaɛnɛmāp!ɛnk·as awâsgɛmas lāxɛns bāʟax. Wä, g·ɪ̂lɛmisē la sēx-
25 ɛwidēda mōkwē bēbɛgwānɛma laē ʟ̣!āqoʟas ʟɛʎts!ōdxa Q!ōmoyâɛyē ʟɛɛwa
Gwētɛla ʟɛɛwa ɛwālas Kwāg·uʎ ʟɛɛwa Q!ōmk·!üt!ɛsē qa lēs ɛwīɛla lāx
g·ōkwas lāx gwēg·ilasasa ʟēʎɛläxa lēlqwälaʟaɛyē, yɪ̂xs laē ɛnɛmsgɛɛ-
makᵘ lēlqwälaʟaɛya mōsgɛɛmakwē Kwākwāg·uʎa qa g·āqalap!ēs lāxa ɛnāxwa
gwaɛyiɛlälatsa ʟēʎɛla. Wä, hëɛm gwēɛyâsa bāk!ümē g·āg·ēxsilaxa ʟēɛla-
50 läxa lēlqwälaʟaɛyē. Wä, g·ɪ̂lɛmisē g·āx ɛwīɛlaēʟēda mōsgɛɛmakwē Kwākwā-

When (1, they had all come in immediately food was given to the
Q!ōmoyâˢyē. There were no speeches made by either side by the Gwētɛla and the Q!ōmoyâˢyē, but they only laughed and joked. As soon
as they had finished eating/ʟ!āqoʟas stood up and spoke, facing the
Q!ōmoyâˢyē, and (5) said: " Am I not going to go, my chiefs? Am I
not going to tell our/chiefs on the far side that the tribes will
quickly come/to this great place here," said he as he turned his
face to the door/of the house, for there were sitting the Gwētɛla
and the ˢwālas Kwāg·uɫ and the/Q!ōmk·!ūt!ɛs, who had all come to sit
in the house. Then he said: " Really this is your mind, (10) chiefs,
that you wish me to warm myself in your/house, chief Nɛqāp!ɛnk·ɛm.
I have come, I have come loaded with the/fifteen hundred blankets
the price of War. Now it is gone down. Now I/hire you Gwētɛla and
ˢwālas Kwāg·uɫ and Q!ōmk·!ūt!ɛs to go and invite the/Mamalēleqala
and the ˢnɛmgis and the Ḻāwits!ēs three days from now when I shall
have finished putting up the (15) watchman's pole on account of him
who is being made a chief, this ʟ!āsotiwalis, for/Yāqoʟasɛmē will
now change his name and you will now call him ʟ!āsotiwalis hereafter./
That is all, chiefs. ..nd now I will hire you, song-makers to sing
the/song of taking care of the salmon trap," said he. Then Nɛqāp!-
ɛnk·ɛm thanked him for his speech./

When they had finished their speeches, they all went out of the
house.(20) When it was day in the morning, ʟ!āqoʟas sent four middle-
aged/men to go paddling looking for four tall young cedar trees./
They were to be two spans in diameter at the/butt end and two were
to be fifteen fathoms in length and two/nine fathoms in length. When
the (25) four men had paddled away, ʟ!āqoʟas called in the Q!ōmoyâˢ
yē and the/Gwētɛla and the ˢwālas Kwāg·uɫ and the Q!ōmk·!ūt!ɛs to
go into his/house in the manner of those who invite the tribes, for
the/four Kwāg·uɫ tribes are now one tribe to help each other in everything in all the/ways of those who invite, and this is referred to
by the Indians as treating as chiefs those who invite the (30)tribes.

10

g·uⱡ lāx g·ōkwas ʟ!āqoʟas laas ʟā̱xᵋwalⱡⱬ ʟ!āqoʟasō̄. Wä, lä gwēg̣ᴇ-

māⱬa lāxēs g·ōkŭlōta Q!ōmoyâᵋyē qaᵋs yāq!ᴇg·a³ⱬē. Wä, lä ᵋnēk·e:

Esᵋmaē̱ᴇn wäg·iʟa, nōs g·Ig·ᴇg̣āmēᵋ mōᵋlaⱬtsᴇns qwēsēg·alⱡⱬē g·Ig·ᴇ-

g̣āmēxs g·āxaēx â̱ⱬalⱡ̱ⱬ qaᵋs g·āxē hōʟōlax gwēbiᵋlälasʟasᴇns wâⱬdᴇmʟa,

5   ᵋnēk·ēxs laē̄ nᴇqᴇmg·alⱡ̱ⱬ lāxa k!ŭdzē̄ᵋlasasa Gwē̄tᴇla lā̱x ōgwiwaᵋlī-

ⱬas g·ōkwas. Wä, lä ᵋnēk·a: ᵋwa, g̣ēlag·a Gwētᴇl; ᵋwa, g̣ēlag·a ᵋwā-

las Kwāg·uⱡ; ᵋwa, g̣ēlag·a Q!ōmk·!ŭt!ᴇs. Hēⱬᵋālē̱ⱬ lāxwa g·ōkwilaᵋ-

yaqᴇn qaᵋs g·āx ᵋnāxōs ᵋwiᵋlaē̱ʟaⱡasa yŭdŭx̣ᵘsᴇᵋmakᵂ ᵋwālas lēlqwalaʟē̄

qaxs k·!ēsaⱬx ā̱ⱬᵋᴇm wāⱬdᴇmaxᴇns g·āxēx gwaēᵋlas lāxwa g·ōkwēx, yîxs

10   k·!ātaᵋyaaxsᴇns g·ālᴇmg·alisa qᴇns nᴇgᴇⱬtawēsᴇᵋwaxᴇns g·āxēx gwaē̄-

lasa qᴇn hawāʟōlag̣âlē lāxᴇns ēg·asʟa qō̄ g·āxʟa lēlqwālaʟaᵋya. Wä,

g·aᵋmisēg·a laᵋmē̄ ā̱xsᴇᵋwa dzōdzoxŭlaʟasa k·!ⱥtᴇlaʟa. Wä, laᵋmᴇns

hёx·ᵋidaᴇⱬⱬ ā̱x̣âlsaⱬtsē̄ lāxwa ʟ!āsanâᵋyaxsa g·ōkwē g·Ig·ᴇg̣āmē̄ᵋqᴇn

ᵋnē̄k·ē̄ qaᵋs q!āq!alaⱡg·ayâosax gwaⱡaasasg·în nâqᴇk·, ᵋnē̄k·ē̄.

15   Wä, la nānaxᵋmayē̄ Nᴇqāp!ᴇnk·ᴇmax wāⱬdᴇmas ʟ!āqoʟas. Wä, lä

ᵋnē̄k·a: Qä̱ʟ, qä̱ʟē̄s wāⱬdᴇmōs g·Ig̣āmē̄ᵋ ʟ!āqoʟas. Lē̄qwaᵋwisē̄s wāⱬdᴇmōs

qaxs gwāⱬᴇlaᵋmayŭⱬa xŭlt!alⱥdzᴇma t!ᴇx·ⱥla qaᵋs nᴇgᴇⱬtawēsᴇᵋwōs.Dâ-

xwa k·!ēsᵋâqōsxwa k·!ⱥtᴇlax. Laᵋmō̄ nēⱬᵋidᴇⱬxwa dâdoq!walap!ēqax

g·āg·ⱥʟᴇla lāxēs nŭyᴇmbaᵋyaōs, g·Īg̣āmēᵋ qᴇn ēt!ēdē̄ x·ⱥts!ax·ⱥlaʟō̱ⱬ

20   g·Īg̣āmē̄. ᵋwa, ᵋwa, qᴇn ᵋnēk·ē̄, ᵋnēk·ēxs laē̄ k!wāg·alⱡⱬa. Wä, lä

ʟā̱xᵋwalⱡⱬē̄ Sēxŭqâlaxa g·Īg̣āmaᵋyasa ᵋnᴇᵋmēmotasa Dzᴇndzᴇnx·q!ayo. Wä,

la yāq!ᴇg·aᵋⱬa. Wä, lä ᵋnēk·a: ᵋya, gwāsēg·alⱥt g·Ig·ᴇg̣āmēᵋ. Wŭla-

ʟᴇnʟaxwa g·Īg̣āmaᵋyēx lāxōx ʟ!āqoʟasēx lāx Wīna. ᵋya, g·Īg̣āmēᵋ ʟ!ā-

qoʟas, lᴇᵋmaē̄ lāxa Wīnaʟ, ᵋnēk·ē̄. Wä, hёx·ᵋidaᵋmisē̄ ʟ!āqoʟas ᵋnē̄-

25   k·a: Laᵋmē̄ lāxa Wīnax·dä. Sᴇk·!ap!ᴇnyag·anâla p!ᴇlxᴇlasgᴇmē k·ilō-

maqē̄, ᵋnēk·ē̄. Wä, la Sēxŭqâla wāwidzōlaqŭla. Wä, lä ᵋnēk·a: La-

ᴇm xōʟᴇns g·ēxtōdᴇx Wīnäxa x̣ŭsᴇläsᴇns g·Īg̣āmaᵋyax lāxōx Yāqoʟasᴇmaᵋ-

yēx g·Īqē̄lasᴇᵋwaqōs, g̣Īg̣āmēᵋ ʟ!āqoʟas. Wä, wäg·iⱬla gwāsēg·alē̄ g·Ig·ᴇ-

As soon as the four Kwāg·uɫ tribes had come (1) into the house of ʟ!āqoʟas, then ʟ!āqoʟas stood up and turned his face/to his tribe, the Q!ōmoyâ⁸yē, and he spoke and said:/ "Am I not going to go on, my chiefs, and thank our chief on the far side/for coming quickly to come and listen from end to end to our speeches?" (5) thus he said and looked straight at the place where the Gwētɛla were sitting in the rear of the/house. Then he said: "Now come, Gwētɛla, come/⁸wālas Kwāg·uɫ, come Q!ōmk·!ūt!ɛs. Be comfortable in this house which I built/that you might always come in, you three great tribes,/for this is no new saying that we come thus into this house. For this (10) is laid down by our ancestors that it shall be followed by us that we come and do this way/to ask each other about what will be good for us to do when the tribes will come./Also now these poles for the watchman's pole are being gotten and/at once we will put them up outside the hous , chiefs. That is what I/say, that you may know what I think in my mind," said he.

(15) Then Nɛqāp!ɛnk·ɛm replied to the speech of ʟ!āqoʟas. He/said: "True, true, it is as you say, chief ʟ!āqoʟas. There is no mistake in your speech,/for already long ago the trail was marked out for you to be followed.Look/at this privilege of the watchman's pole.Now the watchman's pole will show itself,/the one that came from the beginning from your myth, chief, and we shall witness it again, (20) chief. Wa wa.That is what.I say," said he and sat down. Then / Sēxŭqâla arose, the chief of the numaym Dzendzɛnx·q!ayu.Then/he spoke and said: "Chiefs of the other side, I shall ask/this chief ʟ!āqoʟas about (the copper) War. Oh chief ʟ!āqoʟas,/now War has been sold (lit. has gone down)." And at once ʟ!āqoʟas said,(25)"War has been sold. Fifteen hundred blankets was its price," said he. Then Sēxŭqâla shouted. "Wo ho ho",(as though he were lifting a heavy weight). Then he said, " Behold, now/we stand on top of War, the acropolis of our chief Yāqoʟasɛmē/who is being made a chief by you, chief ʟ!āqoʟas. Now go on chiefs of this side,/ (1) you will be happy for

gämē^ε ëk·!ᴅqɛlaʟax qa^εs gwäⱡaⱡaðʋ ^εnäxwa qɛns g·iwälaɛnsasa ^εnäxwa
yä^εwinälasð^εsɛns g·Ig·ɛgämä^εyðx läqoʟasɛma^εyax qð g·äxʟa lðlqwäla-
ʟa^εya läxɛns ^εwälasðx g·ðxᵘdɛmsa, ^εnðk·ð.

Wä, la^εmð ʟ!äqoʟasð äxk·!älaxa ^εnäxwa g·Ig·ɛgämðsa mðsgɛ^εmakwð
5 Kwäkwäg·uⱡ qa ^εnäxwðs gwäⱡaⱡa qa^εs g·äxðⱡ qax^εɛlsaⱡxa k·!ﬁtɛlaxa
läʟa ^εnäx·^εIdɛx gaälaʟas ⱡɛnsʟa ^εnðk·ð. Wä, la^εmð ^εwI^εla hðqüwɛls
läxa g·ðkwa bðbɛgwänɛmð. Wä, la^εmðsð dzⁱqwaxs g·äxaðda mðkwð bð-
bɛgwänɛm däpälaxa mðts!aqð dzɛs^εɛqwa qa^εs lä däp!alIsas läx ʟ!ɛmai-
sas g·ðkwas ʟ!äqoʟasð. Wä, g·ﬁl^εmisð ^εnäx·^εIdxa gaäläxs lað ^εyäla-
10 qð ʟ!äqoʟasasa ma^εlðkwð ha^εyäⱡ^εa qa lðs hðlaxa yüduxᵘsɛ^εmakwð Kwä-
kwäg·uⱡ qa g·äxðs ^εwI^εla qäxɛlsaxa k·!ﬁtɛla. Wä, g·ﬁl^εmisð ^εwI^εl-
xtolsðda ma^εlðkwð ha^εyäⱡ^εaxa g·ig·ðkwasa yüduxᵘsɛ^εmakwð Kwäkwäg·uⱡ-
axs lað nä^εnakwa läx g·ðkwas ʟ!äqoʟas. Wä, lä hälamaxsta gaäxstalð-
da ^εnäxwa bðbɛgwänɛm läxðs g·ig·ðkwð. Wä, g·ﬁl^εmisð gwäⱡa lað ^εwI-
15 ^εla^εmäla qäs^εid qa^εs lð k!üs^εɛls laⱡ ʟ!äsanä^εyas g·ðkwas ʟ!äqoʟasð.
Wä, g·äxð ʟ!äqoʟas g·äxawɛls läxðs g·ðkwð qa^εs ʟäx^εwɛlsð läx ʟ!äsa-
nä^εyasa t!ɛx·ﬂäsðs g·ðkwð. Wä, lä yäq!ɛg·a^εⱡa. Wä, lä ^εnðk·a: ^εwa,
gðlag·a g·Ig·ɛgämð läxwa k·!ðsðx äⱡ^εɛm wäⱡdɛma qɛns gwäyi^εlälasa
läxwa wäⱡdɛmaxsɛn qwðsbalisa wIwðmpaxs g·älaðⱡðx nag·ilðsɛns ^εnälax.
20 Wä, g·äx^εɛms nänagaⱡ^εɛnaⱡqð. Wä, wäg·iⱡla g·Ig·ɛgämð^ε qax^εɛlsaⱡxɛn
k!ðs^εoxwa k·!ﬁtɛlaxwa nüyämbalisð k·!ðs^εowün, ^εnðk·ð.

Wä, hðx·^εida^εmisa ^εnäxwa ⱡðläxsdɛk·!In ha^εyäⱡ^εasa yüduxᵘsɛ^εma-
kwð Kwäkwäg·uⱡ xwänaⱡ^εid qa^εs lälag·I qax^εɛlsaxa k·!ﬁtɛla qaxs k·!ð-
sað la g·iwalðda g·Ig·ɛgäma^εyaxa ha^εyäⱡ^εäxs lað ðaxälaxa dzðngayu
25 qa^εs dzðnqustälayuxa k·!ﬁtɛla. Wä, g·ﬁl^εmisð gwäⱡa mðwð dzðdzɛnga-
yuxa g·a gwäⱡðg·a laðda q!ðnɛmð ha^εyäⱡ^εa nðx^εusdðsaxa mðts!-
aqð dzðdzɛs^εɛqwa qa^εs lä k·at!ɛlsas läx ðxwiwa^εyasa ʟ!äsanä-
^εyas g·ðkwas ʟ!äqoʟasð, yIxa ma^εⱡts!aqð g·ﬂsg·ﬂt!a. Wä, laɛm ða-
ba^εyð ʟɛsʟɛxᵘba^εyas.Wä,lä nðx^εusdðsaxa ma^εⱡts!aqð ts!ɛⱡts!ɛkwaga^εya.
30 Wä,laɛm ʟ!ðʟ!asba^εyð ʟɛsʟɛxᵘba^εya. Wä, laɛm k·ak·ɛtäⱡð wIswüⱡba^εyas
ʟð^ε wIswüⱡba^εyasa g·ﬂsg·ﬂt!a;la ^εnäⱡ^εnɛmp!ɛnk· läxɛns bäʟäqð sðxwa-

you all will be ready to help us now in everything that/is asked
by our chief Yāqoụasɛmē'when the tribes will come/to our great
village site here," said he./

Then ʟ!āqoụas asked all the chiefs of the four (5) Kwāg·uⱡ
tribes to be ready to come and put up the watchman's pole/when day
would come in the morning on the following day, he said. Then all/
the men went out of the house. Now in the evening the four/men
came towing the four poles and they towed them to the beach/of the
house of ʟ!āqoụas. As soon as day cāme in the morning (10) ʟ!āqoụas
sent two young men to hire the three Kwāg·uⱡ tribes/that all should
come and put up the watchman's pole. And when the/two young men
had gone to the houses of the three Kwāg·uⱡ tribes/they went home to
the house of ʟ!āqoụas. Then all the men took a quick breakfast/in
their houses. And when they had finished (15) together all went
and sat doụn outside the house of ʟ!āqoụas./ Then ʟ!āqoụas came out
of his house and stood/outside of the door of his house. Then he
spoke and said:/ "Come now, chiefs, to this speech which is not new
that we may act / according to the words of our distant ancestors
(who lived) when our world was first made long ago. (20) Now come
and follow it. Go on, chiefs, and put up the/watchman's pole which
is my privilege, my privilege from my earliest myth," said he./

Then all the strong young men of the three/Kwāg·uⱡ tribes got
ready to go and put up the watchman's pole,/for/the chiefs were not
going to help the young men when they were working with the levers
(25) for the raising of the pole. As soon as the four levers were
finished/in this way, then many young men hauled up from the beach
the four/poles and they put them down on the bank outside of the/
house of ʟ!āqoụas, that is the two long ones. Now the/butt ends
were landward. Then they hauled up the beach the two shorter ones
(30) and their butt ends were seaward. Now they laid together their
thin ends/and the thin ends of the long poles. One fathom was the

yap!alaɛnaɛyasg·a gwäɫēg·a. Wä, lä äxɛēd-
ēda haɛyäɫɛäxa ʟɛkwē dɛnɛɛn dɛnɛm qaɛs yā-
ʟōdēx(1). Wä, lāxaē hēɛm gwēx·ɛîdxa maɛɫts!aqē la gwäɫaatsa g·ālē
äxäs. Wä, la hayaxk·!ōt!abōt lāxɛns bāʟäqē awâlag·âɫaasas laē k·ît-
5 k·at!asa. Wä, lä äxɛēdxa wâkwē ɫat!aakᵘ k!waxʟäɛwaxa ɛnɛmp!ɛnk·ē
lāxɛns q!wâq!wax·ts!änaɛyē wâdzɛɛwasas.Wä,lä ɛnɛmp!ɛnk·ē wäsgɛmasas
lāxɛns bāʟax.Wä,lä gēg·aaʟɛlōts lāx 1 ,qaɛs yîɫɛaʟɛlōdēs wäx·sbaɛyas
lax 1. Wä, laɛm ɛwîts!â lāx ɛnɛmp!ɛnk· lāxɛns bāʟäqē awâlagâlaasa
dzōdzɛsɛɛqwē. Wä, g·îlɛmisē gwäɫa laē k!wētustolsax 1, qaɛs g·î-
10 buyōdēq qag·äs gwäɫag·a. Wä, lä äxɛēdxa
mōwē dzēngayu qaɛs dzēnqustâlēxa k·!îtɛla.
Wä, g·îlɛmisē gwäɫa laē g·a gwäɫēg·a. Wä,
laɛmē qaxɛâlisa k·!îtɛla. Wä, lä ʟapɛmg·a-
aʟɛladayuwa gēg·idamas. Wä, laɛm yāgwēx·-
15 sa t!ɛx·îɫdɛnaxs laē gwäɫa k·!îtɛla. Wä,
lä päxaʟɛlōdayuwa ʟâdzɛɛwēsɛɛwasa dâdoq!wala bɛgwānɛm lāx ōxtâwaɛ-
yasa k·!îtɛla lāx 1. Wä, g·îlɛmisē gwäɫa laē äxɛētsɛɛwa g·îlt!a
dɛnɛma qaɛs lē yîɫɛaʟɛlōdayu lāx 2, yîx ōbaɛyaṣa g·îlt!a dɛnɛma.
Wä, la äxɛētsɛɛwē äpsbaɛyas qaɛs lē qɛx·sɛmdayu lāxa ɛwälasē t!ēsɛm
20 3 lāxa ʟ!ɛmaisē. Wä, g·îlɛmisē gwäɫa laas yāq!ɛg·aɫē Sēxûqâla.
Wä, lē ɛnēk·a: ɛwa, äɫ.g·îg·ɛgämēɛ. Laɛms gwäɫämasxwa ɛwälasēx
k·!ēsɛosɛn g·îgɛmaɛyaē Yāqoʟasɛmaɛya, ɛnēk·ēxs laē gwēgɛmx·ɛîd lāx
t!ɛx·îläs g·ōkwas ʟ!âqoʟas. Wä, la ɛnēk·a: Gēlag·aɫla g·îgämēɛʟ!â-
qoʟas ʟɛɛwōs g·îqēlasɛɛwaq!ōsxōx Yāqoʟasɛmaɛyax. Laɛmk· gwäɫɛɛlsg·as
25 ɛwälasg·ōs k·!ēsɛâ, g·îgämēxg·ada yaq!wēmag·asēs qwēsbalisaōs gagɛm-
paxs g·âlaōɫē ɛnäg·îlēsɛns ɛnälax. ɛwa, gēlag·a. g·îgämēɛqɛn x·îts!a-
x·ɛîdaōʟ, ɛnēk·ēxs laē k!wäg·aɛlsa.
      Wä, g·äxē g·äxawɛlsē ʟ!âqoʟas lāx t!ɛx·îläsēs g·ōkwē qaɛs lē
ʟâxɛwɛls lāxa nɛxwäɫa lāx ōxʟalasa k·!îtɛla laqēxs gümēkwaasa gümsē.
30 Wä, lä qɛx·ɛmälaxa lälaxwiwaɛyē ts!ōɫdzâ. Wä, lä ʟâsaɫēda maɛɫts!a-
qē ɛmɛla ts!ɛlts!ɛlk·sa kwēkwē lāx aɛwâp!aɛyas x·ōmsas. Wä, lä

(1) amount of their overlapping in this way. Then the young men
took/stout cedar bark rope and/tied them together at 1 And they did
the same with the two others as they had done with the one/they did
first, and half a fathom was the distance between them as they lay/
(5) on the ground. Then they took thick split cedar wood one/span
wide and one fathom long/and they put it across at 1 and they tied
both ends/to 1. Now three-fourths of a fathom was the distance between the/cedar-poles. When it was finished they raised it at 1
and (10) put a support under it in this way. Then they took the/
four levers and raised up the watchman's pole, / and when it was
done it was in this way. Now/the pole had been raised up and they
nailed the/cross bars on to it. Now it was like a (15) ladder when
they were finished. Then/they put on it a flat board as a standing
place for the watchman on top of the/watchman's pole at 1. When
it was finished they took a long/rope and it was tied at 2, namely
the end of the long rope,/and they took the other end and it was
tied to a large stone (20) 3 on the beach. When this was finished Sĕxŭ-
qâla spoke/and said, "Oh new chiefs, you have finished this great/
(watching pole which is) the privilege of our chief Yāqoʟasɛmēᵋ,"
thus he said and turned his face to the/door of the house to ʟ!āqo-
ʟas. Then he said, "Come, chief ʟ!āqoʟas,/and the one whom you are
making a chief, Yāqoʟasɛmēᵋ. Now it is finished, the (25) great
(watchman's pole which is) your privilege, chief, which was given to
you by your grandfather at the far end,/when first our world was
lighted up. Come, chief, and let me watch you,"/said he as he sat
down./

Then ʟ!āqoʟas came out of the door of his house and/stood near
the lower end of the watchman's pole, and he was painted with ochre.
(30) He had around his head a black kerchief and there were standing up two/white tail feathers of the eagle at the back of his head,

nɛxᵋunālaxa qotsɛmē. Wä, lä wŭsēg·oyâlaxēs wŭsēg·ano. Wä, lä hēlo-
kŭᵋyāla ᵋnɛxᵋunālaxa ᵋmɛla ōx̣ᵘsaakᵘ p!ɛlxɛlasgɛma. Wä, lä yāq!ɛg·aᵋ-
ɫa. Wä, lä ᵋnēk·a: Laɛmk·, laɛms gwāɫamasg·în k·!ēsᵋokᵘ, g·Ig·ɛgä-
mēᶜ. Wä, gēlak·asᵋla, wäx·sonōkwasōᵋs g·Ig·ɛgāmēᶜ. Laᵋmēsɛn lāɫ qɛn

5   lē dōx̣ᵋwîdqē qō g·āx̣ᵋɛm.lax wɛyuq!wax·iwaᵋyɛn k·!ōtɛla lāxg·ada k·!î-
tɛlak·xg·ada k·!ēsak· āɫᵋɛm sɛnaᵋyaxg·ada nŭyämbalisɛk· k·!ēsᵋâ,
k·!ēsᵋosɛn gagɛmpaxa g·ālaōɫēx ᵋnāg·flîsɛns ᵋnālax, ᵋnēk·ēxs laē
gwēgɛmx·ᵋîd lāxa k·!îtɛla qaᵋs lē dzɛlx·ustâ lāq qaᵋs lē ḷâdzōdxa
ḷaxwadzaᵋwēg·iᵋlakᵘ lāx ōxtâᵋyasa k·!îtɛla.

10   Wä, lä äxIgiɫtawēsēs hēɫk·!ōts!ānaᵋyē qaᵋs dōqwaḷēxa ʟ!āsakwē.
Wä, laᵋmē ᵋnēk·a häsɛla: Hā, hä, hā, hŭ, ᵋwa. Wä, lä yāq!ɛg·aᵋɫa. Wä,
lä ᵋnēk·a: G·āx̣ᵋɛmk· wɛyuq!wax·Iwēg·în k·!ōtɛlak· lāxg·în ḷāwayukᵘ,
g·Ig·ɛgämēᶜ, ᵋnēk·ēxs laē ēdzaqwa ᵋnēk·a: Hā, hä, hā, hŭ, ᵋwä.Wä,
lāxaē ᵋnēk·a: G·āx̣ᵋɛmk· wɛyuq!wax·Iwēg·în k·!ōtɛlak· lāxg·în ḷāwa-

15 yukᵘ, g·Ig·ɛgämēᶜ. Wä, lä hamōp!ɛnago ᵋnēk·a laas yāq!ɛg·aᵋɫēda g·a-
yōɫē lāxa ᵋnɛᵋmēmotasa Kŭkwāk!ŭmasa Q!ōmoyâᵋyēxa ḷēgadäs Hawîlkŭlaɫ.
Wä, lä ᵋnēk·a: Wäg·adzâ g·Igämē ʟ!āqoḷas, wat!ēdag·a qaᵋs maɫt!ēx·ᵋ-
îdaōsax k·!ōtɛlaēnaᵋyaxsōx mäts!ᴀwäxsōs ʟāwayâqōs, g·Igämēᶜ, ᵋnēk·ē.
Wä, la ʟ!āqoḷas nānaxᵋmēq. Wä, lä ᵋnēk·a: ēx·ᵋmis wāɫdɛmōs, g·Igämēᶜ.

20 Laᵋmɛn wat!ēdeɫ, ᵋnēk·ēxs laē dāx·ᵋîdxa dɛnɛmē,3, qaᵋs nēxᵋîdēq.Wä,
lä yāq!ɛg·aᵋɫa. Wä, lä ᵋnēk·a: ᵋya, g·Ig·ɛgämēᶜ; gŭnt!aɛmg·ada k·!ō-
tɛlak· mäts!âsg·în ḷāwayukᵘ g·ad Wīnak·xg·ada mäts!ᴀk·, ᵋnēk·ēxs
g·āxaē g·āxaxa. Wä, lä ḷāxᵋwɛls lāx ōx̣ᵘsîdzaᵋyasa k·!îtɛla. Wä,lä
ᵋyālagIlasa haᵋyāɫᵋa qa läs gɛmxawɛlsaxa lāk·!ɛndē p!ɛlxɛlasgɛm lāx

25 g·ōkwas. Wä, laɛm wŭsēk·as lāxa Gwētɛla ʟɛᵋwa ᵋwālas Kwāg·uɫ ʟɛᵋwa
Q!ōmk·!ŭt!ɛs lāx gwēk·!ālasasēxs laē yāqwasa p!ɛlxɛlasgɛmē lāxa ᵋnāxwa bēbɛgwānɛma, yîxs ᵋnēk·aē: Laɛms wŭsēg·adɛsēqai ōx̣ᵘsaakᵘ p!ɛlxɛ-
lasgɛm. Wä, la ᵋnāxwaɛm hē gwēk·!ālaxa bēbɛgwānɛmē. Wä, g·flᵋmisē
gwāɫ wŭsēk·asasa p!ɛlxɛlasgɛmaxs laē nēɫaxa yŭduxᵘsēᵋmakwē Kwākwāg·u-

30 ɫaxs lɛᵋmaē q!ɛmdîɫaɫxa dzāqwa. Wä, laᵋmē gwāɫē wāɫdɛmas lāxēq.

and he (1) wore a blue blanket, and he as belted with a belt, and
he had over his/blanket a single white blanket. Then he spoke/and
said, " Now you have finished this that is my privilege, chiefs./
Thank you for what you tried to do, chiefs. Now I will go and (5)
look to see whether my schools of salmon have arrived on this watchman's pole,/this which is not a new device, this privilege which comes
from the very beginning of my myth,/the privilege of my grandfather
when long ago our world first became light." Thus he said and turned
his face to the watchman's pole, and he ran up and stood on the/
place made for standing on at the top of the watchman's pole.

(10) Then he shaded his eyes with his right hand and stood looking seaward./ Then he said aloud, " Hā, hā hā hū, ᵋwā." Then he
spoke and/said, " My schools of salmon are coming to my salmon weir
here,/chiefs.' Thus he said and he said again, "Hā, hā hā hū, ᵋwā."
Then/he said again, " My schools of salmon are coming to my salmon
weir here,(15) chiefs." Four times he said thus. Then spoke/one
who belonged to the nuṃaym Kükwāk!ŭm of the Q!ōmoyāᵋyē and whose name
was Hawīlkŭlaⱡ/and said, " Now go on, chief ʟ!āqoᶸas, haul in hard
that you may ascertain/what kind of salmon it is that you got in your
salmon weir, chief," thus said he./ Then ʟ!āqoᶸas answered him and
said, " Your word is good, chief. (20) Now I will haul it in, " said
he and took hold of the rope 3 and pulled it. Then/he spoke and said,
" Oh chiefs, heavy is this salmon,/caught in my salmon weir here.
This is War, the salmon in it, " said he/as he came down. Then he
stood at the foot of the watchman's pole and/sent the young men into
the house to go and bring out one hundred blankets from (25) his
house. He was going to belt with them the Gwētɛla and the ᵋwālas
Kwāg·uⱡ and the/Qŏmk·!ŭt!ɛs, as they say when they give away blankets
to all the/men. Then he said, " Now you have for a belt this single
blanket,"/he said this to all the men. As soon as he/had finished
giving belts with the blankets, he told the three Kwāg·uⱡ tribes (30)
to sing in the house that evening. Now they finished their speeches

Wä, laᵋmē ᵋwĪᶜla näᵋnakwa bēbɛgwānɛmē lāxēs g·ig·ōkwē qaᶜs lä ʟ!āxwa.

Wä, g·fĪᶜmisē dzāxq!ālaxs laēda maᶜlōkwē q!ŭlsq!ŭlyakᵘ q!ɛm-
dilalaxa Gwētɛla ʟɛᶜwa ᶜwālas Kwāg·uɫē ʟɛᶜwa Q!ōmk·!ŭt!ɛsē. Wä,
g·fĪᶜmisē laēʟ lāxa t!ɛx·flāsa g·ōkwasa Gwētɛla laē ᶜnēk·a ᶜnɛmō-
5 kwē q!ŭlyakwa: Laᶜmɛnuᶜxᵘ q!ɛmdilālaloʟai Gwētɛlai qaɛns g·ĭgāmaᶜ-
yē Yāqoʟasɛmaᶜyai, ᶜnēk·ē. Wä, lēda ᶜnɛmōkwē q!ŭlyakᵘ ᶜnēk·a:
Hălag·fĪiʟasai. Wä, g·fĪᶜmisē lāg·aa lāx g·ōkwasa ᶜwālas Kwāg·uɫ
laē ᶜnēk·a: Laᶜmɛnuᶜxᵘ q!ɛmdilāloʟai ᶜwālas Kwāg·uɫai qaɛns g·ĭgā-
maᶜyē Yāqoʟasɛmaᶜyai, ᶜnēk·ē. Wä, lāxaēda ᶜnɛmōkwē q!ŭlyakᵘ ᶜnēk·a:
10 Hălag·fĪiʟasai, ᶜnēk·ē. Wä, g·fĪᶜmisē lāg·aa lāx g·ōkwasa Q!ōmk·!ŭ-
t!ɛsē laē ɓɛm nɛgɛɫtodxēs gwēk·!ālasaxa Gwētɛla ʟɛᶜwa ᶜwālas Kwā-
g·uɫē. Wä, g·fĪᶜmisē ᶜwĪᶜlxtolsaxa g·ig·ōkŭläxs laē aēdaaqa. Wä,
âᶜmisē nɛxsɛmliɫaxa nēnâgadäxs laē ᶜwĪᶜla k!ŭdzĬɫ lāx g·ōkwas ʟ!ā-
qoʟas. Wä, la ᶜnēk·a nēnâgadē qaᶜs hēᶜmē dɛnxᶜĪdayuwa nŭyämbalisē
15 q!ɛmdɛmsa g·ālōɫa ʟ̣ōgwalaxa k·!Ĭtɛla, yĬx Yĭx·āgɛmaᶜyē, yĬx aᶜwā-
näᶜyasa Yaēx·agɛmaᶜyasa Q!ōmoyâᶜyē. Wä, la hēɫᶜaʟalɛmē wäɫdɛmas
lāx ʟ!āqoʟasē. Wä,.g·fĪᶜmisē g·āx ᶜwĪᶜlaēʟa yŭduxᵘsɛᶜmakwē Kwākwā-
g·uɫ lāx g·ōkwas ʟ!āqoʟas laas ʟaxᶜwāliɫē ʟ!āqoʟas qaᶜs yāq!ɛg·aᶜɫē.
Wä, la ᶜnēk·a gwēgɛmaɫa lāxa Q!ōmoyâᶜyē lāqēxs häē k!ŭdziɫa g·ĭg·ɛ-
20 gɛmaᶜyasēda hēɫk·!ostâliɫasa t!ɛx·flāsa g·ōkwē. Wä, hēt!a lä haᶜ-
yāɫᶜäsēda ōgwiwaᶜliɫasa g·ōkwē: Laᶜmɛn wäg·fĪ nōs g·ĭg·ɛgämēᶜ, mōᶜ-
laɫtsɛns g·ĭg·ɛgämaᶜyaxs g·āxaē lāxwa k·!ēsēx āɫᶜɛm wäɫdɛm qɛns
gwayiᶜlälasaxwa g·āxa qɛns gwaēlas lāxwa g·ōkwēx, ᶜnēk·ēxs laē gwē-
gɛmx·ᶜĬd lāxa gɛmxotstâliɫasa t!ɛx·flāsa g·ōkwē qaxs häē k·!ŭdziɫa
25 g·ĭg·ɛgämaᶜyasa yŭduxᵘsɛᶜmakwē Kwākwäg·uɫa. Wä, lä ᶜnēk·a: ᶜwa, gē-
lag·a, qwēsēg·aliɫ g·ĭg·ɛgämēᶜlāxwa lāxwa k·!ēsēx āɫᶜɛm wäɫdɛmaxwa
wäɫdɛmaxsɛns gagɛmpa lāxa qwēsɛlä ᶜnālaxwa xŭtaᶜyē qɛns ɓɛm nɛgɛɫᶜ-
ɛnēsɛᶜwa, ᶜnēk·ēxs laē gwēgɛmx·ᶜĬd lāxa ōgwiwaliɫasa g·ōkwē. Wä, lä
ᶜnēk·a: Wäg·fĬɫla nēnâgad, dɛnxᶜĬtsɛn gāgayäᶜlayâ k·!āk·!Ĭtɛlak·!āla

with this,(1) and all the men went home to their houses to eat./

As soon as evening came two old men/ asked to sing in the house
the Gwētɛla and the ᵋwālas Kwāg·uł and the Q!ōmk·!ūt!ɛs. When/they
went to the doors of the houses of the Gwētɛla one of the (5) old
men said, " We come to ask you to sing in the house, Gwētɛla, for
our chief/ Yāqoʟasɛmēᵋ, " said he. Then the other old man said,/
" Go there quickly. " And when they came to the houses of the ᵋwālas Kwāg·uł/he said, " We come to ask you to sing in the house,ᵋwā-
las Kwāg·uł, for our/chief, Yāqoʟasɛmēᵋ, " said he, and the other old
man said, (10) " Go there quickly, " said he. And when they arrived
at the houses of the Q!ōmk·!ūt!ɛs / they followed the same way as
they had said to the Gwētɛla and the ᵋwālas Kwāg·uł./ And when
they had gone to all the houses they went back again, and/they just
met the song leaders who were all sitting down in the house of ʟ!ā-
qoʟas./ And the song leaders said that the song of the earliest
myth (15) would be sung, of him who first obtained as a supernatural
gift the watchman's pole, that Yīx·āgɛmēᵋ, the / root of the Yaēx·a-
gɛmēᵋ of the Q!ōmoyạyē. Then their speech was agreeable/to ʟ!ā-
qoʟas. As soon as the three Kwāg·uł tribes had all come into/ the
house of ʟ!āqoʟas,ʟ!āqoʟas arose and spoke./ He said, turning his
face to the Q!ōmoyâᵋyē where the chiefs were sitting (20) at the
right hand side of the door of the house, and the/young men went to
the rear of the house. " Now, my chiefs,/I will thank you, our
chiefs, for coming here. It is not a new saying according to which
we/go when you come to be thus in this house, " thus he said and/
turned his face to the left hand side of the door of the house, for
there were sitting the (25) chiefs of the three Kwāg·uł tribes. And
now he said, "Now/come, you chiefs of the other side of the house.
for this is not a new saying this/saying of our grandfather in the
far end of the world, this that is marked down for us to go by, " /
thus he said and turned his face to the rear of the house and said,
" Now go on, song leaders, sing the song that comes from my grand-

q!ɛmdɛma, εnēk·ēxs laē k!wāg·aliʟa. Wä, hëx·εidaεmisa nâgadē dâqâlasa gagaεyāla k·!āk·!îtɛlak·!āla q!ɛmdɛmaxa εnēk·ē:

Hā, laεmɛn dōxεwaʟɛla lahak·asεmɛn dōxεwaʟɛla lāx mɛyâ.
Hē yā hē yā hâ hâ.
G·āxεmōx g·āxεwɛstahēsɛla q!awap!ɛlahēdzēk·as q!ēq!alanɛmk·asahâ
Hē yā hē yā hâ hâ.
εyäg·anōtâsaēnētsɛnosäyâhâ k·!îtɛlayuk·asεo
Hē yā hē yā hâ hâ.

Wä, maʟp!ɛng·ustâεmisa nēnâgadē dɛnxεīts, laē gwāʟa. Wä, la ʟāxεwalēʟē ʟ!āqoʟas, qäʟaxs lɛεmaē ɛlxᵘsēs xūnōkwē Yāqoʟasɛmaεyē. Wä, lä yāq!ɛg·aεʟa. Wä, lä εnēk·a: Laɛms āʟ g·īg·ɛgămē, gwaʟεalīʟa lāxwa dɛnxaläyâqōsxɛn gagɛmpēxwa q!ɛmdɛmēx. εwa, gēlak·asεlax·ēk·, gēlak·asεlaxa nēnâgadäxs q!ālaεmaaqᵘ. Wä, wëg·a âɛm yāʟ!âq qaεs ăxēlaōsaq; wä, sōεmisʟaʟ g·īg·ɛgămēε, wä, sōdzēmisʟaʟ g·īg·ɛgămēs Gwētel, εwālas Kwāg·uʟ, Q!ōmk·!ūt!ɛs. Laɛms wūʟɛlax. Laɛms wūʟāxεaʟɛlax k·!āk·!îtɛlak·!āla q!ɛmdɛmsɛn nūyămbalisēxɛn gagɛmpē ʟ!āsotiwalisēxɛn g·īqag·iwaεyaxs g·ālaōʟēx εnāg·īlisɛns εnālax, yîx Yîx·āgɛmaεyē, wä, hëɛm la ʟēgadɛs ʟ!āsotiwalisē, Yāqoʟasɛmaεyē, G·īxsēεstalisɛmaεyē ʟ!āqoʟas. Häεstaɛm ʟēʟɛgɛms Yîx·āgɛmaεyē. Wä, laεmēts ʟēqɛlaʟɛs ʟ!āsotiwalisē lāx Yāqoʟasɛmaεyē qaεs gwāʟɛlaεmaōs q!āq!alaʟg·îyuqōxs lɛεmaēx ʟ!āyuxʟä. Wä, laεmɛns lāʟ g·īgɛgămēε. Laεmɛns lāʟax gāālaʟa ʟēʟɛlaʟxa Mamalēleqāla ʟōε εnɛmgisē ʟɛεwa Lāwits!ēs qa g·āxlag·īs lāxwa εwālasēx aεwīnagwisa.

Wä, lä ʟāxεwālīʟē K·!âdēxa g·ayoʟē lāx εnɛεmēmotasa Kūkwāk!ūmasa Gwētɛla qaεs yāq!ɛg·aεʟē. Wä, lä εnēk·a: εwa, g·īgămēε; εwa, laεmē gwāʟēs wāʟdɛmaōs,g·īgămēε ʟ!āqoʟas ʟɛεwūns xūnōkwaxōxda g·īgɛmäεyaxōx ʟ!āsotiwalisaxwa g·īgămäεnaxwäq!ɛns gwāsx·äla g·äg·îlisɛxs g·alaōʟēx εnāg·îlisɛns εnālaxwa nɛnōlâx g·īgămaεyaxwa waεyadäx g·äg·îlis lāxa qwēsɛla εnāla. Wä, laɛms εnēk·ēda g·īgămēε qɛns lā-

fathers, the song of the watchman's pole,"(1)thus he said and sat
down. Immediately the song leaders gave out the song/coming from
the grandfathers, the song of the watchman's pole, which said:/

    1. Now I see it, now I see it, the salmon./

        Hē yā hē yā hâ hâ./

(5) 2. It is coming up stream with a great wave following, what I
                obtained by purifying myself./

        Hē yā hē yā hâ hâ./

    3. You were overcome by me on account of this watchman's pole./(?)

        Hē yā hē yā hâ hâ.

Twice the song leaders sang it and then they stopped. Then (10)
ᴸǃāqoʟas arose, for indeed he was now the attendant of his son Yāqoʟasɛmē./ Then he spoke and said, " Now chiefs, you have finished
in the house/with this that has been sung, the song of my grandfather.
Thank you,/thank you, song leaders, for knowing it. Now go on, take
care and/keep it in mind. And you, great chiefs of the Gwētɛla (15)
and the ᵋwālas Kwāg·uɬ and the Qǃōmk·ǃūtǃɛs, now you hear it, now
you hear it suddenly,/the song of the watchman's pole, which comes
from the oldest myth of my grandfather, ᴸǃāsotiwalis,/the chief ahead
of me (that is in the beginning) when first our world became light,
that Yîx·āgɛmēᵋ,/he whose names were ᴸǃāsotiwalis, Yāqoʟasɛmē, G·îx-
sēᵋstalīsɛmēᵋ,/ᴸǃāqoʟas. All these are the names of Yîx·āgɛmēᵋ.Now
you will call(20)Yāqoʟasɛmēᵋ ᴸǃāsotiwalis for it is known by you
already/that he will change his name. Now let us go, chiefs. Let us
go/in the morning and call the Mamalēleqāla and the ᵋnɛmgis and the
Lāwitsǃēs, that/they may come to this great country."

Then K·ǃâdē arose, who belongs to the Kūkwākǃûm (25) of the
Gwētɛla, and spoke and said, " Oh chief,/now it is finished, your
speech, chief ᴸǃāqoʟas, and our son,/this chief ᴸǃāsotiwalis, this
our chief who comes from the beginning when first/our world became
light, this reckless chief who has no mercy,/from the distant beginning of our world. Now you say,chief,that(1)we shall invite

lag·i ʟēx̣elaxwa lēɛlqwălaʟaɛyax x̣ɛnsʟa. Wä, wĕg·fx̣lax·îns x̂ɛmx̣ gā-
g·ustâʟɛx gaālaʟa g·ōx̣g·ŭkŭlōt, ɛnēk·ē. Wä, laɛm gwāx̣ lāx̣ēq.

    Wä, laɛmē ɛwiɛla hōquwɛls lāxa g·ōkwē qaɛs lē ɛwiɛla nǟɛnakᵘ
lāx̣ēs g·ig·ōkwē. Wä, laɛm hëx·ɛidaɛm xwānax̣ɛidēda ɛnāx̣ɛnɛmōkwē lāx
g·ig·ɛgămaɛyasa q!ɛʟ!ɛsgɛɛmak!ŭs ɛnāx̣ɛnɛɛmēmatsa Gwētɛla,hëɛmisa
ɛnɛmōkwē g·igămēsa ɛnɛɛmēmotasa Dzɛndzɛnx·q!ayo; hëɛmisa ɛnɛɛmōkwē
g·igămēsa Wāwŭlibâɛyē. Wä, la ɛnɛmōkᵘ g·igămaɛyasa ʟ̣ēʟɛgēdē, ɛnē-
ɛnɛmok!wa hägowa g·ig·ɛgămaɛyē lāx̣ k!wēmsa ʟēx̣tsaɛyâs ʟ!āsotiwali-
saxa lēɛlqwalaʟaɛyē lāx gwēg·iɛlasasa g·ālē bāk!umxs ʟēx̣elaēs g·i-
gămaɛyē, yîx lāg·ix̣as hö gwēg·ilēda ɛnāxwa g·ig·ɛgămaɛya,yîxs ɛnē-
k·aē qaɛs g·awālap!ē, yîxs ʟēx̣elaaxa lēɛlqwălaʟaɛyē qaxs ɛnāxwaɛma-
ēda g·ig·ɛgămaɛyē g·ig·aēqɛla qaɛs ʟēx̣qwălaʟaɛyē.

    Wä, g·îlɛmisē ɛnāx·idxa gaāla laē ʟaxɛida. Wä, laɛmē ʟ!ax·ʟ!a-
līdzɛmga, yîx gɛnɛmas ʟ!āqoʟas, yîx lāg·ix̣as ʟ!ax·ʟ!alīdzɛmga qaɛs
haɛmēx·silē qa haɛmāsa g·ig·ɛgămaɛyē k!wēms ʟ!āqoʟas. Wä, hëɛmisē
ʟ!ax·ʟ!alīdzɛmga yîxs hëɛmaē q!äg·ēx wāxaasasa p!ɛlxɛlasgɛmē x̣ādā-
gwayusa ɛnāxwa lēɛlqwālaʟaɛya lāx gwēg·ilasas gɛgɛnɛmasa ɛnāxwa g·i-
g·ɛgămēsa ɛnāxwa lēɛlqwălaʟaɛya lax wāx̣dɛɛmēnaɛyasa bāk!umē, yîxs
ɛnēk·aaq hëɛm nâgats!ēsa g·ig·ɛgămaɛyēs gɛgɛnɛmē. Wä, âlaɛmis lāxɛn
nōsē dōqwaʟaēnēq. Wä, laɛmē lāg·aa lāx ɛyîlīsē hängāmlisēxa g·ōkŭ-
la. Wä, lä ʟāxɛwāʟaxsē ʟ!āqoʟas lāxēs ʟēx̣ɛɛlats!ē xwāk!ŭna. Wä,
lä yāq!ɛg·aɛx̣a. Wä, lä ɛnēk·a꞉ G·āxɛmɛn g·āxɛaʟɛla ɛnɛmgis lāxōs
lax·dɛmsaqōs, ɛnēk·ēxs laē ɛlāqŭlaq. Laɛms x·its!ax·flaʟōlai ɛnɛm-
gisai lāx ʟāʟēliʟai xŭnōkwas ʟ!āsotiwalisai halaxsʟasai; ɛnēk·ēxs
laē k!wāg·aax̣axsa. Wä, lēda bɛgwānɛmē g·āyox̣ lāxa ɛnɛmg·isē ʟāx̣ɛ-
wɛls lāx ʟ!āsanx̣ɛyas g·ōkwas K!wāmaxalasxa g·igămaɛyasa ɛnɛɛmēmotasa G·ig·flgămasa ɛnɛmgis. Wä, lä ɛnēk·a꞉ Laɛmɛn ʟēɛlāloʟai wīnai
qaɛs g·āxaōs tǟlts!a lāxg·a g·ōkwas K!wāmaxalasai. Laɛmk· lâqwiɛla-
kwai, ɛnēk·ē. Wä, hëx·ɛidaɛmisē āʟaxʟax·ɛidēda ʟēx̣ɛɛlats!ē xwāk!ŭ-
na qaɛs ɛmōx̣tâlēxēs ɛmɛmɛwāla qaɛs lē ɛmewiʟɛlas lāx g·ōkwas K!wā-

the tribes tomorrow. Let us arise/early in the morning, tribes,"
he said. Now this is the end./

Then they all went out of the house and went home/to their
houses, and immediately one(5)chief of each of the six numayms of
the Gwētɛla made ready,and also/one chief of the numaym Dzɛndzɛnx·-
q!ayu and also one/chief of the Wāwŭlibᵃᵋyē and one chief of the
ᴸēᴸɛgēd,/nine chiefs in all,and they went as a crew of the inviting
canoe of ᴸ!āsotiwalis,/going to the tribes in the way which was done
by the early Indians when a chief goes inviting.(10)And this is the
reason why all the chiefs do this when they wish/to help one another
when they invite the tribes, for all/the chiefs have it in their minds
to invite the tribes./

As soon as day came in the morning they started. Then ᴸ!ax·ᴸ!a-
lĭdzɛmga,/the wife of ᴸ!āqoᴸas, went, and this was the reason for
ᴸ!ax·ᴸ!alĭdzɛmga that (15) she was going to cook the food to be eat-
en by the chiefs,the crew of ᴸ!āqoᴸas,and also that/ᴸ!ax·ᴸ!alĭdzɛm-
ga counted the number of blankets loaned out by/all the tribes in
the way as it is done by the wives of all the chiefs/of all the
tribes, as it is said by all the Indians. For/they say that the wives
are the receptacles of the wisdom of the chiefs, and this is true
according to what (20) I see among them. Now they arrived at ᵋyflĭs,
and the canoe stopped in front of the village./ Then ᴸ!āqoᴸas stood
up in the inviting canoe./ He spoke and said: " I have come, I have
come, ᵋnɛmgis, to your/camp site," said he as he called out to them.
" Now you will be witnesses, ᵋnɛmgis,/to see ᴸāᴸēlīᴸa, the child of
ᴸ!āsotiwalis. Come quickly in your canoes," said he (25) and he sat
down in his canoe. Then a man belonging to the ᵋnɛmgis stood up/
outside of the house of K!wāmaxalas,chief of the numaym/G·Ig·flgăm
of the ᵋnɛmgis, and said: " I invite you, warriors,/to come and warm
yourselves in the house of K!wāmaxalas. Now the fire has been made
there,"/said he. Immediately the inviting canoe went ashore, stern
first (30) and they unloaded their cargo and they carried it into

maxalas. Wä, g·îlᵉmisē gwāźa laē k!ŭsᵉālîźa ʟēźtsaᵉyu bēbᴇgwanᴇna.

Wä, laᵉmē K!wāmaxalas ᵉyālaqasa haᵉyāźᵉa qa lēᵉs k!wāk!wamilalaxa
ᵉnᴇmgisē qa g·āxēs ᵉwīᶜlaēʟᴇla lāx g·ōkwas. Wä, lēda q!ēnᴇmō hăᵉ-
yāźᵉasa ᵉnᴇmgisē lālaēʟ!a lāxa g·ig·ōkwasa ᵉnᴇmgisē. Wä, lä ᵉnēk·a

5 lāx āᵉwīʟᴇläsa t!ᴇx·îla: G·āxᵉmᴇnuᵉxᵘ k!wăk!wāᵉmilalōʟai ᵉnᴇmgisai
qaᵉs laōs hōʟēlaxōx wāźdᴇmiᵉläläxsa wînax, ᵉnēk·a ᵉnᴇmōkwē. Wä, lä.
ᵉnēk·a waōkwē hăᵉyāźᵉa; Halag·ălîʟasai. ᵉnᴇmp!ᴇnats!axstᴇlaᴇmʟᴇnuᵉxᵘ,
ᵉnēk·ē. Wä, hēx·ᵉidaᵉmisa ᵉnā͟xwa bēbᴇgwānᴇmsa ᵉnᴇmgisē la hōgwîʟ
lāxa g·ōkwas K!wāmaxalasē qaᵉs lē k!ŭsᵉālîʟ lāxa wāx·sanēgwiźasa

10 g·ōkwē qaxs hēē k!udzīźa ʟēźtsayu Kwākŭg·uźa ōgwiwaᵉlîźasa g·ōkwē.
Wä, lēx·aᵉmē ʟ!ax·ʟ!älîdzᴇmga, yîx gᴇnᴇmas ʟ!āqoʟas k·!ēs la k!wā-
gēlîźxa ʟēźtsayu Kwākŭg·uźa wāx·ᵉmaē hēᴇm g·aēʟelē. Wä, laᵉmē ʟ!ᴇ-
xwēda ʟēźtsaᵉyu. Wä, lāxaēda ᵉnᴇmgis ʟ!āʟ!āwāla. Wä, g·îlᵉmisē
gwāź ʟ!ᴇxwaxs laē ᵉwīᵉla g·īxasᴇᵉwa hēᵉmaats!ēxa źōᴇlq!wē. Wä,g·îl-

15 ᵉmisē gᵥ̌āźa laas ʟax̌ŭlîźē ʟ!āqoʟas qaᵉs yāq!eg·aᵉźē. Wä, la ᵉnēk·a
gwēgᴇmāźa lāxēs k!wēmē; Qäʟ̌a g·îg·ᴇgāmēē qäʟ̌ōx nâqaᵉyaxsa g·îgāmaᵉ-
yōx K!wāmaxalasēx, yîxs ᵉnēk·aēx qᴇns g·āxē ts!ᴇlqŭmg·aᵉlîź lāxōx
g·ōkwas ʟ!adâ. Wä, laᵉmēsᴇn wēg·iź. Laᵉmēsᴇn mōᵉlaźtsa ᵉnᴇmgisaxs
g·āxaēx āźtsᴇmō g·āxᴇns, ᵉnēk·ēxs laē gwēgᴇmx·ᵉîd lāxa t!ᴇx·îläsa

20 g·ōkwē. Wä, lä ᵉnēk·a; ᵉwa, g·āxᵉᴇms g·îg·ᴇgāmēs ᵉnᴇmgis ᵉwīᵉlaē-
ʟᴇla laxōxda g·ōkwaxsa g·îgāmaᵉyōx K!wāmaxalasēx. ᵉwa,gēlag·a,ᵉwa,
gēlag·a lāxwa k·!ēsēx āźᵉᴇm wāźdᴇm qᴇns gwayiᵉlälasaxwa gwāźᴇlaᵉmōźē
xŭlt!alîdzᴇms bᴇkwîlēnokwaᴇns qᴇns āᴇm nᴇgᴇźtawēsᴇᵉwa. Wä, g·āxᵉmē-
sᴇn sēxwaźᵉᴇmdᴇxg·a t!ᴇx·îlēg·asᴇn wîwŏmpᵉwŭźa qᴇn nᴇgᴇźtawēsᴇᵉwa

25 lāxwa ʟēźelax·ʟax. Wä, g·āxᵉmēsᴇn ʟ̌ōgŭn g·îg·ᴇgāmēk· ʟēźelōʟ qaᵉs
lālag·aōs lāxᴇn g·ōkwaxg·în ʟ!āsotiwalisēk·. Wä, lāk· sᴇk·!ap!ᴇnya-
g·a p!ᴇlxᴇlasgᴇmg·as nᴇqaᵉyēg·ōs ᵉnᴇmgis. Wä, laᵉmēts wäg·îź źada-
kwaź lāxᴇns k!waēᶜlasēx lāxwa g·ōkwēx ᵉnēk·ē. Wä, lä k!wāg·aliźa.
Wä, lä ʟax̌ᵉwālîźē K!wāmaxalas qaᵉs yāq!ᴇg·aᵉźē. Wä, lä ᵉnēk·a;

30 Qäʟ̌, qäʟ̌ēs wāźdᴇmiᵉläläos, g·îgāmē ʟ!āqoʟas, yūʟaxs sᴇmsaaqōsasᴇns
xŭnōkwaxōx ʟ!āsotiwalisax. Wä, gēlag·ax·1 alōmasax g·îgāmaᵉyaxwa

the house of Kǃwāmaxalas. (1) As soon as they had done so the inviters sat down./ Now Kǃwāmaxalas sent a young man to ask the ᵋnᴇmgis
to sit down with them/and to come all into the house. Then many/
young men of the ᵋnᴇmgis went to the houses of the ᵋnᴇmgis and they
spoke(5)inside of the doorway: "We come to ask you to sit down in
the house, ᵋnᴇmgis,/and to listen to what the warriors have to say,"
thus said one of them. And then/the other young men said: "Come into the house quickly. We come to call only once," said they. Then
immediately all the ᵋnᴇmgis went into/the house of Kǃwāmaxalas and
sat down on each side of the(10)house,for the inviting Kwāg·uⱡ were
sitting in the rear of the house./ Only ʟǃax·ʟǃalīdzᴇmga, the wife
of ʟǃāqoʟas, did not/sit among the inviting Kwāg·uⱡ, although she
was in the house. Now/the inviters ate after their arrival and the
ᵋnᴇmgis ate with them. As soon as/they had eaten,all the dishes
were put away and when (15) they had finished ʟǃāqoʟas arose and
spoke. He said,/turning his face to his crew, "Indeed, chiefs, indeed this is the mind of the chief/Kǃwāmaxalas who wished us to warm
our faces in his/good house. Now they may begin. Now I will thank
the ᵋnᴇmgis./ Come without delay to us," said he and turned his face
to the door (20) of the house. He said: "Now come, chiefs of the
ᵋnᴇmgis, come/to this house of chief Kǃwāmaxalas. Now come, now/
come, for it is not newly said that we should do so. This was long
ago in the beginning/marked down by the one who first made us human
beings to be followed by us. Now I paddle/along the trail of my
forefathers which I follow (25) in this that is called inviting.Now
I come with my chiefs to invite you/to come to my house of this ʟǃāsotiwalis. Now here are five hundred/blankets to cover you, ᵋnᴇmgis.
Now you will lend them out/as we are sitting in this house," said he,
and he sat down.

Then Kǃwāmaxalas arose and spoke and said: (30) "Indeed, true
is your word, chief ʟǃāqoʟas, you the mouthpiece of your/son ʟǃāso-

tiwalis. Welcome to the new chief, (1) the chief with a handsome
complexion, thechief who is a prince all over,/the one who is a
chief all over, the one who is not newly made chief. I mean this,/
my people, you ᵋnɛmgis, to go on and lend out all that has been referred to by this chief/as the amount of your blankets to be loaned
out," said he. (5) Immediately ʟ!āx·ʟ!ālidzɛmga was called to sit
down with/her husband ʟ!āqoᴜas. Then ʟ!āx·ʟ!ālidzɛmga carried/five
hundred split cedar sticks tied in the middle, and the name-keeper/
of the ᵋnɛmgis was called to sit down by the side of ʟ!āx·ʟ!ālidzɛmga
in the/rear of the house. Then ʟ!āx·ʟ!ālidzɛmga untied the tying in
the middle of the (10) cedar sticks for the ᵋnɛmgis and the name-
keeper of the/ᵋnɛmgis called out the name of ʟ!āsotiwalis for he
is the eagle. Then/ʟ!āx·ʟ!ālidzɛmga counted five cedar sticks and
gave them/to the name-keeper and the name-keeper put them on the
floor. And/they kept on doing this until they came to the name of
the last man of the ᵋnɛmgis. And (15) when they finished the cedar
sticks were given out to/all the men of the ᵋnɛmgis as they had been
counted. This is called the giving out of cedar sticks as the means
of loaning out./ When all the men had received their cedar sticks
ʟ!āqoᴜas stood up/and spoke and said: "Oh chiefs of the ᵋnɛmgis,/
now these cedar sticks as a means of loaning out have been given to
you. Now go on and loan out (20) as we are here in the house, for
I am going to the Mamalēleqāla tomorrow."/ Thus he said and sat
down. Immediately all the men of the/ᵋnɛmgis went out of the house
and they went to get the blankets(with)which they were going to loan
out./ And they came and put then down next to the place where ʟ!āx·-
ʟ!alīdzɛmga was sitting/with the name-keeper of the ᵋnɛmgis whose
name is (25) G·ēxk·ín, who belongs to the numaym of the ʟ!āʟ!ɛlamin
of the ᵋnɛmgis. As soon as/all the five hundred blankets which were
to be loaned out by the ᵋnɛmgis were inside,/K!wāmaxalas was told to
take care of them during the tine they were going to invite the/Ma-
malēleqāla and the ʟ̣āwits!ēs. As soon as day came (1) next day

łɛnsa laē ălēxᵉwīdēda ᴌēᴌtsaᵉya qaᵉs lē lāxa Mamalēleqăla laqēxs nɛ-
lalalaasa nɛlalayâsa wīnä̀sa Q!ōmoyâᵉyē yīxs laē ā⫯ax·äla lāxēs ᴌēᴌä-
lasɛᵉwē. Wä̀, laᵉmē ᴀɛm nāqămg·īᴌtawēxēs g·īlē gwēg·iᵉlas qaōda ᵉnɛm-
gēse. Lēx·aᵉmēs ōgüx·ᵉīdayusēxs q!ɛʟ!ăp!ɛnyag·aē k!wāqɛmdayâx łādɛ-
5 gwayu qaxs äwülx·īsɛlasɛᵉwaēda Mamalēleqăläxs nɛkümaᵉyaasa ᵉnɛmgēsē
ᴜɛᵉwa Ꮮāwits!ēsē. Wä̀, g·ĩlᵉmisē gwăᴌ łādɛkwasōsa q!ɛʟ!ăp!ɛnyag·ē
p!ɛlxɛlasgɛma laē lāxa Ꮮāwits!ēsē. Wä̀, laɛm mōp!ɛnyag·a p!ɛlxɛlasgɛ-
mē ładɛgwayâsa Ꮮāwits!ēsē. Wä̀, g·āxᵉmē ᵉmălēᴅa ᴌēᴌtsayâxa łādɛgwayu
p!ɛlxɛlasgɛmxs g·āxaē nä̀ᵉnakᵘ lāxg·a Tsāxisɛk: Wä̀, g·īlᵉmisē g·āx
10 hăngɛmalīsa ᴌēᴌtsayuwats!ē xwāxwăk!üna laqēxs laē mᴀᵉᴌts!aqa ᴜɛᵉwa
xwāk!üna bɛk·ânɛms ʟ!ăqoᴜasē lāx K!wāmaxalas qaᵉs ᵉmaᵉwats!ēxa waōkwē
łādɛgwayu p!ɛlxɛlasgɛma. Wä̀, la ᴜāxᵉwaᴌɛxsē ʟ!ăqoᴜas lāxa ᴌēᴌtsayuwats!ē xwāk!üna qaᵉs yāq!ɛg·aᵉᴌē. Wä̀,lä ᵉnēk·a: Nēᴌamăᴌala Kwăkwăg·u-
ᴌai qaᵉs hōᴌēlaōs g·āxɛn. G·āxᵉmɛn g·āxᵉmɛn laᴌa lāxa lēlqwălaᴜᵃyē.
15 G·āxᵉmɛn ᵉmălaxg·ada łādɛgwayugwas. ᵉnēᵉnak·iᴌē qaᵉs ᴀᵉmēᴌōs yăʟ!ᴀ-
ᴜax qō g·āxᴌō ᵉnēk·ɛxs laē k!wāg·aaᴌaxsa. Wä̀, lä ᴜāxᵉwɛlsē ᴀwadē lāx
ʟ!āsanᴀᵉyasēs g·ōkwēxa g·āyuᴌē lāx ᵉnɛᵉmēmutasa Mǎamtag·ila qaᵉs yā-
q!ɛg·aᵉᴌē. Wä̀, lä ᵉnēk·a: Wa, gēlag·ax·ōs wăᴌdɛmaqōs g·īgămēᵉ. Wä̀,
g·āxᴜɛlāg·ax·a yüduxsɛᵉmakwa lēlqwălaᴜaᵉya qɛnᴌōᵉmaslaxō. ᵉnēᵉnak·i-
20 ᴌēs haᵉyăᴜ!ōlaaqōs g·āxɛnuᵉxᵘ g·īgămēᵉ. Wä̀, laᵉmɛn ᴌēᵉlalōᴜai wīnai,
laɛms g·āx teᴌts!ăᴌ lāxg·a g·ōkwas Mălēdai, ᵉnēk·ē. Wä̀, hēx·ᵉidaᵉmē-
sē ā⫯axᴜax·ᵉīdēda xwāxwăk!üna. Wä̀, lä hēx·ᵉidaɛm ᵉmōᴌᴀlasa łādɛgwayu
p!ɛlxɛlasgɛm qaᵉs lē ᵉmaᵉwīᴌālas lāx g·ōkwas ʟ!āqoᴜasē. Wä̀, g·īlᵉmisē
ᵉwīᵉlusdēsa laas ētsēᵉstēda ᴌēᴌᵉwüᴌtōdɛq. Wä̀, laᵉmē äxsɛᵉwa ᵉnăxwa
25 Kwăkwăg·uᴌ qa lēs k!waᵉmēᴌa qaᵉs lē hōᴜēlax ᵉnăxwa ts!ēts!äk·!ālɛmsa
ᴌēᴌtsayu. Wä̀, g·īlᵉmisē g·āx ᵉwīᵉlaēᴌa lāqēxs häē ᵉwīᵉla k!üdzēᴌa ᴌē-
ᴌtsayuwa ōgwiwiᵉlīᴌasa g·ōkwē. Wä̀, laᵉmē ʟ!ɛxwa. Wä̀, g·īlᵉmisē gwă-
ᴌa laas ᴜaxᵉwalīᴌē ʟ!āqoᴜas qaᵉs yāq!ɛg·aᵉᴌē. Wä̀, lä ᵉnēk·a: Wä̀, gē-
lak·asla g·īgămēᵉ, ᴀwad. Wä̀, gēlak·aslax·ēs ᵉnēk·!ēnaōs g·āxē ts!ɛl-

the inviters started off and went to the Mamalēleqăla as they/were
singing the war songs of the Q!ōmoyáᵋyē, as they were going ashore
to those who were/to be invited by them. And now they did the same
as they had done among the ᵋnɛmgis./ Only this was different, that
six hundred cedar sticks(5)were given as a means of loaning out to
make it clear that the Mamalēleqălaᴊare ahead of the ᵋnɛmgis/and
the Ḻāwits!ēs. As soon as the loaning out of the six hundred blankets was finished/they went to the Ḻāwits!ēs. Then four hundred
blankets/were the means of loaning out of the Ḻāwits!ēs. Now the
inviters loaded the blankets which had been loaned out/and they came
back to Fort Rupert. As soon as they came back the (10) inviting
canoes were in front of the village,for there were now two canoes
and the/canoe borrowed by ʟ!āqoʟas from K!wāmaxalas as a means of
carrying the other/blankets which had been loaned out. Then ʟ!āqoʟas
stood up in the inviting/canoe and spoke and said: "Show your faces,
Kwāg·uⱡ,/and listen to me. I have come, I have come. I have now
obtained all the tribes. (15) I come with the cargo of these loaned
out (blankets). I mean that you shall take care that/they come,"
said he as he sat down in his canoe. Then Áwadē arose/outside of
the house which belonged to the numaym Maᾰmtag·ila./ He spoke and
said: "Thank you for your speech, chief. Now/let the three tribes
come that I may act (?). I mean you(20)ask us to take care, chief.
Now I invite you,warriors./Now come and warm yourself in the house of
Mᾰlet,"said he, and immediately/the canoe went ashore stern first.
At once they unloaded the loaned out/blankets and carried them into
the house of ʟ!āqoʟas. As soon as/they were all carried up the beach,
they went again to invite them out of the canoes. Then all the (25)
Kwāg·uⱡ were told to sit with them and to listen to the reports of
the/inviters. As soon as they had all come in,the/inviters sat down
in the rear of the house and ate after their arrival. When they had
finished/ʟ!āqoʟas arose and spoke. He said:/"Thank you,chief Áwadē,
thank you for asking me to come and warm my face (1) in your house.

qŭmg·alîⱡ lāxōs g·ōkwaqōs g·ĭgamēᵋ aⱡᵋmaⱸ̱ᴏx wâⱡdᴇmaxwa ⸪ālilāläxa
⸪ĕⱡtsayu ⸪ᴇᵋwa âᴇm mēmalēxala; ᵋnēᵋnak·iⱡē g·āxᵋmᴇnuᵋx̱ᵘ g·ĭgamēᵋ lâ⸪-
xa lēlqwǎlaⱡaᵋya, ᵋnēk·exs yūduxᵘp!enēg·imēⱡa g·āxᴇnuᵋx̱ᵘ. Wä, laᵋmēsᴇn ᵋnēx· qäns ēt!ēdē q!ämdēⱡaxwa dzāqwax qa maᵋⱡtsᴇmēs q!ᴇmq!ᴇmdᴇmas
⸪!āsotiwalis ⸪ō̄ᵋ äⱡtsᴇma q!ᴇmdᴇm ōqŭᵋla lāxa gâgayalayu k·!îk·!ᴇtᴇla-
k·!āla q!ᴇmdᴇma, ᵋnēk·exs laē k!wāg·aliⱡa. Wä, lä yāq!ᴇg·aᵋⱡē âwadē.
Wä, lä ᵋnēk·a: Wä, gēlag·a g·ĭgamēᵋ ⸪!āqoⱡas. Wä, gēlag·axēs wâⱡdᴇmōs lāxēs wâⱡdᴇmōsaxs ᵋnēk·aaqōsaqē laᴇm g·āxⱡa lēlqwälaⱡaᵋya. Wä,
g·āxⱡa lāg·ax·ĭ qᴇn wäg·ⱸ̄ᴌᴇn aⱸk·ilaⱡaqē qō g·āxⱡa lāxᴇns q!umx·dᴇmē-
sēx. Wä, hēᵋmisēs wâⱡdᴇmōs g·ĭgamēᵋ ⸪!āqoⱡas yîxs ᵋnēk·aēx qᴇns q!äm-
dēⱡēxwa dzāqwax lāxa äⱡtsᴇmsa q!ᴇmdᴇmⱡtsōxda g·ĭgamaᵋyaxōx ⸪!āsotiwa-
li·sax. Wäg·adzâ ᵋnēk·ᴇx g·ĭgamēᵋ, ᵋnēk·ⱸ̄.

Wä, laᵋmē ᵋwîᵋla hōqŭwᴇls lāxa g·ōkwē lāxēq. Wä, g·îlᵋmisē dzāqwaxs laas ⸪!āqoⱡasē ᵋyālaqasa haᵋyäⱡᵋa qa läs q!ämdeᵋlālaxa Gwētᴇla
⸪ᴇᵋwa ᵋwālas Kwāg·uⱡ ⸪ᴇᵋwa Q!ōmk·!ūt!ᴇsē. Wä, hᴇx·ᵋidaᵋmēsē lēda mōkwē haᵋyäⱡᵋasa Q!ōmoyâᵋyē qaᵋs lē ⸪axstoliⱡaxa t!ᴇx·fläsa g·ōkwasa
Gwētᴇla. Wä, lä ᵋnēk·a ᵋnᴇmōkwē lāq: G·āxᵋmᴇnuᵋx̱ᵘ q!ämdēlalōⱡai Gwē-
tᴇlai qa ⸪!āsōtiwalisai, ᵋnēk·ⱸ̄. Wä, la ᵋnēk·a waōkwas: Halag·aliⱡa-
sai. Wä, la hᴇx·sä gwēk·!āla lāxa ᵋnāxwa g·ig·ōkᵘsa yūduxᵘsᴇᵋmakwē
Kwākŭg·uⱡa. Wä, g·îlᵋmisē ᵋwîᵋlxtolsaxa g·ig·ōkwaxs g·āxaē aēdaaqa.
Wä, laᵋmēda nēnâgadē g·alaēⱡa lāxa g·ōkwas ⸪!āqoⱡasē ⸪ᴇᵋwis k!wēk!wa-
nuⱡᴇmaᵋyē. Wä, laᵋmēda nâgadē wŭnwŭnōsa dᴇnxᴇlasēs q!ᴇmdᴇmg·fⱡts!â-
la. Wä, âᴇmisē k!wēk!wanuⱡᴇmaᵋyas hōⱡēlax lälälasasa q!ᴇmtēlaᵋyasa
nâgadē. Wä, hēⱡomalaᵋmisa k!wēk!wanuⱡᴇmaᵋyas q!äxa äⱡtsᴇmē q!ᴇmdᴇmxs
k·!ēsᵋmaē g·āx hōgwiⱡa yūduxᵘsᴇᵋmakwē Kwākŭg·uⱡa. Wä, g·āxᵋmē lōx-
mâlaxs g·āxaē hōgwiⱡalēda ᵋnāxwa bᴇbᴇgwānᴇma qaᵋs lē k!ūsᵋāliⱡ lāx
wāx·sēgwiⱡasa g·ōkwē. Wä, lēda haᵋyäⱡᵋax·sä lāxa ōgwiwaᵋliⱡasa g·ō-
kwē qaᵋs lē k!ūsᵋāliⱡ lāq. Wä, g·îlᵋmisē g·āx ᵋwîᵋlaēⱡa laas ⸪axᵋū-
liⱡē ⸪!āqoⱡasē qaᵋs yāq!ᴇg·aᵋⱡē. Wä, lä ᵋnēk·a: Qä⸪,qä⸪as ᵋnēg·amaōⱡ
lāxᴇns q!ūlsq!ūlyaxŭla qäns hⱸ̄ gwēᵋnākŭlē lāxwa q!ᴇmdēⱡax. Wä,wⱸ̄g·fⱡ-
la nēnâgad hasustâx yîsōs q!ᴇmtēlaᵋyaq!ōs qa hōⱡēlēsg·ins g·ĭg·ᴇgä-

Is it a new speech to meet to invite the/inviters and let them each
just go somewhere? I mean this,we have arrived,chief. We have obtained/
the tribes. They say that they follow us after three days. Now/I
wish for us to sing again in the house this evening that there may
be two songs of (5) ʟ!ásotiwalis,' and also a new song different from
the watching pole song obtained from the grandfather."/ Thus he said
and sat down. Then Ậwadē spóke/and said: " Now come, chief ʟ!āqoʟas.
Thank you for your speech/that you said that the tribes would come./
Let them come that I may treat them well when they come to our village site. (10) And also this your speech, chief ʟ!āqoʟas, that you
said that we/should sing in your house this evening, the new song of
this chief ʟ!āsotiwalis./ Go on now say this, chief," said he./

Then they all went out of the house. As soon as/it was evening
ʟ!āqoʟas sent young men to ask the Gwētɛla to sing in the house,(15)
and the ᵋwālas Kwāg·uł and the Q!ōmk·!ūt!ɛs. Immediately/the four
young men of the Q!ōmoyāᵋyē went and stood in the doorways of the
house of the/Gwētɛla, and one of them said: " We come to ask you to
sing in the house,/Gwētɛla, for ʟ!āsotiwalis," said he. And the
others said, "Come quickly."/ They said the same in all the houses
of the three Kwāg·uł tribes. (20) And as soon as they had been
to all the houses they came back./ Then the song-leaders went first
into the house of ʟ!āqoʟas and they sat down on each side./ Now the
song-leaders sang secretly the song which they had in mind/and only
those who were sitting on either side listened to the way the song
of the/song-leaders went. And at the right time those who were sitting on either side knew the new song. (25) The three tribes of the
Kwāg·uł had not yet come in. Now all the men came in/together and
sat down on/each side of the house. Then the young men went to the
rear of the/house and sat down there. As soon as they had all come
in/ʟ!āqoʟas arose. He spoke and said: " Now,it is true,what I told
you (30) about our old people of long ago, that we should do
in this way singing in the house. Now go on,/song-leaders, breathe

mēg·axōs wałdɛmʟaxsōs q˙ɛmtēlaᶜyax, ᶜnēk·ēxs laē k˙wāg·alIła. Wä,

lä hĕx·ᶜidaᶜma nâgadē dâqâlasēs q˙ɛmtēlaᶜyē. Wä, laᶜmē k·˙ēs hāsɛla

qa helatâlēsēs k˙wēk˙wanuʟɛmaᶜyax lälälasas qaqáyasasa q˙ɛmdɛmē ałtsɛmaxa ᶜnēk·ē;

5   1. Yē ya ha wâ, yē ya ha wâ.

        Wä, g·uwała qɛn lâst˙aqaᶜyēʟasg·în k·˙āk·˙ēlak·˙ayułxɛn

        g·îg·ɛgāmayūta lâx lēlqwälaʟai. Wâ â hu wā.

    2. Yē ya ha wâ, yē ya ha wâ.

        Ha, gwāla wŭłᶜɛm gâgak·˙ālak·as ɛlᶜɛlqwalak·as ʟālaq˙wāla.

10   Wä, k·˙ēsᶜmaēʟɛn nūnłᶜideaʟa tsolēxaʟa. Wä, k·˙ēsᶜmaē-

        ʟɛn x·āyîmg·ilaʟaxa ʟ̣ēgɛmnuxᵘdzēᶜyaʟax K·înts˙egŭmdzē-

        ᶜyasēs yaēxʟɛndzēᶜyaxa nɛnōlōgēlēdzēxa wāyadag·ilēdzē

        Dzōnoq˙wagēlēdzēs g·îg·ɛgāmēdzēs g·îg·ɛgāmaᶜyas lēlqwä-

        laʟai. Wâ â hu wā.

15   3. Yē ya ha wâ, yē ya ha wâ.

        Laᶜmɛn ᶜya ʟ̣ēqayałtsɛn ʟ̣ēgɛmdzēᶜyaxg·in q˙ûlēx·ʟaᶜyamäx·

        G·Ixsēstalisâmē. Laᶜmɛn ᶜya ʟ̣ēqayałtsɛn ʟ̣ēgɛmdzēᶜyax-

        g·în q˙ûlēx·ʟaᶜyamäx· Yāqoʟasɛmēdzēᶜya. Laᶜmɛn ᶜya ʟ̣ē-

        qayałtsɛn ʟ̣ēgɛmdzēᶜyaxg·în q˙ûlēx·ʟaᶜyamäx· ʟ˙āsotiwali-

20   dzēᶜya. Laᶜmɛn ᶜya ʟ̣ēqayałtsɛn ʟ̣ēgɛmdzēᶜyaxg·în q˙ûlēx·-

        ʟaᶜyamäx· ʟ˙āqoʟadzēᶜya. Laᶜmɛn ᶜya ʟ̣ēqayałtsɛn ʟ̣ēgɛm-

        dzēᶜyaxg·în q˙ûlēx·ʟaᶜyamäx· Ewanuxᵘdzēᶜya. Yûɛm ᶜya

        ʟ̣ēʟ̣ɛgɛmsɛn gagɛmpdzēᶜyaxa q˙ûlēx·ʟaᶜyadzēyuła ʟ˙āʟ˙aqwa-

        ladzēyułaxēs q˙ûlēx·ʟaᶜyamäx· ʟ˙āqoʟasɛmēdzēyuła nɛnōlo-

25   gēlesa g·îgɛmaᶜyōs lēlqwälaʟai. Wâ â hu wā.

    Wä, g·îlᶜmēsē gwāł dɛnxɛlēda ᶜnāxwa nēnâgada yîxs laē ᶜnāxwa

q˙ālēda bēbɛgwānɛmaxa āłtsɛmē q˙ɛmdɛma laas ʟaxᶜwalIłē ʟ˙āqoʟasē qaᶜs

yāq˙ɛg·aᶜłē. Wä, lä ᶜnēk·a; ʟ˙ɛdâ ʟ˙ɛdâ laᶜmas g·îg·ɛgāmē wŭʟɛlax ʟ̣ē-

ʟ̣ɛgɛmasɛn aᶜwānâᶜyē Yîx·āgɛmaᶜyē. Yuwēstaɛm ʟ̣ēʟ̣ɛgɛmsē yux ᶜwālaswIst˙a

30 ʟ̣ēʟ̣ɛgɛma. Wä, yûᶜmēsɛn qâqasIłōx·qa ᶜwIᶜlōʟēsōx ʟ˙āsotiwalisaq. ᶜnē-

out the song that you made that our chiefs may listen (1) to what
you will say in your song that you have made," said he and sat
down./ Immediately the song-leaders began the song that they had
made. They did not sing loud/so that it could be heard well by those
who were sitting on either side, the way of the words of the new song/
which said:/

(5) 1. Yē ya ha wâ, yē ya ha wâ./

Make way and let him have this with which I am always trying to strike my/rival chiefs among the tribes. Wâ â hu wâ./
2. Yē ya ha wâ, yē ya ha wâ./

Do not ask in vain for mercy, putting out your tongues and
pressing back your hands. (10) Am I not going to become
excited and am I not going to cause to/disappear the one
who has the great name the Great-Cause-of-Fear/the great
property, the great one that causes people to lose their
senses, the great one that makes people unmerciful, the/
Dzōnoq!wa among the chiefs of the tribes./Wâ â hu wā./

(15) 3. Yē ya ha wâ, yē ya ha wâ. /

Now I will call your great name, your own name/G·Ixsēᵋstal-
Isεmēᵋ. Now I will call your great name/your own name,
Yāqoւasεmēᵋ. Now I will call your/great name, your own
name, ւ!āsotiwalis. (20) Now I will call your great name,
your own name,/ւ!āqoւas. Now I will call your great name/
your own name, Ewanuxᵘdzē. These are the/names of my great
grandfather whose own great name was ւ!āqoւasεmēᵋ,/the one
who was regardless of all caution(25)among your chiefs,
tribes. Wâ â hu wā./

As soon as all the song leaders had finished singing all/
the men knew the new song, and then ւ!āqoւas arose and/spoke.
He said: "It is nice, it is nice. Chiefs, you have heard the/
names of the root of my family,Yîx·āgεmēᵋ, these names, these
names, these great(30)names. This is my way of going, for all

ᵋnak·ik̉ē g·Īg·ɛgămēyōs mōsgɛᵋmakwē Kwākŭg·uk̉ qɛn wäg·ē ts!ɛk·!āk̉ɛ-
las wăk̉dɛmasɛn nɛgŭmpaēda g·Īgămaᵋyaē Lɛlāk·Īnɪs. Laɛmᵋlaē lâʟɛx
K·Īnts!ēgŭmxa ᵋwālasa ʟ!āqwa. Laɛmᵋlāwɪsē g·āxʟ sɛp!ēdak̉tsē g·ā-
xɛn. Wä, laᵋmēsɛn ʟâʟɛwŭlxsēlak̉tsē lāxōx ʟ!āsotɪwalɪsēx. Wä,
5 laᵋmēsōx k·ōqwaʟaq qa nɛgɛk̉tawēmēsēsōxwaxɛn t!ɛx·Īlaᵋyē qa qāstä-
wēsoxōxgŭn laōk̉g·Īn k·ōqwaxa ʟ̣ēgadōk̉a ʟ!āqwē Aŋwalōk̉a. Wä, wēg·a
âɛm yāʟ!âʟɛx g·ōk̉g·ukŭḷōt qō g·āxʟa yŭduxᵘsɛᵋmakwa lēlqwälaʟaᵋya,
ᵋnēk·ēxs laē k!wāg·ĭlĪk̉a. Wä, lä ʟaxᵋwalĭk̉ē Pɛlᵋnakŭlag·ilĭsxa
g·Īgămaᵋyasa ᵋnɛᵋmēmutasa Kŭkwāk!ŭmasa Q!ōmoyâᵋyē. Wä, lä yāq!ɛ-
10 g·aᵋk̉a. Wä, lä ᵋnēk·a: Häwāk·as gĪgămēᵋ wäk̉dɛmaq!ōs. Laᵋmasēʟ
ʟ!āqoʟaa g·Īgămēᵋ laxōda ᵋwālasa ʟ!āqwē K·Īnts!ēgŭmxa säp!ēdayu-
ʟasa g·Īgămaᵋyaē Lɛlāk·Īnɪsaxa ēk·!ɛlwata lāx k·!ēdadē. Wä, gē-
lak·asʟɛlēx·ē ᵋwālasa wäk̉dɛms nɛgŭmpa, g·Īgămēᵋ ʟ!āqoʟas qaxg·Īn
gwāk̉ɛlaᵋmēk· q!ayāxasa qâᵋyasasa·āk̉tsɛmē q!ɛmtēlaᵋyasa nēnâgadēxa
15 ᵋnēk·ē. Wa, k·!ēsᵋmaēʟɛn x·ayĭmg·Īlaʟaxa ʟ̣ēgɛmnuxᵘdzēᵋyaʟax
K·Īnts!ēgŭmdzēᵋya. Hō hō hō hō, gŭnō k·!ētsēᵋsta lāxō g·Īgămēᵋ
lāxēs wäk̉dɛmōs, g·Īgămēᵋ ʟ!āqoʟas, âʟɛn max·ts!alax, ᵋnēk·ēxs laē
k!wāg·âlĪk̉a. Wä, laᵋmē gwāk̉ lāxēq.

Wä, laᵋmē ᵋwĪᵋla hōqŭwɛlsēda bēbɛgwāmɛm lāxēq. Wä, la mōp!ɛn-
20 xwaᵋsa ᵋnāla g·āx g·aēsa ʟēk̉tsayu lāx Tsāxis g·āxaas nēk̉ᵋidēda
Mamalēleqăla qaᵋs lē q!ap!ēᵋnakŭla K·!āq!a. Wä, hēx·ᵋidaᵋmēsa
yŭduxᵋsɛᵋmakwē Kwākŭg·uk̉ la ᵋwĪᵋla hōgwĪʟ lāx g·ōkwas ʟ!āqoʟasē.
Wä, laᵋmē ʟ!āqoʟas k·ĭlxwaxa gŭmsē lāxa k·ĭlwēlasē qa gŭmsālasa
ᵋnāxwa bēbɛgwānɛma. Wä, laᵋmē ʟ!āqoʟasē ʟ̣ɛᵋwis xunōkwē ʟ!āsotɪ-
25 walɪsē q!wālax·a. Wä, laɛm ʟ̣ēʟaap!ɛlaxa ᵋnāk̉ᵋnɛmts!aqē ᵋmɛla ts!ɛl-
ts!ɛlk·sa naxsdaᵋyasa kwēkwē. Wä, lä qamōkᵘsa qāmxwäsa kwēkwē.
Wä, lä wĭwŭsēg·uᵋyâla. Wä, lä ts!ōts!ɛlqalē gŭmsaᵋyas. Wä, g·ĭl-
ᵋmɪsē ᵋwĪᵋla gwāk̉ q!wālax·ēda ᵋnāxwa bēbɛgwānɛmxs laē ᵋwĪᵋla hōqŭwɛls lāxa g·ōkwē qaᵋs lē k!ŭdzɛxsēg·ēx tsāqamaᵋyasa g·ōkwē.

30 Wä, lēx·aᵋmɪsē ʟ!āqoʟas ʟ̣ōᵋ ʟ!āsotɪwalɪsē la g·aēʟɛla lāxa
g·ōkwē. Wä, k·!ēst!ē gēxgas k!ŭts!ɛsa bēbɛgwānɛmaxs g·axaasa

will be obtained by ʟ!ásotiwaⱡis.(1) My meaning, chiefs, you chiefs
of the four Kwāg·ul tribes, is this. I will report to you/what has
been said by my father-in-law chief Lɛlāk·ɛnis. It is said he ob-
tained/Cause-of-Fear, the great copper. Now it will come and it will
be thrown by me./Now I am going to treat like a prince this ʟ!ásoti-
walis.(5) Now I am going to break it so that he may go straight on
the trail that I made for him to/walk on, when long ago I broke the
copper that had the name Cloudy. Now/just take care, tribes, when
the three tribes will arrive."/ Thus he said and sat down. Then Pɛl-
ᶜnakūlag·ilis arose,/the chief of the numaym Kŭkwāk!ŭm of the Q!ōmoyā-
ᶜyē. Then he spoke(10)and said: "Great is your word chief. Now you/
have obtained the copper,chief, the great copper Cause-of-Fear which
will be thrown/by the chief Lɛlāk·ɛnis who is an expert in having
princesses./Thank you for the great word of your father-in-law, Chief
ʟ!āqoꞮas, for/in the beginning I was startled by the words of the new
song made by the song leaders,"(15) said he: "Am I not going to make
disappear that which has the great name/Cause-of-Fear? Hōhō hō hō.
Do not retract your promise,/Chief ʟ!āqoꞮas, else I shall bé ashamed."
Thus said he and/sat down. That wás finished after this./

    Then all the men went out after this and (20) four days after
the inviters had arrived and stayed at Fort Rupert,/the Mamalēleqāla
came in sight and gathered at K·!āq!a and right away/the three tribes
of the Kwag·uⱡ all went into the house of ʟ!āqoꞮas/and then ʟ!āqoꞮas
bought ochre in the store so that/all the men might paint tnemselves,
and then ʟ!āqoꞮas and his son ʟ!āsotiwalis(25)dressed themselves. And
there stood in the hair behind one white/feather of the tail of the
eagle, and down of the eagle was put on./ They had a belt around the
waist and they were painted with charcoal mixed with ochre. As soon/
as all the men had finished dressing they went/out of the house and
sat down near the house front./

    (30)Only ʟ!āqoꞮas and ʟ!āsotiwalis stayed in the/house. The men
had not been sitting there long(1)before the Mamalēꝇeqāla came, the

Mamalēleqǎla ᵋnɛᵋmāg·iwaɫēs yaᵋyats!ē nāᵋlālasa wᴵnak·!ālaxs g·ā-
xaē tēxᵋwida laqēxs k·!ēsaē yāyaᵋnaxs g·āxaē. Wä, g·ᴵlᵋmisē g·āx
mɛxᵋaɪaᵋya lāx nɛgɛt!äsa g·ōkwas ʟ!āqoɪasē laē q!wēɫᵋid nɛᵋlala.
Wä, âᵋmisē la sɛltâlēda Mamalēleqǎla k·!eâs yāq!änt!ālas.

5   Wä, lä ɪaxᵋwŭlsē Lālak·ots!axa g·āyoɫē lāx ᵋnᴇ́mēmotsa Yaēx·a-
gᴇmaᵋyasa Q!ōmoyâᵋyē qaᵋs yāq!ɛg·aᵋɫē. Wä, lä ᵋnēk·a: Wa, gēla-
g·a Mamalēleqǎl. Wa, gēlag·a lāxwa hänēᵋyaxsa wiwōmpꞓäōs, ᵋwālas
lēlqwǎlaɪē lāxa ɪēɫɛlaxᵘnaxwäsg·ᴵn g·ᴵgämēk· yᴵxg·a ʟ!āsotiwalisɛk·.
Laɛms hēɫâlaɪōʟ qaᵋs x·ᴵts!ax·ᵋᴵdaōsaxg·a ʟ!āsotiwalisak·, ᵋnēk·ēxs
10   laē gwēgɛmx·ᵋᴵd lāxa ᵋnāxwa Kwākŭg·ŭɫa. Wä, lä ᵋnēk·a: ᵋWēg·a
q!wāg·ᴵlsax Kwākŭg·uɫ qɛn ɪēɫɛwɛlsaɛnɪaxwa g·ᴵgämaᵋyax qa g·axla-
g·ᴵsō dōxᵋwᴵdɛxg·as ɪēɫɛlakŭk·, ᵋnēk·ēxs laē hāsɛla ᵃnēk·a: Gē-
lag·a g·ᴵgämaᵋya ʟ!āsotiwalisa, g·āxᵋɛmg·as k·!ōtɛlag·ōsa. G·ā-
xᵋɛmk· wŭyōq!wax·iwayaa ᵋnēk·ē. Wä, hēx·ᵋidaᵋmisē ʟ!āqoɪas g·ā-
15   xawɛls lāx t!ɛx·ᴵläsēs g·okwē qaᵋs ɪaxᵋwɛlsē lāxa ʟ!āsanâᵋyē. Wä,
lä k·ᴵsdǎqǎɫasēs hᵉ̌ɫk·!ōtts!änaᵋyē qaᵋs dōqwāɫēx mɛxâlasasa xwāxwak!ŭna. Wä, lä k·ᴵsäxotsēs aᵋyāsowē qaᵋs yāq!ɛg·aᵋɫē. Wä, lä
ᵋnēk·a hāsɛla: Gēlag·a ʟ!āsotiwalisai, g·āxᵋɛmg·as k·!ōtɛlag·o-
sai, ᵋnēk·exs laē wäxaɫa ᵋnāxwa bēbɛgwānɛm qa lɛmxɛxsēg·ayisē tsā-
20   qamaᵋyasēs g·ōkwē. Wä, lä ᵋnāxwaᵋma bēbɛgwānɛm lɛmxɛxsēg·ēsēs
ē·ᵋeyasowē lāxa tsāqamaᵋyasa g·ōkwē. Wä, hēx·ᵋidaᵋmēsē g·āx g·ā-
xawɛlsē ʟ!āsotiwalisē lāxa t!ɛx·ᴵläsēs g·ōkwē qaᵋs lē dzɛlx·ustâ
lāxa k·!ᴵtɛla ɛlxɪālax ʟ!āqoɪasē qaᵋs lē ɪēɪâdzâwēxa k·!āqaɫa.
Wä, hēᵋmisē ʟ!āqoɪasē ᵋnēk·a: Hā hā hā hū wā. Wä, lä mōp!ɛna
25   hē gwēk·!ɛg·aᵋɫē. Wä, la ᵋmē âɛm nɛgɛɫtɛwēxēs g·ālē g·wēk·!āla-
sɛxs g·ālaē la mɛnsɛxs laē gwāɫa k·!ᴵtɛla.
Wä, g·āxē bǎnēᵋsta qaᵋs ɪāxᵋwɛlsē ʟ!āqoɪasē ɪɛᵋwis xŭnōkwē
ʟ!āsotiwalisē lāx ōxᵘsidzaᵋyasa k·!ᴵtɛla. Wä, la ʟ!āqoɪasē yāq!ɛ-
g·aᵋɫa. Wä, lä ᵋnēk·a: Wēg·ᴵɫla nēnâgat q!ɛmt!ētsa gāgayalä
30   k·!ᴵk·!ᴵtɛlak·!āla q!ɛmdɛma, ᵋnēk·ē. Wä, hēx·ᵋidaᵋmēsa nâgadē
dâqâlas gwɛᵋyâsxa ᵋnēk·a:

bows of their canoes in a straight line, singing their war song/when
they came in sight and they were not going fast when they arrived.
When/they stopped in front of the house of ᴌ!äqoᴜas they stopped/sing-
ing, and the Mamaleleqäla kept quiet. Nobody spoke./

(5) Then Lälak·ots!a arose, who belonged to the numaym Yaĕx·agɛmĕᵋ/
of the Q!ōmoyâᵋyē and spoke. He said: "Come/Mamaleleqäla, come to
this canoe resting place of the forefathers of your/great tribe when
they used to be invited by my chief, this ᴌ!äsotiwalis./ Now you will
sit there comfortably to witness ᴌ!äsotiwalis." Thus he said(10)and
he turned his face to all the Kwāg·uᴌ tribes and said,/"Stand up, Kwä-
g·uᴌ, that I may call out of the house this chief that he may come/and
look at his guests." Thus he said and then he said aloud,/"Come, chief
ᴌ!äsotiwalis, now your salmon have come;/they have come in great
schools," said he. and immediately ᴌ!äqoᴜas came(15)out of the door
of his house and stood outside. Then/he put his right hand over his
eyes and looked at the canoes that were stopping outside./ Then he put
down his hand and he spoke and/said aloud, "Come, ᴌ!äsotiwalis, your
salmon has arrived,"/ said he as he told all the men to beat fast time
(20)on the front of his house. Then all the men beat fast time/with
their hands on the front boards of the house and immediately/ᴌ!äsoti-
walis came out of the door of his house and ran up/the watchman's pole
behind ᴌ!äqoᴜas and he stood on the platform./ Then ᴌ!äqoᴜas said "Hä
hä hä hü wä." Four times/(25)he cried this way. Then he did as he
had done when he first cried out this way/when he first tried it when
the watchman's pole was finished./

Then he came down and ᴌ!äqoᴜas and his son/ᴌ!äsotiwalis stood
outside at the foot of the watchman's pole. And then ᴌ!äqoᴜas spoke/
and said, "Now song leaders, sing our grandfather's(30)song of the
watchman's pole," said he. And immediately the song leaders/gave
out what he referred to which said:/

Ha, laᵋmɛn dōxᵋwaʟɛla, lahak·asᵋmɛn dōxᵋwaʟɛla lax mɛyâ.

Hē yā hē yā hâ hâ.

G·āxᵋmōx g·āxᵋũstahēsɛla q!awap!alahedzēk·as q!ōqɛlanɛm-
k·asa hâ.

Hē yā hē yā hâ hâ.

ᵋyäg·ɛnutâsaēnētsɛn ōsäyâhâ k·!ɪtɛlayuk·asᵋō.

Hē yā hē yā hâ hâ.

Wä, g·āxᵋmē wũq!äs ʟ!āsotiwalis yɪx Q!ēx·ʟālaga ʟậʟaxōdɛx
ʟ!āsotiwalisē ʟ̣ōᵋ ʟ!āqoʟasē qaᵋs ᵋnɛmālē yɪxᵋwɪdaxs laē nɛxsɛmā-
las dɛnxɛlēda ᵋnāxwa Kwākũg·uła. Wä, laɛm yɪxwɪwalē Q!ēx·ʟagäxa
yɪxwɪwaᵋyaxs yɪxwaē. Wä, g·ɪlᵋmisē q!ũlbēda q!ɛmdɛmaxs laē
Q!ēx·ʟālaga laēʟ lāxa g·ōkʷē. Wä, laᵋmē gɛmxawɛldzɛma lāk·!ɛn-
dē p!ɛlxɛlasgɛma qaᵋs lē gɛmxɛldzɛm lāx ōxᵘsidzaᵋyasa k·!ɪtɛla
qaxs hᴕx·säᵋmaē ʟậx·ʟosē ʟ!āqoʟas ʟɛᵋwis xunōkwē ʟ!āsotiwalisē.
Wä, g·ɪlᵋmisē g·āx ᵋwɪᵋla gämxasa lāk·!ɛndē p!ɛlxɛlasgɛmxs laē
yāq!ɛg·aᵋłē ʟ!āqoʟasē. Wä, lä ᵋnēk·a:

Wa, gēlag·a Mamalēleqăl. Wa, gēlag·a ᵋwālas lēlqwălaʟē.
G·āxᵋɛms g·āxᵋaʟɛla lāxɛn q!umx·dɛmsēx. Laɛmʟas wũʟậxᵋaʟɛlaxɛn
gâgaᵋyāla k·!ɪk·!ɪtɛlak·!āla q!ɛmdɛma. Hᵉ́ɛm q!ɛmdɛmsɛn aᵋwanâ-
ᵋyē Yɪx·āgɛmaᵋyē. Wä, g·āxᵋmēsōx äxᵋētsōsg·ɪn ʟɛwũlgɛmēk· yɪs-
g·a ʟ!āsotiwalisɛk· qaᵋs x·ɪts!ɛnłōs Mamalēleqăl. Wä, laᵋmēṭs
x·ɪts!anānamałg·ada lāk·!ɛndɛk· p!ɛlxɛlasgɛma yũdzäᵋwēsōs Q!ēx·-
ʟālaga xũnōkwas ʟ!āsotiwalisē. Wä, laɛm ēaxᵋɪts lāxa Mamalēleqăla. Wä, laɛm maēmogũdzâya bēbɛgwānɛm lāxa ᵋnậłᵋnɛmxsa p!ɛlxɛ-
lasgɛmaxs laē ʟ!āqoʟas yāqwaq lāqēxs k!ũdzɛxsālaē lāxa xwâxwäk!ũ-
na. Wä, g·ɪlᵋmisē ᵋwɪᵋla yäxᵋwitsa p!ɛlxɛlasgɛmē laē ᵋnēk·a:
Wa sōxwä.

Wä, lä ʟ̣āxᵋũłaxsē Gũyōłɛlasxa g·ɪgāmaᵋyasa ᵋnɛᵋmēmutasa

Now I see it, now I see it, the salmon./

    Hē yā hē yā hâ hâ./

It is coming up stream with a great wave following, what

    I obtained by purifying myself./

    (5)Hē yā hē yā hâ hâ./

You were overcome by me on account of this watchman's

    pole. (?)/

    Hē yā hē yā hâ hâ./

Then the sister of ʟ!āsotiwalis, Q!ēx·ᴌālaga, came and stood
between/ʟ!āsotiwalis and ʟ!āqoᴌas and they danced together while
they were standing together in the middle of(10)all the Kwāg·uᴌ
who were singing. And Q!ēx·ᴌālaga had on her head the/dancing-
headdress with ermine skins. As soon as they had finished their
singing/Q!ēx·ᴌālaga went into the house. Then they brought out
one hundred/blankets and put them down at the foot of the watchman's pole/while ʟ!āqoᴌas and his son ʟ!āsotiwalis were still
standing there.(15)As soon as they had carried out all the
hundred blankets/ʟ!āqoᴌas spoke and said:/

"Now come, Mamalēleqāla, come great tribe./Now you have
arrived at this my rich village site. Now you will hear my/grand-
father's song, the song of the watchman's pole, this is the song of
my root,(20)Yīx·āgāmēᵋ. Now it comes to be taken by my prince, this/
ʟ!āsotiwalis, that it may be seen by you Mamalēleqāla. Now you
will receive/for witnessing this the one hundred blankets which
were danced upon by Q!ēx·ᴌālaga/the daughter[1]of ʟ!āsotiwalis. "
Then he handed them to the Mamalēleqāla./Now there were four men
to each pair of (25) blankets as ʟ!āqoᴌas gave them to them while
they were still sitting in the canoes./As soon as he had given
away the blankets he said:/"Now it is done."/

Then arose Gūyōᴌᴇlas, chief of the numaym(1)Mamalēleq!ām and

---

[1]A woman dancing on behalf of a person is always called his
daughter because it is properly the function of a daughter to dance.

Mamalēleq!ăm qaᵋs yāqǃɛg·aᵋ⅄ē. Wä, lä ᵋnēk·a: Hăwādzēk·as, hă-
wādzēk·asōs k·ǃēsᵋâqōs, g·Igāmēᵋ ʟǃāsotiwalis, G·āxdzēᵋmō g·āx-
ᵋaʟɛla lâʟxwa k·ǃēsᵋx qǃūnâla nē⅄ᵋĪda lāxwa wâyats!âlax ăxnōgwa-
tsōxda k·ǃĪtɛlax. Wäg·Ī⅄la äwāsâl g·Ig·ɛgamēᵋ qaᵋnuxᵘ ĕx·ᵋak·ē-
5 ʟōʟ ᵋnēk·ēxs laē kǃwâg·aa⅄ɛxsa.

   Wä, laᵋmē Lālak ots!a ᵋnēk·a: Laᵋmɛn ʟēᵋlalōʟai Mamalēle-
qālai qa Qǃēx·ʟālagai xŭnōkwas ʟǃāsotiwalisai. Laɛms g·āxʟa
tɛ⅄tsǃa⅄ lāxg·a g·ōkᵘgwas. Laɛmk· lɛqwēlakwai, ᵋnēk·ē. Wä, hĕx·-
ᵋida ᵋmisē gwē⅄aʟaᵋya xwāxwâk!ūna yaēᵋyats!ēsa Mamalēleqála qaᵋs
10 lē lɛmg·alis lāx ʟǃɛmaisas g·ig·ōkwasēs gwɛᵋyâ qaᵋs g·aēʟɛlasa.
   Wä, laᵋmēda ᵋnāxwa Kwākŭg·u⅄ ᵋmāᵋmawālax ᵋmâmwäläs qaᵋs lē ᵋmāwĪ-
ʟɛlas lāxa g·ig·ōkwē. Wä, g·Īlᵋmisē ᵋwĪᵋlōsdēsa laē watᵋwŭsdēsax
xwāxwak!unäs. Wä, g·Īlᵋmisē ᵋwĪᵋla la wādɛkwa laas hĕx·ᵋidaɛm
ētsēᵋstēda qǃēmâla haᵋyā⅄ᵋasa Kwākŭg·u⅄ᵋxa pǃēkwē Mamalēleqāla
15 qa läs ʟǃɛxwa lāx ʟǃāsotiwalisē. Wä, la hĕᵋmɛnā⅄aɛm hĕg·ĪlĪ⅄a
pǃēkwaxs ʟē⅄wŭ⅄totsɛᵋwaē qaxs âlak·ǃālaē pōsqǃa.

   Wä, g·Īlᵋmisē g·āx ᵋwĪᵋlaēʟa laē hĕx·ᵋida xämsxasᵋĪdxa xaᵋmasē. Wä, g·Īlᵋmisē gwā⅄ xämsxasxa xaᵋmasē laas äxᵋētsɛᵋwa mɛnatsǃē qaᵋs lē xämsᵋalĪlɛm lāx hĕ⅄k·ǃōtiwali⅄as g·ōkwē qaxs hēē
20 kǃŭdzĪ⅄Īda Mamalēleqālē ōgwiwalĪ⅄asa g·ōkwē. Wä, g·Īlᵋmisē xämsa-
lēlɛma mɛnatsǃē laas ʟaxᵋwalĪ⅄ē Lālak·otsǃaxa g·āyo⅄ē lāx ᵋnɛᵋmēmotas ʟǃāqoʟasēxa Yaɛx·agāmaᵋyē. Wä, lä yāqǃɛg·aᵋ⅄a. Wä, lä
ᵋnēk·a: Wĕg·Ī⅄la lāg·ustâʟɛx Mamalēleqāl nē⅄a⅄xɛns ᵋnālax. Ā⅄-
ᵋmaêʟōx wā⅄dɛma dādɛnxa⅄g·ulĪ⅄ēx kǃwē⅄axwa ᵋnēg·ɛmŭ⅄ēx lāxɛns wĪ-
25 wompᵋwŭ⅄a qa kǃwēᵋlālēs dɛnxɛla nē⅄axɛns ᵋnāläxs kǃwē⅄aē. Wä,
wĕg·Ī⅄la ᵋnēk·ēxs laē kǃwâg·ĪlĪ⅄a.

   Wä, hĕx·ᵋidaᵋmisē ʟāxᵋwalĪ⅄e Gŭyō⅄ɛlasxa g·Igāmaᵋyasa ᵋnɛᵋmēmutasa Mamalēleqǃăm qaᵋs yāqǃɛg·aᵋ⅄ē. Wä, lä ᵋnēk·a: Qäʟ,
qäʟēs wā⅄dɛmōs g·Igāmēᵋ Lālak·otsǃ qäʟaxs hĕᵋmaēx gwä⅄ēxwa ʟēqwi-
30 ᵋläla xŭtēs bɛkwēlēnokwasɛns lāx nɛgɛĪᵋnēsɛᵋwa, lāg·i⅄aɛns k·ǃēs
âɛm sɛna qɛn gwēyiᵋläsa. ᵋnēᵋnak·i⅄ē nōs g·ōkŭlōt Mamalēleqāl.

spoke. He said, "Mighty,/really mighty are your privileges, chief
L!ãsotiwalis, which have come/to you, this what is not often shown
by those who are unable (to do so although) they are owners of this/
watchman's pole. Go on now, chiefs, you with your father, that we
may be kindly disposed towards you,"(5)said he, and sat down.

Then Lālak·ots!a said: "I invite you, Mamaēleqãla/on account
of Q!ēx·ᴌãlaga, the daughter of L!ãsotiwalis. Now come/and warm
yourselves in his house here. Now the fire has been built!" said
he. Immediately/the canoes of the Mamaēleqãla scattered and(10)
they went ashore at the beach of the houses of those with whom they
wanted to stay./ Then all the Kwãg·uᴌ carried up the load and carried it/into the houses. As soon as everything had been carried
up/the canoes were hauled up. When they had been hauled up/many
young men of the Kwãg·uᴌ went to the invited Mamaēleqãla(15)who
were to eat after their arrival at(the house of)L!ãsotiwalis. Gen-
erally/the guests go immediately when they are invited, for they
are really hungry./

When they had all gone into the house, they ate dried salmon/
and after they had eaten dried salmon, the drum was taken/and was
put down on the right hand side in the rear of the house for(20)
the Mamaēleqãla were sitting down in the rear of the house. As
soon as they had put down the/drum, Lālak·ots!a arose who belonged
to the numaym/of L!ãqoᴌas, the Yaēx·agɛmēᵋ. Then he spoke and/
said: "Now go on and sing, Mamaēleqãla, and tell our world.
It is not a new way that feasters should sing first. This was
said long ago to our(25)ancestors to sing a feasting song to tell
our world we are feasting. Now/go on," said he and sat down./

Immediately arose Gūyōᴌɛlas, chief of the/numaym Mamaēleq!ãm.
He spoke and said: "Indeed/true is your word, chief Lālak·ots!a.
Indeed,different ways(30)were marked out by our Creator to be fol-
lowed. I do not/just plan that it should be done in this way.
That is my meaning, my tribe Mamaēleqãla. (1)Go on and sing

12

Wĕg·a lāg·ustâsɛn k!wēlaᵋyalä q!ɛmdɛma, ᵋnĕk·ē. Wä, hᵕx·ᵋida‐
ᵋmēsa nâgadäsa Mamalēleqäla dâqâlas k!wēlaᵋyäla q!ɛmdɛmsxa ᵋnĕ‐
k·ēda k!wēlaᵋyaᵋlayu q!ɛmdɛms:

1. Wâ hū wa hâ yä ha.

Ẏawehᵕx·flēdzōlɛns g·Īgämaᵋyᵕx. Wädzōlàg·a. Yawehᵕ‐
x·flēsʟa yāyaᵋwēnqɛlēsʟa g·Īgämaᵋyᵕx lēlqwälaʟaí.

Lādzeᵋya laᵋmɛn ʟ̥ēqayaⱡtsɛn ʟ̥ēgɛmdzēᵋyasɛn gagɛmpdzē‐
ᵋyaxēxs q!ûlēxʟeᵋyadzēᵋya Kwākwax·âlasa, Kwāx·fla‐
nōkumēdzēs g·Īgämaᵋyas lēlqwälaʟaí.

Lādzeᵋyaᵋmɛn ʟ̥ēqayaⱡtsɛn ʟ̥ēgɛmdzēᵋyasɛn gagɛmpdzēᵋyaxēxs
q!ûlēxʟeᵋyadzeᵋya ʟ!âʟ!aqwalaⱡa, ʟ!âqwag·iladzēs
g·Īgämaᵋyas lēlqwälaʟaí.

Ladzēᵋyaᵋmɛn ʟ̥ēqayaⱡtsɛn ʟ̥ēgɛmdzeᵋyasɛn gagɛmpdzeᵋyaxa
q!ûlēxʟeᵋyadzeᵋya Lᵕx·sᵋɛndālaⱡa Q!âq!âltalaⱡdzēs
g·Īgämaᵋyas lēlqwälaʟaí.

Ladzēᵋyaᵋmɛn ʟ̥ēqayaⱡtsɛn ʟ̥ēgɛmdzeᵋyasɛn gagɛmpdzeᵋyaxa
q!ûlēxʟeᵋyadzeᵋya P!ēp!adzayusa P!āsälaⱡdzēs g·Īgä‐
naᵋyas lēlqwälaʟaí.

Ya wâ hu wä haᵋyē.

Ẏūɛmya ʟ̥ē̥ɛgɛmdzeᵋyasɛn g·Īqag·iwaᵋya lēlqwälaʟaí.

Ya wâ hu wä.

2. Wâ hū wa hâ yä.

Lādzēɛm lālâx ōxwayaʟa dzōnoqwayaʟa dzōnoq!wagēledzes
g·Īgämaᵋyas lēlqwälaʟaí.

Ladzēɛm lālâx ʟēnag·ilaʟa qaᵋs ᵋwĪᵋwūlsgɛᵋmakwa lēɛlqwä‐
ⱡaʟaí lāx gwegwäla g·flēdzēᵋyasɛn gagɛmpdzeᵋyaxa
q!ûlēxʟeᵋyadzeᵋya Mɛlnasdzēyuⱡas g·Īgämaᵋyōs lēlqwä‐
laʟaíxa hamanēkwila dzōnoq!wadzeᵋya ⱡōqûlĪⱡasɛn
gagɛmpdzeᵋyaxa q!ûlēxʟeᵋyadzeᵋya Kwax·flanokumēdzē
Kwākwax·âlats g·Īgämedzeᵋya lēɛlqwälaʟaí.

our feasting song," said he. Immediately/the song leaders of
the Mamaléleqala started the feasting song, and this is what says/
the feasting song:/

1. Wâ hū wa hâ yä ha./
(5) Now our great chief will begin to move;/ he will begin to
       move in the world, the chief,tribes./
    Now I shall name the great name of our great grandfather,/
       whose own name was Kwākwax·âlas, the great Kwāx·îla-
       nōkǔmēᶜ,/the chief of the tribes./
(10) Now I shall name the great name of my great grandfather,/
       whose own name is ʟ!āʟ!aqwalaɬ,the great ʟ!āqwag·ila,/
       the chief of the tribes./
    Now I shall name the great name of my great grandfather,/
       whose own name is Lāx·sᴇ́ndalaɬ, the great Q!āq!ālta-
       laɬ,(15)the chief of the tribes./
    Now I shall name the great name of my great grandfather,/
       whose own name is P!ēp!ādzɛyōs, the great P!āsālaɬ,
       the chief/of the tribes./
    Ya wâ hu wä haᶜyē./
(20) These are the great names of my chief before me, tribes./
    Ya wâ hu wä./

2. Wâ hū wa hâ yä./
    Now he will shout the Dzōnoq!wa shout of the/chiefs of
       the tribes./
(25) Now he will give a great grease feast to all the tribes,/
       as was done by my great grandfather/whose own name
       was Mᴇlnas, your chief, tribes;/the great terrifying
       Dzōnoq!wa was the feasting dish of my/great grand-
       father whose own name was the great Kwāx·îlanōkǔmēᶜ,/
       Kwākwax·âlas, the great chief, tribes./

12*

Ya wâ hu wä haᵋyē.

Yuᴇmya ʟᵉ̆ᒷᴇɢᴇmdzeᵋyasᴇn g·iqag·iwaᵋya lēlqwalaʟai.

Ya wâ hu wä.

3. Wâ hū wa hậ yä ha.

Gwāłaᴇmx·dᴇn k·!ēk·!esnēqäla k·ēk·alēqalasōx k·āk·alᴇᵋma-
yusa k·flᴇmgēlēdzēx g·Igämaᵋya lēlqwälaʟai. Läex·de-
ᵋyax k·!āk·!ēlak·!āyasōs yflyflkwalag·ilaxwa ʟᵉ̆gᴇm-
nuxᵘdzē̆ᵋyax Dᴇnt!ālayudzeᵋyax yaēxʟᴇnasᴇn·g·Igämaᵋyē̆
lēᴇlqwälaʟai.

Ya wâ hu wä.

Wä, g·flᵋmisē q!ūlbēda q!ᴇmdᴇm dᴇnxᴇlayusa k!wō̆łē Mamalēleqậ-
la laas G̱ūyōłᴇlas ōxwa·dzōnoqwa. Wä, lä yāq!ᴇg·aᵋła. Wä, lä
ᶜnēk·a lāqēxs ʟaᵋwfłtsämaē lāx wāwasälīlasas dᴇnxᴇlayuwē q!ᴇmdᴇ-
mas. Laᴇms nōs g·ōkŭlōt,laᵋmē wŭʟāxᵋaʟała ēt!ēdaxwa ᵋwālasēx k!wē-
laᵋyala q!ᴇmdᴇmᴇn qaᵋs Kwākŭguł lāx Dzāwadē̆ layułg·în ʟ!ēnag·ila,
ᵋnēᵋnak·ʔłaxg·în laᵋmēk· qāsō qaᵋs Gwētᴇl ʟōᵋs Q!ōmayậᵋyē ʟōᵋs ᵋwalas Kwāg·uł ʟoᵋs Q!ōmk·!ūt!ᴇs yfsg·ada xwāk!ŭnak·, yfx sᴇk·!ax·so-
k!uxwēk· p!ᴇlxᴇlasgema, ᶜnēk·ē. Wä, laᵋmē k!wāg·flîł lāxēq.

Wä, laᴇm ᶜnᴇmsgᴇmōdxa q!ᴇmdᴇm, wä, lä äxᵋēîsᴇᵋwa mᴇnats!ē
qaᵋs g·āxē xämsᵋalīlem lāx max·stâlīłasa t!ᴇx·fläsa g·ōkwē. Wä,
laᵋmē hŏleg·întsōsa t!ᴇqa. Wä, g·flᵋmisē gwāł t!ᴇxt!aqxa q!wēdzᴇ-
kwē t!ᴇqaxs laē yāq!ᴇg·aᵋłē ʟ!āqoʟasē. Wä, lä ᶜnēk·a: Q̱âʟ, qâ-
ʟas g·Igämēᵋ G̱ūyōłᴇlas laxēs läyōs wāłdᴇmaxwa k·!ēsēx q!ūnēnēᵋ
wāłdᴇms g·Igämaᵋya qāsō, lāg·iłas q!ēnᴇma aētaxaläsa g·Ig·ᴇgämaᵋya
lāqᵘ. Xᴇnyasawēsᴇnʟasēs wāłdᴇmōs g·Igämēᵋ qaxs yŭmaaqōs ēaxēna-
ᵋyōxda k!wēlasēx g·Igämēᵋ, ᶜnēk·ēxs laē nᴇxbag·flîłē wāłdᴇmas lāxa ᶜnāxwa k!wēłaxa Mamalēleqäla. Wä, lä ᶜnēk·a: Wäk·as, g·Ig·ᴇ-
gämēs Mamalēleqậl. Wäk·as lāg·aqō hēłtalaqō. Laᵋmō aĕk·!aakᵘxwa

Ya wâ hu wä ha^εyē./

These are the great names of my chief before me, tribes./

Ya wâ hu wä./

3. Wâ hū wa hâ yä ha./

(5) Already I was scared! I was afraid of the/Cause-of-Fear, the
    great chief, tribes, as he was about/to strike with
    that which hurts that has the great name/Dεnt!a^εlayu,
    the property of my chief,/tribes./

(10)Ya wâ hu wä./

As soon as was finished the song sung by the feasting Mamalēleqâla,/then Ǧûyōᶻεlas uttered the Dzōnoq!wa cry. Then he spoke and/
said as he was standing still while they were singing their song:/
"Now, you my tribe, now is heard again this great feasting(15)song
for you, Kwāg·uᶻ, at Dzāwadō, where long ago I gave a grease feast./
I mean that I promise a feast for you Gwētεla, and you Q̓!ōmoyaᶜyē,
and you/ᶜwālas Kwāg·uᶻ,and you Q!ōmk·!ūt!εs,with this canoe which is
worth fifty/blankets." Thus he said and sat down after this./

Now they sang one song. Then the drum was taken(20)and put
away down next to the door of the house./ Now they were given as a
second course dried berries,and after they had eaten the squeezed
berries,/ʟ!āqoᶅas spoke and said:"Indeed,indeed,/chief Ǧûyōᶻεlas,
true is your word which is not often(25)said by chiefs, 'I promise
a feast.' Therefore many chiefs go down in rank/on account of this.
Am I not startled by your speech, chief? For this is your kind of
work, the/feast-giving, chief." Thus he said and he directed his
speech to/all the feasting Mamalēleqäla and he said: "Go on, chiefs/
of the Mamalēleqala, go on with this which is done right. Now it is
well done. (1)This is not a new saying, the giving of three courses

k·ꞏēsēx āɫꞓɛm wāɫdɛmaxa hёleg·ꞏîndäsa hāsaꞓyē lāxēs hämg·ꞏîlasɛꞓwē
yîxs ꞓnēk·aēda qꞏûlsqꞏûlyaxᵘdä ꞓyäx·sɛmxꞇäɛns kꞏwēꞓlēnaꞓyē lāxa
g·ꞏîgämaꞓyē qaxs hёwäxaē hёleg·ꞏînts ꞓnɛmsgɛma wāɫdɛm g·āxɛns qꞏû-
nālax·dɛn wûʟɛlaxa ꞓnēk·ē, ꞓnēꞓnak·iɫē wäk·as, wäk·as, ꞓnēk·ēxs
5 laē kꞏwäg·ꞏflîɫa. Wä, lä k·ꞏēs ʟāxꞓwalîɫa g·ꞏîgämaꞓyē Yāqaɫꞓɛn-
lidzēxa g·āyuɫē lāx ꞓnɛꞓmēmutasa ꞓwālasēxa k·ꞏēsꞓōnokwasa nāꞓnax-
maꞓyaxa hёleg·ꞏîndäsa yāqꞏänt!äla lāxa kꞏwēɫē. Wä, lä ꞓnēk·a:
Qäꞇēs wāɫdɛmōs, g·ꞏîgämēꞓ ʟꞏäqoꞇas. Laꞓmɛnuꞓxᵘ ёx·pꞏasɛꞓwasg·as
ʟēꞓlälayug·ōs g·āxɛn, g·ꞏîgämēꞓ qag·as hёleg·ꞏîndaẏug·ōsxg·ada ёx·-
10 pꞏak· hāsaꞓyōs, g·ꞏîgämēꞓxwa k·ꞏēsēx āɫꞓɛm wāɫdɛm qɛns gwēk·ꞏäla-
saxwa gwaɫālamulēx wāɫdɛmxɛns g·ꞏîg·ꞏîlɛmg·ꞏîlēsaxg·ꞏîns ꞓnâxwēk·
lēlqwälaʟaꞓya, qɛns gwēk·ꞏälasa. Wä, yuꞓmēsɛns Ꞑɛm la nɛgeꞒēnē-
sɛꞓwōx.ꞓnēꞓnak·iɫē âla âlaʟasēs wāɫdɛmiꞓlälayōs g·ꞏîgämēꞓ ꞓnēk·ēxs
laē gwēgɛmx·ꞓîda lāxa Mamalēleqäla. Wä, lä ꞓnēk·a: Qɛn ꞓnēk·ē
15 Mamalēleqäl; ёx·laxaēʟa qō k·ꞏeâs sɛbats ёk·ē wāɫdɛmiꞓlälasa g·ꞏî-
gämaꞓyē g·āxɛns. Wa, wa, ꞓnēk·ē. Wa, laꞓmē ꞓwîꞓla hōꞐûwɛlsa
kꞏwēɫdē lāxēq.
      Wä, lä ꞓnäx·ꞏꞓîdxa gaālaxa ɫɛnsē. Wä, laꞓmēsē ёxaɫa qaꞓs nɛ-
qälēxs g·āxaēda ꞓnɛmgēs ꞇɛꞓwa Ɫāwitsꞏꞏēsē g·āxandālax ʟꞏɛmaisas g·ꞏō-
20 kwas ʟꞏäqoꞇasē. Wä, laɛmxaē qꞏapꞏēx·ꞓîd la ꞓnaꞓnämuɫꞓîdēda Gwētɛla ꞇɛꞓwa ꞓwālas Kwäg·uɫ ꞇɛꞓwa Qꞏōmk·ꞏutꞏɛs ꞇɛꞓwa Mamalēleqäla,
wä, hёꞓmisꞇēda Qꞏōmoyäꞓyē. Wä, laɛm la sɛk·ꞏäsg·ɛꞓmakᵘ lēlqwälaʟaꞓya la qꞏapꞏēs lāx ōxʟaꞓyasa k·ꞏîtɛla. Wä, Ꞑꞓmisē la nɛqɛmg·ꞏîɫ-
tɛwēxēs ꞓnâxwa gwayiꞓlälas qaēda Mamalēleqäläxs g·ālaē g·āxalisa
25 ꞇōxs laē dɛnxɛlasa qꞏɛmdɛmasa k·ꞏîtɛla. Wä, hёɛmxaäwis gwēx·ꞏꞓîdē-
da ꞓnɛmgēsē ꞇɛꞓwa Ɫāwitsꞏꞏēsē yîxs ꞓnāɫꞓnɛmōkwaēs qäsō qaēda mōs-
gɛꞓmakwē Kwäkûg·uɫa laqēxs g·ālaē la kꞏwēɫa. Wä, laɛm gwäɫ dɛnxɛ-
layuwē qꞏɛmdɛmasa k·ꞏîtɛla laxēq. Wä, lēx·aɛm ōgûx·ꞏꞓîdaꞓyōs wāɫdɛmasa Ɫāwitsꞏꞏēsaxs laē kꞏwēɫa, yîxs laēda g·ꞏîgämaꞓyē Lɛlak·ꞏînis
30 sɛpꞏēts Dɛntꞏälaꞓyuxa qꞏäyōxwē ʟꞏäqwa lāxēs nɛgûmpē ʟꞏäqoꞇasē.
Wä, la ʟꞏäqoꞇasē ꞇäꞇɛwɛlxsîlas Dɛntꞏälaꞓyu lāxēs g·ꞏîqēlasɛꞓwēs

with breath (i.e. a speech) to those who are given to eat,/ for it
is said by the old people that very bad is our feasting of a/chief,
for never is there one word of giving a third course to us./ I
have often heard them say it. I mean,go on,go on,"said he(5)and
sat down. Then stood up chief Yāqaɫ^ɛɛnlis/who came from the numaym
^ɛwālas, whose privilege it is to answer the/third course with a
speech at the feast. He said:/ "Indeed true is your word, chief
ʟ!āqoʟas. Now we are made happy (sweet) by the/means by which you
invite us, chief, for this your third course, this your (10) sweet
breath, (i.e. speech) chief. This is not a new saying, for this is
the way we spoke/in the beginning, this word of our ancestors of all
the/tribes. This we were to say. And now we just follow this./ I
mean this, true, true is your saying, chief." Thus he said/and
turned his face to the Mamāleleqāla and he said: "I say,(15)Mamāle-
leqala, would it be good if the kind words of the chiefs did not
strike us? Wa wa," said he. And then all the feasters went out
of the house/after this./

Day came the next morning and when it was almost noon/the ^ɛnɛm-
gis and the Ɫāwits!ēs came in front of the beach of the house(20)of
ʟ!āqoʟas. Then assembled the Gwētɛla/and the ^ɛwālas Kwāg·uɫ and the
Q!ōmk·!ūt!ɛs and the Mamāleleqala/and also the Q!ōmoyā^ɛyē. There
were five tribes/gathered at the lower end of the watchman's pole,
and now they just did/everything they had done for the Mamāleleqāla
when they first came to the beach(25)and when they sang the song of
the watchman's pole. And the/^ɛnɛmgis and Ɫāwits!ēs each also did
the same when they promised a feast for the four/Kwāg·uɫ tribes
when they first went to the feast. Then they stopped singing /the
song of the watchman's pole after this. And only this was different in the speech/of the Ɫāwits!ēs when they feasted that chief
Lɛlak·ɛnis(30)gave Dɛnt!ala^ɛyu,the expensive copper, to his son-
in-law, ʟ!āqoʟas./ Then ʟ!āqoʟas treated as a prince with Dɛnt!a-
la^ɛyu his prince, whom he was making a chief, (1) ʟ!āsótiwalis,

ʟawɛlgǎmaᵋyē ʟ!ǎsotiwalisē, qaxs hꝡᵋmēʟē ʟ!ǎsotiwalisē k·ōqwaɫ-
xa q!ǎyōxwē ʟ!ǎqwē Dɛnt!alaᵋyu qō lǎɫ yǎqwasa p!ɛlxɛlasgɛmē lǎxa
yǔduxᵘsɛᵋmakwē ʟēɫɛᵋlakᵘ lēlqwǎlaʟaᵋya. Wä, laɛm dzǎqwaxs laē
ᵋwīᵋla hōqǔwɛls lǎxa ʟēɫɛᵋlats!ē g·ōkwa. Wä, laᵋmē gwǎɫē g·ā-
5   lō ēaᵋxēnēsa mōsgɛᵋmakwē Kwǎkǔg·uɫ lǎxēq··.

Wä, g·īlᵋmēsē ᵋnǎx·īdxa gaāla laēda g·īgǎmaᵋyē Gǔyōɫɛlasxa Mamalēleqǎla ʟēᵋlǎlaxa mōsgɛᵋmakwē Kwǎkǔg·ǔɫa qa läᵋs k!wē-
ɫa. Wä, hëx·ᵋidaᵋmēsa mōsgɛᵋmakwē Kwǎkǔg·ǔɫ k!wāx·ᵋida lǎx g·ō-
kwas ʟ!ǎqoʟas qaᵋs hawaʟēlagâlē lǎx qāsowēxsdlǎxasa ᵋnǎxwa g·ī-
10   g·ɛgǎmēᵋ ʟō dzōxwaēxsdlǎxas, qaxs hꝡᵋmaᵋ qǎdatsa ᵋnǎxwa lēlqwǎ-
laʟaᵋ, qaᵋs k·!ēsē wǎlɛm la k!wēɫ lǎxa g·ālē k!wēlatsa ʟēɫɛᵋla-
kwē ʟōxs g·ālaē k!wēɫa ʟēɫɛlǎxa lēlqwǎlaʟaᵋyē qaᵋs qāsonukwē
ʟōᵋ qa dzōxwēsa· ᵋnǎɫᵋnɛmōkwē lǎxa ᵋnǎɫᵋnɛmsgɛᵋmakwē lēlqwǎlaʟaᵋya,
qō k·!eâslax qāsō ʟōᵋ dzōxwas la ᵋnēk·a bǎk!umaq ᵋyāg·aᵋyu lǎxa ʟē-
15   ɫɛla ʟɛᵋwa k!wēɫē. Wä, hëᵋmis lāg·iɫasa Kwǎkǔg·uɫē ʟēɫts!ōd lǎx
g·ōkwas ʟ!ǎqoʟas qaᵋs yäq!ɛntuwēsōx.

Wä, g·īlᵋmisē ᵋnǎɫᵋnɛmōkwa g·īg·ɛgǎmaᵋyasa mōsgɛᵋmakwē Kwǎ-
kǔg·ǔɫ ᵋnēk·ɛxs lɛᵋmaē qāsōɫ lǎxa k!wēlasʟasa Mamalēleqǎla yîx
ᵋnēᵋnak·īɫas yîxs q!ǎlaᵋmaēda mōsgɛᵋmakwē Kwǎkǔg·uɫaxs ᵋnǎɫᵋnɛms-
20   gɛmaēs k!wēlalaᵋyuʟa q!ɛmdɛm. Wä, hëᵋmis lāg·iɫas ɫâk!wēmas qa
mōkwēsēs qāsō. Wä, g·īlᵋmisē gwǎɫē wǎɫdɛmas laē ᵋwīᵋla la hōgwiʟa lǎxa k!wēlaᵋyats!ē g·ōxᵘsa g·īgǎmaᵋyē Gǔyōɫɛlas. Wä, g·īl-
ᵋmisē g·āx ᵋwīᵋlaēʟa mōsgɛᵋmakwē Kwǎkǔg·ǔɫa lāqēxs lɛᵋmaē ᵋwīᵋla
k!wamēɫa Mamalēleqǎla ʟɛᵋwa ᵋnɛmgēsē ʟɛᵋwa Ɫāwits!ēsē qaxs hëᵋmaē
25   nǎqaɫap!ōtsa Mamalēleqalēda Gwētɛla; wä, hëᵋmis nǎqaɫap!ōtsa
ᵋnɛmgēsēda Q!ōmayâᵋyē; wä, hëᵋmis nǎqaɫap!ōtsa Ɫāwits!ēsēda
ᵋwālas Kwāg·uɫa, laas äxᵋētsɛᵋwa mɛnats!ē qaᵋs lē xǎmsᵋalēlɛm
lǎxa hëɫk·!ōtiwalɫasa g·ōkwē.

Wä, lä ʟaxᵋwalɫa ōmpas Gǔyōɫɛlasxa ʟēgadäs Kwāx·īlanokǔ-
30   maᵋyē. Wä, lä yäq!ɛg·aᵋɫa. Wä, lä ᵋnēk·a gwēgɛmāɫa lǎxa Mamalēleqǎla: Laᵋmɛn wēg·īɫ nōs g·īg·ɛgǎmēᵋ lǎx gwēk·!ǎlasē lǎqᵘ

for his name was to be ʟ!āsotiwalᴉs after breaking the/expensive
copper Dᴇnt!alaᶜyu, when were to be given away blankets to the/
three invited tribes. It was evening when/they all went out of the
inviter's house. Then the(5)Kwāg·uⱡ tribes finished the first
work with this./

As soon as daylight came in the morning,then chief Gŭyōⱡᴇlas/
of the Mamaⱡeleq́ala invited the four Kwāg·uⱡ tribes to a feast./
Immediately the four tribes sat down in the house/of ʟ!aqoᵢas to
listen to each other, as to who wanted to promise a feast among all
the chiefs,(10)and who wanted to give a potlatch. For it is the
custom (lit. support) of all the tribes/that they should not in
vain be guests in the first feast. of the invited ones,/and when
first the one who invites the tribes gives a feast, then they have
someone to promise a feast/and a potlatch, one in each tribe./ If
they do not promise a feast and a potlatch, then the Indians say
that it is bad treatment in the(15)invitation and at the feast.
Therefore, the Kwāg·uⱡ were called together in the/house of ʟ!ā-
qoᵢas to talk it over./

As soon as one chief of each of the four Kwag·uⱡ tribes/said
he would promise a feast to the feasters of the Mamaⱡeleq́ala,-for
this/is what it means, the four Kwāg·uⱡ tribes know that they will
each(20)sing one feasting song, and this is the reason why they are
strong, that / four of them promise a feast; - and after they
had finished speaking, then all went into/the feasting house of
chief Gŭyōⱡᴇlas. As soon as/the four Kwāg·uⱡ tribes came in they
all went and/sat next to the Mamaⱡeleq́ala and the ᶜnᴇmgᴉs and Lawi-
ts!ēs, for(25)the Gwētᴇla are paired with the Mamaⱡeleq́ala and the
ᶜnᴇmgᴉs are paired with the/Q!ōmoyáᶜyē and the Ⱡawits!ēs are paired
with the/ᶜwālas Kwāg·uⱡ. Then the drum was taken and was put down/
in the right hand rear corner of the house/

Then arose the father of Gŭyōⱡᴇlas, whose name was Kwāx·flanō-
kŭmēᶜ,(30)and he spoke and said, turning his face to the Mamaⱡeleq́ala:/

lāxwa k!wēlasēx wāⱡdɛma, ᶜnēk·exs laē g̱wēgɛmx·ᶜĪd lāxa ōgwi-
walĪⱡasa g·ōkwē qaxs hēē k!ŭdzĪⱡa Gwētɛla. Wä, lä hö̆ k!ŭdzĪ-
ⱡa Q!ōmoyᾰᶜya hö̆ⱡk·!ōdɛnēg̱wĪⱡ; wä, lä hö̆ k!ŭdzĪⱡa ᶜwālas Kwāg·-
g·uⱡa gɛmᶜxōdɛnēg̱wĪⱡasa g·ōkwē. Laɛms wö̆g·aⱡōⱡ Gwētɛl, Q!ōmo-
yawē, ᶜwālas Kwāg·uⱡ, Q!ōmk·!ŭt!ɛs lāg·ustᾰⱡax. Laɛms k!wēᶜlā-
laⱡōⱡ qaᶜs nēⱡaōsaxɛns ᶜnāläxs k!wēlaēx. Āⱡᶜmaēⱡōx wāⱡdɛm qɛns
g̱wēk·!ālasaxwa lä qɛns wāⱡdɛmaxwa ᶜnēg·ɛmaxɛns ēʼwanᾰʼyaxg·Ī ns
ᶜnāxwēk· lēlqwǎlaⱡaᶜyaxs g·ālaōⱡēx ᶜnāg·alĪsɛns ᶜnālax qɛns ᶜnē-
k·ē Mamalēleqǎl, ᶜnɛmg̱ās, Ⱡawits!ēs, lāxōx wāⱡdɛᶜmēnaᶜyēx lāqᵘ,
ᶜnēk·ēxs laē k!wāg·alĪⱡa.

Wä,hö̆x·ᶜidaᶜmisē Q!ōmogwēxa g·ayuⱡē lāx ᶜnɛᶜmēmutasa Maᾰm-
tag·ila ⱡaxᶜwalĪⱡa qaᶜs yāq!ɛg·aᶜⱡē. Wä, lä ᶜnēk·a꞉ Qᾰ̱ⱡ, qā-
ⱡaxs hö̆ᶜmaēx gwǎlasēxɛns g·āxēx gwaēlas lāxōx g·ōkwaxsa g·Īgā-
maᶜyaqōs Mamalēleqǎlax bɛxᶜŭnālag·ilaēⱡēda ᾰlakwē g·Īgāmēxs
yāq!ɛg·aᶜⱡaē lāxwa k!wēlasⱡax wāⱡdɛmaxōs wāⱡdɛmaqōs g·Īgāmēᶜ
G̱ŭyōⱡɛlas. ᶜmāsɛnlag·Īⱡⱡa yax·q!āsɛlaⱡ ⱡōᶜgŭn g·ōⱡg·ɛkulōtak·,
ᶜnēᶜnak·iⱡē wö̆g·a lāg·ustᾰsɛn k!wēᶜyālalä q!ɛmdɛma qɛn ⱡalogwa-
daē lāxa g·Īgāmaᶜyē ᶜnēk·ē. Wä, hö̆x·ᶜidaᶜmisē dɛnxᶜēdēda Gwē-
tɛläs q!ɛmdɛmasxa ᶜnēk·ē꞉

1. Wᾰ hᾰ yä hᾰ yä hā hā.
Lādzēᶜmālᾰx yawix·flēsⱡa yayawinqɛlēsⱡa wāladzɛgēlē-
dzēx g·Īgāmaᶜyɛns lēɛlqwǎlaⱡai.
Lādzeᶜmālᾰx g·Īqǎmx·ᶜĪdēᶜyaⱡa ᶜnɛmōkŭmaᶜyēx g·Īgāma-
ᶜyaxg·Īns lēɛlqwalaⱡai.
Yā wᾰ hᾰ wä.

2. Wᾰ hᾰ yä hᾰ yä hā hā.
Māx·ts!ag·ilaᶜlaᾰx gwǎlag·flēdzadzēᶜyaxsɛns g·Īgāma-
ᶜyēx lēɛlqwǎlaⱡai.

"Now let me go on, my chiefs, according to the way of speaking/in
the feasting house," said he, and turned his face to the rear of
the/house, for there the Gwētɛla were sitting down, and the/Q!ōmo-
yâɛyē were sitting on the right hand side and the ɛwālas Kwāg·uⱡ
were sitting/on the left hand side in the rear of the house. "Now
go on, you Gwētɛla, Q!ōmoyâɛyē,(5)ɛwālas Kwāg·uⱡ,Q!ōmk·!ūt!ɛs, and
sing your feasting songs/and tell our world about this feasting.
Is it a new saying that we/say thus when we are speaking, this saying that was said by the ancestors of/all our tribes, when first
light came into our world? That is what I say,/Mamalēqăla, ɛnɛmgis,
Ⱡāwits!ēs, according to the way of saying about this."/10)Thus he
said and sat down./

Immediately Q!ōmogwē who came from the numaym Maămtag·ila/arose
and spoke. He said: "Indeed, indeed,/that is the way it is done,
the way we are in this house of your chief,/Mamalēleqăla, he who
was really made a chief, who made the souls go out(15)when he spoke
in this that is called a feast, your word that you say, chief/Gŭ-
yōⱡɛlas. Why should I be lowered together with my tribe?/ I mean,
go on and sing your feasting song that I may obtain a dish/from
the chief,"said he. And immediately the Gwētɛla sang/their song
which said:/

(20) 1. Wâ hâ yä hâ yä hā hā./

        Now this great one will move; he will move about this
            greatest/chief of our tribes./

        Now this great one will(show)the face of a great chief,
            this head chief,/our tribes./

(25)   Yā wâ hâ wä./

   2. Wâ hâ yä hâ yä hā hā./

        It is said they cause people to be ashamed, the ways of
            our great chief,/tribes./

Ôdzɛgag·ila^ɛlaâx gwälag·flēdzadzē^ɛyaxsa ōdzɛgamēdɛdzēx

wŭlgâma^ɛya g·ĭgäma^ɛyēx lēɛlqwälaʟai.

Layōłg·ɛns g·ĭgäma^ɛyēx ämaxodēyaxa ʟ̣ēgɛmnuxᵘdzēyaʟax

Lētax·ʟadzēyaxa ʟ! äʟ!aqwa qa^ɛs lēɛlqwälaʟai.

Layōłg·îns g·ĭgäma^ɛyēx ämaxodēyaxa ʟ̣ēgɛmnuxᵘdzēyaʟax

Nɛngɛmäladzēyaxa ʟ!äʟ!aqwa ḍa^ɛs lēɛlqwälaʟai.

Layōłg·îns g·ĭgäma^ɛyēx ämaxodēyaxa ʟ̣ēgɛmnuxᵘdzēyaʟax

Ângwälax·ʟadzēyaxa ʟ!äʟ!aqwa qa^ɛs lēɛlqwälaʟai.

Layōłg·îns g·ĭgäma^ɛyēx ämaxodēyaxa ʟ̣ēgɛmnuxᵘdzēyaʟax

Wâx·sē^ɛstalax·ʟadzēyaxa ʟ!äʟ!aqwa qa^ɛs lēɛlqwälaʟai.

Layōłg·îns g·ĭgäma^ɛyēx ämaxodēyaxa ʟ̣ēgɛmnuxudzēyaʟax

Mauak·!ax·ʟadzēyaxa ʟ!äʟ!aqwa qa^ɛs lēɛlqwälaʟai.

Layōłg·îns g·ĭgäma^ɛyēx nūnł^ɛēdēyak·as tsōlexayak·as x·ā-

yɛmg·ĭlaxa ʟ̣ēgɛmnuxᵘdzēyaʟax Adɛmgŭlēx·ʟadzēya ʟ!ä-

ʟ!aqwa qa^ɛs lēɛlqwälaʟai.

Layōłg·îns g·ĭgäma^ɛyēx nūnł^ɛēdēyak·as tsōlexayak·as x·ā-

yɛmg·ĭlaxa ʟ̣ēgɛmnuxᵘdzēyaʟax Qōlōmax·ʟadzēya ʟ!ä-

ʟ!aqwa qa^ɛs lēɛlqwälaʟai.

Yŭɛmya ʟ!äʟ!aqwa g·ĭsa^ɛwēsɛns g·ĭgäma^ɛyēx qa^ɛs lēɛlqwä-

laʟai.

Yā wâ hâ wä::

3. Wâ hâ yä hâ yä hä hä.

La^ɛmɛn nūsayaʟas ʟ̣ēʟɛgɛmasɛns g·ĭgäma^ɛyēx qa^ɛs lēɛlqwä-

laʟai.

Yŭ^ɛmɛnya ʟ̣ēgɛmaxg·în q!ŭlēxʟēya^ɛmēk· ^ɛmäxŭyalidzē ^ɛmäxŭ-

lag·flidzēs g ĭgäma^ɛyōs lēɛlqwälaʟai.

Yŭ^ɛmɛnya ʟ̣ēgɛmaxg·în q!ŭlēxʟēya^ɛmēk· ^ɛmäx·mɛwēsa mäx·mɛ-

wĭsagämēdzēs g·ĭgäma^ɛyōs lēɛlqwälaʟai.

Yŭ^ɛmɛnya ʟ̣ēgɛmaxg·în q!ŭlēxʟēya^ɛmēk· Gŭyōłɛlasa ǧŭyōłɛ-

lasɛmēdzēs g·ĭgäma^ɛyōs lēɛlqwälaʟai.

It is said he makes people jealous,the great high one who has
a face of which people are jealous,/the greatest chief,
tribes./

Long ago this,our great chief,gave away in a potlatch the one
that has the name/Lēta,the copper for you,tribes./

(5)   Long ago this,our great chief,gave away in a potlatch the one
that has the name/Bear Face,the copper for you,tribes./

Long ago this,our great chief,gave away in a potlatch the one
that has the name/Cloudy,the copper for you,tribes./

Long ago this,our great chief,gave away in a potlatch the one
that has the name(10)Thick-All-Around,the copper for
you, tribes./

Long ago this,our great chief,gave away in a potlatch the one
that has the name/Sea-Lion,the copper for you,tribes./

Long ago this,our great chief,became extravagant,broke and
made disappear/the one that has the great name Crane,the
copper(15)for you,tribes./

Long ago this,our great chief,became extravagant,broke and
made disappear/the one that has the great name Beaver-
Face,the copper/for you,tribes./

These are the coppers given away by our chief,for you,(20)
tribes./

Yā wâ hâ wä./

3. Wâ hâ yä hâ yä hā hā./

Now I will tell the myth of the names of our chief, for you,/
tribes./

(25) This is my name, my own name, ᶜmāxŭyalidzē, the great ᶜmāxŭ-
lag·ilis,/your chief, tribes./

This is my name,my own name, ᶜmax·mɛwis, the great ᶜmāx·mɛ-
wisagãmēᶜ,/your chief, tribes./

This is my name, my own name, Gŭyōɫɛlas, the great Gŭyōɫɛla-
sɛmēᶜ,/your chief, tribes./

Yū^εmεnya ḷēǥεmaxg·ĭn q̓ü̓lēxʟēya^εmēk· ʟ̓āqwag·iladzē
ʟ̓āqō̓ṵ̄āladzē ʟ̓ä̓ʟ̓aqwaladzē ʟ̓āqoʟasεmēdzē g·īgä-
ma^εyōs lēεlqwä̓laʟai.

G·adzēyaεm mεnmεnx̓axʟäyu ḷē̓ḷεǥεmas wiwōmpdzēyaxa q̓ü-
lēxʟēya^εmēk· Mεnlēdēya Mεnlēdεnü̓x̓dzē g·īgäma^εyōs
lēεlqwä̓laʟai.

G·adzēyaεm mεnmεnx̓axʟäyu ḷē̓ḷεǥεmas wiwōmpdzēyaxa q̓ü-
lēxʟēya^εmēk· Kwāx·flanōkümē Kwākwax·âladzē Kwāx·-
sē^εstaladzē g·īgäma^εyōs lēεlqwä̓laʟai.

Yūεmya ḷē̓ḷεǥεmdzēyasεn g·īqag·iwa^εyεn gagεmpdzēyaxa q̓ü-
lēxʟēya^εmēk· Mātag·iladzēs g·īgäma^εyōs lēεlqwä̓laʟai.
Yā wâ hâ wä.

Wä, g·fl^εmisē q̓ü̓lbēda q̓εmdεmē laas Q̓ōmogwē xāxalolaqwa
laqēxs ḷa^εwē̓x̓tsämaē lāx wāwasεlīlasasa dεnxεla. Wä, lä yāq̓ε-
g·a^εx̓a. Wä, lä ^εnēk·a: Wa, wa, laεms ēt̓ēd wü̓ʟ̓āx^εaʟεlaxwa ^εwā-
la^εyālax q̓εmdεmaxεn q̓εmdεmēx qa^εs ha^εmā̓x̓εl lēlqwä̓laʟai. ^εnē-
^εnak·ix̓ē la^εmεn qāsō qa^εs Mamalēleqä̓l, ^εnεmgēs, x̓awits̓ēs,^εnēk·ē.

Wä, lä ḷāx^εwalīx̓ē x̓ālak·ots̓a qa^εs yāq̓εg·a^εx̓εxa g·āyux̓ē
lāx ^εnε^εmēmutasa Yaēx·agema^εyasa Q̓ōmoyâ^εyē. Wä, lä ^εnēk·a:
Qä̓ʟ, qä̓ʟaxs hē^εmaē wāx̓dε^εmēnē lāq^u qaεns g·īg·flgowēk· ḷε^εwa ^εwā-
lasēx lēlqwä̓laʟa^εyaxg·īns ^εnēx·sō^εmēk· yīsεns wīsōmp^εwü̓x̓a qεns
â^εmē nεgεx̓tεwēx t̓εx·īla^εyas qεns qāstawēsε^εwa lāxwa g·āxa qεns
gwaēlas lāxwa g·ōkwaxsa g·īgäma^εyāx Gü̓yōx̓εlasēx. ^εnē^εnak·ix̓ē wä-
g·a ēk·̓ēqεlax Kwāküg·ü̓x̓ qa^εs dεnx^εidaōsasεn q̓εmdεma, ^εnēk·ē.
Wä, hē̓x·^εida^εmisē dâqâlēda nâgadäs q̓εmdεmasxa ^εnēk·ē.

1. Wâ hâ hâ yä, wâ hâ hâ yä, hēla ha hâ wâ hō wa.
Ladzē^εmalōx ētalēsʟεns g·īgäma^εyēx ḷēlax̓εwax̓xa ^εwī^εwεls-
gε^εmakwa lēlqwä̓laʟai.
^εya wâ hâ yä xwa ämā̓xwalax̓εx g·īgäma^εyεns lēlqwä̓laʟai.

191

This is my name,my own name,the great ʟ!āqwag·ila,/the great
     ʟ!āqoʟāla,the great ʟ!āʟ!aqwala,the great ʟ!āqoʟasɛmēᵉ,
     your chief,/tribes./
And these are the feast names of my own great ancestors(5),
     whose own names were Mɛnlēd,the great Mɛnlēdɛnuɫ, your
     chief,/tribes./
And these are the feast names of my own great ancestors,/whose
     own names were Kwāx·ꜩlanokŭmēᵉ,the great Kwākwax·âla,/the
     great Kwax·sēᵉstāla, your chief,tribes./
(10) These are the names of my chief before me,my great grandfather/
     whose own name is the great Mātag·ila of your chief,tribes./
     Yā wâ hâ wä./

As soon as the song was at an end Q!ōmogwa shouted "ha ha ha!"/
while he was standing still during the time that they were singing.
Then he spoke(15)and said: "Wa wa. Now you have heard again the/
great sound of this song,my song for every tribe./ I mean I promise
a feast for you, Mamalēleqāla, ᵉnɛmgis, Ḻāwits!ēs," said he./
     Then Ḻālak·ots!a arose and spoke. He belonged/to the numaym of
the Yaēx·agɛmēᵉ of the Q!ōmoyâᵉyē. He said(20),"Indeed,indeed,that
is the speech to(make at)the first meeting of these great/tribes,
for we are told by our ancestors that we/are to follow the road
they made for us to be walked on. In this way/we come and are in
this house of this chief Gŭyōɫɛlas. I mean this,go on/and be happy,
Kwāg·uɫ,and sing my song," said he.(25)Immediately, the song leaders
began the song which said:/

     1.Wâ hâ hâ yä, wâ hâ hâ yä, hēla hā hâ wâ hō wā./
     Now our chief will be again great when he invites all the/
          tribes./
     ᵉyā wâ hâ yä. The chief,Potlatch Dancer,our tribes./

ᵋya wâ hâ yä xwa ᴌēlaᴌawaēnōxᵘdzēx g·Ȋgāmaᵋyᴇns lēlqwälaᴌai.

ᵋya wâ hâ yä lāx gwēgwälag·ȋlēdzēyasᴇns wȋwōmpdzēyaxa
q!ülēxᴌaᵋyadzē ᴌālēᴌalaᴌdzēs g·Ȋgāmaᵋyōs lēlqwälaᴌai.

ᵋya wâ hâ yä ᴌēgᴇmdzēyasᴇn wiwōmpdzēyaxa q!ülēxᴌäᵋya-
dzē P!āsᴇlaᴌdzē P!ēp!ādzäyudzēs g·Ȋg·ᴇgāmaᵋyōs lēlqwälaᴌai.

ᵋya wâ hâ yä ᴌēgᴇmdzēyasᴇn wiwōmpdzēyaxa q!ülēxᴌaᵋya-
dzē Lāk·usaᵋyadzē Lālak·uts!adzēs g·Ȋg·ᴇgāmaᵋyōs
lēlqwälaᴌai.

ᵋya wâ hâ yä ᴌēgᴇmdzēyasᴇn wiwōmpdzēyaxa q!ülēxᴌäᵋya-
dzē Haēᴌᴇkᵘdzē Haēᴌᴇkümēdzēs g·Ȋgagāmaᵋyōs lēlqwälaᴌai.

ᵋya wâ hâ yä yūdzēᴇm ᴌēᴌᴇgᴇmdzēyasᴇn g·Ȋqag·iwē qaᵋs
lēlqwälaᴌai.

ᵋya wâ ha hä.

2.Wâ hâ hâ yä, wâ hâ hâ yä, hēla ha hâ wâ hō wa.

Ladzēᵋma lāx q!ayâlaᴌa nūsaᵋyaᴌᴇns g·Ȋgāmēdzēsēs nūᴌa-
g·iwēdzēxa q!ülēxᴌäᵋyadzē Nᴇnōlᴇyōdzē Nᴇnōlōgᴇmē-
dzēs g·Ȋg·ᴇgāmaᵋyōs lēlqwälaᴌai.

Lāyuᴌa lax·sᵋᴇndēyaxa ᴌēgᴇmnuxᵘdzēyuᴌa Adᴇmgüli ᴌ!āqwa-
ya qaᵋs lēlqwälaᴌai.

ᵋya wâ hâ yä lāyuᴌa lāx·sᵋᴇndēyaxa ᴌēgᴇmnuxᵘdzēyuᴌa ᴌ!ēx-
ts!ᴇm ᴌ!āqwaya qaᵋs lēlqwälaᴌai.

ᵋya wâ hâ yä lāyuᴌa lāx·sᵋᴇndēyaxa ᴌēgᴇmnuxᵘdzēyuᴌa Q!ᴇ-
datâla ᴌ!āqwaya qaᵋs lēlqwälaᴌai.

ᵋya wâ hâ yä lāyuᴌa lāx·sᵋᴇndēyaxa ᴌēgᴇmnuxᵘdzēyuᴌa Ōba-
laa ᴌ!āqwaya qaᵋs lēlqwälaᴌai.

ᵋya wâ hâ yä. The great one who always invites our chief,/
tribes./

ᵋya wâ hâ yä. As it was always done by my great ancestors,/
whose own name is the great ʟalêʟalaⱡ, your chiefs,
(5) tribes./

ᵋya wâ hâ yä. The great name of my ancestors, whose own
name was/great P!asɛlaⱡ, the great P!êp!ādzäyōs, your
chiefs,/tribes./

ᵋya wâ hâ yä. The great name of my ancestors, whose own
name was(10)Lāk·us , the great Lālak·ots!a, your
chiefs,/tribes./

ᵋya wâ hâ yä. The great name of my ancestors, whose own
name was/HaêʟakU; the great Haêʟakûmêᵋ, your chiefs,/
tribes./

(15) ᵋya wâ hâ yä. These are the great names of my chief who
lived before me, for you,/tribes./

ᵋya wâ ha hä./

2. Wâ hâ hâ yä, wâ hâ hâ yä, hâla ha hâ wâ hō waⱡ/
Now I will tell the history, the myth of our great chief,
of this great extravagant one(20)whose own great name
was the great Nɛnōlɛyos, Nɛnōlōgɛmêᵋ,/your chief,
tribes./

How long ago he broke the copper which had the name Crane,
the copper/for you, tribes./

ᵋya wâ hâ yä. Long ago he broke the copper which had the
name Sea Lion Flipper,(25)the copper for you,tribes./

ᵋya wâ hâ yä. Long ago he broke the copper which had the
name Patched Ear,/the copper for you, tribes./

ᵋya wâ hâ yä. Long ago he broke the copper which had the
name Point of Rock,/the copper for you, tribes./

ᵉya wâ hâ yä lāyuƚa lāx·sᵉɛndēyaxa ʟ̣ēg̣ɛmnux̣ᵘdzēyuƚa
Sɛwa ʟ!āqwaya qaᵉs lēlqwälaʟai.

ᵉya wâ hâ yä lāyuƚa lāx·sᵉɛndēyaxa ʟ̣ēg̣ɛmnux̣ᵘdzēyuƚa
Qolōma ʟ!āqwaya qaᵉs lēlqwälaʟai.

5 ᵉya wâ hâ yä lāyuƚa lāx·sᵉɛndēyaxa ʟ̣ēg̣ɛmnux̣ᵘdzēyuƚa
Q!ōq!ŭs·ʟ!āqwaya qaᵉs lēlqwälaʟai.

ᵉya wâ hâ yä lāyuƚa lāx·sᵉɛndēyaxa ʟ̣ēg̣ɛmnux̣ᵘdzēyuƚa
Nusē ʟ!āqwaya qaᵉs lēlqwälaʟai.

ᵉya wâ hâ yä yŭdzēɛm lɛlax·sᵉɛmut ʟ!āʟ!aqwayasɛn wi-
10 wōmpdzēya qaᵉs lēlqwälaʟai.

ᵉya wâ hâ yä yŭdzēyaᵉmɛn nŭƚag·iwē qaᵉs lēlqwälaʟai.

ᵉya wâ ha hä.

3. Wâ hâ hâ yä, wâ hâ hâ yä, hēla ha hâ wâ hō wa.

Māx·ts!ag·ilōx k·!ēsᵉōxʟäyēx ʟ̣ēʟ̣ɛg̣ɛmaxsa âla g·îgāma-
15 ᵉyîns lēlqwälaʟai.

ᵉya wâ hâ yä māx·ts!ag̣ɛmg·ilōx k·!ēsᵉoᵉwilas g·ōx̣ᵘdzē-
yaxsɛns g·îgāmaᵉyɛns lēlqwälaʟai.

ᵉya wâ hâ yä ōdzɛg̣ɛmg·ilōx gwälag·flidzadzēyaxsɛns g·î-
gāmaᵉyɛns lēlqwälaʟai.

20 ᵉya wâ hâ yä gwāla wŭƚᵉɛmaik·as hāyōtɛlaʟa wŭnwŭnk·!ā-
laʟōƚ g·îgabewēsɛns g·îgāmaᵉyēx lēlqwälaʟai.

ᵉya wâ hâ yä ᵉnɛmōxdzēyaᵉmēk· āmāx̣ŭlaƚ qaᵉs lēlqwälaʟai.

ᵉya wâ hâ yä.

Wä, g·îlᵉmisē q!ŭlbē q!ɛmdɛmas laas Lālak·ots!a dzōnoqwa.
25 Wä, lä yāq!ɛg·aᵉƚa. Wä, lä ᵉnēk·a: Qāʟ, qāʟa wāƚdɛmasa q!ɛm-
dɛ̣ɛnxɛn q!ɛmdɛm qaᵉs hamāƚel lēlqwälaʟai. Wä, hēᵉmisɛn lāg·iƚa
k·!ēs bɛnsasg·în wāƚdɛmbidoᵉʟɛk· ʟâʟ lēlqwälaʟai. Laɛm haᵉmäƚ
qᵉs Mamalēleqal, ᵉnɛmg̣ēs, Ƚawits!ēs lāqag·axs lāk·!ɛndēk· p!ɛl-
ᵉ lasg̣ɛma,ᵉnēk·ēxs laē k!wāg·flîƚa.

ᵋya wâ hâ yä. Long ago he broke the copper which had the
    name Sɛwa,/the copper for you, tribes./

ᵋya wâ hâ yä. Long ago he broke the copper which had the
    name/Beaver Face,the copper for you,tribes./

(5) ᵋya wâ hâ yä. Long ago he broke the copper which had the name/
    Mountain on the Ground,the copper for you,tribes./

ᵋya wâ hâ yä. Long ago he broke the copper which had the
    name/Moon, the copper for you, tribes./

ᵋya wâ hâ yä. These are the coppers which were broken(10)by
    my ancestors for you, tribes./

ᵋya wâ hâ yä. This is my great extravagant one, who lived be-
    fore me, for you, tribes./

ᵋya wâ ha hä./

3. Wâ hâ hâ yä, wâ hâ hâ yä, hēla ha hâ wâ hō wa./
    Making Ashamed, this is the privilege name, the names of the
        true chiefs,(15)our tribes./

    ᵋya wâ hâ yä. Causing to look ashamed,this is the great privi-
        lege,the great house of our/chief,our tribes./

    ᵋya wâ hâ yä. Causing the face to look different,this is the
        manner of our/chief, our tribes./

(20) ᵋya wâ hâ yä. Do not try in vain to talk loud and to talk
        secretly,/you chief under our chief, tribes./

    ᵋya wâ hâ yä. This is the only potlatch dancer for you,tribes./

    ᵋya wâ hâ hä.

As soon as the song was ended Lālak·ots!a uttered the Dzōnoq!wa
cry.(25) Then he spoke and said: "Indeed, true are the words of the
song,/my song for you,(various)tribes. Therefore/I am not ashamed
of the little speech that I am going to(address to)you, tribes. Indeed this will be food/for you,Mamalēleqala,ᵋnɛmgis,Lāwits!ēs,these
hundred blankets."/ Thus he said and sat down.

Wä, lä ʟā̆xᴇwalĪ̆ē Lāxsō̆dᴇlasᴇᴄwēxᴀ g·āyuƚe lāxa ᴄnᴇᴄmēmutasa
Wāwŭlibā̆ᴄyasa ᴄwālas Kwāg·uƚ. Wä, lä yāq!ᴇg·aᴄƚa. Wä, lä ᴄnēk·a:
Wāg·a dᴇnxᴄētsᴇn q!ᴇmdᴇmaxa ᴄwālaᴄyalä q!ᴇmdᴇmᴇn qag·ada lēlqwāla-
ʟēk·,ᴄnēk·ē. Wä, heᴄx·idaᴄmisa nā̆gadē dā̆qā̆lasa ᴄnēk·ē:

5   1. Hă̆wᴉlkŭlaƚg·ᴉns g·Ĭg̱āmēg·ᴉns lēlqwālaʟai.
        Wā̆ ā̆ ā̆ hā̆ ho wā yā wā̆ ho wā.
        Hă̆wᴉlkŭlaƚg·ᴉns g·Ĭg̱āmēg·ᴉns lēlqwālaʟai.
        Wāwistālax˺dzēg·ᴉns g·Ĭg̱āmēg·ᴉns lēlqwālaʟai.
        Xwa gwā̆ƚᴇlamuƚēx g·Ĭg̱āmēsᴇn nŭyᴇmbālisa qaᴄs lēlqwālaʟai.
10   ᴄya wā̆ ho wä.

        2. ʟā̆kŭlaƚg·ᴉns g·Ĭg̱āmēg·ᴉns lēlqwālaʟai.
        Wā̆ ā̆ ā̆ hā̆ ho wā yā wā̆ ho wa.
        ʟā̆kŭlaƚg·ᴉns g·Ĭg̱āmēg·ᴉns lēlqwālaʟai.
        Ā̆ladzēᴇmᴄla lōx nŭyᴇmbalis g·Ĭg̱āmēᴄyᴇns g·Ĭg̱amaᴄyēx lēlqwā-
15   laʟai.
        Nō̆gwaᴇm ʟē̆ʟᴇgᴇmalasa g·ᴉlō̆ʟaxalasxēs ʟē̆ʟᴇgᴇmosai lēlqwāla-
        ʟaimᴇnēᴄxᵘ.
        Nō̆gwaᴇms k·!ak·!esᴄā̆lasō̆sai lēlqwālaʟaimᴇnēᴄxᵘ.
        Nō̆gwaᴇms ʟ!ā̆ʟ!aqwālasō̆sai lēlqwālaʟaimᴇnēᴄxᵘ.
20   Ā̆g·iƚdzēyaᴄmᴇn dāsdalᴇmnuxᵘ wā̆ƚdᴇmmᴇnēᴄxwas g·Ĭg·ᴇg̱āmmᴇnē̆x-
        ᴎasa lēlqwālaʟai.
        Xō̆xs ᴄnēk·amēᴄstālaēx g·Ĭg̱āmaᴄyᴉn g·Ĭg̱āmaᴄyᴉn.
        Nō̆gwadzēwēsʟa ā̆laya g·Ĭg̱āmaᴄyō̆s lēlqwālaʟai.
        ᴄya wā̆ ho wä.

25   3. Hă̆wᴉlkŭlaƚg·ᴉns g·Ĭg̱āmēg·ᴉns lēlqwālaʟai.
        Wā̆ ā̆ ā̆ hā̆ ho wā yā wā̆ ho wa.
        Hă̆wᴉlkŭlaƚg·ᴉns g·Ĭg̱āmēg·ᴉns lēlqwālaʟai.
        G·āxdzēᴇmk· ēt!alisg·ᴉns g·Ĭg̱āmēg·ᴉns lēlqwālaʟai.

Then arose Laxsõdɛlasõᵋ who belonged to the numaym/Wãwũlibã-ᵋyẽ of the ᵋwãlas Kwãg·uⱡ. He spoke and said:/"Go on and sing my song,my great sounding song,for these tribes."/said he. Immediately the song leaders began with these words:/

(5) 1. A great cedar dancer is our chief, our tribes./

Wâ â â hâ ho wã yã wâ ho wã./

A great cedar dancer is our chief, our tribes./

It cannot be spanned, our great chief, our tribes./

My chief here from long ago, from the beginning of the myth

time, for you, tribes./

(10) ᵋya wâ ho wä.

2. A big (tree) dancer is our chief, tribes./

Wâ â â hâ ho wã yã wâ ho wa.

A big tree dancer is our chief, our tribes./

It is said truly great is he from the beginning of the myth

time, our chief, (15) tribes./

I am the one from whom you took the names, from whom you

stole your names,/little tribes./

I am the one from whom you took the crests,little tribes./

I am the one from whom you took the coppers,little tribes./

(20) Therefore I have it as a matter for laughing, the little

words you say, little chiefs/of the tribes./

For you say all around that I am a chief,I am a chief.

I am thoroughly great, truly your chief, tribes./

ᵋya wâ ho wä./

(25) 3. A great cedar dancer is our chief, our tribes./

Wâ â â hâ ho wã yã wâ ho wa.

A great cedar dancer is our chief, our tribes./

He comes again,the great one,our chief,our tribes./

Laɛmxaak· ētalisᴌa ᴌēlaᴌawaᴌôᴌ lēlqwälaᴌai.

ᴊēgɛmqꜞälɛmᴌai ᴊēgɛmdzēyasɛn gagɛmpdzēyaxa qꜞülēxᴌēyadzēyuᴌa Yāqoᴌadzēya Yaqoᴌalasɛmēdzēs g·Ig·ɛgāmaᶜya qaᶜs
lēlqwälaᴌai.

5   Gagɛmpqꜞälɛmᴌɛn gagɛmpdzēyaxa qꜞülēxᴌēyadzēyuᴌa Yāqaᴌᶜɛnā-
ladzē, Yāqaᴌᶜɛnlidzēs g·Ig·ɛgāmaᶜya qaᶜs lēlqwälaᴌai.

Gagɛmpqꜞälɛmᴌɛn gagɛmpdzēyaxa qꜞülēxᴌēyadzēyuᴌa Yäqawidzē
Yäqukꜞwālag·flidzēs g·Ig·ɛgāmaᶜya qaᶜs lēlqwälaᴌai.

Gagɛmpqꜞälɛmᴌɛn gagɛmpdzēyaxá qꜞülēxᴌēyadzēyuᴌa ᴌꜞālidzē

10   ᴌꜞālisk·asᶜodzēs g·Ig·ɛgāmaᶜya qaᶜs lēlqwälaᴌai.

Yūɛmya ᴊēᴌɛgɛmdzēyasɛn gagɛmpdzēyaxa K·flɛmdzē K·Ik·f-
ᴌalayudzēs g·Ig·ɛgāmaᶜyas lēlqwälaᴌai.

ᶜya wâ ho wä.

Wä, g·flᶜmisē qꜞülbē qꜞɛmdɛmas laē hāsɛla dāᴌᶜɛla. Wä, g·fl-

15   ᶜmisē gwāᴌ dāᴌalaxs laē ᴌꜞôlapsamēxs laē yāqꜞɛg·aᶜᴌa. Wä, lä ᶜnē-
k·a: Hëᶜmɛn lāg·iᴌa âɛm dāsdaᴌas wâᴌdɛmasa bɛgwānɛm, yîxs laē g·f-
lôᴌaxɛn ᴊēᴌɛgɛm qaᶜs lē ᴌɛmqꜞāla ᶜnēx· gāgayatsɛn gagɛmpē k·ꜞeâsaaᴌaᴌ
gwɛᶜyâ. ᶜnēnak·iᴌē g·Ig·ɛgāmēs Mamalēleqāl, ᶜnɛmᵷis, Ꝇāwitsꜞēs, ha-
ᶜmāᴌa qaᶜs lāk·ꜞɛndē pꜞɛlxɛlasgɛma, ᶜnēk·ēxs laē kꜞwag·alîᴌa.

20   Wä, lä ᴌāxᶜwälîᴌē Kwāgwaᶜnoxa g·āyuᴌē lāxa ᶜnɛᶜmēmutasa ᴊēᴌɛ-
gēdäsa Qꜞômk·ꜞütꜞɛs. Wä, lä yāqꜞɛg·aᶜᴌa. Wä, lä ᶜnēk·a: Nôgwaɛm
Kwāgwaᶜnâ ᴊēᴌɛlaēnoxᵘ lâᴌ hamäᴌɛl lēlqwälaᴌaᶜya. Wä g·a dôqwäᴌa g·ā-
xɛn. Ā, maᴌtꜞälag·anɛmaôs g·āxɛn hamäᴌɛl lēlqwälaᴌai. Wäg·a, lā-
g·ustâsɛn qꜞɛmdɛma ᶜnēk·ē. Wä, hëx·ᶜidaᶜmēsē dâqâlēda nâgadēxa ᶜnē-

25   k·a g·fldzaᶜyala qꜞɛmdɛms:

1. Wâ â â â a; wâ wâ hâ ho wā ā a ho wa â ā ā hā.
    ᶜmāx·mɛwäsax ôdamuᴌahax nôhogwä.
Wâ â â â a; wâ wâ hâ ho wā ā a hô wa ā ā ā hā.
    ᴌēx·ᴌɛlîsax ôdamuᴌahax nôhogwä.

Now you will be again invited, tribes./

The true name of my great grandfather, whose own name is/Yā-
qoḷas,Yāqoḷālasɛmēᶜ,the great chief,for you/tribes./

(5)   It is truly my grandfather,whose own name was Yāqaⱡɛnāla,/
Yāqaⱡᶜɛnlis, chief,for you tribes./

It is truly my grandfather,whose own name was Yāqawid/Yāqu-
k!wālag·ilis, chief for you, tribes./

It is truly my grandfather,whose own name was ʟ!ālis,(10)
ʟ!ālisk·asᶜo,chief for you, tribes./

These are the great names of my great grandfather,K·ilɛm,
K·ik·iⱡɛlayu,/chiefs of the tribes./

ᶜya wâ ho wä./

As soon as the song was finished he laughed loud and(15)after
he had laughed, he spoke angrily and said:/"This is the reason why
I laugh at the words of the man who stole/my names,and who brags,
saying that he has for his grandfather my grandfather,but it is not/
(true)what he claims. I mean this, chiefs of the Mamalēleqala,ᶜnɛm-
gis,Lāwits!ēs,/this will be food for you,these one hundred blankets,"
thus he said and sat down./

(20)Then arose Kwāgwaⁿo,who belonged to the numaym of the ʟē-
ʟɛgēd/of the Q!ōmk·!ūt!ɛs. Then he spoke and said, "I am Kwagwaᶜno,
I know/how to invite you,(various)tribes. Now look at me./ Oh, you
may know me, all you tribes. Now go on/sing my song," said he. And
immediately the song leaders began the words(25)of the song of the
ancestors./

1. Wâ â â â a; wâ wâ hâ ho wā ā a ho wa ā ā ā hā./
Give a potlatch to those who suddenly came to me./
Wâ â â â a; wâ wâ hâ ho wā ā a hō wa ā ā ā hā./
Invite those who come suddenly to me./

WäꞆɛlag·a g·Ig̃ãmḗdzē ꞆēqayaꞘtsēs Ꞇēgɛmdzē yūsaxs q!ǔ-
lēxꞆeya^ɛmax HaēꞆ.ɛk^u, HaēꞆ.ɛkǔmḗdzē.

WäꞆɛlag·a g·Ig̃ãmḗdzē ꞆēqayaꞘtsēs Ꞇēgɛmdzē yūsaxs q!ǔ-
lēxꞆeya^ɛmax Yãyagalas, YäquꞆ!ēqɛladzē.

5   WäꞆɛlag·a g·Ig̃ãmḗdzē ꞆēqayaꞘtsēs Ꞇēgɛmdzē yūsaxs q!ǔ-
lēxꞆeya^ɛmax Gwãgǔng·ilalis, Gǔnãxaladzē.

WäꞆɛlag·a g·Ig̃ãmḗdzē ꞆēqayaꞘtsēs Ꞇēgɛmdzē yūsaxs q!ǔ-
lēxꞆeya^ɛmax Kwãg·uꞘdzēyag·în Kwãgwa^ɛnodzē.

WäꞆɛlag·a g·Ig̃ãmḗdzē ꞆēqayaꞘtsēs Ꞇēgɛmdzē yūsaxs q!ǔ-
10   lēxꞆeya^ɛmax ^ɛnãx·nag·ɛm, ^ɛnãx·nag·ɛmgãmē^ɛdzē.

Yūɛmya ꞆēꞆ.ɛgɛmdzēyasɛn wiwõmpdzēya qa^ɛs lēlqwãlaꞆai.
^ɛya wâ hēla hã wâ ho wä.

2. Wâ â â â a; wâ wâ hâ ho wã ã a hõ wa ã ã ã hã.

La^ɛmɛnya q!ɛyâlaꞘtsg·a Ꞇ!ãꞆ.!aqwayasa g·Ig̃ãma^ɛyēx lâꞘ lēɛl-
15   qwãlaꞆai.

G·aɛmg·a Sɛ^ɛwax·Ꞇadzē Ꞇ!ãqwayasɛns g·Ig̃ãma^ɛyēx lēɛlqwãlaꞆai.

G·aɛmg·a Adɛmgulix·Ꞇadzē Ꞇ!ãqwayasɛns g·Ig̃ãma^ɛyēx lēɛlqwãlaꞆai.

G·aɛmg·a LõbiꞘilax·Ꞇadzē Ꞇ!ãqwayasɛns g·Ig̃ãma^ɛyēx lēɛlqwã-
20   laꞆai.

G·aɛmg·a Dɛnt!ãlayux·Ꞇadzē Ꞇ!ãqwayasɛns g·Ig̃ãma^ɛyēx lēɛlqwãlaꞆai.

G·aɛmg·a Qõlomax·Ꞇadzē Ꞇ!ãqwayasɛns g·Ig̃ãma^ɛyēx lēɛlqwãlaꞆai.

25   G·aɛmg·a Q!õq!ǔsx·Ꞇadzē Ꞇ!ãqwayasɛns g·Ig̃ãma^ɛyēx lēɛlqwãlaꞆai.

G·aɛmg·a yūdux^usɛmdzē Nūsēx·Ꞇadzē Ꞇ!ãqwayasɛns g·Ig̃ãma^ɛyēx
lēɛlqwãlaꞆai.

Yūɛm Ꞇ!ãꞆ.!aqwayasɛns g·Ig̃ãma^ɛyēx, lēɛlqwãlaꞆai.
30   ^ɛya wâ hēla hã wâ ho wä.

Go on, great chief, call your great name,/your own name,
    Haêḷᴇkᵘ, Haêḷᴇkŭmêᵋ./

Go on, great chief, call your great name,/your own name,
    Yāyagalas, YᾱquʟꞋêqᴇla./

(5) Go on, great chief, call your great name,/your own name,
    Gwāgŭng·ilalis, Gŭnāxalas./

Go on, great chief, call your great name,/your own name,
    Kwāg·uɫ, Kwāgwᴀ́no./

Go on, great chief, call your great name,(10) your own name,
    ᵋnāx·nag·ᴇm, ᵋnāx·nag·ᴇmgᾰmêᵋ./

These are the great names of my ancestors, for you, tribes./
ᵋya wâ hêla hā wâ ho wä./

2. Wâ â â â a; wâ wâ hâ ho wā ā a hō wa ā ā ā hā.

Now I will tell the tale of those coppers of this chief to
    you, (15) tribes./

This is named Sᴇᵋwa, the great copper of our chief, tribes./

This is named Crane, the great copper of our chief,/tribes./

This is named the Great-House-Emptier, the copper of our
    chief (20) tribes./

This is named Means-of-Strife, the great copper of our
    chief,/ tribes./

This is named Beaver-Face, the great copper of our chief,/
    tribes./

(25) This is named Mountain-on-the-Ground, the great copper of
    - our chief,/ tribes./

These are the three great ones, named Moon, the great copper
    of our chief,/ tribes./

These are the coppers of our chief, tribes./

(30) ᵋya wâ hêla hā wâ ho wä.

3. Wâ â â â a; wâ wâ hâ ho wā ā a hō wa â ā ā hā.

Māx·ts!ag·ila lâx māx·ts!agɛmg·ila lâx ʟ!âʟ!aqwayaxsɛns
g·īgāmaᶜyēx lēɛlqwālaʟai.

Māx·ts!ag·ila lâx māx·ts!agɛmg·ila lâx ʟêʟɛgɛmdzēyaxsɛns
5   g·īgāmaᶜyēx lēɛlqwālaʟai.

Yūɛmya ʟ!âʟ!aqwadzēyasɛn wiwōmpdzēyaxa q!ülêxʟēyadzē G·ā-
laxaakᵘ G·ālaxaakwiᶜlakᵘdzē g·īgāmaᶜyēx lēɛlqwālaʟai.

Nōgwadzēyaɛm ʟɛᶜwɛlgāmēsɛn ōmpk·asᶜowaxa q!ülêxʟēyadzē G·ā-
yusdēyadzē, G·āyusdēyadzēsɛmēᶜdzē g·īgāmaᶜyēx lēɛlqwā-
10   laʟai.

ᶜya wâ hēla hā wâ ho wä.

Wä, g·îlᶜmisē q!ülbē q!ɛmdɛmas laē Kwāgwaᶜno xāxalolāqwa qaᶜs
dzōnoqwē. Wä, lä yāq!ɛg·aᶜła. Wä, lä ᶜnēk·a; Lɛᶜmas wüʟɛlaxɛn
q!ɛmdɛm. Hěᶜmɛn q!ɛmdɛmxg·în g·ālaōłg·în ʟêłɛla lâʟ Mamalēleqâl,
15 ᶜnɛmgēs, Łāwits!ēs. Małt!älag·anɛmaōs g·āxɛn. Nōgwaɛm Kwāgwaᶜnâ,
q!âʟɛlax ʟêłɛla lâʟ yūduxᵘsɛᶜmakᵘ lōlqwālaʟē. Nōgwaɛm māx·ts!ag·i-
la g·īgāmēᶜ qaᶜs hamałɛl lōlqwālaʟē; ᶜnēnak·iłē laᶜmɛn qāsō qaᶜs
Mamalēleqâl. Laᶜmɛn qasō qaᶜs ᶜnɛmgēs. Laᶜmɛn qāsō qaᶜs Łāwits!ēs
yîsg·ada lāk·!ɛndē p!ɛlxɛlasgɛma. Wa, wa, ᶜnēk·ēxs laē k!wāg·alîlₐ.
20 Wä, lä ʟâxᶜwalîłē Gǔyôʟɛlasxa k!wēlasēxa g·īgāmaᶜyasa Mamalēleqāla qaᶜs yāq!ɛg·aᶜłē. Wä, lä ᶜnēk·a, Qäʟ g·īg·ɛgāmēᶜ qäʟēs wäł-
dɛmōs laxwa ʟeqwiᶜlälax wäłdɛms äxänokwasɛns lax gwaᶜyiᶜlälasa.
Nōsaêʟɛnsäx· wäłdɛmaxwa ᶜnēk·amōsɛlayâsɛns gaāgɛmpᶜwüła qɛns âɛm
nānagałᶜɛnēsɛᶜwa. Wä, hěᶜmēsɛns lāg·iła k·!eâs āłilaᶜya. ᶜnē-
25 ᶜnak·iłē laᶜmɛns g·āg·ixsilaxwa āłax g·īgāmaᶜya lāxōx ʟ!âsotiwali-
saxōs g·îqēlasɛᶜwaq!ōs g·īgāmēᶜ ʟ!âqoʟas. ᶜwa, gēlak·asᶜla Kwākǔ-
g·uł, g·āxaaqōs ěk·!ēqägilēłxɛn łōɛlq!wēx, ᶜnēk·ēxs laē wäxaxa hä-
ᶜyäłᶜäsa Mamalēleqāla ʟɛᶜwa ᶜnɛmgēs ʟɛᶜwa Ławits!ēsē qa k·āx·ᶜi-
dēsēsa k!wēladzɛmē lāxa Kwākǔg·ułē. Wä, g·îlᶜmisē ᶜwîᶜla la k·ax·-

3. Wâ â â â a; wâ wâ hâ ho wā ā a hō wa ā ā ā hā.

    This is causing shame, that causes us to look ashamed, the
        coppers of our/chief, tribes./

    This is causing shame, causing us to look shamed, the great
        names of our(5)chief, tribes./

    These are the great coppers of our ancestors, whose own
        names were G·ālaxaaku,/G·ālaxaakwiᶜlaku, the great chief,
        tribes./

    I am the great one,the prince of my excellent father whose
        own name is G·āyusdēᶜyas,/G·āyusdēᶜyadzēsɛmēᶜ, the
        great chief,(10) tribes./

    ᶜya wâ hēla hā wâ ho wä.

As soon as the song was at an end,Kwāgwᴉno cried,"Haha haha,"
uttering the/Dzōnoq!wa cry. Then he spoke and said: "Now you have
heard my/song. This is my song,this one when I first invited you,
Mamalēleqàla,(15)ᶜnɛmgis,Lāwits!ēs. You may know me. I am Kwāgwaho,/
who knows how to invite you three tribes. I am the/chief who makes
ashamed all you tribes. I mean this. I promise a feast to you,/Mama-
lēleqala. Now I promise a feast to you,ᶜnɛmgis. Now I promise a
feast to you,Lāwits!ēs/with these hundred blankets. Wa wa," said he
and he sat down./
(20) Then Gûyōłɛlas arose,the host,the chief of the Mamalēleqàla/
and he spoke and said,"Indeed, chiefs, true are you words,/these
different kinds of words which are the work of him who may do what
we are now doing./Are these our words? We were told to do this by
our grandfathers of olden times. We were just told/to follow it,and
therefore it is no new saying, I mean(25)we are treating now as a
chief this new chief ʟ!āsotiwalis/who is being made a chief by you,
chief ʟ!āqoᴜas. Now thank you,Kwag·uł./Now come and be happy alongside of my feast dishes." Thus he said and told the/young men of the
Mamalēleqala and the ᶜnɛmgis and the Lāwits!ēs to put down the/feast-
ing dishes before the Kwag·uł. And as soon as the(1)dishes had been

dzaᶜmoliⱡxa ⱡōɛlq!wē lāxa Kwākūg·uⱡ, laas ᶜnaxwa hāmx·ᶜİda laqēxs
ᶜnɛmp!ɛnēⱡaᶜmaē hāmg·İlēda ᶜwālasē k!wēlasa qaxs h̓ēᶜmaē gɛlōkwē
k·ɛlxwäsa lāk·!ɛndē p!ɛlxɛlasgɛm qaᶜs k!wēladzɛma. Wä, la k·!ēs
gɛlōkwa hōlaⱡagawaᶜyasa lāk·!ɛndē p!ɛlxɛlasgɛm laōxsa k!wēladzɛmē.
5 Wä, hēɛm ʟ̣āyuwa laōxwadäsa lāk·!ɛndē p!ɛlxɛlasgɛm k!wēladzɛmsa g·ⱡ-
g·ɛgāmaᶜyaxs ʟ̣āp!aasēs k!wēlats!ɛdzaᶜyē ʟɛᶜwis p!ēdzaᶜyē ʟ̣ɛᶜwis qō-
tēndzaᶜyē ʟɛᶜwis lōp!ɛdzaᶜyē.
    Wä, g·İlᶜmisē gwāⱡ haᶜmāpa k!wēⱡē laas ʟ̣āxᶜwalİⱡē Gūyōⱡɛlasē
qaᶜs yāq!ɛg·aᶜⱡē. Wä, lä ᶜnēk·a gwēgɛmāⱡa lāxēs g·ōkūlōta Mamalē-
10 leqäla. Qäʟ, qäʟaxs nēg·İmᶜmaōⱡēx lāxɛns wiwōmpᶜwüⱡasa g·İlg·ilōⱡa
qaᶜs gwēk·!älas lāxwa ʟēqwiᶜlälasa qɛn gwayiᶜlälasa. ᶜnēᶜnak·iⱡax-
g·İns k·!eásēk· äⱡelaya qɛn wäⱡdɛma. Laᶜmēsɛn hōleg·İndɛⱡtsg·ada
hasēk· laxg·ada g·İg·ɛgāmēxg·İn ʟēlānɛma, ᶜnēk·exs laē gwēgɛmx·ᶜİt
lāxa ōgwiwaᶜlİⱡasa k!wēlayats!e g·ōkwa. Wä, lä ᶜnēk·a, Qäʟ, qäʟ
15 mōsgɛᶜmakᵘ Kwākūg·uⱡ; äⱡᶜmɛwİsō wäⱡdɛma qɛns gwēk·!älasa lāxwa g·ā-
xa qɛns gwaēlas lāxwa g·ōkwēxwa ʟ̣ɛxsᶜālayâxɛns qwēsbalisaxs g·alaō-
ⱡēx ᶜnāg·ilēsɛns ᶜnālax yİs bɛkwēlēnokwasɛns g·ālɛmg·İlisaxg·ɛns ha-
maⱡalēk· lēlqwälaʟaᶜya; ᶜnēnak·iⱡē, wäk·as Gwētɛl, wäk·as Q!ōmoyâ-
ᶜyē, wäk·as ᶜwälas Kwāg·uⱡ, wäk·as Q!ōmk·!ūt!ɛs. Laᶜmō aēk·!aak·ōs
20 k·axstalİⱡax. Wäk·as, wäk·as, wa, wa, ᶜnēk·exs laē k!wäg·alİⱡa.
    Wä, lä yāq!ɛg·aᶜⱡē ⱡwaxɛlag·İlisxa xamagɛmaᶜyē g·İgāmēsa ᶜnɛ-
ᶜmēmutasa Maämtag·ila. Wä, la ᶜnēk·aɩ Ēx·ᶜmaas wäⱡdɛmasa g·İgāmaᶜyē
Gūyōⱡɛlas. ⱡlasēs wäⱡdɛmōs g·İgāmēxwa k·!ēsēx äⱡilē wäⱡdɛmaxwa ʟ̣ā-
gūnsäxēs k!wēlēkwē. (Maᶜⱡē wäⱡdɛᶜmēnaᶜyē ʟ̣ōᶜ hēlēg·İndēda k!wēlasa-
25 sēs hasaᶜyē lāxēs k!wēlēkwēxa ëx·p!a.) Wä, laᶜmɛnuᶜxᵘ ëx·p!asɛᶜwa
g·İgāmēᶜ. ᶜnēᶜnak·iⱡē nōs g·ōⱡg·ɛkūlōt; ēslaxɛns ëx·lax qänsō k·!ēs-
lax sɛbaslaxs wäⱡdɛmasa g·İgāmaᶜyē, wa. Wä, ladzâlaᶜmē ᶜwİᶜla hō-
qüwɛlsa k!wēⱡdē lāxēq qaxs lɛᶜmaē k!wäg·ila dzāqwa.

put down before the Kwāg·uⱡ,then all began to eat,as there is/only
one course given as food at a great feast,for this is counted/
buying with one hundred blankets the giving of a feast; and it is
not/counted less than one hundred blankets,this giving of a feast,
(5)and these hundred blankets are exchanged for the feast given by
the chief, when they discuss about the number of feasts given and
of blankets given and of/marriage-payments and the number of giving
away of spread-out blankets./

As soon as the guests had finished eating Gūyōⱡɛlas arose/
and spoke. He said,turning his face to his tribe,the Mamalēleqăla,/
(10) "Indeed, it is true what was said by our ancestors who first
spoke/in the way we speak in the various ways we are now doing. I
mean/there is nothing new in what we are saying. Now I give a second course with this/breath(speech)here to these chiefs whom I invited." Thus he said and turned his face/to the rear of the feast-
ing-house. Then he said: "Indeed, it is true,(15)you four Kwāg·uⱡ
tribes. Are these new words which we, are saying in this way/when
we come as we are here in this house? This advice was given to us
in the far away time when first/daylight came into our world,sent
by the one who made our ancestors, our/tribes. This is what I
mean. Go ahead,Gwētɛla, go ahead,Q!ōmoyâ⁵yē,/go ahead,⁵wālas Kwā-
g·uⱡ, go ahead Q!ōmk·!ūt!ɛs. Now it is well placed/in front of you.
Go ahead. Wa wa," said he and sat down./

(20)Then spoke Â⁵waxɛlag·ilis,head chief of the numaym/of the
Maămtag·ila. He said: "Good are your words,chief/Gūyōⱡɛlas. True
it is what you say,chief. For these are not new words,this/pressing
down(the food of)the guests,(which has two names,also the second
course is the feast-giving with the(25)breath to the guests,the
sweet taste). Now we are treated with sweet things,/chief. I mean
this,my tribes; it would not be good if we did not/reply with a
speech of a chief. Wa." Finally all the/guests went out after this
for now it was late in the evening./

(Qasō qǃämax·tsǃēxa ᵋnāx̣waᴇm ꜞlak·ǃāla g·Ɪg·ᴇg̑āmēsa mōsgᴇᵋmakwē
Kwākŭg·uƚa mōkwē qēqāsꜞ, yꞮx lāg·iƚas hë gwēx·ᵋidē qaxs x̣āmagᴇma-
ᵋyaē g·ꞯgāmaᵋyē Gŭyōƚᴇlasasa ᵋnāx̣wa Mamalēleqǎla. Wä, qō bᴇgwanᴇm-
qǃalᴇmēda kǃwēlasasa Mamalēleqǎla,lālaxē mōkᵘ bēbᴇgwanᴇmqǃālᴇmē qā-
5 sꜞsa mōsgᴇᵋmakwē Kwākŭg·uƚa qaxs ᵋnāx̣waᵋmaē qǃämdadxa bēbᴇgwānᴇm-
qǃālᴇmē. Wä, hꞋᵋmis lāg·iƚasa g·ꞯgāmaᵋyē Gŭyōƚᴇlas hë g·Ɪl qāsoxs
qǃālaᵋmaax ʟǃāsotiwalisax ᵋwālasēƚ g·ꞯgāmᴇʟ qaēs ōmpē ʟǃāqoʟasaxs
ꜞlak·ǃālaē g·ꞯgāmēsēs ᵋnᴇᵋmēmuta Yaēx·agᴇmaᵋyasa Qǃōmoyꜞᵋyē. Wä,
laᵋmēs lꜞsᴇlasēs ᵋnāx̣wa gwayiᵋlälatsa ᵋwāᵋwilōʟǃäx lābᴇndālaēnaᵋya-
10 sa g·ꞯgāmaᵋyaa g·äg·Ɪʟᴇlaxs g··ālaē māᵋyoʟᴇmsēs g·ꞯqǃēdzaᵋyē abᴇmpa
lāg·aa lāqēxs laē gwᴇᵋyꜞsa bākǃümē ᵋwꞮᵋlōƚᵋalisa. ᵋnēᵋnak·iƚē qaᵋs
qǃālaōsaq. Wä, g·aᵋmēsēg·a g·Ɪlᵋmaē g·ꞯgāmaᵋya yäwix·Ɪläsa Gwētᴇla
laē nᴇqōgwilē yäwix·Ɪlē g·ꞯgāmaᵋyasa Qǃōmoyꜞᵋyē. Wä, hꞋᴇmxaāwisē
gwēx·ᵋidēda ᵋwālas Kwāg·uƚ ʟᴇᵋwa Qǃōmk·ǃütǃᴇsē. Wä, g·Ɪlᵋmisē bᴇ-
15 gwānᴇmqǃālᴇᵋmē yäwix·Ɪlasa Gwētᴇla lä ᵋnāx̣waᴇm bᴇgwānᴇmqǃālᴇmē yä-
wix·Ɪläsa Qǃōmoyꜞᵋyē ʟᴇᵋwa ᵋwālas Kwāg·uƚ ʟᴇᵋwa Qǃōmk·ütǃᴇsē. Wä,
g·aᵋmēs ʟōma ōgŭqāƚa gwēg·ilatsa bākǃümē yꞮxs g·Ɪlᵋmaē bābagŭxa
tsǃᴇdāqa qāsꜞ ʟōxs dzōx̣waēxa g·äyoƚē lāxa Gwētᴇla lāxaē nᴇqōgwila-
sōs bābagŭxa tsǃᴇdāqsa Qǃōmoyꜞᵋyē ʟᴇᵋwa ᵋwālas Kwāg·uƚ ʟᴇᵋwa Qǃōm-
20 k·ǃütǃᴇsē. Wä, ᵋnāx̣wa hë gwēg·ilēda ᵋnāx̣wa lēᴇlqwālaʟaᵋya. ꜞᵋmᴇn
ᵋnēx· qᴇn ʟax·dzaqwē gwagwēx·sᵋaēd lāq qaxg·ꞯn hꞋwäxaᵋmēk· gwagwēx·-
sᵋāla lāq. Wä, laᵋmēsᴇn ēdzaqwaƚtsᴇn hꞋnoma k·ǃätasᴇᵋwa.)

Wä, lä mopǃᴇnxwaᵋsē ᵋnäläsa Kwākŭg·uƚē ʟᴇᵋwa Mamalēleqǎla ʟᴇᵋwa ᵋnᴇmgēsē ʟᴇᵋwa Ƚawitsǃēsē gwāgwaᵋlaxēs kǃwēkǃülasē. Wä, g·Ɪl-
25 ᵋmisē ᵋwꞮᵋla gwäƚa laasē ʟǃāqoʟas ʟēᵋlālaxa qǃāqǃasto bᴇgwānᴇmsa
Mamalēleqǎla ᵋnᴇmōkwē ʟᴇᵋwa qǃāqǃasto bᴇgwānᴇmsa ᵋnᴇmgēsē ʟᴇᵋwa qǃā-
qǃastǃo bᴇgwānᴇmsa Ƚawitsǃēsē qa läs ʟᴇlqumasa ƚādᴇgwaᵋyꜞsa ᵋnāx̣wa

(If you take notice, all the real chiefs of the four/Kwāg·uⱡ
tribes promise four feasts. This is the reason why they did so,/
that Gŭyōⱡɛlas was the head chief of all the Mamalēleqǎla. If he
were a common man,/the Mamalēleqǎla host, then four common men of
the (5) four Kwāg·uⱡ tribes would promise feasts, for all the common
men own songs./ Therefore chief Gŭyōⱡɛlas was the first to promise
a feast/because he knew that ⱡ!āsotiwⱥlis was to be a great chief
on account of his father ⱡ!āqoⱡas,/for he was a real chief of the
numaym Yaēx·agɛmē^ε of the Q!ōmoyâ^εyē. Now/he passed all the rules
of one who tries to come to the end of becoming a(10)chief, begin-
ning from the time when he was first born by his mother, who belongs to a chief's family,/until he comes to what is referred to
by the Indians as "having obtained everything". This is what I
mean that/you may remember this. And this also: As soon as a chief
of the Gwētɛla gives a winter ceremonial,/then a chief of the Q!ō-
moyâ^εyē rivals him in giving a winter ceremonial, and this is also/
done by the ^εwālas Kwāg·uⱡ and the Q!ōmk·!ūt!ɛs. And as soon as
(15)a common man of the Gwētɛla gives a winter ceremonial, then
only common men/of the Q!ōmoyâ^εyē and the ^εwālas Kwāg·uⱡ and the
Q!ōmk·!ūt!ɛs give each a winter ceremonial. And/this is a very
different rule of the Indians: If a/woman who has a man's seat
promises a feast or a potlatch, one who belongs to the Gwētɛla,
then also/a woman who has a man's seat among the Q!ōmoyâ^εyē does
the same, and also of the ^εwālas Kwāg·uⱡ and the Q!ōmk·!ūt!ɛs.(20)
They all do this, all the tribes. I only wish/to speak about this
because I never talked about/it. Now I will speak again about what
I am really writing about,)/

   After four days, the Kwāg·uⱡ and the Mamalēleqǎla and the/
^εnɛmgis and the Ⱡāwits!ēs finished their feasts. As soon as (25)
they had all finished, ⱡ!āqoⱡas called the tally keeper of the/
Mamalēleqǎla and the tally keeper of the ^εnɛmgis and the/tally
keeper of the Ⱡāwits!ēs to put together the loaned out blankets

bēbɛgwānɛmsēs g·ig·ōkūlōtē. Wä, g·flᵋmisē la k!ūsᵋāliⱡ lāx g·ōkwas
ⱡ!āqoⱡasē g·āxaas ⱡ!ax·ⱡ!alIdzɛmga, yĭx gɛnɛmas ⱡ!āqoⱡasē dālaxa
ⱡ!āⱡ!axɛmē g·Its!ɛᵋwatsa xōkwē k!waxⱡāwaxa k!waxⱡāwasa ⱡādɛgwaᵋyâsa
ᵋnāxwa bēbɛgwānɛma. Wä, laᵋmē ⱡ!ax·ⱡ!alIdzɛmga k!wāgālIⱡaq qaᵋs

5   āxᵋwūⱡts!âlēxa k!waxⱡāwe qaᵋs dāⱡēqēxs laēda q!āq!astowē bɛgwānɛm
ⱡēxᵋēdɛx ⱡēgɛmasa kwēkwē. Wä, la ⱡ!ax·ⱡ!alIdzɛmga ⱡēxᵋēdɛx wāxaasas
ⱡādɛgwaᵋyâs. Wä, la ⱡ!ax·ⱡ!alIdzɛmga hōsᵋIdxa sɛk·!ats!aqē lāxa
k!waxⱡāwē qaᵋs ts!ɛᵋwēs lāxa q!āq!astowē bɛgwānɛm. Wä, lā ⱡɛxᵘᵋwā-
liⱡas. Wä, g·flᵋmisē ᵋwIᵋla la ⱡɛxwIⱡa k!waxⱡāwē ⱡādɛgwayusa Ma-

10   malēleqāla laē g·Inwēda q!āq!asto bɛgwānɛmsa sɛk·!ats!aqē k!waxⱡā-
wa lāxa sɛk·!āts!aqē k!waxⱡâ ⱡādɛgwayâ. Wä, laɛm nɛqaxsa p!ɛlxɛ-
lasgɛmē yaq!wēmāsa sɛk·!āts!aqas k!waxⱡāwäs ⱡādɛgwayuwē hägâ lāxēq.
ᵋnāⱡᵋnɛmōkwa g·Igāmēᵋ ⱡādɛkwasa nɛqasa p!ɛlxɛlasgɛma. Wä, lā maᵋⱡ-
tsogûxsa p!ɛlxɛlasgɛmē yaq!wēmäs, ᵋnɛmāx·fs ⱡōᵋ gwānaxᵋida ⱡɛᵋwis

15   päg·aᵋya ⱡādɛgwayuwē p!ɛlxɛlasgɛma. Wä, g·āxᵋmēda p!ɛlxɛlasgɛmē
q!ɛnēpoxᵋwidēda ⱡādɛgwayu ⱡɛᵋwa yaq!wēma p!ɛlxɛlasgɛm qaᵋs lä qa-
t!alIlɛm lāqēxs laē lēx·ᵋɛna. Wä, hēɛm ⱡēgadɛs ⱡɛlqumakwa ⱡādɛgwayu p!ɛlxɛlasgɛm ⱡɛᵋwa hēnōma yaq!wēma p!ɛlxɛlasgɛma. Wä, la hēx·-
sāɛm gwēg·ila lābɛndālaxˈwāxaasas bēbɛgwānɛmasa ᵋnāxwa lēɛlqwāla-

20   ⱡaᵋya. Wä, āⱡ!misē gwāⱡxa la gāⱡa gānuⱡa.

    Wä, g·flᵋmisē ᵋnāx·ᵋIdxa gaālāxs laē ⱡ!āqoⱡas ᵋyālaqasa q!ē-
ᵋmāla haᵋyāⱡᵋasa Q!ōmoyâᵋyē ga lēs qāsaxa Gwētɛla ⱡɛᵋwa ᵋwālas Kwā-
g·uⱡ ⱡɛᵋwa Q!ōmk·!ūt!esē qa g·āxēs ᵋwIᵋlaēⱡɛla lāx g·ōkwas hoᵋmāⱡa-
qēxs yāqumaasa p!ɛlxɛlasgɛmē lāxēs ⱡēⱡɛᵋlakwa lēlqwālaⱡaᵋyē. Wä,

25   lä ᵋwIᵋla hōquwɛlsa haᵋyāⱡᵋa lāx g·ōkwas ⱡ!āqoⱡas qaᵋs lē ⱡaxstol-
sax t!ɛx·flās g·ōkwasa Gwētɛla. Wä, lā ᵋnēk·a ᵋnɛmōkwē lāq, G·āx-
ᵋmɛnuᵋxᵘ qāsoⱡai Gwētɛlai qaᵋs laōs hoᵋmāⱡaxwa yāqumaxōx ⱡ!āsotiwa-
lisexai lāxos ⱡēⱡɛᵋlakwa lēlqwālaⱡaᵋyēx, ᵋnēk·ē. Wä, lā ᵋnɛmādzaqwēda waōkwē haᵋyāⱡᵋa ᵋnēk·a, Hālāg·flilⱡasai, ᵋnēk·ē yĭxs k·!ēsᵋmaē

30   gaāxstalēda ᵋnāxwa bēbɛgwānɛma. Wä, lä häᵋstaɛm gwēk·!āla lāxa

of all the(1)men of their tribes. After they had sat down in the
house of/ʟ!āqoʟas,ʟ!ax·ʟ!alĪdzɛmga came,the wife of ʟ!āqoʟas,car-
rying a/small basket in which were split cedar sticks,the cedar
sticks which were given as a sign of their advance payments by/all
the man. Then ʟ!ax·ʟ!alĪdzɛmga sat down among them and(5)she took
out the cedar sticks and she held them while the tally keeper/called
out the name of the Eagle. Then ʟ!ax·ʟ!alĪdzɛmga named the amount of
the/advance payment,and then ʟ!ax·ʟ!alĪdzɛmga counted five/cedar
sticks and she gave them to the tally keeper,and he put them down./
And when all the cedar sticks(representing)the advance payments(10)
of the Mamalēleqǎla had been put down,then the tally keeper added
five cedar sticks/to the five cedar sticks of the advance payment.
Now there were ten pairs of blankets/to be given for the five cedar
sticks of the advance payment after this./Sometimes a chief advances
ten pairs of blankets and then/twenty pairs of blankets are to be
given in the same way(15)added on to the blankets given in advance.
Now the blankets/were gathered together,those that were advanced and
those that were to be given./They were put down and rolled up. This
is called "pressing together the advanced/blankets and the blankets
really given away." They kept on/doing this until they came to the
end of the total number of men of all the tribes,(20)and they only
finished late at night./

As soon as day came in the morning,ʟ!āqoʟas sent many/young
men of the Q!ōmoyâᵋyē to go to call the Gwētɛla and ᵋwālas Kᴎāg·uⱡ/
and Q!ōmk·!ūt!ɛs to come into his house to watch when the/blankets
were given out to the invited tribes.(25)Then all the young men went
out of the house of ʟ!āqoʟas and they stood in the/doors of the
houses of the Gwētɛla,and one of them said,/"We come to call you,
Gwētɛla,to watch the giving out to the names/by ʟ!āsotiwalis/to the
invited tribes." Thus he said. Then said together the/other young
men,"You are to go quickly," they said,(30)for all the men had not
yet eaten breakfast. Now they said this in/all the houses of the

ᵉnāx̱wa g·ig·ōkwasa ᵉwālas Kwāg·uⱡ ʟɛᵉwa Q!ōmk·!ūt!ɛsē. Wä,g·fⁱᵉmisē
ᵉwⁱᵉlxtolsaxa ᵉnāx̱wa g·ig·ōkwa g·āxaē aēdaaqwa.qaᵉs lē hōgwiʟa hä⟶
ᵉyāⱡᵉa lāx g·ōkwas ʟ!āqoʟas. Wä, lä äx̱k·!ālasɛᵉwa häᵉyāⱡᵉa qa lēs
lāxa āʟ!ē sōp!ēdɛx mōts!aqa ëx·ᵉɛn wⁱswűⱡᵉɛn q!waxasa qa yaēyuduxᵘ-
5   p!ɛnk·ēs äᵉwâsgɛmasas lāxɛns bāʟax.
     Wä, hëx·ᵉidaᵉmisa häyāⱡᵉa la dag·fⁱqɛlaxa sōbayu. Wä, ᴋ·!ēs-
t!ē gäⱡaxs g·āxaē wⁱwik·ɛlaxa mōts!aqē q!wēq!waxas. Wä, lä wⁱx·ᵉa-
lⁱⱡas lāxa max·stâlⁱⱡasa t!ɛx·fla qaᵉs dzōdzōx̱ᵘbɛndëx ʟɛx̱ᵘbaᵉyas.
Wä, lä äx̱ᵉēdxa ᵉnɛmts!aqē lāxa ʟ!ɛbɛmē q!wɛxasa qaxs hëᵉmaē ʟēgɛms ⁱ
10   qaᵉs lē ʟāg·fⁱⱡas lāxa ōgwiᵉwalⁱⱡasa g·ōkwē qaᵉs dëx̱ᵉwalⁱⱡēs. Wä,
laɛm qādɛdzâyē ōxtâᵉyas lāx ⁱᵉwābâᵉyasa säläsa g·ōkwē. Wä, g·fⁱᵉmisē
gwāⱡa laē äx̱ᵉēdxa ᵉnɛmts!aqē ʟ!ɛbɛmē q!waxasa qaᵉs lē ʟāg·fⁱⱡas lāxa ᵉnɛmp!ɛnk·ē lāxɛns bāʟēqē äᵉwâlagâⱡaasas. Wä, lä ᵉwⁱᵉla dëx̱ᵉwa-
lⁱⱡtsa mōts!aqē ʟ!ɛbɛmē q!wēq!waxasa. Wä, g·fⁱᵉmisē gwāⱡ g·āxaas
15   ᵉwⁱᵉla hōgwiʟēda Gwētɛla ʟɛᵉwa ᵉwālas Kwāg·uⱡ ʟɛᵉwa Q!ōmk·!ūt!ɛsē.
Wä, g·fⁱᵉmisē g·āx ᵉwⁱᵉlaēʟa laē hëx·ᵉidaɛm gaāxstāla. Wä, g·fⁱᵉmi-
sē gwāⱡ haᵉmāpa laas ʟēᵉlālasɛᵉwa yūdukwē q!ēq!aq!asto bēbɛgwānɛmsa
yūduxᵘsɛᵉmakwē lēlqwālaʟaᵉya. Wä, g·aɛm ⱡax̱waⱡa gwēg·ilatsē g·ada-
xa q!āq!astowē bɛgwānɛma, yⁱxs laē g·āyaxsdɛndxa ʟēgɛmasa ᵉnɛmox̱uᵉɛm
20   la māk·!ɛxsdēsa gūnxaᵉyē ᵉnɛᵉmēmota qa lē g·fⁱⱡts!â lāxa ʟ!ɛbɛmē q!wa-
xasa. Wä, lä ʟēx̱ᵉēdɛx ʟēgɛmas ᵉnālaᵉyas qa lē k·!ēgɛg·atsa p!ɛl-
xɛlasgɛmē lāxa g·fⁱⱡts!âx·dē hë gwēᵉnāküla ëk·!ōⱡɛlēda yaēq!wēma p!ɛl-
xɛlasgɛm lāg·aa lāx ʟâx̱ûmaᵉyasa ᵉnɛᵉmēma. Wä, g·fⁱᵉmisē ᵉwⁱlxtowa
māk·!ɛxsdē ᵉnɛᵉmēmaxs laē k·ātɛᵉyⁱntsa k!waxʟâᵉwē lāx ōküᵉyaᵉyasa
25   p!ɛlxɛlasgɛmē. Wä, lēda q!āq!astowē bɛgwānɛm ʟēx̱ᵉēdɛx ʟēgɛmas bɛgwānɛmē māk·!ɛxsdēsa ᵉnālēʟɛla ᵉnɛᵉmēma. Wä, lä k·!fⁱqɛᵉyⁱndayuwa
p!ɛlxɛlasgɛm yaq!wēmas lāxa k!waxʟâᵉwē la k·ātēᵉyōx yaq!wēmäsa mā-
k·!ɛxsdēlas ᵉnɛᵉmēma. Wä, hëᵉm ʟēgadēda k!waxʟâᵉwē la k·āk·ɛʟawēxa
p!ɛlxɛlasgɛmē yaēq!wēmäsa ᵉnāⱡᵉnɛᵉmēmasas ʟōᵉ aᵉwɛlgâᵉwē k!waxʟâsa
30   yaēq!wēmäsa ᵉnāⱡᵉnɛᵉmēmas lāx ᵉnɛmts!aqustâlaēda p!ɛlxɛlasgɛmē la
ʟüxts!âxa ʟ!ɛbɛmē q!waxasa nɛqaᵉyēsa Mamalēleqâla. Wä, lä ᵉnɛmts!a-

ᵋwālas Kwāg·uł and the Q!ōmk·!ut!ɛs,and as soon as/ they had gone to
all the houses they went back and all the young men went/ into the
house of ʟ!āqoʟas. Then the young men were told to go/ inland to chop
down four straight young hemlock trees,three fathoms(5)in length./

Immediately the young men went and took along an axe. They had
not/ been away long before they came carrying the four hemlock poles.
They put them down/ near the door and they sharpened the butt ends./
Then they took one of the holding hemlock poles,for this is their
name,(10)and put it up in the rear of the house and rammed it into
the ground./ Then they placed the top under the roof of the house,
and as soon as/ this was done,they took another holding hemlock pole
and put it up/ one fathom away from the first one and they drove into the ground the/ four hemlock poles. When this was done(15) the Gwētɛla came in and the ᵋwālas Kwāg·uł and the Q!ōmk·!ut!ɛs./ As soon
as they were all inside,they had breakfast at once and after/ they
had eaten,the three tally keepers/ of the three tribes were called.
Now this is difficult work for the/ tally keeper,for he must begin
with the last one of the names of the numaym,(20) the last one at the
edge of the numaym,for that goes first between the holding hemlock
poles./ Then he calls the name of the next one above,so that the
blanket is put on top/ of the one that was put in first. They go on
doing this,going up with the blankets to be given away/ until they
come to the one who stands at the head of a numaym. As soon as all
the names are gone to the/ last one in the numaym,they put a cedar
stick on top of the(25)blankets. Then the tally keeper calls out
the name of the/ last man of the next higher numaym, and the/ blankets to be given away are put on top of the cedar stick,which is on
top of the(blankets)given away to the/ last numaym. The name of this
cedar stick is "lying between the/ blankets to be given away to the
numayms" or "separating cedar stick of the(30)gifts for the numayms".
The blankets go up one tier/ piled up inside of the holding hemlock
poles to be given away to the Mamalēleqāla. Then another pile of/

14*

qustâlēda p!ɛlxɛlasgɛmē la ʟüxts!âxa ᶜnɛmts!aqē ʟ!ɛbɛmɛ q!waxasa
nɛqaᶜyēsa ᶜnɛmɢ·ōs. Wä, lāxaē hēɛm gwäɫē nɛqāᶜyasa ʟawits!ēsō. Wä,
g·flᶜmisē ᶜwīᶜlxtowa ᶜnāxwa bēbɛgwānɛmsa lēlqwalaʟaᶜyē la ʟüxts!â
lāxa ʟ!ɛbɛmē q!waxasa laē ʟēgadɛs ʟ!ɛbɛgwēlkᵘ p!ɛlxɛlasgɛma lāxēq.

5 Wä, laᶜmē ᶜnāxwaɛm la ᵉk·!ɛnxaᶜyē yaēq!wēmäsa g·ig·alaxäsa ᶜnāɫᶜnɛ-
ᶜmēmasēxa p!ɛlxɛlasgɛmē lāxa la ʟ!ɛbɛgwēlkᵘ p!ɛlxɛlasgɛma. Wä, g·fl-
ᶜmisē gwāɫa laas ʟ!āqoʟas ʟaxᶜwālīɫa qaᶜs yāq!ɛg·aᶜɫē. Wä, lä ᶜnē-
k·a: Laᶜmō lādzēmo gwāɫa wāɫdɛmʟa q!ɛsa g·īgāmaᶜyax ʟ!āsotiwalisax.
Wä, wäg·iɫla mōsgɛᶜmakᵘ Kwāküg·uɫ ts!ɛk·āɫaʟax gaālaʟa qɛn yāxᶜwida-

10 g·ʼɫtsa p!ɛlxɛlasgɛmēx lāxa lēlqwālaʟaᶜyax qa lālag·iɫtso näᶜnaxᵘʟax
dzāqwaʟax ɫɛnsʟa, ᶜnēk·ē. Wä, laᶜmēsɛns q!ɛmdiɫaɫxwa gānuʟēx yīsɛn
lax·ᶜidɛᶜma q!ɛmdīlɛma āɫtsɛma q!ɛmdɛma, ᶜnēk·ē. Wä, laɛm ᶜnāxwa
mōᶜlēda g·īg·ɛgāmaᶜyas wāɫdɛmas. Wä, laᶜmē yāwasᶜīt hōqüwɛls lāxa
g·ōkwē.

15   Wä, g·flᶜmisē p!ɛdɛx·ᶜīda laasa q!ēnɛmē häᶜyāɫᶜasa Q!ōmayaᶜyᵊ
hōqüwēls lāx g·ōkwas ʟ!āqoʟasē qaᶜs lē qāsaxa yüduxᵘsɛᶜmakwē Kwā-
küg·uɫ qa lēs hōʟēlax wāɫdɛmiᶜlälaʟas ʟ!āsotiwalisē. Laɛm k·!ēs
q!ɛmdilāla qaxs âᶜmaē ᶜnēk·a ᶜnɛmōkwē lāxa qāsɛlg·īsē häᶜyāɫᶜa:
G·āxᶜmɛnuᶜxᵘ qasai Gwētɛlai qaᶜs laōs hōʟēlax wāɫdɛmiᶜlälaʟas ʟ!ā-

20 sotiwalisē, ᶜnēk·ē. Wä, lä ᶜnɛmādzaqwa ᶜnēk·a häᶜyāɫᶜa: Hälag·ī-
līʟasai. Wä, lä hēᶜstaɛm gwēk·!āla lāxa ᶜnāxwa g·ig·ōkwa. Wä,hēɛm
lāg·iɫasa qāsɛlg·īsē häᶜyāɫᶜa k·!ēs nɛgɛltawēxēs g·flx·ᶜidä wāɫ-
dɛmxs g·ālaē qāsaxa Kwāküg·uɫaxs g·ālaē q!ɛmdēɫasa āɫtsɛmē q!ɛm-
dɛmxs k·!ēsᶜmaē la ʟēɫɛlaxa lēlqwalaʟaᶜya qaxs lɛᶜmaē ʟ!āqoʟasē

25 gwāgwēx·sᶜālaɫ qaēda mōsgɛᶜmakwē Kwāküg·uɫaxs lɛᶜmaē k·oqwaɫxa ʟ!ā-
qwa qō lāɫ yaxᶜwītsa p!ɛlxɛlasgɛmē lāxa lēlqwälaʟaᶜyē. (Wä, âᶜmɛn
ᶜnēx·qa q!āɫēs lāg·iɫas k·!ēs q!ɛmdilalēda häᶜyāɫᶜaxs laē qāsa.)

        Wä, g·flᶜmisē g·āx ᶜwīᶜlaēʟeda Kwāküg·uɫē laas ʟ!āqoʟasē ʟāx-
ᶜwālīɫ qaᶜs yāq!ɛg·aᶜɫē. Wä, lē ᶜnēk·a: Qāʟ, qāʟas Kwāküg·uɫ; qā-

30 ʟaxs hēᶜmaēx gwēk·!ālasē lāx wāɫdɛᶜmēnaᶜyaxsɛns wiwōmpᶜwüɫaxɛns g·ā-
xēx gwaēlas lāxwa g·ōkwaxsa g·īgāmaᶜyaē ʟ!āsotiwalisa. Wä, wēg·a

blankets is piled up inside the other(pair of)holding poles/for the
ᶜnɛmgis,and then they do the same for the Ḷāwits!ōs./And as soon as
(the names of)all the men of the tribes have been given and they
have been put between/the holding hemlock poles,then this is called
after this "blankets piled up between the holding poles in the house."
(5)Now everything that is to be given away first to the first numaym/
is on top of the blankets piled up between the holding poles in the
house. And when/they had finished,ʟ!āqoḷas stood up and spoke. He
said:/"Now this great work is done, his word that he will be a chief,
this ʟ!āsotiwalis./ Now go on, you four Kwāg·uł tribes, stay awake
early that I may give away the(10)blankets to the tribes that they may
go home/tomorrow evening," said he. "Now we will learn the song to-
night, the/new song that we have been learning," said he. Then all
the/chiefs thanked him for what he had said and for a short time they
all went out of the/house./

(15)When it became dark many young men of the Q!ōmoyᵃᵉyē/went
to the house of ʟ!āqoḷas together to call the three/Kwāg·uł tribes
to listen to what ʟ!āsotiwalis would say. Now they did not/learn
the song,for only one of the young men inviters spoke,/"We come to
call you,Gwētɛla,to listen to what ʟ!āsotiwalis will say,"(20)said
he. Then the other young men said together,"You are to go quickly."/
Then they said the same in all the houses. And this/is the reason
why the young men inviters did not say the same words they first
said/when they went to call the Kwāg·uł tribes,when they first came
to learn the new song/when they had not yet invited the tribes,that
now ʟ!āqoḷas(25)was going to talk about it to the four Kwāg·uł tribes,
that he was going to break a copper/when they were going to give away
the blankets to the tribes. (I only/wish it to be known,why the
young men did not call to learn the song,when they went to invite.)/

As soon as all the Kwāg·uł had come in ʟ!āqoḷas stood up/and
spoke. He said,"Indeed, it is true,Kwāg·uł.(30)This is truly the
way of speaking of our ancestors as we come/to stay in this house

dɛnxᵋîtsa ā̱tsɛma q!ɛmtîlaᵋya qa hôᴸēlēsg·ada g·îgǟmēg·aqē yîxg·a
ʟ!ā̱sotiwalisɛk·, ᵋnēk·ē.

Wä, hëx·ᵋidaᵋmisē Ōmx·ᵋidēxa nâg̱adē g·āyu̱ʟ lāxa ᵋnɛᵋmēmutasa
Hāanaᴸenâsa Q!ōmoyâᵋyē dâq̱âlasēs ā̱tsɛmē q!ɛmtilaᵋya. Wä, laᵋmē

5   ᵋṉāxwa dɛnxᵋidēda Q!ōmoyâᵋyē yîsɛn lāx·ᵋidɛᵋma k·!ā̱t!ēdaᵋyē ā̱tsɛm
q!ɛmdɛma. Wä, g·îlᵋmisē nɛxsᵋɛg·ilalî̱ʟ dɛnxɛlaxs g·āxaē ʟ!ā̱sotiwa-
lisē g·āxᵋu̱̱ʟts!â̱lî̱ʟ lāxa ōts!â̱lî̱ʟē dālax Dɛnt!ālá̱yuxa ʟ!āqwa qaᵋs
lē ᴸā̱ᴸā̱xu̱g̱u̱lî̱ʟ ᴸɛᵋwis ōmpē ʟ!āqo̱ᴸasē. Wä, lä yîxᵋwîdɛx·daᵋxwa. Wä,
k·!ēst!a gēg·îlî̱ʟ yîxwaxs laē ʟ!ā̱sotiwalisē ēpā̱ʟax bɛnbaᵋyē ōnu-

10   ts!ɛxsdēsa ʟ!āqwa qa bɛnxtâ̱ʟisēxs yîxwax·säᵋmaē. Wä, g·îlᵋmisē
q!u̱lbēda q!ɛmdɛmē laas yaq!ɛg·aᵋʟē ʟ!āqo̱ᴸasē. Wä, lä ᵋnēk·a: Âdzē-
k·asōᴸ g·îgǟmēᵋ ʟ!ā̱sotiwalis âlaᵋmasēᴸ ᵋnēk·aa, âladzēᵋmasēᴸ ᵋnēx·
qaᵋs yāg̱u̱nōlisaōsaxwa ᴸēg̱adē ʟ!āqwaa lāxōx Dɛnt!ālá̱yudzēx. Wä, wä-
g·î̱ʟla, qā̱ᴸaxs nu̱̱ʟag·iᵋwālaaqōs ᴸāxa hëx·dä gwēg·ilaxwa ᴸēᴸɛg̱adēx

15   ʟ!ā̱ᴸ!aqwa.

Laɛm â̱ɛm ᴸā̱ᵋwî̱ʟē ʟ!ā̱sotiwalisē pāq!â̱bä̱lî̱ʟxa ʟ!āqwa. Wä, lä
ʟ!āqo̱ᴸasē dāx·ᵋîdxa ʟ!āqwa lāx Dɛnt!ālayu qaᵋs xāxalolāqwē. Wä,lä
yāq!ɛg·aᵋʟē. Wä, la ᵋnēk·a: Wēg·a yā̱ʟ!â̱ʟɛx g·îg·ɛgǟmēs lēlqwāla-
ᴸaᵋya; k·!ēsᴸɛs hayōtɛlaᴸōᴸ, ā̱las yāxᵋwitsōsg·ada k·ōqwa̱ʟg·ada g·î-

20   gǟmēk·, yîxg·a ʟ!ā̱sotiwalisg·axg·ada ᴸēg̱addzē Dɛnt!alayukᵘ. ᵋnē-
ᵋnak·î̱ʟē g·îg·ɛgǟmēs Kwāku̱g·u̱ʟ. Wä, gēlag·a g·îgǟmēᵋ â̱ᵋwaxɛlag·îlis
(xa xāmag̱āmaᵋyē g·îgǟmēsa ᵋnɛᵋmēmutasa Maämtag·ila ᴸēᵋlālasōᵋs). Wä,
lä ᵋnēk·a: Wa gēlag·a g·îgǟmēᵋ Nɛqāp!ɛnk·ɛm (xa xāmag̱āmaᵋyē g·îgǟ-
mēsa ᵋnɛᵋmēmutasa Ku̱̱kwāk!u̱masa Gwētɛla); sōᵋmaas âla k·îk·ōq!wēnoxᵘ-

25   xa ᴸēᴸɛg̱adē ʟ!ā̱ᴸ!aqwa. Wa, gēlag·a g·îgǟmēᵋ Nɛg·ädzē (xa xāmag̱āma-
ᵋyē g·îgǟmēsa ᵋnɛᵋmēmutasa G·îg·îlg̱āmasa ᵋwālas Kwāg·u̱ʟē), sōᵋmaas
âla k·îk·ōq!wēnoxᵘxa ᴸēᴸɛg̱adē ʟ!ā̱ᴸ!aqwa. Wa, gēlag·a g·îgǟmēᵋ Wā-
k·adzē (xa xāmag̱āmaᵋyē g·îgǟmēsa ᵋnɛᵋmēmutasa Wāwu̱libâᵋyēsa ᵋwālas
Kwāg·u̱ʟ), sōᵋmaas âla k·îk·oq!wēnoxᵘxa ᴸēᴸɛg̱adē ʟ!ā̱ᴸ!aqwa. Wa, gē-

of chief ʟ!ásotiwalis. Now go on(1)and sing the new song which is
made,and that they listen to this chief/ʟ!ásotiwalis," he said./

Immediately Ōmx·ᵉĩd the song leader who belonged to the num-
aym/Hāǎnaʟēno of the Q!ōmoyáᵉyē took up the new song made by him and
then(5)all the Q!ōmoyáᵉyē sang the new song which I have written
down.[1]/And when they were half through singing ʟ!ásotiwalis/came out
of the bedroom carrying the copper Dɛnt!alaᵉyu and/he went and stood
with his father ʟ!áqoʟas. Then they danced and/they had not been
dancing long before ʟ!ásotiwalis held with his fingers the lower
corner of the(10)copper so that its head was downward while he was
dancing,and after the/song was finished ʟ!áqoʟas spoke and said:
"Ah,you are great,/chief ʟ!ásotiwalis. Do you really wish it? Is it
really your great wish/to let it lie dead by the side of the fire,
this copper that has a name,this Dɛnt!alaᵉyu? Now/go on with it. Indeed,for you are descended from those who are extravagant,from those
who did so with(15)coppers that had names."/

Now ʟ!ásotiwalis was just standing in the house holding the
copper over his chest. Then/ʟ!áqoʟas took the copper Dɛnt!alaᵉyu
and cried out,"ha ha". Then/he spoke and said: "Indeed take care,
chiefs of the tribes./ Do not talk against me,else you will be giv-
en a piece of what will be broken by this chief,(20)ʟ!ásotiwalis,
this one which has the name Dɛnt!alaᵉyu./ That is what I mean,chiefs
of the Kwāg·uⱡ. Now come here,chief Áᵉwaxalag·ĩlĩs."/(The head chief
of the numaym Maǎmtag·ila was called by him.)/Then he said,"Now come
chief Nɛqap!ɛnk·ɛm,(the head chief of the/numaym Kükwāk!ŭm of the
Gwētɛla). You are the true breakers of(25)coppers that have names.
Now come,chief Nɛg·ädzē,(the head/chief of the numaym G·ĩg·ĩlgăm of
the ᵉwālas Kwāg·uⱡ). You are the/real breakers of coppers that have
names. Now come,chief/Wāk·as,(the head chief of the numaym Wāwŭli-
báᵉyē of the ᵉwālas Kwāg·uⱡ)./ You are the real breakers of coppers

216

lag·a lāxg·as k·ǃōtɛlag·ōs g·Ig·ɛgāmēᵋ. Laɛms xǔltaʟōɫ waōyad g·Ig·ɛgāmēᵋ lāxa Dɛntǃãlayuxᵘdɛk· , ᵋnēk·ē.

Wä, hᵋx·ᵋidaᵋmisa mōkwē g·Ig·ɛgāmēᵋ qǃwāg·ɪlɪɫ qaᵋs lē qǃwāg·ɪlɪɫ lāx ʟaᵋwēlasas ʟǃāsotiwalisē. Wä, lä yāqǃɛgaᵋɫē Ã́waxɛlag·ɪ̄-
5   lisē; wä, lä ᵋnēk·a: Qä̱ʟ, qä̱ʟēs wāɫdɛmōs g·Igāmēᵋ ʟǃāqoʟas, yü̱ʟaxs sɛmsaaqōs yɪsg·ada g·Igāmēk· , yɪxg·as g·Iqēlasōgwōs lāxg·a ʟǃāsotiwalisɛk· . Wä, laɛms hᵋ̄ɫaxamasa g·Igāmēᵋ ʟǃāqoʟasxwa k·ǃēsēx qǃūnāla hᵋ̄ɫaxamatsɛᵋwa xǔnōkwaxs lāloʟǃasɛᵋwaē qaᵋs ᵋwāᵋwilōʟǃēx k·ātā-
ᵋyas äxänuxᵘᵋwǔɫasōxɛns lālabaasɛᵋwēx. ᵋnēᵋnak·ɪɫē g·Igāmēᵋ ʟǃāso-
10 tiwalidzē, lᵋᵋmas nɛnōlōɫ g·Igāmēᵋʟa. Laᵋmas ã́la ᵋnēx· qaᵋs k·ōqwaōsaxg·ada ʟēgadɛk· lāxg·a Dɛntǃalã́yudzē, ᵋnēk·ē.

Wä, lä ɾ̃aᵋnaxmaᵋyē ʟǃāsotiwalisaq. Wä, lä ᵋnēk·a: Laᵋmɛn wayadagāmɛlkwa. Wēg·a ã̂ɛmx g·Ig·ɛgāmēᵋ xǔltǃēdɛq qɛn wēg·iɫ k·ōqwaɫqōx ɫɛnsʟa, ᵋnēk·ē.
15 Wä, la Nɛqāpǃɛnk·ɛm yāqǃɛg·aᵋɫa. Wä, lä ᵋnēk·a: ã́laʟã̱s wāɫdɛmasa g·Igāmaᵋyēx. Wä, lä dāx·ᵋIdɛx Dɛntǃalã́yuxa ʟǃāqwa. Wäʺ lä dōqǔmēxa ʟǃāqwa. Wä,lä ᵋnēk·a: Nōsʟawisē nã̂qaᵋyaxɛn gwēx·ᵋidaasʟaōʟ qāst Dɛntǃalã́yudzē qaxg·anuᵋxᵘ ã̂mēʟa k·ǃāk·ǃēsᵋoxᵘsilaxg·anu-
ᵋxᵘ k·ǃēsᵋōxᵘg·ada xǔltak· k·ǃēsᵋã̂ ʟ̱ōgǔn yǔdukǔk· ᵋnēᵋnɛmōkwa. Wä,
20 hālādzēʟalag·a qāst Dɛntǃalã́yudzē, ᵋnēk·ēxs laē paxēāliɫas. Wä, lä kǃǔtsēᵋstalēda mōkwē g·Ig·ɛgāmēᵋxa ʟǃāqwa. Wä, la ʟǃāqoʟasē dālaxa k·ǃāwayu qaᵋs lē ʟ̱āxᵋwalɪɫ lāx ʟǃāsaliɫas. Wä, lä yāqǃɛg·aɫa. Wä, lä ᵋnēk·a: Wēg·a ã̂ᵋmasʟ hōʟēlaʟɛx g·Ig·ɛgāmēᵋ Ã́waxɛlag·ɪlis, Nɛqāpǃɛnk·ɛm, Nɛg·ädzē, wä, sōmēs Wāk·adzē, qa lālag·Isg·ada nuyɪmbali-
25 sak· nānuɫx·ä k·ǃāwayu xǔldayuxa k·ōqwasōʟē ʟǃāʟǃaqwasɛn wiwōmpᵋwǔɫa, ᵋnēk·ēxs laē tsǃās lāx Nɛqāpǃɛnk·ɛm. Wä, hᵋ̄ᵋmis la xǔltɛlax ã́ᵋwɪg·aᵋyas Dɛntǃalã́yã̂xa xǔltaᵋyē qa nɛgɛɫᵋɛnēsōɫts qō k·ōqwāʟaq.
Wäʺ laᵋmē ʟǃāqoʟas kǃwāgēliɫxa mōkwē g·Ig·ɛgāmaᵋya qaᵋs ʟ̱ɛxsᵋālēxēᵤ gwɛᵋyō qa k·ōqoyōɫ lāxa ʟǃāqwa. Wä, la k·ǃeã̂s gwēx·ᵋidaasē ʟǃɾ̃qo-
30 ʟasē nēɫax ᵋnɛmōkwa bɛgwānɛm lāxa Kwākǔg·uɫasēs yāxᵋwitsōʟasa k·ōgǔkwē ʟǃāqwa. Wä, lāxaē k·ǃeã̂s ᵋnɛmōkᵘ bɛgwānɛm nāla wǔʟāq, wāx·-ᵋmaēs ᵋnāɫᵋnɛmᵋwyōtē k·ǃēs qǃālaq.

that have names. Come(1)to this,your salmon,chiefs. Now you will
mark it, unmerciful chiefs, this Dɛnt!alaᵋyu," said he.

Immediately the four chiefs arose and stood/at the place where
ʟ!ãsotiwalis was standing.Then Aᵋwaxalag·flis spoke(5)and said: "Indeed,true is your word,chief ʟ!ãqoʟas. You are the/mouthpiece of this
chief here whom you are making a chief,this ʟ!ãsotiwalis./Now you have
done well,chief ʟ!ãqoʟas. For not always/is the child successful when
the attempt is made to get for him everything that is marked out in
the/rules when we are trying to go to the end. I mean this, chief
ʟ!ãsotiwalis.(10)Will you now become an extravagant chief? Do you
really wish to/break this great Dɛnt!alaᵋyu that has a name?' said he./

Then ʟ!ãsotiwalis answered and said: "Now/I have been made
unmerciful. Go on,chief,mark it that I may/break it to-morrow,"
said he./

(15)Then Nɛqap!ɛnk·ɛm spoke and said: "True is your word/
chief." Then he took Dɛnt!alaᵋyu the copper,and/he looked at the
face of the copper and said: "Is it my wish what I am going to do/
to you,friend Dɛnt!alaᵋyu? For we are just using our privileges/
this privilege of marking, I and my three friends. (20)Good bye,
great friend Dɛntalaᵋyu," said he. Then he put it down and the/four
chiefs sat down around the copper. Then ʟ!ãqoʟas took his/knife
and stoo͡ outside of them. He spoke/and said: "Now listen,chief
Aᵋwaxalag·flis,/Nɛqap!ɛnk·ɛm,Nɛg·ãdzē and you,Wãk·as. Now take this
large knife which belongs to the beginning of myth time(25)with the
mad edge for marking the coppers that were to be broken by my ancestors."/Thus he said,and gave it to Nɛqap!ɛnk·ɛm. Then he marked a
line/on the back of Dɛnt!alaᵋyu,the marks to be guides when it was
to be broken./ Then ʟ!ãqoʟas sat down among the four chiefs to ad-
vise them/what he wanted to be broken off from the copper. Then
there was no way in which ʟ!ãqoʟas(30)could tell any one man among
the Kwãg·uⱡ to whom he was going to give the/broken copper, and
also no man dared ask him./ Even his brothers did not know about it.

Wä, g·îlᵉmisē la xŭldɛkwē Dɛnt!alaᵘyu laē ᵉwîᵉla q!wāg·flîƚa
mōkwē g·Ig·ɛgămaᵉya. Wä, laᵉmē Nɛqāp!ɛnk·îmē dālaxa ʟ!āqwa. Wä,
lä yāq!ɛg·aᵉƚa; wä, lä ᵉnēk·a: Laɛmk· xŭldɛkᵘg·as ʟ!āqwag·ōs g·I-
gămēᵉ ʟ!āsotiwalis. Gŭᵉnō hălxwa lāxō āʟanuᵉxᵘ max·ts!ālax. ᵉnē-
5   ᵉnak·iƚē mōsgɛᵉmakᵘ Kwākŭg·uƚ, laɛms ᵮɛm ᵉnāxwaƚ gwāƚaƚaʟɛx qaᵉs
g·ōxᵉwidēlāxōs qō nɛqōgwilasō lāxē gwēx·ᵉidaasʟasg·ɛns g·Igămēk·,
ᵉnēk·ē. Wä, laɛm gwāƚē wāƚdɛmas lāxēq. Lēx·aɛm āƚālxsdē wāƚdɛms
ʟ!āqoʟasaxs ᵉnēk·aē laɛm gaāxalaƚ yāqwaƚtsa p!ɛlxɛlasgɛmē lāxa lēl-
qwālaʟaᵉyax gaālaʟa. Wä, lāwisʟē gwāƚ lāxēq. Wä, laᵉmē ᵉwîᵉla hō-
10   qŭwɛls lāxa g·ōkwaxa la gäƚa gānuʟa.

Wä, g·îlᵉmisē ᵉnāx·ᵉidxa gaāläxs laē ʟ!āqoʟas ᵉyālaqasa hä-
ᵉyāƚᵉāsa Q!ōmoyāᵉyē qa lēs qāsaxa Gwētɛla ʟɛᵉwa ᵉwālas Kwāg·uƚ ʟɛᵉwa Q!ōmk·!ût!ɛsē qa g·āxēs ᵉwîᵉla ʟɛᵉwa bābagŭxa ts!ēdaq lāx g·ō-
kwas; yîx lāg·iƚas ᵉnēk·ē ʟ!āqoʟasē qa g·āxēs ᵉwîᵉlaēʟɛla lax g·ō-
15   kwasēxs ᵉnēk·aē qaᵉs hāwāxɛlēxa Kwākŭg·uƚē qa ᵉnāxwaᵉmēs gwāƚaƚasēs
ʟ!āʟ!ɛqwa qō k·āk·ōgwalasōlaxs yāxᵉwidaasʟasa k·ōqwasōʟas ʟ!āqwa.
Wä, hēᵉmis lāg·iƚas ʟ!āqoʟasē wāƚaqēla qa g·āxēs ᵉwîᵉlēda yūduxᵘsɛᵉmakwē Kwākŭg·uƚ lāx g·ókwas. Wä, laᵉmēda hāᵉyāƚᵉa qāsa. Wä,g·îl-
ᵉmisē ᵉwîlxtōdxa g·ig·ōkwē g·āxaē aēdaaqa lāqēxs ᵉnēk·aēda hāᵉyāƚ-
20   ᵉāxs laē qāsa,G·āxᵉmɛnuᵉxᵘ qāsoʟai Gwētɛlai qa ʟ!āsotiwalisai. Wä,
lä ᵉnɛmādzaqwa ᵉnēk·a waōkwas: Halāg·flēʟāsai. ᵉnɛmp!ēnats!axsta-
ɛmʟɛnuᵉxwai, ᵉnēx·daᵉxwē. Wä, g·āxē ᵉwîᵉla hōgwiʟɛla lāxa g·ōkwē.
Wä, g·îlᵉmisē g·āx ᵉwîᵉlaēʟa laas ᵮɛm ᵉnāxwa tētɛk!walēda g·Ig·ɛ-
gămaᵉyē. Wä, lāxaē ōgwaqa tētɛk!walēda bēbɛgwānɛmq!ālɛmē laaʟas
25   xwānaƚɛlēda hāᵉyāƚᵉäx gaaxstēʟasa g·āxē ᵉwîlaēʟɛla lāxa g·ōkwē. Wä,
g·îlᵉmisē gwāƚē haᵉmōx·silaᵉyasa hāᵉyāƚᵉäxs laē ƚuxts!ōᵉyo lāxa ƚōɛlq!wa. Wä, lä k·āgɛmlēlɛm lāxa ᵉnāxwa bēbɛgwanɛma. Wä, g·îl-
ᵉmisē ᵉwîla la k·āgɛmalîƚa ƚōɛlq!wāxs laē hālɛmq!ɛsᵉîdēda ᵉnāxwa
bēbɛgwānɛma qaxs ᵉnāxwaᵉmaē q!ēq!aēqɛîa, lāg·iƚa k·!ēs nɛqɛlqɛlaxs
30   wāx·aē haᵉmāpa.

As soon as Dɛnt!alaᵋyu was marked, all the/four chiefs arose
and then Nɛqap!ɛnk·ɛm took the copper/and spoke and said: "Now
your copper here has been marked,/chief ʟ!āsotiwalis. Do not kill
it else we are going to be ashamed.(5)I mean you, four tribes of the
Kwāg·uɫ. Indeed you will all be ready to/help if someone should
match our chief in what he is going to do."/Thus he said. Then
their speeches were finished after this, only this was the last word
of/ʟ!āqoʟas who said, "Now you will give away the blankets to the/
tribes early in the morning." And at last he finished after this,
and then they all(10)went out of the house late at night./

As soon as it was daylight in the morning, ʟ!āqoʟas sent the/
young men of the Q!ōmoyâᵋyē to go and invite the Gwētɛla and ᵋwālas
Kwāg·uɫ/and Q!ōmk·!ūt!ɛs to come, all the men and the women who had
men's seats, to his house./ The reason why ʟ!āqoʟas wished that all
should come into his house was that he(15)wished to ask the Kwāg·uɫ
that all should get ready with their/coppers, in case any should be
broken to match him when he should give away the pieces of the copper that was to be broken./ Therefore ʟ!āqoʟas wished all the three
tribes of the/Kwāg·uɫ to come to his house. Now the young men went
(to call them) and as soon as/they had been to all the houses they
came back again, and the young men said(20)as they went (to call),
"We come to call you, Gwētɛla, on behalf of ʟ!āsotiwalis," and then
the others said, "Come quickly, we are calling only once,"/ they
said. Then they all came into the house/and when they had all come
in, the chiefs joked one another,/and also the common men joked one
another, while(25)the young men got ready the breakfast for those
who had come into the house./ As soon as the food cooked by the
young men was finished, they put it into the dishes/and put them before all the men. As soon as/the dishes had been put in front/of
them, all the/men ate quickly, for they had much to think. There-

Wä, g·îlᵋmisē gwăɫa lăxēs haᵋmaēnaᵋyaxs laēda hăᵋyăɫᵋa q!ap!ēg·îlîɫaxa ɫōɛlq!wē qaᵋs lē g·ēxaq lăxa onᵋēgwiɫasa g·ōkwē. Wä, g·îlᵋmisē gwăɫa laas ᴌ!āqoᴌasē ᴌăxᵋwalîɫa qaᵋs yāq!ɛg·aᵋɫē. Wä, lä ᵋnēk·a: Qăᴌ, qăᴌax hꝺᵋmaēx gwēk·!ālasē g·îg·ɛgămēxwa hꝺleg·în-

5 dăsa hăsāᵋyē lăxēs ᴌēlănɛmē lăxɛn wŭᴌɛɫē lăxɛns wîwōmpꝺ̈wŭɫa. Wäk·as, wäk·asōᴌ g·îg·ɛgămēᵋ, laᵋmō aꝺk·!aakwaxōs k·ăxstalîɫaqōs g·îg·ɛgămēᵋ. Wa, wa, ᵋnēk·ē. Wä, la ēdzaqwa yāq!ɛg·aᵋɫa. Wä, lä ᵋnēk·a: Laɛm ᴌēqwalîɫᴌɛn wăɫdɛm lăᴌ g·îg·ɛgămēᵋ laxg·în ᵋnēk·ꝺk· qaᵋs ᵋnăxwaᵋmaōs gwăɫaɫa qaᵋs g·ōxᵋwidaōsasēs ᴌ!āᴌ!aqwăyōs g·āxɛn qō k·āk·ogwala

10 lăxɛn yāxᵋwitsōᵋᴌasa k·ōqoyoᴌa lăxōx Dɛnt!alaᵋyux ᵋnēk·ē. Wä, hꝺᵋmisa qaᵋs wäg·aōs ᵋnăxwa q!wälax·ᵋida ᴌōᵋ qaᵋs gŭmsᵋidaōs g·ōɫg·ŭkŭlōt, ᵋnēk·ē. Wä, hăg·axōx Maēmaɫp!ɛngāmaᵋyē ᴌaxᵋwɛls lăxg·ada ᴌ!āsanᴂᵋyax qaᵋs lāqwaläxwa lēlqwălaᴌaᵋyax. Wä, lä ᴌꝺᴌɛqɛlax ēᵋaɫtsɛmē ᴌꝺᴌɛgɛmsa maᵋlōkwē ts!ēdaq sāsɛms. Wä, hꝺᵋmisē ᴌꝺgɛmᴌas ᴌō-

15 ᵋlēᵋyas ᴌ!āqoᴌasē. Wä, lä lāwɛlsē Maēmaɫp!ɛngāmaᵋyē lăxa g·ōkwē qaᵋs lē ᴌăxᵋwɛlsa, yîxs g·āyoɫaē lăx ᵋnɛᵋmēmoqtasa ꝺ·îg·îlgāmasa Q!ōmoyᴂᵋyē. Wä, lä ᵋnēk·a: Laɛms ʌ·îts!ax·îlaᴌai Mamalēleqălai. lăx Q!ēx·ᴌalagai xŭnōkwas ᴌ!āsotiwalisai. Laɛms x·îts!ax·îlaᴌai ᵋnɛmgēsai lăx ᴌăᴌeliᴌ!ai xŭnōkwas ᴌ!āsotiwalisai. Laɛms x·îts!ax·îlaᴌai Ɫāwits!ēsai lăx Gŭyōlsɛlasai xŭnōkwas ᴌ!āsotiwalisai. Hä-

20 laxsᴌasai, ᵋnēk·ē. Wä, hꝺɛm k·!ēsᵋōs Maēmaɫp!ɛngamaᵋya lāqwala qaēda p!ɛsäxa lēlqwălaᴌaᵋyē g·äg·îᴌɛla lăxēs awᴂᵋyē Ōmaxt!ālaᴌaᵋyē.

Wä, g·îlᵋmisē gwăɫa g·āxaē g·āxēᴌa lăxa t!ɛx·îla. Wä, lä ᵋnēk·a: Laᵋmē lāg·aɛlsɛns wăɫdɛma, g·îgămēᵋ ᴌ!āsotiwalis, ᵋnēk·ē.

25 Wä, laᵋmē ᵋnăxwa q!wälɛnkwa bēbɛgwānɛm lăxēq. Wä, laᵋmē k!ŭsᵋaliɫa nēnᴂgadē ᴌɛᵋwa ēᵋaɫostă lăxa ōgwiwaᵋliɫasa g·ōkwē qaᵋs ɑɛnxālēsa g·îg·îldzɛyāla q!ɛmq!ɛmdɛmasa ᵋnɛᵋmēmotasa Yaēx·agɛmaᵋyē, yîx ᵋnɛᵋmēmotas ᴌ!āsotiwalisē. Wä, g·îlᵋmisē wŭᴌăxᵋaᴌɛlēda lēlqwălaᴌaᵋyaxa dɛnxk·!ālaxs laē hōgwiᴌa ᵋwîᵋla. Wä, hꝺɛm ᴌꝺgadɛs dɛhxdɛn-

30 xîɫaxa dɛnxɛläsa g·îldzɛyāla q!ɛmdɛma lăxa p!ɛsa. Wä, hꝺᵋmis ᴌꝺᵋlalayuxa ᵋnăxwa lēlqwălaᴌaᵋyē qa g·āxlag·is hōgwîᴌ lăxa ᴌꝺɫɛlats!ē

As soon as they had finished eating,the young men/gathered up
the dishes and put them away in the corner of the house,/and when
that was done,ᴸ!āqoᴸas arose and spoke./ He said: "Indeed, it is
true,this is the way of speaking,chiefs, this second course with a
speech(the(5)breath)for the guests,according to what was learned
from our ancestors. Go on/now,go on,chiefs. It is well done,what
is placed before you,chiefs./ Wa wa," said he. Then he spoke again
and said: "Now/I shall change my speech to you,chiefs. I wish all
of you to/get ready to help me with your coppers,in case the one
may match me(10)to whom I am going to give away the broken copper
Dᴇnt!alaᵋyu," said he. "And this also,/that you go on and dress
yourselves and paint yourselves with ochre,tribes,"/said he. "Now
let Maēmaᵋx̣p!engᴇmēᵋ go on and stand/outside of the house to call
the tribes." Then he named/the two new names of his two daughters,
and also the name of the(15)nephew of ᴸ!āqoᴸas. And then Maēmaᵋx̣-
p!engᴇmēᵋ went out of the house/and stood outside,for he belonged
to the numaym G·ɪg·îlg̱ăm/of the Q!ōmoyâᵋyē. And he said: "Now Mamalēleqăla,you will witness/Q!ēx·ᴸālag̱a,the daughter of ᴸ!āsotiwalis.
Now ᵋnᴇmgis,you will witness ᴸᴀᴸilɪᴸ!a,the daughter of ᴸ!āsotiwa-
lis. Now(20)Lāwits!ēs, you will witness G̱ŭyōlsᴇlas, the child of
ᴸ!āsotiwalis./Go aboard quickly," said he. This is the privilege
of Maēmaᵋx̣p!engᴇmēᵋ,to call the people for the/potlatch(given)to
all the tribes,beginning from his first ancestor,Ōmaxt!ālaᴸēᵋ./

As soon as he had finished,he came into the doorway and said:/
"Now our word has gone out,great chief ᴸ!āsotiwalis," said he.(25)
Then all the men were dressed after this. The/song leaders and the
young men sat down in the rear of the house and they sang/the old
songs of the numaym Yaēx·agᴇmēᵋ,the/numaym of ᴸ!āsotiwalis. As soon
as the tribes heard the/sound of singing,they all came in. This is
called "singing on the floor,"(30)the singing of the ancestral
songs in the potlatch,and this is/the means of inviting all the

g·ōkwa. Wä, g·îlᵋmisē g·äx ᵋwÎᵋlaêʟa yŭduxᵁsɛᵋmakwê lêlqwälaʟaᵋya
laas qǃwêłᵋidēda dɛnxdɛnxÎła.

Wä, lä ʟaxᵋwalÎłē Pɛlᵋnäkŭlag·îlisxa xämagämaᵋyê g·Îgämēsa
ᵋnɛᵋmēmutasa Kŭkwäkǃŭmasa Qǃōmoyâᵋyê qaᵋs yäqǃɛg·aᵋłē. Wä, lä ᵋnê-
k·a gwêgɛmäła läxa mōsgɛᵋmakwê Kwäkŭg·uła: Laᵋmɛn wäg·Îł nōs g·Î-
g·ɛgämêᵋ mōᵋmałk·ǃälałtsɛns g·Îg·ɛgämaᵋyaxs g·äxaê ᵋwÎᵋlaêʟa läxwa
g·ōkwêx ᵋnêk·êxs laê gwêgɛmx·ᵋÎt läxa kǃŭdzōlasasa lêlqwälaʟaᵋya
wäx·saᵋnêgwiłasa g·ōkwê. Wä, lä ᵋnêk·a: Wa, gêlag·a Mamalêlᵋqäl;
wa gêlag·a ᵋnɛmgês; wa, gêlag·a Łäwitsǃês. HêłᵋalÎł läxwa läx hê-
łiᵋlälakwa qaᵋs g·Îg·ɛgämêk·as läx wäłdɛᵋmênaᵋyê läqᵁ yîsa ʟôłɛläxa
lêlqwälaʟaᵋyêxwa k·ǃêsêx ałᵋɛm äxä qän gwêk·ǃälasaxwa wäłdɛmaxsɛns
nenŭyɛmbalisaxg·îns ᵋnäxwêk· lêlqwälaʟaᵋya. Wä, hêᵋmisɛns k·ǃeâsi-
ła äłelaᵋya ᵋnêᵋnak·iłê laɛms hêlêʟôʟ g·Îg·ɛgämêᵋ, ᵋnêk·exs laê
gwêgɛmx·ᵋÎt läxa nênâgadê. Wä, lê yäqǃɛg·aᵋła. Wä, lä ᵋnêk·a: Laɛms nɛxbag·fïlêʟôʟ nênâgada laxɛns g·äxêła läxwa g·ōkwaxs ʟǃâsotiwalisê, ᵋnêk·êxs laê däk·ǃälaxa tɛlgŭmʟa pǃɛlxɛlasgɛmxa nâgadê qaᵋs
qǃɛmtêlaᵋyas.ʼ Wä, hêx·ᵋidaᵋmisê ʟǃâqoʟas tsǃâsa sɛk·ǃaxsa pǃɛlxɛlasgɛm läq. Wä, lä däx·ᵋÎdxa ᵋnɛmxsa läq qaᵋs ʟɛpǃêdêq. Wä, lä
ᵋnêk·a: Laᵋmɛn tɛlqwasêqai sɛk·ǃäxsak· pǃɛlxɛlasgɛma lâʟ nâgadä
qaês qǃɛmtêlaᵋyas qag·în g·Îgämêk·, ᵋnêk·ê. Wä, la hêx·ᵋidaᵋma
ᵋnäxwa êᵋałâstâ qǃwäg·fïiła qaᵋs ʟax·ʟaᵋwÎłê gwêgɛmäła läxa ōgwiwa-
ᵋlÎłasa g·ōkwê. Wä, laᵋmêda nâgadê dâqâlasês qǃɛmtêlaᵋyê äłtsɛm
qǃɛmdɛma (xɛn läx·ᵋidaᵋma häłaxdzɛm lâʟa qǃɛmdêlɛmê äłtsɛm qǃɛmdɛma). Wä, laᵋmê ᵋnäxwa dɛnxᵋêdêda êᵋałostâ. Wä, g·äxê ʟǃâqoʟas g·ä-
lag·iwis ʟǃâsotiwalisêxa däläxa ʟǃâqwa läx Dɛntǃalaᵋyu. Wä, lä mä-
k·fïlê Qǃêx·ʟalaga ʟôᵋ ʟäʟiliʟǃa. Wä, lä ɛlxʟaᵋyê Gŭyōlsɛlas qaᵋs lê
yîpɛmg·fïlÎł läxa ʟǃâsaliłasa êᵋałostâxa dɛnxɛla. Wä, laᵋmê ᵋnɛmä-
gɛlÎł yîxᵋwÎd ʟôᵋ ʟǃâqoʟas ʟôᵋ ʟǃâsotiwalisêxa däläxa ʟǃâqwa.

Wä, g·îlᵋmisê qǃŭlbêda qǃɛmdɛmaxs laê ʟǃâsotiwalisê xäxalōla-
qwa. Wä, laᵋmê yäqǃɛg·aᵋła. Wä, lä ᵋnêk·a: Wäg·ax·în gŭnx·ᵋÎda
wîwomp ʟôᵋs qǃwêqǃŭlêᵋ qɛn wäg·i g·îldzaqwa yäqǃɛg·aᵋła. Wä, lä

tribes to come into the feasting(1)house. As soon as the three
tribes were in,/they stopped singing on the floor./

Then Pɛlᵉnākŭlag·ílis arose,the head chief/of the numaym Kŭkwāk!ŭm of the Q!ōmoyáᵉyē,and spoke. He said,(5)turning his face to
the four Ḵwāg·uⱡ tribes, "Now I will go ahead,my chiefs,/and speak
gratefully to our chiefs as they all have come into this/house,"
thus he said as he truned his face to the place where the tribes
were sitting/on each side of the house,and he said: "Now come,Mama-
lēleqāla,/come ᵉnɛmgis,come Ɫāwits!ēs. Sit down comfortably in this
place(10)which is well prepared for you,chiefs,as is said by the
one who invites/the tribes. This is not new,that we should say so.
These are the words of our/myths from the beginning,all our tribes,
and we do not make anything/new. I mean this. Now sit down well,
chiefs." Thus he said and/turned his face to the song leaders. Then
he spoke and said:(15)"Now begin what we are here for,song leaders,
the reason for which we have come into this house of Ɫ!āsotiwalis."/
Thus he said and he asked for the blankets which were to be a pil-
low for the song leader for the/song which he had made. Immediately
Ɫ!āqoⱡas gave five pairs of blankets/to him. Then he took one pair
and spread it out and/he said: "I make a soft layer with these five
pairs of blankets for you,song leader,(20)for the song you made for
my chief here," said he,and immediately/all the young men stood up
and they stood on the floor facing the rear/of the house,and the
song leader began the new/song. (I have already sent you the new
song they made.)/Then all the young men sang, and Ɫ!āqoⱡas came(25)
leading Ɫ!āsotiwalis and carrying the copper Dɛnt!alaᵉyu. And next
to him were/Q!ēx·Ⱡālaga and ⱠāⱡilîⱢ!a,and last Gŭyōlsɛlas. And/they
stood in a row outside of the young men who were singing,and now
they/danced together with Ɫ!āqoⱡas and Ɫ!āsotiwalis who was holding
the copper.

As soon as the song was at an end,Ɫ!āsotiwalis shouted,"Ha ha!"
(30)Then he spoke and said: "Let me now try,/fathers and uncles,to

ᵉnāxwaᵉma g·Ĩg·ᴇgãmaᵉyasa Kwākũg·u̓x̌ē ᵉnēk·a. Wâg·adzēlag·a g·Ĩ-
g̣āmēᵉ. Lᴇᵉmaaqōs ᵉwĨᵉlō̧ᵗᵉnākũlax q̣wāq̣uxēx̌asa hēx̌axa g·Ĩgãmaᵉya.
Qā̧ᒐaxs âyadaaqōsxwa ṭᴇx·Ĩlax qaᵉs qōqãsĨx̌ōs g·Ĩgãmēᵉ, ᵉnēk·a bᴇ-
bᴇgwānᴇmē. Wä, âᵉmisē ᒐ̣āsotiwalisē la ̧ᒐāᵉwix̌ qaᵉs hōᒐēlāx wāx̌-
dᴇmas. Wä, g·Ĩᵉmisē q̣ũlbē wāx̌dᴇmas laas ᒐ̣āsotiwalisē ēdzaqwa
yāq̣ᴇg·aᵉx̌a. Wä, lä ᵉnēk·a: Ãla, âlasēs wāx̌dᴇmōs g·Ĩg·ᴇgãmēᵉ lāxwa g·Ĩgᴇmaᵉya qᴇn ōmpa yĨx·sṭaᒐᴇn ̧ᒐōᵉ ᵉwĨᵉlōᒐax gwāyiᵉlälasaxsᴇn
g·Ĩgãmaᵉyēx ōmpax ̧ᒐōᵉ k·̣ēs. Wä, lā̧ᒐaᒐᴇn gũnx·ᵉ̧Ĩdaᴇmᒐ qãsaᒐ lāxōx
ṭᴇx·Ĩlaᵉyaxs qᴇn qãstawēsᴇᵉwa. Wä, lᴇn k·ōtaᴇm lābᴇndaᴇmᒐaq. ᵉnē-
ᶠnak·ix̌ē, wä, gēlag·a g·Ĩg·ᴇgãmēᵉ Âwaxᴇlag·ᶠlis ̧ᒐōᵉs Nᴇqãp̣ᴇnk·ᴇm
̧ᒐōᵉs Nᴇg·ädzē; wä, sōᵉmēs Wāk·adzē. G̣ēlag·a qaᵉs k·̣ēlax·ᵉidaōsax-
g·a Dᴇnṭalaᵉyu, yũᒐaxs k·̣ēsᵉonukwaaqōsas, ᵉnēk·ē.

Wä, hēx·ᵉidaᵉmisa mōkwē g·Ĩg·ᴇgãmēᵉ q̣wāg·ᶠlĨx̌ qaᵉs lē lāx ̧ᒐā-
ᵉwilasas ᒐ̣āsotiwalisē qaᵉs q̣wäᵉstālaq. Wä, laᵉmēda yũduxsᴇᵉmakwē
ᒐēx̌ᶠlakᵘ lēlqwālaᒐēᵉ äkũᵉnēg·alix̌a qaxs âlaē k·Ĩxᴇlas yāxᵉwitsōᒐas
ᒐ̣āsotiwalisasa k·ugᴇkwē ᒐ̣āqwa. Wä, laᵉmē Nᴇqãp̣ᴇnk·ᴇm dāx·ᵉĨdᴇx
Dᴇnṭalaᵉyu qaᵉs yāq̣ᴇg·aᵉx̌ē. Wä, lä ᵉnēk·a: Qä̧ᒐ, Âwaxᴇlag·ᶠlis,
Nᴇg·ädzē; wä, sōᵉmis Wāk·adzē. NōsᒐawĨsᴇnsax nâq̣ēᒐᴇns gwēx·ᵉidaas-
ᒐaxᴇns ᵉnᴇmōxᵘdzēx lāxōx Dᴇnṭalaᵉyux. Häsᵉmēᒐaxsōxwaxōxda g·Ĩgã-
maēx wāx̌dᴇma qᴇns k·̣āk·̣ēsᵉox·sĨlēxᴇns k·̣ēsᵉōx. ᵉnēᵉnak·ix̌ē. Wä,
wēg·axᴇns âᴇm halōsṭaqa k·̣ēlax·ᵉĨdᴇqᵘ, ᵉnēk·ēxs laē ᶠnᴇmāx·ᵉĨdᴇxs
laē ḳũsᵉālix̌a.

Wä, la ᒐ̣āqoᒐas tṣâsa dzādzax·silaᵉyu q̣ᴇldayu ̧ᒐᵉᵉwa ãmaᵉyē
sōbayu lāx Nᴇqãp̣ᴇnk·ᴇmē. Wä, lä äxᵉētsᴇᵉwa tṣᴇq̣ũltsᴇmē ṭēsᴇma
qaᵉs lē mᴇxᵉwalĨlᴇm lāx ᒐ̣āsalĨx̌asa mōkwē q̣ēq̣ᴇltᴇlg·Ĩsxa ᒐ̣āqwa
g·Ĩg·ᴇgamaᵉya. (Māᵉx̌ē ̧ᒐēgᴇmasa q̣ēq̣ᴇltᴇlg·Ĩsē ̧ᒐōᵉ k·ēk·oqũlg·Ĩsē.)
Wä, la Âᵉwaxᴇlag·ᶠlis dāx·ᵉĨdxa ᒐ̣āqwa qaᵉs pāxᵉaᵉlōdēs lāxa q̣ᴇldᴇ-
ma tṣᴇq̣ũltsᴇm ṭēsᴇma. Wä, la Nᴇg·ädzē dāx̌axa q̣ᴇltoyuᒐē. Wä,
la Nᴇqãp̣ᴇnk·ᴇmē q̣ᴇltōdxa gᴇmᵉxanũᒐᴇmaᵉyasa ᒐ̣āqwa. Wä, la Nᴇg·ä-
dzē tṣâsa q̣ᴇlṭaᵉyē lāx Wāk·adzē. Wä, lä dāx·ᵉidē Nᴇg·ädzäxa
ēk·̣ᴇnxaᵉyasa hēx̌k·̣ōdᴇnuᒐᴇmaᵉyasa ᒐ̣āqwa. Wä, lāxaē Nᴇqãp̣ᴇnk·ᴇm

speak my first speech." Then(1)all the chiefs of the Kwāg·uⱡ said:
"Go on,great chief./ Now you are obtaining everything. You should
grow up well,chief./ Indeed you have a father who made a road for
you to follow,chief,"said the/men. Now ⱡ!āsotiwalis was just standing on the floor and he listened to their words.(5)As soon as they
had finished speaking,then ⱡ!āsotiwalis/spoke again and said:"It is
true what you say,chiefs,of this/chief my father. I may succeed in
obtaining all the different ways of my/chief,my father,or I may not.
I shall try hereafter to walk the/way made by him for me to follow.
I think I shall go the the end.(10)That is what I mean. Now chiefs
Ꞓᵋwaxɛlag·ilis and you Nɛqap!ɛnk·ɛm/and you Nɛg·ädzē and you Wāk·as,
come and strike this/Dɛnt!alaᵋyu. You are the owners of this privilege," said he./

Immediately the four chiefs stood up and went to the place
where/ⱡ!āsotiwalis was standing and they stood around him. Now the
three(15)invited tribes kept quiet,because they were really afraid
that/ⱡ!āsotiwalis would give away the broken copper. Then Nɛqap!ɛn-
k·ɛm took/Dɛnt!alaᵋyu and spoke. He said: "Indeed Ꞓᵋwaxɛlag·ilis,/
Nɛg·ädzē and you Wāk·as, is it our wish what we do/to our great
friend,this Dɛnt!alaᵋyu? It is the(20)wish of this chief that we
use our privilege. I mean this./ Now let us only be quick and strike
him," said he and together they all/sat down./

Then ⱡ!āqoⱡas gave a chisel and a small/axe to Nɛqap!ɛnk·ɛm
and then was taken a diorite stone(25)and put down in front of the
four chiefs whose business it was to cut the copper./(They have two
names,the "copper cutters"and the "copper breakers.")/Then Ꞓᵋwaxɛla-
g·ilis took the copper and laid it down on the/diorite stone on
which it was to be cut and Nɛg·ädzē held what was to be cut/and Nɛqap!ɛnk·ɛm cut off the left hand corner of the copper. Then Nɛg·ä-
dzē(30)gave the piece cut off to Wāk·as and Nɛg·ädzē took the/upper
corner of the right hand side of the copper and Nɛqap!ɛnk·ɛm(1)qut

15

qᴊɛltōdɛq. Wä, lāxaē Nɛg·ädzē ts!âsa qᴊɛlt!ɛᶜyē lāx Wāk·adzē. Wä,
lāxaē Nɛg·ädzē dāx·ᶜidxa hễłk·!ōdɛnuts!ɛxsdaᶜyasa ʟ!āqwa. Wä, lāxaē Nɛqāp!ɛnk·ɛm q!ɛltōdɛq. Wä, lāxaē Nɛg·ädzē ts!âsa qᴊɛlt!ɛᶜyē
lāx Wāk·adzē; Wä, g·îlᶜmisē lawäyēda yūduxwē q!ɛltoyo lāxa ʟ!ā-
5 qwa laas Áᶠwaxɛlag·îlisē ʟ̣āxᶜwalîła dālaxa q!ɛldɛkwē ʟ!āqwa qaᶜs
yāq!ɛg·aᶜła. Wä, lä ᶜnēk·a dzōxwałas: Wa, dōxᶜwit, g·îg·ɛgāmēs
lēlqwälaʟai lāxg·a lāx· gwäłaatsg·a Dɛnt!alaᶜyukᵘ lāxg·ada ᶜwāla-
sɛk· xūsɛlag·îlisg·în g·îgāmēk· lāxg·a ʟ!āsotiwalisak:. Wä, laᶜmēsɛn lāł g·ēxałqɛk·, ᶜnēk·ēxs laē lats!âliłasa q!ɛldɛkwē ʟ!āqwa qaᶜs
10 lē äxᶜāliłas. Wä, k·!ēst!ē gäłaxs g·āxaē aēdaaqa qaᶜs lē ʟ̣ᾷgelîła-
xēs waōkwē. Wä, lä yāq!ɛg·aᶜłē Wāk·adzē. Wä, lä ᶜnēk·a: Hễq!ɛ-
maaxs gwälasē lāxg·în k·!ēsᶜokᵘ yînʟaxg·în k·!ēsᶜonukwēg·asa däg·a-
ᶜyaxa q!ɛltasɛᶜwē lāxa ʟ̣ẹ̄ʟɛgadx·dä ʟ!āʟ!aqwa g·äg·îʟɛlaxs g·ālaōłē
ᶜnāg·îlisɛns ᶜnālax. ᶜnēᶜnak·iłē g·îg·ɛgāmēs lēɛlqwälaʟai. ᶜnē-
15 ᶜnak·iłē, wä, laᶜmēsɛk· lāłg·ada yūduxūk· q!ɛltaxoyu lāxōx Dɛnt!a-
laᶜyuxᵘdä laxōxda łaᶜwisēx nɛnōlox g·îgāmaᶜyōx ʟ!āsotiwalidzēx qa
wäg·isōxwasɛk· lāxēs gwaēxsdaasasɛsɛk·, ᶜnēk·ēxs laē ts!âs lāx
ʟ!āsotiwalisē.

Wä, laᶜmēda mōkwē g·îg·ɛgāmē bâs lāxēq qaᶜs lē k!ūsᶜāliła. Wä,
20 laᶜmē ʟ!āsotiwalisē la ᶜnɛmōxᵘᶜɛm la ʟ̣aᶜwîła. Wä, lä yāq!ɛg·aᶜła.
Wä, lä ᶜnēk·a: Áq!amîłg·în nɛgɛłtewēʟɛx t!ɛx·îlaᶜyasɛn g·îgāmaᶜyēx
ōmp qɛn qāstewēsō t!ɛx·îlaxwa nɛnōlōx wāyäd g·îgāmaᶜyaxwa k·!eâsēx
k·îlɛm g·îgāmaᶜyas.ᶜnēᶜnak·iłē g·îg·ɛgāmēᶜ. Laᶜmɛn yîxsᶜɛndɛxg·a
Dɛnt!alaᶜyuxᵘdɛk· qaᶜs yūduxᵘsɛᶜmakᵘ lēlqwälaʟai. ᶜnēᶜnak·iłē, wä,
25 laᶜmēsɛn yāxᶜwidɛłtsak·, ᶜnēk·ēxs laē dzōxwałasēs hễłk·!ōtts!ānaᶜyē
dāłaxa ᶜnɛmē lāxa q!ɛldɛkwē ʟ!āqwa. Wä, lä ᶜnēk·a: Wa, g·îgāmaᶜyai
Wānidai,ᶜnēk··ē ʟ!āsotiwalisaxs laē hễɛm la ts!âsa q!ɛldɛkwē gɛmᶜxa-
nūʟɛmēᶜ lāx Wānidēxa g·āyułē lāx ᶜnɛᶜmēmutasa ᶜwālasasa Mamalēleqāla. Wä, lä ᶜnēk··ē Wānidē, laē dāx·ᶜîdxa yāxᶜwidayâq q!ɛldɛkᵘ ʟ!ā-
30 qwa: Gēlak·asᶜla g·îgāmēᶜ ʟ!āsotiwalis qaxs k·!ēsaaqōs k·!ōta yāx-
ᶜwîtsg·ada g·āyułɛk· lāxwa ʟ̣ēgadäx ʟ!āqwa lāxox Dɛnt!alaᶜyudzäx.

it off also,and Nɛg·ädzē gave the piece cut off of Wāk·as./ And Nɛg·ädzē took the right hand lower corner of the copper and/Nɛqapǃɛnk·ɛm cut it off also and Nɛg·ädzē gave the piece cut off to Wāk·as. As soon as the three pieces were off from the copper(5)AᵉwaxɛlagˑƗlis stood up and took the copper which had been cut and/spoke. He said holding it up, "Look here, chiefs of the/tribes,at the way in which Dɛntǃalaᵉyu is,this great/acropolis made by my chief here,ʟǃāsotiwalis. Now/I will put this away," said he and he went into the room with the copper that had been cut and(10)put it down there. He had not been away long before he came back and stood/among the others. Then Wāk·as spoke and said: "This is the way/our privilege is used, for I have this privilege of holding the/pieces cut off from the copper that has a name, beginning from the time when/light came into our world. I mean this, chiefs of the tribes.(15) I mean this, now these three pieces cut off from Dɛntǃalaᵉyu will go/to this angry extravagant chief,the great ʟǃāsotiwalis,so that/he may go on and do with this whatever he wishes." Thus he said and gave them to/ ʟǃāsotiwalis./

Now the four chiefs left him and they went and sat down.(20) Then ʟǃāsotiwalis was standing alone on the floor and he spoke/and said: "I am just going to follow the road made by my chief,/my father,the road to walk on,extravagant merciless chief,/the chief who is not afraid of anything. I mean this,chiefs,I have danced to pieces/Dɛntǃalaᵉyu for you,three tribes. I mean this,(25)now I am going to give this away," said he,holding up in his right hand/one of the broken pieces of copper. Then he said, "Now,chief/Wanēd," said ʟǃāsotiwalis,and then he himself gave the broken piece/from the left hand side of the copper to Wanēd,who belonged to the numaym ᵉwālas of the Mamalēleqǎla./ Then said Wanēd,as he took the broken piece of the copper that was given to him,(30)"Thank you, chief ʟǃāsotiwalis,that you do not think me too small/to give this that comes from the copper that has a name,Dɛntǃalaᵉyu.(1)Thank you," said

ᵋwa, gēlak·asᵋla ᵋnēk·ē. Wä, la ʟ!ásotiwalisē ēt!ēd dzōxᵋwaɫa dā-
ɫaxa hēɫk·!ōdɛnuts!ɛxsdaᵋyasa ʟ!aqwa. Wä, lä ᵋnēk·a: Wa, g·Igāma-
ᵋyai Q!ōmx·ɫlag·ɫlisai, ᵋnēk·ē ʟ!ásotiwalisaxs laē hēɛm la ts!ậsa
q!ɛldɛkwē hēɫk·!ōdɛnuts!ɛxsdē lāx Q!ōmx·ɫlag·ɫlisēxa g·ayuɫē lāx
5   ᵋnɛᵋmēmutasa Ts!ōts!ɛlwālagɛmaᵋyasa ᵋnɛmgēsē. Wä, lāxaē yāq!ɛg·a-
ᵋɫēda g·Igāmaᵋyē Q!ōmx·ɫlag·ɫlisē. Wä, lä ᵋnēk·a: Qäʟ, qäʟ g·I-
g·ɛgāmēs lēlqwälaʟai. ᵋyāx·sɛmɛwɪsē yɛg·āyậwēsa ᵋyāxᵋwɪdäsa q!ɛl-
dɛkwē ʟ!āqwa. Aᵋmaaxs hēɛm ᵋyāxᵋwidaatsa q!ɛldɛkwē ʟ!āqwēda hēnoma
ma g·Igāmēsa lēlqwälaʟaᵋya. ᵋnēᵋnak·iɫē g·Igāmēᵗʟ!ásotiwalis. Gē-
10   lak·asᵋla, gēlak·asᵋla, wa, wa, ᵋnēk·ē. Wä, ᶅa ʟ!ásotiwalisē dā-
ɫaxa q!ɛldɛkwē ʟ!āqwaxa g·āyuɫē lāxa hēɫk·!ōdɛnuʟɛmaᵋyē. Wä, lä
ᵋnēk·a: Wa, xamalai, Lɛᵋwag·ilai (xa gwaᵋwina gwɛᵋyậs). Laɛms
q!wēɫᵋidʟōʟ ᵋnēk·ēxs laē ts!ɛxᵋālɪɫaq. Wä, laᵋmē k·ōtēda ᵋnāxwa
bēbɛgwanɛmx ʟ!ásotiwalisē q!ālaxa ᵋnɛᵋmōkwa bɛgwānɛm ᵋyax·p!axstaq.
15   (Wä, hēᵋmis gwɛᵋyōs xamala Lɛᵋwag·ilē.)

       Wä, laᵋmē gwäɫa. Wä, laᵋmē ʟ!ásotiwalisē wäxaxa Kwākǔg·uɫē
qa ᵋyāxᵋwidēsēsa p!ɛlxɛlasgɛmē lāxa yūduxᵘsɛᵋmakwē lēlqwälaʟaᵋya.
Wä, hēx·ᵋidaᵋmisē ʟ!āqoʟas yāq!ɛg·aᵋɫa. Wä, lä ᵋnēk·a: ʟ!ɛdậ,
ʟ!ɛdậ hēɫaxamaswɪst!ɛnʟaxɛn g·Iqēlasɛᵋwa qɛn xǔnōkwōx ʟ!ásotiwa-
20   lisēx qaᵋs haᵋmaɫɛl lēɛlqwälaʟē. ᵋnēᵋnak·iɫē g·Ig·ɛgāmēs Kwākǔg·uɫ.
Laɛm lāʟɛn ʟậxwaᵋyē lāxōx ʟ!ásotiwalisēx ʟɛᵋwǔn yāq!äntp!ēqē qa wä-
g·isōx yāq!ɛnt!āla; wä, hēᵋmēsɛn dāgɛmaᵋyē·lāxɛn ᵋnɛᵋmēmuta Hāānaʟēᵋnậ. Wä, Aɛmɫwisɛn lāɫ ʟậxsdēsɛn ᵋnɛᵋmēmutasa Hāānaʟēᵋnậ. Wä,
g·āxlậg·ax·i mɛnats!ä q!ōxᵋwāliɫa qa k!wāsgɛmēsōsg·a ʟ!ásotiwali-
25   sɛk·, ᵋnēk·ē.

       Wä, lä äxᵋētsɛᵋwa mɛnats!ē qaᵋs lē quxᵋwalɪlɛm lāxa ōgwiwalɪ-
ɫasa g·ōkwē lāx ʟāsaliɫasa nēnậgadē. Wä, la ʟ!ásotiwalisē k!wās-
gāmlɪɫaq. Wä, lä ʟēᵋlālasɛᵋwē q!āq!asto bɛgwānɛmsa Mamalēleqāla.
Wä, la k!wāg·ɫlɪɫa q!āq!astowē bɛgwānɛm lāx hēɫk·!ōtagaᵋwalɪɫas
30   ʟ!ásotiwalisē. Wä, lēda hāᵋyāɫᵋa ʟ!ɛpōstậ lāxa ʟ!ɛbɛg·ɪ̄ɫē p!ɛl-
xɛlasgɛma qaᵋs lē k!waxtɛwēq. Wä, lä lēx·axōtsa ᵋnɛmts!aqē q!ɛnē-

he. Then again ᴸ!āsotiwalis held up/the right hand side bottom
piece of the copper and he said, "Oh,chief/Q!ōmx·flag·flis,"said
ᴸ!āsotiwalis,when he gave the/broken piece from the lower right
hand side to Q!ōmx·flag·flis,who belonged to the(5)numaym Ts!ēts!ɛᴸ-
wālagɛmēᵉ of the ᵋnɛmgis. Then spoke/chief Q!ōmx·flag·flis and said:
"Indeed,indeed,/chiefs of the tribes,is it not bad,the giving of
the/broken pieces of copper,just that they give the broken pieces
of copper to the real/chiefs of the tribes. This is what I mean,
chief ᴸ!āsotiwalis,(10)thank you,thank you, Wa wa," said he. Then
ᴸ!āsotiwalis held up the/broken piece of copper from the right hand
upper side and/he said: "Now Orphan, World-Maker,(he meant the Ra-
ven)now/you will stop talking," said he as he threw it down. Then
all the/men guessed that ᴸ!āsotiwalis knew that one man had spoken
badly of him.(15) (This is what is called "Orphan World-Maker".)

Now he finished. Then ᴸ!āsotiwalis told the Kwāg·uᴸ/to go ahead
and to give away the blankets to the three tribes,/and immediately
ᴸ!āqoᴸas spoke and said, "It is nice./ It is nice. It is well done,
what I did in my chief making for my son ᴸ!āsotiwalis,(20)for you,
tribes. I mean this,chiefs of the Kwāg·uᴸ./ Now my seat will go to
this ᴸ!āsotiwalis,and my speaker's staff,for/he will be speaker,and
my office of giving away property in my numaym,the Hāānaᴸēᵐno./Now
I shall stand at the end of my numaym,the Hāānaᴸēᵐno. Now/bring the
drum and put it on its side so that ᴸ!āsotiwalis may ᴣit on it,"
(25) said he.

Then the drum was taken and was put on its side in the rear of
the/house in front of the song leaders, and then ᴸ!āsotiwalis sat
down on it./ Then they called the tally keeper of the Mamalēleqāla/
and the tally keeper sat down on the right hand side of(30)ᴸ!āso-
tiwalis. Then the young men climbed on the blankets that were piled
up/and sat down on top of them. Then they rolled down one(1)bundle

p!ɛnāla ë̆k·!ɛnxē p!ɛlxɛlasgɛma. Wä, lēda waōkwē hä̆ᵋyäⱡᵋa dādalaq
qaᵋs lē k·āt!alǐⱡas lāx gɛmᵋxagawalǐⱡas ʟ!āsotiwalisē. Wä, lä
qwē̆ⱡk·!ɛwēᵋstɛntsɛᵋwa q!ɛnēp!ɛnāla p!ɛlxɛlasgɛma. Wä, lēda ts!ā-
ts!ậmē̆ⱡē hë̆ⱡᵋa dāx·ᵋIdxa ᵋnɛmxsa p!ɛlxɛļdsgɛm qaᵋs ʟɛpsēᵋstɛndēq

5   qaᵋs ts!ậwēs lāx ʟ!āsotiwalisē Wä, lä dāgɛmdē ʟ!āsotiwalisaxa ᵋnɛmxsa p!ɛlxɛlasgɛm qaᵋs ʟɛpk·äx·ɛndēs. Wä, lä yāq!ɛg·aᵋⱡa. Wä, lä
ᵋnēk·a; Qäļ, ōmp ʟ!āqoļas, qäļēs wā̆ⱡdɛmōs, qäļaxs lɛᵋmaaqōs ë̆g·osọ̄
g·āxɛn. Qäļaxs lɛᵋmaaqōs g·Iqēla g·āxɛn qɛn ʟ!āyustoliⱡaōʟ lāxēs
k·!ēsᵋowǐlasōs k!waᵋya, g·Igᵌ̈mēᵋ ōmp. Qäļ, qäļaxs lɛᵋmaēx hë̆ⱡᵋaʟɛ-

10   laⱡ g·āxɛnxōs ᵋnä̆xwiᵋläläqōs g·āxōdzɛm g·āxɛn. Wä, laᵋmēsɛn ậɛm
lāⱡ nōmadziladʟōs qaᵋs ậᵋmēʟōs ļēxsᵋālaⱡ g·āxɛn qɛn ë̆k·ë̆ⱡ g·Igᵌ̈ma-
ᵋya. ᵋnēᵋnak·iⱡē laᵋmɛn dāgɛnʟa. Wä, laᵋmē dzō̆xwaⱡasa ᵋnɛmxsa
p!ɛlxɛlasgɛma. Wä, lēda q!āq!astowē bɛgwānɛm ļēxᵋēdɛx kwēkwasa
ᵋnä̆xwa lēlqwä̆laʟaᵋyē ʟ!āsotiwalisasa ᵋnɛmgēs. Wä, la ʟ!āsotiwalitsa

15   Q!ōmoyậᵋyē ᵋnēk·a; ʟ!āsotiwalisexai sɛk·!axsa p!ɛlxɛlasgɛma. Wä,
lēda ts!āts!ậmiⱡē hë̆ⱡᵋa äxᵋē̆dxa waōkwasa la ᵋyāxᵋwidayậ qaᵋs ts!ɛx-
ᵋwuⱡt!āliⱡēq lāx la x·ǐlalǐlats ʟ!āsotiwalisaxa ᵋnɛmxsa p!ɛlxɛlasgɛ-
ma. Wä, laᵋmēda ōgǔᵋlamē hë̆ⱡᵋa la äxᵋaliⱡaxa sɛk·!axsa p!ɛlxɛlas-
gɛm qaᵋs ļē äxᵋāliⱡas lāx ʟ!āsalǐⱡas ʟ!āsotiwalisasa ᵋnɛmgēs.(Hö̆ɛm

20   ļē̆gadɛs ļāxstalǐⱡa hö̆ⱡᵋa la ts!ậsa ᵋyaq!wē̆ma p!ɛlxɛlasgɛma.) Wä,
hö̆x·sä̆ᵋmēs gwēg·ilaxs ᵋyāqwaē ʟ!āsotiwalisaxs ᵋyāqwaasa p!ɛlxɛlas-
gɛmē. Wä, g·ǐlᵋmisē ᵋwǐlxtowa yǔduxᵘsɛᵋmakwē lēlqwä̆laʟaᵋyaxs laē
ᵋwǐᵋla hōqǔwɛls lāxa ʟē̆ⱡᵋlats!e g·ōkwa. Wä, hö̆x·ᵋidaᵋmisē ᵋnä̆xwa
xwānaⱡᵋIda qaᵋs lē wǐᵋxstɛndxēs xwä̆xwak!ǔna qaᵋs ᵋmō̆xsēsēs dēda-

25   ᵋmāla lāq. Wä, laᵋmē ᵋwǐᵋla nä̆ᵋnakwa.

         Wä, hö̆t!a la mō̆xsa ᵋnälä̆sa lēlqwä̆laʟaᵋyē la bậsg·a Tsä̆xisɛk·
laas ʟ!āqoļasē ᵋyālaqasa mō̆kwē hä̆ᵋyä̆ⱡᵋasēs ᵋnɛᵋmēmuta Yaēx·agɛmaᵋyē
qa lēs qāsaxa Gwētɛla ļɛᵋwa ᵋwālas Kwāg·uⱡ ļɛᵋwa Q!ōmk·!ǔt!ɛsxa ᵋnē-
k·a qasɛlg·ǐsē mō̆kᵘ hä̆ᵋyä̆ⱡᵋa lāx ä̆ᵋwǐʟɛläs t!ē̆t!ɛx·ǐlä̆sa g·Ig·ōkwa-

30   sa Gwētɛla; G·āxᵋmɛnuᵋxᵘ qāsoʟai Gwētɛlai qaēda lō̆lapmutilaʟɛ ʟ!ā-
sotiwalis qaᵋsai, ᵋnēk·ē. Wä, lēda waōkwas ᵋnēk·a; Halag·ǐlē̆ʟɛsai,

from the top of the blankets,and then the other young men took hold
of it/and put it down on the left hand side of ʟ!āsotiwalis. Then/
the bundle of blankets was unrolled. Then the/young man who had to
give them out took one pair of blankets and spread it out(5) and
gave it to ʟ!āsotiwalis. Then ʟ!āsotiwalis took hold of the one
pair of/blankets and spread it on his knees and he spoke and/said:
"Indeed,father ʟ!āqoʟas,true is your word. Truly you brought me up
well./ Truly now you made me a chief and I take in exchange your/
privileges and your seat,chief father. Now it is true,you acted
properly(10)to me in all your ways which you gave to me. Now you
will only be/the old man of the house,for you will just give me advice that I may be a good chief./ I mean this. Now I will take hold."
Then he held up one pair of/blankets and the tally keeper named the
eagle of/all the tribes, ʟ!āsotiwalis of the ᵋnɛmgis. Then ʟ!ā-
sotiwalis(15)of the Q!ōmoyâᵋyē said, "ʟ!āsotiwalis, five pairs of
blankets."/ Then the young man who gave them out took the others
that were now being given away,and/threw them out at the place where
ʟ!āsotiwalis had put down the one pair of blankets./ Then another
young man took up from the floor the five pairs of blankets/and put
them down in front of ʟ!āsotiwalis of the ᵋnɛmgis. (This(20)is called
"Standing on the floor", namely the young man who gives away the
presents of blankets)/ And ʟ!āsotiwalis continued giving away the
blankets./ As soon as they had been all given to the three tribes,
then/all went out of the house into which they had been invited,and
immediately/all got ready and pushed their canoes into the water
and loaded them with things,(25)and now they went home./

　　　Four days after the tribes left had Fort Rupert,/ʟ!āqoʟas sent
four young men of his numaym,the Yaēx·agɛmēᵋ,/to go and call the
Gwētɛla and ᵋwālas Kwāg·uⱡ and Q!ōmk·!ūt!ɛs,/and the inviters,the
four young men,said inside the doorways of the houses of the (30)
Gwētɛla, "We come(to call)you,Gwētɛla,for ʟ!āsotiwalis is emptying
for/you what is left," said he,and the other said,"You will go

ᵋnēk·exs laē hōqŭwɛls qaᵋs lē lāxa ăpsālasē g·ōkwa. Wä, ᴀ̂ɛmxaāwi-

sē nɛqɛmg·ꞮⱢtewēxēs g·Ɪlx·dē wăⱢdɛma. Wä, g·flᵋmisē ᵋwꞮlxtolsaxa

g·ig·ōkwē g·āxaē ᵋwꞮᵋla aēdaaqēda mōkwē hăᵋyāⱢ·ᵋa qáᵋs lē ᵋwꞮᵋla

hōgwiⱢ lāx g·ōkwas ⱢꞮāsotiwalisē. Wä, lä hᵉ̈x·ᵋidaᵋmē ⱢꞮāsotiwali-

5   sē ăxk·Ꞩālaxa hăᵋyāⱢᵋa qa lēs ăxᵋwŭⱢtꞩalꞮⱢaxa xēxɛtsɛm ꞱEᵋwa Ɫꞩā-

Ɫꞩābate, yꞮx g·āyꞮmtsꞩEᵋwasdäsa pꞩɛlxɛlasgɛmēxa la ᵋyāxᵋwidayusē-

xa yŭdux̣ᵘsEᵋmakwē lēlqwălaⱢaᵋya. Wä, g·āxᵋmē qꞩŭlyaēꞱɛlēda Qꞩōmoᵉᵋ-

yâᵋyē qaᵋs g·āg·awālēxa hăᵋyāⱢᵋa; hᵉ̈ᵋma Ɫēɛlᵋwaᵋyē ꞱEᵋwa sēsɛwayu

g·āx ăxᵋālꞮlɛms. Wä, g·flᵋmisē g·āx ᵋwꞮᵋlᴀ ăxᵋālilɛma laasa mōkwē

10 hăᵋyāⱢᵋa la qatsēᵋstaxa yŭdux̣ᵘsEᵋmakwē Kwākŭg·uⱢa. Wä, g·flᵋmisē

ᵋwꞮlxtolsaxa g·ig·ōkwē g·āxaē ᵋwꞮᵋla aēdaaqēda mōkwē hăᵋyāⱢᵋa qaᵋs

lē ᵋwꞮᵋla hōgwiⱢ lāx g·ōkwas Ɫꞩāsotiwalisē. Wä, laᵋmē ēsⱢɛla qa g·ā-

xēs ᵋwꞮᵋla hōgwiⱢa bēbɛgwānɛmasa yŭdux̣ᵘsEᵋmakwē Kwākŭg·uⱢa. Wä,

g·flᵋmisē g·āx ᵋwꞮᵋlaēⱢa laas Ʇ̣āxᵋwaliⱢē Ɫꞩāsotiwalisē qaᵋs yāqꞩE-

15 g·aᵋⱢē. Wä, lä ᵋnēk·a: Wa, gēlag·a, yŭdux̣ᵘsEᵋmakwē Kwākŭg·uⱢ lāx-

wa Ʇēgadɛx, yūɛm Ʇēgadɛs lōlapmutilax yꞮsa ꞱēⱢɛläxa lēlqwălaⱢaᵋyē.

Wä, hᵉ̈ᵋmaa qɛnⱢo k·Ꞩēslax lōlapmutilalax qaᵋs g·ig·ɛgämēᵋ lālaxɛn

qꞩŭlēx·sᵋɛm lāx qꞩämēg·ila qa qꞩämēsɛn sāsɛmlaxa. Wä, lālaxɛn

ᵋnēx·sōᵋlax wꞮbɛnd lābɛndālaēnaᵋyasa gwaᵋyiᵋlälasasa ꞱēⱢɛlax·däxa

20 lēlqwălaⱢaᵋyē. ᵋnēᵋnak·iⱢē g·ig·ɛgämēᵋ. Gēlag·a ăxᵋēdxēs ăxēxstsE-

ᵋwaōs lāxg·ada ᵋmōᵋmagawalꞮⱢak· lāxōx gwēgwasaxs, ᵋnēk·ē. Wä, lä

hᵉ̈x·ᵋidaᵋma ᵋnāxwa bēbɛgwānɛm qꞩwāg·flꞮⱢ qaᵋs lē ăxᵋēdxa ᵋnāⱢᵋnɛms-

gɛmē xɛtsɛm ăxāsa waōkwē Ʇ̣ōxs ᵋnāⱢᵋnɛmaē Ɫꞩābatē Ʇ̣ōxs ᵋnāⱢᵋnɛmaē Ɫē-

ᵋwaᵋyē Ʇ̣oxs ᵋnāⱢᵋnɛmēxⱢaē Ɫōqꞩwäs Ʇ̣ōxs axᵋēdaaxa ᵋnāⱢᵋnɛmēxⱢaē k·ā-

25 tsꞩɛnaqē ăxᵋētsEᵋwasa waōkwē bɛgwānɛmaxa sēsɛwayuxa ᵋnāxwa g·ēx·g·a-

āⱢ lāxa g·ōkwē dāg·flx̣Ʇ̣ēsa bēbɛgwānɛmaxs laē hōqŭwɛls lāxa g·ōkwē.

Wä, laɛm ᴀ̂lak·Ꞩāla la lōptsꞩālꞮⱢa g·ōkwē lāxēq.

Wä, g·flᵋmisē mōxsa ᵋnāläs Ɫꞩāsotiwalisē hē gwēx·ᵋidē laē ētꞩē-

da ᵋyālaqasa mōkwē hăᵋyāⱢᵋa qa lēs qāsaxa Gwētɛla ꞱEᵋwa ᵋwālas Kwā-

30 g·uⱢ ꞱEᵋwa Qꞩōmk·Ꞩŭtꞩɛsē qa g·āxēs ᵋwꞮᵋla lāx g·ōkwasēx, laē k·ōtaq

laɛm ᵋwꞮᵋla gwăⱢ gaāxstālaxa gaāla. Wä, laɛmxaē ōgŭxᵋꞮdē wăⱢdɛmasa

quickly."(1)Thus they said as they went out. And they went to the
next house and they just/followed with the same words as before.
And when they had been in all the/houses,the four young men went
back and they all/went into the house of ʟ!āsotiwalis. Then ʟ!āso-
tiwalis(5)called the young men to bring out of the room all the
boxes and/cedar bark baskets in which the blankets had been that
were given away to the/three tribes. Then the Q!ōmoyâᵋyē came on
their own accord/to help the young men,and the mats and paddles/were
put on the floor by them. And when they all had been put down on the
floor,the four (10)young men went back to call the three Kwāg·uʟ
tribes,and as soon as/they had gone to all the houses,the four young
men came back again and/went into the house of ʟ!āsotiwalis. Now
they were waiting for/all the men of the three Kwāg·uʟ tribes to
come in,/and as soon as they had all come and had gone in,ʟ!āsotiwa-
lis arose. He spoke(15)and said, "Welcome, you three Kwāg·uʟ tribes,/
to this that has the name, this name ʰgiving away the empty things
left over after the inviting of the tribes'./ If I should not give
away the empty things left over to chiefs,I should/bring disgrace
upon myself and disgrace on my children. It would be/said that I did
not go to the end of our rules of inviting the(20)tribes. I mean this,
chiefs. Come now and take what is wanted by you/among that which is
piled up in the middle of the house,as it is done," said he, and/
immediately all the men stood up and each took one/box and others
each took a basket and others a mat/and others a dish,and one spoon
(25)was taken by other men and paddles. Everything that was/in the
house was taken by the men as they went out of the house./Now after
this the house was really empty./

Now four days after ʟ!āsotiwalis had done so he sent/again four
young men to go and call the Gwētɛla and ᵋwālas Kwāg·uʟ(30)and Q!ōm-
k·!ūt!ɛs,all to go to his house,when they thought/they had finished
that morning eating their breakfast. Now it is also different, the
word of the(1)oldedst of the young men who said: "We come to call

q!ŭlᵉyak!ŭga bɛgwānɛmsa hãᵉyāɫᵉaxa ᵉnēk·ē: G·āxᵉmɛnuᵉx̣ᵘ qāsōʟ
Gwētɛl qa ʟ!āsotiwalisxa ʟ!ɛmkwaʟē qaᵉs g·Īg·ɛg̣ãmē, ᵉnēk·ē. Wä,
lä ᵉñēk·a hãᵉyāɫᵉa; Halag·flïʟasai. ᵉnɛmp!ēnats!axstaɛmʟɛnuᵉx̣ᵘ
ᵉnēk·ē. Wä, la hƀx·sāɛm gwēk·!āla lāxa ᵉnāxwa g·Īg·ōkwa. Wä,g·fl-

5 ᵉmisē ᵉwĪĪxtulasaxa g·Īg·ōkwaxs g·āxaē aēdaaqa qaᵉs lē hōgwïʟ lāx
g·ōkwas ʟ!āsotiwalisē. Wä, hƀx·ᵉidaᵉmēsē ʟ!āsotiwalisē ᵉyālaqasa
la q!ɛyōkᵘ hãᵉyāɫᵉasa Q!ōmoyãᵉyē qa lēs ᵉwĪlg·ustã lāx ōgwäsasēs
g·ōkwē qa ᵉwĪᵉlēs sēg·fɫtsɛmdɛx säläsēs g·ōkwē qa wĪqŭmaxōdēsēq.
Wä, hƀx·ᵉidaᵉmisē la ᵉwĪlg·ustãwēda hãᵉyāɫᵉa qaᵉs sēg·fɫtsɛmdēxa

10 sälax·däsa g·ōkwē qaᵉs wĪqŭmãxōdēq. ãᵉmis la ƀk·!äbɛlsa saōkwē lāx
ᵉwāx·sanãᵉyasa g·ōxᵘdē. Wä, g·flᵉmisē ᵉwĪᵉlaxaxs g·āxaēda hãᵉyāɫᵉa
hōqwaxa. Wä, g·āxᵉɛm ᵉwĪᵉlēda Gwētɛla ʟɛᵉwa ᵉwālas Kwāg·uɫ ʟɛᵉwa
Q!ōmk·!ūt!ɛsē k!ūts!ɛs lāx ʟ!āsanãᵉyas g·ōxᵘdäs ʟ!āsotiwalisē. Wä,
hƀt!a ʟ!āqoʟasē ʟāxᵉwɛls qaᵉs yāq!ɛg·aᵉɫē. Wä, lä ᵉnēk·a: Wä,g·ā-

15 xᵉms g·Īg·ɛg̣āmēs Gwētɛl, ᵉwālas Kwāg·uɫ, Q!ōmk·!ūt!ɛs. Wa, gēlag·a
gēladzēlag·a lāxwa ɛlxʟaᵉyaxs gwaᵉyiᵉlälasasa ʟēɫɛläxa lēlqwāʟaʟa-
ᵉyēxwa ʟēgadēx; yūɛm ʟēgadɛs ʟ!ɛmkwa yĪxōx gwēx·ᵉidaasaxsɛn g·Īg̣ā-
maᵉyēx xŭnōkwa; yūɛm k·!ēs q!ūnāla gwēx·ᵉidaatsa ʟēɫɛläxa lēlqwälaʟaᵉyē qaxs wāyats!ãlaē ēt!ēd g·ōkwēlaxa āɫtsɛmē g·ōkwa. ᵉnēᵉna-

20 k·iɫē g·Īg·ɛg̣ãmē. Laᵉmɛn wäxaɫxōx ʟ!āsotiwalisēx qa dōxᵉwidag·isōx
lāxwa k·!ēsk·!ɛdēɫaxsa g·Īg·ɛg̣āmaᵉyaxsa lēlqwāɫaʟaᵉyax qaᵉs gāgak·!a-
sɛᵉwa, ᵉnēx·ʟɛns Q!ōmoyãᵉyē qa g·āx lāg·iɫtsē k!wāg·alĪɫʟa lāxōx ʟ!ā-
sotiwalisēx. ᵉnēᵉnak·iɫē Q!ōmoyãᵉyē qaᵉs q!ãlaōsax gwäɫaasasɛn nãqaᵉyē. Wa, wa, ᵉnēk·ēxs laē k!wāg·aɛlsa.

25   Wä, lä ʟāxᵉwɛlsē ʟ!āsotiwalisē qaᵉs yāq!ɛg·aᵉɫē. Wä, lä ᵉnē-
k·a: Qãʟ,qāʟa wäɫdɛmasɛn g·Īgāmaᵉyē ōmpa qaxs ᵉnēk·aē qɛn dōxᵉwi-
dag·ē qɛn gɛnɛma. Wä, laᵉmis ƀx· lāxɛn nãqaᵉyē wäɫdɛmas. ᵉnēᵉna-
k·iɫē, ᵉnēᵉnak·iɫē Gwētɛl, ᵉwālas Kwāg·uɫ, Q!ōmk·!ūt!ɛs, laᵉmɛn hƀɫ-
dɛk·a. Ladzēᵉmɛn hƀɫdɛk·a lāxwa k·!ēsēx q!ūnāla hƀɫdɛg·atsa ʟēɫɛ-

30 läxa lēlqwälaʟaᵉyē. Wä, ladzēᵉmɛn ᵉwĪᵉlōʟɛx gwɛᵉyãsɛn ōmpēx gwaᵉyi-
ᵉlälatsa ʟēɫɛläxa lēlqwälaʟaᵉyē. Laᵉmɛn gwäɫxa lōlapmutēla, lälasa

you,/GwētɛLa,for ʟ!āsotiwalis who will give away the boards to you,
chiefs," said he./ Then the young men said: "You will go quickly,we
call only once,"/said they. They continued saying this in all the
houses. As soon as(5)they had been in all the houses,they came back
and went into the/house of ʟ!āsotiwalis. Immediately ʟ!āsotiwalis
sent/many young men of the Q!ōmoyᵃᵉyē to go up to the roof of his/
house and to take off all the roof planks of his house and to push
them down./ Immediately all the young men went up,and took off the
(10)roof planks of the house and pushed them down. Now the boards
stood on end on/each side of the house. As soon as they were all
down,the young men/came down. Now all the GwētɛLa and ᵉwālas Kwāg-
g·uⱡ and/Q!ōmk·!ūt!ɛs sat down outside of the house of ʟ!āsotiwa-
lis./ Now ʟ!āqoʟas arose and spoke and said: "You have come, (15)
chiefs of the GwētɛLa and ᵉwālas Kwāg·uⱡ and Q̇!ōmk·!ūt!ɛs. Now
come,/come,great ones to this,the last of our ways of inviting the
tribes,/this which has a name,the name 'poking with boards'. That
is what is being done by the chief,/my son. This is not often done
by the inviter of the tribes,/for he is not brave enough to make a
new house. I mean this,(20)chiefs. I am going to say to ʟ!āsotiwalis
to go ahead to look/among the princesses of the chiefs of the tribes
to be married./ We are going to say this,Q!ōmoyᵃᵉyē,that she may
come and sit down here in the house with ʟ!āsotiwalis./ I mean this,
Q!ōmoyᵃᵉyē,that you may know the ways of my heart./ Wa wa," said
he and sat down./

Then ʟ!āsotiwalis arose and spoke. He said,/ "Indeed,true is
your word,my chief,father,for he said I should look/for a wife. Now
his word is good in my mind. I mean this./I mean this,GwētɛLa,ᵉwā-
las Kwāg·uⱡ,Q!ōmk·!ūt!ɛs. I have succeeded./ I have succeeded great-
ly in this that is not done often by those who invite the(30)tribes.
Now I got everything that was mentioned by my father,the different
ways in which/he invited the tribes. Now I have finished the giving
away of the empty boxes and then finally the(1)poking with boards.

ɛlx̣ʟaɛya ʟ!ɛmkwa. Laɛmōx x·͡ɪsɛlsɛn ʟē̆ʟɛɛlats!ēx·däxa lēlqwälaʟaɛyē g·ōkwa. Wä, hĕdzēɛmisa ʟ̣ēgadɛx·däē Dɛnt!aláyudzēx·dä. ɛnē-
ɛnak·iʟ̆ē. Laɛmɛn lābɛnd ɛw͡Iɛlōʟax gwaɛyiɛlälasasa ʟē̆ʟɛla. Wä, wä-
g·iʟ̆la q!wāg·͡ɪlsʟɛx g·͡Ig·ɛgāmēs Gwētɛl, ɛwälas·Kwāg·uʟ, Q!ōmk·!ū-
5   t!ɛs qaɛs ä̆xɛēdaōsaxwa sälä̆xsɛn g·ōxᵘdēx, ɛnēk·ē, qaxs k·!ēsaē ɛyā-
q!ūlayа̂ saōkwaxs hä̆ē gwēx·ɛidayuwē. Wä, hɛ̆x·ɛidaɛmisē ɛnäxwa q!wā-
g·͡ɪlsa bēbɛgwānɛmē qaɛs lē w͡Ix·ɛIdxa ɛnäʟ̆ɛnɛmxsa saōkᵘ qaɛs lē nä-
ɛnakᵘ lä̆xēs g·ig·ōkwē. Wä, â̂ɛmisē ʟ!āsotiwalisē ʟɛɛwis ōmpē ʟ!ā-
qoʟas la ɛmaɛwa lä̆x g·ōkwasēs māg·iʟ̆ē ʟ̣ē̆ʟɛʟâla. Wä laɛm gwāʟ̆ lä̆xa
10   ʟē̆ʟɛlá̆xa lēlqwälaʟaɛyē lä̆xēq.

10. Marriage.

Wä, la mā̆ɛʟ̆ɛɛnxē ts!ɛwŭnxas ʟ!āsotiwalisē x·ōsä̆ʟa qaxs lɛɛmaē
wŭnä̆ʟa g·ayâlax Q!ēx·ʟālagaxa k·!ēdeʟ̆as Aɛmä̆xŭlaʟaxa g·ayuʟ̆ē lä̆x
ɛnɛɛmēmutasa Kŭkwāk!ŭmasa Gwētɛla, y͡ıxs ɛnɛmgɛɛyaxsɛmaē Ōɛmag·͡ɪɛyē-
15   gaxa ä̆bɛmpas Q!ēx·ʟālaga, y͡ıxs k·!ēdēʟ̆aē Ōɛmag·͡ɪɛyēgä̆s ɛnɛmōgwisxa
xä̆magɛmaɛyē g·͡Igā̆mēsa ɛnɛɛmēmutasa ʟ!āʟ!ɛlä̆minasa ɛnɛmgēsē.

Wä, la maɛʟ̆ɛɛnxē ts!ɛwŭnxas g·ayâlē ʟ!āsotiwalisax Q!ēx·ʟālaga
laas ʟē̆ʟɛlēda g·͡Igā̆maɛyasa ɛnɛɛmēmutasa G·͡Ig·͡ɪlgā̆masa ɛnɛmgēsēxa
ʟ̣ēgā̆dä̆s Lɛlā̆k·͡ɪnx·ɛidä̆xa mōsgɛɛmakwē Kwākŭg·uʟ̆ ʟɛɛwa Mamalēleqāla
20   ʟɛɛwa Qwēqᵘsōt!ēnoxwē ʟɛɛwa ʟāwits!ēsē ʟɛɛwa Mād͡ıʟ̆bēɛ ʟɛɛwa Dɛnax·-
daɛxᵘ ʟɛɛwa Ā̆ɛwa͡ɪʟɛla ʟɛɛwa DzāwadɛɛnoxwēS ʟɛɛwa Hä̆xwāmisē. Maɛʟ̆tsɛ-
magŭg·ɛyo lēɛlqwälaʟaɛyē ʟē̆ʟɛlasɛɛwas Lɛlā̆k·͡ɪnx·ɛIdē lä̆x ɛy͡ɪl͡ɪsē.
Wä, g·͡ɪlɛmisē la ɛw͡Ilg·͡ɪlisa lēɛlqwälaʟaɛyē laas hɛ̆x·ɛidaɛmē ʟ!āso-
tiwalisē xwānaʟ̆ɛid qaɛs gwēgŭnēxēs g·ig·ä̆ʟa p!ɛlxɛlasgɛm lä̆xa ɛnäx-
25   wa bēbɛgwānɛma. Wä, g·͡ɪlɛmisē la ɛw͡Ila gŭnēda bēbɛgwānɛmaxēs dē-
danɛmē p!ɛlxɛlasgɛm lä̆x ʟ!āsotiwalisē laas ʟ!āsotiwalisē ʟēɛlālaxa
g·ä̆xsaxa g·ayuʟ̆ē lä̆xa ɛnä̆xwa lēɛlqwälaʟaɛya qa lēs ɛw͡Iɛla lax g·aē-
ʟɛlasa lä̆x g·ōkwas Mâ̂ɛnākŭlaxa g·ä̆yuʟ̆ē lä̆x ɛnɛɛmēmutasa Ts!ēts!ē̆ʟ̆-
wälagāmaɛyasa ɛnɛmgēsē. Wä, g·͡ɪlɛmisē g·ä̆x ɛw͡Ilaēʟa g·ä̆xsä̆ laas
30   ʟ!āqoʟas â̂ɛm k!waēʟ̆tsä̆xs laē yā̆q!ɛg·aɛʟa. Wä, lä̆ ɛnēk·a: Wa, gē-
lag·a g·͡Ig·ɛgāmēɛ. Wä, g·ēlag·a lä̆xwa lä̆xwa k·!ēsēx ā̆ʟ̆ɛɛm wäʟ̆dɛma-

Now my feasting house has disappeared,my house for the tribes,/and
this great one that has the name Dɛnt!alaᶜyu./ I mean this. I have
gone to the end. I have gone through all the rules of the inviter.
Now/go on and stand up,chiefs of the Gwētɛla,ᶜwālas Kwāg·uⱡ,Q!ŏm-
k·!ūt!ɛs,(5)and take the roof of my house," said he, for the/boards
are not given away to each singly when they do this. Immediately
all the/men stood up and carried on their shoulders each one board,
and they went home/to their houses. Only ʟ!āsotiwalis and his father
ʟ!āqoⱡas/went into the house of their near relative. Now this is the
end of the(10)inviting of the tribes.

10. Marriage

Then for two winters ʟ!āsotiwalis took a rest,for he was/se-
cretly engaged to marry Q!ēx·ʟālaga,the princess of Aᶜmāxŭlaⱡ,who
belonged to the/numaym Kŭkwāk!ŭm of the Gwētɛla. For Ōᶜmag·îyēga,(15)
the mother of Q!ēx·ʟālaga was a Mamālēleqāla woman. Ōᶜmag·îyēga was
the princess of ᶜnɛmōgwis,/the head chief of the numaym ʟ!āʟ!ɛlāmin
of the ᶜnɛmgis./

After two winters,ʟ!āsotiwalis asked Q!ēx·ʟālaga in marriage./
Then the chief of the numaym G·îg·îlgām of the ᶜnɛmgis,/whose name
was Lɛlāk·înx·ᶜît invited the four Kwāg·uⱡ tribes, the Mamālēleqāla,
(20) the Qwēqᵘsōt!ēnoxᵘ and the Lāwits!ēs and the Mādiⱡbēᶜ and the
Dɛnax·daᶜxᵘ/and the Aᶜwaîⱡɛla and the Dzāwadɛēnoxᵘ and the Hăxwamis.
Twelve/tribes were invited by Lɛlāk·înx·ᶜît at Alert Bay./ As soon
as all the tribes had arrived,right away ʟ!āsotiwalis/made ready and
asked payment of all those who had borrowed blankets from him.(25)
As soon as all the men had paid their debts for the/blankets borrowed
from ʟ!āsotiwalis,then ʟ!āsotiwalis invited/all the chiefs belonging
to all the tribes,that all should stay/in the house of Mᾶᶜnākŭla who
belonged to the numaym Ts!ēts!ēⱡwālagāmēᶜ/of the ᶜnɛmgis. As soon
as all the chiefs were in,(30)ʟ!āqoⱡas was just sitting down as he
spoke. He said: "Now/come,chiefs,come to this which is not a new
saying.(1)This was already said by our ancestors,to be said in this

xwa gwālɛlaᶜmuⱡēx wāⱡdɛmxɛns wīwōmpᶜwüⱡa qa gwēk·!ālas lāxwa gāga-
k·!ax wāⱡdɛma. ᶜnēᶜnak·iⱡē g·īg·ɛgämä qaxs lɛᶜmaē gwāⱡilänuᶜxᵘ
wāⱡdɛmē ʟɛᶜwa g·īgāmaᶜyaē Aᶜmāxülaⱡē qaēs k·!ēdēⱡē Q!ēx·ʟālaga.
Wä, laᶜmēts lāx·daᶜxᵘʟōʟ g·īg·ɛgämēᶜ ᶜyālagɛmⱡtsg·a ʟ!āsotiwalisɛk·
5   yālasōs ʟēʟaxsᶜalakwa lāxōx gwēk·!ālasēx lāqᵘ, ᶜnēk·ē.

Wä, hёx·ᶜidaᶜmisē la ᶜwIᶜla hōqüwɛls lāxa g·ōkwa g·äxsä qaᶜs
lē hōgwiʟ lax g·ōkwas ᶜnɛmōgwis. Wä, laᶜmē ᑫɛm nɛgɛⱡtɛwayē wāⱡdɛmas yāq!ɛnt!āläsa ᶜyālagɛmē g·äxsä lāxɛn laᶜma k·!āt!ēdayu qaᶜsxa
k·!ēsaʟāⱡ q!ēᶜmâla, yîxs ᑫᶜmaē mōkwa bēbɛgwānɛm ᶜyālagɛmsa gāgak·!a.
10 Wä, hёɛm ᶜnɛmx·ᶜidāⱡasa yüduxᶜwidāⱡa ʟēqwiᶜlälatsaᨳgāgak·!ax. Wä,
yüᶜmis gwɛᶜyᑫsa bāk!ümē ᶜwāᶜwalatsīla k·!ēsᶜōⱡt!ɛnda qādzīʟa qaxs
hёᶜmaē ʟēgɛmsē gwēx·ᶜidaasʟasa g·īg·ɛgāmaᶜyasa lēɛlqwālaʟaᶜyaxs qā-
dziʟēⱡē qa ʟ!āsotiwalisē, qaxs g·īgāmaᶜyaē lāg·iⱡas hё gwēx·ᶜidē dᑫ-
xa q!ēᶜmâla g·äxsä la ᶜyālagɛma lāx Aᶜmāxülaⱡē. Wä, hёᶜmis la ᶜnā-
15 xwaɛm la ᶜyāxᶜwitsɛᶜwa g·äxsäsa ᶜnāⱡᶜnɛmxsa p!ɛlxɛlasgɛms Aᶜmāxülaⱡ
laē gwāⱡē wāⱡdɛmas. Wä, laɛm hёx·ᶜidaɛm g·āx hōqüwɛls lāx g·ōkwas
ᶜnɛmōgwisē qaᶜs lē ᶜwIᶜla näänxᶜünālaxa ᶜnāⱡᶜnɛmxsa p!ɛlxɛlasgɛmxs
laē hōgwIʟ lāx g·ōkwas Mᑫᶜnäküla. Wä, lä k!üsᶜāliⱡa lax wāx·saᶜnē-
gwiⱡasa g·ōkwē. Wä, lä ʟāxᶜwalIⱡē Güyōⱡɛlasēxa xāmagɛmaᶜyē g·īgä-
20 mēsa ᶜnɛᶜmēmutasa Mamalēleq!āmē. Wä, lä yāq!ɛg·aᶜⱡa. Wä, lä ᶜnē-
k·a: Wёg·a hёⱡgämg·alIⱡax g·īgämēᶜ ʟ!āsotiwalis. G·āxᶜmɛnuᶜxᵘ hä-
lä g·āxdzēᶜmɛnuᶜxᵘ q!ɛⱡɛlqālaxg·as gɛnɛmⱡg·ōs, g·īgämēᶜ, ᶜnēk·ēxs
laē k·!ōxsɛmdxa ᶜnɛmxsa p!ɛlxɛlasgɛm qaᶜs q!ɛⱡāⱡēq, hё gwäⱡēda ts!ɛ-
dāqaxs q!ɛⱡālaaxēs xünōkwē. Dᑫxg·a Q!ēx·ʟalagɛk·xg·a k·!ēdēⱡg·as
25 Aᶜmāxülaⱡē. G·āxᶜmɛnuᶜxᵘ q!ɛⱡɛlqālaxg·as gɛnɛmg·ōs, g·īgämēᶜ. ᶜnē-
ᶜnak·iⱡē, wäg·iᶜlaɛns ᑫɛm qādzēʟax ⱡɛnsʟa qaɛns g·īgāmaᶜyōx ʟ!āso-
tiwalisēx, ᶜnēx·sɛᶜwün qɛn ᶜnēk·aōʟ g·īgämēᶜ. Wa, wa, ᶜnēk·ēxs laē
k!wāg·alIⱡa.

Wä, lä ʟāxᶜwalIⱡē ʟ!āqoʟasē yîx ōmpas ʟ!āsotiwalisē. Wä, lä
30 yāq!ɛg·aᶜⱡa. Wä, lä ᶜnēk·a: Ādzēk·asōʟ g·īg·ɛgämēᶜ; ādzēk·atsēs
wāⱡdɛmōs. Hёⱡᶜodzēlaxas wīyōʟaa qadzēyōs ᑫᶜwāwaasaqōs. K·!ēᑫs yɛ-

way in marrying./ I mean this, chiefs, for we are agreed in talking together/with chief Aᵉmax̣ŭlax̣ on account of his princess Q!ēx·-ᴌālaga./ Now go on, you chiefs sent by chief ᴌ!āsotiwalis,(5)you are already advised what is to be said about this," said he./

Immediately all the chiefs went out of the house and they/went into the house of ᵉnᴇmōgwis. Now they just followed the words of the/speech (that is used) when chiefs are sent, as I have written for you before./ Not many of them went, for there are only four men sent by the one who asks in marriage,(10) and this is one of the three different ways of asking in marriage and/this is called by the Indians "great work in bringing out the privileges in marriage," for/this is the name of what was going to be done by the chiefs of the tribes when they/were about to arrange the marriage for ᴌ!āsotiwalis,for he is a chief./ Therefore they did so./ Look at the many chiefs that were sent to Aᵉmāx̣ŭlax̣! Then each one(15) of the chiefs was given one pair of blankets by Aᵉmāx̣ŭlax̣/when they finished their speeches. And immediately they came out of the house of/ᵉnᴇmōgwis and they were wearing each one pair of blankets/as they went into the house of Mâᵉnākŭla. Then they sat down on each side of the/house. Then Ḡŭyōx̣ᴇlas arose, the head chief(20)of the numaym Mamalēleq!am, and he spoke and said:/ "Turn your face this way, chief ᴌ!āsotiwalis. We come back,/we great ones come carrying in our arms this, your wife chief," said he, as he folded up one pair of blankets and carried it in his arms in the manner of a/woman carrying her child. "Look at this Q!ēx·ᴌalaga, the princess of(25)Aᵉmāx̣ŭlax̣. We come carrying in our arms your wife, chief./ I mean this. We are just told to go on to marry tomorrow for our chief here, ᴌ!āsotiwalis,/this I was told to tell you chief. Wa wa," said he and sat down./

Then arose ᴌ!āqoᴊas, the father of ᴌ!āsotiwalis. (30)He spoke and said: "You are really great, chief; really great is your/speech. You are so great that you could not help getting there on account of your greatness. For there is nothing (1) impossible for a chief

yōḷánɛms g·ȋgɛmaᵋyaxs yāq!ɛg·aᵋɫaē. Ꞵa, gēlak·asᵋlax·i wāɫdɛmas
Aᵋmāxǔlaɫaxa g·ȋgāmaᵋya. ᵋnēᵋnak·iɫē g·ȋg·ɛgāmēᵋ, laᵋmɛn ᵋnēx· qɛns
nānagēg·iᵋmēx wāɫdɛmasa g·ȋg·ɛgāmaᵋyaō ᚸᵋmāxǔlaɫa yɫxs ᵋnēk·aē qɛns
qādzēɫaᵋmēx ɫɛnṣɫa, Ꞷā, laᵋmēsɛn ᵋnēx· qaᵋs dōqwaɫaōs lāxɛns āxᵋē-

5 tsōɫa lāx ɫēqwiᵋlāla qādzēɫ!ēnēsɛns wiwōmpᵋwǔɫa lāqōxs yūduxᵋwȋdā-
ɫaēx, ᵋnēk·ē.

Ꞷā, 1ᴵ yāq!ɛg·aᵋɫē Lɛlāk·inisxa g·ȋgāmaᵋyasa Ꞥāwits!ēsē, yɫx
gagɛmpas ɫ!āsotiwalisē. Ꞷā, la ᵋnēk·a: Hēᵋmaxɫᵢns qādzēɫ!ēnaᵋya
ᵋwāᵋwalatsēla k·!ēsᵋōɫt!ɛnd qādzēɫa, qaɛn g·ȋxsēᵋstɛlax ts!ōxᵘɫɛma.

10 ᵋnēᵋnak·iɫē laɛms g·ȋg·ɛgāmēs hamaᵶɛl lēɛlqwālaɫēᶘ nēɫēᵋdamasɫɛxs
k·!ēk·!ɛsᵋōs qaxg·ȋn k·!ēsēk· wāwaɫ!axa g·ȋgāmaᵋyē Aᵋmāxǔlaɫē q!ē-
q!ādaas g·ȋgāmaᵋya. ᵋnēᵋnak·iɫē, laɛms āɛm yāɫ!āɫōɫ g·ȋg·ɛgāmēᵋ
qansō amaqasō lāxō ᵋnēk·ē. Ꞷa, wa, ᵋnēk·ē. Ꞷā, lā nāᵋnaxmaᵋyē Nɛ-
g·äxa xāmagɛmaᵋyē g·ȋgāmēsa ᵋnɛᵋmēmutasa Tɛmɫtɛmɫɛlsasa Mamalēleqā-

15 laxa ᵋnēk·ē: Yūɛm yūdzēᵋmōs wāɫdɛmaqōs g·ȋgāmēᵋ Lɛlak·ɛnis, yɫxs
ᵋnēk·aaqōs qa ᵋwȋᵋlēs g·āx ɫ!āstaɫɛns k·!ēk·!ɛsᵋōx lāxwa ᵋwālasē
g·ȋxsēᵋstāla g·ȋgāmaᵋyaxwa qādzēɫaɫōx ɫ!āsotiwalisē. Ꞷā, wā-
g·iɫlax·ɛns g·ȋg·ɛgāmēᵋ. Ꜳlag·aᵋmax·ȋns gāg·ustâx gaālaɫa, ᵋnēk·ē .
Ꞷā, laᵋmē gwāɫ lāxēq. Ꞷā, laᵋmē ᵋwȋᵋla hōqǔwɛls lāxa g·ōkwē.

20   Ꞷā, g·iɫᵋmisē ᵋnāx·ᵋidxa gaāla laas āɛm ēsɛla ɫ!āsotiwalisē qa
ᵋwȋᵋlēs gwāɫ gaaxstalēda ᵋnāxwa bēbɛgwānɛma. Ꞷā, g·iɫᵋmisē k·ōta
ɫ!āsotiwalisaq laɛm ᵋwȋᵋla gwāɫ haᵋmāpa laē ᵋyālaqasa g·ayuɫē lax hāᵋyāɫᵋāsa Q!ōmoyāᵋyē qa lēs qāsaxa hāᵋyāɫᵋāsa ᵋnāxwa lēɛlqwālaɫaᵋya
qa g·āxēs ᵋwȋᵋla hōgwiɫ lāx g·ōkwas Māᵋnakǔla qaxs hēᵋmaē g·aēɫɛlē

25 ɫ!āsotiwalisē. Ꞷā, g·iɫᵋmisē g·āx ᵋwȋᵋlaēɫēda hāᵋyāɫᵋa laē ɫ!āsoti-
walisē āxᵋēdxa yāsɛkwē qaᵋs ts!awānaqēs lāxa hāᵋyāɫᵋa qa yāsɛkǔmdēs.
Ꞷā, g·iɫᵋmisē gwāɫ yāsɛkǔmaxs laē ɫ!āsotiwalisē ts!āsa gǔmsē qa gǔm-
gǔmsɛmdēs. Ꞷā, g·iɫᵋmisē gwāɫ gǔmsa laē āxᵋēdē ɫ!āqoɫasaxēs qāmxwā-
sa kwēkwē qaᵋs ᵋwȋᵋlē qāmxᵋwidxa hāᵋyāɫᵋa. Ꞷā, g·iɫᵋmisē gwāɫa laas

30 ɫ!āqoɫasē ōgwaqa q!wālax·ᵋida qaxs lāɫē qāgēxa hēlɛlg·isɫē hāᵋyāɫᵋa.

when he speaks. Thank you for the saying of/Aᵉmāxŭlaɫ, that great
chief. I mean this, chiefs. I wish to/obey what is said by chief
Aᵉmāxŭlaɫ,as he told us to/get married tomorrow. Now I wish it to be
seen by you what we are going to use,(5) all the different ways of
marrying of our forefathers, as there are three ways,"/ said he./

Then spoke Lɛlāk·ɛnis, the chief of the Lāwits!ēs, the/grand-
father of ʟ!āsotiwalis. He said, "Let this be our way of marrying,/'working something great for bringing out the privileges in
marriage', for my grandson, this one who is all over a chief.(10)
I mean this. Now you chiefs of the tribes, show your/privileges
for I have no mercy on chief Aᵉmāxŭlaɫ,/the chief who has much property. I mean this. Now you will only take care, chiefs,/if we
should be met in sham fight," said he. "Wa wa," said he. Then Nɛ-
g·ä,/the head chief of the numaym Tɛmɫtɛmɫɛls of the Mamaleleqāla,
answered and(15)said, "This is your great word, chief Lɛlāk·ɛnis,
for/you said that we all should come out and show our privileges
for this great one/who is a chief all over, the chief who will be
married, ʟ!āsotiwalis. Now/let us do it, chiefs, only let us get up
early in the morning," said he./ Then they finished after this and
they all went out of the house./

(20) As soon as day came in the morning, ʟ!āsotiwalis just waited
for/all the men to finish eating their breakfast, and as soon as/
ʟ!āsotiwalis thought that all had finished eating, he sent young
men of the/Q!ōmoyâᵉye to go to call the young men of all the tribes/
to come into the house of Mâᵉnākŭla,for that was where(25) ʟ!āsoti-
walis was staying. And as soon as all the young men were in,ʟ!āsoti-
walis/took tallow and distributed it among the young men to put it on
their faces./ And after they had greased their faces, ʟ!āsotiwalis
gave them ochre to put on their faces,/and when they had finished
putting on ochre, ʟ!āqoʟas took his/eagle down and put down on all
the young men and after they had finished(30)ʟ!āqoʟas also dressed
himself, for he was going to walk among the young men who were hired./

Wä, g·îlᵋmisē gwäⱡa laē ᵋwⁱᵋla hōqŭwɛls lāxa g·ōkwē. Wä, hëᵋnäkŭla
lāxa ᵋnɛlbaᵋyē g·ōkwa qaᵋs ᵋwⁱᵋlē hōg̱wiⱢ lāq. Wä, lä ᵋnɛmädzaqwa
ᵋnēk·a häᵋyāⱡᵋa; Hēlai, hēlai, hēlai, hēlai. Wä, g·îlᵋmisē q̣wēⱡ-
ᵋida laas Ɫ̣äqoⱢasē ᵋnēk·a; Laɛms lāⱡ ᵋwɛxēⱢaⱡ g·āxɛnⱢaxg·ɪn Ɫ̣ä-
sotiwalisēk·, ᵋnēk·ē. Wä, g·îlᵋmisē q̣ŭlba wäⱡdɛmas Ɫ̣äqoⱢasaxs
laē ᵋwⁱᵋla hōqŭwɛls lāxa g·ōkwē qaᵋs lē hōg̱wiⱢ lāxa äpsälasē g·ō-
kwa. Wä, ĝɛmxaāwisē nɛqɛmg·îⱡtɛwēxēs g·îlx·dē gwēk·ⱡālasa. Wä,
g·îlᵋmisē ᵋwⁱlxtolsaxa g·ig·ōkwē laē ᵋwⁱᵋla la hōg̱wiⱢ lāx g·ōkwas
Mĝᵋnakŭla. Wä, hëx·ᵋidaᵋmisē Ɫ̣äsotiwalisē äxk·ⱡälaxa häᵋyāⱡᵋa qa
10 hōsᵋidēsēxa p̣ɛlxɛlasgɛmē qa sēsɛk·ⱡaxsaⱡⱡēs gwēliⱡaxa sɛk·ⱡäp̣ɛn-
ᵋyag·i p̣ɛlxɛlasgɛm qädzēⱢɛmⱡ lāx Aᵋmāx̱ŭlaⱡē. Wä, g·îlᵋmisē gwäⱡa
häᵋyāⱡᵋa laē ḳŭsᵋäliⱡa qaᵋs ēsɛlēxa g·Ig·ɛgämaᵋyasa lēɛlqwälaⱢaᵋyē
qa g·āxēs hōg̱wiⱢa lāxa g·ōkwē. Hēda lāg·iⱡas gäⱡa k·ⱡēs g·āx hō-
g̱wiⱢa g·Ig·ɛgämaᵋyē lāxa g·ōkwaxs q̣wälax·aē. Wä, g·āxᵋmē hōg̱wiⱢɛ-
15 lēda g·Ig·ɛgämaᵋyasa lēɛlqwälaⱢaᵋyēxa hälsɛlaᵋmē k·ⱡēs ᵋnāxwa xē-
xugɛkᵘsa äᵋwāᵋwē ëx·tṣɛm Ɫōxs k·ēdziⱡbalaēda waōkwaxa aēdzɛmē. Wä,
lä ᵋnāxwaɛm dālaxēs yⁱyaq̣ɛntp̣ēqē tṣōtṣɛⱡɛmakwa q̣ēq̣ɛltⱡɛsɛläxa
Ɫ̣äqwa. Wä, lä gŭmēkwa k·ⱡeĝs q̣ēq̣ɛltⱡɛdzēxa Ɫ̣äqwa. Wä, lä ᵋnä-
xwaɛm tⱡ̣ētⱡ̣ɛⱡᵋalaxēs naɛnxᵋŭnaᵋyē la wⁱᵋwŭsēg·akwa. Wä, lāxāē ᵋnä-
20 xwa qämōkᵘsa qämxwäsa kwēkwē. Wä, la qēqɛx·ɛmälaxa lāɛlāxwiwaᵋyē.
Wä, laɛm ḳŭsᵋäliⱡa lāx wäx·sahēgwⁱⱡasa g·ōkwē. Wä, laɛm k·ⱡēs g·āx
ḳwägēlⁱⱡa waōkwē lāxa Gwētɛla lāq, qaxs laēda waōkwē lāx g·ōkwas
ᵋnɛmōgwisē qaxs häē g·aēⱢɛlē Aᵋmāx̱ŭlaⱡē g·ōkwas. Wä, g·îlᵋmisē la
ᵋwⁱᵋlaēⱢa g·Ig·ɛgämaᵋyē lāx g·ōkwas Mĝᵋnäkŭla laas Ɫ̣āxᵋwäliⱡⱡē Ɫ̣ä-
25 qoⱢasē. Wä, lä yāq̣ɛg·aᵋⱡa. Wä, lä ᵋnēk·a; Wä, gēlag·a, gēladzē-
lag·a g·Ig·ɛgämēs lēɛlqwälaⱢēᵋ. G·āxᵋɛms lāxwa xŭltaᵋyēx qɛns gwē-
ᵋnäkŭlasa yⁱsɛns wⁱwōmpᵋwŭⱡa. Wä, laᵋmēsɛns nänagɛⱡᵋɛnaⱡqē lāx
gwēᵋnäkŭlasasa qädzēⱢax·Ɫax.NⁱsaēⱢɛnsaqᵘ wäⱡdɛma. Häsᵋmaaxsōxwaqē
wäⱡdɛma yⁱx bɛkwēlēnukwaɛns lāg·iⱡaɛns k·ⱡeĝs āⱡēlaᵋya. ᵋnēᵋnak·i-
30 ⱡē g·ig·ɛgämēs lēɛlqwälaⱢēᵋ. Wäg·îⱡla Ɫ̣āxᵋwäliⱡⱡɛx g·Igämē Âwaxɛ-
lag·îlisxa xämagɛmaᵋyē g·Igämēsa ᵋnɛᵋmēmutasa Maämtag·ila gwēᵋyâs,

(1) And when they had finished, all went out of the house, and they
went straight/to the house at the upper end of the village and they
went in. And the/young men said together, "Hire, hire, hire, hire!"
As soon as they stopped speaking/then ʟ!āqoʟas said, "Now you will
go and take pity on me, that I am ʟ!āsotiwalis,"(5)said he. As soon
as ʟ!āqoʟas finished his speech/then all went out of the house and
they went into the next house,/and they just said again the same
they had said before, and/after they had gone to all the houses, they
all went into the house of/Mā͡ᵋnākŭla. Immediately ʟ!āsotiwalis asked
the young men to (10)count the blankets, for there were in five piles
distributed five hundred/blankets meant as a marriage gift to Aᵋmāxŭlaɬ. After they had done so/the young men sat down and waited for
the chiefs of the tribes/to come into the house. This is the reason
that it takes a long time, that the chiefs do not come/to the house,
because they were dressing. And now there came in (15) the chiefs of
the tribes almost all/wearing in their ears large abalone shells
and nose ornaments, and others small abalone shells,/and all carrying speakers' staffs, and the faces were blackened of those who had
broken/coppers and painted red of those who had not broken any coppers, and all of them/having their blankets over one shoulder, and
belted, and all (20) covered with down of the eagle, and wearing kerchiefs around their heads./ Then they sat down on each side of the
house. Now/some of the Gwētɛla did not sit down among them for some of
them were in the house of/ᵋnɛmōgwis, for Aᵋmāxŭlaɬ was staying in his
(ᵋnɛmōgwis's) house. As soon as/all the chiefs were in the house of
Mā͡ᵋnākŭla, ʟ!āqoʟas arose(25)and spoke and said, "Now come, come
great ones,/chiefs of the tribes. Come that we may thus move on the
line marked out for us/by our forefathers. Now we will follow it, as
is/done in this marriage name. Will it be our wish? It is what he/
said, he who made us. Therefore we do nothing new. I mean this,(30)
chiefs of the tribes. Now stand up, chief Āᵋwaxalag·îlis/(he meant
the head chief of the numaym Maᴀmtag·ila)(1) that you may go and

qaᵋs laōs wāꜹaqag·fllⱵɛla lāxa g·Igāmaᵋyaē Aᵋmāxŭlaⱡa. Wäg·fⱵla
ꜹāxᵋwälIⱵʟɛx g·Igāmēᵋ Q!āq!uᵋyalagŭmxa xāmagɛmaᵋyē g·Igāmēsa ᵋnɛᵋmēmutasa ᵋwālasasa Mamalēleqāla gwɛᵋyâs, qaᵋs laōs wāꜹaqag·fllⱵɛ-
la lāxa g·Igāmaᵋyaē Aᵋmāxŭlaⱡa. Wäg·fⱵla ꜹāxᵋwälIⱵʟɛx g·Igāmēᵋ
5 Q!ŭmx·ɛlag·fllsxa xāmagɛmaᵋyē g·Igāmēsa ᵋnɛᵋmēmutasa G·Ig·flgāmasa
ᵋnɛmgēs gwɛᵋyâs, qaᵋs laōs wāꜹaqag·fllⱵɛla lāxa g·Igāmaᵋyaē Aᵋmāxŭlaⱡa. Wäg·fⱵla ꜹāxᵋwⱥlIⱵʟɛx g·Igāmēᵋ Ōdzēᵋstalisxa xāmagɛmaᵋyē g·I-
gāmēsa ᵋnɛᵋmēmutasa Nŭnɛmasɛqâlisasa Ⱡāwits!ēs gwɛᵋyâs, qaᵋs laōs
wāꜹaqag·fllⱵɛla lāxa g·Igāmaᵋyaē Aᵋmāxŭlaⱡa. Wa, laɛms lāⱡ lādzē-
10 ɛms lāʟ̣ōʟ g·Ig·ɛgāmēᵋ lāxōs k·!ēk·!ɛsᵋâqōsa wāꜹaqag·fllⱵɛla. Wa,
wa, ᵋnēk·ē.

Wä, hᵋx·ᵋidaᵋmisa mōkwē g·Ig·ɛgāmēᵋ q!wāg·fllⱵa qaᵋs lē q!wāg·-
g·fllⱵ yfpɛmlIⱵ lāxa ōgwiᵋwallⱵasa g·ōkwē. Wä, lä yāq!ɛg·aᵋⱡē Awa-
xɛlag·fllsē. Wä, lä ᵋnēk·a: Qāꜹ, qāꜹēs wāⱡdɛmōs g·Igāmēᵋ ʟ!āqoꜹas.
15 Qāꜹaxs q!ālalēsᵋmaaqōs lāxɛnuᵋxᵘ k·!ᴈsᵋōxwa ⱡāxwāⱡaxwa q!ŭnālax yflg-
gwasa wāꜹaqag·fllⱵɛla. ᵋnēᵋnak·iⱡē lāmɛnuᵋxᵘ lāⱡ, ᵋnēk·ēxs laē dɛ-
nōxꜹalēda mōkwē âlakŭxs laē hōquwɛls lāxa g·ōkwē qaᵋs lē hōgwIʟ lāx
g·ōkwas ᵋnɛmōgwisē. Wä, lä k!ŭsᵋâllⱵa yŭdukwē g·Ig·ɛgāmēᵋ lax aᵋwI-
ʟɛläsa t!ɛx·fla. Wä, lēx·aᵋmisē la ꜹaᵋwIⱡē Awaxɛlag·fllsē dālaxēs
20 yāq!ɛntp!ēqē. Wä, lä yāq!ɛg·aᵋⱡa. Wä, lä ᵋnēk·a: Wäg·a hēlatoleʟ̣ōʟ
g·Igāmēᵋ Aᵋmāxŭlaⱡ qaᵋs hōʟ̣ēlaōsaxg·anuᵋxᵘ qậts!ēnēk·. G·āxᵋmɛnuᵋxᵘ
g·Ig·âmēᵋ wāꜹaqag·fllⱵɛla g·Igāmēᵋ. G·āxᵋɛmk· q!ap!äg·ada hēlanɛm-
k·g·ada g·āxʟɛk· qâdzēʟaʟɛxs k·!ēdēⱡaqōs, g·Igāmēᵋ, ᵋnēk·ē. Wä,
lä k!wāg·fllⱵa laas ꜹāxᵋwällⱵa g·Igāmaᵋyē Q!āq!uᵋyalagŭmē. Wä, lä
25 yāq!ɛg·aᵋⱡa. Wä, lä ᵋnēk·a: G·āxᵋmɛn g·Igāmēᵋ lāxwa k·!ēsēx āⱡēlē
wāⱡdɛma. G·āxᵋmɛn wāꜹaqag·fllⱵɛla g·Igāmēᵋ. Laɛmᵋlaɛnuᵋxᵘ g·āxꜹa
qâdzēʟaʟɛxs k·!ēdēⱡaqōs g·Igāmēᵋ Aᵋmāxŭlaⱡ qa ʟ!āsotiwallsē. ᵋnē-
ᵋnak·iⱡē g·Igāmēᵋ Aᵋmāxŭlaⱡ qaᵋs gwālilⱡaōs, ᵋnēk·ēxs laē k!wāg·allⱵ-
ⱡa. Wä, lä ꜹāxᵋwällⱵa g·Igāmaᵋyē Q!ŭmx·ɛlag·fllsē. Wä, lä yāq!ɛ-
30 g·aᵋⱡa. Wä, lä ᵋnēk·a: G·āxᵋmɛn ts!ōxᵘʟɛm Aᵋmāxŭlaⱡ. G·āxᵋmɛn
wāꜹaqag·fllⱵɛla, g·Igāmēᵋ. G·āxᵋmɛn q!āq!alaⱡg·ɛyōsg·ada lāk· q!a-

ask in the house about chief Aᵋmāxŭlaⱡ. Now/stand up, chief Q!āq!uᵋyalagŭm (he meant the head chief of the/numaym ᵋwālas of the, Mamalēleqāla) that you may go and ask in the house/about chief Aᵋmāxŭlaⱡ. Now stand up, chief (5) Q!ŭmx·ɛlag·îlis, (he meant the head chief of the numaym G·îg·îlgăm of the/ᵋnɛmgis) that you may go and ask in the house about chief/ Aᵋmāxŭlaⱡ. Now stand up, chief Ödzēᵋatalis (he meant the head chief/of the numaym Nŭnɛmasɛqâlis of the Ⱡāwits!ēs) that you may go/ and ask in the house about chief Aᵋmāxŭlaⱡ. Now you will go, great ones, (10) you chiefs who have this privilege to ask in the house. Wa,/ wa." said he./

Immediately the four chiefs stood up and they stood/ in a row in the rear of the house and then/ Aᵋwaxalag·îlis spoke and said, "Indeed, true is your word, chief Ⱡ!āqoⱡas. (15) Indeed you know that these are our privileges which are difficult, for often they are/ hurt who are asked in the house. I mean this. Now we shall go," said he, as they/ went one after another, the four true men, as they went out of the house and went into the/house of ᵋnɛmōgwis. And the three chiefs sat down/ inside the door. Now Aᵋwaxalag·îlis was standing on the floor of the house, carrying his (20) speaker's staff. He spoke and said, "Go on, set your ear right,/ chief Aᵋmāxŭlaⱡ, and listen to the reason why we are walking here. We come,/ chief, to inquire in your house, chief. Those who have been hired come jointly./ They will come to get married to your princess, chief,"said he./ Then he sat down and chief Q!āq!uᵋyalagŭm arose and (25) spoke. He said, "Chief, this is not a new way/ of speaking to come to inquire in the house, chief. Now we will come / to get married to your princess, chief Aᵋmāxŭlaⱡ, for chief Ⱡ!āsotiwalis./ I mean this, chief Aᵋmāxŭlaⱡ. You will be ready," said he and he sat down./ Then arose chief Q!ōmx·îlag·îlis and (30) spoke and said, "I come, grandson Aᵋmāxŭlaⱡ, I come/ to inquire in the house, chief. I come, assembling these (1) who will come to marry your princess, chief Aᵋmāxŭlaⱡ./

p!ḗg̣·ada g·ā̱xʟɛk· q!adzêʟaʟɛxs k·!ēdêłaqōs g·Ig̱āmēᶜ A̱ᶜmāxū̱lał.

Hōᶜmôsɛn g·āxêʟa ʟ̣ōg̱ū̱n ᶜnēᶜnɛmōkū̱k· qa tɛmsx·ɪ̣g·flɪ̱łêsōs k·!ēdē̱-
łaqōs g·Ig̱āmēᶜ A̱ᶜmāxū̱laλ, ā̱łê̱lawɪ̄sɛs yɪ̄xg·ɪn wā̱łdɛmk· lā̱ʟ g·Ig̱ā̱-
mēᶜxg·ada wā̱ʟaqag·flɪ̱łɛlaxg·ada wā̱łdɛmg·asɛns gaāg̱ɛmpᶜwū̱ła. Wa,

5 wa, ᶜnēk·ôxs laē k!wāg·flɪ̱ła. Wä, lä ʟ̣ā̱xū̱lɪ̱ła g·Ig̱āmaᶜyē Ōdzɛ̱ᶜsta-
lɪs. Wä, lä yāq!ɛg·aᶜła. Wä, lä ᶜnēk·a łā̱wits!axsdā̱łaxs yāq!ɛn-
t!ā̱laē. G·āxᶜmɛn g·Ig̱āmēᶜ, g·ā̱xᶜmɛn wā̱ʟaqag·flɪ̱łɛla g·Ig̱āmēᶜ A̱ᶜmā̱-
xū̱lał lāxwa ʟ̣ē̱gadē qa ʟ̣ē̱g̱ɛms qa ʟ̣ē̱g̱ɛms Wāwałk·inē lāxa xunōxᶜwid-
lāxasōs k·!ēdēłaqōs ʟ̣ᶜᶜwa g·Ig̱āmaᶜyaē ʟ!ā̱sotiwalisa qaxg·ɪn q!u-

10 nā̱lēk· wū̱ʟɛlaxa q!ā̱mōdē̱da xomā̱łᶜidē ts!ē̱dā̱qaxa ᶜnēk·axēs hayōtē
šg·anɛmē g·ā̱xsä wā̱ʟaqag·flɪ̱łɛlax ā̱bā̱saxēs g·āxê̱łōs g·ɪ̄nā̱nɛma. Wä,
yūᶜmôsɛn ᶜnēᶜnak·ɪ̄łōʟ·g·Ig̱āmēᶜ, laɛmk· wɪwū̱lg̱āmɛ̣ g·Ig·ɛg̱āmēᶜg·ada
g·ā̱xɛk· wā̱ʟaqag·flɪ̱łɛla qa tɛmsx·ɛg·flɪ̱łêsōs k·!ēdē̱łaqōs g·Ig̱āmēᶜ.
Wa, wa, ᶜnēk·ôxs laē k!wag·flɪ̱ła.

15 Wä, lä, ʟ̣ā̱xᶜwallł̄ē Ōdzēᶜstalisē̱xa g·āyu̱łē̱ lāx ᶜnɛᶜmēmutasa
Kū̱kwāk!ū̱masa Gwē̱tɛla yɪ̄xs hōᶜmaē ᶜnɛᶜmēmuts A̱ᶜmāxū̱laλ̄ē. Wä, lä
yāq!ɛg·aᶜła. Wä, lä ᶜnēk·a: A̱lasēs wā̱łdɛmōs g·Ig̱āmēᶜ Ōdzēᶜsta-
lisxa ʟ̣ē̱q̱ēla qa ʟ̣ē̱g̱ɛmsa ᶜnā̱xwaɛmʟaɛns ᶜnāk·!ā̱łʟa xū̱nōxᵘᶜwidlaxasg·ɪn
k·!ēdē̱łɛk· ʟ̣ᶜᶜwēs łā̱ᶜwū̱nɛmʟaē̱da g·Ig̱āmaᶜyaē ʟ!ā̱sotiwalisa qä̱ʟaxs

20 lɛᶜmaēx lā̱ʟa g·Ig̱āmēᶜ lā̱xg·a k·!ēdē̱łg·ɪsg·ɪn g·Ig̱āmēk·, ᶜnēᶜnak·iłē
g·Ig·ɛg̱āmēᶜ ᶜnōᶜnak·iłē ᶜnēk·ôxs laē dā̱x·ᶜɪdᴋa ᶜnɛmxsa lāxa p!ɛlxɛ-
lasg̱ɛm g·ā̱x ᶜāxā̱lilɛms A̱ᶜmāxū̱laλ̄ē. Laɛm lā̱lg·ada mɛxstawēg·ā̱sg·ada
k·!ēdē̱łɛk·. Laɛms lā̱ł qä̱q̱ā̱la̱łqä̱k·, ᶜnēk·ôxs laē ᶜyā̱xᶜwitsa mā̱ᶜła̱-
xsa p!ɛlxɛlasg̱ɛm lāx A̱waxalag·flisē. Wä, la ᶜnā̱xwa mēmaᶜła̱xsa p!ɛl-

25 xɛlasg̱ɛmē ᶜyā̱xᶜwidayâsēxa yū̱dukwē g·Ig·ɛg̱āmaᶜya ōg̱ū̱ᶜla lāx A̱waxala-
g·flisē. Wä, g·flᶜmisē gwā̱ł ᶜyā̱qwaxs laē ᶜnēk·ō Ōdzēᶜstalisē: Wa,
wa, g̱ēlag·a g·Ig·ɛg̱āmēᶜ qā̱dzē̱lax·, ᶜnēk·ō. Wä, hᴏ̈x·ᶜidaᶜmisē̱da
mōkwē g·Ig·ɛg̱āmēᶜ q!wāg·flɪ̱ła qaᶜs ᶜnā̱xwē yā̱laqwasēs yiyā̱laxʟɛnaxs
laē hōqū̱wɛls lāxa g·ōkwē qaᶜs lä hōg̱wɪ̄ʟ lāx g·ōkwas ᶜnɛmōg̱wisē

30 yiyā̱lag̱ū̱tɛᶜwaya qaᶜs lē q!wāg·flɪ̱ł lāx ā̱wɪ̄ʟɛlāsa t!ɛx·flā̱sa g·ōkwē.

Wä, laᶜmē A̱waxalag·flisē yāq!ɛg·aᶜlaxs laē ᶜnɛmā̱xᶜid

This is why I come with our friends to shake off the floor of the
house your princess,/ chief Aᵋmāx̱ŭlaⱡ. This is no new way of
speaking to you, chief,/ this inquiring in the house. It is the
way of saying of our grandfathers. Wa (5) wa," said he and sat
down. Then arose chief Ōdzēᵋstalis/and spoke. He said, speaking angrily,/ "I come, chief, I come to inquire in the house,
chief Aᵋmāx̱ŭlaⱡ/ in this which has a name, the name Wāwaⱡk·ĭn,
when your princess will have a child/ with chief ʟ!āsotiwalis,
for I have (10) often heard that a quarrelling woman brought disgrace when she said to her rival,/ ʰmay be those who inquired in
the house about your mother who was the reason of your being a
child, were not chiefs from both sides! /This is what I mean,
chief. These are high chiefs/ who come to inquire in the house,
to shake from the floor your princess, chief./ Wa, wa", said he
and he sat down. (15)

Then Ōdzēᵋstalis arose. He comes from the numaym/ Kŭkwā-
k!ŭm of the Gwētɛla, for that is the numaym of Aᵋmāx̱ŭlaⱡ, and he/
spoke and said, "True, true is your saying, chief Ōdzēᵋstalis,/ ʰhe
giving a name when she expects a child, in case/ your princess here
should have for her husband chief ʟ!āsotiwalis. Indeed, (20) you
got her, chief, this princess of my chief here. I mean this,/
chiefs, I mean this," said he. Then he took one pair of blankets/
and put them down by Aᵋmāx̱ŭlaⱡ "Now this will go to this repre-
sentative of this/princess. Now you will let these walk with you,"
said he as he gave the/ two pairs of blankets to Aᵋwaxalag·ĭlis.
Then he gave two pairs of (25) blankets to the three other chiefs
beside/ Aᵋwaxalag·ĭlis. As soon as he had finished giving away
Ōdzēᵋstalis said,/ ʰWa, wa. Come chief, get married now," said he
and immediately/ the four chiefs arose and they all sang their sacred
songs/as they went out of the house, and they went into the house
of ᵋnɛmōgwis (30) singing as they were walking. And they stood
inside of the door of the house.

And now Aᵋwaxalag·ĭlis spoke as they all (1) stopped singing

q!wēx̣ᵉîdɛxs yiyälaqwalaē. Wä, lä ᵉnēk·a꞉ Wäg·îx̣la hōᴌōlaᴌɛx.
g·îgämēᵉ ʟ!āsotiwalis. G·äxᵉmɛnuᵉx̣ᵘ qàqɛlaxg·as gɛnɛmg·ōs, ᵉnē-
k·ēxs laē x·îlxᵉalîx̣asa maᵉx̣axsa p!ɛlxɛlasgɛma. Dậqɛk·, ᵉnēᵉna-
k·îx̣ē laᵉmɛns ʟēlēg·ēsō qɛns lālag·i g·îg·ɛgämēᵉ qädzēᴌaxa k·!ē-
5 dēx̣asa g·îgämaᵉyē A̋ᵉmax̣ûlax̣ē, ᵉnēk·ē. Wä, hɛx·ᵉidaᵉmisa ᵉnax̣wa hä-
ᵉyax̣ᵉa äxk·!ālasōᵉ qa ᵉnax̣waᵉmis gämxalaxa sēsɛk·!axsa p!ɛlxɛlasgɛm
qaᵉs lē gämxɛlsalas läx ʟ!āsanậᵉyas g·ōkwas ᵉnɛmōgwisē. Wä,g·îl-
ᵉmisē ᵉwîᵉlaᵉwɛlsa qädzēᴌayuᴌē p!ɛlxɛlasgɛmxs laē ᵉwîᵉla hōqûwɛlsa
ᵉnax̣wa lēᴇlqwälaᴌaᵉya qaᵉs lē ᵉwîᵉla k!ûsᴇls läx ᵉmōdzasasa p!ɛl-
10 xɛlasgɛma. Wä, g·îlᵉmisē ᵉwîlg·aᴇlsa laas ᴌax̣ᵉwûlsē Lälak·ots!axa
xämagɛmaᵉyē g·îgämēsa ᵉnᴇᵉmēmutasa Hāanaᴌēᵉnậ. Wä, laɛm yāyaq!ɛn-
tēmsᴌasa qädzēʟa. Wä, laɛm k·!ēsᵉonux̣ᵘsa yāyaq!ɛntēmtsa ᵉwäᵉwala-
tsila qädzēʟa.
Wä, lä yāq!ɛg·aᵉx̣a. Wä, lä ᵉnēk·a꞉ G·äxdzēᵉmɛns g·ax̣aᴌäla
15 g·îg·ɛgämēs lēᴇlqwälaᴌḗ läxwa ᴌēgadēx. Yūɛm ᴌēgadᴇs ᵉwäᵉwala-
tsila qädzēʟa. Yūɛm g·äx nēlatsɛns k·!ēk·!ɛsᵉōx qa tɛmsx·ɛg·îlî-
lɛms k·!ēdēx̣asa âlakwē g·ēxsēᵉstäla g·îgämaᵉya.ᵉnēᵉnak·îx̣ē.g·ägɛm-
dälaɛmʟɛnʟɛxs ᴌēᴌax̣ûmaᵉyaqōs. ᵉnēᵉnak·îx̣ē. Wa, gēlag·a g·îgämēᵉ ʟ!ā-
qwadzē (xa g·îgämaᵉyasa ᵉnᴇᵉmēmutasa Ts!ēx̣ts!ɛx̣wälagậmaᵉyasa ᵉnɛm-
20 gēsē, yîxs hēᵉmaē kwēk̶ᵘsa ᵉnax̣wa lēᴇlqwälaᴌaᵉya) qaᵉs g·äxaōs ᴌax̣-
ᵉwɛls läxg·a ᴌāᵉwasg·asēs nūyɛmbalisaē K!wāqaxsaᵉno, hēᵉmaas k·!eᵉ-
âs wɛyōᴌänɛmē, ᵉnēk·ē. Wä, hɛx·ᵉidaᵉmisē ᴌax̣ᵉwɛlsē ʟ!āqwadzē, yîxa
maᵉx̣ᵉidäx̣äs k·!ēsᵉō ᴌōᵉ Kûnōsila qaᵉs lē ᴌax̣ᵉwɛlsa. Wä, lä yāq!ɛg·a-
ᵉx̣a. Wä, lä ᵉnēk·a꞉ Lāʟɛn yāwasᵉîdᴌa läxɛn g·ōkwa. Qäᴌas lāq!ama-
25 ēx ᵉnēk·a qa ᵉwîᵉlēs g·äx nēx̣ᵉidɛns k·!ēk·!ɛsᵉō, ᵉnēk·ɛxs laē dzɛlx-
ᵉwîda qaᵉs lē laᴇl läxēs g·ōkwē. Wä, k·!ēst!ē gäx̣axs g·äxaē g·ä-
xawɛls läx t!ɛx·îläsēs g·ōkwē dälaxa x̣ɛk!wisē. Wä, lä ᵉnēk·a ʟē-
xax̣alai. Wä, lēda bēbᴇgwänɛmē ʟēxadzɛwēx tsägɛmas g·ōkwas ᵉnɛmōgwisē. Wä, g·äxē ʟ!āqwadzē hᴇkwäx̣a g·îldᴇkûlēs gaxᵉmisē gälpstɛ-
30 wēxa x̣ɛk!wisē hanaʟ!äla. Wä, g·äxē g·äxᵉaʟɛla läx t!ɛx·îläsa g·ō-
kwas ᵉnɛmōgwisē laē ᴌax̣ᵉwɛlsa. Wä, lä yāq!ɛg·aᵉx̣a. Wä, lä, ᵉnēg·e-

their sacred songs, all stopping at the same time. He said, "Now
listen to me,/ chief ʟ!ā́sotiwalis. We come and your wife walked
with us,"/ said he as he threw down the two pairs of blankets.
"Look at her. I mean this./ Now we have been called to go, chief,
to get married to the (5) princess of chief Aᵋmā́x̣ū́laⱡ," said he.
Immediately all the/ young men were asked to carry five pairs of
blankets/ and to go and put them down outside the house of ᵋnɛmṓ-
gwis. As soon/ as all the blankets to be used for the wedding were
carried out, all the tribes went out./ They sat down where the
blankets had been piled up (10) and when they were all on the
ground Lā́lak·ots!a,/ the head chief of the numaym Hā́ā́naⱡēno arose.
He was going to be the speaker/for the wedding. He owned the privilege of being the speaker at the/great wedding./

Then he spoke and said, "We have come, (15) chiefs of the
tribes, to this which has a name, which is named a great/ wedding.
This is where we show our privileges, to shake from the floor/ the
princess of this one who is through and through a chief. I mean
this. I shall/ begin with your head chief for he is standing first
among you. I mean this. Now come, chief/ ʟ!ā́qwadzē,(the chief of
the numaym Ts!ḗⱡts!ɛⱡwā́lagā́mē of the (20) ᵋnɛmgis,for ne is the
eagle among all the tribes) come and/ stand by this place where the
one at the beginning of your myth, K!wā́qaxsaᵋno, stood. For/ there
was nothing that he did not overcome," said he, and immediately ʟ!ā́-
qwadzē arose, for he/has two privileges, also that of Kū́nṓsila, and
he stood up. Then he/ spoke and said, "Now I will go for a short
time to my house. Indeed you wish (25) that we all show our privileges," said he and he/ ran into his house. Before long he came out
of/ the door of his house carrying a bow and he said,/ "Beat fast
time." Then the men beat fast time on the front boards of the house
of ᵋnɛmṓgwis,/ and ʟ!ā́qwadzē came stooping with long steps(30) span-
ning his bow to shoot. And he came to the door of the/ house of
ᵋnɛmṓgwis and stood there. Then he spoke and he (1) said, speaking

ʟalaxa g·ōkwaxs laē yāqǃɛg·aᵋʟa, wä la ᵋnēk·a: G·āxᵋmɛn, g·āxᵋmɛn
g·ῑgämēᵋ Ӽᵋmāxŭlaⱡ ʟōᵋgŭn kⱷǃēsᵋokᵘxag·ada k·ǃēsɛk· aōms ⱡɛkǃwisax‑
g·ada k·ǃeậsɛk· wɛyōʟānɛm ⱡɛkǃwῑtsɛn äwānậᵋyēda naulakᵘᵋwŭⱡa bɛ‑
gwānɛmē Kǃwāqaxsaᵋnὸ. ᵋnēᵋnak·iⱡē g·ῑgämēᵋ, g·āxᵋmɛn wāwixaliᵋlaxs
5 k·ǃēdeⱡaqǃōs lāxōx Qǃēxʟālagax. G·āxᵋmɛn qādzēʟaqō qag·ada g·ῑgä‑
mēk· lāxg·a ʟǃāsotiwalisak·, ᵋnēk·exs laē gwēgɛmx·ᵋῑt lāxa ᵋnāxwa
lēɛlqwälaʟaᵋya. Wä, lä ᵋnēk·a: Laᵋmē laēʟɛn wāⱡdɛma lāx g·ōkwasa
g·ῑgämaᵋyē Ӽᵋmāxŭlaⱡē. Wä, laɛmɪ̱as dōxᵋwaʟɛlaxg·ada naualakŭk· ⱡɛ‑
kǃwῑts Kǃwāqaxsaᵋnoxa ʟō̱ʟɛgwalɛntsǃēsɛlaxa k·ǃeậsᵋwŭⱡa k·ǃēs yāk·ậ‑
10 matsōᵋ lāxēs dōxᵋwŭ̱ʟɛⱡē, ᵋnēk·ē. (Hё̈ɛm ᵋnēᵋnak·iⱡtsē Tǃēsɛmg·itē.)
Wä, gῑlᵋmisē qǃŭlbē wāⱡdɛmas g·ȃxaas Ōdzēᵋstalis g·āxawɛls lāxa tǃɛ‑
x·ῑläsa g·ōkwē dālaxa maᵋⱡexsa pǃɛlxɛlasgɛma. Wä, lä yāqǃɛg·aᵋⱡa.
Wä, lä ᵋnēk·a: Wäg·aamasʟ ʟā̱ʟaxbalax g·ῑgämēᵋ. Wa, gēlag·a, g·ῑgä‑
mēᵋ, g·āxaaqōs g·āxaaqōs wāwixɛlῑᵋlaxg·ɛn k·ǃēdēⱡɛk· yῑsa k·ǃēsēx
15 aōms ⱡɛkǃwῑs yῑsēs äwanậᵋyosē Kǃwāqaxsaᵋno. ᵋnēᵋnak·iⱡē lɛᵋmōx qǃŭ‑
nēqwaliⱡa k·ǃēdēⱡaxsa g·ῑgämaᵋyōx Ӽᵋmāxŭlaⱡēx. Laᵋmisɛk· lāⱡg·ada
maᵋⱡäxsa pǃɛlxɛlasgɛm qaēs hasāyōs, g·ῑgämēᵋ, ᵋnēk·exs laē tsǃậsa
maᵋⱡäxsa pǃɛlxɛlasgɛm lāx ʟǃāqwadzē. Wä,laᵋmē Ōdzēᵋstalisē xwēla‑
gῑʟ lāxa g·ōkwē. Wä, g·āxē ʟǃāqwadzē kǃwāg·aɛlsa.
20
Wä, lä ʟā̱xᵋwɛlsē Lālak·otsǃaxa yāyaqǃɛntēms. Wä, lä yāqǃɛg·aᵋⱡa
Wä, lä ᵋnēk·a: ʟǃɛdậ, g·ῑgämēᵋ ʟǃāqwadzē. Hēⱡolaxaē bɛnyɛm laxōs ᵋwä‑
lasaqōs k·ǃēsᵋậa. Wa, gēlak·asᵋla g·ῑgämēᵋ. ᵋnēᵋnak·iⱡē, wa, gēlag·a
g·ῑgämēᵉ Mậᵋnakŭl qaᵋs lālag·aōs wāwixɛliᵋlax k·ǃēdēⱡasa g·ῑgämaᵋyē
25 Ӽᵋmāxŭlaⱡē, ᵋnēk·ē, (yῑxs g·āyuⱡaē Mậᵋnakŭla lāx ᵋnɛᵋmēmutasa ᵋnē‑
ᵋnɛlk·ǃēnoxwasa ᵋnɛmgēsē) Wä, hёx·ᵋida ᵋmisē Mậᵋnakŭla ʟā̱xᵋwɛlsa qaᵋs
yāqǃɛg·aᵋⱡē. Wä, lä ᵋnēk·a: Wäg·a hōʟēlax g·ῑg·ɛgämēᵋ qä̱ʟēs wāⱡdɛ‑
mōs, yῑxs ᵋnēk·aēx qa nēⱡᵋidēsɛns k·ǃēk·ǃɛsᵋōx qadzēyῑns g·āxeⱡa lāqᵘ.
Nōgwaɛmʟa̱ⱡ nŭyɛmbalisax Kŭnōsila. Wä, hētǃaʟɛn g·āx nēⱡᵋidämatsōᵋʟɛn
30 k·ǃēsᵋo lāxɛn äpsōtǃɛna·ya Mậtsǃadɛx, ᵋnēk·exs laē ʟēᵋlālax ʟǃāsabo‑
lisxa g·āyuⱡē lāx ᵋnɛᵋmēmutas Mậᵋnakŭla. Wä, lāx·daᵋxwē qāsᵋit,
qaᵋs·lē hōgwiʟ lāx g·ōkwas Mậᵋnakŭla. Wä, k·ǃēstǃē gäⱡaxs g·āxaē

into the house as he was talking; He said: "I come, I come/ chief
Aᵉmāxŭlaⱡ with my privilege. This is no ordinary bow/ for there is
nothing that it did not get, the bow of my ancestor, the supernatural/
man K!wāqaxsano, I mean this chief. I come to lift (5) your princess
Q.!ēx·Lālaga. I come to marry her to this/ chief here, L!āsotiwalis."
Thus he said and turned his face to all the/ tribes. Then he said:
"Now my word has gone into the house of/ chief Aᵉmāxŭlaⱡ. Now you
have seen the supernatural/ bow of K!wāqaxsaᵉno who long ago obtained supernatural power, for there was nothing that was not vanquished
(10) that was seen by him," said he. (This refers to T!ēsɛmg·it.)/
As soon as his speech was finished, Ōdzēᵉstalis came out of the/ door
of the house carrying two pairs of blankets, and he spoke/ and said,
"Stand there for a while, chief. Now come, chief/ and come, and come
and try to lift my princess with this (15) supernatural bow of your
ancestor, K!wāqaxsaᶜno. I mean that now the/ princess of this chief
Aᵉmāxŭlaⱡ is on the floor. Now these/ two pairs of blankets will go
for your breath, chief," said he as he gave the/ two pairs of blankets to L!āqwadzē. Now Ōdzēᵉstalis went back (20) into the house,
and then L!āqwadzē came and sat down.

Then Lālak·ots!a arose, the speaker at the wedding. He spoke/
and said, "It is well, chief L!āqwadzē. Why should you be ashamed
of your great/privilege? Now thank you, chief. I mean this. Come/
chief Māᶜnākŭla and go and lift the princess of chief (25) Aᵉmāxŭlaⱡ," said he. (For this belongs to Māᶜnākŭla of the numaym/ᶜnēᶜnɛl·
k·!ēnoxᵘ of the ᶜnɛmgis.) Immediately Māᶜnākŭla arose and/spoke. He
said: "Now listen, chiefs. True is what you say,/ for you wish that
we shall show our privileges, the great ones for which we come here./
I am the one who has at the beginning of his myth Kŭnōsila. I am going to show this my (30) privilege from the other side of my body,
the Māts!adɛx." Thus he said and he called L!āsabolis,/ the one who
belongs to the numaym of Māᶜnākŭla. Then they walked/and went into
the house of Māᶜnākŭla, and they were not long before (1)Māᶜnakŭla

g·āxăwɛlsē Mâ°nakŭla lāxa g·ōkwē dālaxa gwāgwēk·!ayu mastâ. Wä,
g·āxē ʟ!āsabolisē ɛlxʟēᵉ q!ɛlxŭlaxa sɛg·aānâᵉyē dɛnɛma. Wä, laᵉmē ʟēxɛdzodēda ᵉnāxwa bēbɛgwānɛm lāxa tsāgɛmasa g·ōkwas ᵉnɛmōgwisē.
Wä, la Mâᵉnākŭla ᵉnēg·ɛtɛwēxs g·āxaē gwāsoʟɛla; hē hē hē hē ē, la-
5 qēxs sāyak·!ālaasēs gwāgwēk·!ayuwē māstō nâʟax t!ɛx·flās g·ōkwas ᵉnɛmōgwisē. Wä, laᵉmē ʟ!āsabolisē q!ɛlxŭlaxa sāg·aano dɛnɛm la mōkwāʟē
ōbaᵉyas lāx ōxʟaᵉyasa māstowē. Wä, g·flᵉmisē lāg·aa lāx ʟ!āsanâ-
ᵉyasa t!ɛx·flāsa g·ōkwē laē hāyaʟp!aʟtɛwabuʟa qēʟiᵉlālaxēs x·ōmsaxs
laē sɛg·īla ᵉmaᵉmaq!axʟasēs māstowē lä dāk·!ɛndxa dɛnɛmaxs laaxat!
10 ᵉnēk·a; hē hē hē hē ē. Wä, lä gwēgɛmx·ᵉīt lāxa lēɛlqwălaʟaᵉyē qaᵉs yāq!ɛg·aᵉʟē. Wä, lä ᵉnēk·a; Hēɛm k·!ēsᵉōsɛn nūyɛmbalisē Ts!ax·sōt-
xa ᵉnɛmōxᵉŭm g·fl ʟōgwalaxg·ada gwāgwēk·!ayukᵘ mastō lāxa āʟanɛm.
Wä laᵉmē hēʟbata sɛx·īdayâxg·ada ᵉwālasɛk· gweᵉyîma. Hēɛm k·!eâs wɛyō-
ʟānɛmēda māstō. Laᵉmē lāg·aaʟɛla lāx k·!ēdeʟasa g·īgāmaᵉyaē Aᵉmā-
15 xŭlaʟ, ᵉnēk·ēxs laē nēxaᵉwɛlsaxēs māstowē.

Wä, g·āxē g·āxawɛlsē Ōdzēᵉstalisē lāxa t!ɛx·fla dālaxa p!ɛlxɛ-
lasgɛmē. Wä, lä yāq!ɛg·aᵉʟa. Wä, lä ᵉnēk·a; Wäg·aamasʟ ʟâʟaxbalax
g·īgāmēᵉ Mâᵉnakŭl. Wa, gēlag·a g·īgāmēᵉ g·āxaaqōs g·āxaaqōs wāwixɛli-
ᵉlaxg·în k·!ēdēʟɛk· yîsa k·!ēsēx aōms gwāgwēk·!ayu māstō yîsōs āwanâ-
20 ᵉyaōsē Ts!ax·sōt. ᵉnēᵉnak·iʟē laᵉmōx qūnēquliʟa k·!ēdēʟaxsa g·īgā-
maᵉyōx Aᵉmāxŭlaʟēx. Laᵉmēsɛk· lāʟg·ada maᵉʟɛxsɛk· p!ɛlxɛlasgɛm qaēs
hasāyōs g·īgāmēᵉ, ᵉnēk·ēxs laē ts!âsa maᵉʟɛxsa p!ɛlxɛlasgɛm lāx Mâᵉnakŭla. Wä, lä āxᵉēdxa ᵉnɛmxsa p!ɛlxɛlasgɛm. Wä, lä ᵉnēk·a; Lāʟg·a-
da ᵉnɛmxsak· p!ɛlxɛlasgɛm qaēs daanâyaaxa dɛnɛmē yŭʟ ʟ!āsabolis, ᵉnē-
25 k·ēxs laē ts!âsa ᵉnɛmxsa p!ɛlxɛlasgɛm lāq. Wä, g·āxē Mâᵉnakŭla ʟōᵉ
ʟ!āsabolis k!ūsᵉɛlsa.

Wä, laᵉmē Ōdzēᵉstalisē xwēlagēʟ lāxa g·ōkwē. Wä, lä ʟâxᵉwɛlsē
Lālak·ots!axa yāyaq!ɛntēms. Wä, lä yāq!ɛg·aᵉla. Wä, lä ᵉnēk·a; ʟ!ɛ-
dâ. g·īgāmēᵉ Mâᵉnakŭl. Hēʟolaxaē bɛnyɛm laxōs ᵉwālasaqōs k·!ēsᵉâa
30 Wa, gēlak·asᵉla g·īgāmēᵉ. ᵉnēᵉnak·iʟē. Wa, gēlag·a g·īgāmēᵉ ᵉwālas
Kwāx·flanōkŭmēᵉ (xa xāmagɛmaᵉyē g·īgāmēsa ᵉnɛᵉmēmutasa Tɛmʟtɛmʟɛlsasa

came out of the house carrying the whaling harpoon, and/ʟ!asabolis
came behind him carrying the coiled harpoon line. Then/all the men
beat fast time on the boards of the house of ᵋnɛmōgwis./ Then Mâᵋnākŭla said, while he was coming along, "Hē hē hē hē,ē," (5) as he pretended to spear with the whaling harpoon at the door of the house of/
ᵋnɛmōgwis. Then ʟ!āsabolis carried the coiled harpoon line which
was tied to the/end on the butt end of the harpoon and as soon as he
arrived at the outside/of the door of the house he pretended to see
distinctly. He bent his head/to one side and he threw the harpoon
into the door. He held on to the harpoon line and (10) cried out "Hē
hē hē hē, ē," Then he turned his face to the tribes and/spoke. He
said, "This is the privilege of my earliest myth, Ts!ax·sōt/ the
only one who first obtained a supernatural gift, the whaling harpoon,
from the Wolf./ Indeed, my harpoon went right to the end of this
great whale. There is nothing that the/ harpoon does not get. Now
it has reached the princess of chief Aᵋmāxŭlaɫ." (15) Thus he said
and then he pulled out his harpoon./

Then Ōdzēᵋstalis came out of the door carrying a blanket./ Then
he spoke and said, "Now stand here for a while,/ chief Mâᵋnākŭla.
Now come, chief. You will try to lift from the floor/ this princess
with this unusual whaling harpoon of your ancestor (20) Ts!ax·sōt.
I mean this. Now has been moved from the floor the princess of/this
chief Aᵋmāxŭlaɫ. Now these two pairs of blankets will go for your/
breath, chief." Thus he said as he gave the two pairs of blankets to
Mâᵋnākŭla./ Then he took one pair of blankets and he said,/ "This
one pair of blankets will go for your holding the rope, ʟ!āsabolis."
(25) Thus he said and gave one pair of blankets to him. Then Mâᵋna-
kŭla and/ʟ!āsabolis came and sat down.

Now Odzēᵋstalis went back into the house. Then arose/Lālak·o-
ts!a, the speaker, and spoke and said,/"It is nice, chief Mâᵋnākŭla.
Why should you be ashamed of your great privilege. (30) Thank you,
chief. I mean this. Now come, chief ᵋwālas/ Kwāx·ilanōkŭmēᵋ. (The

Mamalēleqāla g̱wɛᵋyōs) qaᵋs lālag·aōs wāwixɛlIᵋlax k·!ēdeɫasa g·Ī-
g̱amaᵋyē Aᵋmāx̱ŭlaɫ, ᵋnēk·ē.

Wä, hëx·ᵋidaᵋmisē ̩ɫāxᵋwɛlsē ᵋwālas Kwāx·flanokŭmaᵋyē qaᵋs yā-
q!ɛg·aᵋɫē. Wä, lä ᵋnēk·a: Ēsaēɭa ëx·ᵋmaa g·ᵂg̱āmēᵋ Lālak·ots!a,
5 ēsaēɭa ëx·ᵋmaa laaqōs ̩ɭēxᵋēt g·āxɛn. ᵋwIᵋlaqwē aōmsɛn äwānᴀᵋyē
ōg̱waqa. ᵋnēᵋnak·iɫē laᵋmɛn lāɫ, ᵋnēk·exs laē qāsᵋida. Wä, hëᵋmis
āɫēs nɛg̱ōᵋyolsa lāxēs qāts!ēnaᵋyē lāᵋlaa lāxa t!ɛx·flās g·ōkwas X̱-
ᵋmāx̱ŭlaɫaxs laē g̱āmōt!ag·aᵋɫa hāsɛla lāx g̱wēk·!ālasasa ōlēg·In (xa
āɭanɛmaxs) g̱āmōtaē. Wä, g·flᵋmisē q!ŭlbē g̱āmōt!ēnaᵋyas laē ᵋnēk·a
10 hŭä, hŭä, hŭä, hŭä, g̱ŭyōɫɛla lāx t!ɛx·flās g·ōkwas Aᵋmāx̱ŭlaɫē. Wä,
g·flᵋmisē lāg·aa lāx max·stᴀᵋyas laē yāq!ɛg·aᵋla. Wä, lä ᵋnēk·a:
G·āxᵋmɛn, g·āxᵋmɛn g·āxᵋaɭɛla g·Īg̱āmēᵋ Aᵋmāx̱ŭlaɫ. G·āxᵋmɛn wāwixɛ-
lIᵋlaxs k·!ēdeɫaqōs g·Īg̱āmēᵋ Aᵋmāx̱ŭlaɫ, yIsg·ada k·!eâsɛk· wɛyōɭā-
nɛma yIsɛn nŭyɛmag·iwaᵋyax bāk·âē ̩ɭɛᵋwa ōlēg·In lāx Mēt!apēᵋ. Wä,
15 lä hōxᵋwidēda ōlēg·Inasa xwēᵋlē qaᵋn g·flg·flisaxg·In ᵋwālasēk·
Kwāx·flanokŭmaᵋya. Wä, yŭᵋmisɛn lāg·iɫa hōɫɛmalaxɛn ᵋnāxwa äxɛxs-
dɛsɛᵋwa. Wa, wa, ᵋnēk·ē. Wä, g·āxē Ōdzēᵋstalis g·āxawɛls lāxa
t!ɛx·fla dālaxa maᵋɫɛxsa p!ɛlxɛlasgɛm. Wä, lä yāq!ɛg·aᵋɫa. Wä,
lä ᵋnēk·a: Wäg·aamasɭ ̩ɭāɭaxbalax g·Īg̱āmēᵋ ᵋwālas Kwāx·flanokŭmēᵋ.
20 Wa, g̱ēlag·a g·Īg̱āmēᵋ, g·āxaaqōs wāwixɛliᵋlaxg·In k·!ēdēlɛk· yIsa
k·!ēsēx aōmsa ōlēg·ɛnēx yIsōs awānᴀᵋyōsē ᵋwālas Kwāx·flanokŭmaᵋyē.
ᵋnēᵋnak·iɫē laᵋmōx qŭnēqŭlIɫa k·!ēdēɫaxsa g·Īg̱amaᵋyōx Aᵋmāx̱ŭlaɫēx.
Laᵋmēsɛk· lāɫg·ada maᵋɫäxsɛk· p!ɛlxɛlasgɛm qaēs hasāᵋyōs, g·Īg̱āmēᵋ,
ᵋnēk·ēxs laē ts!âsa maᵋɫɛxsa p!ɛlxɛlasgɛm lāq. Wä, laᵋmē Ōdzēᵋsta-
25 lis xwēlagēɭ lāxa g·ōkwē. Wä, g·āxē ᵋwālas Kwāx·flanokŭmaᵋyē k!wäg·aɛlsa. (Wä, g·aɛm ɫāxwāɫa wāɫdɛmsa bāk·!ŭmaxs ɫēnamap!aaxēs k·!ē-
sᵋo.)

Wä, hëᵋmaaxs g·ālaē k!wäg·aɛlsē ᵋwālas Kwāx·flanokŭmaᵋya laas
̩ɭaxᵋwɛlsē Wāk·asxa g·āyuɫē lāx ᵋnɛᵋmēmutas ᵋwālas Kwāx·flanokŭmä.
30 Wä, lē Wāk·as yāq!ɛg·aᵋɫa. Wä, lä ᵋnēk·a: Hëdɛn lāg·iɫa ̩ɭāxᵋwɛl-

head chief of the numaym Tᴇmⱡ̣ᴛᴇmⱡ̣ᴇls/ (1) of the Mamalēleqāla was
the one he referred to.) Now try to lift the princess of chief/
Aᵋmāx̣ülaⱡ," said he./

Immediately ᵋwālas Kwāx·flanōkümēᵋ arose and spoke./ He said,
"Is it not kind of you, chief Lālak·ots!a? (5) Is it not good that
you name me. Not common is my ancestor/also. I mean this. I will
go," said he as he started. He/ walked along only half way towards
the door of the house of/ Aᵋmāx̣ülaⱡ, when he howled like a wolf,
loud with a noise like a wolf (a/ wolf)¹ as he was howling. As soon
as he had finished howling he said, (10) "Hūā, hūā hūā hūā," going towards the door of the house of Aᵋmāx̣ülaⱡ./ When he came near it he
spoke and said,/ "I come, I come. I have reached chief Aᵋmāx̣ülaⱡ.
I come to lift/ your princess, chief Aᵋmāx̣ülaⱡ, with this that cannot
be withstood,/ that belongs to the beginning of my myth that my ancestor made who lived at Mēt!apē. (15) Then the wolf vomited the
quartz for my first ancestor, ᵋwālas/Kwāx·flanōkümēᵋ, and this is why
I obtain everything that I want to get./ Wa wa," said he. Then Ōdzēᵋstalis came out of the/ door carrying two pairs of blankets, and he
spoke and/ said, "Stand there for a while, chief ᵋwālas Kwāx·flanō-
kümēᵋ, (20) Come now, chief, and come and lift my princess by means
of the/ supernatural wolf of your ancestor, ᵋwālas Kwāx·flanōkümēᵋ./
I mean this, that now has been moved on the floor the princess of
this chief Aᵋmāx̣ülaⱡ./ Now these two pairs of blankets will go for
your breath, chief,"/ said he as he gave the two pairs of blankets
to him. Then Ōdzēᵋstalis (25) went back into the house and ᵋwālas Kwā-
x·flanōkümēᵋ came and sat down/.(This is the most difficult speech of
the Indians, when each one speaks about his/ privileges.)/

And as soon as ᵋwālas Kwāx·flanōkümēᵋ had sat down/Wāk·as arose,
the one who belongs to the numaym of ᵋwālas Kwāx·flanōkümēᵋ, (30)
and then Wāk·as spoke and said: "This is the reason why I arise,/

---

(1) The writer uses here first the Mamalēleqāla term for wolf, then the
Kwāg·uⱡ term.

sē g·Ig·ɛgämēs lēɛlqwälaLēᶜ qɛn wüʟēxwa g·Igämaᶜyōx ᶜwälasēx Kwāx·ilanokumaᶜya, ᶜmādzēs bɛnyɛmaōs g·Ig·āmēᶜ lāxɛns k·!ēsᶜoxa Hōʟagɛnus laē laēʟē xɛns awānᴀ̂ᶜyē lāx g·ōkwas Hōʟagɛnus lāxōx Dɛmlēwasēx qaxs ᶜnɛmwɛyōtâlaē Hōʟagɛnus ʟōᶜ ᶜwālas Kwāx·îlanokumaᶜyēxa k·!eâsē

5   wɛyōʟānɛma. ᶜnēᶜnak·iƶē hâsaâsēx Qawadiliqala k·!ēsᶜowa ōlēg·în.
ᶜnēᶜnak·iƶē, laɛms ʟēxʟēqwäliƶa, ᶜnēk·ēxs laē k·!wāg·aɛlsa. Wä,
laᶜmē ᶜwālas Kwāx·îlanokümaᶜyē hĕwäxa nāᶜnaxmēx wäƶdɛmas Wāk·asxa
nɛwēᶜlēnoxwasa Mamalēleqäla.

    Wä, lä ʟaxᶜwɛlsē Lālak·ots!axa yāyaq!ɛntēms. Wä, lä yāq!ɛg·a-
10 ᶜƶa. Wä, lä ᶜnēk·a: ʟ!ɛdâ g·Igämēᶜ ᶜwālas Kwāxîlanokümēᶜ. Hĕƶo-
laxaē bɛnyɛm lāxōs ᶜwālasaqōs k·!ēsᶜâa. Wa, gēlak·asᶜla g·Igämēᶜ.
ᶜnēᶜnak·iƶē. Wa, gēlag·a g·Igämēᶜ Q!āq!uyalagum (xa g·ayuƶē lāx ᶜnɛ-
ᶜmēmutaṣa ᶜwālasäsa Mamalēleqäla gwɛᶜyōs.) qaᶜs lālag·aōs wāwixɛlî-
ᶜlax k·!ēdēƶasa g·Igämaᶜyē Aᶜmāxülaƶ, ᶜnēk·ē. Wä, hĕx·ᶜidaᶜmisē,
15 ʟāxᶜwɛlsē Q!āq!uyalagum. Wä, lä yāq!ɛgaᶜƶa. Wä, lä ᶜnēk·a: Qäʟ,
qäʟaxs hĕᶜmaᴣx gwēg·ilasēxwa ʟēgadäxs ᶜwāᶜwatsila qādzēʟa. Qäʟ lāq!a-
mēg·îns g·āg·ēxsilaxɛn g·Igämaᶜyax laxōx ʟ!āsotiwalisaxwa gɛg·adʟɛxsa
k·!ēdēƶax laxōx Q!ēxʟālagax. ᶜnēᶜnak·iƶē, laᶜmɛn lāƶ laēʟ qɛn dōxᶜwi-
dēqō laɛmlax k!wēmg·aliƶlaxō, ᶜnēk·ēxs laē qāsᶜida qaᶜs lē laēʟ lāxa
20 t!ɛx·îläsa g·ōkwē. Wä,k·!ēst!ē gäƶ̣axs g·āxaē g·āxawɛls lāxa t!ɛx·î-
la qaᶜs ʟāxᶜwɛlsē. Wä, lä xwäk!üg·aᶜƶ laqēxs Nɛnstâliƶaas Baxᵘba-
kwälanuxᵘsIwaᶜyē. Nan, nan, nan, ᶜnēk·ē. Wä, lä yāq!ɛg·aᶜƶa. Wä,
lä ᶜnēk·a: Wä, hĕᶜmɛn ᶜnēᶜnak·iƶē qaxg·în k·!eâsēk· k·îlɛma. Dâxɛn
ᶜwālasē läda. ᶜnēᶜnak·iƶē, g·Igämēᶜ ʟ!āsotiwalis. Laɛm k·!aniᶜläla-
25 g·îliƶg·a Q!ēxʟālagak·g·as gɛnɛmƶg·ōs,·g·Igämēᶜ, ᶜnēk·ē.

    G·āxē Odzēᶜsʟalis g·āxawɛls lāxa t!ɛx·îla dālaxa sɛk·!axsa p!ɛl-
xɛlasg·ɛm. Wä, lä yāq!ɛg·aᶜƶa. Wä, lä ᶜnēk·a. Wäg·aamasʟ ʟāʟaxbalax
g·Igämēᶜ Q!āq!uyalagum. Wa,gēlag·a g·Igämēᶜ g·āxaaqōs g·āxaaqōs wāwixɛ-
liᶜlaxg·în k·!ēdēƶɛk· yîsa k·!ēsēx aōms ᶜwālas lādaxwa Nɛnstâliƶaxs

(1) chiefs of the tribes, that I may ask this chief ᵋwālas/Kwāx·ꜰlano-
kūmēᶜ, is there any reason, chief why you should be ashamed of our
crest/Hōʟagᴇnus when our first ancestor entered the house of Hōʟagᴇ-
nus at Dᴇmlēwas?/ For Hōʟaganus and ᵋwālas Kwāx·ꜰlanōkūmēᶜ were brothers so that there was nothing (5) that they could not get. I mean
this that belongs to Qawadiliqala, the wolf crest./ I mean you have
made a mistake," said he as he sat down./ Now ᵋwālas Kwāx·ꜰlanōkūmēᶜ
never answered the speech of Wāk·as/ for he is the myth keeper of the
Mamalēleqȧla./

Then Lālak·ots!a arose, the speaker. He spoke (10) and said,
"It is nice, chief ᵋwālas Kwax·ꜰlanōkūmēᶜ./ Why should you be ashamed
of your great crest. Indeed I thank you, chief./ I mean this, now
come, chief Q!āq!oyalagum. (He belonged to the/ numaym ᵋwālas of the
Mamalēleqala, the one to whom he referred.) Now come and try to
lift the/ princess of chief Aᵋmāxūlaʟ," said he. Immediately (15)
Q!āq!oyalagum arose. He spoke and said, "Indeed/ it is true This
is the way it is done in this that has the name great marriage. Indeed,/ now we are treating like a chief our chief, ʟ!āsotiwalis, the
one who will have for his wife this/ princess, Q!ēx·ʟālaga. I mean
this, now I will go in and look at her/ to see if she has moved,"
said he, as he started. He went into the (20) door of the house ȧnd
it was not long before he came out of the door/ and he stood up and
he became excited as a bear of the Cannibal-of-the-North-End-of-the-
World/ and cried, "Nan nan nan." Then he spoke/ and said, "This is
what I mean. There is nothing that I am afraid of. Look/ at my
great dance. I mean this, chief ʟ!āsotiwalis. Now is beginning to
move on the ground (25) Q!ēx·ʟālaga. She will be your wife, chief,"
said he./

Then Ōdzēᵋstalis came out of the door carrying five pairs of
blankets/and he spoke and said, "Go on, stand there a while/ chief
Q!āq!oyalagum. Come, chief, you come, you come to lift from the floor/
the princess with his supernatural great dance, 'Grizzly Bear of the

Baxⁿbakwālanuxⁿsiwaᵋya yîsōs gɛg·adānɛmōx lāxa g·Īgāmaᵋyaē ʟ!āqwa-
g·ilāsa nauałakwē lēlqwālaʟaᵋya Nōxŭnts!Ĩdɛxwas Awĩk·!ēnoxⁿ. ᵋnēᵋ-
nak·iłē, laɛms dāqaq lāxēs k·!ēsᵋosē Hānaʟēᵋnâ lāxēs âbāsk·!ōtōsa
Haânaʟēᵋnâsa Q!ōmoyâᵋyē. Wä, laɛmxaas dâqaxa ᵋwâlasē lädē lāxēs

5   k·!ēsᵋosē sĩsɛyūʟē lāxēs âsk·!ōtōs lāxwa ᵋnɛᵋmēmutaqōsa Tɛmłtɛmłɛls
lāxwa Mamalēlexk·!ōt!ɛnaᵋyaqōs, g·Ĩgāmēᵋ.ᵋnēᵋnak·iłē, laᵋmōx k!wäg·flił
qŭnēqŭllła k·!ēdēłaxsa g·Īgāmaᵋyōx Aᵋmâxŭlałēx. Laᵋmēsɛk·
lāłg·ada sɛk·!axsak· p!ɛlxɛlasgɛm qaēs hasāᵋyōs (qaēs yāq!ânt!ālayu,
ᵋnēk·exs ᵋnēk·aē qaēs hasāᵋyōs), g·Ĩgāmēᵋ, ᵋnēk·ēxs laē ts!âsa sɛk·!a-

10 xsa p!ɛlxɛlasgɛm lâq. Wä, laᵋmē Ōdzēᵋstalisē xwēlagēʟ lāxa g·ōkwē.
Wä, g·āxē Q!âq!uyalagum k!wāg·aɛlsa.
   Wä, lä ʟāxᵋwɛlsē Lālak·ots!axa yāyaq!ɛntēms. Wä, lä yāq!ɛg·a-
ᵋła. Wä, lä ᵋnēk·a: ʟ!ɛdâ g·Ĩgāmēᵋ Q!âq!uyalagum hēłodzēlaxaē
bɛnyɛm laxōs ᵋwālasaqōs lādaaxwa gâg·adānɛmēxwa ʟēgadäxs wĩnānɛm.

15 Wa, gēlak·asᵋla g·Ĩgāmēᵋ. ᵋnēᵋnak·iłē. Wa, gēlag·a g·Ĩgāmēᵋ Ōdzēᵋstalis qaᵋs lālag·aōs wāwixɛllᵋlax k·!ēdēłasa g·Ĩgāmaᵋyē Aᵋmâxŭlał
ᵋnēk·ē. Wä, hᵘx·ᵋidaᵋmisē ʟāxᵋwɛlsē Ōdzēᵋstalis (xa xāmagɛmaᵋyē
g·Ĩgāmēsa ᵋnɛᵋmēmutasa Nūnɛmasɛqâlitsa Lāwits!ēse)qaᵋs yāq!ɛg·aᵋłē.
Wä, lä ᵋnēk·a: Yūmawisʟaʟɛn wáłdɛmʟɛn ʟ!ōᵋlēyōx ʟ!âsotiwalisēxwa

20 g·Ĩgāmaᵋyēx qa wäg·ēsōx dōqwałaxɛns ᵋnāxwax mayax·ālasxōx ʟēgɛmdzä-
xs lāxɛns lālōʟ!aasāxwa gɛnɛmʟaq!ɛs. ᵋnēᵋnak·iłē,g·Ĩgāmēᵋ ʟ!âsoti-
walis qaᵋs awɛlx·ayaᵋmaōsax nâxsâlaaqōs qaᵋs k·!ēsaōs bâbakwayōsala
qaēs bɛxᵋutōs, hᵘᵋmis qaᵋs k·!ēsaōs ʟɛmlɛmsɛma, hᵘᵋmis qaᵋs k·!ēsaōs
nɛx·sōkwä qaxs hᵘᵋmaē ᵘx· g·Ĩgāmaᵋya ᵘk·alaxa ēaxk·!alāxēs g·Ĩgēdē

25 qaᵋs âlaōs aᵘk·ila g·āg·ēxsilasōsēs g·Ĩgēdōs. ᵋnēᵋnak·iłē g·Ĩgāmēᵋ
qaᵋnuxⁿ la gwegwälag·fldzasa ʟēqēla qa ʟēgɛmsēs xŭnōxⁿlaxaōs ʟōgwada
k·!ēdēłg·asg·ada g·Ĩgāmēg·a. ᵋnēᵋnak·iłē g·Ĩg·ɛgāmēs lēɛlqwālaʟēᵋ.
Nōgwaɛm nŭyɛmbalis Nōmasa, lāg·iłasg·În ᵋnɛᵋmēmutɛk· lɛguxʟâlax Nunɛ-
masɛqâlisē. Wä, laᵋmēsɛn lāł lāxēs wáłdɛmōs, g·Ĩgāmēᵋ Lālak·ots!a,

30 ᵋnēk·ēxs laē hâkwâła sēk·!aqaxēs sēk·!aganâxs laē k·!ēs yāyaᵋnaxs

Door of the (1) Cannibal-of-the-North-End-of-the-World, which you obtained in marriage from chief ʟ!áqwag·ila/of the supernatural tribe Nōxŭnts!idɛx of the Awɪk·!ēnoxᵘ./I mean this. Now you took first the crest of Hāᵋnaᴛēnâ from your mother's side,/the Hāǎnaᴛēno of the Q!ōmoyâᵋyē. Now you also took the great dance as your (5) privilege, the double headed serpent from your father's side from the numaym Tɛmᴌtɛmᴌɛls/of your Mamalēleqǎla side, chief. I mean now has moved/ quite a distance the princess of this chief Aᵋmāxŭlaᴌ. Now/these five pairs of blankets will go for your breath, (instead of "for your speech"/said he "for your breath") chief," thus he said as he gave him the five pairs of (10) blankets. Then Ōdzēᵋstalis went back into the house/and Q!āq!oyalagum came and sat down./

Then Lālak·ots!a, the speaker arose. He spoke/ and said: "It is nice, chief Q!āq!oyalagum. Why should you be/ashamed of your great dance which you obtained by marriage,and the name that you have obtained in war? (15) Now thank you, chief. I mean this, come chief Ōdzēᵋstalis/and go now and try to lift the princess of chief Aᵋmāxŭlaᴌ,"/ said he. Immediately Ōdzēᵋstalis arose (the head/chief of the Nŭnɛmasɛqâlis of the Ɫāwits!ēs) and spoke./ He said, "This will be my speech to my nephew,ʟ!āsotiwalis,(20) the chief. Let him see that we all respect this his great name/in the way in which we try to get the one who will be his wife. I mean this, chief ʟ!āsotiwalis,/that you may show that you are noble, that you may not look angrily/upon your fellow men and also that you may not speak proudly and that you may not/ be childish,for he is a good chief who is kind, speaking kindly to the people,(25) that you may really be treated nicely like a chief by your people. I mean this, chief,/what we are now doing is giving a name to be the name of your child,this/princess,chief. That is what I mean, chiefs of the tribes./ I have at the beginning of my myth Nōmas. Therefore, my numaym have the tribe name Nŭnɛmasɛqâlis./ Now I will do according to your word, chief Lālak·ots!a,"/said he as he stooped down

laē qāᵋnakŭla gwɛyōⱡɛla lāx t!ɛx·îläs g·ōkwꜳs Aᵋmāxŭlaⱡō Laɛm nā-
ɛnaxts!ɛwax qāts!ắts!ēnaᵋyꜳsa nōmasē bɛgwānɛma. Wä, g·îlᵋmisē lāg·aa
lāxa t!ɛx·îla laē nɛgɛtōx̣ᵋwit ʟ̂âsa. Wä, lä yāq!ɛg·aᵋⱡa. Wä, lä
ᵋnēk·a: G·āxᵋmɛn, g·āxᵋmɛn g·āxᵋaʟɛla lât g·Îgāmēᵋ Aᵋmāxŭlaⱡ. Nō-
5 gwaɛm Odzēᵋstalisa, nōgwaɛm naualak·ustâlis Nōmasa. G·āx̄ᵋmɛn wāwi-
xɛliᵋlaxs k·!ēdēⱡaq!ōs, g·Îgāmēᵋ. ᵋnēᵋnak·îⱡē g·Îgāmēᵋ Aᵋmāxŭlaⱡ.
Wǟg·iⱡla wǟg·îdzɛⱡla hḗⱡq!ɛg·alîⱡaxs k·!ēdēⱡaq!ōs g·Îgāmēᵋ qɛn nō-
gwaᵋmē lâʟqō qag·în g·Îgāmēk· lāxg·a ʟ!āsotiwalisɛk̦, ᵋnēk·ē. Wä,
g·îlᵋmisē q!ŭlbē wāⱡdɛmas g·āxē Odzēᵋstalisē g·āxawɛls lāxa t!ɛx·îla
10 dālaxa maᵋⱡaxsa p!ɛlxɛlasgɛm. Wä, lä yāq!ɛg·aᵋⱡa. Wä, lä ᵋnēk·a:
Wǟg·aāmasʟ ʟ̂âʟaxbālax, g·Îgāmēᵋ Odzēᵋstalis. Qǟʟ, qǟʟēs wāⱡdɛmōs,
gÎgāmēᵋ. Âla, âlasēs wāⱡdɛmōs yîxs laaqōs ʟēxsᵋālaxwa g·Îgāmaᵋyax
lāxōx ʟ!āsotiwalisax qa k·!ēsēsōᵋ bābakwayōsɛla qaēs g·ōkŭlōtē lāx
gwēg·ilasasa âɛm äwɛlqɛla qaᵋs g·Îgāmaᵋyēxa k·!eâsē g·Îqag·iwaᵋyaxa
15 k·!eâsē gagɛmpa. Wä, hᵋɛm ʟɛmqē qaēs g·ōkŭlōtē, lāg·iⱡas ʟ!ēdzɛⱡē,
wäx·i nŭyɛmbalis g·Îgāmaᵋya g·Îgāmeᵋyᵋ lä k·flɛmsa ʟɛmqag·iⱡä. ᵋnē-
ᵋnak·iⱡē, wa gēlag·a g·Îgāmēᵋ, g·āxaaqōs g·āxdzēaqōs wāwixɛliᵋlaxgîn
k·!ēdēⱡɛk· yîsa k·!ēsēx aōmsa Nōmasēx yîsōs awānâᵋyōsē Odzēᵋstalis
Aōdziᵋlālag·flis. Hᵋɛms nŭyɛmbalis ʟᵋʟɛgɛmē, g·Îgāmēᵋ. ᵋnēᵋnak·iⱡē,
20 laᵋmōx qŭnēqwaliⱡa k·!ēdēⱡaxsa g·Îgāmaᵋyōx Aᵋmāxŭlaⱡēx. Laᵋmēsɛk·
lāⱡg·ada maᵋⱡắxsɛk· p!ɛlxɛlasgɛm qaēs hasāᵋyōs, g·Îgāmēᵋ, ᵋnēk·ēxs
laē ts!âsa māᵋlăxsa p!ɛlxɛlasgɛm lāq. Wä, lä Odzēᵋstalis xwēlagēʟ
lāxa g·ōkwē. Wä, g·āxē Odzēᵋstalis k!wāg·aɛlsa.

Wä, lä ʟ̂āxᵋwɛlsē Lālak·ots!axa yāyaq!ɛntēms. Wä, lä yāq!ɛg·aᵋⱡa.
25 Wä, lä ᵋnēk·a: ʟ!ɛdâ, g·Îgāmēᵋ Odzēᵋstalis. Laɛmxaē dōxᵋwaʟɛⱡaxēs
ᵋwālasōs k·!ēsᵋâ. Hᵋⱡolaxaē k·!ēs yālaxsɛmyâaxa naualak·ustâlisē

carrying his cane. And he did not go fast (1) when he was walking
towards the door of the house of Aᵉmāx̆ūlaɫ. Then/ he imitated the
way of walking of an old man, and when he arrived/ at the door he
stood up straight and he spoke and/ said: "I came, I came and
reached you, chief Aᵉmāx̆ūlaɫ. (5) I am Ȯdzēᵉstalis. I am Nōmas
who came up with supernatural power. I came to try to/lift up/
your princess, chief. I mean this, chief Aᵉmāx̆ūlaɫ./ Now go on,
go on great one, let her come right off from the floor your princess,
chief, that I may/ get her for my chief here, for ʟ!āsotiwalis,"
said he./ And as soon as his speech was ended Odzēᵉstalis[1] came out
of the door (10) carrying two pairs of blankets and he spoke and
said,/ "Stand here for a while, chief Odzēᵉstalis[2]. Indeed, your
word is true,/ chief. It is true, it is true what is said when you
give advice to this chief/ ʟ!āsotiwalis that he should not look
angrily upon his tribe/ in the way of those who just want to be
chiefs and who have no chief ancestors, (15) who have no grandfathers
They are proud in (their dealings with) their tribe and therefore
they are hated./ But if a chief begins from the myth times, then he
is afraid to be proud./ I mean this. Now come, chief, you great one,
come and lift/this my princess with the supernatural Nōmas, the
first ancestor of Ȯdzēᵉstalis,/ Aōdziᵉlālag·ilis. That is the name
at the beginning of myth time, chief. I mean this. (20) Now
has been moved on the floor this princess of chief Aᵉmāx̆ūlaɫ. Now/
will go these two pairs of blankets for your breath, chief." Thus
he said/ as he gave him the two pairs of blankets. Then Ȯdzēᵉstalis
went back/ into the house and Ȯdzēᵉstalis came and sat down./

Then Lālak·ots!a, the speaker, arose and spoke (25) and said, "It
is nice, chief Odzēᵉstalis. Now has been seen again/your great privilege. Why should you not be proud of the supernatural (1) privilege

---

1. This is Ȯdzēᵉstalis of the numaym Kᵘkwāk!ūm of the Q!ōmoyāᵉyē.
2. This is Ȯdzēᵉstalis of the numaym Nūnᴇmasᴇqⱥlis of the Ɫāwits!ᴇs.

nûyᴇmbalis k·!ēsᵉōs, g·Igāmēᵉ.Wa, gēlak·asᵉla g·Igāmēᵉ.ᵉnēᵉnak·iⱡē.

Wa, gēlag·a g·Igāmēᵉ Yāxyᴇgas (xa xāmagᴇma'yē g·Igāmēsa ᵉnᴇᵉmēmutasa
Sîsᴇnʟ!ēsa ʟāwits!ēsē gwᴇᵉyōs) qaᵉs lālag·aōs wāwixᴇliᵉlax k·!ēdēⱡasa
g·Igāmaᵉyē Aᵉmāx̣ūlaⱡ, ᵉnēk·ē. Wä, hēx·ᵉidaᵉmisē Yāxyᴇgas ʟaxᵉwᴇlsa.

5 Wä, lä yāq!ᴇg·aᵉⱡa. Wä, lä ᵉ nēk·a: Qäʟ qäʟaxs lᴇᵉmaaqōs ᵉnēk·a,
g·Ig·ᴇgāmēdzē āwāsâl ʟ!āqoʟas ʟᴇᵉwa g·Igāmēdzēx xūnōkwas ʟ!āsotiwa-
lidzäxwa âlak·!āläx g·Ixsēᵉstāla ʟᴇwᴇlqiᵉlakᵘ g·Igāmaᵉya. Wa, laᴇms
yāʟ!Âʟᴇx g·Igāmēᵉ ʟ!āsotiwalis, ladzēᴇms yāʟ!Âʟᴇx lāxg·as g·igēdg·ōs,
g·Igāmēᵉ, qaxg·anuᵉxᵘ laᵉmēk· g·āg·ēxsila lâʟ, g·Igāmēᵉ ʟ!āsotiwalis

10 lāxwa k·!ēsēx q!ūnāla nēⱡᵉēdxwa ᵉwāᵉwalatsilax k·!ēsᵉoⱡt!ᴇn qādzēʟa
ᵉmᴇnmᴇsōdᴇs lāxōs ᵉwālasaqōs ʟēgᴇma g·Igāmēᵉ ʟ!āsotiwalis, G·Ixsēᵉsta-
lisᴇmēᵉ, Yāqoʟasᴇmaᵉyē, dâxs läqōs lâʟānᴇm ʟēʟᴇgᴇmdzē. Laᴇms k!wā-
yuʟa lāxēs qāqᴇsîⱡōs g·Igāmēᵉ. Laᴇms g·ik·!uⱡts!ᴇnda lāxa t!ᴇxîla-
ᵉyasōx âdzēx. ᵉnēᵉnak·iⱡē g·Ig·ᴇgāmēᵉ. Laᵉmᴇn läⱡtsg·în ᵉwālasᴇk·

15 k·!ēsᵉâxg·ada k·!eâsᴇk· wᴇyōʟānᴇm k·!ēsᵉâ wāwixᴇliᵉlax k·!ēdēⱡasa
g·Igāmaᵉyaē Aᵉmāx̣ūlaⱡa, ᵉnēk·ᴇxs laē qāsᵉida qaᵉs lē ʟaxstolsaxa t!ᴇx·
flās g·ōkwas Aᵉmāx̣ūlaⱡ. Wä, lä dōgwiʟᴇlaxa g·ōkwaxs laē wâk!wāla
lāx gwēk·!ālasasa ᵉwats!e, ᵉwo,ᵉwo,ᵉwo,ᵉwo,hē ō, ᵉnēk·ē qaxs ᵉwᴇts!a-
ēs k·!ēsᵉo. Wä, lä yāq!ᴇg·aᵉⱡa. Wä, lä ᵉnēk·a: ᵉyâ ᵉyâ, g·Igāmē Aᵉma-

20 x̣ūlaⱡ. G·āxᴇn wāwixᴇliᵉlaxs k·!ēdēⱡaqōs, g·Igāmēᵉ Aᵉmaxūlaⱡ qag·ada
g·ayâlaqōxada g·Igāmēk·xg·a ʟ!āsotiwalisᴇk·. Nōkᵘ K·!âda, nōkᵘ ʟāʟēliʟ!a, nōkᵘ Yāxyagasg·în ᵉyālagᴇmēk· lâʟ, g·Igāmēᵉ Aᵉmāxūlaⱡ. G·āxᵉmᴇn
qādzēʟaxs k·!ēdēⱡaq!ōs, ᵉnēk·ē. Wä, gāxē Odzēᵉstalis g·āxawᴇls lāxa
t!ᴇx·fla dālaxa sᴇk·!axsa p!ᴇlxᴇlasgᴇm. Wä, lä, yāq!ᴇg·aᵉⱡa. Wä, lä

25 ᵉnēk·a: Wâg·aâmasʟ ʟâʟaxbālax g·Igāmēᵉ Yāxyagas. Wa, gᴇlag·a g·Igāmēᵉ
g·āxaaqōs, g·āxaaqōs wāwixᴇliᵉlaxgîn k·!ēdēⱡᴇk· yîsa k·!ēsēx aōmsa ᵉwā-
lasēx k·!ēsᵉâ ᵉwats!ēx yîsōs âwānâᵉyōsē K·!âdē. ᵉnēᵉnak·iⱡē g·Igāmēᵉ,
laᵉmōx k!wāg·fl1ⱡ ʟᴇqūlîⱡa k·!ēdēⱡaxsa g·Igāmaᵉyōx Aᵉmāxūlaⱡōx. Laᵉmē-
sᴇk· lāⱡg·ada sᴇk·!axsak· p!ᴇlxᴇlasgᴇm qaᵉs hasāᵉyōs, g·Igāmēᵉ, ᵉnēk·ēxs

30 laē ts!âsa sᴇk·!axsa p!ᴇlxᴇlasgᴇm lāq. Wä, laᵉmē Odzēᵉstalis xwîlagēʟ
lāxa g·ōkwē. Wä, g·āxē Yāxyagasē k!wāg·aᴇls.

which came up at the beginning of the myth time, chief. Now thank you,
chief. I mean this./ Now come, chief Yaxyāgas,(the head chief of the nu-
maym/SīsɛnⱢ!ēᶜ of the Ⱡāwits!ēs is the one he meant) and try to lift off
the· floor the princess/of chief Aᶜmāxūlaⱡ," he said. Immediately arose
Yaxyāgas (5) and he spoke and said, "Indeed, it is true. Now you say
it,/these are great chiefs,father and son,Ⱡ!āqoⱢas and this great chief
your son,the great Ⱡ!āsotiwalis,/who is really a chief all over, the
chief who is made a prince. Now/take care, chief Ⱡ!āsotiwalis, take
great care of those who have you as a chief,/ chief,that we may treat
you as a chief,chief Ⱡ!āsotiwalis (10) at this great marriage at which
the crests are brought out of the woods, which is not often shown,/
which is equal to the greatness of your name, chief Ⱡ!āsotiwalis,
G·ĩxsēᶜstalisɛmēᶜ,/YāqoⱢasɛmēᶜ. Look at these your great names that
you have obtained. Now you got much/that you went out to. get, chief.
Now you have passed half the road/made by your great father. I mean
this, chiefs. Now I will go with my great (15) privilege, the crest
which nothing can withstand,and try to lift up the princess of this/
chief,Aᶜmāxūlaⱡ," Thus he said and he started,and he stood in the door/
of the house of Aᶜmāxūlaⱡ and he looked into the house and he barked
in/the way a dog barks,"ᶜwo ᶜwo ᶜwo ᶜwo,hē ē," said he,for the dog/is
his crest. Then he spoke and said,"Oh chief Aᶜmāxūlaⱡ,(20) I come to
lift your princess,chief Aᶜmāxūlaⱡ,for this one/who wants to marry her,
this chief Ⱡ!āsotiwalis. I am K·!âdē, I am ⱠālēlīⱠ!a,/ I am Yaxyāgas.
I am sent to you, chief Aᶜmāxūlaⱡ. I come/ to marry your princess," said
he. Then Ōdzēᶜstalis came out of the/ door carrying five pairs of blankets and he spoke and (25) said: "Stand there for a while, chief Yaxyāgas
Now come, chief./ You came, you came to lift this princess with the
supernatural great/crest, the dog of your ancestor K·!âdē. I mean this,
chief./ Now a long way has moved this princess of this chief Aᶜmāxūlaⱡ.
Now/ these five blankets will go for your breath, chief," said he (30)
as he gave the five pairs of blankets to him. Then Ōdzēᶜstalis went
back/ into the house and Yaxyāgas came and sat down./

(1) Then arose Lālak·ots!a, the speaker. He spoke/ and said ,
"ɪt is true, it is true what you say, chief/Yaxyăgas. Why should
you be ashamed of your crest? Look at your/great names. Thank you,
ohief. That is what I mean. Now come,(5) ohief Mōkwētɛlasōgwiᵋlakᵘ,
(the head chief of the numaym/ Qaqawatiliqala is the one he meant)
come and lift the princess/of chief Aᵋmāxūlaⱡ," said he. Immediately
arose chief/Mōkwētɛlasōgwiᵋlakᵘ and spoke. He said, "Great,/it is
great,chiefs of the tribes. Great are these which are not often shown,
(10) these crests and this great marriage at which a name is given to
be the/name of the son of this chief,this great ʟ!āsotiwalis. Now go
on, chief/ʟ!āsotiwalis, take care. Now on account of this, chiefs of
the different/tribes, there is nothing too heavy for your great speech
chief./ I mean this.I am Mōkwētɛlasōgwiᵋlakᵘ, the one who at the beginning of myth time was (15) Qawadiliqala, the great supernatural
one,the only one who had the dance brought down from above/now scattered among you,all you tribes. For this reason I am imitated by you./
I mean this. Now I will go. Now I will go and try to lift the princess
of/ chief Aᵋmāxūlaⱡ," thus he said and he went and stood near the/door
of the house of Aᵋmāxūlaⱡ. Then he howled like a wolf in the doorway.
(20) As soon as he had howled four times, he spoke and said,/ "Now
listen well,chief Aᵋmāxūlaⱡ. I came, I brought/my great supernatural
treasure. I am Mōkwētɛlasōgwiᵋlakᵘ. I am he who came/from our first
myth, Qawadiliqala. I came, chief, holding before me/ my great crest
this G·flālaⱡit,trying to lift up (25) your princess,chief Aᵋmāxūlaⱡ,"
said he. Then Ōdzēᵋstalis came/ to the door carrying five pairs of
blankets. He spoke/ and said, "Now stand there for a while, chief
Mōkwētɛlasōgwiᵋlakᵘ./Now come,chief. You came to lift my princess/here
with the supernatural Qawadiliqala, your root, the one who has the
dance brought down from above. (30) I mean this. Now a long way has
moved on the floor the princess of this / chief Aᵋmāxūlaⱡ. Now these
five pairs of blankets (1) will go for your breath, chief." Thus he

qaēs hasā⁶yōs, g·Ígämē⁶, ⁶nēk·exs laē ts!ȃsa sɛk·!axsa p!ɛlxɛlasgɛm
lȃq. Wä, la⁶mȱ Odzē⁶stalisē xwēlagȱʟ lȃxa g·ōkwē. Wä, g·āxē Mōkwē-
tɛlasōgwi⁶lakwē k!wȃg·aɛls.

Wä, lä ʟȃx⁶wɛlsē Lȃlak·ōts!axa yȃyaq!ɛntēms. Wä, lä yȃq!ɛg·a-
5 ⁶ȧa. Wä, lä ⁶nēk·a: ʟ!ɛdȃ g·Ígämē⁶ Mȱkwētɛlasōgwi⁶lak⁴ hēȧōdzēlaxaē,
hēȧōdzēlaxaē bɛnyɛm lȃxōs ⁶wȃlasaqōs k·!ēs⁶ȃaxwa ȃlax g·Îlōʟaxalasō⁶
lȃʟ, g·Ígämē⁶ yîsa g·Íg·ɛgäma⁶yasa lēlqwȃlaʟa⁶yē, dȃxēs ʟȇʟɛ⁶gɛmdzē-
yōs g·Ígämē⁶. ⁶nē⁶nak·iȧē. Wa, gēlak·as⁶la g·Ígämē⁶, gēlaq!ȃnakü⁶la.
⁶nē⁶nak·iȧē. Wa, gēlag·a g·Ígämē⁶ ⁶māxwaq!ōȧɛl qa⁶s lȃlag·aōs wȃ-
10 wȧxɛli⁶lax k·!ēdēȧasa g·Ígäma⁶yē Ȧ⁶mȃxülaȧ, ⁶nēk·ē.Wä, hȇx·⁶ida⁶misa
g·Ígäma⁶yē ⁶māxwaq!ōȧɛla ʟȃx⁶wɛlsa qa⁶s yȃq!ɛg·a⁶ȧē. Wä, lä ⁶nēk·a
(xa g·āyuȧȇ lȃx ⁶nɛ⁶mēmutasa Nȃx·naxülasa Qwēq⁴sōt!ēnox⁴ gwɛ⁶yōs).
Qȃʟ, qȃʟēs wȃȧdɛmōs, g·Ígämē⁶ Lȃlak·ōts!· Laɛms nȃx·nȃqȃlÍȧa g·Ígämē⁶
laaqōs ʟȇx⁶ēt g·āxɛn, yînʟaxg·în awȃnȃlēg·axɛn nüyɛmbalisē ʟ!ȃʟ!a-
15 xwasdēxa xüngwadäs Odzē⁶stalis. Wä xüngwadɛx·⁶Ídē Odzē⁶stalisas Yȃ-
qaȧ⁶ȃnlidzē. Hȃ, qȃnʟo hȃnaȧlax ʟȇqɛlax ʟȇʟɛgɛmdzäsɛn g·Íg·ɛqaȵ·iwax-
g·a, läk· ʟȇgad ⁶māxwaq!ōȧɛla. ⁶nē⁶nak·iȧē g·Íg·ɛgämēs lē⁶lqwȃlaʟē⁶.
Yü⁶mɛn gwasx·älag·flis ēa⁶xēna⁶yōx lȃxɛns ⁶wȃlasēx gēnat!ɛsa. ⁶nē⁶na-
k·iȧē. Wȃg·a ⁶nȃxwa yȃʟ!ȃʟɛx g·Íg·ɛgämē⁶ ȃʟɛns wɛyōʟlax. Wä, la⁶mēsɛn
20 lȃȧ,⁶nēk·ēxs laē qās⁶idᵃa qa⁶s lä ʟȃxstolsaxa t!ɛx·flȃsa g·ōkwas Ȧ⁶mȃxü-
laȧȇ. Wä, lä dzōnoqwa ȱ ȱ ȱ lȃx gwɛ⁶yȃ gwēk·!ȃlats ʟ!ȃʟ!axwasdäxs
wînaȱ. Wä, lä yȃq!ɛg·a⁶ȧa. Wä, lä ⁶nēk·a: G·āx⁶mɛn g·Ígämē⁶, g·āx-
⁶mɛn g·āx⁶aʟɛlasg·în ⁶wȃlasɛk· k·!ēs⁶ȃ wȃwixɛli⁶laxs k·!ēdēlaqōs
g·Ígämē⁶ Ȧmȃxülaȧ. Nōgwaɛm nüyɛmbalisax ʟ!ȃʟ!axwasdēxa xüngwadäs,
25 Odzē⁶stalisēxa k·!eȃsē wɛyōʟȃnɛma, ⁶nē⁶nak·iȧē, g·Ígämē⁶ Ȧ⁶mȃxülaȧ.
Wȃg·ax·ōx nōsila qɛn nōgwē⁶mē lȃʟɛxs k·!ēdēȧaqōs g·Ígämē⁶ qag·ada
g·Ígämēk· lȃxg·a ʟ!ȃsotiwalisɛk·, ⁶nēk·ē. Wä, g·āxē Odzē⁶stalis g·ā-
xawɛls lȃxa t!ɛx·flȃsa g·ōkwē dälaxa sɛk·!axsa p!ɛlxɛlasgɛm. Wä, lä
yȃq!ɛg·a⁶ȧa. Wä, lä ⁶nēk·a: Wȃg·aamasʟ ʟȃʟaxbȃlax, g·Ígämē⁶ ⁶māxwa-
30 q!ōȧɛl. Wa, gēlag·a, wa, gēladzēlag·a g·Ígämē⁶, g·āxaaqōs g·āxdzȧaqōs

said as he gave the five pairs of blankets/ to him. Then Ōdzēᵋstalis went back into the house and/Mōkwētɛlasōgwiᵋlakᵘ came and
sat down.

Then the speaker Lālak·ots!a arose and spoke (5) and said, "It
is nice, chief Mōkwētɛlasōgwiᵋlakᵘ. Why should you/ be ashamed of
your great crest that has just been stolen from you,/ chief, by the
chiefs of the tribes. Look at your great names,/chief. I mean this.
Thank you, chief. Thank you indeed./ I mean this. Now come, chief
ᵋmāxwaq!ōʼɛla and try (10) to lift up the princess of chief A̱ᵋmāxū-
laʼ," said he. Immediately/ chief ᵋmāxwaq!ōʼɛla arose and spoke and
said, /(The one who came from the numaym Nāx·naxūla of the Qwēqᵘsō-
t!ēnoxᵘ he referred to.)/ "Indeed, true is your word, chief Lālak·o-
ts!a. You hit it, chief,/when you named me. I own as my ancestor
at the beginning of my myth ʟ!āʟ!axwas. (15) He had as his child
Ōdzēᵋstalis, and Ōdzēᵋstalis had for his child Yāqałᵋɛnlis./ Oh, if
I should continue to name the great names of my chief-ancestors!/
Now my name is ᵋmāxwaq!ōʼɛla. I mean this, chiefs of the tribes.
This my/work comes from long ago in the great dance that we are
carrying out. I mean this./ Now go on, take care, chiefs, else
we may not get this. Now I will go," (20) said he. Then he started
and stood in the door of the house of A̱ᵋmāxūlał./ Then he uttered
the Dzōnoq!wa cry, "O o o," in the way, it is said, ʟ!āʟ!axwas cried
when he/ went to war. Then he spoke and said, "I have come, chief.
I have come./ I reached here with my great crest, and I try to lift
your princess,/ chief A̱ᵋmāxūlał. I am the one who is from the beginning of myth times ʟ!āʟ!axwas.   He had as his child (25) Ōdzēᵋstalis. There is nothing he could not get. I mean this, chief
A̱ᵋmāxūlał./ Let me be the one to get her so that I may get your princess chief, for this/ chief ʟ!āsotiwalis." Thus he said. Then Ōdzēᵋstalis came/ out of the door of the house carrying five pairs of
blankets./ He spoke and said, "Stay there for a while, chief ᵋmāxwa-
q!ōʼɛla (30) Now come, now come, great chief. You have come, great

q!wālɛnkᵘsōs nūyɛmbalisaqōsxōx ʟ!āʟ!axᵂasdē. G·āxdzǎaqōs wǎwixɛli-
ᵋlaxg·ɪn k·!ēdēʟɛk·, yɪ́dzēsōs ʟ̱ē̱gɛmdzǎqōs, ᵋmāxᵂaq!ōʟɛl. Laᵋmōx
g·āx nēʟᵋēdōs ᵋwālasēx k·!ēsᵋā̱, g·ɪ́gǎmēᵋ. ᵋnē̱ᵋnak·iʟ̄ē, g·āxdzāᵋmōx
ēx·astōliʟa lāxwa t!ɛx·flaxwa k·!ēdēʟaqɛn g·ɪ́gǎmēᵋ, qaxs k·!ēsaaqōs
5 aōmsa, g·ɪ́gǎmēᵋ. ᵋnē̱ᵋnak·iʟ̄ē laᵋmēsɛk· lāʟg·adu sɛk·!axsak· p!ɛlxɛ-
lasgɛm qaēs hasāᵋyōs, g·ɪ́gǎmēᵋ, ᵋnē̱k·ēxs laē̱ ts!ā̱sa sɛk·!axsa p!ɛlxɛ-
lasgɛm lā̱q. Wä, laᵋmē̱ Ōdzēᵋstalisē̱ xᵂē̱lagē̱ʟ lāxa g·ōkwē̱. Wä,g·āxē̱
ᵋmāxᵂaq!ōʟɛla k!wāg·aɛls.

      Wä, lä ʟ̱āxᵋwɛlsē̱ Lālak·ots!axa yāyaq!ɛntēms. Wä, lä yāq!ɛg·a-
10 ᵋʟa. Wä, lä ᵋnē̱k·a: Ādzēk·as, g·ɪ́gǎmēᵋ, ādzēk·atsēs wāʟdɛmōs g·ɪ́-
gǎmēᵋ ᵋmāxᵂaq!ōʟɛlxwa q!ūnālax dōxᵋwaʟɛʟaxwá ᵋwālasaqōs k·!ēsᵋāxōx
ʟ̱!āʟ!axᵂasdē. Wa, gēlak·asᵋla, Wa, gēlaq!anakᵘᵋla, g·ɪ́gǎmēᵋxɛn
ᵋnē̱ᵋnak·iʟ̄ē, g·ɪ́gǎmēᵋ ᵋmāxᵂaq!ōʟɛl, g·āxᵋmē̱ g·āxstoliʟa lāxa t!ɛx·flē̱
k·!ēdēʟasa g·ɪ́gǎmaᵋyē̱ Λᵋmāxᵘ̱laʟa. ᵋnē̱ᵋnak·iʟ̄ē. Wa, gēlag·a, g·ɪ́gǎ-
15 mēᵋ Q!ōmoqā̱ (xa xāmagɛmaᵋyē̱ g·ɪ́gǎmēsa ᵋnɛᵋmē̱mutasa G·ɪ́g·flgɛmasa Gwa-
waē̱noxᵘ gwɛᵋyōs) qaᵋs lālag·aōs g·āg·axstōliᵋlax k·!ēdēʟasa g·ɪ́gǎma-
ᵋyaē̱ Λᵋmāxᵘ̱laʟē̱, naualakwaxalisaasēs g·flg·ālesōs, g·ɪ́gǎmēᵋ, ᵋnē̱k·ē̱.
Wä, hēx·ᵋidamisē̱ Q!ōmoqā̱ ʟ̱āxᵋwɛlsa qaᵋs yāq!ɛg·aᵋʟē̱. Wä. lä ᵋnē̱k·a: Āla,
g·ɪ́gǎmēᵋ, ā̱lasēs wāʟdɛmōs, g·ɪ́gǎmē̱ Lālak·ots!. . Λlaᵋmē̱ naualakwaxa-
20 lisɛn nūyɛmbalisē̱ ᵋnālanokū̱mg·iᵋlakwē̱xa k·!eā̱sᵋwū̱ʟa k·!ēs laasaxa
lāʟa laē̱ʟ lāx g·ōkwas Q!ōmogwayē̱ lāx Ts!ē̱gwats!ē̱. Wä, laᵋmē̱ ʟ̱ōgwalaxa
ᵋnāxwa qaᵋs gwēx·sdɛm yäxʟɛnaxa ᵋyāᵋyag·adelaʟ ʟ̱ɛᵋwa hā̱māxālaʟ ʟ̱ɛᵋwa
ᵋwālasa k·!ōᵋma. Wä, hē̱ᵋmisɛn lāg·iʟa ʟ̱ē̱gadɛs ʟ!ā̱qwag·ila ʟ̱ōᵋ Q!ō-
moqā̱. Wä, nōgwaᵋmis ᵋnālanokū̱mg·iᵋlakwa. Wä, laᵋmē̱sɛn lāʟ, g·ɪ́gǎ-
25 mēᵋ Lālak·ōts! g·āg·axstoliᵋlax Q!ēx·ʟālagäxa k·!ēdēʟas Λᵋmāxᵘ̱laʟa,
ᵋnē̱k·ēxs laē̱ qāsᵋida qaᵋs lē̱ lāxa t!ɛx·flä̱sa g·ōkwas Λᵋmāxᵘ̱laʟ. Wä
lä ʟ̱āxstolsaxa t!ɛx·fla. Wä, lä yāq!ɛg·aᵋʟa. Wä, lä ᵋnē̱k·a: Wäg·fla
hē̱latolē̱ʟɛx g·ɪ́gǎmēᵋ Λᵋmāxᵘ̱laʟ. G·āxᵋmɛn g·āxᵋaʟɛla lā̱ʟ, g·ɪ́gǎmēᵋ,
Nōgwaɛm Q!ōmoqā̱ awā̱nā̱ʟaxɛn nūyɛmbalisē̱ ᵋnālanōkū̱mg·iᵋlakwē̱xa xūngwa-
30 dä̱s Q!ōmoqā̱xɛn lē̱ ʟ̱ē̱qasɛᵋwa. ᵋnē̱ᵋnak·iʟ̄ē, g·āxᵋmɛn wǎwixɛliᵋlaxs k·!ē-

one, (1) dressed in what belonged to the beginning of your myth,
ᴌ!āᴌ!aᵡwas, come great one and try to lift / this great princess with your great name, ᵋmāᵡwaq!ōᴌala. Now/ you have come and
shown your great crest, chief. I mean this, now/ she has moved near
to the door, this princess of my chief, for you are (5) supernatural,
chief. I mean this, these five pairs of blankets will go/for your
breath, chief." Thus he said as he gave the five pairs of blankets/
to him. Then Ōdzēᵋstalis went back into the house, and/ ᵋmāᵡwaq!ō-
ᴌala came and sat down./

        Then arose Lālak·ots!a the speaker. He spoke (10) and said,
"Ah, chief, great is what you said, chief/ ᵋmāᵡwaq!ōᴌala, this what
is often seen, your great crest,/ ᴌ!āᴌ!aᵡwas. Thank you, thank you
indeed, chief./ I mean this, chief ᵋmāᵡwaq!ōᴌala, she has come towards
the door,/ the princess of chief Aᵋmāᵡŭlaᴌ. I mean this. Now come,
chief (15) Q!ōmoqā (The head chief of the numaym G·Ig·flgām of the
Gwawaēnoxᵘ/was the one he meant.) Come, and make come to the door
the princess of chief/Aᵋmāᵡŭlaᴌ. Your ancestors, chief, came down
with supernatural power," said he./ Immediately Q!ōmoqā arose and
spoke. He said, "True/ chief, true is your word, chief Lālak·ots!a.
My ancestor,(20) according to the myth from the beginning, ᵋnālanō-
kŭmg·iᵋlakᵘ came down with supernatural power. There was nothing
that he went for in vain/when he went into the house of Q!ōmogwa
at Ts!ēgwats!e. Then he obtained supernatural power/ all kinds of
dancing paraphernalia, the sea-monster dance, and the killer-whale
dance and the/ great bullhead, and therefore his name was ᴌ!āqwag·ila
and Q!ōmoqā./ I am ᵋnālanōkŭmg·iᵋlakᵘ. Now I will go, chief (25)
Lālak·ots!a, and try to bring to the door Q!ēx·ᴌālaga, the princess
of Aᵋmāᵡŭlaᴌ."/ Thus he said and he started to the door of the house
of Aᵋmāᵡŭlaᴌ./ Then he stood outside of the door and spoke. He said,
"Now/listen well, chief Aᵋmāᵡŭlaᴌ. I have come. I reached you,
chief./ I am Q!ōmoqā. My ancestor at the beginning of my myth was ᵋna-
lanōkŭmg·iᵋlakᵘ. He had for his child (30) Q!ōmoqā and I am named thus.

dēłaq!ōs g·Ꭵgămēᶜ, qa g·āxlag·isō g·āxawɛlsa lāxs g·ōkwaqōs, g·Ꭵgă-
mēᶜ. G·āxᶜmɛn ᶜyālagɛmsg·ada g·Ꭵgămēk·xg·a ʟ!āsotiwalidzēk·xg·as
ʟɛwŭlqōtʟɛg·ōs Q!ēx·ʟālagaxwa k·!ēsēx q!ŭnāla hᵉłaxaakᵘ ʟɛwŭlqōx.
ᶜnᵉᶜnak·iłē. Wa, gēlałlag·ax·ō g·Ꭵgămēᶜ Aᶜmāxŭlał k·!ēdēłaq!ōs,

5   ᶜnēk·ē. Wä, g·āxē Ōdzēᶜstalis g·āxawɛls lāxa t!ɛx·îla dālaxa sɛ-
k·!axsa p!ɛlxɛlasgɛma. Wä, lä yāq!ɛg·aᶜła. Wä, lä ᶜnēk·a: Wäg·a-
āmasʟ ʟaʟaxbalax, g·Ꭵgămēᶜ Q!omoqâ. Wa, gēlag·a g·Ꭵgămēᶜ, g·āxa-
aqōs ᶜnɛᶜmāᶜnakŭla ʟɛᶜwōs naualakwag·iwaᶜyaqōsōx ᶜnālanokŭmg·iᶜla-
kwēx, lāg·iłaōs lag·iłaōs laɛm lâʟg·în k·!ēdēlɛk·. ʟaᶜmēsɛk· lāl-

10   g·ada sɛk·!axsak· p!ɛlxɛlasgɛm qaēs hasāᶜyōs, g·Ꭵgămēᶜ, ᶜnēk·ēxs
laē ts!âsa sɛk·!axsa p!ɛlxɛlasgɛm lāq.

Wä, lä ᶜnēk·ē Ōdzēᶜstalisaq; Hāg·a nēłaxa g·Ꭵgămaᶜyaē ʟ!āso-
tiwalisa qa wäg·isē qādzēłᶜida, ᶜnēk·ēq. Wä, hēx·ᶜidaᶜmisē Q!ō-
mōqâ yālaqwas yālaxʟɛnalas ᶜnālanōkŭmg·iᶜlakᵘᶜwŭłaxa ᶜnēk·ē yîxs

15   hᵉᶜmaē āłē hē ʟâsē ʟ!āsanâᶜyasa t!ɛx·îlās g·ōkwas Aᶜmāxŭlałē:

    1. Lāx·dɛn bēbɛnadzɛlēdzɛms lāx bēbɛnagâwalits lōwa, ha wo.
    2. Lāx·dɛn laēʟɛm lāx g·ōxᵘg·ōkŭlēg·is Q!ōmogwaᶜya, ha wo.
    3. G·āxᶜɛmx·dᵉwÏsɛn ᶜwÏᶜlōʟɛlisaxg·a q!ōmałayuwahak·ats ʟ!ā-
       qwag·ila, ha wo,

20   ᶜnēk·exs g·āxaē gwasōłɛla lāx k!ŭts!ɛdzasa ᶜnʌ̀xwa lēlqwălaʟaᶜya.
Wä, g·îlᶜmisē g·āxᶜaʟɛlaxs laē yāq!ɛg·aᶜła. Wä, lä ᶜnēk·a: G·āx-
ᶜmɛn, g·Ꭵgămēᶜ ʟ!āsotiwalis, laᶜmɛn lâʟa lāxēs gɛnɛmōs, g·Ꭵgămēᶜ.
Laᶜmɛns wäxasōᶜ qɛns qādzēʟalag·i, ᶜnēk·ē.

Wä, hēxᶜidaᶜmisē xwānałᶜidē Lālak·ots!axa yāyaq!ɛntēmsdē

25   qaᶜs hᵉᶜmaē lâł hōsałxa qadzēʟɛmʟē p!ɛlxɛlasgɛma. Wä, laᶜmē Lā-
lak·ots!a dāx·ᶜÏdxa ᶜnɛmxsa p!ɛlxɛlasgɛm qaᶜs ʟɛp!Ïdēq. Wä, lä
ʟēᶜlālasɛᶜwa q!āq!astowē bɛgwānɛm qa lēs k!wäᶜs lāxa nɛxwâła lāx
ʟâdzasas Lālak·ots!a. Wä, lä yāq!ɛg·aᶜła yîx Lālak·ots!a. Wä,
lä ᶜnēk·a: Qâʟaʟɛns g·Ꭵg·ɛgămēs lōlqwălaʟēᶜ lāxwa ʟēgādē qādzē-

30   ʟ!ēnaᶜya. Yŭɛm k·!ēs q!ŭnāla nēłᶜēdōx. Wä, laᶜmɛns g·āg·ēxsila-
xwa g·Ꭵgămaᶜyōx ʟ!āsotiwalisēx. ᶜnᵉᶜnak·iłē, laᶜmēsɛns qādzē-

I mean this. I come to try to lift your princess,(1) chief, that
she may come outside of your house, chief./ I come, sent by this
great chief, ʟ!ās̱otiwalis,/who, as a prince, marries your princess,
Q!ḗx·ʟālaga. Not often comes down by good luck the marriage between
princes./ I mean this. Now, chief Aᵋmāx̆ŭlaⱡ, let your princess come,"
(5) said he. Then Odzēᵋstalis came out of the door carrying/five
pairs of blankets. He spoke and said,/"Stand there for a while,chief
Q!ōmoqā. Now come,chief, you came/together with your supernatural
ancestor, ᵋnālanōkŭmg·iᵋlakᵘ./ Therefore you have now obtained my
princess. Now (10) These five pairs of blankets will go for your
breath, chief." Thus he said/as he gave the five pairs of blankets
to him./

    Then Odzēᵋstalis said to him,"Go now and tell chief ʟ!ās̱otiwa-
lis/that he may be married now," said he to him. Immediately Q!ōmo-
qā/sang the sacred song of ᵋnālanōkŭmg·iᵋlakᵘ, while (15) he was
still standing outside of the door of the house of Aᵋmāx̆ŭlaⱡ:/

    1. " I was carried down to the lowest world. Ha wo./

    2. I was taken down into the house of Q!ōmogwa. Ha wo./

    3. So I obtained everything, this wealth-bringer of/Copper-
        Maker. Ha wo."/

(20) Thus he said as he came towards the place where were sitting
all the tribes./ As soon as he reached them he spoke and said, "I
have come,/chief ʟ!ās̱otiwalis. Now I got your wife, chief./ Now we
are told to get married," said he./

    Immediately Lālak·ots!a, the speaker, got ready,(25) for he
was the one who was to count the marriage gift blankets. Then/Lā-
lak·ots!a took one pair of blankets and spread it out. Then/the
tally keepers were called and they went and sat down near/the place
where Lālak·ots!a was standing Then spoke Lālak·ots!a and/he said,
"Now, chiefs of the tribes,in this what is called a great wedding,(30)
this is not often shown. Now we shall treat as a chief/this chief
ʟ!ās̱otiwalis. I mean this. Now we shall get married (1) with this,"

ʟasēqai, ᵋnēk·ōxs laē x·ᶠlxsayap!ɛntsa ᵋnɛmxsa p!ɛlxɛlasgɛm lāxa

hёʟᵋa g·āx k!wāᶜs lāx ʟ!āsaᶜlasas Lālak·ots!a. Wä, laᶜmēda q!ā-

q!astowē bɛgwānɛm hāsɛla ᵋnēk·a, ᵋnɛmxsa, maᶜʟɛxsa, yūduxuxsa, mō-

xsa, lastâai. Hёɛm hōsalatsa q!āq!astowē bɛgwānɛmqēxs laē Lālak·ots!a

5   x·ᶠlxsayap!ɛndālasa p!ɛlxɛlasgɛm lāxa hёʟᵋa. Wä. g·ᶠlᶜmisē sɛk·!axsa

p!ɛlxɛlasgɛm la x·ᶠlxsayap!ēxa hёʟᵋäxs laē taōdaēʟas lāx g·ōkwas

Áᶜmāxŭlaʟē. Wä, lä ēt!ēdē Lālak·ots!a dāx·ᶜldxa ᵋnɛmxsa p!ɛlxɛlas-

gɛma. Wä, lä ᵋnēk·a, dālaxēqai lāxaē x·ᶠlxsayap!ɛndālasa sɛk·!axsa

p!ɛlxɛlasgɛm lāxa ōgŭᶜlaᶜmē hёʟᵋa. Wä, lä Lālak·ots!a ᵋnēk·a la-

10   stâai. Wä, lēda q!āq!astowē bɛgwānɛm ᵋnēk·a la maᶜʟtsokwai. Wä,

laᶜmē hёx·säɛm wāʟdɛms Lālak·ots!a, Dālaxēqai, lāxa p!ɛlxɛlasgɛm.

Wä, āʟᶜmisē gwāʟ dālaxaxs laē ᵋwIᶜlg·ᶠlsa maᶜʟp!ɛnyag·i p!ɛlxɛlas-

gɛm daaxᵘs. (Maᶜʟē ʟēgɛmas ʟōᶜ qādzēʟɛm.) Wä, la Lālak·ots!a dā-

x·ᶜldxa ᵋnɛmxsa p!ɛlxɛlasgɛm. Wä, lä yāq!ɛg·aᶜʟa. Wä, lä ᵋnēk·a:

15   Laᶜmē gwāʟxa maᶜʟp!ɛnyag·ä' p!ɛlxɛlasgɛm daākwasg·ín g·Igāmēk·, yíxg·a

ʟ!āsotiwalisɛk·. ᵋnēnak·iʟē, g·Ig·ɛgāmēs lēɛlqwalaʟai. Nōsaᶜwi-

sɛnsax wāʟdɛmaxɛns gwēᶜnakŭlasēx lāxwa ōgwaqāʟax ᶜwāᶜwalatsila gā-

gak·!a qaxg·íns âᶜmēk· nɛgɛʟᶜɛnēx t!ɛx·Ilaᶜya qɛns nɛgɛʟᶜɛnēsɛᶜwa

yísɛns awānâᶜyē. ᵋnēᶜnak·iʟē. Laᶜmɛn ʟâg·ᶠlIʟasēqai lāx k·!ēdēʟasa

20   g·Igāmaᶜyē Áᶜmāxŭlaʟ, ᵋnēk·ōxs laē x·ᶠlxsayap!ɛndālasa sɛk·!axsa

p!ɛlxɛlasgɛm lāxa hёʟᵋaxa la taōdaēʟas lāx g·ōkwas Áᶜmāxŭlaʟē. Wä,

la maᶜʟp!ɛnyag·i p!ɛlxɛlasgɛma ʟâg·alIlɛmasēx k·!ēdēʟas Áᶜmāxŭlaʟ.

Wä, g·ᶠlᶜmisē ᶜwIᶜlēda maᶜʟp!ɛnyag·i ʟâg·ᶠlēlɛm p!ɛlxɛlasgɛma laas

Lālak·ōts!a dāx·ᶜldxa ᵋnɛmxsa p!ɛlxɛlasgɛm. Wä, lāxaē yāq!ɛg·aᶜʟa.

25   Wä, lä ᵋnēk·a: Qãʟ, qãʟaxg·ín lālōʟ!ɛᶜmēk· lāxa k·!ēdēʟē qa laᶜmēs

qãgē g·āxɛns g·Ig·ɛgāmēs lēɛlqwälaʟēᶜ qãnsō lāʟ lax g·ōkwasg·ín g·I-

gāmēk· lāxg·a ʟ!āsotiwalisɛk·. ᵋnēᶜnak·iʟē, laᶜmɛn ʟēᶜlalasēqaʟ,

ᵋnēk·ɛxs laē x·ᶠlxsayap!ālasa sɛk·!axsa p!ɛlxɛlasgɛm lāxa hёʟᵋa. Wä,

lä, hёx·säɛm gwēk·!āla. Áʟᶜmisē gwāʟɛxs laē ᶜwIᶜlg·ɛlsa lak·!ɛndē

30   p!ɛlxɛlasgɛm ʟēᶜlalayâ. Wä laɛm sɛk·!āp!ɛnyag·i hãgawēda p!ɛlxɛ-

lasgɛm.

said he as he threw one pair of blankets on the shoulders of/ one
young man who came and sat down in front of Lālak·ots!a. Then the/
tally keeper said aloud,"One pair, two pairs, three pairs, four
pairs,/ ten!" (This is what the tally keepers count while Lālak·ots!a
(5) is throwing the blankets on the shoulders of the young man,) and
when five pairs of/ blankets were on his shoulders, the young man
took them into the house of/ Aᵋmāxūlaɫ. Then Lālak·cts!a took
again one pair of blankets/ and said: "Carry this now," and he threw
on the shoulders/ of another young man five pairs of blankets. Then
Lālak·ots!a said, "Ten!" (10) and the tally keeper said, "Twenty!"/
Lālak·ots!a continued saying "Carry this now," about the blankets /
and he only stopped saying "Carry this," when the two hundred blankets were "all off the ground" and/ carried up. (These are two
names for the wedding gift.) Then Lālak·ots!a/took one pair of
blankets and he spoke and said,(15)"Now the two hundred blankets are
finished which were carried by this my chief, this/ ʟ!āsotiwalis. I
mean this, chiefs of the tribes. Is this not our/ saying that we
act thus in the various ways of great works,/ when we are trying to
get a wife, for we are only following the road made for us to walk
on/ by our ancestors. I mean this. Now I lift from the floor with
this the princess of (20) chief Aᵋmāxūlaɫ." Thus he said and put
five pairs of/ blankets on the shoulders of a young man who took them
into the house of Aᵋmāxūlaɫ./ Now there were two hundred blankets to
lift off from the floor the princess of Aᵋmāxūlaɫ./ As soon as all
the two hundred blankets for lifting her up were taken in,/ Lāla-
k·ots!a took one pair of blankets. Then he spoke (25) and said,
"Indeed it is true that I try to get the princess to/ walk among us,
chiefs of the tribes, when we go to the house of my chief/ ʟ!āsoti-
walis. I mean this, with this I call her,"/ said he, as he put the
five pairs of blankets on the shoulders of a young man./ He continued saying this and he only stopped when one hundred (30) blankets
were all taken away as the means of calling. Now in all there were
five hundred/ blankets.

Wä, la⁵mē Lālak·ots!a nēɫaxa g·ῑg·ɛgᾱma⁵yaxs la⁵mē gwāɫa.

Wa, la⁵mēsɛns ᾶɛmɫ ōlastogwaɛlsʟ, ⁵nēk·ēxs laē k!wᾱg·aɛlsa.

Wä, g·āxē Ōdzē⁵stalis g·āxawɛls lāxa t!ɛx·fläsa g·ōkwas ᾶ⁵maxūlaɫē. Wä, lä yāq!ɛg·a⁵ɫa. Wä, lä ⁵nēk·a: Wa, laɛms gwāɫa, la-

5 dzēɛms gwāɫa, g·ῑg·ɛgᾱmē⁵. Wᾱg·a hēlsɛx, g·ῑg·ɛgᾱmē⁵, lāq!ama-
aqōs lᾶɫg·ada k·!ēdēɫɛk· lāxg·a Q!ēx·ʟᾱlagak· lāxg·a k·!ēdēɫg·as-
g·ῑn g·ῑgᾱmēk· qɛn lālag·i laēʟ ʟē⁵lāla qag·a gɛnɛmg·aōs, g·ῑgᾱ-
mē⁵ ʟ!ᾱsotiwalis, ⁵nēk·exs laē laēʟē Ōdzē⁵stalisē lāxa g·ōkwas
ᾶ⁵māxūlaɫ. Wä, k·!ēst!ē gaēʟɛlaxs g·āxaē xwɛlaqawɛlsa. Wä, la-

10 ⁵mē g·ālabēs ᾶ⁵maxūlaɫē ʟō⁵ Q!ēx·ʟᾱlagaxa pāq!ᾱpɛlä Sɛ⁵waxa q!ɛ-
yōxwē ʟ!āqwa. Wä, la ɛlxʟᾱlaxa g·ῑg·ɛgᾱmᾶ⁵yē P!ᾱsɛlaɫ xa xᾱmagɛ-
ma⁵yē g·ῑgᾱmēsa ⁵nē⁵mēmutasa Laᾱlax·s⁵ɛndayu, wä hē⁵misē K·!ᾶdēxa
gagɛmpas ᾶ⁵māxūlaɫē. Wä, lä q!wᾱg·aɛls lāx ʟ!ᾱsanᾶ⁵yasa t!ɛx·fläsa
g·ōkwē. Wä, lä yāq!ɛg·a⁵ɫē Ōdzē⁵stalisē. Wä, lä ⁵nēk·a: Gwāɫlas

15 hē gwēsē g·ῑgᾱmē⁵ ʟ!ᾱsotiwalis ʟō⁵s g·ῑgᾱmē⁵ ʟ!āqoʟas, wä, sōdzē-
⁵mēs g·ῑg·ɛgᾱmēs lēlqwᾱlaʟai . Wᾱg·adzᾶ q!wᾱg·aɛlsɛx. G·āx⁵ɛmg·as
gɛnɛmg·ōs g·ῑgᾱmē⁵ ʟ!ᾱsotiwalis. G·āx⁵ɛmk· q!wᾱlɛnkwa. Laɛm q!wᾱ-
lɛnkᵘsg·a Sɛ⁵wak·xg·ada wīwɛnxɛk· ʟ!āqwa lᾶʟ bɛgwānɛm, ⁵nēk·ē. Wä,
g·āx⁵mēda q!ēnɛmē hᾱ⁵yāɫ⁵a ⁵mō⁵wɛlsɛlaxa yūduxᵘp!ɛnyag·i p!ɛlxɛlas-

20 gɛma. Wä, g·fl⁵misē ⁵wi⁵lg·aɛlsa laᾱs Odzē⁵stalisē yāq!ɛg·a⁵ɫa. Wä,
lä ⁵nēk·a: Wᾱg·fɫla g·ῑgᾱmē⁵ P!ᾱsɛlaɫ lāxōs k·!ēs⁵ᾶqōs qaxs k·!ē-
saēx nūnaxᾶlag·fn ʟᾱxwᾱɫaasɛk· ʟɛ⁵wōs hōsaqōs ʟᾱxwᾱɫaasa, g·ῑgᾱmē⁵,
⁵nēk·ē. Wä, lä P!ᾱsɛlaɫē dāx·⁵ῑdxa ʟ!āqwa dāaxᵘs Q!ēx·ʟᾱlaga. Wä,
lä yāq!ɛg·a⁵ɫa. Wä, lä ⁵nēk·a: Qᾱʟ, qᾱʟaxs ⁵nēgɛmaēx lāxɛns wiwōmp-

25 ⁵wūɫa qa k·!eᾶsēs alēg·fntsɛ⁵wɛns lāxa ʟēxs⁵ala⁵yᾶq qa ⁵gwayi⁵lä-
lats lāxwa gᾶ⁵gak·!ax. Wä, la⁵mēsɛn q!ᾱmx·ts!ēxēs ⁵nāxwayōs gwa-
yi⁵lälasa g·āxbɛndālaq. Wä, lɛn k·!eᾶs dōgūɫ alēg·ɛnda⁵yusaq.
Wä, las k·!eᾶs ʟ!ɛlēwēsɛ⁵wa. Wa, gēlak·as⁵la g·ῑg·ɛgᾱmē⁵. Laɛms
hēɫaxamasa. ⁵nē⁵nak·iɫē g·ῑg·ɛgᾱmē⁵ awasᾶɫ ʟ!ᾱsotiwalis ʟɛ⁵wōx

30 ᾶdzäx ʟ!āqoʟasax. Wᾱg·a dōx⁵widɛxg·fn daᾱkūk· lāxg·ada ʟēgadɛk·
g·aɛm Sɛ⁵wak·! . Laɛmk· sayabalag·as gɛnɛmg·ōs, g·ῑgᾱmē⁵ ʟ!ᾱso-

(1) Then Lālak·ots!a told the chiefs that it was finished./
"Now we shall just wait on the ground," said he and he sat down./
Then Ōdzēᶜstalis came out of the door of the house of Kᵉma-
xūlaȴ./ He spoke and said, "Now you have finished, (5) you have
finished a great thing, chiefs. Now sit down well, chiefs./ Now
you have got this princess Q!ēx·ᴸālaga, the princess/ of my chief
here. I will go in and call this your wife, chief/ ᴸ!āsotiwalis."
Thus he said, and Ōdzēᶜstalis went into the house of/Kᵉmāxūlaȴ. He
was not long inside when he came out again (10) leading Kᵉmāxūlaȴ
and Q!ēx·ᴸālaga, who held lying on her chest Sɛᶜwa, the/ expensive
copper, and behind them came chief P!asɛlaȴ (the/head chief of the
numaym Lāālax·sᶜɛndayu) and also K·!ā̀dē,/ the grandfather of Kᵉmāxūlaȴ. Then they stood outside the door of the/ house, and Ōdzēᶜstalis spoke and said, "Do not sit (15) this way, chief ᴸ!āsoti-
walis, and you, chief ᴸ!āqoᴸas, and you, great/ chiefs of the tribes.
Now go on and stand up. Now has come/ the wife of your chief ᴸ!ā-
sotiwalis. She comes dressed up. Now/ she is dressed with this
Sɛᶜwa, this Wīwûnx copper[1], to you, man," said he./ Then many young
men came who carried out three hundred blankets, (20) and when they
were all on the ground, Ōdzēᶜstalis spoke and/ said, "Now go on,
chief P!asɛlaȴ, according to your privilege, for it is not/ in
doubt my standing and your standing, chief,"/ said he. Then P!a-
sɛlaȴ took the copper carried by Q!ēx·ᴸālaga./ Then he spoke and
said, "Indeed, indeed, for this was told to our (25) ancestors
for we add on nothing new to what we were advised to/ do when we
try to get a wife. Now I notice everything/ that we are doing
coming up to this point. There were no new ways added on/and nothing was forgotten. Now thank you, chiefs, you/ have done well.
I mean this, chiefs, father and son, ᴸ!āsotiwalis and (30) great
ᴸ!āqoᴸas. Now look at this that I am holding, this which has the
name/ Sɛᶜwa. Now it is the return gift of your wife, chief ᴸ!ā-

---

1.) This designation of the copper is not clear.

tiwalis, yîsg·a Sεᶜwak·. Wa, gēlag·a g·Ǐgămēᶜ ʟ!ăqoʟas, dāx·ᶜǏd-
qεk·, ᶜnēk·ē. Wä, hëx·ᶜidaᶜmisē ʟ!ăqoʟas la qaᶜs dāx·ᶜidēxa
ʟ!āqwa. ·Wä, lä yāq!εg·aᶜƚa. Wä, lä ᶜnēk·a dōqümēxa ʟ!āqwa ; Wa,
gēladzēla Sεᶜwa, q!ālax·st!aakuᶜεmsaxg·în sēxwätâyēk· wǐnaxa g·Ǐ-
5   gămaᶜyē Xᶜmāx̣ülaƚ qεn ʟ!ăqoʟēxsâ ᶜwālasas Sεᶜwa,⸰ᶜnēᶜnak·iƚē, g·Ǐ-
g·εgămēs lēεlqwālaʟai. G·āxᶜεmg·ada ʟēgadεk·, g·āxᶜεmg·a Sεᶜwak·.
Laεm sayabalayusa g·Ǐgămaᶜyē Xᶜmāx̣ülaƚ qaᶜēs k·!ēdēƚē Q!ēx·ʟālaga
lāxwa k·!ēsēx q!ūᶜnēnaᶜya sāyabaläxsa ƚaōxüla ʟ!āqwa. Hëεm ᶜwaᶜlē
wāƚdεmasēxs laē bεlasōs P!asεlaƚē qa q!wēƚᶜidamawēsʟēs. Wä, g·iƚ-
10 ᶜmisē q!wēƚᶜēda laas ēdzaqwa yāq!εg·aᶜƚē P!āsεlaƚaxs laē dālaxa
ᶜnεmxsa p!εlxεlasgεma. Wä, lä ᶜnēk·a: Qäʟaxs hëᶜmaēx gwēg·iᶜlatsa
ᶜnεmōkwē lāxa xεnʟyεnx̣ubasaxēs k·!ēdēƚa g·Ǐgămaᶜyä. ᶜnēᶜnak·iƚē
g·Ǐg·εgămēs lēεlqwālaʟē. Hëεm lāg·iƚas q!ēnεma ētaxasa g·Ǐg·ε-
gămaᶜyaxs wāx·aē nānaxts!εᶜwaxg·a lax gwēx·ᶜidaatsg·ada g·Ǐgă-
15 măk· yîxg·a Xᶜmāx̣ülaƚεk·. ᶜnēᶜnak·iƚē g·Ǐg·εgămēᶜ awasâl ʟ!āso-
tiwalis, sōdzēᶜmits ʟ!āqoʟas. Laεm aōxʟaatsēs gεnεmōs g·Ǐgămēᶜ
ʟ!āsotiwalisxg·ada yüdux̣up!εnyag·εk· p!εlxεlasgεma. Wä, laᶜmēsεk·
lāƚg·ada ʟēgεmk·. Laεms ʟēgadεƚ Äwidē, g·Ǐgămēᶜ. Wa, gēlag·a
lāxg·as gεnεmg·ōs g·Ǐgămēᶜ ʟ!āsotiwalis qaᶜs laōs näᶜnaku lāxēs
20 g·ōkwaōs, ᶜnēk·ē. Wä, hëx·ᶜidaᶜmisē lēda q!ēmâla g·Ǐg·εgămēᶜ
qaᶜs lē q!wäᶜstālax Q!ēx·ʟālaga qaᶜs lē taōts lāx g·ōkwas Mâᶜnaküla qaxs häē g·aēʟεlē ʟ!āsotiwalisē g·ōkwas.

Wä, g·îlᶜmisē laēʟēda g·äxsa la qâyōdεx Q!ēx·ʟālaga laē
Q!ēx·ʟālaga äxk·!ālasōᶜ qaᶜs lē k!wanōdzεlǏƚax ʟ!āsotiwalisaxs
25 âx·säᶜmaē t!ēg·iƚ lāxēs g·ōkwaxs laē qadzēʟēda ᶜnāx̣wa lēεlqwā-
laʟēᶜ qaē. Wä, g·āxē ᶜwǏᶜla hōqüwεls lāxa g·ōkwa qayōdεx·dē
g·äxsä Q!ēx·ʟālaga. Lāx·daᶜxwaē x̣wēlaqa k!üsᶜεlsa lāx ʟ!āsanâ-
ᶜyas g·ōkwas Mâᶜnaküla.

sotiwalis, (1) this Sεᵋwa. Now come, chief ʟ!āqoⱢas and take it,"/ said he. And immediately ʟ!āqoⱢas went and took the/ copper. Then he spoke and said, looking at the face of the copper:/ "Now come, great Sεᵋwa. It seems that you know that I am paddling upward to make war on chief (5) Aᵋmāxŭlaⱡ, for me to obtain a copper of the size of Sεᵋwa. I mean this, chiefs/ of the tribes. Come now, this one that has a name. Come now, Sεᵋwa./ Now it is the return gift of chief Aᵋmāxŭlaⱡ, on account of his princess Q!ēx·Ɫālaga,/ in this that is not often done, the return gift of an expensive copper." This was the end/ of his speech, for he was stopped by P!asεlaⱡ that he might be quiet for a while. When (10) he stopped speaking P!āsεlaⱡ spoke again, holding/ one pair of blankets. He said, "Indeed, this is the way it is done/ by one of those who really love their daughter, a chief. I mean this,/ chiefs of the tribes. This is the reason why many times the chiefs fall back,/ who try to imitate this that is now being done by this chief., (15) this Aᵋmāxŭlaⱡ. I mean this, chiefs, father and son,/ ʟ!āsotiwalis and you, great ʟ!āqoⱢas. Now this is the carrying strap of your wife, chief/ʟ!āsotiwalis, these three hundred blankets. Now/this name will go. Now your name will be Awidē, chief. Now come/to your wife, chief ʟ!āsotiwalis, and go home to your (20) house," said he. Immediately the many chiefs went/and stood around Q!ēx·Ɫālaga, and they took her to the house of/Mâᵋnākŭla, for ʟ!āsotiwalis was staying in his house./

As soon as the real chiefs had gone in, walking home with Q!ēx·Ɫālaga, then/ Q!ēx·Ɫālaga was asked to sit down by the side of ʟ!āsotiwalis, (25) for he had just been lying on his back in his house while the marriage was arranged by all the tribes/ for him. Then came out of the house again all the chiefs who had taken home/ Q!ēx·Ɫālaga and they sat down again outside of the/ house of Mâᵋnākŭla./

Wä, g·îlᵋmisē ᵋwîᵋla la k!ûts!ᴇsa laas yāq!ᴇg·aᵋ𝑥ē ʟ!āqo-
ʟas. Wä, lä ᵋnēk·a: Wa, gēlag·a g·îg·ᴇgämēs lēᴇlqwälaʟai, Wä-
g·adzâx·îns gāgasōd mōlasg·ada ᵋwälasä wä𝑥dᴇmxa g·îgämaᵋyaē ʟ!ā-
sotiwalisa, ᵋnēk·ē. Wä, hëx·ᵋidaᵋmisē nâgadē dâqâlasa ᵋnēk·ē:

5   1. Wâ â huwa yēya a a, wâ hu wa a a ä.
         Ladzēᵋmaha laōx yawix·îlahadzēʟᴇns g·îgämahaᵋyēx lēlqwä-
         lahaʟai.
         Wâ â wâ huwä.

     2. Wâ â huwa yēya a a, wâ hu wa a a ä.

10   Ladzēᵋmaha laōx ētalᴇhedzēʟa ʟēla𝑥ᵋwahadzē𝑥xa ᵋwîᵋwᴇlsgᴇ-
         ᵋmahakwēx lēlqwälahaʟai, anaxʟahän g·îqag·iwaᵋyahänxa
         ʟ̣ōgwalayaxa q!ōmä𝑥ag·ilahayaxa bâxûlalî𝑥iladzēyahax
         yaēxʟahändzēyasᴇn ōmpk·asᵋowaxa q!ülēxʟēyahadzēyaʟax
         G·îxsēᵋstalîsᴇmēᵋdzēs g·îgämaᵋyas lēlqwälahaʟai.

15   Wâ â wâ huwä.

     3. Wâ â huwa yēya a a, wâ hu wa a a ä.
         Ladzēyahamähän ʟ̣ēqayaha𝑥tsᴇn ʟ̣ēgᴇmdzēyahasᴇn wiwōmpdzē-
         yahaxaha q!ülēxʟēyahadzēya Yāqoʟadzē, Yāqoʟasᴇmēdzē,
         ʟ!āqoʟadzē, ʟ!āqoʟasᴇmēdzē, ʟ!āsodēts ᵋnāladzē, ʟ!ā-
20   sotiwalidzē, Bᵋwanuxᵘdzēs g·îgämaᵋyas lēlqwälaʟa.Yū-
         ᴇmya ʟ̣ēᵋʟᴇgᴇmdzēyasᴇn wiwōmpdzēya qaᵋs lēlqwälaʟai.
         Wâ â wâ huwä.

Wä, laᴇm yîxwē ʟ!āqoʟasē dālax Sᴇᵋwaxa ʟ!āqwa. Wä, g·îlᵋmisē
q!ülbēda q!ᴇmdᴇm laē yāq!ᴇg·aᵋ𝑥ē ʟ!āqoʟas. Wä, lä, ᵋnēk·a:
25   Qäʟ, qäʟag·ada ᵋwälasᴇk· ʟ!āqwa g·âxᵋᴇmk· g·âxᵋaʟᴇla läxa g·î-
gämaᵋyē ʟ!āsotiwalisē. ᵋnēᵋnak·i𝑥ē g·îg·ᴇgämēs lēᴇlqwälaʟēᵋ.
Wäg·a mōsgᴇᵋmakᵘ Kwäkûg·u𝑥, wäg·a q!ap!ēg·aᴇlsᴇx qa hawasiᵋlä-
laōsaxwa aōxʟaasēx p!ᴇlxᴇlasgᴇm qaᵋs wûsēx·ᵋidaōsasōx läxwa lē-
ᴇlqwälaʟaᵋyēx, ᵋnēk·ē. Wä, hëx·ᵋidaᵋmisē hawasiᵋlälasᴇᵋwa aō-
30   xʟaasē p!ᴇlxᴇlasgᴇma yîsa q!ēq!aq!asto bēbᴇgwänᴇmsa lēlqwälaʟaᵋyē.
Wä, g·îlᵋmisē gwä𝑥a laas Lälak·ots!axa yāyaq!ᴇntēmsdē ʟ̣âxᵋwᴇls

As soon as they had all sat down, ʟ!áqoʟas spoke/ and said,
"Now come, chiefs of the tribes./ Let us sing the grandfather's
song, to thank for the great words, for chief/ʟ!ásotiwalis," said
he. And immediately the song leader took up the song which said,/

(5)   1. Wâ â huwa yēya a a, wâ hu wa a a ā./

          Now the great one will move, our great chief,/tribes./
          Wâ,â wâ huwä./

      2. Wâ â huwa yēya a a, wâ hu wa a a ā./

(10)   Now the great one will invite all/the tribes, for my
          ancestor, the chief,/ obtained as his treasure the
          Wealth Maker, the great Rising Property/of my excellent
          father whose own name will be/G·Ixsēᵉstalisamēᵉ, the
          great chief of the tribes./

(15)   Wâ â wâ huwä./

      3. Wâ â huwa, yēya a a, wâ hu wa a a ā./

          Now I shall call the great name of my forefathers,/
          whose own name is the great Yāqoʟas, the great Yā-
          qoʟasɛmēᵉ,/ the great ʟ!áqoʟas, the great ʟ!áqoʟa-
          sɛmēᵉ, the great ʟ!ásōdēts ᵉnāla, (20) the great
          ʟ!ásotiwalis, the great Êwanuxᵘdzē, the chief of the
          tribes./These are the names of my great ancestors, for
          you, tribes./

          Wâ â wâ huwä./

Then ʟ!áqoʟas danced carrying Sɛᵉwa, the copper, and as soon as/
the song was at an end ʟ!áqoʟas spoke and said, (25) "Indeed it
is true, this great copper came. Now it came up to/ chief ʟ!á-
sotiwalis. I mean this, chiefs of the tribes./ Go on, four Kwā-
g·uⱡ tribes, assemble and count/ the packstrap blankets to put a
belt about those tribes,"/said he, and at once were counted the (30)
packstrap blankets by the tally keepers of the tribes./As soon as
they finished L!álak·ots!a, the speaker, arose (1) and spoke,

qaᶜs yāq!ɛg·aᶜⱡē dālaxa ᶜnɛmxsa p!ɛlxɛlasgɛm. Wä, lä ᶜnēk·aː Laᶜmɛn wǐsēk·aⱡōⱡ, g·Ig·ɛgāmēᶜ lāxōx gwälasēx lāqᵘxwa ᶜnālɛnxayōxsɛns
gāgak·!aēnaᶜyē(laqōxs mōxᶜwidalaēxɛns gāgak·!aēnaᶜyēx k!wāsaxala
ōgǔᶜla lāxa q!āq!āk!wa Ɫɛᶜwa dāx·sidzɛndē Ɫɛᶜwa xwēsa. Wä, yuwiᶜ-
5 staɛm ōgǔqāⱡa lāxwa lāqɛns gwāⱡ wāⱡdɛma ᶜwāᶜwalatsilax k·!ēsᶜoⱡ-
t!ɛnt qādzēⱢa. Wä, laɛm k·!eâs qautēx·a lāqᵘ qaēda g·Igāmaᶜyē
Xᶜmāxǔlaⱡaxs sayabalaas Sɛᶜwaⱡlāxēsnɛgǔmpē Ɫ!āsotiwalisē. Wä,
laɛm nēnaq!ɛxᶜēd lāxēq. K·!eâs la q!ēq!aēgɛma. Wä, lālasa ōgǔ-
qāⱡaxa qadzēⱢɛmxa qādzēⱢāxēs gɛnɛmē qaᶜs qautēx·sɛᶜwēⱡtsēs nɛgum-
10 pē. Wä, lāⱡ Ɫāk·ɛyālaⱡxa Ɫ!āqwa. Hēɛm gäⱡa k·!ēs gǔnasɛᶜwa qa-
dzēⱢɛm p!ɛlxɛlasgɛm. Wä, lālasa qaqadzēⱢɛma. Hēɛm k·!ēs q!ǔnā-
la hēⱡaxē qaxs k·!ēsaē q!ǔnāla qāqotēnɛmasɛᶜwa qaqadzēⱢayu. Wä
lālasaxa ⱢāⱢēk·ɛwaxa p!ɛlxɛlasgɛm qaᶜs qadzēⱢɛmbuⱡa. Wä, hēɛm
q!āmäg·ila qa q!āmäsēs sāsɛm Ɫɛᶜwēs gɛnɛmē qaxs âᶜmaē la ᶜwIᶜla
15 aēdaaqēda qadzēⱢɛmbuⱡa p!ɛlxɛlasgɛmxs laē gānuⱡᶜida lāx ēxnogwa-
däs. ᶜnēᶜnak·iⱡē mōxᶜwidaⱡōx.) Wä, laᶜmēsɛn wǐsēk·asg·ada ᶜnɛm-
xsak· p!ɛlxɛlasgɛm lâⱢ, g·Igāmēᶜ Ɫ!āqwadzē qaxs ⱡāxǔmx·ɛidaaqōs,
g·Igāmēᶜ, ᶜnēk·ē Lālak·ots!a. Wä, la häᶜstaɛm gwēk·!ālaxs laē
ᶜyāqwasa p!ɛlxɛlasgɛmē lāxa lēlqwälalaᶜyē. Wä, g·Ilᶜmisē ɛlāq
20 ᶜwIᶜlxtō ᶜyāxᶜwitsɛᶜwa Mamalēleqāla, laas yāq!ɛg·aᶜⱡē Ɫ!āqoⱢas
dālax SɛᶜwaxaⱢ!āqwa. Wä, lä ᶜnēk·aː Wäg·a hōⱢēlaxg·In wāⱡdɛm-
Lɛk· g·Ig·ɛgamēs lēlqwälaⱢēᶜxɛn lāg·iⱡa mōlasg·a Sɛᶜwak·xg·ada
sayabalayugwax Ɫ!āsotiwalisa. ᶜnēᶜnak·iⱡē, g·Ig·ɛgāmēs lēlqwä-
laⱢēᶜ. Wä, lä dzōxwäⱡas Sɛᶜwa. Wä, lä ᶜnēk·aː Ɫ!ēnä qaᶜs Mama-
25 lēleqālai,Ɫ!ēnä qaᶜs ᶜnɛmgēsai, Ɫ!ēnä qaᶜs Ⱡāwits!ēsai, Ɫ!ēnä qaᶜs
Maämtag·ilai. Laᶜmɛn qāsōsg·a Sɛᶜwak· qaᶜs mōsgɛᶜmakᵘ lēɛlqwälaⱢai,
yInⱢaxg·In Ɫ!āsotiwalisēk·. ÂlaxutⱢɛn lāxutⱢɛxg·a Sɛᶜwa, ᶜnēk·ēxs

holding one pair of blankets. He said, "Now/I put a belt on you,
chiefs, for in this way it is done in the greatest way of our/
wooing." (For there are four ways of wooing,going downward,/dif-
ferent from the "obtaining of a slave,"[1] and "taking hold of the
foot,"[1] and the "exchange marriage."[1] And all of these (5) are
different from what we are now finishing, that we call the "great
bringing out of the crest/in marriage." Now there is no repay-
ing of the marriage debt in this, for Chief/Aᵋmax̣ulaⱡ gave as a return gift Sᵋwa to his son-in-law,ʟ!asotiwalis./ Now this is
settled after/this. There is nothing now to trouble him. And there
is another way/of marrying, when a man marries his wife and the
marriage debt is repaid by the father-in-law.(10) Now the copper
will stand as a mast, for a long time are not paid back the marriage gift/blankets. Then there is the small marriage. This does
not often/come out well for the little marriage debt of the little
marriage is not often rapaid./ Then there is borrowing of blankets
for the pretended marriage, and/this brings disgrace to the children and wife, for all just (15) go back, the pretended marriage
gift blankets when it gets evening, to their owners./ I mean,
these are the four ways.) "Now I shall put on the belt with this
one pair/of blankets on you, chief ʟ!aqwadzē,for you had hard work,/
chief," said Lālak·ots!a,and he continued to say the same as he/gave
out the blankets to the tribes. When they were nearly (20) all given
away to the Mamaleleqala,then spoke ʟ!aqoʟas/holding the copper Sᵋwa.
He said, "Now listen to my word,/chiefs of the tribes. This is the
reason that I am glad of this Sᵋwa,/the return gift to ʟ!asotiwalis.
I mean this, chiefs of the tribes,"/and he held up Sᵋwa and said,
"Grease for you, Mamaleleqala,(25) grease for you, ᵋnɛmgis, grease
for you, Lāwits!ēs, grease for you,/Maǎmtag·ila. Now I promise a
feast with this Sᵋwa, for you, four tribes,/I who am ʟ!asotiwalis.
Indeed, I shall sell Sᵋwa," said he (1) as he laid it down in the

1) Terms for different forms of marriages.

laē pāx̣ᵉalị̑ɫɛq lāxa ōgwiᵉwalị̑ɫē. Wä, wäg·a äx̣ᵉēdnōküqɛk·, ᵉnē-
k·ēxs laē bᾶs qaᵉs lē k!wäg·ị̑lị̑ɫa.

Wä, lä ʟᾳ̈x̣ᵉwalị̑ɫē g·ị̑gämaᵉyasa Mamalēleqala yị̑x Gᴜ̈yōɫelasē
qaᵉs lē dāg·alị̑ɫax Sɛᵉwa qaᵉs yāq!ɛg·aᵉɫē. Wä, lä ᵉnēk·ē: G·äx̣-
5 ᵉmɛn dāx̣·ᵉidɛxg·as ʟ!ạ̄qwag·ōs, g·ị̑gämēᵉ. Laᵉmēsɛn yäq!ɛntōɫ
ʟɛᵉwᴜ̈n g·ōkulōtēx qaēs wᾶɫdɛmōs g·ị̑gämēᵉ ʟ!ạ̄qoʟas, ᵉnēk·ēxs laē
k!wäg·alị̑ɫa.

Wä, laᵉmē Lᾱlak·ots!a ētị̑ēda ᵉyax̣ᵉwitsa p!ɛlx̣ɛlasgɛmē lāxa
ᵉnᾶx̣wa bēbɛgwänɛma. Wä, g·ị̑lᵉmisē ᵉwilx̣toxs laē ᵉwị̑ᵉla ᵉnᾶᵉnakᵘ
10 lāx̣ēs g·ig·ōkwē. Wä, laɛm gwᾶɫa qādzēʟa lax̣ēq.

11. Purchase of a Copper.

Wä, maᵉɫɛnx̣ēlaxa ts!ᾶwɛnxas ʟ!ạ̄sotiwalis x·ōsᾶɫa, laɛm k·!ēs-
p!ɛsa lēx·aɛm gwēg·iᵉlatsēxs ᾶᵉmaē hēmɛnaɫa k!wäk!wēladzɛma. Wä
g·āx̣ēda g·āx̣ᾶ lāx Dzāwadēxa g·āx̣ē ᾼxk·!ạ̄lax ʟ!ạ̄sotiwalisē ʟɛᵉwis
ōmpē ʟ!ạ̄qoʟas qa lēs lāx Dzāwadē qaxs lɛᵉmaē k·ị̑lx̣wasōʟē Sɛᵉwasa
15 ʟ!ēna yị̑s ʟaēdzēxa g·ị̑gämaᵉyasa ᵉnɛᵉmēmutasa Wị̑womasgɛmasa Mama-
lēleqᾶla qaēs nɛgᴜ̈mpē Gᴜ̈yōɫelas qaxs gɛg·adaas K·!ạ̄sogwiᵉlakᵘxa
k·!ēdēɫas ʟaēdzē. Wä, hᵉ̈x̣·ᵉidaᵉmisē ʟ!ạ̄sotiwalis ʟēɫts!ōdxa mōᵇ-
gɛᵉmakwē Kwᾶkᴜ̈g·uɫ qa lēs ᵉwị̑ᵉla hōxts!ᾶ lāx g·ōkwas. Wä, g·ị̑l-
ᵉmisē g·ᾱx ᵉwị̑ᵉlaēʟa Kwᾶkᴜ̈g·uɫaxs laē ʟ!ạ̄qoʟas ts!ɛk·!ạ̄ɫelasa g·ᾱ-
20 x̣ē dāq qa lēs lāx Dzāwadē qaxs laᵉmē k·ị̑lx̣wasōʟē Sɛᵉwa yị̑s ʟaēdzē.
Wä, g·ị̑lᵉmisē gwᾶɫ ts!ɛk·!ạ̄ɫelaxs laē Lᾱlak·ots!a yāq!ɛg·aᵉɫa.
Wä, lᾶ ᵉnēk·a: Wa, gēlak·asᵉlaxa ēk·ēx wᾶɫdɛma, g·ị̑gämēᵉ ʟ!ạ̄qoʟas.
Gēlaq!ạ̄nax̣ᵘ laxōx. ᵉnēᵉnak·iɫē g·ị̑g·ɛᵉgämēs Kwᾶkᴜ̈g·uɫ. Wäg·ax·ị̑ns
q!ạ̄mdēɫa k!wēlaᵉyalä ᾶɫtsɛma q!ɛmdɛmax̣wa dzäqwaʟēx, ᵉnēk·ē. Wä,
25 lä ᵉnᾶx̣waɛm ᵉ̈x·ᵉak·a bēbɛgwänɛmax wᾶɫdɛmas. Wä, g·ị̑lᵉmisē gwᾶɫē
wᾶɫdɛmas laē ᵉwị̑ᵉla hōqᴜ̈wɛls lāxa g·ōkwē. Wä, lēx·aᵉmēs la k!ᴜ̈-
dzị̑ɫa mōkwē nēnᾶgadā qaxs laᵉmē ᵉwᴜ̈nᵉwᴜ̈nōsä dɛnx̣ɛlēda ᵉnɛmōkwē
nᾶgadēsēs q!ɛmdɛm g·ị̑ɫts!ᾶla. Wä, laᵉmē k!wägeliɫē ʟ!ạ̄qoʟasaq
qaxs laē ᵉnēx·ᵉalị̑ɫɛlasēs gwɛᵉyō qa qāyatsa ᾶɫtsɛmē k!wēᵉyalᾱla
30 q!ɛmdɛmʟas ʟ!ạ̄sotiwalisē. Wä, g·ị̑lᵉmisē ᾶlak·!ạ̄la la q!ạ̈da mōkwē
nēnᾶgadxa q!ɛmdɛm laē ᵉwị̑ᵉla hōqᴜ̈wɛls lāxa g·ōkwē.

rear of the house. "Now go on, will one of you take it up?" said
he/as he left it and sat down./

Then arose the chief of the Mamalēleqǎla, Gŭyōx̣ᴇlas./ Then
he took up Sᴇᵋwa and spoke. He said, (5) "Icome and take up this
your copper, chief. I shall talk/ to my tribe on account of what
you said, chief ʟ!āqoḺas," said he and/ sat down./

Then Lālak·ots!a again gave away blankets to/ all the men and
when they had all been given they all went home (10) to their
houses. And after this the marriage was at an end./

      11.   Purchase of a Copper.

Now for two winters ʟ!āsotiwalis rested. He did not/ give
away property, the only thing he did was always to give small
feasts. Then/those came who came out from Knight Inlet and told
ʟ!āsotiwalis and his/father, ʟ!āqoḺas, to go to Knight Inlet, that
Sᴇᵋwa was going to be bought (15) with grease by Ḻaēdzē, the chief
of the numaym Wīwomasgᴇm of the Mamalēleqǎla,/ for his son-in-law
Gŭyōx̣ᴇlas, for he had as his wife K·!äsogwiᵋlakᵘ,/ the princess of
Ḻaēdzē. Immediately ʟ!āsotiwalis called in the four/ Kwāg·ux̣ tribes
to go into his house. And/as soon as all the Kwāg·ux̣ tribes were
in, ʟ!āqoḺas told them (20) that they had come to get him to go to
Knight Inlet, for now Sᴇᵋwa was to be bought by Ḻaēdzē./ As soon
as he had finished telling them, Lālak·ots!a spoke/ and said "Thank
you for this good word, chief ʟ!āqoḺas./ Thank you very much, for
I mean this, chiefs of the Kwāg·ux̣. Now go on,/ let us sing in the
house a new feasting song this evening," said he./ (25) Then all the
men agreed to what he said, and when they had finished/ speaking
they all went out of the house and only/the four song leaders sat
down, for one song leader sang secretly/the new song that was in him.
Then ʟ!āqoḺas sat down among them,/ for he told them what to refer
to in the words in the new feasting (30) song of ʟ!āsotiwalis. And
when the four/ song leaders knew well the song, they went out of
the house./

Wä, g·îlᵋmîsē dzāqwaxs laas ᵋyālaqē ʟ!āqoʟasaxa häᵋyāɫᵋa
maᵋlōkwa qa lēs qāsaxa yūduxᵘsᵋᵋmakwē Kwākŭg·uɫ ōgŭᵋla lāxa Q!ō-
moyâᵋyē qa g·āxēs ᵋwĪᵋla lāx g·ōkwas ʟ!āsotiwalisē, yîxs ᵋnēk·aē-
da maᵋlōkwē häᵋyāɫᵋa lāx äᵋwĪʟɛläs t!ɛx·flāsa g·Īg·ōkwē: G·āxᵋmɛ-
5   nuᵋxᵘ q!ɛmdîᵋlaloʟai Gwētɛlai qa ʟ!āsotiwalisai. Hālag·alēʟasai,
ᵋnēk·ō. Wä, la häᵋstaɛm gwēk·!āla lāxa ᵋnāxwa g·ig·ōkwa. Wä,
g·îlᵋmîsē ᵋwĪlxtolsaxa g·ig·ōkwaxs g·āxdaᵋxwaē aēdaaqa qaᵋs lē
xwēlag·ēʟ lāx g·ōkwas ʟ!āsotiwalisē qaᵋs ēxᵋwidēx äwĪnagwiɫas.
Wä, g·îlᵋmîsē gwāɫ laē lāqolĪɫaq. Wä, g·îlᵋmîsē gwāɫa g·āxaas
10   g·ālaēʟa mōkwē nēnâgada qaᵋs lē k!ŭsᵋālĪɫ lāx nɛqēᵋwalĪɫasa g·ōkwē.
Wä, hёx·ᵋidaᵋmîsē ᵋwŭnᵋwŭnōsa dɛnxᵋētsa āɫtsɛmē q!ɛmdɛma. Wä,
g·āxᵋmē hōgwiʟelēda k!wēk!wanuʟemaᵋyasa nēnâgadē qaᵋs lē k!ŭsᵋā-
lĪɫ lāx ᵋwāx·sbalĪɫasa mōkwē nēnâgadâ. Wä, g·îlᵋmîsē g·āx ᵋwĪ-
ᵋlaēʟa ᵋnāxwa bēbɛgwānɛmsa mōsgɛᵋmakwē Kwākŭg·uɫa laas ʟāxᵋwalĪɫē
15   Lālak·ots!a, wä, lä yāq!ɛg·aᵋɫa. Wä, lä ᵋnēk·a: Qāʟ, qāᴸ, mōsgɛᵋmakᵘ Kwākŭg·uɫ. Ɛts!ēᵋmawĪsɛns ёx·q!ɛsɛla qaɛns g·āxēx q!āɫa
g·āxdzāqɛns q!āɫaxa g·Īgāmaᵋyaē ʟaēdzäxa k·flxwaʟɛx Sɛᵋwä ʟ!āqwā-
sɛns g·Īgāmaᵋyaōx ʟ!āsotiwalisēx. Wa, gēlak·asᵋlax·i wāɫdɛmasa
g·Īgāmaᵋya. Gēlaq!anakᵘ lax·i wāɫdɛmasē. ᵋnēᵋnak·iɫē, g·Īg·ɛgāmēs
20   Kwākŭg·uɫ, laᵋmɛn ᵋnēx· qɛns ᵋwĪᵋlaᵋmē la lāx Dzāwadē lāsgɛmēxɛns
g·Īgāmaᵋyōx ʟ!āsotiwalisēx, ᵋnēk·ō. Wä, lä wāxaxa nēnâgadē qa wā-
g·Īs dɛnxᵋētsa āɫtsɛmē k!wēlaᵋyāla q!ɛmdɛma. Wä, hёx·ᵋidaᵋmisa
nâgaaē dâqâlasēs q!ɛmtēlaᵋyēxa ᵋnēk·ō:

1. Yā ha wâ yeya ha.
25   Wa ᵋyāx·ᵋidg·iladzēyɛn.
       Wa ᵋyāx·ᵋidg·iladzēyîn g·în ᵋyāx·ᵋidg·iladzēyaq!amē-
           g·în yîmg·flĪsē, laē lāx g·āg·igāmmɛnēxwas lēɛlqwā-
           laʟai.
       ʻYa ha wâ yeya ha wâ huwä.

(1) As soon as it was evening ʟ!āqoʟas sent two young men/ to walk calling the three Kwāg·uⱡ tribes besides the Q!ōmoyaᵋyē,/ that all should come to the house of ʟ!āsotiwalis. And the/ two young men said inside the doors of the houses, "We come (5) to ask yoᵘ to sing in the house, Gwētɛla, on behalf of ʟ!āsotiwalis. Go there quickly,'/ they said, and they kept on saying the same in all the houses./ As soon as they had been in all the houses they went back again and/ went into the house of ʟ!āsotiwalis to clear the floor./ When they had finished, they made a fire in the middle of the house. After this was done (10) the four song leaders came in and sat down in the middle of the rear of the house./ At once they sang secretly the new song./ Now came in those who were sitting on the sides of the song leaders and they sat down/ on each side of the four song leaders. As soon/ as all the men of the four Kwāg·uⱡ tribes were in, arose (15) Lālak·ots!a and spoke. He said: "Indeed it is true, you four/ Kwāg·uⱡ tribes. Should we not be happy about this, that we have/ learned that chief ʟaēdzē will buy Sɛᵋwa the copper/ from our chief ʟ!āsotiwalis. Thank you for the words of the/ chief. Thank you indeed for what you have said. I mean this, chiefs (20) of the Kwāg·uⱡ. Now I wish that you all go to Knight Inlet following/ our chief ʟ!āsotiwalis," said he. Then he told the song leaders to go ahead/ and sing the new feasting song, and immediately/ the song leaders began the song which said,/

1. Ya ha wâ yeya ha./

(25) I am the great one who causes them to be bad.[1]/

I am the great one who causes them to be bad.

I am the great one who causes them to be bad,/ to give

up, the little chiefs of the/ tribes./

Ya ha wâ heya ha wâ huwä./

---

1. That means "to lose in rank."

2. Kwāg·uʌdzɛmskün^ɛwa̱.

Kwāg·uʌdzɛmskün^ɛwa

Kwāg·uʌɛn ^ɛnēk·aēx sŏxwamē^ɛstāla lāx lēɛlqwälaʟai:

Nōgwaɛms yāyagalasō^ɛsä lēɛlqwälaʟai.

5   Nōgwaɛms ʟ!āʟ!aqwaalasō^ɛsä lēɛlqwälaʟai,

Nōgwaɛms ʟ̯ā̯ʟ̯ēgɛmālasō^ɛsä lēɛlqwälaʟai.

Nōgwaɛms k·!āk·!ōs^ɛâlasō^ɛsä lēɛlqwälaʟai.

Ya ha wâ yeya ha wâ huwä.

3. Ya ha wâ yeya ha.

10   Wa, la^ɛmɛn ya ʟ̯ēqa^ɛyaʌtsɛn mɛnmɛnʌɛxʟäyasɛn gagɛmpdzēyaxa

q!ülēxʟēyadzēya Kwākúx·âladzē, Kwāx·flanōkümē^ɛ, g·Igämē^ɛ

qa^ɛs lēɛlqwälaʟai.

Layuʌa lāx·s^ɛɛndēyaxa ʟ̯ēgɛmnuχ^udzēyaʟɛx Ángwalax·ʟadzē

ʟ!āqwasɛns gagɛmpdzēyaxa q!ülēxʟēyadzēya K!wāk!wabalas,

15   K!wāk!wabalasɛmē^ɛ g·Igämē^ɛ qa^ɛs lēɛlqwälaʟai.

Layuʌa lāx·s^ɛɛndēyaxa ʟ̯ēgɛmnuχ^udzēyaɪɛx Nɛngɛmālax·ʟadzē

ʟ!āqwasɛn gagɛmpdzēyaxa q!ülēxʟēyadzēya Mālēdeäs g·I-

gämē qa^ɛs lēɛlqwälaʟai.

Läyuʌa lāx·s^ɛɛndēyaxa ʟ̯ēgɛmnuχ^udzē∀aɪɛx Māx^ɛēnoxúx·ʟadzē

20   ʟ!āqwasɛn gagɛmpdzēyaxa q!ülēxʟēyadzēya Ɛwanuχ^u, Ɛwanu-

χ^udzēs g·I^ɛgämē^ɛ qa^ɛs lēɛlqwälaʟai.

Ya ha wâ yeya ha wâ huwä.

Wä, g·fl^ɛmisē ^ɛnāxwa q!ālēda bēbɛgwānɛmaxa āʌtsɛmē k!wē-

la^ɛyāla q!ɛmdɛma, wä, la^ɛmē gwāʌ dɛnxɛla laas ʟāx^ɛwaliʌē ʟ!ā-

25   qoʟasē qa^ɛs yāq!ɛg·a^ɛʌē. Wä, lä ^ɛnēk·a: La^ɛmō gwāʌtsɛma q!ɛm-

dɛmaxsɛn g·Igāma^ɛyēx. Ladzē^ɛmō gwāʌtsɛma. Wä, lɛ^ɛmas wüʟɛlax

g·Ig·igɛxʟäyâsɛn gaagɛmp^ɛwüʌaxa ^ɛnāxwa^ɛmē âla ^ɛwI^ɛlōʟɛx q!wāxa-

g·iʌasa g·Igāma^ɛyē. Wa, gēlak·as^ɛlax·ōx wāʌdɛmaqōs Lāx·sodālasō^ɛ,

^ɛnēk·ē (ʟ̯ēx^ɛēdxa nâgadēxa âxēnukwasa k!wēla^ɛyāla q!ɛmdɛma gwɛ^ɛyōs)

30   Laɛms hēʌaxāmasa. ^ɛnēɛnak·iʌē, g·ōʌg·ōkülōt. La^ɛmɛn häwāxɛlōʟ

qɛns lē lāx Dzāwadē qa hē^ɛmēsōx ʟ!ēnag·ila k!wēlasōx ʟ!āsotiwali-

2. I am the great Kwāg·uł/

    I am the great Kwāg·uł/

    I, the Kwāg·uł say this as you are paddling about among
        the tribes.(?)/

    I am the one from whom property is obtained by the tribes./

(5) I am the one from whom coppers are obtained by the tribes./

    I am the one from whom names are obtained by the tribes./

    I am the one from whom crests are obtained by the tribes./

    Ya ha wâ he ya wâ hu wä./

3. Ya ha wâ he ha ha./

(10) Now I will name the feasting names of my great grandfather/
        whose own name was Kwākwax·âlas, Kwāx·ɫanōkŭmēᵋ, the
        chief,/ for you, tribes./

    Long ago he broke the copper that had the great name Cloudy,/
        that belonged to my grandfather whose own name was K!wā-
        k!wabalas,(15) K!wāk!wabalasɛmēᵋ,the chief,for you,tribes./

    Long ago he broke the copper that had the name Bear Face,/
        that belonged to my grandfather whose own name was
        Mälet, the chief,/ for you, tribes./

    Long ago he broke the copper that had the name Killer Whale/
        (20) that belonged to my grandfather whose own name was
        Ēwanuxᵘ, Ēwanuxᵘdzē,/ the chief, for you, tribes./

    Ya ha wâ heya ha wâ huwä./

As soon as all the men knew the new feasting/ song, they stopped
singing and then ʟ!āqoʟas arose (25) and spoke. He said, "Now is
finished/ the song of my chief, the great one is finished and you
have heard/ the chief-names of my grandfathers, all of which were
obtained by/ this chief who has grown up for them. Thank you for
these your words, Läx·sodālasōᵋ,"/ he said. (He named the song
leader who made the feasting song.) (30) "Now you made it well. I
mean this, tribes. I beg you/ to go to Knight Inlet, for this is
where ʟ!āsotiwalis gave a grease feast (1) Now his feasting name

sēxa laᵋmēx k!wēladzɛxʟälaʟɛx Ēwanukwē. Wä, laᵋmēsɛn lâsaⱡtsɛn
āʟanɛmēx ⱡoqwalIⱡ ʟɛᵋwa nānēx ʟɛᵋwa mēgwatēx, wä, yūᵋmēsa ts!āwēx
ⱡēⱡōqwaⱡē lāxōx Ēwanukwēx. Wä, laᵋmēsɛns lāⱡ ᵋmâlaʟɛqᵘ,Kwākŭg·uⱡ
yIxs ĕk·ēʟa ᵋnäläx ⱡɛnsʟa, ᵋnēk·ē. (Wä, laᵋmɛn k!wâgeliⱡɛq. Wä

5   lɛn k·!ēs lāsgɛmxa mōsgɛᵋmakwē Kwākŭg·uⱡaxs laē lāx Dzāwadē qaɛn
ᵋnā̱xwaᵋmēk· dōqŭlaxɛn k·!ātasɛᵋwē qaᵋs.)

Wä, g·Ilᵋmisē gwāⱡē wâⱡdɛmas laē ᵋwIᵋla hōqŭwɛls lāxa g·ōkwē
qaᵋs xwānaⱡᵋidē. Wä, g·Ilᵋmisē ᵋnāx·ᵋidxa gaāläxs laē ᵋwIᵋla wI-
xᵘstɛndxēs xwāxwāk!ŭna qaᵋs ᵋmōxsēsēs dēdamāla lāq. Wä, g·Ilᵋmisē

10 ᵋwIlxsē dēdamālâs laē ʟɛxᵋēda. (Wä, laᵋmɛn k·!ēs la lāq. Laᵋmɛn
āmlē̱xᵘ lāxg·a Tsāxisɛk·.)

Wä, yāyŭduxᵘsɛmg·ustâlē ᵋnālasēsa q!ɛʟ!ɛxsa (yIxs ᵋnēk·aēda
wāokwē bāk!ŭma q!ɛʟ!ɛxsagâla ᵋnäläsēxs) g·āxaē hâla lāxg·a Tsā-
xisɛk·xa mōsgɛᵋmakwē Kwākŭg·uⱡa. Wä, hĕᵋmisē ʟ!āqoʟas ts!ɛk·!ā-

15 ⱡɛlaxs q!ɛʟ!ɛp!ɛnyag·aē k·!ɛwɛlxᵘsɛm ʟ!ēnē k·flōmax Sɛᵋwa. Wä,
hĕᵋmis la ᵋwIᵋla k!wēlasᵋidayus ʟ!āsotiwalisxa la k!wēladzɛxʟälax
Ēwanukwaxa lēɛlqwälaʟaᵋyē, ᵋnēk·ēxs laē ts!ɛk·!āⱡɛla g·āxɛn.

12. Continuation of Marriage Ceremonies

Wä, maᵋⱡᵋɛnxēlēxa ts!āwŭnxē q!ap!ā̱xa yāqɛlaxa p!ɛlxɛlasgɛmē
ʟ!āsotiwalis qaxg·In hēx·säᵋmēʟɛk· ʟēqalayuʟɛqēs ʟēgɛmaxs lāx·dē

20 ʟēⱡɛlaxa lēlqwälaʟaᵋyē. Wä, laᵋmē ᵋnēx· qaᵋs k!waapēxēs gɛnɛmē
Q!ēx·ʟālaga lāxēs ōmpē Aᵋmāxŭlaⱡē ʟōᵋ g·Igâmaᵋyasa ᵋnɛᵋmēmutasa
ʟ!āʟ!ɛlaminasa ᵋnɛmgēsē. Wä, g·āxᵋɛmxaa ʟēⱡɛlakwa ᵋnā̱xwa lēlqwäla-
ⱡēs ᵋnɛmōgwisxa g·āyuⱡē lāxa ᵋnɛᵋmēmutasa Sēnʟ!ɛmasa Gwētɛla. Wä,
lä ʟ!āsotiwalisē ʟēⱡts!ōdxa mōsgɛᵋmakwē Kwākŭg·uⱡa qa lēs ᵋwIᵋla

25 hōgwiʟ lāx g·ōkwas. Wä, laᵋmē ᵋnēk·a maᵋlōkwē bēbɛgwānɛmxa qāsɛl-
g·Isē: G·āxᵋmɛnuᵋxᵘ qasai Gwētɛlai qaᵋs laōs hōʟēlax wâⱡdɛmʟas
ʟ!āsotiwalisē. Hâlag·flēʟasai, ᵋnēk·ē lāx āᵋwIʟɛläs t!ɛx·flāsa
ᵋnā̱xwa g·ig·ōkwa. Wä, g·Ilᵋmisē ᵋwIlxtolsaxa g·ig·ōkwaxs g·āxaē
aēdaaqa. Wä, g·āxē hōgwiʟēda ᵋnā̱xwa bēbɛgwānɛm. Wä, g·Ilᵋmisē

30 g·āx ᵋwIᵋlaēʟa laas ʟā̱xᵋwalIⱡē Lālak·ots!a qaᵋs yāq!ɛg·aᵋⱡē. Wä,
lä ᵋnēk·a: Wa, gēlag·a mōsgɛᵋmakᵘ Kwākŭg·uⱡ. Wa, gēlak·asᵋlaxs

will be Ewanuk^u. Now I will turn over/my Wolf house dish, and
the Bear and the Seal and also the Beaver/house dish to Ewanuk^u.
Now we will take them there, Kwāg·uł/if it is a good day tomorrow,"
said he. (I was sitting among them, but (5) did not follow the
four Kwāg·uł tribes when they went to Knight Inlet,for/ I saw all
that has been written by me for you.)/

After they had finished speaking, then they all went out of
the house/ and got ready, and as soon as it got day in the morning,
they all/ launched their canoes and they loaded them with their goods
and when (10) all the goods were aboard they started. (Now I did
not go there, I stayed/ at home here at Fort Rupert.)/

Now there were six of the third ten days, as they say,/(or as
other Indians say, six between twenty days, twenty-six). Then
they came back to Fort Rupert,/ the four Kwāg·uł tribes, and ʟ!ā-
qoʟas reported (15) that six hundred coal oil tins of grease had
been paid for Sɛˤwa,/ and this was all given in a feast by ʟ!āsoti-
walis, whose feasting name/ was Ewanuk^u, to all the tribes, said
he as he told me the news./

12. Continuation of Marriage Ceremonies.

For two winters ʟ!āsotiwalis collected property, namely blank-
ets/ (for I will continue to call him by this name after (20) he
had invited all the tribes). Now he wished to "sit under" his
wife/Q!ēx·ʟālaga, on account of her father, Aˤmāxūlał, and the
chief of the numaym/ ʟ!āʟ!ɛlamin of the ˤnɛmgis. Now also came
all the tribes invited/ by ˤnɛmōgwis who belongs to the numaym Sēnʟ!em of the Gwētɛla . / Then ʟ!āsotiwalis invited in the four Kwā-
g·uł tribes to go (25) into his house, and two men, the inviters,
said,/ "We come walking, Gwētɛla, that you may go and listen to the
words of/ʟ!āsotiwalis. You will go quickly," said they in the door-
ways/ of all of the houses. And after they had been to all the houses
they went/ back. Then all the men came into the house, and as soon
as (30) they were all in,Lālak·ots!a arose and spoke./ He said,"Now

g·āxaēx g·āxēʟ·lāxwa ᴇwālasēs g·ōkwa, g·ōkwaxsg·ɪn g·ɪgāmēk·
lāxg·a ʟ!āsotiwalisɛk· laxg·ada ᴇnēkɪ́k· qaᴇs ᴇwāᴇwɪᴇlōʟ!ēx
xúltaᴇya qa labɛndalasa g·ɪgāmaᴇyē g·ãg·ɪ̓ʟɛlaxs g·ālaē māᴇyō-
ʟᴇmsēs ābᴇmpē. ᴇnēᴇnak·iɫē g·ɪgᵛᴇgāmēᴇ ēɛng·a ʟ!āsotiwalisɛk·
5   ʟōgwas gɛnᴇmg·ēg·a Q!ēx·ʟālaǥa. Laᴇmēsōx k·!ǥsâla. Lɛn k·!ēs
ᴇnēx· qa xɛk·!axap!ēsōx. ᴇnēᴇnak·iɫē, laᴇmēsɛns lāɫ k!waap qaxs
laᴇmɛn g·ɪgāmaᴇyōx ʟ!āsotiwalisēx k!waapaɫxēs gɛnᴇmē qaēda gēga-
k·!ōmas ʟᴇᴇwē ᴇyāk·!ɛlwasē qaxs lᴇᴇmaē ᴇnēk·a g·ɪgāmaᴇyēx qaᴇs
günx·ᴇɪdē lalōʟ!a qaᴇs ᴇyāg·ɪ̓ʟɛlaxōdē qag·ada lēᴇlqwālaʟaᴇya. Wä,
10   laᴇmēsɛns lāɫ g·ɪg·ᴇgāmēs mōsgeᴇmakᵘ Kwāküg·uɫ k!waāpaxa gɛnᴇmas
ʟ!āsotiwalis. Wä, hāg·a g·ɪgāmēᴇ ᴇmāxüyālisᴇmēᴇ, op!ēdxa g·ɪgā-
maᴇyaē Aᴇmāxülaɫ, nēɫaqēxg·ɪns laᴇmēk· lāɫ k!waapaʟɛx gɛnᴇmasōx
ʟ!āsotiwalisēx.

      Wä, laᴇmē ᴇmāxüyālisᴇmaᴇyēxa g·āyuɫē lāx ᴇnᴇ́mēmutasa Hā-
15   ānaʟēᴇnâsa Q!ōmoyâᴇyē. Wä, k·!ēst!a gàɫaxs g·āxaē aēdaaqa. Wä
âᴇmisē ᴇnēk·ᴇxs lᴇᴇmaē Aᴇmāxülaɫē âᴇm la nāk·!âɫaq qa lēs hali-
ᴇlāla k!waāpax gɛnᴇmas ʟ!āsotiwalis.

      Wä, hēx·ᴇida ᴇmisa q!ēnᴇmē hāᴇyāɫᴇa sēsɛk·!axsɛnkülaxa
p!ɛlxɛlasgᴇmaxs laē hōqüwᴇls lāxa g·ōkwas ʟ!āsotiwalisē qaᴇs lē
20   k·!ɛxᴇɛlsɛlas lāx ʟ!āsanâᴇyas g·ōkwas Aᴇmāxülaɫē. Wä, lã ᴇwɪᴇla
lāsgᴇmaᴇyē bēbɛgwānᴇmaq qaᴇs lē k!üsᴇɛls lāq. Wä, hēᴇmxaāwisē
Lālak·ots!a ʟāxᴇwɛls qaᴇs yāq!ᴇg·aᴇɫē. Wä, lã ᴇnēk·aɪ G·āxᴇmᴇn,
g·ɪgāmēᴇ Aᴇmāxülaɫ. G·āxᴇmɛn g·āxᴇaʟᴇla g·ɪg·ᴇgāmēᴇ Aᴇmāxülaɫ
sōdzēᴇmēs g·ɪgāmēᴇ ᴇnᴇmōgwis. G·āxᴇmɛnʟaxg·ɪn ʟ!āsotiwalisēk·
25   k!waāpaxɛn gɛnᴇmax lāxōx Q!ēxʟālaǥäx k·!ēdēɫaq!ōs, g·ɪgāmēᴇ
Amāxülaɫ. ᴇnēᴇnak·iɫē, ᴇnēk·ᴇxs laē ʟēᴇlālaxa q!āq!astowē bɛ-
gwānᴇma qa lēs hōdzēg·ēxa p!ɛlxɛlasgᴇmē. Wä, g·ɪ̓lᴇmisē k!wā-
g·aɛlsa q!āq!astowē bɛgwānᴇm lāx gᴇmᴇxagawalasas Lālak·ōts!a
laē Lālak·ōts!a dāx·ᴇidxa ᴇnᴇmxsa p!ɛlxɛlasgᴇm lāx ᴇnāxwaᴇmaē
30   sēsɛk·!axsasa āɫᴇosgᴇmalsa lōsᴇmx·ᴇɪdē p!ɛlxɛlasgᴇm k!waābayōs

come, you four Kwāg·uł tribes. Thank you (1) for coming inside this
great house, the house of this your chief/ ʟ!āsotiwalis, for he said
that he will do all/ that is marked down for a chief to go through
to the end, beginning from the time when he was first born/by his
mother. I mean this, chiefs. Now have quarreled ʟ!āsotiwalis (5)
and his wife, Q!ēx·ʟālaga, and now they will part. I do not/ wish
them to part for good. I mean this. Now we will go and 'sit below,' for/ my chief ʟ!āsotiwalis will 'sit under' (his wife) on
account of his wife's property/and 'trifles,ᴸ for now this chief
says that he will/try to obtain 'trifles' to be given away to these
tribes. Now (10) we shall go, chiefs of the four Kwāg·uł tribes
and 'sit under' the wife of/ʟ!āsotiwalis. Now go, chief ᵋmāx̣ūyāli-
sɛmēᵋ, whisper to chief/Aᵋmāx̣ūlał, and tell him that we shall now
go and 'sit under' the wife of/ʟ!āsotiwalis."/

Then ᵋmāx̣ūyālisɛmēᵋ, who belongs to the numaym Hāānaʟēnō (15)
of the Q!ōmoyâᵋyē went, and it was not long before he came back
and/ he just said that Aᵋmāx̣ūlał was just waiting for them to go
quickly/ and "sit under" the wife of ʟ!āsotiwalis./

Immediately many young men carried each five pairs of/ blank-
kets as they went out of the house of ʟ!āsotiwalis, and (20) they
put them down outside of the house of Aᵋmāx̣ūlał. All the/ men followed them and sat down there outside, and/ Lālak·ots!a also stood
up outside and spoke. He said, "I have come,/chief Aᵋmāx̣ūlał, I
have come up, chief Aᵋmāx̣ūlał,/ and you, great chief ᵋnɛmōgwis. I
come that ʟ!āsotiwalis (25) may 'sit under' my wife, Q!ēx·ʟālaga
here, your princess here, chief/ Aᵋmāx̣ūlał. I mean this," said he as
he called the tally keeper/ to count the blankets. As soon as the/
tally keeper sat down at the left hand side of Lālak·ots!a,/ Lālak-
k·ots!a took up one pair of blankets. And they were all in (30)
five pairs in each pile on the ground, one thousand blankets, the

_____

1) All property except blankets is called "trifles," literally
   "bad things."

ʟ!āsotiwalisaxēs gᴇnᴇmē. Wä, lä ᵋnēk·ē Lālak·ots!a dzŏx̣ustŏdxa
ᵋnᴇmxsa p!ᴇlxᴇlasgᴇm: Laᵋmᴇn k!waāpasēqä laxᴇn gᴇnᴇmax lâʟ, g·Ī-
gämēᵋ Aᵋmāx̣ŭlaⱡ sᴇk·!axsa p!ᴇlxᴇlasgᴇm, ᵋnēk·ē. Wä, lēda hēⱡᵋa
gᴇmxᴇlsaxa sᴇk·!axsa p!ᴇlxᴇlasgᴇm qaᵋꜱ lē gᴇmxēʟas lāx g·ŏkwas
5   Aᵋmāx̣ŭlaⱡ. Wä, lä hᵆx·sãᴇm gwēk·!ãlaxs laē ᵋwĪᵋlēda sᴇk·!ap!ᴇn-
yag·i pᴇlxᴇlasgᴇm k!waābᴇm lāx Aᵋmāx̣ŭlaⱡ. Wä, g·f1ᵋmisē ᵋwi-
ᵋlēda sᴇk·!āp!ᴇnyag·i p!ᴇlxᴇlasgᴇmxa k!waābᴇmax Aᵋmāx̣ŭlaⱡ lāxaē
Lālak·ots!a dãx·ᵋfdxa ᵋnᴇmxsa p!ᴇlxᴇlasgᴇm. Wä, lä yāq!ᴇg·aᵋⱡa.
Wä, lä ᵋnēk·a dzŏx̣ustŏdxa ᵋnᴇmxsa p!ᴇlxᴇlasgᴇm: Laᵋmᴇn k!waāpa-
10   sēqä lāxᴇn gᴇnᴇmax lâʟ g·Īgämēᵋ ᵋnᴇmŏgwis, sᴇk·!axsa p!ᴇlxᴇlasgᴇm ,
ᵋnēk·ē. Wä, lēda hēⱡᵋa gᴇmxᴇlsaxa sᴇk·!axsa p!ᴇlxᴇlasgᴇm qaᵋs
lē gᴇmxēʟas lāx g·ŏkwas Aᵋmāx̣ŭlaⱡ qaxs hᵆᵋmãe g·aēʟelē ᵋnᴇmŏgwisē.
Wä, lä hᵆx:sãᴇm gwēk·!ālē lãg·aa laqēx lāaxat! ᵋwĪᵋlēda sᴇk·!ā-
p!ᴇnyag·i p!ᴇlxᴇlasgᴇmxa k!waābᴇmax ᵋnᴇmŏgwis. Wä, g·Īg·ᴇgämēᵋ
15   Aᵋmāx̣ŭlaⱡ sŏdzēᵋmē g·Īgämēᵋ ᵋnᴇmŏgwis. Hãloxsᴇmx·ᵋidgŏxda ʞ!wa-
ābᴇmēx p!ᴇlxᴇlasgᴇm lâʟ g·Īg·ᴇgämēᵋ. Wa, wa, ᵋnēk·exs laē k!wãg·-
g·aᴇlsa.

Wä, g·āxē P!āsᴇlaⱡ g·āxawᴇls lāxa g·ŏkwas Aᵋmāx̣ŭlaⱡ qaᵋs
ᴌāxᵋwᴇlsē lāx ʟ!āsanâᵋyasa t!ᴇx·fla. Wä, lä yāq!ᴇg·aᵋⱡa. Wä,
20   lä ᵋnēk·aɪ Qãʟ, qãʟ,adzēxaēs wãⱡdᴇmōs, g·Īgämēᵋ, yŭʟ ʟ!āsotiwa-
lis. Ladzēᴇmxaē gwãⱡa. Wãg·axᴇn q!ālaxēs gwᴇᵋyãōs qaᵋs lālŏ-
ʟ!asōs lāxg·a nᴇgŭmpᴇk· qaᵋs g·Īgämēᵋ ʟ!āsotiwalis qaxs lᴇᵋmaē
Sᴇᵋwa lâʟ, g·Īgämēᵋ, ᵋnēk·ē.

Wä, lä ᴌāxᵋwᴇlsē ʟ!āqoʟas, yfx ōmpas ʟ!āsotiwalisē qaᵋs yā-
25   q!ᴇg·aᵋⱡē. Wä, lä ᵋnēk·aɪ Ex·ᵋmēs wãⱡdᴇmōs, g·Īgämēᵋ P!āsᴇlaⱡ,
âla g·āxᵋmē Sᴇᵋwa, g·āxdzēᵋmēxa lä ʟ!ēnaxasg·fn g·Īgämēk·. Wä,
laᵋmē lāxa. Wä, hᵆt!ᴇn la gwᴇᵋyō qaᵋs lalŏt!asōsa g·Īg·ᴇgäma-
ᵋyaxŏx Aᵋmāx̣ŭlaⱡax ʟ,ŏdzēya g·Īgämaᵋyax ᵋnᴇmŏgwisaxa ãpsâᵋyas
Sᴇᵋwaxa gēgak·!ōmasa ʟᴇᵋwa ᵋyãk·!ᴇlwasa, ᵋnēk·ēg·a ʟ!āsotiwa-
30   lisᴇk·, qaᵋs ᵋyãg·aʟᴇlaxŏdē qaŏxda lēᴇlqwãlataᵋyēx ᵋnēk·ē. Wä,
lä ᴌâtsäᵋma laas ēdzaqwa yāq!ᴇg·aᵋⱡē P!āsᴇlaⱡ. Wä, lä ᵋnēg·ē-

means of (1) ʟ!āsotiwalis of "sitting under" his wife. Then Lāla-
k·ots!a said holding up/one pair of blankets, "Now with this I 'sit
under' my wife, for you, chief/Aᵉmāx̣ŭlaɬ, five pairs of blankets,"
said he. Then a young man/took up the five pairs of blankets and
carried them into the house (5) of Aᵉmāx̣ŭlaɬ. He kept on saying
this until all five hundred/blankets,the means of "sitting under"
Aᵉmāx̣ŭlaɬ, were at an end. And when the/five hundred blankets,
the means of "sitting under" Aᵉmāx̣ŭlaɬ were at an end, then/Lāla-
k·cts!a took up one pair of blankets. He spoke/and said, holding
up one pair of blankets, "Now I sit (10) with this under my wife,
for you, chief ᵉnɛmōgwis, five pairs of blankets,"/said he. Then the
young men took up five pairs of blankets and/carried them into the
house of Aᵉmāx̣ŭlaɬ, for that was where ᵉnɛmōgwis was living./ And
he kept on saying this and taking up again the five hundred/blankets
given to "sit under" ᵉnɛmōgwis. "It is done, chiefs (15) Aᵉmāx̣ŭlal
and you also, great chief ᵉnɛmōgwis. These in all are one thousand
blankets as a means of sitting under/you chiefs. Wa wa," said he
and/sat down./

Then came P!asɛlaɬ out of the house of Aᵉmāx̣ŭlaɬ and/he stood
outside of the door. He spoke (20) and said, "Indeed, it is true
what you say, chief ʟ!āsotiwalis./ Now this great thing is finished.
Now go on,that I may know what you want to get/from your father-in-
law,chief ʟ!āsotiwalis,for/Sɛᵉwa has gone to you,chief," said he./

Then arose ʟ!āqoʟas, the father of ʟ!āsotiwalis. He spoke (25)
and said, "God is what you say, chief P!āsɛlaɬ./ It is true. Sɛᵉwa
came, the great one came that had been sold for grease by my chief
here./ Now it has been sold. Now I wish to get from you, chiefs,/
great Aᵉmāx̣ŭlaɬ, and you, great chief ᵉnɛmōgwis,the other part of/
Sɛᵉwa, the wife's property and the 'trifles.'" He said this,(ʟ!āso-
tiwalis),(30) that he would give away trifles to the tribes, said
he./ Now he was standing still, and while he was there P!asɛlaɬ

ʟɛlax t!ɛx·ᴬlasa g·ōkwas Aᵉmāx̣ǔlaⱡē: Wǎg·a hĕlatâlaxi̯ɛx g·ɪ̇g·ɛ-
gǎmēᵉ Aᵉmāx̣ǔlaⱡ ꞁōdzēs g·ɪ̇gǎmēᵉ ᵉnɛmōgwis. Laɛms wāwaⱡk·inǎla
g·ɪ̇g·ɛgǎmēᵉ. Laɛms qautēx·aꞁōꞁ ᵉyǎg·ai̯ɛlaxōdɛⱡ lag·a nɛgǔmpē
Aᵉmāx̣ǔlaⱡ. Laɛmlas lǎlōꞁ!ɛⱡxa gēgak!ōmaᶊa ꞁɛᵉwa ᵉyǎk·!ɛlwas,
5   g·ɪ̇g·ɛgǎmēᵉ, ᵉnēk·ē.
      Wǎ, laᵉmē gwǎⱡē wǎⱡdɛmas lāxēq. Wǎ, laᵉmē ᵉwɪ̄ᵉla la·nǎ-
ᵉnakwa bēbɛgwanɛm lāxēs g·ig·ōkwē.
      Wǎ, laɛm hewäxa ēɛnē ʟ!āsotiwalisē ꞁɛᵉwis gɛnɛmē Q!ēx·ʟā-
laga qaxs ⱥᵉmaē ꞁēgadɛs ēɛn qaxs ᵉnēk·aē ʟ!āsotiwalisē qaᵉs
10   k!waāpēxēs gɛnɛmē ᵉnɛmāx·ᴬs ꞁ̓ōᵉ ōt!ēdē qādzōꞁaxēs gɛnɛmē lāxēs
gwēx·ᵉidaasē qaxs lɛᵉmaē gǔnaᵉyē Sɛᵉwa lāxa g·ālē qādzōꞁɛm p!ɛl-
xɛlasgɛm sɛk·!ap!ɛnyag·a. Wǎ, la ꞁēgɛmsa k!waāpäxēs gɛnɛmē qa
hĕⱡaxaⱡts!ɛlēs wǎⱡdɛmasa yāq!ɛnt!ālaxa ᵉnēk·aq ēɛnēda bɛgwānɛm
ꞁɛᵉwis gɛnɛmēxa k·!ēsaꞁaⱡ ēɛna. Wǎ, hĕt!a q!ēnɛma g·ɪ̇g·ɛgāmaᵉyē-
15   xwa āⱡēx ᵉnāla qādzōꞁasa g·inǎla lāxa lōxsɛmx·ᵉidē p!ɛlxɛlasgɛm
lāx ōmpasēs gɛnɛmē. Wǎ, lax ⱡēᵉwēnukwa gɛnɛmasa sɛk·!axsugǔg·ō-
yuwē p!ɛlxɛlasgɛm qa wǔsēk·alaxa ᵉnāxwa bēbɛgwānɛmxa hēlānɛmē
qa qādzōꞁax gɛnɛmasa g·ɪ̇gāmaᵉyē. Wǎ, lä ᵉnāⱡᵉnɛmp!ɛna sɛk·!a-
xɛnxē ts!ɛwǔnxas k·!ēs qautēx·ēda bɛgwānɛmaxēs nɛgǔmp. Wǎ, laɛm
20   ꞁak·ɛyālaxa ʟ!āqwa. Wǎ, laɛm ōgǔqǎⱡa lāxa sāyabalǎsa ʟ!āqwaxa
ⱥɛm la gǔnasa ʟ!āqwa lāxa qādzōꞁɛmē p!ɛlxɛlasgɛma.
      Wǎ, laɛm ⱥɛm la ĕk· hayāsɛk·ǎlē ʟ!āsotiwalisē ꞁɛᵉwis gɛnɛmē
Q!ēx·ʟālaga lāxēq. Laɛm hĕwäx·a k·!āsⱥ. Wǎ, laɛm ēsɛlē ʟ!āso-
tiwalisaxa mōxᵉǔnxē ts!ɛwǔnx qa qautēx·adɛms Aᵉmāx̣ǔlaⱡē ꞁ̓ōᵉ ᵉnɛ-
25   mōgwisaq.

      13. Maturity of the Chief's Sister.

      Wǎ, la maᵉlōkwē ts!ēdaqē wɪ̄waq!was ʟ!āsotiwalisēxa ꞁēgadǎs
Q!ēx·ʟālaga ꞁɛᵉwa āmāᵉyᴬnxaᵉyē ꞁāꞁēliꞁ!a. Wǎ, hĕt!a ʟ!āqoꞁas
k·!ēdadɛs Q!ēx·ʟālaga qaxs ᵉnōlaē. Wǎ, laɛm hĕ qādzōꞁasē ʟ!ā-
qoꞁasax Q!ēx·ʟālaga. Wǎ, laɛm qautēx·ax ⱡaᵉwǔnɛmasē Gǔyōⱡɛlasxa
30   g·ɪ̇gāmaᵉyasa Mamalēleqāla. Wǎ, la ꞁ!āsotiwalisē k!ēdadɛs ꞁāꞁē-

spoke again. He talked (1) into the door of the house of Aᵋmāx̣ŭlał.
"Go on and listen chief/ Aᵋmāx̣ŭlał, and you great chief ᵋnᴇmōgwis.
Now by luck you got everything,/great chiefs. Now you will pay
the marriage debt, he will give away trifles, your son-in-law,/
Aᵋmāx̣ŭlał. Now you will try to get the wife's property and the
trifles, (5) chiefs," said he./

Then they finished their speeches after this and all/ the men
'went home to their houses./

Now ʟ!āsotiwalis and his wife Q!ēx·ʟālaga never quarrelled/
for it is only called quarreling between husband and wife, for ʟ!āso-
tiwalis wished to (10) "sit under" his wife, just as if he was marrying again his wife in the/ way he did, for they had already paid with
Sᴇᵋwa the first/ five hundred marriage blankets. And this is named
"sitting under" the wife, so that/ the words of the speaking may be
right, they say that the man quarreled/ with his wife, but they did
not really quarrel. And there are many chiefs (15) in recent days
who give in marriage more than a thousand blankets/ to the father
of the wife, and the wife has as a mat one hundred and fifty/ blankets and as a belt for all the men who are hired/ for marrying the
wife of a chief. And sometimes it takes five/ winters for a man
to repay the marriage debt to his son-in-law and then (20) they use
as a mast the copper. And this is different from the return gift
of the copper,/ when they just pay back with the copper the marriage
blankets./

Now ʟ!āsotiwalis was just well married after this, with his
wife/ Q!ēx·ʟālaga, and they never parted. Now ʟ!āsotiwalis was
waiting/ four years to be paid back by Aᵋmāx̣ŭlał and (25) ᵋnᴇmōgwis./

13. Maturity of the Chief's Sister.

ʟ!āsotiwalis had two sisters who were named/Q!ēx·ʟālaga and
the other ʟaʟᵋlīʟ!a. Now ʟ!āqoʟas had/ for his princess Q!ēx·ʟālaga
for she was the elder one. Now she was given in marriage by ʟ!ā-
qoʟas, that is Q!ēx·ʟālaga, and he paid back the marriage debt to
her husband G̣ŭyōłᴇlas, (30) the chief of the Mamaleleqala. Then

liɫꜝaxēs āmaᵋyᷫnxaᵋyē wɛqꜝwa qaxa k·ꜝeᷠsaē xŭnōx̣ᵘs ʟᵋwis gɛnɛmē
Qꜝēx·ʟālaga. Wä, hēᵋmis lāg·iꝏas ʟꜝāsotiwalisē la k·ēdadɛs
ʟāʟēliʟꜝa. Wä, laᵋmē ēxɛntē ʟāʟēliʟꜝa. Wä, la hēx·ᵋidaᵋmē ʟꜝāsotiwalis gwēgŭgwanaxēs g·ig·äꝏaxa ᵋnāxwa bēbɛgwānɛmaxa tsꜝōtsꜝo-

5   xōᵋmatsꜝe ʟᵋwa dzēdzɛx·sɛm ʟᵋwa xēxɛtsɛm ʟᵋwa k·āk·ätsꜝɛnaqē
ʟᵋwa ꝏēꝏōqꜝwa ʟᵋwa ꝏēɛlᵋwaᵋyē ʟᵋwa k·ōkwäxtâla ʟᵋwa pꜝɛlxɛ-
lasgɛmē ʟᵋwa hänᵋxatsꜝe. Wä, g·ᷫlᵋmisē ᵋwᷫla gŭnasɛᵋwa dēdanɛm-
x·dē, wä, g·ᷫlᵋmisē mōpꜝɛnxwaᵋsē ᵋnāla g·äg·ᷫʟɛla·lāx g·ᷫlx·dɛ-
mas ēxɛntꜝēdē ʟāʟēliʟꜝa laas ʟꜝāsotiwalisē ʟēꝏtsꜝōdxa Qꜝōmoyâ-

10   ᵋyaxa gaāla qa lēs ᵋwᷫla lāx g·ōkwas. Wä, maᵋlōkwē ᵋyālagɛmas
häᵋyäꝏᵋa qa lēs ʟēᵋlālaxa Qꜝōmoyâᵋyēxa ᵋnēk·ē. Qâsanuᵋx̣ᵘ qa ʟꜝāsotiwalis qâns lē hawâʟēlagâla lāx g·ōkwas qaōxda ēxɛntax. Halāg·ᷫ-
lēʟasai, ᵋnēk·ē. Wä, la âlaɛm hēx·ᵋidaɛm lax·daᵋx̣ᵘ ᵋwᷫla hōgwēʟa Qꜝōmoyâᵋyēxa bɛgwānɛmx·sä. Wä, g·ᷫlᵋmisē g·āx ᵋwᷫlaēʟa laas

15   ʟāxᵋwalᷫꝏē Lālak·otsꜝa qaᵋs yāqꜝɛg·aᵋꝏē Wä, lä ᵋnēk·a: Wa,
gēlag·a Qꜝōmoyŭᵋwē lāxwa k·ꜝēsēx āmʟa wâꝏdɛmaxwa k·ꜝālapᷫlax·ʟax
qag·ᷫns g·ᷫgāmēᵋ lāxg·a ʟꜝāsotiwalisɛk·. Laɛmk· g·āxâlᷫꝏtsōgwa
ʟāʟēliʟꜝak· k·ꜝēdꝏg·asōx ʟꜝāsotiwalisēx. ᵋnēᵋnak·iꝏē g·ᷫg·ᵋɛgāmēᵋ.
Laᵋmēsōx k·ꜝālapᷫᵋlayuʟa lāqōs dōgwaꝏ ᵋmɛᵋwᷫꝏ qag·ada Gwētɛla,

20   ᵋwālas Kwāg·uꝏ ʟᵋwa Qꜝōmk·ꜝūtꜝɛs. ᵋnēᵋnak·iꝏē. Wä, laᵋmēsɛn
hēꝏaꝏ qa lēꝏ qâsaxg·ada yŭduxᵘsɛᵋmakᵘg·a, ᵋnēk·exs laē häsɛla
ᵋnēk·a dālaxa ᵋnɛmxsa pꜝɛlxɛlasgɛma : Laᵋmɛn hēloʟai, g·ᷫgāmaᵋyai
âwadai, qaᵋs laōs qâsaxa Gwētɛla, ᵋwālas Kwāg·uꝏ, Qꜝōmk·ꜝūtꜝɛs
qag·ada g·ᷫgāmēk· ʟꜝāsotiwalis g·āxâlᷫꝏtsugwa k·ꜝēdꝏg·as. Laᵋmits

25   wŭsēg·adɛꝏtsa ᵋnɛmxsa pꜝɛlxɛlasgɛm, ᵋnēk·exs laē x·ᷫlxᵋalᷫꝏas. Wä
lä dāx·ᵋidxa ōgŭᵋlamaxat! ᵋnɛmxsa pꜝɛlxɛlasgɛma, wä, lä ᵋnēk·a:
Laᵋmɛn hēloʟai g·ᷫgāmaᵋyai Ōmx·ᵋidai qaᵋs laōs qâsaxa Gwētɛla, ᵋwālas Kwāg·uꝏ ʟᵋwa Qꜝōmk·ꜝūtꜝɛs qag·ada g·ᷫgāmēk· ʟꜝāsotiwalis
g·āxâlᷫꝏtsōgwa k·ꜝēdꝏg·as. Laᵋmits wŭsēg·adɛꝏtsa ᵋnɛmxsa pꜝɛl-

30   xɛlasgɛma ᵋnēk·exs laē x·ᷫlxᵋalᷫꝏas. Wä, lä ᵋnēk·a: Hāg·a g·ᷫ-
g·ᵋɛgāmēᵋ. Hēᵋems wâꝏdɛmʟēda. Qâsanuᵋx̣ᵘ Gwētɛl qaɛns g·ᷫgāmaᵋyōx

ʟ!ásotiwalis had for his princess ʟāʟēliʟ!a,(1) his younger sister, for he had no child with his wife/ Q!ēx·ʟālaga, and therefore ʟ!āsotiwalis had for his princess/ ʟāʟēliʟ!a. Now ʟāʟēliʟ!a grew up and immediately ʟ!ásotiwalis/ asked all the men to pay their debts, wash basins (5) and buckets and boxes and spoons/ and dishes and mats and button blankets and blankets/ and looking glasses. When they had paid their debts/ then after four days from the beginning of her/menstruation ʟ!ásotiwalis invited in the Q!ōmoyâᶜyē (10) in the morning to come into his house, and two/ young men were sent to invite the Q!ōmoyâᶜyē, saying,"We walk for ʟ!ásotiwalis,/ that we discuss in his house on account of his sister who is menstruating. You will come quickly,"/ said they, and really immediately went in all the/men of the Q!ōmoyâᶜyē. As soon as they were all in (15) Lālak·ots!a arose and spoke. He said, "Now/come, Q!ōmoyâᶜyē, to this speech which is not surprising, which is called 'making steam underneath'/ for our chief ʟ!ásotiwalis. Now has grown up ʟāʟēliʟ!a, the princess of ʟ!ásotiwalis. I mean this, chief. Now this is the means of 'making steam underneath,' what is seen by you heaped up on the floor for the Gwētɛla (20) and the ᶜwālas Kwāg·uⱡ and the Q!ōmk·!ût!ɛs. I mean this. Now/ I will hire you to go and call these three tribes.'⁴ Thus he said and he said aloud/ holding one pair of blankets,"I hire you, chief/ Awadē to go and call the Gwētɛla, ᶜwālas Kwāg·uⱡ and Q!ōmk·!ût!ɛs/on behalf of this chief ʟ!ásotiwalis, and the maturity of this princess. Now/ (25) you wear as your belt this one pair of blankets,"said he as he threw it down./ Then he took up another pair of blankets and said,/"With this I hire you,chief Omx·ᶜîd to go and invite the Gwētɛla/and ᶜwālas Kwag·uⱡ and Q!ōmk·!ût!ɛs for this chief,ʟ!ásotiwalis/and the maturity of this princess. You will have as your belt one pair of blankets,"(30) he said as he threw them down. Then he said, "Go, chiefs./ You will say, 'We walk to call you, Gwētɛla for

our chief,(1) ʟ!āsotiwalis,and the maturity of ʟāʟēliʟ!a, ʟ!āsoti-
walis' princess./ You will come quickly,' thus you will say," said
Lālak·ots!a, giving instructions to Âwadē what/he was to say./

Then the two chiefs who were hired went inviting. (5) As soon
as they had gone out of the house, Âwadē and Ōmx·ᵋĪd, Lālak·ots!a /
said that all the things were to be put in separate piles./ Then
the young men piled up separately the whole amount that was to be
given to the/ three Kwāg·uⱡ tribes, and when each kind was gathered
up,/ then Lālak·ots!a told four young men (1Q) to go to call the three
Kwāg·uⱡ tribes and/ the four young men of the Q!ōmoyâᵋyē went out
of the house into/ the house of the head tribe, the GwētƐla, and
one of the/inviting young men said, "Now we come to invite you,Gwē-
tƐla for ʟ!āsotiwalis."/ Thus he said, and then the three young men
said, "Come quickly,"(15) Thus they said as they went out of the
house and they kept on/ saying this as they entered all the houses
of the three Kwāg·uⱡ tribes./ As soon as they had gone into all the
houses they went back and entered/ his house. Then the GwētƐla came
in and sat down/ in the rear of the house and the ᵋwālas Kwāg·uⱡ
came in (20) and sat down in the right hand corner of the house and/
the Q!ōmk·!ūt!Ɛs came in and sat down in the left hand corner/ of
the house. When the men and the women with men's seats/had all
come into the house, Lālak·ots!a sent for the four young men/ who
had been inviting (the people) to look for the last one (to look
for a face of) the one who had not yet come of the men who belonged
to the (25) three Kwāg·uⱡ tribes. Then the four young men went again/
those that were now called "sent to look for a face." They went
out of the house and entered/ the house of the GwētƐla. Then they
all said, "We come/to 'look for a face,' GwētƐla. that may not have
gone into the/ house of chief ʟ!āsotiwalis," they said. Then they
arrived (30) at the house of the ᵋwālas Kwāg·uⱡ and went into the/
door of the house and they said again, "We come to 'look for a face,'

(1) ᵋwālas Kwāg·uⱡ, that may not have gone into the house of chief/ ʟ!āsotiwalis," they said. They went out of the/ house and they went into the house of the Q!ōmk·!ūt!ɛs and/ they said, "We come to look for a face , Q!ōmk·!ūt!ɛs, that may not have gone (5) in-to the house of chief ʟ!āsotiwalis,"/ they said. And as soon as they had gone into the houses they came/ back and went into the house in which the three Kwāg·uⱡ tribes had gone./ And when they had all gone in, they said, "Now/ the tribes are all inside," they said./

(10) Then arose Lālak·ots!a and spoke./ He said, turning his face to the Q!ōmoyaᵋyē who were sitting down inside of the/ door-way of the house, "Now, my chiefs, I shall speak and/ I shall speak gratefully of the chiefs of the three Kwāg·uⱡ tribes, for they have come/ quickly," said he as he turned his face to the rear of the house. And (15) he spoke and said, "Now welcome, Gwētɛla, ᵋwālas Kwāg·uⱡ,/ Q!ōmk·!ūt!ɛs. Welcome to this that is not often shown/ for the princess of a chief, what is called 'taking out the steam,' the maturing of / the princess, for they cannot stand the amount it costs of trifles given away/for they are never returned when a man gives a potlatch with blankets (20) and trifles. It is only shown when/ the princesses of chiefs grow up, I mean this," said he/ as he took up a wash basin. And then he said aloud,/ "This is the wash basin for the maturing ʟāʟēliʟ!a, the princess of ʟ!āsotiwalis/ one hundred," said he as he put it down among the others. (25) Then he took up one kettle and he said aloud, "This is/ the wash basin for the maturing ʟāʟēliʟ!a, the princess of ʟ!āsotiwalis/ one hundred. Now this is for you Gwētɛla, ᵋwālas Kwāg·uⱡ, Q!ōmk·!ūt!ɛs,"/ thus he said as he put it down among the others. Then he took one/box and he said aloud, "This is the recep-tacle for time beating for the maturing (30) ʟāʟēliʟ!a, the prin-cess of ʟ!āsotiwalis, one hundred. Now this is going to you, Gwē-tɛla,ᵋwālas Kwag·uⱡ,Q!ōmk·!ūtɛs," he said as he put it down (1)

lāxēs waōkwē. Wä, lä dāx·ᵋidxa ᵋnɛmēxʟa k·āts!ɛnaq. Wä, lä
hāsɛla ᵋnēk·a: G·aɛm yūyats!e k·āts!ɛnaqsa g·axᴀlil̓tsɛᵋwē
ʟᴀʟēliʟ!a k·!ēdēl̓as ʟ!āsotiwalis, sɛk·!ax·sok·ᴀla. Laɛm lāl̓
lᴀ̂ʟ, Gwētɛl, ᵋwālas Kwāg·ul̓, Q!ōmk·!ūt!ɛs, ᵋnēk·exs laē hänqas
5   lāxēs waōkwē. Wä, lä dāx·ᵋidxa ᵋnɛmēxʟa l̓ōq!wa. Wä, lä hāsɛla
ᵋnēk·a. G·aɛm hamaats!e l̓ōq!wasa g·axᴀlil̓tsɛᵋwē ʟᴀʟēliʟ!a k·!ē-
dēl̓as ʟ!āsotiwalis sɛk·!ax·sōgŭg·ɛyu. Laɛm lāl̓ lᴀ̂ʟ Gwētɛl, ᵋwālas
Kwāg·ul̓, Q!ōmk·!ūt!ɛs, ᵋnēk·exs laē hänqas lāxēs waōkwē. Wä, lä
dāx·ᵋidxa ᵋnɛmxsa l̓ēᵋwaᵋya. Wä, lä hāsɛla ᵋnēk·a: G·aɛm k!wä-
10 dzᴀᵋlil̓tsōsa g·axᴀlil̓ts!ɛᵋwē ʟᴀʟēliʟ!a k·!ēdēl̓as ʟ!āsotiwalis sɛ-
k·!asgɛmg·ustᴀxsa. Laɛm lāl̓ lᴀ̂ʟ, Gwētɛl, ᵋwālas Kwāg·ul̓, Q!ōmk·!ū-
t!ɛs, ᵋnēk·exs laē pāq!ᴀ̈qas lāxēs waōkwē.

Wä, lä dāx·ᵋidxa ᵋnɛmxsäxat! l̓ēᵋwaᵋyaxa ōgŭgēl̓ᵋmē lāxa g·il-
xdē wäl̓dɛms. Wä, lä hāsɛla ᵋnēk·a: G·aɛm kwädzɛdzōsa g·axᴀlil̓-
15 tsɛᵋwē ʟᴀʟēliʟ!a k·!ēdēl̓as ʟ!āsotiwalis sɛk·!asgɛmg·ustᴀxsa. Laɛm
lāl̓ lᴀ̂ʟ, Gwētɛl, ᵋwālas Kwāg·ul̓, Q!ōmk·!ūt!ɛs, ᵋnēk·exs laē p!ā-
q!ᴀ̈qas lāxēs waōkwē.

Wä, lä dāx·ᵋidxa ᵋnɛmē k·ukwäxtᴀla. Wä, lä ᵋnēk·a: G·aɛm
ᵋnɛxᵋūnēsa g·axᴀlil̓tsɛᵋwē ʟᴀʟēliʟ!a k·!ēdēl̓as ʟ!āsotiwalis, mᴀᵋl̓-
20 tsōgŭg·ɛyu. Laɛm lāl̓ lᴀ̂ʟ, Gwētɛl, ᵋwālas Kwāg·ul̓, Q!ōmk·!ūt!ɛs,
ᵋnēk·exs laē x·îlq!ɛqas lāxēs waōkwē.

Wä, lä dāx·ᵋidxa ᵋnɛmxsa p!ɛlxɛlasgɛma. Wä, lä ᵋnēk·a:
G·aɛm ēdɛm k·ādzɛkᵘsa g·axᴀlil̓tsɛᵋwē ʟᴀʟēliʟ!a k·!ēdēl̓as ʟ!ā-
sotiwalis sɛk·!ax·sōk·ᴀla p!ɛlxɛlasgɛma. Laɛm lāl̓ lᴀ̂ʟ, Gwētɛl,
25 ᵋwālas Kwāg·ul̓, Q!ōmk·!ūt!ɛs, ᵋnēk·exs laē x·îlq!ᴀ̈qas lāxēs waōkwē.

Wä, lä dāx·ᵋidxa ᵋnɛmē hänᵋxats!e. Wä, lä ᵋnēk·a: G·aɛm
hänxɛla hänᵋxats!ēsa g·axᴀlil̓tsɛᵋwē ʟᴀʟēliʟ!a k·!ēdēl̓as ʟ!āsoti-
walis maᵋl̓tsogŭg·eyē. Laɛm lāl̓ lᴀ̂ʟ, Gwētɛl, ᵋwālas Kwāg·ul̓, Q!ōm-
30 k·!ūt!ɛs, ᵋnēk·ēxs laē pāq!ᴀ̈qas lāxēs waōkwē.

among the others. Then he took up one spoon and/said aloud, "This is the spoon for eating of the maturing/LᴀLēlιʟ!a, the princess of ʟ!ásotiwalis. One hundred and fifty. Now it is going/ to you Gwētɛla, ᵋwālas. Kwāg·uⱡ, Q!ōmk·!ūt!ɛs." Thus he said and put it down (5) among the others. Then he took up one (wooden) dish and said aloud,/ "This is the eating dish of the maturing Lᴀlēlιʟ!a the princess/ of ʟ!ásotiwalis, one hundred and fifty. Now it goes to you, Gwētɛla, ᵋwālas/ Kwāg·uⱡ, Q!ōmk·!ūt!ɛs." Thus he said and put it down among the others. Then/ he took a mat and said aloud, "This is (10) the seat of the maturing Lᴀlēlιʟ!a, the princess of ʟ!ásotiwalis,/ fifty. Now it goes to you, Gwētɛla, ᵋwālas Kwāg·uⱡ, Q!ōmk·!ūt!ɛs."/ Thus he said and he put it down among the others./

Then he also took one mat from another pile different from the one/ just mentioned and he said aloud, "This is the mat on which washes herself the maturing (15) Lᴀlēlιʟ!a, the princess of ʟ!ásoti- walis, fifty. Now/ it goes to you, Gwētɛla, ᵋwālas Kwāg·uⱡ, Q!ōm- k·!ūt!ɛs." Thus he said and/ he put it down among the others./

Then he took a button blanket and he said, "This is/ the blanket of the maturing Lᴀlēlιʟ!a, the princess of ʟ!ásotiwalis. (20) One hundred and twenty. Now it is going to you, Gwētɛla, ᵋwālas Kwāg·uⱡ, Q!ōmk·!ūt!ɛs."/ Thus he said and put it down among the others./

Then he took one pair of blankets and he said,/ "This is the cedar bark napkin of the maturing Lᴀlēlιʟ!a, the princess of ʟ!á- sotiwalis,/two hundred and fifty blankets. Now it is going to you, Gwētɛla,(25) ᵋwālas Kwāg·uⱡ, Q!ōmk·!ūtɛs." Thus he said and he put it down among the/others./

Then he took a looking-glass and he said, "This is/ the look- ing-glass of the maturing Lᴀlēlιʟ!a, the princess of ʟ!ásotiwalis./ One hundred and twenty. Now it will go to you, Gwētɛla, ᵋwālas Kwāg·uⱡ, Q!ōmk·!ūt!ɛs (30) Thus he said and he put it down among the others./

Wä, lä dāx·ᵉidxa ᵉnɛmē xɛgɛm. Wä, lä ᵉnēk·a: G·aɛm xāqɛla
xɛgɛmsa g·axᴀliᴧtsɛᵉwē ʟᴀʟēliʟ!a k·!ēdēᴧas ʟ!āsotiwalis sɛk·!as-
gɛmg·ustᴀ. Laɛm lāᴧ lᴀ̂ʟ, Gwētɛl, ᵉwālas Kwāg·uᴧ, Q!ōmk·!ût!ɛs,
ᵉnēk·exs laē pāq!āqas lāxēs waōkwē.

5   Wä, lä dāx·îdxa q!ɛʟ!ɛts!āqē xōkᵘ k!waxʟᴀ̂ᵉwa. Wä, lä ᵉnēk·ᴀ:
G·aɛm dzēg·ats!e ꭓwāk!ūnasa g·āxᴀliᴧtsɛᵉwē ʟᴀʟēliʟ!a k·!ēdēᴧas
ʟ!āsotiwalis q!ɛʟ!ɛts!āqa ꭓwāxwāk!ūna sēsɛk·!ax·sōk!ûx p!ɛlxɛlas-
gɛm. Laɛm lāᴧ lᴀ̂ʟ, Gwētɛl, ᵉwālas Kwāg·uᴧ, Q!ōmk·!ût!ɛs, ᵉnēk·exs
laē ꭓwēlaqa ʟoxᵉwalîʟɛq.

10   Wä, lä dāx·ᵉidxa sēwayu. Wä, lä ᵉnēk·a: G·aɛm sēꭓûla sēwa-
yusa g·axᴀliᴧtsɛᵉwē ʟᴀʟēliʟ!a k·!ēdēᴧas ʟ!āsotiwalis ʟaxût!aaxa
g·āwēq!ānɛmē, yūduꭓᵘsɛmg·ustᴀ̂ sēsɛwayá. Laɛm lāᴧ lᴀ̂ʟ, Gwētɛl,
ᵉwālas Kwāg·uᴧ, Q!ōmk·!ût!ɛs, ᵉnēk·exs laē pāq!āqas lāxēs waōkwē.

Wä, lä dāx·ᵉîdxa gwēᴧgwälaxa sāxsdaᵉyē ʟɛᵉwa häxa gweᵉyōs
15 gwēᴧgwäla. Wä, lä ᵉnēk·a: G·aɛm q!ōxts!ɛᵉwēsa g·axᴀliᴧtsɛᵉwē
ʟᴀʟēliʟ!a k·!ēdēᴧas ʟ!āsotiwalisē, sɛk·!ax·sogûg·ɛyōkᵘ sēsaxsda-
ᵉya ʟɛᵉwa hēhäxa ʟɛᵉwa tētɛlgwabᴀ̂ᵉyē ʟɛᵉwa ts!ēts!ɛts!ɛsɛlax·si-
dzēᵉ ʟɛᵉwa t!ēt!ɛᵉbayu. Laɛm lāᴧ lᴀ̂ʟ, Gwētɛl, ᵉwālas Kwāg·uᴧ, Q!ōm-
k·!ût!ɛs, ᵉnēk·exs laē x·flq!āqas lāxēs waōkwē.

20   Wä, lä dāx·ᵉidxa ᵉnɛmsgɛmē kwᴀ̂ᵉlōg·a k·!ōkûla. Wä, lä ᵉnēk·a:
G·aɛm qēqax·ts!anē dalēg·a k·!ōkûlasa g·axᴀliᴧtsɛᵉwē ʟᴀʟēliʟ!a
k·!ēdēᴧas ʟ!āsotiwalisē, maᵉᴧtsɛm kwēkwᴀ̂ᵉlōg·a k·!ōkûla g·aᵉmēsēg·a
sɛk·!asgɛmgᴀ̂lak· dēdaᵉlōg·a k·!ōkûla. Laɛm lāᴧ lᴀ̂ʟ, Gwētɛl, ᵉwālas
Kwāg·uᴧ, Q!ōmk·!ût!ɛs, ᵉnēk·exs laē g·îqas lāxēs waōkwē.

25   Wä, lä dāx·ᵉidxa ᵉnɛmē kûskwᴀ̂ᵉla gāsgɛʟ!a Wä, lä ᵉnēk·a:
G·aɛm mōsmaᵉlasa g·axᴀliᴧtsɛᵉwē ʟᴀʟēliʟ!a k·!ēdēᴧas ʟ!āsotiwa-
lisē, sɛk·!āk!wēma kûskwᴀ̂ᵉla gāsgɛʟ!a Laɛm lāᴧ lᴀ̂ʟ, Gwētɛl,
ᵉwālas Kwāg·uᴧ, Q!ōmk·!ût!ɛs, ᵉnēk·exs laē g·îqas lāxēs wāokwē.

Wä, lä dāx·ᵉidxa ᵉnɛmē dāsdälaa tēstɛk!wa (maᵉᴧē ʟēgɛmas
30 ʟōᵉ ts!āᴧts!ɛmāq!a). Wä, lä ᵉnēk·a: G·aɛm ts!aᴧts!ɛmāq!asa
g·axᴀliᴧtsɛᵉwē ʟᴀʟēliʟ!a k·!ēdēᴧas ʟ!āsotiwalisē, yūduꭓᵘsɛmg·ustᴀ̂

(1) Then he took up a comb and he said, "This is the comb/ of the maturing ᴸāᴸēliᴸ!a, the princess of ᴸ!āsotiwalis, fifty./ Now it will go to you, Gwēᴛɛla, ᵋwālas Kwāg·uⱡ, Q!ōmk·!ūt!ɛs,"/ Thus he said and put it down among the others./

(5) Then he took up six split cedar sticks and he said,/ "These are the clam digging canoes of the maturing ᴸāᴸēliᴸ!a, the princess/ of ᴸ!āsotiwalis. Six canoes,'each valued at fifty blankets./ Now they are going to you, Gwēᴛɛla, ᵋwālas Kwāg·uⱡ, Q!ōmk·!ūt!ɛs." Thus he said/ and put them down./

(10) Then he took up a paddle and he said, "This is the paddle used/by the maturing ᴸāᴸēliᴸ!a, the princess of ᴸ!āsotiwalis, when she goes out/ after clams, thirty paddles. Now they are going to you, Gwēᴛɛla,/ ᵋwālas Kwāg·uⱡ, Q!ōmk·!ūt!ɛs." Thus he said and put it down among the others./

Then he took up clothing,(skirts and women's shirts are referred to (15) as clothing) and he said, "This is worn by the maturing/ᴸāᴸēliᴸ!a, the princess of ᴸ!āsotiwalis, one hundred and fifty skirts/ and petticoats and undershirts and stockings/ and shoes. Now they are going to you, Gwēᴛɛla, ᵋwālas Kwāg·uⱡ, Q!ōmk·!ūt!ɛs."/ Thus he said and he put them down among the others./

(20) Then he took up one gold bracelet and he said,/ "This is the silver bracelet of the maturing ᴸāᴸēliᴸ!a/the princess of ᴸ!āsotiwalis. Two gold bracelets and/twenty-five silver bracelets. Now they are going to you, Gwēᴛɛla, ᵋwālas/Kwāg·uⱡ, Q!ōmk·!ūt!ɛs," And he put it down among the others./

(25) Then he took up one gold earring and he said,/ "This is the ear ornament of the maturing ᴸāᴸēlíᴸ!a, the princess of ᴸ!āsotiwalis,/ five pairs of gold earrings. Now they are going to you Gwēᴛɛla,/ ᵋwālas Kwāg·uⱡ, Q!ōmk·!ūt!ɛs," said he and put them down among the others./

Then he took up one silver ear ornament (they have two names,/ (30) also "ear icicles") and he said, "These are the ear icicles of/

dāsdᾱlaa tēstɛk!wa. Laɛm lāx̣ lᾶʟ, Gwētɛl, ᵋwālas Kwāg·ux̣, Q̣!ōm-
k·!ūt!ɛs, ᵋnēk·exs laē g·Ꞁqas lāxēs waōkwē.

Wä, lᾶ dāx·ᵋidxa ᵋnɛmē ëx·ts!ɛma. Wä, lᾶ ᵋnēk·a: G·aɛm xō-
xoqṹla ëx·ts!ɛmsa g·axᾶlix̣tseᵋwē ʟᾱlēlіʟ!a k·!ēdēx̣as ʟ!āsotiwalisē,
5   maᵋx̣gṹnāx̣tsɛmg·ustᾶ k!wēma. Laɛm lāx̣ lᾶʟ, Gwētel, ᵋwālas Kwāg·ux̣,
Q̣!ōmk·!ūt!ɛs, ᵋnēk·exs laē g·Ꞁqas lāxēs waōkwē.

Wä, lᾶ dāx·ᵋidxa ᵋnɛmē ʟ!ōxɛkᵘ k·flx·sɛm yāsɛkᵘsa ᵋmɛlxʟọwē.
Wä, lᾶ ᵋnēk·a: G·aɛm yāsɛkṹla yāsɛkᵘsa g·axᾶlix̣tsɛᵋwē ʟᾱlēlіʟ!a
k·!ēdēx̣as ʟ!āsotiwalisē, sɛk·!ax·sōgṹg·ɛyu ʟ!ōxɛkwa. Laɛm lāx̣
10 lᾶʟ, Gwētɛl, ᵋwālas Kwāg·ux̣, Q̣!ōmk·!ūt!ɛs, ᵋnēk·exs laē ᾶxᾱqas
lāxēs waōkwē.

Wä, lᾶ dāx·ᵋidxa ᵋnɛmē dēgɛmᵋyᾶ. Wä, l⸬ ᵋnēk·a: G·aɛm
k·ᾱk·adzɛkṹmᵋyu k·ᾱdzɛkᵘsa g·axᾶlix̣tsɛᵋwē ʟᾱlēlіʟ!a k·!ēdēx̣as
ʟ!āsotiwalisē, lᾱk·!endē dēgɛmᵋyᾶ. Laɛm lāx̣ lᾶʟ, Gwētɛl, ᵋwālas
15 Kwāg·ux̣, Q̣!ōmk·!ūt!ɛs, ᵋnēk·exs laē x·flq!ᾱqas lāxēs waōkwē.

Wä, lᾶ yāq!ɛg·aᵋx̣a. Wä, lᾶ ᵋnēk·a: Wa, wadzēsōx wᾶx̣dɛm-
ʟɛxsg·fn g·Ꞁgāmēk·xwa k·!ēsēx q̣!ṹnāla nēx̣ᵋid lāxa waōkwē g·Ꞁ-
g·ɛgᾱmaᵋya qaēs k·!ēdēx̣axs g·axᾶlix̣tseᵋwaē. Wä, yūɛm ʟ̣ēgadɛs
k·!ālapodäxēs k·!ēdēx̣axs g·ālaē ēxɛnta. Ladzēᵋmē ᵋwIlg·flix̣axen
20 ʟ̣ēʟɛqɛlaseᵋwēxa k·!ālapoᵋdayuʟɛxg·ada g·axᾶlix̣tsōkᵘxg·a ʟᾱlēli-
ʟ!ak· k·!ēdēx̣g·as ʟ!āsotiwalisxg·ada ʟ̣āwūlsēᵋstāla g·Ꞁgāmaᵋya.
ᵋnēᵋnak·ix̣ē. Wäg·a Q̣!ōmoyūwē. ᵋwIlg·flIx̣ɛlaɛmʟᾱs ts!awānaēsa
ᵋnᾱxwax qaᵋs ᵋgwēgṹx·sdɛm lāxwa yūduxᵘsɛᵋmakwē qaxs k·!eᾶsaē
ʟ̣ēʟɛgɛmsōx lāxwa k·!ālapēlax. Wä, la k·!eᾶs q̣!ɛmdɛm lāqᵘ,
25 ᵋnēk·ē.

Wä, hᵉ̈x·ᵋidaᵋmisa ᵋnᾱxwa bēbɛgwānɛmsa Q̣!ōmoyᾶᵋyē q̣!wāg·f-
lix̣ qaᵋs lē ᾶx·ᵋēdxa ᵋnᾱxwa qaᵋs gwēx·sdɛᵋma qaᵋs lē ts!awānaēsas
lāxa Gwētɛla g·āla qaxs hᵉ̈ᵋmaē mɛkṹmēsa ᵋnᾱxwa lēlqwālaʟaᵋya.
Wä, g·flᵋmisē ᵋwIlxtoxs laē ts!awānaēsasɛᵋwa ᵋwālas Kwāg·ux̣. Wä
30 g·flᵋmisē ᵋwIlxtoxs laē ʟ̣āx̣x̣walix̣ō ʟālak·ots!a qaᵋs ēdzaqwē yāq!ɛ-
g·aᵋx̣a. Wä, lᾶ ᵋnēk·a: ᵋya, g·Ꞁg·ɛgᾱmēs Gwētɛl, ᵋwālas Kwāg·ux̣,

ʟāʟēliʟ!a, the princess of ʟ!āsotiwalis, thirty (1) silver ear ornaments. Now they are going to you, Gwētɛla, ᵋwālas Kwāg·uⁱ, Q!ōmk·!ū-
t!ɛs."/ Thus he said and put them down among the others./

Then he took up one abalone shell and he said, "This is/ the
head ornament of the maturing ʟāʟēliʟ!a, the princess of ʟ!āsotiwalis
(5) eighty pairs. Now they are going to you, Gwētɛla, ᵋwālas Kwāg·uⁱ,/
Q!ōmk·!ūt!ɛs." Thus he said and put them down among the others./

Then he took up one cake of tallow of the mountain goat/ and he
said, "This is the tallow for greasing (the face) of the maturing
ʟāʟēliʟ!a/ the princess of ʟ!āsotiwalis, one hundred and fifty cakes.
Now they are going (10) to you, Gwētɛla,ᵋwālas Kwāg·uⁱ,Q!ōmk·!ūt!ɛs,"
Thus he said and put them down/ among the others./

Then he took up one towel and he said, "This is/ the cedar bark
face towel of the maturing ʟāʟēliʟ!a, princess of/ ʟ!āsotiwalis, one
hundred towels. Now they are going to you, Gwētɛla, (15) ᵋwālas Kwā-
g·uⁱ,Q!ōmk·!ūt!ɛs." Thus he said and put it down among the others./

Then he spoke and said; "Now this is the great word/ of my chief,
this that is not often shown by other chiefs/ when their princesses
mature. This is named/ 'taking out the steam of his princess when
she menstruates the first time.' Now it is at an end (20) what I have
named taking out the steam of this maturing ʟāʟēliʟ!a/ the princess of
ʟ!āsotiwalis, this chief who is all over first born./ I mean this,
Q!ōmoyâᵋyē. You shall all go and give out/ all these kinds of things
to the three tribes," (for they do not/ use the names for this "taking
out of the steam" and there is no song with it)(25) said he./

At once all the men of the Q!ōmoyâᵋyē arose/ and took up all
the kinds of things and distributed them/ among the Gwētɛla first, for
they are the head of all the tribes,/ and when they had finished
with them they distributed them among the ᵋwālas Kwāg·uⁱ (30) and
when they had finished with them, Lālak·ots!a arose and spoke again./

Q!ōmk·!ūt!ɛs. Wäg·a, dōqwaƚaxwa ᵉwālasᵉx k·!älapōᵉdayuxa g·a-
xᴀ́liƚtsɛᵉwē ʟᴀ̄ʟēliʟ!a k·!ēdēƚas ʟ!ᴀ̄sotiwalis. ᵉnēᵉnak·iƚē
yūduxᵘsɛᵉmakᵘ Kwākŭg·uƚ, laɛms ʟ̱ēqɛlaʟɛs ʟᴀ̄ʟēliʟ!adzē lāxa
g·axᴀ́liƚtsɛᵉwē ʟᴀ̄ʟēliʟ!axa k·!ēdēƚiᵉlakwēxa k·!ēdēƚtsēᵉstāla
5   qa äxäsg·a lak· k·!ēdadɛsēg·ɪn g·ɪgᴀ̄mēk·xg·a ʟ!ᴀ̄sotiwalisɛk·.
ᵉnēᵉnak·iƚē g·ɪg·ɛgᴀ̄mēs yūduxᵘsɛᵉmakᵘ Kwākŭg·uƚ, 'lēx·adzᴀ́ᵉmaɛn
hᵍ gwēx·sēxg·ɪn nänukwēg·asa ēxɛntɛmƚa ʟɛtɛmƚtsa g·axᴀ́liƚtsɛᵉwē
ʟᴀ̄ʟēliʟ!adzē, ᵉnēk·ē. Wä, hᵍx·ᵉidaᵉmisē ʟ!ᴀ̄sotiwalisē ʟ̱ᴀ̄xᵉwaliƚa
qaᵉs yāq!ɛg·aᵉƚē. Wä, lä ᵉnēk·a: Wäxq!ŭnēxsʟ̱ēda ʟēʟɛtɛmƚa. Hāg·a
10   äxᵉēdqē lāxa ōts!ᴀ́liƚē, ᵉnēk·ē. Wä, lēda hᴀ́ᵉyāƚᵉa lats!ᴀ́liƚ lāxa
ōts!ᴀ́liƚē qaᵉs g·äxē dālaxa sɛk·!asgɛmg·ustᴀ́ ʟɛtɛmƚ qaᵉs g·äxē
ᵉmōgŭᵉliƚas lᴀ̈x ʟ̱aᵉwilasas Lālak·ots!a. Wä, hᵍx·ᵉidaᵉmisē yᴀ̱-
q!ɛg·aᵉƚē Lālak·ots!a Wä, lä ᵉnēk·a: ᵉwālasᵉwɪst!a ʟ!ɛlēƚawa
ᵉyaēxg·ada ēxɛntɛmƚɛk· ʟɛtɛmƚa. Wa, gɛlak·asᵉlax·ɛn laēnaᵉyē
15   mɛlxᵉwaʟɛlaqɛk· qaxs ᵉwālasēlaxsdē q!ämēsᵉns ᵉnɛᵉmēmuta Yaēx·a-
gɛmaᵉyē. ᵉnēᵉnak·iƚē. G·aɛm ēxɛntɛmƚ ʟɛtɛmƚtsa g·axᴀ́liƚtsɛᵉwē
ʟᴀ̄ʟēliʟ!adzē k·!ēdēƚas ʟ!ᴀ̄sotiwalisē, sɛk·!asgɛmg·ustᴀ́ ʟēʟɛtɛmƚa.
Laɛm lāƚ lᴀ̂ʟ, g·ɪg·ɛgᴀ̄mēs Gwētɛl, ᵉwālas Kwᴀ̄g·uƚ, Q!ōmk·!ūt!ɛs,
ᵉnēk·ɛxs laē g·ɪqasa ᵉnɛmsgɛmē lax·dᴀ̈ daakᵘs. Wä, lä ᵉnēk·a: Wä-
20   g·a ēt!ēd ts!awänaēsax Q!ōmoyŭwē, ᵉnēk·ɛxs laē k!wäg·alƚa. Wä,
laᵉmē ts!awänaēsasɛᵉwa Q!ōmk·!ūt!ɛs. Wä, g·ɪlmisē ᵉwɪᵉla ts!a-
wänaēsasɛᵉwa Q!ōmk·!ūt!ɛsē laas äxᵉētsɛᵉwa ʟēʟɛtɛmƚē qaᵉs lē
ts!awänaēdzɛm lāxa g·ig·ɛgᴀ̄maᵉyasa yūduxᵘsɛᵉmakwē Kwākŭg·uƚa.
Wä, g·ɪlᵉmisē ᵉwɪᵉla ts!awänaēdzɛma ʟēʟɛtɛmƚē lāxa g·ɪg·ɛgᴀ̄ma-
25   ᵉyasa yūduxᵘsɛᵉmakwē Kwākŭg·uƚa laas ᵉnɛmᴀ̄x·ɪs ʟ̱ōᵉ ts!ɛx·ᵉidēda
g·ɪg·ɛgᴀ̄maᵉyasa yūduxᵘsɛᵉmakwē Kwākŭg·uƚa. Wä, laᵉmē yaēq!ɛnta-
lēda k·!alapōdē qaēs k·!ēdēƚaxs g·ālaē g·äxᴀ́liƚtsɛᵉwa. Wä, laɛm
nēᵉnas yāq!ɛnt!ala. Wä, lä k·fƚɛla yāq!ɛnt!alēda hᵍwäxa q!asɛ-
laxēs k·!ēdēƚaxs g·axᴀ́liƚtsɛᵉwaē.
30   Wä, hᵍɛm gwɛᵉyōsa bäk!umē wɪx·sᴀ́ g·ɪgᴀ̄maᵉyē wäx·ᵉmaē p!ɛsasa
p!ɛlxɛlasgɛm lāxēs g·ōkŭlōtē. Wä, wäx·ᵉɛmxaäwisē ʟēƚɛlaxa ᵉnᴀ̱xwa

He said, "Oh chiefs of the Gwētɛla,ᵋwālas Kwāg·uɫ,(1) Q!ōmk·!ut!ɛs,
look at this great 'taking out the steam'/of the maturing ʟāʟēliʟ!a,
the princess of ʟ!āsotiwalis. I mean this,/ chiefs of the three
Kwāg·uɫ tribes. Now you will call her great ʟāʟēliʟ!a,/ the maturing ʟāʟēliʟ!a who has been made a princess, who is a princess all
over (5) on account of what has been done by the one who has now a
princess, my chief ʟ!āsotiwalis here./ I mean this, chiefs of the
three Kwag·uɫ tribes. Now there is only/one thing that is missing,
the menstruation hat of the maturing/great ʟāʟēliʟ!a," said he. Immediately ʟ!āsotiwalis arose/and spoke. He said, "I forgot the hats.
Now (10) get them from the bedroom," said he. Then the young men
went into the/bedroom and they came carrying fifty hats and they/put
them down where Lālak·ots!a was standing. Immediately/Lālak·ots!a
spoke and said, "Very great is/this menstruation hat which was forgotten by you. Now thank you.(15) For it occurred to me that it
would be a great disgrace for our numaym,the Yaēx·agɛmēᵋ./ I mean
this, this the menstruation hat of the great maturing/ʟāʟēliʟ!a, the
princess of ʟ!āsotiwalis,fifty hats./ Now they are going to you,
Gwētɛla, ᵋwālas Kwāg·uɫ,Q!ōmk·!ut!ɛs."/ Thus he said and put down the
one that he was holding. Then he said,(20)"Go on,Q!ōmoyâᵋyē, and distribute them," said he as he sat down. / Then they were distributed
among the Q!ōmk·!ut!ɛs, and as soon as all/ the Q!ōmk·!ut!ɛs had
been given, then the hats were taken and/ distributed among the chiefs
of the three Kwāg·uɫ tribes./ And as soon as all the hats had been
distributed among the chiefs(25) of the three Kwāg·uɫ tribes, then
it was as though had waked up/the chiefs of the three Kwāg·uɫ tribes
and now were talking/ those who had "taken out the steam" for the
princess who had grown up. Now/ they dared to talk. Those are
afraid to talk who do not take notice/ of their princess when she
grows up./

(30) This is referred to by the Indians as "chiefs not going
through", although they give away/ blankets to their tribes and also

lēlqwǎlaʟaᵉya, wä, g·îlᵉmisē k·ǃēs k·ǃālapōda qaᵉs k·ǃēdēᴌaxs
g·ālaō g·axᴂliᴌtsɛᵉwa, wä, laᵉmē ʟēgadɛs wîx·sᴂ g·îgǎmä lāxēq.
Wä, lāxaō hᵂɛm gwǎᴌa wǎᴌdɛmō qaōda k·ǃēs qautōx·ax ᴌāᵉwǔnɛmasēs
k·ǃēdēᴌō. Laɛmxaa ʟēgadɛs wîx·sᴂ g·îgāmaᵉya lāxēq. Wä, hōᵉmis
5   ʟēgadɛs xāmagɛmǎ ᵉwîᵉlōʟɛlēs g·îgǎmaᵉyō ʟǃāsotiwalisō qō lāᴌ
ᵉwîᵉlōʟɛx qǃwāxag·iᴌasa wǎᴌaqēla qaᵉs nɛgɛᴌtōdēx gwǎlag·îlidza-
ᴂasēs gagɛmpaxa qwēsɛlä ᵉnālaxa ᵉnǎxwaᵉma ᵉwîᵉloʟɛx wǎx·a ʟēgwē-
tsōsa g·îg·ɛgǎmaᵉyō qaᵉs ᵉwîᵉla lǎʟǎnᵉmaxɛn lāx k·ǃātasɛᵉwaxa
gwǎᴌɛlaᵉma wǔlgǎmō g·îgǎmōᵉg·îlisō Yîx·āgɛmaᵉyōxa ǎᵉwǎnᴂlisas
10   ʟǃāsotiwalisō lax ʟɛx·sîwaᵉyō. Wä, lāᵉlaō ᵉnǎxwaɛm xēxāmagɛmd
g·îg·ɛgǎmaᵉyōda la ʟǃāyōs g·äg·îʟɛla lāx Yîx·āgɛmaᵉyō, g·āxᵉa -
ʟɛla lāx ʟǃāsotiwalisō. Wä, hōᵉmis lāg·iᵉᴌas ʟǃāqoʟasō ᴌâkǃwō-
mas ᵉnōx· qa hālabalēsēs ʟɛwɛlgamaᵉyō ʟǃāsotiwalis ᵉwāᵉwiᵉlō-
ʟǃax gwayiᵉlǎlasasa ᵉnōk·ō qaᵉs xāmagɛmaᵉyō g·îgǎmaᵉya. Wä,
15   laᵉmisō kǃwāyōʟɛq. K·ǃēsō la qǃōx·ᵉidǎᴌō lä lālōʟǃasōs ʟǃāsotiwalisō qo lāᴌ ᴂlak·ǃālaᴌ xāmagǎmēᵉ ᵉwîᵉlōʟɛlēs g·îgǎmēᵉ
lāxēq.

     Wä, laᵉmō ᵉwîᵉla hōqǔwɛlsa yǔduxᵘsɛᵉmakwō Kwǎkǔg·uᴌ lāxēq.
Wä, lāʟa ʟāʟēliʟǃadzō kǃwatsǃǎliᴌtsäɛm lāxēs ōxɛndatsǃō g·aōlas
20   lāxa onōgwiᴌas g·ōkwas ʟǃāsotiwalisōxa āmaᵉyō g·ōkwa. Laɛm
lālōʟǃa qaᵉs mōpǃɛnō kwäsaxēs qǃāᴌᵉmōsō gwayiᵉlälasaxa g·ālō
ōxɛnta tsǃātsǃadagɛma. Wä laɛm lāba lāxa gwǎgwōx·sala lāxa
g·ālō ōxɛnta. Hōɛm gwɛᵉyōsa g·āᴌō bākǃum g·axᴂliᴌtsɛᵉwa.

                    14. Building of a House.

     Wä, laᵉmō ʟǃāsotiwalisō ᵉnōx· qaᵉs g·ōkwōlōx g·ōkwa qaᵉs
25   wǎg·i ʟēᴌɛlaxa lēlqwǎlaʟaᵉyas qautēnayuʟɛs Aᵉmǎxǔlaᴌ ʟōᵉ ᵉnɛmōgwisaq. Wä, laᵉmō ʟēᴌtsǃōdē ʟǃāsotiwalisaxēs g·ōkǔlōta
Qǃōmoyǎᵉyō. Wä, g·îlᵉmisō g·āx ᵉwîᵉlaōʟa laas nēᴌaxēs g·ōkǔ-
lōtaxs lɛᵉmaō nak·ǃāᴌaxēs nɛgǔmpō Aᵉmǎxǔlaᴌō ʟōᵉ ᵉnɛmōgwisēxa
g·îgǎmaᵉyasa ᵉnɛmgēsō. Laɛm gwǎᴌaᴌa qaᵉs qautōx·ēq. Wä, hō-
30   ᵉmisɛn lāg·iᴌa ᵉnōx· qɛn g·ōkwōlōx g·ōkwa qɛn ʟēᴌɛᵉlatsǃexa lēl-

although they invite all the (1) tribes, if they do not "take out the steam" for their princess/when she grows up, then they have the name "chief not going through" after that./ That is the same word as for one who has not paid the marriage debt to the husband of his/ princess. He also has the name "chief who does not go through" after that. But this is (5) the name of the head chief, "the one who went through everything," chief ʟ!ãsotiwalis, if he/obtains everything, he, who grows up according to those who wish him to follow the ways/ of his grandfathers of long past days, who all obtained everything/ that chiefs try to obtain what has been written by me, about the/ one who is made the highest chief, Yîx·ãgɛmēᵋ, the ancestor (10) of ʟ!ãsotiwalis at ʟɛx·sîwēᵋ. They all were head / chiefs and they took the place of Yîx·ãgɛmēᵋ coming down/ to ʟ!ãsotiwalis, and therefore ʟ!ãqoḷas wished strongly / that his prince ʟ!ãsotiwalis should quickly try to get all the ways / of those who wished that he should become head chief. (15) Now he got almost all, not many more were tried for by ʟ!ãsotiwalis / when he really was going to be head chief/after this./

Now all the three Kwag·uⱡ tribes went out after this/and then the great ʟãʟēliʟ!a was sitting still in her menstruation room in (20) the corner of the house of ʟ!ãsotiwalis, the small house. Now/she tried to get the four washings, about which you know, the doings of the/ girl who menstruates for the first time. Now this is the end of talking about the/maturing girl. This is called by the Indians g·ãxâlîⱡtsōᵋ./

14. Building of a House

Now ʟ!ãsotiwalis wished to build a house to (25) invite the tribes when the marriage debt was paid by Aᵋmãxŭlaⱡ and ᵋnɛmōgwis./ Then ʟ!ãsotiwalis called his tribe/ the Q!ōmoyâᵋyē into his house and as soon as they were all in, he told his tribe/ that he was expecting his father-in-law, Aᵋmãxŭlaⱡ and ᵋnɛmōgwis/ the chief of the ᵋnɛmgis, who was ready to pay the marriage debt to him. "And (30) this is why I wish to build a house as an inviting house for the

qwălaʟaᵋyē. Wä, laᵋmēts dōqwaⱡaⱡ qa gwäⱡaatsēs wäⱡdɛmʟaōs,
g·ōкŭlōt, ᵋnēk·exs laē k!wäg·flⱡa.

Wä, lä ʟāxᵋwaliⱡō Lālak·ots!a qaᵋs yāq!ɛg·aᵋⱡē. Wä, lä
ᵋnēk·a꞉ Qǎʟag·a wäⱡdɛmg·asg·ɛns g·Igǎmēk·, Q!ōmoyŭwē. Laɛm
5 ᵋnēx· qaᵋs g·okwēlēx äⱡewakwa g·ōkwaxwa k·!ēsēx nēnēda g·ōkwi-
läxa äⱡewakwē g·ōkwa qa x·ɛdzeⱡmaᵋyas läxwa dādɛk·asēx qaēda
hēlānɛmʟa q!ēnɛm bēbɛgwānɛmⱡ. ᵋnēᵋnak·iⱡē Q!ōmoyŭwē, gwālaxɛns
g·Igǎmaᵋyōx ʟ!āsotiwalisēx hēla g·äxɛns qa laǎns ēaxɛlaxa gwēⱡgwä-
10 laʟasa äⱡewexᵘʟa g·ōxʟ qaxs q!ēx·ᵋidǎⱡaē ēaxɛlasōʟasa hēᵋlānɛmʟa.
ᵋnēᵋnak·iⱡē Q!ōmoyŭwē. Hǎg·a häᵋyäⱡᵋas Q!ōmoyŭwē, hǎg·a qǎsaxa
Gwētɛla ʟɛᵋwa ᵋwälas Kwäg·uⱡ ʟɛᵋwa Q!ōmk·!ŭt!ɛs qa g·äxēs ᵋwIᵋla
hōʟēlaxōx wäⱡdɛmaxsɛns g·Igǎmaᵋyōx ʟ!āsotiwalisēx. Ʌɛmʟɛs ᵋnēx·-
ʟōʟ, häᵋyäᵋⱡä꞉ Qǎsanuᵋxᵘ Gwētɛl qaᵋs laōs hōʟēlax wäⱡdɛmas
15 ʟ!āsotiwalisē. Hālag·flēʟɛsai, ᵋnēx·ʟɛs, ᵋnēk·ēda ʟēxsᵋaläxa
häᵋyäⱡᵋa qa. wäⱡdɛms.

Wä, hěx·ᵋidaᵋmisē la hōqŭwɛls läxa g·ōkwas ʟ!āsotiwalisē
qaᵋs lē hōgwIʟ läx g·ōkwasa Gwētɛla. Wä, laᵋmē ᵋnēk·a꞉ Qǎsanuᵋxᵘ Gwētɛl qaᵋs laōs hōʟēlax wäⱡdɛmas ʟ!āsotiwalisē. Hālag·flē-
20 ʟɛsai, ᵋnēk·exs laē hōqŭwɛls läxa g·ōkwē. Wä, âx·sämisē hě gwē-
k·!äla läxa ᵋnäxwa g·ig·ōkwa. Wä, g·flēᵋmisē ᵋwIlxtolsaxa g·I-
g·ōkwasa Gwētɛla ʟɛᵋwa ᵋwälas Kwäg·uⱡ ʟɛᵋwa Q!ōmk·!ŭt!ɛs g·äxaē
aēdaaqa qaᵋs lē hōgwiʟ läx g·ōkwas ʟ!āsotiwalisē. Wä, lä ᵋnē-
x·daᵋxᵘ꞉ Laɛmx·dɛnuᵋxᵘ ᵋwIlxtolsaxa g·ōкŭla, ᵋnēk·exs laē k!ŭs-
25 ᵋāliⱡa.

Wä, laᵋmē Lālak·ots!a ᵋnēx· qa gwäⱡelaᵋmisē ʟ!āsotiwalisē
ʟēʟɛqɛla ʟēʟēgɛmasēs hēᵋlānɛmʟa läxa yŭduxᵘsɛᵋmakwē Kwäкŭg·uⱡa.
Wä, hěᵋmis qa ᵋnäxwaᵋmisē ʟēqɛlax ēaᵋxēnēʟas läx gwēⱡgwälasa
g·ōxᵘʟa, ᵋnēk·ē. Wä, hěx·ᵋidaᵋmisē ʟ!āsotiwalisē nēⱡas waxŭgwas –
30 ʟasē bēbɛgwānɛmē hēᵋlānɛmʟa.

(1) tribes. Now you will see what you will say,/ tribes," said he
as he sat down./

Then arose Lālak·ots!a and spoke./ He said, "True is the
saying of our chief, Q!ōmoyâᵉyē,(5) He says he wants to build a
new house. This is not dared (by all),the building / of a new
house on account of the disappearance of property among/those who
are hired, many men. I mean this, Q!ōmoyâyē, do not let our/
chief ʟ!āsotiwalis hire us to work on the timbers (10) of the new
house, for there are many kinds of work to be done by the hired
men./ I mean this, Q!ōmoyâᵉyē. Go on, young men of the Q!ōmoyâᵉyā
go now and call the/ Gwētᴇla and the ᵉwālas Kwāg·uɫ and the Q!ōm-
k·!ūt!ᴇs to come/ and listen to the words of our chief, ʟ!āsotiwa-
lis. You will just say,/ young men, 'We invite you, Gwētᴇla, to
go and listen to the words of (15) ʟ!āsotiwalis. Come quickly,'
you shall say," said he, giving advice to the/ young men ·as to
what they were to say./

Immediately they went out of the house of ʟ!āsotiwalis/ and
went into the houses of the Gwētᴇla and they said: "We invite
you,/ Gwētᴇla, to listen to the words of ʟ!āsotiwalis. You shall
come quickly," (20) said they as they went out of the house. And
they just continued saying this/ in all the houses, and when they
had been to all the/ houses of the Gwētᴇla and ᵉwālas Kwāg·uɫ and
Q!ōmk·!ūt!ᴇs they went/ back and entered the house of ʟ!āsotiwalis.
Then they said:/ "We have been to all the houses," said they as
they (25) sat down.

Then Lālak·ots!a said that ʟ!āsotiwalis should be ready/ to
name the names of those whom he would hire among the three Kwāg·uɫ
tribes,/ and also that they should name all those who should work
at the timbers of the/ house, said he. Immediately ʟ!āsotiwalis
told him how (30) many men would be hired./

Wä, g·îlɛmisē gwāɫē wāɫdɛmas laē ɛyālagɛma hāɛyāɫɛa qa

lēs qātsēɛsta. Wä, hɛ̈x·ɛidaɛmisa hāɛyāɫɛa la hōqŭwɛls lāxa g·ō-

kwē qaɛs lē hōgwiʟ lāx g·ōkwasa Gwētɛla. Wä, lä ɛnēk·a: G·āx-

ɛmɛnuɛxu qātsēɛsta Gwētɛl. ʟɛxɛwĭt, ʟɛxɛwĭt, ʟɛxɛwĭt, wŭ, wŭ, wŭ,

5   ɛnēk·exs laē hōqŭwɛls lāxa g·ōkwē. Wä, lä hɛ̈x·sä̈ɛm gwēk·!āla

lāxa ɛnāxwa g·ig·ōkwa. Wä, g·îlɛmisē ɛwĭlxtolsaxa g·ig·ōkwaxs

g·āxaē aēdaaqa qaɛs lē hōgwiʟ lāx g·ōkwas ʟ!āsotiwalisē. Wä, g·āx-

ɛmē hōgwiʟɛlēda bēbɛgwānɛmē lāxa g·ōkwē qaɛs k!ŭsɛāl[iɫ]ɛlē lāx

wax·saɛnēgwiɫasa g·ōkwē. Wä, g·îlɛmisē g·āx ɛwĭɛlaēʟa bēbɛgwānɛ-

10   masa yŭduxusɛɛmakwē Kwākŭg·uɫa laas ʟᴀ̄xɛwaliɫē Lālak·ots!a. Wä,

lä yāq!ɛg·aɛɫa. Wä, lä ɛnēk·a: Wa, gēlag·a Gwētɛl, wa, gēlag·a

ɛwālas Kwāg·uɫ, wa, gēlag·a Q!ōmk·!ŭt!ɛs lāxwa ladzōxwa ɛwālasēx

wāɫdɛmsg·în g·îgāmēk·xg·a ʟ!āsotiwalisɛk·xg·ada laɛmk· ɛnēx· qaɛs

g·ōkwēlēx āɫāwakwa g·ōkwaxwa k·!ēsēx nēnēda qa x·ɛdzɛɫmaɛyas lā-

15   xwa· yāqɛlax, lāg·iɫas k·îlɛma g·ōkwēlaxa āɫāwakwē g·ōkwa. Wä, la-

ɛmēsɛn hēlaɫ lâʟ, yŭduxusɛɛmaku Kwākŭg·uɫ qa ēaxālēsēxa gwēɫgwē-

laʟasa g·ōxuʟa, ɛnēk·exs laē ä̈xk·!ālax ʟ!āsotiwalisē qa ä̈xɛwŭɫ-

t!āliɫēsēxa p!ɛlxɛlasgɛm lāxa ōts!āliɫēxa hālāgɛmʟaxa ɛwāɛwiɛla-

ʟaxa maɛɫts!aqʟa wilku qa k·ik·atēwēɫāsa g·ōxuʟa.

20   Wä, hɛ̈x·ɛidaɛmisa hāɛyāɫɛāsa Q!ōmoyāɛyē la ɛmōɫts!āliɫɛlaxa

p!ɛlxɛlasgɛmē lāxa ōts!āliɫē qaɛs g·āxē ɛmōgŭliɫas lāx ʟawilasas

Lālak·ots!a lāx ōgwiɛwaliɫasa g·ōkwē. Wä, g·îlɛmisē g·āx ɛwiʟ-

g·îliɫa p!ɛlxɛlasgɛmē laas ēdzaqwa yāq!ɛg·aɛɫē Lālak·!ots!a. Wä

lä ɛnēk·axs laē dāx·ɛidxe ɛnemxsa p!ɛlxɛlasgɛma. Laɛmɛn wäg·îl

25   hēlaɫ lâʟ Gwētɛl qaɛs laōs ä̈xʟɛxa lēɛlx·ɛnʟasa g·ōxʟasg·în g·îgā-

mēk·, ɛnēk·exs laē hōsɛidxa nɛqaxsa p!ɛlxɛlasgɛm. Wä, lä ɛnēk·a:

Laɛmɛn hēloʟ ʟ!āqwag·il qaɛs laōs sōp!ēdxa ɛnɛmts!aqa k·ātewaɛya

nɛqaxsak· p!ɛlxɛlasgɛmg·as tɛlxts!anēɫg·ōs, g·îgāmēɛ, ɛnēk·ē.

Wä, lēda g·ayuɫē lāx hāɛyāɫɛāsa Q!ōmoyāɛyē ä̈xɛāliɫaxa nɛqaxsa p!ɛl-

30   xɛlasgɛm qaɛs lē ɛmōgwaliɫas lāx k!wāēlasas ʟ!āqwag·ilaxa xāmagɛ-

maɛyē g·îgāmēsa ɛnɛɛmēmutasa Maāmtag·ila.

(1) When they had finished talking, the young men were sent to/ invite again, and immediately the young men went out of the house/and went into a house of the Gwētɛla. They said, "We come/ to invite again, Gwētɛla. Get up, get up, get up! Wū wū wū," (5) said they as they went out of the house. And they continued saying this/ in all the houses. And as soon as they had been to all the houses/ they came back and went into the house of ᴌ!ā́sotiwalis. Then/ the men went into the house and sat down on/ each side of the house. And when all the men of the (10) three Kwāg·uⱡ tribes were in, Lālak·ots!a arose/ and spoke. He said: "Come, Gwētɛla, come,/ᵉwālas Kwāg·uⱡ, come, Q!ōmk·!ū́tɛs to (hear this) great / word of my chief ᴌ!ā́sotiwalis, who wishes to/ build a new house, which nobody dares on account of the property that is lost by it. (15) Therefore people are afraid to build a new house./ Now I will hire from among you, three Kwāg·uⱡ tribes, (men) to work on the timbers of the/ house that is to be," said he, and he asked ᴌ!āsotiwalis to bring out/ of the bedroom the blankets which were to, be paid to those who were going to get/ two cedar trees for the beams of the future house./

(20) Immediately the young men of the Q!ōmoyâᵉyē brought out the/ blankets from the bedroom and put them down in front of/ Lālak·ots!a in the rear of the house. When/ the blankets were piled up, Lālak·ots!a spoke again/ and said, as he took up one pair of blankets, "Now let me (25) hire you, Gwētɛla, to get the thick posts of the future house of my chief,"/ said he counted out ten pairs of blankets. Then he said,/"Now I thire you, ᴌ!ā́qwag·ila to go and chop down one beam./ Ten pairs of blankets as a protection for your hands, chief," said he,/ and a young man of the Q!ōmoyâᵉyē took up ten pairs of blankets (30) and put them down at the place where was sitting ᴌ!ā́qwag·ila, the head/chief of the numaym Maᾱmtag·ila./

Wä, la ēt.!ēdē Lālak·ots.!a hōsᵋidxɒ nɛqaxsa p.!ɛlxɛlasgɛm.

Wä, lä ᵋnēk·a: Laᵋmɛn hēlōʟ Wādzē qaᵋs laōs sōp.!ēdxa ᵋnɛmts.!aqa k·ātawaᵋya, nɛqaxsɛk· p.!ɛlxɛlasgɛmg·as tɛlxts.!anēẑg·ōs,
g·ɨgámēᵋ, ᵋnēk·ē. Wä, lēda g·ayuẑē lāxaax hēẑᵋä·sa Q.!ōmoyaᵋyē
5 äxᵋāliẑaxa nɛqaxsa p.!ɛlxɛlasgɛm qaᵋs lē ᵋmōgwaliẑas lāx k.!waē-
lasas Wadẑēxa g·ayuẑē lāx ᵋnɛᵋmēmutasa Dzɛndzɛnx·q.!ayâsa ᵋwālas
Kwāg·uẑ.

Wä, la ēt.!ēdē Lālak·ots.!a hōsᵋidxa nɛqaxsa p.!ɛlxɛlasgɛm. Wä,
la ᵋnēk·at Laᵋmɛn hēlōʟ Ts.!ōxᵘts.!aēsgämēᵋ qaᵋs laōs sōp.!ēdxa ma-
10 ᵋẑts.!aqa ʟēʟāma, nɛqaxsak· p.!ɛlxɛlasgɛmg·as tɛlxts.!anēẑg·ōs, g·ɨgämēᵋ,
ᵋnēk·ē. Wä, lēda hēẑᵋa äxᵋāliẑaxa nɛqaxsa p.!ɛlxɛlasgɛm qaᵋs lē
ᵋmōgwaliẑas lāx k.!waēlasas Ts.!ōxᵘts.!aēsagɛmaᵋyēxa g·āyuẑē lāx
ᵋnɛᵋmēmutasa Kükwāk.!ûmasa Gwētɛla.

Wä, la ēt.!ēdē Lālak·ots.!a hōsᵋidxa nɛqaxsa p.!ɛlxɛlasgɛm. Wä,
15 lä ᵋnēk·a: Laᵋmɛn hēlōʟ Pɛngwit qaᵋs laōs sōp.!ēdxa maᵋẑts.!aqa ʟēʟāma, nɛqaxsak· p.!ɛlxɛlasgɛmg·as tɛlxts.!anēẑg·ōs, g·ɨgämēᵋ, ᵋnēk·ē.
Wä, lēda hēẑᵋa äxᵋāliẑaxa nɛqaxsa p.!ɛlxɛlasgɛm qaᵋs lē ᵋmōgwaliẑas
lāx k.!waēlasas Pɛngwidēxa g·āyuẑē lāx ᵋnɛᵋmēmutasa Dzɛndzɛnx·q.!a-
yâsa ᵋwālas Kwāg·uẑē.

20 Wä, la ēt.!ēdē Lālak·ots.!a hōsᵋidxa nɛqaxsa p.!ɛlxɛlasgɛm, lä
ᵋnēk·a: Laᵋmɛn hēlōʟ, G·ɨgämēᵋ qaᵋɛ laōs k·!ōẑax ᵋnɛmxsä k·!ōk.!ux-
ʟaᵋya, nɛqaxsak· p.!ɛlxɛlasgɛmg·as tɛlxts.!anēẑg·ōs, g·ɨgämēᵋ ᵋnēk·ē.
Wä, lēda hēᵋẑᵋa äxᵋāliẑaxa nɛqaxsa p.!ɛlxɛlasgɛm qaᵋs lē ᵋmōgwaliẑas
lāx k.!waēlasas G·ɨgämaᵋyēxa g·āyuẑē lāx ᵋnɛᵋmēmutasa ʟōʟɛᵋgēdäsa
25 Q.!ōmk·!ût.!ɛsasa ᵋwālas Kwāg·uẑ.

Wä, la ēt.!ēdē Lālak·ots.!a hōsᵋidxa nɛqaxsa p.!ɛlxɛlasgɛm. Wä,
lä ᵋnēk·a: Laᵋmɛn hēlōʟ Nuẑnuẑelig·ē qaᵋs laōs k·!ōẑax ᵋnɛmxsä
k·!ōk.!üxʟaᵋya, nɛqaxsak· p.!ɛlxɛlasgɛmg·as tɛlxts.!anēẑg·ōs, g·ɨ-
gämēᵋ, ᵋnēk·ē. Wä, lēda hēẑᵋa äxᵋāliẑaxa nɛqaxsa p.!ɛlxɛlasgɛm qaᵋs
30 lē ᵋmōgwaliẑas lāx k.!waēlasas Nuẑnuẑelig·aᵋyēxa g·āyuẑē lāx ᵋnɛᵋmēmutasa Wāwülibâᵋyasa ᵋwālas Kwāg·uẑ.

(1) And then Lālak·ots!a counted again ten pairs of blankets/ and said, "Now I hire you, Wādzē,to chop down one beam. Ten pairs of blankets for a protection for your hands,/chief," said he. Then a young man of the Q!ōmoyâᶜyē (5) took the ten pairs of blankets and put them down at the place where was sitting/Wādzē who belonged to the numaym Dzɛndzɛnx·q!ayu of the/ ᶜwālas Kwāg·uł./

And Lālak·ots!a counted again ten pairs of blankets/ and said, "Now I hire you, Ts!ōxᵘts!aēsgāmēᶜ, to chop down two (10) posts. Ten pairs of blankets as a protection for your hands, chief,"/said he. Then a young man took the ten pairs of blankets and/ put them down at the place where was sitting Ts!oxᵘts!aēsgāmēᶜ, who belonged to the/ numaym Kŭkwāk!ŭm of the Gwētɛla./

Then Lālak·ots!a counted again ten pairs of blankets (15) and said, "With these I hire you, Pɛngwit, to chop down two posts./ Ten pairs of blankets as a protection for your hands, chief," said he./ Then a young man took the ten pairs of blankets and put them down/ at the place where was sitting Pɛngwit who belonged to the numaym Dzɛndzɛnx·q!ayu of the/ᶜwālas Kwāg·uł./

(20) Then Lālak·ots!a counted again ten pairs of blankets/ and said, "I hire you, G·Igāmēᶜ, to go and hew one side bar./ Ten pairs of blankets for a protection for your hands, chief," said he./ Then a young man took the ten pairs of blankets and put them down/ at the place where was sitting G·Igāmēᶜ of the numaym Lēᵘɛᶜgēd of (25) the Q!ōmk·!ūt!ɛs of the ᶜwālas Kwāg·uł./

Then Lālak·ots!a counted again ten pairs of blankets/ and said, "Now I hire you, Nŭłnŭłɛlig·ē, to go and hew one/side bar. Ten pairs of blankets as a protection of your hands, chief,"/said he. Then a young man took the ten pairs of blankets and (30) put them down at the place where was sitting Nŭłnŭłɛlig·ē who belonged to the numaym/Wāwŭlibâᶜyē of the ᶜwālas Kwāg·uł./

Wä, lä ēt!ēdē Lālak·ots!a hōsᵋidxa nɛqaxsa p!ɛlxɛlasgɛm. Wä,
lä ᵋnēk·a: Laᵋmɛn hēlōʟ Gwɛᵋyîmdzē qaᵋs laōs sōp!ēdɛx äʟɛbōts!aqa
pēpüx̣ᵘbala,nɛqaxsak· p!ɛlxɛlasgɛmg·as tɛlxts!anēłg·ōs, g·îgämēᵋ,
ᵋnēk·ē. Wä, lēda hēłᵋa äxᵋāliłaxa nɛqaxsa p!ɛlxɛlasgɛm qaᵋs lē
5 ᵋmōgwalîłas läx k!waēlasas Gwɛᵋyîmdzēxa g·āyułē läx ᵋnɛᵋmēmutasa
Laālax·sᵋɛndayuwē.

Wä, lä ēt!ēdē Lālak·ots!a hōsᵋidxa nɛqaxsa p!ɛlxɛlasgɛm. Wä,
lä ᵋnēk·a: Laᵋmɛn hēlōʟ Haēʟɛkᵘ qaᵋs laōs sōp!ēdɛx aʟɛbōts!aqa
pēpüx̣ᵘbāla, nɛqaxsak· p!ɛlxɛlasgɛmg·as tɛlxts!anēłg·ōs, g·îgämēᵋ,
10 ᵋnēk·ē. Wä, lēda hēłᵋa äxᵋāliłaxa nɛqaxsa p!ɛlxɛlasgɛm qaᵋs lē
ᵋmōgwaᵋlîłas läx k!waēlasas Haēʟɛkwēxa g·āyułē läx ᵋnɛmēmutasa Wä-
wülibâᵋyasa ᵋwālas Kwāg·uł.

Wä, lä ēt!ēdē Lālak·ots!a hōsᵋidxa nɛqaxsa p!ɛlxɛlasgɛm. Wä,
lä ᵋnēk·a: Laᵋmɛn hēlōʟ ʟ!ālis qaᵋs laōs sōp!ēdɛx sɛk·!ats!aqa
15 sēx·dɛmāla, sɛk·!axsak· p!ɛlxɛlasgɛmg·as tɛlxts!anēłg·ōs, g·îgämēᵋ,
ᵋnēk·ē. Wä, lēda hēłᵋa äxᵋāliłaxa sɛk·!axsa p!ɛlxɛlasgɛm qaᵋs lē
ᵋmōgwalîłas läx k!waēlasas ʟ!ālisxa g·āyułē läx ᵋnɛᵋmēmutasa ʟōya-
lałaᵋwäsa Gwētɛla.

Wä, lä ēt!ēdē Lālak·ots!a hōsᵋidxa sɛk·!axsa p!ɛlxɛlasgɛm.
20 Wä, lä ᵋnēk·a: Laᵋmɛn hēlōʟ ᵋnāx̣ülalis qaᵋs laōs sōp!ēdɛx sɛk·!a-
ts!aqa sēx·dɛmāla, nɛqaxsak· p!ɛlxɛlasgɛmg·as tɛlxts!anēłg·ōs, g·î-
gämēᵋ, ᵋnēk·ē. Wä, lēda hēłᵋa äxᵋāliłaxa sɛk·!axsa p!ɛlxɛlasgɛm qaᵋs
lē ᵋmōgwalîłas läx k!waēlasas ᵋnāx̣ülalisxa g·āyułē läx ᵋnɛᵋmēmutasa
ʟēq!ɛmasa Q!ōmk·!üt!ɛsē.

25 Wä, lä ēt!ēdē Lālak·ots!a hōsᵋidxa sɛk·!axsa p!ɛlxɛlasgɛm. Wä,
lä ᵋnēk·a : Laᵋmɛn hēlōʟ Ts!ōx̣ᵘts!aēsa qaᵋs laōs k·!ōłax ᵋnɛmxsä
tɛgwaq, sɛk·!axsak· p!ɛlxɛlasgɛmg·as tɛlxts!anēłg·ōs g·îgämēᵋ,
ᵋnēk·ē. Wä, lēda hēłᵋa äxᵋāliłaxa sɛk·!axsa p!ɛlxɛlasgɛm qaᵋs lē
ᵋmōgwalîłas läx k!waēlasas Ts!ōx̣ᵋts!aēsaxa g·āyułē läx ᵋnɛᵋmēmutasa
30 G·ēxsɛmasa Gwētɛla.

(1) Then Lālak·ots!a counted again ten pairs of blankets/ and
said, "Now I hire you, Gwɛᵋyîmdzē, to go and chop seven/rafters.
Ten pairs of blankets as a protection for your hands, chief,"/said
he. Then a young man took the ten pairs of blankets and (5) put
them down at the place where was sitting Ĝwɛᵋyîmdzē who belonged to
the numaym/Laãlax·sᵋɛndayu./

Then Lālak·ots! counted again ten pairs of blankets/ and he
said, "Now I hire you, Haêʟɛkᵘ to chop seven/ rafters. Ten pairs
of blankets as a protection for your hands, chief," (10) said he.
Then a young man took the ten pairs of blankets and/ put them down
at the place where was sitting Haêʟɛkᵘ who belonged to the numaym/
Wāwŭlibâᵋyē of the ᵋwālas Kwāg·uł./

Then Lālak·ots!a counted again ten pairs of blankets/ and
said, "Now I hire you, ʟ!ālis to chop down five (15) roof beams.
Five pairs of blankets as a protection for your hands, chief,"/said
he. Then a young man took the five pairs of blankets and/ put them
down at the place where was sitting ʟ!ālis who belonged to the nu-
maym/ʟōyalała ᶜwa of the Gwētɛla./

Then Lālak·ots!a counted again five pairs of blankets (20) and
said, "Now I hire you, ᵋnāx̣ŭlalis, to chop down five/ roof beams.
Five pairs of blankets as a protection for your hands, chief,"/said
he. Then a young man took the five pairs of blankets and/ put them
down at the place where was sitting ᵋnāx̣ŭlalis who belonged to the
numaym/ʟ̣ēq!ɛm of the Q!ōmk·!ūt!ɛs./

(25) Then Lālak·ots!a counted again five pairs of blankets/ and
said, "Now I hire you, Ts!ōx̣ᵘts!aēs to hew one/retaining plank.[1]
Five pairs of blankets as a protection for your hands, chief," said
he. Then a young man took the five pairs of blankets and/put
them down at the place where was sitting Ts!ōx̣ᵘts!aēs who belonged
to the numaym·(30) G·ēxsɛm of the Gwētɛla./

---

1) These are the planks that retain the soil of the platform that
   runs around the walls of the house inside. In feasts the people
   sit leaning against these planks.

Wä, lä ēt!ēdē Lālak·ots!a hōsᵋidxa sɛk·!axsa p!ɛlxɛlasgɛm.
Wä, lä ᵋnēk·a: Laᵋmɛn hēlōᴸ ᵋmāx·ᵋmɛwisa qaᵋs laōs k·!ōⱬax ᵋnɛmxsä tɛgwāq, sɛk·!axsak· p!ɛlxɛlasgɛmg·as tɛlxts!anēⱬg·ōs, g·ĭ-
gämēᵋ, ᵋnēk·ē. Wä, lēda hëⱬᵋa äxᵋāliⱬaxa sɛk·!axsa p!ɛlxɛlasgɛm

5   qaᵋs lē ᵋmōgwalĬⱬas lāx k!waēlasas ᵋmāx·ᵋmɛwisaxa g·ayuⱬē lāx
ᵋnɛᵋmēmutasa G·ĭg·ĭlgämasa ᵋwālas Kwāg·uⱬ.

Wä, lä ēt!ēdē Lālak·ots!a hōsᵋidxa sɛk·!axsa p!ɛlxɛlasgɛm.
Wä, lä ᵋnēk·a : Laᵋmɛn hēlōᴸ Hämdzit qaᵋs laōs k·!ōⱬax ᵋnɛmxsä
tɛgwāq, sɛk·!axsak· p!ɛlxɛlasgɛmg·as tɛlxts!anēⱬg·ōs, g·ĭgämēᵋ,

10   ᵋnēk·ē. Wä, lēda hëⱬᵋa äxᵋāliⱬaxa sɛk·!axsa p!ɛlxɛlasgɛm qaᵋs
lē ᵋmōgwalĬⱬas lāx k!waēlasas Hämdzidxa g·āyuⱬē lāx ᵋnɛᵋmēmutasa
Sēnᴸ!ɛmasa Gwētɛla.

Wä, lä yāq!ɛg·aⱬē Lālak·ots!a. Wä, lä ᵋnēk·a laē gwāⱬ hōsᵋidxa sɛk·!axsa p!ɛlxɛlasgɛm: Laɛms g·ig·ɛgämēs Kwāküg·uⱬ. Dō-

15   qwaⱬaxg·ĭn g·ĭgämēk·, lāxg·a ᴸ!āsotiwalisɛk· laxg·ada g·ōkwēlag·ax
äⱬɛwaxᵘsɛma g·ōkwa. Hᵕɛm lāg·iⱬasōx k·ᴉlɛma g·ōkwēlax aⱬtsɛma g·ō-
kwa qa ᵋwaxax·staᵋyālasasa dādak·asē lāqᵘ. ᵋnēᵋnak·iⱬē ! Laᵋmɛn
hēlōᴸ Haēᴸɛ kumēᵋ qaᵋs laōs k·!ōⱬax ᵋnɛmxsä tɛgwāq, sɛk·!axsak· p!ɛl-
xɛlasgɛmg·as tɛlxts!anēⱬg·ōs, g·ĭgämēᵋ, ᵋnēk·ē. Wä, lēda hëⱬᵋa

20   äxᵋāliⱬaxa sɛk·!axsa p!ɛlxɛlasgɛm qaᵋs lē ᵋmōgwalĬⱬas lāx k!waēlasas
Haēᴸɛkümaᵋyē.

Wä, lä ēdzaqwa yāq!ɛg·aᵋⱬē Lālak·ots!a. Wä, lä ᵋnēk·a : Wa, wa
yũduxᵘsɛᵋmakᵘ Kwāküg·uⱬ ladzēᵋmo gwalēk·in wäⱬdɛmaxɛn hēhelānɛmēx.
Laɛms lax·daᵋxᵘ hahalōᴸ!aⱬxa lēlēx·ᵋɛnᴸa yũᴸaxg·ĭn hēhelānɛmēg·ōᴸ.

25   ᵋnēᵋnak·iⱬē,Gwētɛl, ᵋwālas Kwāg·uⱬ, Q!ōmk·!üt!ɛs. Laᵋmɛn hēlaagwi -
ⱬōᴸ qaᵋs lēⱬōs lēx·ᵋwüⱬt!alaxa lēlēx·ᵋɛnᴸa sōbanɛmsɛn hēhelanɛmēx.
Wä, g·āxᴸɛs dāpɛlaᴸɛq, ᵋnēk·ē. Wä, laɛm gwäⱬē wäⱬdɛmas laxēq.

Wä, laᵋmē ᵋwĬᵋla hōqũwɛlsa bēbɛgwānɛm qaᵋs lē xwānaⱬᵋidēda
hēhelānɛmaxēs sēsōbayuwē ᴸɛᵋwis xwäxwaxwagũmē. Wä, g·ᴉlᵋmisē

30   ᵋnäx·idxa gaāläxs laē ᵋwĬᵋla alēxᵋwidēda hēhelānɛm bēbɛgwanɛm qaᵋs
lē lāxēs wiᵋwĬᵋla wilkwa laxēs ᴸēᴸāⱬaasē qaᵋs âᵋmē hëx·ᵋidaɛm sō-

(1) Then Lālak·ots!a counted again five pairs of blankets/ and
said, "Now I hire you, ᵋmāx·ᵋmɛwis , to hew one/ retaining plank.
Five pairs of blankets as a protection for your hands, chief,"/ said
he. Then a young man took the five pairs of blankets (5) and put
them down at the place where was sitting ᵋmāx·ᵋmɛwis who belonged
to the/ numaym G·Ig·ilgăm of the ᵋwālas Kwāg·uł./

Then Lālak·ots!a counted again five pairs of blankets/ and he
said, "Now I hire you, Hămdzit, to hew one/ retaining plank. Five
pairs of blankets as a protection for your hands, chief," (10) said
he. Then a young man took the five pairs of blankets and/ put them
down at the place where was sitting Hămdzit who belonged to the nu-
maym/ Sēnʟ!ɛm of the Gwētɛla./

Then Lālak·ots!a spoke and said after he had finished counting/
five pairs of blankets, "Now, chiefs of the Kwāg·uł,(15) look at my
chief, here, at ʟ!āsotiwalis, who is building a/ new house. Therefore the building of a new house is dreaded/ on account of the un-
counted property. I mean this./ I hire you, Haēʟɛkŭmēᵋ to go and hew
one retaining plank. Five pairs of blankets/ for a protection for
your hands, chief," said he. Then a young man (20) went and took
the five pairs of blankets and put them down at the place where was
sitting/ Haēʟɛkŭmēᵋ.

And Lālak·ots!a spoke again and said, "Wa,wa./ You three Kwāg·uł
tribes, now my great speech is finished with which I hire you./ Now
you will go quickly to get the thick timbers for which I have hired
you. (25) I mean this, Gwētɛla, ᵋwālas Kwāg·uł, Q!ōmk·!ŭtɛs. I
hire you/ to roll out of the woods the round timbers that will be
chopped down by those whom I have hired./ Now you will come and tow
them," said he. Now his speech was finished after this./

Then all the men went out and the/hired men made ready their
axes and their small canoes. And as soon as (30) day came in the
morning the hired men started and/ went to where cedar trees were
standing. And immediately (1) they chopped them down and when a

p!äxōłɛq. Wä, g·îlᶜmisō t!äx·ᶜidɛxs laō sāq!wag·it!ēdɛq qa ᶜwī-
ᶜlâwēs ts!äxᶜanaᶜyas. Wä, lä bäłᶜidxa ᶜnäᶜnɛmāp!ɛnk·ē läxɛns
bāʟax qa äwâsgâmatsa k·ēk·ätēwaᶜyaxs laō sōpsᶜɛndxa wīłɛtâᶜyas.
Wä, hēɛm ᶜwälōxᶜwidēda hēlänɛmē bɛgwānɛmxs laō näᶜnakᵘ läxēs g·ō-
5 kwē. Wä, läʟa g·awaʟâlē G·îgämēᶜ ʟōᶜ Nūłnułɛlig·ēxa maᶜlōkwē bēbɛgwānɛm hēlänɛm qa k·!ōłaxa maᶜłɛxsa k·!ōk!ûʟēᶜ qaxs kûxsᶜɛndaaxa
wilkwē. Wä, lä äxᶜēdē G·îgämaᶜyaxa äpsōdiłē. Wä, lä äxᶜēdē Nūł-
nułɛg·aᶜyaxa äpsōdiłē qaᶜs pats!âlēx äᶜwîg·aᶜyas qa ᶜnɛmp!ɛnk·ēs
wûgwâsas läxɛns ts!ɛxᵘts!änaᶜyēx. Wä, lä ᶜnäłᶜnɛmp!ɛna yūduxᵘp!ɛn-
10 k·ē ᶜwädzawasas läxɛns q!wäq!wax·ts!änaᶜyēx. Wä, lä ᶜnäᶜnɛmap!ɛnk·ē
ᶜwäsgɛmasas läxɛns bāʟax.

Wä, hēɛmxaäwis g·äwalap!ē Ts!ōxᵘts!aēsa ʟōᶜ ᶜmäx·mɛwisaxa
maᶜlōkwē bēbɛgwānɛm hēlänɛm qa k·!ōłaxa maᶜłaxsa tɛgwäq qaxs
kûxsᶜɛndaaxa wilkwē. Wä, la äxᶜēdē Ts!ōxᵘts!aēsäxa äpsōdiłē.
15 Wä, lä äxᶜēdē ᶜmäx·mɛwisaxa äpsōdiłē qaᶜs pats!âlēx äᶜwîg·aᶜyas
qa ᶜnɛmp!ɛnk·ēs wâgwasas läxɛns ts!ɛxᵘts!änaᶜyēx. Wä, lä ᶜnäłᶜnɛmp!ɛna yūduxᵘp!ɛnk· ʟōxs mōp!ɛnk·aēs ᶜwädzɛwasas läxɛns q!wä-
q!waxts!änaᶜyēx. Wä, lä aʟɛbōp!ɛnk·ē ᶜwäsgɛmasas läxɛns bāʟax.

Wä, läxaē g·äwalap!ē Haēʟɛkumaᶜyē ʟōᶜ Hämdzidē qaēda maᶜłɛ-
20 xsaᶜmaxat! tɛgwäqa. Wä, laɛm q!ɛʟ!ɛp!ɛnk·ē ᶜwäsgɛmasas läxɛns
bāʟax qaxs hēᶜmaē ts!ɛg·ōłasa tɛgwäqasa g·ōxᵘʟē qaxs hēᶜmaē tɛ-
säłaats äᶜwîg·aᶜyasa bēbɛgwānɛmax k!wēłaēxa tɛgwäqē läx äᶜwîᶜsta-
līłasa g·ōkwē.

Wä, g·îlᶜmisē ᶜwîᶜla gwäłē äxsɛᶜwasa mōgûg·ɛyuwē bēbɛgwānɛm
25 hēlänɛms ʟ!äsotiwalisē g·äxaē ᶜwîᶜla näᶜnakwa. Wä, hēx·ᶜidaᶜmisē
ʟ!äsotiwalisē ᶜyälaqasa mōkwē häᶜyäłᶜa qa lēs ʟēᶜlälaxa mōgûg·ɛyuwē
wē bēbɛgwānɛm hēlänɛms qa lēs ʟ!ɛxwa läx g·ōkwas. Wä, laɛm ᶜnēk·a
mōkwē häᶜyäłᶜa läx äᶜwîʟɛläs t!ɛx·fläsa g·ig·ōkwasa Gwētɛla: G·äx-
ᶜmɛnuᶜxᵘ ʟēᶜlälōʟaixwa hēlänɛmaxs ʟ!äsōtiwalis qaᶜs laōs ʟ!ɛxwa
30 läx g·ōkwas. Läʟɛs k!wamēłʟōʟ, Gwētɛl. Halag·fliʟasai, ᶜnēk·exs
laō hōqûwɛls läxa g·ōkwē. Wä, g·îlᶜmisē ᶜwîlxtolsax g·ig·ōkwasa

tree fell down they peeled it so that the/ bark came off. Then they
measured the length of nine/ fathoms for the length of the beams
and they chopped off the thin end./ And all this was done by the
hired men before they went home to their houses. (5) Then G·Ígămēᵉ
and Nūᶻnuᶻɛlig·ēxa helped each other, the two/ men who were hired
to hew the two side bars, for they split/ a cedar tree, and then
G·Ígămēᵉ took the one side and Nūᶻnuᶻɛlig·ēxa took the/ other side.
Then they split off the back so that it was one/ span thick. Sometimes it is three (10) spans wide and it is nine/ fathoms long./

Then also Ts!ōxᵘts!aēs and ᵉmāx·ᵐɛwis helped each other,/ the
two men hired to hew out the flat retaining planks, for/ they split
a cedar tree in two and Ts!ōxᵘts!aēs took one half (15) and ᵉmāx·ᵐɛ-
wis took the other and split off the back/ so that it was one span
thick./ Sometimes it is three spans or four spans wide/ and it is
is seven fathoms long./

And Haēᶫɛkŭmēᵉ and Hāmdzit helped each other with the two (20)
retaining planks and their length is six/ fathoms, for thus is the
width of the retaining planks of the house, for that is the/ back
support of the men who sit feasting around the inside/ of the house./

When the work of the fourteen men (25) hired by ᴌ!āsotiwalis
was finished they all went home. Then/ ᴌ!āsotiwalis sent four young
men to call the fourteen/ men hired by him to go and eat in his
house. Then said the/ four young men and stood inside of the doors
of the houses of the Gwetɛla,/ "We come to invite those hired by ᴌ!ā-
sotiwalis to go and eat (30) in his house. You will go and sit next
to them, Gwētɛla. You will go quickly," said they/ as they went out
of the house. When they had been to all the houses (1) of the Gwētɛla

Gwētɛla laē hōgwiʟ lāx g·ōkwasa ᵋwālas Kwāg·uⱡē ʟ̣ōᵋ g·ig·ōkwasa
Q!ōmk·!ūt!esē. Wä, laɛm ᴀ̱ɛm nᴇgɛⱡtewēxēs g·ālē wāⱡdɛma lāx g·ī-
g·ōkwasa Gwētɛla. Wä, g·fiᵋmisē ᵋwīlxtolsaxa g·ig·ōkwaxs laē
aēdaaqa qaᵋs lē hōgwiʟa hä̆ᵋyāⱡᵋa.lāx g·ōkwas ʟ!āsotiwalisēxa k!ēsē
5 ᵋwālas g·ō̱xᵘs. Wä, laᵋmēda mōkwē hä̆ᵋyāⱡᵋa nēⱡaxs ʟᴇᵋmaē ᵋwīlxtolsaxa g·ig·ōkwasa yūduxᵘsɛᵋmakwē Kwākūg·uⱡa. Wä, k·!ēst!a gä̆ⱡa
x·ōsaⱡaxs laē ētsēᵋsta. Wä, laᵋmē ᵋnēk·a mōkwē hä̆ᵋyāⱡᵋa lāx ä̆ᵋwī-
ʟɛlä̆s t!ɛx·fläsa g·ōkwē: G·āxᵋmɛnuᵋx̱ᵘ ētsēᵋstai Gwētɛl qaᵋs laōs
halaēʟa, ᵋnēk·ō. Wä, laɛm hēx·sä̆ gwēk·!āla lāxa ᵋnā̱xwa g·ig·ōkwa.
10 Wä, g·fiᵋmisē ᵋwīlxtolsaxa g·ig·ōkwaxs g·āxaē aēdaaqa qaᵋs lē hōgwiʟ lāx g·ōkwas ʟ!āsotiwalisē. Wä, g·āxᵋmē hōgwiʟɛlēda mōgŭg·ɛyuwē
bēbɛgwānɛm qaᵋs lē ᵋwīᵋla k!ŭsᵋāliⱡ lāxa ōgwiwaliⱡasa g·ōkwē, yīx
lāg·iⱡas ᵋnex·sōᵋ qa hēs k!ŭsᵋāliⱡa ōgwiwaliⱡasa g·ōkwē qaxs hēᵋmaē ᴀ̱lak·!āla ʟēlānɛma ēaxɛlāxa gwēⱡgwälasa g·ō̱xᵘʟē. Wä, lä̆ ᴀ̱ɛm
15 k!wamēⱡa yūduxᵘsɛᵋmakwē Kwākūg·uⱡa. Wä, g·āxᵋmē hōgwiʟɛlē ᵋnā̱xwa
bēbɛgwānɛm. Wä, lä̆ k!ŭsᵋāliⱡa Gwētɛla lāx hēⱡk·!ōdɛnēgwiⱡasa
g·ōkwē. Wä, lēda ᵋwālas Kwāg·uⱡ ʟ̣ᴇᵋwa Q!ōmk·!ūt!ɛs k!ŭsᵋāliⱡ lāxa
gᴇmᵋxōdɛnēgwiⱡē. Wä, laᵋmē ᵋyālagᴇmē mōkwē hä̆ᵋyāⱡᵋa qa lēs dādaqu-
ᵋma. Wä, lēda mōkwē hä̆ᵋyāⱡᵋa hōqŭsɛls lāxa g·ōkwē qaᵋs lē lāxa
20 g·ōkwasa Gwētɛla. Wä, lä̆ ᵋnēk·a: G·āxᵋmɛnuᵋx̱ᵘ dādoqŭᵋma Gwētɛlai-
lax k·!ēsᵋɛmlaxa lālax, ᵋnēx·daᵋxwē. Wä, laɛm ᵋnā̱xwaɛm hē gwēk·!ā-
la lāxa g·ig·ōkwasa yūduxᵘsɛᵋmakwē Kwākūg·uⱡa. Wä, g·fiᵋmisē ᵋwīlxtolsaxa g·ōkŭla laē aēdaaqa qaᵋs lē hōgwiʟ lāx g·ōkwas ʟ!āsoti-
walisē. Wä, lä̆ ᵋnēk·a: Lᴀ̱ɛmx·dɛnuᵋx̱ᵘ wax· dādoquᵋma. Laᵋmᴇns
25 ᵋwīᵋlaēʟa, ᵋnēx·daᵋxwē. Wä, hēx·ᵋidaᵋmisē ä̆xᵋētsɛᵋwa xamasē qaᵋs
ts!ɛx·ä̆sɛᵋwēsa ᵋnā̱xwa hä̆ᵋyāⱡᵋasa Q!ōmoyᴀ̱ᵋyē laaʟasa waōkwē ä̆xᵋēdxa
ⱡōɛlq!wē ʟ̣ᴇᵋwa ts!ɛbats!e ʟ̣ᴇᵋwa ʟ!ōᵋna. Wä, laᵋmē k·!ŭpts!ᴀ̱layuwa
ts!ɛnkwē xamas lāxa ⱡōɛlq!wē. Wä, lēda waōkwē hä̆ᵋyāⱡᵋa k!ŭxts!ᴀ̱lasa
ʟ!ōᵋna lāxa ts!ɛbats!e. Wä, g·fiᵋmisē ᵋwīᵋla gwäⱡa laē ä̆xᵋētsɛᵋwa

they went into the house of the ᵋwālas Kwāg·uł and the houses of
the/ Q!ōmk·!ūt!ɛs and they only said the same as their first speech
in the/ houses of the Gwētɛla. As soon as they had been to all
the houses they went/ back and the young men entered the house of
ʟ!āsotiwalis which was not (5) a large house. And now the four
young men told them that they had been to all the/ houses of the
three Kwāg·uł tribes. They did not/ rest long before they went
back to them and now the four young men said inside the/ doorways
of the houses, "We come to call again, Gwētɛla, that you may go/
quickly into the house," they said, and they kept on saying this
in all the houses. (10) As soon as they had gone to all the houses
they came back and entered/ the house of ʟ!āsotiwalis. Then the
fourteen/ men were coming in and they all sat down in the rear of
the house for/ they were told to sit down in the rear of the house
because/ they were the real guests, those who were making the timbers of the house. (15) The three Kwāg·uł tribes just sat down
in a feast. Now all the men were coming in./ And the Gwētɛla
sat down on the right hand side of the/ house, and the ᵋwālas
Kwāg·uł, and the Q!ōmk·!ūt!ɛs sat down on the/ left hand side of
the house. Then four young men were sent to try "to see a face,"[1]/
and the four young men went out of the house and went into the (20)
house of the Gwētɛla and said, "We come to look for a face, Gwētɛla,
in case he should not have gone in," they said and they all said
the same/ in the houses of the three Kwāg·uł tribes. And as soon
as/ they had been in all the houses, they went back and entered the
house of ʟ!āsotiwalis./ Then they said again, "We have tried to see
a face. Now (25) we are all in," they said. And right away dried
salmon was taken and/ it was blistered by the young men of the
Q!ōmoyāᵋyē. and others took/ dishes and grease dishes and oil and
they broke the/blistered dried salmon into pieces in the dishes and
other young men poured/oil into the grease dishes and when all of

---

1) That means to call those who had delayed coming.

ƚōɛlq!wē qaᶜs lō k·ax·dzamōliƚas lāxa mōgŭg·ɛyuwē hēlānɛm bēbɛgwānɛm lāxa ōgwiwaliƚasa g·ōkwē. Wä, g·flᶜmisē gwäƚa laē äxᶜētsɛᶜwa
waōkwē ƚōɛlq!wa qaᶜs lō k·ax·dzamōliƚas lāxa Gwētɛla ʟɛᶜwa ᶜwālas
Kwāg·uƚ ʟɛᶜwa Q!ōmk·!ût!ɛsē. Wä, g·flᶜmisē ᶜwilg·aliƚa ƚōɛlq!wē
5   laē hëx·ᶜidaɛm ᶜnäxwa xämsxasᶜidēda bēbɛgwānɛmxa hēlānɛmē. Wä,
g·flᶜmisē ᶜnäxwa la haᶜmāpa laasa Gwētɛla ʟɛᶜwa ᶜwālas Kwāg·uƚ
ʟɛᶜwa Q!ōmk·!ût!ɛs ōgwaqa hämx·ᶜĪda. Wä, g·flᶜmisē ᶜnäxwa gwäƚ
xämsxasxa xamasē laē tsēx·ᶜĪtsɛᶜwa äƚta ᶜwāpa qa nāgēg·ēs. Wä,
g·flᶜmisē gwäƚa laē höleg·Intsɛᶜwa. Wä, laᶜmē hëwäxa k!wēᶜlāla
10   dɛnxɛla qaxs halak·!aē qaxs q!ēnɛmaēs wäƚdɛmʟa. Wä, g·flᶜmisē
gwäƚ haᶜmāpxa hēlēg·ano laas q!ap!ēg·fliƚasɛᶜwa ƚōɛlq!wē qaᶜs lō
mɛxᶜālĪlɛm lāxa max·stäliƚas äᶜwĪʟɛläsa t!ɛx·fla.

Wä, g·flᶜmisē gwäƚa laasa g·äyuƚē lāxa hēlānɛmē bɛgwänɛm,
yĪx Ts!ōxᵘts!aēsaxa g·äyuƚē lāxa ᶜnɛᶜmēmutasa G·ēxsɛm yāq!ɛg·aᶜƚa.
15   Wä, lä ᶜnēk·a : G·äxᶜmɛn, g·äxᶜmɛnuᶜxwaxg·anuᶜxᵘ hēlānɛmēg·ōs,
g·Igämēᶜ ʟ!äsotiwalis. Laɛm ᶜwĪᶜla gwāgŭƚäxēs gweᶜyōs qänuᶜxᵘ
la äxsɛᶜwa. Wäg·a hēla qa lēs lēx·ᶜüƚt!älaq, ᶜnēk·ē. Wä, hëx·ᶜi--
daᶜmisē Lālak·ots!a ʟaxᶜwaliƚa qaᶜs yāq!ɛg·aᶜƚē. Wä, lä ᶜnēk·a:
Åla, älaʟasēs wäƚdɛmōs, g·Igämēᶜ Ts!ōxᵘts!aēs. Wa, gēlak·asᶜlax·ēs
20   wäƚdɛmōs, g·Igämēᶜ. ᶜnēᶜnak·iƚē, g·Ig·ɛgämēs Kwākŭg·uƚ, laᶜmɛn
hēlōʟ yūduxᵘsɛᶜmakᵘ Kwākŭg·uƚ qaᶜs lālag·iʟōs lēx·ᶜüƚt!alaƚxa
äxänɛmasa hēlānɛmasg·Ĭn g·Igämēk· lāxg·a ʟ!äsotiwalisɛk·, läx
gaālaʟa qaᶜs g·äxᶜmēʟōs ᶜnäxwa däpɛlaʟqēx dzāqwaʟas ƚɛnsʟa, ᶜnē-
k·ō. Wä, g·flᶜmisē gwäƚē wäƚdɛmas laē ᶜwĪᶜla hōqŭwɛls lāxa
25   g·ōkwē.

Wä, lä hëx·ᶜidaɛm ᶜnäxwa xwänaƚɛlōda bēbɛgwänɛmaxēs dɛnɛmō
qa danuƚt!alayuʟaxa lēɛlx·ᶜɛnō wilkwa ʟɛᶜwa äwäwē xwäxwak!Ĭna
qaxs wĪxstɛnaᶜmaaqēxa dzāqwa. Wä, g·flᶜmisē ᶜnäx·ᶜidxa gaäläxs
laē Lālak·ots!a läʟ!ɛsɛlaxa g·ig·ōkwē qaᶜs mɛx·stewēx t!ɛx·fläs
30   gwäxa ᶜnäxwa bēbɛgwänɛm qa ʟaxᶜwidēs qa hēyäsɛlēs lāxēs g·ig·ō-
kwē. Wä, g·flᶜmisē gwäƚ hēyäsɛlaxs laē ᶜwĪᶜla la hōgŭxs lāxa

this was done the (1) dishes were taken and put down in front of
the fourteen hired men/ in the rear of the house. When they had
finished they took/ other dishes and put them down in front of the
Gwētɛla, ᵋwālas/Kwāg·uⱡ and Q!ōmk·!ūt!ɛs. When the dishes had been
put down (5) all the hired men ate the dried salmon,/ and as soon
as all had eaten, then the Gwētɛla, ᵋwālas Kⱡāg·uⱡ/ and Q!ōmk·!ū-
t!ɛs also ate, and as soon as all had finished/ eating the dried
salmon, then they went to draw water to drink after the food./
After they had finished they were given a second course. Now they
never sing a (10) feasting song for they are in a hurry for there
is much to be said. When/ they finished eating the second course
the dishes were gathered up and/ were put away near the inside of
the door./

As soon as they had finished then one who belonged to the
hired men,/ that is, Ts!ōx̣ᵘts!aēs who belongs to the numaym
G·ēxsɛm, spoke (15) and said, "I come. We come who were hired
by you,/ chief ʟ!āsotiwalis. Now it is finished what you wanted
us/ to do. Go on and hire people to roll them out of the woods,"
said he. Immediately/ Lālak·ots!a arose and spoke. He said,/ "True
is what you say, chief Ts!ōx̣ᵘts!aēs. Thank you for your (20)
speech, chief. I mean this, chiefs of the Kwāg·uⱡ. Now/ I will
hire you, three Kwāg·uⱡ tribes to go and roll out of the woods/
what has been worked by those hired by my chief, this ʟ!āsotiwalis./
In the morning you will come and tow them in the evening tomorrow,"
said he./ As soon as he had finished his speech, they all went out
of the (25) house./

Immediately all the men prepared their ropes/ for hauling out
of the woods the round cedar trees, and the large canoes,/ for
they launched them that evening. As soon as daylight came in the
morning,/ Lālak·ots!a went to the houses and knocked on the doors
(30) waking up all the men to get up to eat in their houses before
starting./ As soon as they had finished eating before starting,

x̱wāx̱wak!ŭna qaᵋs Ḻɛxᵋēdē. Wä, laᵋmē lāƛ lāx ᾱxasasa wilkwē.

Wä, laᵋmē lēx·ᵋwŭƛt!alaq qaxs ᵋnāx̱waᵋmaō mɛmg·axstalisē ēxasas.

Wä, g·flᵋmisē ᵋwɪᵋlastaxs g·āxaē dāpɛlaq qa g·āxēs k·atk·ɛdēs lāx
Ḻ!emaisas g·ōkwas Ḻ!āsotiwalisē. Wä, g·flᵋmisē ᵋwɪlg·alisa laas
5 ᵋwɪᵋla hōxᵋwŭƛtâwa bēbɛgwānɛmē. Wä, la Lālak·ots!a äxk·!ālaq qa
lēs ᵋwɪᵋla hōgwēḺ lāx g·ōkwas Ḻ!āsotiwalisē qaᵋs lax·daᵋxwē Ḻ!ɛ-
x̱wa lāq. Wä, g·flᵋmisē g·āx ᵋwɪᵋlaēḺa bēbɛgwānɛm laē hëx·ᵋidaɛm
Ḻ!ɛx̱wēlasɛᵋwa. Wä, laɛmx̱aō maᵋƛp!ɛnōƛaxs laō Ḻ!ɛx̱wa. Wä, g·fl-
ᵋmisē gwāƛa laas Lālak·ots!a Ḻāxᵋwaliƛa qaᵋs yāq!ɛg·aᵋƛō. Wä,
10 lä ᵋnēk·aꞁ Wa, gēlag·a, wa, gēlag·a g·ɪg·ɛgāmēs Gwēƛɛl, ᵋwālas
Kwāg·uƛ, Q!ōmk·!ŭt!ɛs, g·āxᵋmō g·āxᵋmɛns g·ōx̱ᵘḺɛx g·āxalis lāx̱wa
Ḻ!ɛmaisax. ᵋnēᵋnak·iƛē. Laɛms lēx·ᵋŭsdēsaƛqōx ƛɛnsḺa qa g·āx-
lag·iƛtsō k·ātɛmg·aɛls lāxōs ᾱxāsḺēxs, ᵋnēk·ē. Wä, laᵋmē ᵋwɪᵋla
hōqŭwɛls lāxa g·ōkwē lāxēq.

15   Wä, g·flᵋmisē ᵋnāx·ᵋidxa gaālāxs laēda hāᵋyāƛᵋāsa Q!ōmoyaᵋyē
la māmɛx·stɛwax t!ōt!ɛx·flās g·ig·ōkwasa Gwēƛɛla Ḻɛᵋwa ᵋwālas
Kwāg·uƛ Ḻɛᵋwa Q!ōmk·!ŭt!ɛsēxa ᵋnēk·ēꞁ Ḻāxᵋwit, Ḻāxᵋwit, Gwēƛɛl,
qaᵋs laōs gaaxstāla lāx Ḻ!āsotiwalis. Wa. (Maᵋƛō gwēk·!ālasasa
hāᵋyāƛᵋāxs laō māmɛx·stɛᵋwa t!ōt!ɛx·flās g·ig·ōkwasa Gwēƛɛlaxa
20 ᵋnōg·ɛtậyaxs laō mɛx·aꞁ gaāxstalaḺɛns Gwēƛɛl lāx Ḻ!āsotiwalisē.
Ḻāxᵋwit, Ḻāxᵋwit, ᵋnēk·ē.) Wä, g·flᵋmisē ᵋwɪlxtolsaxa g·ig·ōkwēsa
yudux̱ᵘsɛᵋmakwē Kwākŭg·uƛaxs g·āxaēda hāᵋyāƛᵋa aēdaaqa. Hēɛm
Ḻēgadɛs gwāyɛḺ!āsɛlaxa g·ōkulōtē qa hēyasɛlēsēxs ēaxɛlēḺē. Wä
laɛm Ɪɛm hayîmg·flɪ̄ƛ Ḻāxᵋwidēda ᵋnāx̱wa bēbɛgwānɛm qaᵋs lō hōgwiḺ
25 lāx g·ōkwas Ḻ!āsotiwalisē qaxs q!ậḺɛlaᵋmaēda ᵋnāx̱wa bēbɛgwānɛmqēxs
k·!ēsaē ētsēᵋstaakwa hēlānɛmō bēbɛgwānɛm qa lēx·ᵋŭsdēsɛlaxa wilkwē.
Wä, hēᵋmis lag·iƛas hëx·ᵋidaɛm q!wāg·flɪ̄ƛ qaᵋs lō ᵋwɪᵋla hōgwiḺ
lāxa g·ōkwas Ḻ!āsotiwalisē.

Wä, g·flᵋmisē g·āx ᵋwɪᵋlaēḺa laas halamaxsta gaāxstalax·ᵋida.
30 Wä, g·flᵋmisē gwāƛ hēyāsɛlaxs laō ᵋwɪᵋla hōqŭwɛls lāxa g·ōkwē qaᵋs
lō lēx·ᵋŭsdēsaxa wiwilkwē. Wä, hēᵋmisa k·!ōk·!amḺētɛlaq Ḻɛxsᵋāla

they went aboard their (1) canoes and started. Then they went to
the place of the cedar trees/ and they rolled them out of the
woods, for they were all near the water./ As soon as all were in⁴
the water, they came towing them and brought them to the/ beach
of the house of ʟ!āsotiwalis. As soon as they were all on the
beach, (5) the men all went ashore. Then Lālak·ots!a asked them
to/ come into the house of ʟ!āsotiwalis to eat/ there. As soon as
all the men were in/ they were given to eat. They were given two
courses, and after/ they were done Lālak·ots!a stood up and spoke.
(10) He said, "Welcome, welcome, chiefs of the Gwētɛla, ᵋwālas Kwā-
g·uⱡ,/ Q!ōmk·!ūt!ɛs. It has arrived, our house at this/beach. I
mean this, now you will roll them up tomorrow so that/ they may
come and lie on the ground where they are to be put," said he. Then
they all went/out of the house after this./

(15) As soon as day came in the morning the young men of the
Q!ōmoyᵋᵋyē went/and knocked at the doors of the houses of the Gwētɛla and ᵋwālas Kwāg·uⱡ/and Q!ōmk·!ūt!ɛs, saying, "Get up, get up,
Gwētɛla,/to go and eat breakfast with ʟ!āsotiwalis." (There are two
ways in which/the young men speak when they are knocking at the
doors of the houses of the Gwētɛla. (20) They say while they are
knocking, "Let us eat breakfast, Gwētɛla, with ʟ!āsotiwalis./ Get
up, get up," they say.) As soon as they had gone to all the houses
of the/three Kwag·uⱡ tribes the young men came back. This is/called
"waking the tribes to eat breakfast when they are going to work."/
Now all the men immediately arose and went into (25) the house of
ʟ!āsotiwalis, for all the men knew/that they would not call again the
men hired to roll up the beach the cedars,/and therefore they arose
right away and went into/the house of ʟ!āsotiwalis./

As soon as they had all come in they ate breakfast quickly (30)
and after they had finished eating breakfast they all went out of
the house and/ went and rolled up the cedars, and those who were
going to adze them advised them (1) where to put them down. When

qa k·atɛmg·aɛlsalats. Wä, g·îlᶜmisē ᶜwĩᶜlusdēsa lēx·ᶜusdēsa wi-
wilkwaxs laē Lālak·otsˈa ʟ̣āxᶜwɛls qaᶜs yāqˈɛg·aᶜɫē. Wä, la ᶜnēk·a:
Wa, g·Îg·ɛgämēᶜ g·āxᶜmō g·āxᶜûsdesaxɛns g·ōx̣ᵘʟɛx. Hǟsʟaēḷōx g·ōx̣ᵘ-
ʟasg·a ʟˈāsotiwalisɛk·, nōsᶜmēɫg·änsɛqᵘ g·ōx̣ᵘʟ, ᶜnēᶜnak·iɫē,
5   g·Îg·ɛᶜgämēᶜ. Wäg·a, kˈwāɫax qɛn wǔsēx·ᶜîdaōʟ yîsg·ada mōpˈɛnya-
g·ɛk, pˈɛlxɛlasgɛma, ᶜnēk·ē.

Wä, g·āxᶜmēda hǟᶜyāɫᶜǟsa Qˈōmoyâᶜyē ᶜmōᶜwēsɛlaxa pˈɛlxɛlasgɛmē lāx g·ōkwas ʟˈāsotiwalisē qaᶜs lē ᶜmogwaɛlsɛlas lāx ʟ̣âdzasas
Lāĺak·otsˈa. Wa, lä dāx·ᶜidē Lālak·otsˈäxa ᶜnɛmxsa pˈɛlxɛlásgɛm.
10 Wä, lä ᶜnēk·a: Laɛms wǔsēg·adɛsēqaî Ăwaxɛlag·îlisai ᶜnɛmxsa pˈɛl-
xɛlasgɛm láᶜs ʟ̣āʟaxbēᶜ ʟ̣ōᶜ ʟˈāqwag·ila, ᶜnēk·ē. Wä, lä hëx·säɛm
gwēk·ˈāla laxtōdālaxa yûduxᵘsɛᶜmakwē Kwākûg·uɫa. Wä, g·îlᶜmisē
gwāɫ ᶜyāqwasa pˈɛlxɛlasgɛmē laē ēdzaqwa yāqˈɛg·aᶜɫa. Wä, lä ᶜnēk·a:
Qäʟ̣, qälaxs gwāɫɛlaᶜmaōɫēx wāɫdɛms bǎkwēlēnukwasɛns āᶜwǎnâᶜyaxg·îns
15 ᶜnāxwēk· lēlqwǎlaʟaᶜya qɛns gwaᶜyilälas lāxwa g·ōkwēläxa āɫɛwaxᵘ-
sɛmē g·ōkwa. Wä, hëᶜmisɛns lāg·iɫa k·ˈeâs āɫēlaᶜya qɛns gwēᶜnakû-
lasa. Wä,lāg·a ʟˈāsotiwalisɛk· ᶜnēx· qaᶜs nɛgɛɫtâᶜyē ʟ̣ēxᶜalayâsēs
gagɛmpēda g·ālä G·ēxsēᶜstalisɛmaᶜyaxa ᶜnēk·ē gwāla g·āᶜyûɫ ᶜnēnk·ˈē-
qɛla qaᶜs g·ōkwēlaōsax āɫawɛxᵘsɛma g·ōkwa, Dōgɛgwiɫalalax wāxaasas
20 haɫaqiᶜlälayâxa hēlänɛma qa hēɫᶜalēsēs dādɛk·asōs lāq qaxs qˈwē-
lēx·sᶜmaē qˈämäg·iĵēda ᶜwäläs dǎdɛk·asē lāqēxs k·ˈēsᶜmaē gwāɫa
g·ōkwē. Wä, yûᶜmēsɛn ᶜnēᶜnak·iɫōx g·Îg·ɛgämēᶜ laɛm hēlᶜnäkûlag·a
ʟˈāsotiwalisɛk·. ᶜnēᶜnakiɫē, laᶜmɛn hēlōʟ k·ˈÎmk·ˈɛmʟˈēnōxᵘs
Gwētɛl, maᶜlōx̣ᵘʟē. Laᶜmɛn hēlōʟ k·ˈÎmk·ˈɛmʟˈēnoxᵘs ᶜwälas Kwāg·uɫ,
25 maᶜlōx̣ᵘʟē. Laᶜmɛn hēlōʟ k·ˈÎmk·ˈɛmʟˈēnoxᵘs Qˈōmk·ˈût·ˈɛs, maᶜlōx̣ᵘʟē.
Wä, laɛms gag·îlsɛlax gaālaʟa, ᶜnēk·ē. Wä, laᶜmē gwāɫē wāɫdɛmas
lāxēq. Wä, laᶜmē ᶜwĩᶜla näᶜnakwa bēbɛgwänɛmē lāxēs g·ig·ōkwē
lāxēq.

Wä, g·îlᶜmisē ᶜnāx·ᶜîdxa gaāla laēda k·ˈÎmk·ˈɛmʟˈēnoxwē hē-
30 laxēs gwɛᶜyuwē qa g·iwālēsēq lāxēs ʟ̣ēḷɛḷâla. Wä, hëᶜmis g·îl äxᶜē-
tsosēs sōbayuwē qaᶜs lē sōpâlax xudzēg·aᶜyasa wilkwē qa ᶜwiᶜlâwēs

all the cedars had been rolled up the beach,/ Lālak·ots!a stood up
and spoke and said,/ "Chiefs, it has come up the beach, what is
going to be our house. It will not be the house of/ this ᴌ!āso-
tiwalis, it will be our house. I mean this,(5) chiefs. Remain
seated and let me put a belt on you with these four hundred/ blankets," said he./

Then the young men of the Q!ōmoyâꞒyē came carrying the blankets/
out of the house of ᴌ!āsotiwalis and they piled them up on the
ground where was standing/Lālak·ots!a. Then Lālak·ots!a took one
pair of blankets (10) and said, "Now you have a belt, ÂꞒwaxalag·îlis,
one pair of blankets/with which you stand at each end with ᴌ!āqwa-
g·ila," said he and then he kept on/saying this, going through the
three Kwāg·uᴌ tribes. As soon as/he had finished giving away the
blankets he spoke and said,/ "Indeed, truly long ago it was said by
the creator of the ancestors (15) of all the tribes that we should
do this way when we build houses when a new house is made,/and therefore we are not doing anything new./ Now this ᴌ!āsotiwalis shows
that the advice given by/his grandfather, the first G·îxsēꞒstalisɛ-
mēꞒ, whould be followed,who said, Do not be too quick/when you plan
to build a new house. Look out before how much property (20) you
have to pay those whom you hire so that you may have enough property
for it,/for you will bring disgrace upon yourself if the property
gives out before you finish/the house.' Yes, this is what I mean,
chiefs. Now he is going on in the right way, this/ ᴌ!āsotiwalis.
I mean this. Now I hire you, adzers of the/Gwētɛla. There will
be two. Now I hire you, adzers of the Ꞓwālas Kwāg·uᴌ, (25) there
will be two. I hire you, adzers of the Q!ōmk·!ūt!ɛs, there will
be two./ Now arise early in the morning," said he and he finished
his speech./ Then all the men went back to their houses/ after that./

As soon as day came in the morning the adzers hired (30) the
men whom they wanted to help among their relatives and first they
took/ their adzes and they chopped off the sap of the cedar tree

ʟō̆xs laē̆ aĕk·!a sopấlaxa quᴸɛla qa nɛqalē̆sa k·ấtē̆wē̆ʟē̆. Wä̆, g·flᵋ-
ᵋmisē̆ ᵋwī̆ᵋlâwa xudzē̆g·aᵋyas laē̆ ä̆xᵋē̆dxē̆s k·!ĭ́mᶫᵤayuwē̆ qaᵋs k·!ɛmᴸē̆-
t!ē̆dē̆xa k·atē̆wē̆ʟē̆. Wä̆,lä̆ ᵋnä̆ᴸᵋnɛmp!ɛna maᵋ×p!ɛnxwaᵋsē̆ ᵋnäläs k·!ĭm-
ᴸaqē̆xs laē̆ gwä̆ᴸa.

5   Wä̆, g·fl ᵋmisē̆ gwä̆ᴸ k·!ĭmᴸ!ē̆noxᵘ laas ᵋláp!ē̆dē̆da waō̆kwē̆ bē̆bɛ-
gwä̆nɛmxa ᴸaxᴸadzasᴸasa mō̆ts!aqē̆ ᴸē̆ᴸama. Wä̆, g·fl ᵋmisē̆ ᵋnä̆x̱wa la
ᵋlē̆ᵋlabɛkwa mō̆dzɛqē̆ ᴸē̆ᴸä̆ᴸaasᴸtsa ᴸē̆ᴸä̆mē̆ ᴸɛᵋwa mō̆kwē̆ q!ē̆q!ats!ē̆noxᵘ
bē̆bɛgwä̆nɛmx ō̆xtấᵋyasa mō̆ts!aqē̆ ᴸē̆ᴸä̆maxa k·adɛtấᵋyaasᴸtsa k·atē̆waᵋyē̆
laas ᵋwī̆ᵋlē̆da bē̆bɛgwä̆nɛmē̆ lē̆x·ᵋidxa mō̆ts!aqē̆ ᴸē̆ᴸä̆m qa lē̆s gwä̆ᴸɛla-
ɛm ᵋnä̆x̱waᴸa lä̆xē̆s ᴸē̆ᴸä̆x·ᴸadzasᴸē̆. Wä̆, laɛm gwɛls qō̆ ᵋnä̆x·ᵋidɛᴸxa
10   ᴸɛnsᴸa. Wä̆, g·fl ᵋmisē̆ gwä̆ᴸa ē̆axɛläxs laē̆ ʟ!ấsotiwalis ᴸē̆ᵋlē̆ᴸaxa
ᵋnä̆x̱wa bē̆bɛgwä̆nɛm lä̆xē̆s g·ō̆kwē̆ qa lē̆s ᴸ!ɛxwa lä̆q. Wä̆, g·fl ᵋmisē̆
gwä̆ᴸ ᴸ!ɛxwa laas ᴸä̆x̱ᵋwaliᴸē̆ Lä̆lak·ots!a qaᵋs yä̆q!ɛg·aᵋᴸē̆. Wä̆,
lä̆ ᵋnē̆k·a: Wa, gē̆lag·a yŭduxᵘsɛᵋmakᵘ Kwä̆kŭg·uᴸ. Laɛms hō̆×p!ä̆ᴸ-
tấlaxg·ĭn g·Ĭgä̆mē̆k· lä̆xg·a ᴸ!ấsotiwalisɛk·. Laɛmk· hē̆lᵋnä̆kŭla
15   lä̆xwa k·!ē̆sē̆x q!ŭnä̆la hē̆ᴸdɛg·asa g·ō̆kwē̆lä̆xa aᴸewɛxᵘsɛmē̆ g·ō̆kwa.
ᵋnē̆ē̆nak·iᴸē̆, g·Ĭg·ɛgä̆mē̆ᵋ, wä̆g·iᴸla ts!ɛk·ä̆ᴸax gä̆älaᴸa qaᵋs wä̆g·i-
ᴸō̆s ᴸ!ɛlä̆ᴸxwa k·ē̆k·atē̆waᵋyax ᴸɛnsᴸa qaᵋs haliᵋlä̆laᵋmē̆ʟō̆s gwä̆ᴸä̆mas-
xwa ᴸō̆ᴸɛᵋlats!ē̆ᴸɛ̆x g·ō̆xᵘᴸɛsg·ĭn g·Ĭgä̆mē̆k·, ᵋnē̆k·ē̆xs laē̆ k!wä̆g·allᴸ-
ᴸa. Wä̆, laᵋmē̆ ᵋwī̆ᵋla hō̆qŭwɛlsa Kwä̆kŭg·uᴸē̆ lä̆xē̆q.

20   Wä̆, g·fl ᵋmisē̆ ᵋnä̆x·ᵋidxa gä̆äläxs laē̆ hē̆x·ᵋidaᵋma mō̆kwē̆ hä̆ᵋyä̆-
ᴸᵋasa Q!ō̆moyä̆ᵋyē̆ la ᴸē̆ᵋlälaxa yŭduxᵘsɛᵋmakwē̆ Kwä̆kŭg·uᴸ qa g·ä̆xē̆s
hē̆yä̆sɛla lä̆x g·ō̆kwas ᴸ!ấsotiwalisē̆. Wä̆, g·fl ᵋmisē̆ ᵋwī̆lxtolsaxa
g·ĭg·ō̆kwasa yŭduxᵘsɛᵋmakᵘ Kwä̆kŭg·uᴸaxs g·ä̆xaē̆ aē̆daaqa qaᵋs lē̆ hō̆-
25   gwiᴸ lä̆x g·ō̆kwas ᴸ!ấsotiwalis qaᵋs lē̆ g·ä̆g·awä̆laxa haᵋmē̆x·silä̆x
hē̆yadzō̆ᴸasa yŭduxᵘsɛᵋmakwē̆ Kwä̆kŭg·uᴸa. Wä̆, g·ä̆xᵋmē̆ q!ŭlyaō̆ᴸɛlē̆da
yŭduxᵘsɛᵋmakwē̆ Kwä̆kŭg·uᴸa. Wä̆, lä̆ hälɛmq!ɛsᵋĭt hämx·ᵋĭda. Wä̆,
g·fl ᵋmisē̆ gwä̆ᴸaaxs laē̆ ᵋwī̆ᵋla hō̆qŭwɛls lä̆xa g·ō̆kwē̆ qaᵋs lē̆ hē̆ɛm
g·fl ᴸɛmg·aɛldzɛmsē̆da mō̆ts!aqē̆ ᴸē̆ᴸä̆ma. Wä̆, laᵋmē̆ ấɛm gwē̆ᴸɛlsa
30   ᵋnä̆x̱wa bē̆bɛgwä̆nɛm ē̆axɛlaxē̆s gwɛᵋyō̆ qaᵋs ē̆axɛlasɛᵋwa. Wä̆, g·fl ᵋ-
ᵋmisē̆ ᵋnä̆x̱wa la ᴸax·ᴸasa mō̆ts!aqē̆ ᴸē̆ᴸä̆m laas ᴸ!ɛlx·ᵋidxa maᵋ×ts!a-
qē̆ k·ē̆k·atē̆waᵋyē̆.

so that it all came off. (1) Then they chopped off the crooked
parts so that the beam might be straight, and when/ all the sap
was off they took their small adzes and adzed what was going to
be/ the beam. Sometimes it takes four days adzing/ before it is
finished./

(5) As soon as the adzers finished, other men dug/holes in
which the four posts were to stand. When all the/ four holes had
been dug, where the posts were to stand, then the four fitters/ were
going to place on top of the four poles the beams./ Then all the
men rolled the four posts so that they were ready (10) near the
place where they were to stand, and they were ready on the ground
when day came/ the following morning. And when they had finished
working ʟ!āsotiwalis called/ all the men to his house to eat after
working. And after they had/finished eating Lālak·ots!a arose and
spoke/ and said, "Come, you three Kwāg·uł tribes. Now you see
clearly (15) this my chief ʟ!āsotiwalis, who is going on in the right
way./ Not often this building of a new house comes out in the right
way./ I mean this, chiefs. Now wake up in the morning and/ place
the beams tomorrow that you may finish in one day/ what will be the
inviting house of my chief here." Thus he said and sat down. (20)
Then all the Kwāg·uł tribes went out after this./

As soon as day came in the morning four young men of the/ Q!ō-
moyâᵉyē went out to call the three Kwāg·uł tribes to come/ to eat
breakfast in the house of ʟ!āsotiwalis. When they had gone into all
the/ houses of the three Kwāg·uł tribes, they came back and went (25)
into the house of ʟ!āsotiwalis to go and help cooking the/ breakfast
for the three Kwāg·uł tribes. Now the/ three Kwāg·uł tribes came in
of their own accord, and they ate hurriedly./When they had finished
they all went out of the house and/first they put up the four posts
and then (30) all the men scattered, each going to work at his work,
and after/the four posts had been put up, then they raised the two/
beams./

Wä, lä mōp!ɛnx̣waᵋsē ᵋnäläs ēaxɛlaqēxs laē gwäᵵa g·ōkwē
ᵋnäx̣wa ᴜɛᵋwis säla. Wä, g·f1ᵋmisē gwäᵵa laē Lälak·ots!a äxk!ä-
laxa ᵋnäx̣wa bōbɛgwänɛm qa k!üsᵋäliᵵēs läxa äᵵewɛxᵘsɛmē g·ōkwa.
Wä, g·f1ᵋmisē ᵋwĪᵋla k!üsᵋäliᵵa laas Lälak·ots!a äxk·!älaxa hä-
5 ᵋyäᵵᵋäsa Q!ōmoyäᵋyē qa lēs gɛmxaxa p!ɛlxɛlasgɛmē qa g·äxēs gɛm-
xēᴜas läxa äᵵewɛxᵘsɛmē g·ōkwa. Wä, lä ᵋwĪᵋlēda häᵋyäᵵᵋa hōqüwɛls.
Wä, k·!ēst!ē gäᵵaxs g·äxaē hōgwiᴜa, ᵋnäx̣waɛm gɛmsɛᵋyap!ɛlaxa p!ɛl-
xɛlasgɛmēᵋ qaᵋs lē gɛmxᵋaliᵵas läxa ōgwiwaliᵵasa g·ōkwē qaxs hēē
ᴜäwiᵵē Lälak·ots!a. Wä, g·fl ᵋmisē g·äx ᵋwĪlg·äliᵵa p!ɛlxɛlasgɛmaxs
10 laē Lälak·ots!a äxk·!älaxa häᵋyäᵵᵋa qa hōsᵋaliᵵēsēx q!ɛᴜ!ɛx·ᵋidaē-
ᵵa naɛnqaxsa p!ɛlxɛlasgɛma. Wä, hēᵋmis mōxᵋwidaēᵵa sēsɛk·!axsaēᵵ
p!ɛlxɛlasgɛma. Wä, g·fl ᵋmisē gwäᵵa häᵋyäᵵᵋa hōsᵋaliᵵɛlaxa p!ɛlxɛ-
lasgɛmē laas yäq!ɛg·aᵋᵵē Lälak·ots!a. Wä, lä ᵋnēk·aː Qäᴜ, qäᴜaxs
gwäᵵelaᵋmaōᵵēx wäᵵdɛmxɛns wiwōmpᵋwüᵵa qa gwayiᵋläᵋlats läxwa lä-
15 dzēxwa g·ōkwēläxa äᵵewɛxᵋsɛm g·ōkwa. Wä, hēᵋmis la nänagɛlᵋɛnē-
sōsg·ĭn g·ĭgämēk·, yĬxg·a ᴜ!äsotiwalisɛk· qa ᵋnäx̣wēsōx nēᵵᵋĭdxwa
xültaᵋyēx qa gwayiᵋläᵋlatsa g·ōkwēla, xɛn ᵋnēᵋnak·iᵵēː Laᵋmɛn
tɛlxts!änɛntsg·ada nɛqaxsak· p!ɛlxɛlasgɛm läᴜ, ᵋnēx· ᴜēxᵋēdɛx ᴜē-
gɛmasa k·!ĭmk·!ɛmᴜ!ēnoxwasa Gwētɛla, yĬx Häᵋmidē. Wä, lēda hēᵵᵋä-
20 sa Q!ōmoyäᵋyē gɛmxɛliᵵaxg·a nɛqaxsak· p!ɛlxɛlasgɛm qaᵋs lē gɛmxᵋaliᵵas läx k!waōlasas Häᵋmidē. Wä, läxaē Lälak·ots!a ᵋnɛk·aː Laᵋmɛn tɛlxts!änɛntsg·ada nɛqaxsak· p!ɛlxɛlasgɛm läᴜ, Ts!ōxᵘts!aēsa-
gämēᵋ, ᵋnēk·ē. Wä, laxaēda hēᵵᵋa gɛmxɛliᵵaxa nɛqaxsa p!ɛlxɛlasgɛm
qaᵋs lē gɛmxᵋaliᵵas läx k!waōlasas Ts!ōxᵘts!aēsagɛmä. Wä, laɛm
25 ᵋwĪᵋla la tɛlgɛkwa Gwētɛla. Wä, la Lälak·ots!a ᵋnɛk·aː Laᵋmɛn
tɛlxts!änɛntsg·ada nɛqaxsak· p!ɛlxɛlasgɛm läᴜ, Wadzē, ᵋnēk·ē. Wä,
laxaēda hēᵵᵋa gɛmxɛliᵵaxa nɛqaxsa p!ɛlxɛlasgɛm qaᵋs lē gɛmxᵋaliᵵas
läx k!waōlasas Wadzē. Wä, la Lälak·ots!a ᵋnēk·aː Laᵋmɛn tɛlxts!ä-
nɛntsg·ada nɛqaxsak· p!ɛlxɛlasgɛm läᴜ, G·äyusdäs, ᵋnēk·ē. Wä,
30 laxaēda hēᵵᵋa gɛmxɛliᵵaxa nɛqaxsa p!ɛlxɛlasgɛm qaᵋs lē gɛmxᵋalĪ-
ᵵas läx k!waōlasas G·ayusdäs. Wä, lä ōgwaqa tɛlxts!änɛntsa naɛn-

(1) For four days they worked and then the house was entirely finished,/also the roof. When they had finished, Lālak·ots!a asked/all the men to sit down in the new house./ And when they were all seated Lālak·ots!a asked all the young men (5) of the Q!ōmoyâᵉyē to bring the blankets and come and put them/ in the new house. Then all the young men went out/ and it was not long before they came in all carrying blankets on their shoulders/ and they put them down in the rear of the house, for there/ Lālak·ots!a was standing. And when the blankets had been put down (10) Lālak·ots!a asked the young men to count six piles/ each of ten pairs of blankets, and also four piles each of five pairs of/blankets and when the young men had counted the blankets,/ Lālak·ots!a spoke and said, "Indeed/ it was rightly said by our forefathers what to do about this (15) great building of a new house, and this is the way it has been followed/ by my chief here, ʟ!āsotiwalis, for all this shows/ the way that has been marked down for the house building. I mean this,/ I give these ten pairs of blankets as a protection for your hands to you," said he as he called the name of the/ adzers of the Gwētɛla, Hāᵉmid. And then a young man of the (20) Q!ōmoyâᵉyē took ten pairs of blankets and put them down/ at the place where Hāᵉmid was sitting, and then Lālak·ots!a said again, "Now/ I give these ten pairs of blankets as a protection for your hands to you, Ts!oxᵘts!aēsagɛmēᵉ,"/ said he. Then a young man took up ten pairs of blankets/ and put them down at the place where was sitting Ts!oxᵘts!aēsagɛmēᵉ./ Now (25) all the Gwētɛla had been softened (i.e. given a protection for the hands). Then Lālak·ots!a said, "Now I give these ten pairs of blankets as a protection for your hands to you,Wādzē," said he/and again a young man carried the ten pairs of blankets and put them down/at the seat of Wādzē. Then Lālak·ots!a said, "Now/I give these ten pairs of blankets as a protection for your hands to you,G·āyusdäs," said he.(30)Then a young man took up again ten pairs of blankets and put them down/at the

qaxsa p!ɛlxɛlasgɛm lāxa k·!îmk·!ɛmʟ!ēnoxwasa Q!ōmk·!ūtɛsēxa ma-
ɛlōxᵘmaxat! bēbɛgwānɛma. Wä, lāxaē Lālak·ōts!a tɛlxts!ānɛntsa
sēsɛk·!axsa p!ɛlxɛlasgɛm lāxa q!ɛʟ!âkwē bēbɛgwānɛm ɛlēɛlapɛlg·îs-
xa ʟax·ʟadzasasa ʟēʟāmē.

5   Wä, g·îlɛmisē gwāɫa laē wūsēk·asa māmop!ɛnyag·aläsa maɛɫtsō-
kwē p!ɛlxɛlasgɛm lāxa yûduxᵘsɛɛmakwē Kwākûg·uɫa. Wä, laɛm ʟâʟɛx-
baɛya maɛlōkwē bēbɛgwānɛmxa ɛnɛmxsa p!ɛlxɛlasgɛma läx gwēk·!älasas
Lālak·ots!äxs laē wūsēk·axēs la ɛyāqwasōsa p!ɛlxɛlasgɛmē, yîxs ɛnē-
k·aaxs laē dzōxwaɫasa ɛnɛmxsa p!ɛlxɛlasgɛma: Laɛms wūsēg·atsē qaí
10   ꞓwaxɛlag·îlisai ʟâʟɛxbēs ʟōɛ ʟ!āqwag·íla, ɛnēk·ē. Wä, hɛ̈x·säɛmisē
gwēk·!älaxs ɛyāqwaē. Wä, g·îlɛmisē gwāla laēda ɛnāɫɛnɛmōkwē läx
g·îg·ɛgāmaɛyasa Gwētɛla ʟɛɛwa ɛwālas Kwāg·uɫ ʟɛɛwa Q!ōmk·!ūt!ɛs
yāq!ɛg·aɛɫa ɛnāɫɛnɛmōk!ûmk·axa ɛnēk·axēs g·ōkûlōtē qa wäg·ēs sēx·-
ɛîdxa g·ōkwē qa hālabalēs gwāɫa qaxs lɛɛmaē ɛwîɛla ʟ!ɛlkwa k·ē-
15   k·atewaɛyē ʟɛɛwa k·!ēk·!ōk!waxʟaɛyē, wä, hɛ̈ɛmē qa g·āxēs ēaxɛlas
saōkwa läx ʟ!āsotiwalisē qa sälasēs g·ōkwē, ɛnēk·a g·îg·ɛgāmaɛya-
xēs g·ig·ōkûlōtē. Wä, g·îlɛmisē gwāɫa laē ɛwîɛla hōqûwɛls lāxa
g·ōkwē.

       Wä, g·îlɛmisē ɛnāx·ɛîdxa gaāläxs laē ɛwîɛla halamaxsta gaāxs-
20   talēda bēbɛgwānɛmē lāxēs g·ig·ōkwē. Wä, g·îlɛmisē gwāɫa laasa
ɛnāxwa bēbɛgwānɛm lāg·äs lāxēs g·ig·ōkwē qaɛs wîqwaxōdēxa âlä la
äwâdzō saōkwa. Wä, laɛm ɛnāɫɛnɛmxsa saōkwē la wîg·ɛkᵘsa ɛnāɫɛnɛmōkwē bēbɛgwānɛmxs laē lāxa g·ōkᵘʟɛs ʟ!āsotiwalisē qaɛs lē pāxɛ-
ɛlsas lāq. Wä, hɛ̈x·ɛidaɛmisē la ēaxɛlēda ɫēlâkwē bēbɛgwānɛmxa
25   pēpûxᵘbala qaɛs lē k·atɛmg·aaʟɛlōts lāxēs k·ēk·atɛlāʟɛlasʟē. Wä,
g·îlɛmisē gwāɫa laasa waōkwē bēbɛgwānɛm k·ādēg·ɛndalasa sēx·dɛmala
lāxa pēpûxᵘbala. Wä, g·îlɛmisē gwāɫa laēda waōkwē bēbɛgwānɛm wî-
qustōdxa saōkwē. Wä, laɛmē sēx·ɛidayuxs laaʟēda waōkwē bēbɛgwānɛm
q!wäɛstɛntsa q!wäɛsta saōkᵘsa g·ōkwē ʟɛɛwa q!wāgɛmaɛyas. Wä, g·îl-
30   ɛmisē ɛlāq dzāqwaxs laē gwāɫa g·ōkwē.

seat of G·āyusdäs. Then he also (1) gave ten pairs of blankets as
a protection for the hands to the adzers of the Q!ōmk·!ūtɛs,/also
two men, and Lālak·ots!a gave also / five pairs of blankets as a
protection for the hands to the six men who had dug the/ holes for
erecting the posts./

(5) As soon as this was finished he used as a belt the three
hundred and twenty/ blankets for the three Kwāg·uł tribes, and now/
they made two men stand at the ends of each pair of blankets, according to the way in which/ Lālak·ots!a spoke when he gave the blankets
out as a belt, and as he said/ when he was holding up one pair of
blankets, "This you will have as a belt (10) Aɛwaxalag·flis. You
stand at the ends with L!āqwag·ila,"said he, and he kept/ on saying this as he was giving them out. When he had finished, one/ chief
each of the Gwētɛla, and ɛwālas Kwāg·uł and Q!ōmk·!ūt!ɛs/ spoke,
one at a time and said to his tribe to go out and put the roof on
the/ house and to finish quickly, for now they had put on the beams
(15) and the side timbers and also they all came and worked on the/
roof boards for the roof of L!āsotiwalis' house. Thus.said the
chiefs/to their people, and when they had finished they all went
out of the/house./

When day came in the morning the men had breakfast quickly (20)
in their houses and when they had finished/all the men went up to
the roof of the house to push down the really/broad planks. One
roof board each carried each of the/ men and they went to the house
of L!āsotiwalis and put them down on the ground,/ and immediately
strong men worked on (25) the rafters and put them on where they
lie above./ And after they had finished, other men put the cross
bars on which the roof boards lie/on the rafters. When this was
done other men pushed up the/roof boards and now they put on the
roof while other men/put around the boards of the house and the front
boards, and when (30) it was nearly evening the house was finished./

Wä, laᵋmē Lēlēᴸē ʟ!āsotiwalisaxa ᵋnāxwa bēbɛgwānɛm qa lēs
ʟ!ɛxwa lāx g·ōkwas. Wä, laᵋmē hamg·ǐlaqēxs g·āxaē ᵋwǐᵋlaēʟa. Wä,
g·ǐlᵋmisē gwāᴸ haᵋmāpa laas ʟaxᵋwiliᴸē Âwaxalag·ǐlisxa xāmagɛmaᵋyē g·ǐgämēsa ᵋnɛᵋmēmutasa Maämtag·ila qaᵋs yāq!ɛg·aᵋᴸē. Wä, lä
5 ᵋnēk·a: Laᵋmō, g·ǐgämēᵋ, ladzēᵋmō gwāᴸaxwa g·ōxᵘʟɛxsa hamaᴸɛläx
lēlqwälaʟaᵋya. Laɛmk·, ladzēɛmk· g·āg·ēxsilag·ǐn g·ōkǔlōtɛk· lâʟ,
g·ǐgämēᵋ ʟ!āsotiwalis yǐsōs ᴸādɛkwēx qaᵋs ʟēᴸēᵋlats!eyōs läxwa
hamaᴸɛläx lēlqwälaʟaᵋya. ᵋnēᵋnak·iᴸē. Wäg·fᴸla q!ɛmdēᴸaʟɛx dzā-
qwaʟɛs ᴸɛnsʟa qa lälag·iᴸtsēs ʟēᴸtsaᵋyoʟɛxa hamaᴸɛla lēlqwälaʟaᵋya
10 qa g·āxlag·iᴸtsē, ᵋnēk·ē. Wä, hᵋɛmxaāwis wāᴸdɛmsa waōkwē g·ǐg·ɛ-
gämaᵋya.

  · Wä, g·fᴸᵋmisē gwāᴸē wāᴸdɛmas laē ʟaxᵗwäliᴸē Lälak·ots!a qaᵋs
nänaxmaᵋyēx wāᴸdɛmasa g·ǐg·ɛgämaᵋyē. Wä, lä ᵋnēk·a: Âla, g·ǐg·ɛ-
gämēᵋ, âlasēs wāᴸdɛmōs. Laɛms g·āg·ēxsilaxg·a ʟ!āsotiwalisɛk·xg·a-
15 da ēak·ostâ q!wäxa g·ǐgämaᵋyaxg·ada laɛmk· dādoq!wälaxa g·ǐg·ɛgä-
maᵋyaē Âᵋmāxǔlaᴸa ʟɛᵋwa g·ǐgɛmaᵋyaē ᵋnɛmōgwisaxa hāᵋnak!wala qa ha-
labalēsōx gwāᴸɛlsa g·ōkwēx qaᵋs lɛᵋmaa ōdzɛq!āla qaᵋs g·āxlag·ǐ
qautēx·axg·ǐn g·ǐgämēk· laxg·a ʟ!āsotiwalisɛk·. ᵋnēᵋnak·iᴸē g·ǐg·ɛ-
gämēᵋ. Laɛms lāʟɛx ᴸɛnsʟa qaᵋs lälag·aōs ʟēᴸtsayōsg·ǐn g·ǐgämēk·-
20 xg·a ʟ!āsotiwalisɛk· läxwa hamaᴸɛläx lēlqwälaʟaᵋya qa g·āxlag·isō
läxɛns q!ōmx·dɛᵋmēsēx, ᵋnēk·ē. Wä, laᵋmē ᵋnāxwa mōlēda g·ǐg·ɛgäma-
ᵋyas wāᴸdɛmas. Wä, laᵋmē ᵋwǐᵋla hōqǔwɛlsa bēbɛgwānɛm läxēq.

  Wä, g·fᴸᵋmisē ᵋnāx·ᵋǐdxa gaālāxs laē wǐxstɛndēda Q!ōmoyâᵋyaxa
ᵋwälasē qautēnɛlats!e ʟēᴸtsayoats!ēʟɛxa lēlqwälaʟaᵋyē xwāk!ǔna.
25 Wä, lēda g·āyoᴸē läx g·ǐg·ɛgämaᵋyasa Gwētɛla ʟɛᵋwa ᵋwälas Kwäg·uᴸ
ʟɛᵋwa Q!ōmk·!ǔt!ɛs hōgǔxsɛla läxa xwāk!ǔna. Wä, hᵋɛmisa·hāᵋyaᴸ-
ᵋäsa Q!ōmoyâᵋyē ʟ̣ōᵋ Lälak·ots!a. Wä, laɛmxaāwisē ʟ!āsotiwalis
ʟɛᵋwis gɛnɛmē Q!ex·ᴸälaga qaxs hᵋɛmaē haᵋmēx·silɛlg·ǐtsa k!wēmasa
ʟēᴸtsayo xwāk!ǔna. Wä, g·fᴸᵋmisē ᵋwǐlg·aaᴸɛxs läxa xwāk!ǔna laas
30 ʟaxᵋwaᴸɛxsē Lälak·ots!a qaᵋs yāq!ɛg·aᵋᴸē. Wä, lä ᵋnēk·a āʟɛgɛmaᴸa
läxa g·ig·ōkwasa Kwäkǔg·uᴸē. Laᵋmɛn lāᴸ, g·ǐg·ɛgämēs Gwētɛl, ᵋwälas

(1) Now ʟ!ásot̯iwalis called all the men to/ eat in his house,
and he gave them to eat when they had all come in./ After they had
eaten Âᶜwaxalag·flis arose, the head/chief of the numaym Maǎmtag·ila,
and spoke and (5) said, "Indeed, chief, indeed, the great house is
finished for all the different/ tribes. Now this my tribe has treated
you as a chief,/ chief ʟ!ásotiwalis, with split boards for your feasting house for/all the different tribes. I mean this, go on and sing in
the house/tomorrow evening, and let the inviting canoes go to all the
different tribes (10) so that they may come," said he. This was also
the speech of other/ chiefs./

When they had finished their speeches Lälak·ots!a arose to/reply
to the speeches of the chiefs. He spoke and said, "Really, chiefs,/
true is your word, Now you have treated ʟ!ásotiwalis like a chief,(15)
this chief who is well growing up. This one who expects to see the
chiefs/Aᶜmǎxǔlaⱡ and ᶜnɛmōgwis. Therefore he asked to/ have the house
finished quickly in case they should come at once to/pay the marriage
debt to my chief, ʟ!ásotiwalis. I mean this, chiefs,/ now you will go
tomorrow as inviters of my chief,(20) ʟ!ásotiwalis, to all the different tribes that they may come/to our rich village site," said he.
Then all the chiefs thanked him/for his speech and all the men went out
after this./

As soon as day came in the morning the Q!ōmoyâᶜyē launched/ the
great canoes for the payment of the marriage debt, those which were
to be the inviting canoes for the tribes. (25), Then chiefs belonging
to the Gwētɛla and ᶜwālas Kwāg·uⱡ/ and Q!ōmk·!ût!ɛs went aboard the
canoes and also the young men/of the Q!ōmoyâᶜyē and Lälak·ots!a and
also ʟ!ásotiwalis/ with his wife Q!ēx·ʟālaga, for she was to cook the
food for the crew of the/ inviting canoes. As soon as they had all
gone aboard the canoes (30) Lälak·ots!a arose in the canoe and spoke.
He said, looking landward/at the houses of the Kwāg·uⱡ, "Now I
will go, chiefs of the Gwētɛla, ᶜwālas Kwāg·uⱡ,(1) Q!ōmk·!ûtɛs.

Kwāg·uⱡ, Q̣ǃōmk·ǃūṭǃɛs. Laᵋmɛn lāⱡ sēxstōdɛⱡg·a ṭǃɛx·fflēg·asɛn
gaāg̣ɛmpaxg·ín ʟǃāsotiwalisēk·xa ʟēʟēⱡɛlaēnox⁴ᵋwūⱡa g·íg·ɛg̣āmēxa
hamaⱡɛla lēlqwālaʟaᵋya. Wä, laɛmxaāwisɛnʟaxg·ín ʟǃāsotiwalisɛk·
qautēnɛlaⱡxa g·íg̣āmaᵋyasa ᵋnɛmg̣ēs lāx ᵋnɛmōgwisa ʟ̣ōᵋ Ăᵋmāx̣ūlaⱡa,
5 ᵋnēk·exs laē wäxaxēs kǃwēmē qa daxtōdēsēxēs sēsɛwayu qa sēxᵋwidēs.
   Wä, laᵋmē ʟɛxᵋēda, k·ǃēsᵋmisē ʟ̣âla qaᵋs dzāqwēxs laē lāg·aa
lāx ᵋyfflisē. Wä, g·fflᵋmisē lāg·alis lāx ʟǃɛmaisas nɛqɛtsɛmaᵋyasa
g·ōkūla laas ʟ̣āxᵋwaⱡɛxsē Lālak·otsǃa lāxa xwāḳǃūna. Wä, lä yāq̣ǃɛ-
g·aᵋⱡa. Wä, lä ᵋnēk·aǃ G·āxᵋmɛn g·āxᵋaʟɛla ᵋnɛmg̣ēs. Laᵋmɛn nɛ-
10 gɛⱡtōdxwa ṭǃɛx·ílaᵋyēx ṭǃɛx·íla qɛn sēxûⱡtɛwēsɛᵋwa yís gaāg̣ɛmpas-
g·ín ʒ·íg̣āmēk· lāxg·a ʟǃāsotiwalisɛk·. Laɛms x·ítṣǃax·fflaʟōʟai
ᵋnɛmg̣ēsai lāx Q̣ǃēx·ʟālagai xūnōkwas ʟǃāsotiwalisai. Halaxsʟɛsai,
ᵋnēk·ē. Wä, hë̆x·ᵋidaᵋmisa bɛgwānɛm g·āyuⱡ lāxa ᵋnɛmg̣ēsē ʟ̣âs lāx
ʟǃāsanâyas g·ōkwas ʟǃāqo̧ʟas, ᵋnēk·aː Laᵋmɛn ʟēlaloʟai winai qa
15 Oᵋmag·fflisai xūnōkwas ʟǃāqo̧ʟasai. Laɛms g·āxʟ tɛⱡtṣǃaⱡ. Laɛmk·
lɛqwēlakwai, ᵋnēk·ē. Wä, g·āxēda g·ayuⱡē lāxa ᵋnɛmg̣ēsē ᵋmāᵋmawa-
laxa ʟēⱡtsaᵋyo. Wä, laᵋmē ᵋwíᵋla hōxᵋwûⱡtâwa bēbɛgwānɛm lāxa xwā-
ḳǃūna qaᵋs lē lāx g·ig·ōkwasēs ʟ̣ēʟɛʟ̣âla. Wä, g·fflᵋmisē gwāⱡ ᵋmōⱡ-
tâlaxēs ᵋmɛmᵋwāla g·āxaasa hăᵋyāⱡᵋäsa ᵋnɛmg̣ēsē ētsēᵋṣaxa ʟēⱡtsa-
20 ᵋyō. Wä, laᵋmē ʟǃāsotiwalisē hö̆ɛm g·aēʟɛlē g·ōkwas ᵋnɛmōgwisē.
   Wä, laᵋmē qǃēqǃɛyōdē Lālak·otsǃa ʟ̣ōᵋ ᵋnɛmōgwis gwāgwēx·sᵋāla̧ lāx
ʟǃāsotiwalisaxs lɛᵋmaē hö̆ɛm ʟēⱡᵋᵋlayoxa lēlqwālaʟaᵋyē qautēnɛmʟasēç.
Wä, laɛm ᵋnēg·ɛgwiⱡē Lālak·otsǃäx ᵋnɛmōgwisē qa qǃāqǃalaⱡg·ɛyowēsēx
wāⱡdɛmʟɛs lāxa la ʟēᵋlālaq yîxs wäx·ᵋmaē Lālak·otsǃa qǃâʟɛlax ᵋnɛ-
25 mōgwisē ʟ̣ōᵋ Ăᵋmāx̣ūlaⱡaxs lɛᵋmaē ᵋnɛmālaɛm la gwāⱡaⱡa qaᵋs qautē-
x·ēx ʟǃāsotiwalisē. Wä, g·fflᵋmisē gwāⱡē wāⱡdɛmas laē Lālak·otsǃa
lāxa ʟēᵋlalāq. Wä, laᵋmē ᵋwíᵋla kǃwamēⱡa ᵋnɛmg̣ēsē. Wä, g·fflᵋmisē
g·āx ᵋwíᵋlaēʟa ʟēⱡtsaᵋyo Kwākūg·uⱡa ʟɛᵋwa ᵋnɛmg̣ēsaxs laē hö̆x·ᵋida-
ɛm hămg·fflasōsa tṣǃɛnkwē xamasa. Wä, g·fflᵋmisē gwāⱡ xɛmsxasxa xa-
30 masē laē hö̆lēg·íntsɛᵋwa.

Now I will paddle along this road of/ my grandfathers, my ʟ!āsotiwa-
lis who knew how to invite the chiefs of the/ different tribes. Now
also my ʟ!āsotiwalis/ asks for the repayment of the marriage debt
of the chiefs of the ᵋnɛmgis, ᵋnɛmōgwis and Aᵋmāx̣ūlaⱡ." (5) Thus he
said and told the crew to go ahead and to take hold of the ends of
the paddles and to paddle./

Then they started and it was not yet nearly evening when they
arrived/ in Alert Bay. As soon as they arrived at the beach in the
middle of the/ village, Lālak·ots!a arose in the canoe and spoke/
and said, "I come. I arrive, ᵋnɛmgis. Now (10) I will follow the
road made along which I was to paddle by the grandfathers of my/
chief here, ʟ!āsotiwalis. Now you will witness,/ᵋnɛmgis, Q!ēx·ʟā-
laga, the daughter of ʟ!āsotiwalis. You will quickly go aboard,"/
said he. Immediately a man belonging to the ᵋnɛmgis stood up/ outside of the house of ʟ!āqoʟas and said, "I invite you in, warriors,
on account of (15) Ōᵋmag·flis the child of ʟ!āqoʟas. Now you will
come and warm yourselves. Now/ the fire has been made," said he.
Then those who belonged to the ᵋnɛmgis carried up the cargo of the/
inviters. All the men went out of the canoes/ and went into the
houses of their relatives. As soon as the load had been taken up,/
the young men of the ᵋnɛmgis came back to call again the inviters
(20) and then ʟ!āsotiwalis stayed in the house of ᵋnɛmōgwis/ and
Lālak·ots!a and ᵋnɛmōgwis were talking much about/ ʟ!āsotiwalis,
that he was soon to invite the tribes for the payment of the marriage
debt./ Now Lālak·ots!a told in advance ᵋnɛmōgwis that he might know
before hand/ what he was going to say when he was inviting, although
Lālak·ots!a knew that ᵋnɛmōgwis (25) and Aᵋmāx̣ūlaⱡ both were ready
to repay the marriage debt/ to ʟ!āsotiwalis. As soon as they had
finished talking Lālak·ots!a went/ to invite them in. Now they all
sat down with the ᵋnɛmgis and when/ all the inviting Kwāg·uⱡ and the
ᵋnɛmgis had come in,/ they were given blistered dried salmon, and
when they had finished eating the dried salmon, (30) they were given
a second course.

Wä, g·îlᵉmisē ɛlāq gwäɫ hӓᵉmāpxa hӗlēg·ano laas ʟ̣ӓxᵉwaliɫē
Lālak·otsꜣa qaᵉs yāqꜝɛg·aᶜɫē gwēgɛmāɫa lāxa Kwäkŭg·uɫē. Wä, lä
ᵉnēk·a: Laᶜmɛn wäg·îɫ, nōs g·Ig·ɛgämēᵉ, nēɫaxg·ada ᵉwālasɛk· lēlqwälaʟaᵉya yîsɛns ᵉnɛmx·ᵗidäɫax g·âxēɫa, ᵉnēk·exs laē gwēgɛmx·ᵉId
lāxa max·stâliɫasa tꜝɛx·flӓsa g·ōkwē. Wä, lä ᵉnēk·a: G·âxᵉmɛn,
g·âxᵉaʟɛla yînʟaxg·în ʟꜝāsotiwalisɛk· qautēᵉnɛlōʟ, g·Ig·ɛgämēᵉ ᵉnɛmōgwis, sōdzēᵉmēs g·Igämēᵉ Aᵉmāxŭlaɫ. Hӗɛm ᵉwālē wäɫdɛmas laē ᵉnɛmōgwisē yāqꜝɛg·aᵉɫa. Wä, lä ᵉnēk·a: Hӗɛmax·i ᵉwālēs wäɫdɛmōs,
g·Igämēᵉ Lālak·otsꜣa, yūʟaxs sɛmsaaqōs yîsa g·Igɛmaᵉyaxōx ʟꜝāsoti-
walisax. ᵉmadzâsōsʟas gɛyōɫēg·în wäx· nɛnkōʟ qaᵉs g·āxaōs qautē-
ᵉnɛla g·āxɛn. ᵉnēᵉnak·iɫē, laᵉmōxᵘ gwaaliɫnuxᵘ qautēnayoʟēx lâʟ,
g·Igämēᵉ ʟꜝāsotiwalis. Âlag·aᵉmax·i ӗak·ēs nâqaᵉyōs, g·Igämēᵉ.
Laᵉmɛnuxᵘ lâɫ qautēx·ɛlɛlaʟōʟ ʟ̣ōgŭn ᴣ·ōkŭlōtɛk·, ᵉnēk·exs laē kꜝwä-
g·aliɫa.

Wä, lä Lālak·otsꜣa mōlas wäɫdɛmas lāxēq. Wä, laᵉmē gwäɫē
wäɫdɛmas. Wä, laᵉmē ᵉwIᵉla hōqŭwɛls lāxa g·ōkwē. Wä, laɛm hӗwäxa
dɛdābeng·alē ʟꜝāsotiwalisē lāxa ᵉnɛmgēsē qaxs ᵉyāg·ɛlɛlaxōdeʟasa
daᵉlēg·a ʟɛᵉwa k·âᵉlēg·a k·ꜝōkwäla ʟɛᵉwa ᵉnāxwa ᵉyäk·ꜝɛlwasa.

Wä, lä lāxa Mamalēleqäla ʟēɫɛlaq ʟɛᵉwa Ɫäwitsꜝēs lāxēs qꜝwaɫ-
xoᵉmaē xaᵉmāla lāxa ᵉnɛmsgɛᵉmakwē lēlqwälaʟaᵉya. Wä, g·āxē lāxa
Dɛnax·daᵉxᵘ ʟɛᵉwa Madiɫbēᵉ. Wä, lä laᵉwiɫ lāx G̱wayasdɛms ʟēɫɛlaxa
Dzawadɛēnoxᵘ ʟɛᵉwa Qwēqᵘsōtꜝēnoxᵘ ʟɛᵉwa Hāxwāmis ʟɛᵉwa Gwawaēnoxᵘ
ʟɛᵉwa Aᵉwaiʟɛla. Wä, nɛqasgɛᵉmakwē lēlqwälaʟaᵉyē ʟēɫɛlakᵘʟas ʟꜝāsotiwalisē. Wä, g·îlᵉmisē ᵉwilxtōdxa ᵉnāxwa lēlqwälaʟēxs g·āxaē
nâᵉnakᵘ lāɫg·a Tsāxisɛk·. Wä, g·îlᵉmisē g·āxᵉaʟɛlaxs laē Lâlēᵉla-
lasōsa âmlēxwasa G̱wētɛla, qa lēs ʟꜝɛxwa lāx g·ōkwas Ōdzēᵉstalisxa
g·āyuɫē lāx ᵉnɛᵉmēmutasa Kŭkwäkꜝŭmasa G̱wētɛla. Wä, g·îlᵉmisē ᵉwI-
ᵉlaēʟa ʟēɫtxaᵉyoxᵘdē laasa âmlēxᵘdē bēbɛgwānɛm tsꜝɛk·ꜝâɫɛlaxa ʟēɫ-
tsaᵉyoxᵘdē qa wäg·is tsꜝɛk·ꜝâɫɛlas wäɫdɛmasa g·Ig·ɛᵉgämaᵉyasa lē-

(1) When they had nearly finished eating the second course
arose/Lālak·ots!a and spoke, turning his face to the Kwāg·uł,and/
said, "Now I will go on, my chiefs, and tell this great/tribe about
the kind of thing that brought us here," said he and turned his face
(5) to those near the door of the house. He said, "I came./ I arrived for my ʟ!āsotiwalis to ask for the payment of the marriage
debt, chiefs ᵋnɛmōgwis/and you, great chief Aᵋmāxūlał." Then he
stopped his speech and ᵋnɛmōgwis/spoke and said, "Now stop your
great speech,/chief Lālak·ots!a, you who are the mouthpiece of
chief ʟ!āsotiwalis.(10) What is it? Long ago we sent a message to
you that you should come and ask me to pay the marriage debt./ I
mean this, this repayment is ready for you,/chief ʟ!āsotiwalis. Now
your heart may really be glad,chief./We are going to pay the marriage
debt to you,with this my tribe," said he and/he sat down.

(15) Then Lālak·ots!a thanked him for his speech and now were
finished/the speeches and they all went out of the house. Now/
ʟ!āsotiwalis never asked for the return of the loan from the ᵋnɛm-
ǥis, for he was going to give trifles[1],/ silver and gold bracelets
and every kind of trifles./

Then they went to the Mamalēleqāla to invite them and to the
Lāwits!ēs and (20) every time they stayed one night with each
tribe. Then they went to the/Dɛnax·daᵋxᵘ and the Mādiłbēᵋ and they
crossed over to Gwayasdɛms to invite the/Dzāwadɛēnoxᵘ and the Qwēqᵘsot!ēnoxᵘ and the Hāxwāmis and the Gwawaēnoxᵘ/and the Aᵋwaiʟɛla.
Ten tribes were invited by ʟ!āsotiwalis./ And as soon as they had
been to all the tribes they came (25) back to Fort Rupert. When
they arrived they were invited/by the Gwētɛla,who had stayed at
home,to eat in the house of Ōdzēᵋstalis/who belongs to the numaym
Kūkwākūm of the Gwētɛla. And as soon as they had all gone in,/the
inviters,then the men who had stayed at home asked the inviters/to
report to them and to tell them what the chiefs of the tribes had

---

1.) Literally, "bad things," any property not blankets.

ɛ̓ı̣qwälaʟaᵉyē. Wä, lä Lālak·ots!a ts!ɛk·!ăᵹᴇlas ᵉnᴇmō̆gwisē ʟ̣ō̆ᵉ
Ăᵉmăx̣ülaᴸaxs lɛᵉmaē ᵉnᴇmāla ts!ăsaᴸa qaᵉs qautēx·ē lax ʟ!ăsotiwa-
lisē. Wä, hɵ̈ᵉmisa ɴᴇqasgᴇᵉmakwē lēlqwälaʟaᵉyaxs ᵉnēk·aē mōp!ᴇnxwa-
ᵉdzᴇxʟäᵉyēʟaxa ʟēᴸtsaᵉyo,ᵉnēk·ē. Wä, laᴇm ᵉnēkē Ōdzēᵉstalı̄s qaᵉs
5 gᴇyōᴸē ts!ɛk·!ăᵹᴇlasōxs k··!ēsᵉmaē hămx·ᵉı̄dēda ʟēᴸtsaᵉyoxᵘdäxa lēlqwälaʟaᵉyē. Wä, g·ı̄lᵉmisē gwăᴸ ts!ɛk·!ăᵹᴇlē Lālak·ots!a laas hămx·-
ᵉı̄da. Wä, lä maᵉᴸp!ᴇnēᴸa hămg·ı̄lasᴇᵉwa. Wä, g·ı̄lᵉmisē gwāᴸa laas
yāq!ᴇg·aᵉᴸē Ōdzēᵉstalisē. Wä, lä ᵉnēk·a: Wa, gēlag·a‚wa gēlag·a
g·ı̄g·ᴇgămēᵉ laᴇmx·dᴇs ʟēᴸtsaᵉyosa ᵉwālasʟēx ᵉyāg·ı̄ʟᴇlaxōdᴇʟᴇns,
10 g·ı̄gămaᵉyōx ʟ!ăsotiwalisēx lāxg·ada hamaᴸelag·a lēlqwälaʟaᵉya. ᵉnē·-
ᵉnak·iᴸē, g·ı̄g·ᴇgămēs Kwăküg·uᴸ. Wäg·ax·ı̄ns ᵉnāx̣waᴇm hashēnaqaxᴇns
g·ig·ōkwēx qaēda q!ēnᴇma lēlqwälaʟaᵉya qa·kwēkwalats qo g·ăxʟō,
ᵉnēk·ē. Wä, gēlak·asᵉlax·ı̄ʟᴇs wᴇlx̣ᵘlaēx g·āxa g·ı̄g·ᴇgămēᵉ ᵉnēk·ē.
Wä, g·ı̄lᵉmisē gwăᴸa laē ᵉwı̄ᵉla hōqū̆wᴇls lāxa g·ōkwē qaᵉs lē ēkwaxa
15 g·ig·aēlasē qa kwālats ʟ̣ēʟ̣ᴇʟ̣ālăs qọ̄ g·āxʟō. Wä, g·ı̄lᵉmisē gwăᴸaxs
laē ᵾ̆ᴇm la nak·!ăᴸa qa g·āxēs nēᴸᵉidēda hɵ̈ᵉmᴇnāᴸaᴇm g·ālabaᵉya
Mamalēleqălasa ᵉnāx̣wa lēlqwälaʟaᵉyaxs ʟēᴸ̌ᵉlakwaē. Ϣä, la măk·ı̄-
lēda ᵉnᴇmgēsaq. Wä, lä măk·ı̄lēda Ᵹāwits!ēsaxa ᵉnᴇmgēsē. Wä, lä
ɛlxʟ̣aᵉyēda Mādiᴸbē lāxᴇn la ʟ̣ēʟ̣ᴇqᴇlasᴇᵉwa mōsgᴇᵉmakwē lēlqwälaʟē
20 qō g·āxʟō.

Wä, g·ı̄lᵉmisē mōp!ᴇnxwaᵉsē ᵉnāläsa ʟēᴸtsaᵉyo g·āx nă̆ᵉnakwaxs
g·āxaēda˙Mamalēleqăla nēᴸᵉida. . Wä, g·ı̄lᵉmisē ᵉwı̄ᵉlōᴸtă̂ lāxēs ẙaē-
yats!ē x̣wāx̣wak!ūnaxs g·āxaē nēᴸᵉidēda ᵉnᴇmgēsē. Wä, g·ı̄lᵉmisē
ᵉwı̄ᵉloᴸtă̂ lāxēs yaēyats!e x̣wāx̣wak!ūnaxs g·āxaē nēᴸᵉidēda Ᵹāwits!ē-
25 sē. Wä, g·ı̄lᵉmisē ᵉwı̄ᵉloᴸtă̂ lāxēs yaēyats!ē x̣wāx̣wak!ūnaxs g·āxaē
nēᴸᵉidēda Madiᴸbaᵉyē laqēxs q!wăᴸxoᵉmaē ʟāliᵉlālasōxs g·ālaē g·āx-
ᵉalisa yı̄s Lālak·ots!a qa ʟ!ăsotiwalisē. Ϣä, laᵉmē hɵ̈x·ᵉidaᴇm ētsē-
ᵉstasᴇᵉwa mōsgᴇᵉmakwē lēlqwälaʟaᵉya qa ʟ!ăsotiwalisē, wä laᵉmē
k!wēᴸa. Wä g·ı̄lᵉmisē gwăᴸa laē ᵉwı̄ᵉla hōqū̆wᴇls lāxa g·ōkwē qaᵉs
30 lē lāxēs g·ig·aēʟᴇlasēs ʟ̣ēʟ̣ᴇʟ̣āla.

Wä, g·ı̄lᵉmisē ᵉnāx·ᵉidxa gaāla laas ʟēᵉlalē Nᴇqāp!ᴇnk·ᴇmaxa
mōsgᴇᵉmakwē lēlqwälaʟaᵉya qa lēs gaāxstala lax g·ōkwas. Wä, laᴇm

said.(1) Then Lālak·ots!a reported about ᵋnɛmōgwis and/Aᵋmaxūlaɬ,
that they had resolved to pay the marriage debt to ʟ!āsotiwalis/and
also about the ten tribes that said that they would follow the inviters after four days,/ said he. Then Ōdzēᵋstalis said they should
(5) report early, before eating, to the tribes./ And after Lālak·o-
ts!a had reported they ate./ Then they were given two courses to eat.
When they had finished/Ōdzēᵋstalis spoke and said, "Now come, now
come,/ chiefs, you who want to invite for the great giving away of
trifles (10) by our chief ʟ!āsotiwalis, to all the different tribes./
I mean this, chiefs of the Kwag·uɬ. Let us now prepare our/houses
for the many tribes as their sleeping places when they come,"/
said he. "Now thank you, for they will come soon, chiefs," said
he./ As soon as he finished they all went out of the house and they
cleared (15) their houses for sleeping places for their relatives
when they should come. As soon as they had finished/they just waited
that those should come in sight who always come first/ among all the
tribes invited, the Mamalēlaqǎla. Next after them/ (come) the ᵋnɛmgis and next the Ḻāwits!ēs after the ᵋnɛmgis and/ last the Mādiɬbēᵋ
among the four different tribes whom I have mentioned (20) who were
coming./

Four days after the inviters had come home/ the Mamalēlaqǎla
came in sight and as soon as they were all out of the/ canoes the
ᵋnɛmgis came in sight and when/ they were all out of the canoes
the Ḻāwits!ēs came in sight (25) and when they were all out of the
canoes/the Mādiɬbēᵋ came in sight, and every time one of them arrived
they were invited first/ by Lālak·ots!a on behalf of ʟ!āsotiwalis
and immediately/ the four tribes were called again on behalf of ʟ!ā-
sotiwalis. Now/they were given a feast After they finished they
all went out of the house to the (30) places where they stayed with
their relatives./

As soon as daylight came in the morning Nɛqāp!ɛnk·ɛm
called the/ four tribes to eat breakfast in his house. Then (1)

ᵋnãᶜnᴇmõɫᵋidēda mõsgᴇᵋmakwē Kwãküg·uɫ lãxēq, yîxs g·ãyuɫaē Nᴇqãp!ᴇnk·ᴇm lãx ᵋnᴇᵋmēmutasa Kükwãk!ümasa Gwētᴇla. Wä, hᵋᵋmis
lãg·iɫa hᵋᵋm ʟēᵋlalᴇlg·îsa ᵋnãxwa hãᵋyãɫᵋa Kwãküg·uɫxa mõsgᴇᵋmakwē lēlqwãlaʟaᵋya. Wä, g·flᵋmisē g·ãx ᵋwⁱᵋlaēʟa laē hᵋx·ᵋidaᴇm
5 hãmg·îlasᴇᵋwa. Wä, g·flᵋmisē gwãɫ hãᵋmãpa ḳ!wēɫē laas ʟaxᵋwãliɫē
ᵋnᴇmõgwisxa g·îgãmaᵋyasa ᵋnᴇmgēs. Wä, laᵋmē mõlas gwēx·ᵋidaasas
Nᴇqãp!ᴇnk·ᴇm qaxs ʟēᵋlãlaaxa mõsgᴇᵋmakwē lēlqwãlaʟaᵋya qa lēs k!wēɫ
lãx g·õkwas. Wä, lä ʟēqwaliɫē wãɫdᴇmas. Wä, laᵋmē gwⁱgügüᵋnaxa
k·!ēsᵋᴇm günaxēs dēdēdãnᴇm lãq ʟõᵋ Aᵋmãxülaɫē qaēxs ᵋnᴇmalēʟē qau-
10 tēx·aɫtsa ᵋyãk·!ᴇlwasē lãx ʟ!ãsotiwalisēxa ʟēɫᴇlãxg·anuᵋxu lēlqwã-
laʟaᵋyēk·, ᵋnēk·ē. Wä, laᵋmē ᵋnãxwa ʟãsʟawãlēda bēbᴇgwãnᴇm qaᵋs
hãlabalē günaq. Wä, g·flᵋmisē gwãɫē wãɫdᴇmas laē ᵋwⁱᵋla hõqüwᴇlsa
bēbᴇgwãnᴇm qaᵋs lē k!üsᵋᴇls lãxa ãᵋwãgwasē lãx ʟ!ãsanãᵋyas g·õkwas
ʟ!ãsotiwalisē. Wä, laᵋmē gügünap!ēda günaʟax ᵋnᴇmõgwisē ʟõᵋ Aᵋmã-
15 xülaɫaxēs g·ig·ãɫa qaᵋs günãᵋyaxa sēsak·ᴇlisē ʟᴇᵋwa xwãxwak!üna
ʟᴇᵋwa hãnxasiwãla ʟᴇᵋwa yîxwⁱwaᵋyē ʟᴇᵋwa ēx·ts!ᴇmē ʟᴇᵋwa mᴇsēᵋnē
ʟᴇᵋwa dᴇnxts!ᴇwaku ʟᴇᵋwa q!ᴇng·axtãla ʟᴇᵋwa dãᵋlēg·a k·!õküla
ʟᴇᵋwa kwãᵋlēg·a k·!õküla ʟᴇᵋwa küskwãᵋla, wä, hᵋᵋmisa lãᵋxusᴇm.
Wä, hᵋᵋstaᴇm gwēgügünasõᵋ lãxa ᵋnãxwa bēbᴇgwãnᴇma. Wä, lä ᵋnãɫ-
20 ᵋnᴇmp!ᴇna maᵋɫp!ᴇnxwaᵋsē ᵋnãlas gwēgügüᵋnaxs laē ᵋwⁱᵋla günēda
bēbᴇgwãnᴇmaxēs dēdãnᴇmx·dē.

    Wä, g·flᵋmisē ᵋwⁱᵋla günaxs laē hᵋx·ᵋidaᵋmē ᵋnᴇmõgwisē ʟõᵋ
Aᵋmãxülaɫē xwãnaɫᵋid qaᵋs wãg·iɫ qautēx·aɫ qo ēx·ʟa ᵋnãlax ɫᴇnsas
günaxdᴇᵋaq. Wä, g·flᵋmisē ᵋnãx·ᵋidxa gããlaxs laēda hãᵋyãɫᵋãsa
25 ᵋnãxwa lēlqwãlaʟēᵋ ᵋmõwᴇlsᴇlaxa ᵋnãɫᵋnᴇmx·ᵋidaɫa qaᵋs lē q!ap!ē-
gaᴇlsᴇlaxa hãnxasiwala. Wä, g·flᵋmisē ᵋwⁱᵋlawᴇlsa laē ᵋmõwᴇlsaxa
g·flg·fldas qa lēs q!ap!ēsa. Wä, lä hᵋsᵋstaᴇm gwēg·ilaxa wãokwē.
Wä, lãxaē hᵋᵋm gwēg·ilaxa qautēnayuʟᴇs Aᵋmãxülaɫē. Wä, g·ilᵋmisē
ᵋwⁱᵋla la ãxᴇsa laasa hãᵋyãɫᵋãsa mõsgᴇᵋmakwē lēlqwãlaʟēᵋ qãsaxa mõs-
30 gᴇᵋmakwē Kwãküg·uɫ qa g·ãxlag·is k!üsᵋᴇlsa. Wä, laᵋmē ᵋnᴇmp!ᴇna-

the four Kwāg·uł tribes became one, for Nɛqāp!ɛnk·ɛm belonged/ to
the numaym Kŭkwāk!ŭm of the Gwētɛla./ Therefore his inviters were
all the young men of the four Kwāg·uł/ tribes. As soon as they had
all come into the house they were given (5) to eat and after the
guests had eaten arose/ ᶜnɛmōgwis, the chief of the ᶜnɛmgis, and
thanked/ Nɛqāp!ɛnk·ɛm for what he had done and he invited the four
tribes to a feast/ in his house. Then he changed his speech and he
asked/ those who had not paid their debts which were loaned to them
to repay him and Aᶜmāxŭlał, for both of them together were going to
pay the marriage debt (10) with trifles to ʟ!āsotiwalis, "who invited
us, tribes,'/ said he. Then all the men were willing to/ pay quickly
their debts to him. As soon as he had finished his speech all the
men went out of the house/and sat down on the summer seat outside
the house of/ʟ!āsotiwalis. Then they asked one another to pay their
debts to ᶜnɛmōgwis and Aᶜmāxŭlał (15) and to pay boats and canoes/
and dressers with looking-glasses and forehead masks and abalone
shells and sewing machines/and phonographs and button blankets and
silver bracelets/and gold bracelets and gold ear ornaments and
shawls,/all this was asked by him to be paid by all the men. Sometimes (20) it takes four days for the payment of these debts. Then
all the/men finished paying what had been loaned to them./

When all the debts had been paid then ᶜnɛmōgwis and/ Aᶜmāxŭlał
were ready to pay the marriage debt if the next day were fine, the
day after/ the debts had been paid to them. As soon as daylight
came in the morning the young men (25) of all the tribes carried out
everything and they put together the/ dressers with looking-glasses,
and when these were all out they carried out the/boxes and put them
together,and with all the others they did the same way,/and they did
this in the same manner with all that was used as a payment of the
marriage debt to Aᶜmāxŭlał. As soon as/this was done the young men
of the four tribes were asked to call the four (30) Kwag·uł tribes.

ᵋma hǎᵋyāⱡᵋa la qāsaxa Kwākŭg·uⱡaxs laē k!ŭsᵋɛlsa. Wä, lä dɛnxᵋidēda mōsgɛᵋmakwē lēlqwālaʟēᵋsēs g·ĩg·ỉldzɛᵋyala qēqautēᵋnāla q!ɛm-
q!ɛmdɛma. Wä, g·āxēda mōsgɛᵋmakwē Kwākŭg·uⱡ k!ŭsᵋɛls lāxa qwēsāⱡe
lāx nɛqɛmāᵋyasa qautēx·a. Wä, laxaēda Kwākŭg·uⱡ dɛnxᵋĨtsēs g·ĩg·ỉl-
5   dzɛᵋyāla qēqautēᵋnāla q!ɛmq!ɛmdɛmē laqēxs naqûlaaxē dɛnxɛlaē.

Wä, g·ĩlᵋmisē gwāⱡ dēdɛnxɛla laēda ᵋnɛmōkwē lāx nēnᴀ̂gadāsa
ᵋnɛmgēsē ᵋnēk·a: Hū ū ū. Wä, la ᵋnāxwa ᵋnɛmādzaqwēda ᵋnēk·a hū ū.
Wä, la mōp!ɛndzaqwa hǒ gwēk·!ɛg·aᵋⱡē k·!ōlēsa gwɛᵋyĩma. Wä, lä
ʟāxᵋwɛlsa yāyaq!ɛntēmsas ᵋnɛmōgwisē ʟ̣ōᵋ Aᵋmāxŭlaⱡē qaᵋs yāq!ɛg·aᵋⱡē
10   gwēgɛmaⱡa lāxēs la q!ap!ēx·ᵋidōta mōsgɛᵋmakwē lēlqwālaʟaᵋya. Wä,
lä ᵋnēk·a: Qāⱡaʟɛns qāⱡaʟɛns yūⱡ g·Ĩg·ɛgāmēs lēlqwālaʟēᵋ lāxwa
k·!ēsēx lāxwa k·!ēsēx q!ûnāla nēⱡᵋidamatsōsa wāx·ᵋɛm wŭlgɛmē g·Ĩ-
gāmaᵋyaxwa ᵋwālasēx qautēx·a qaēs k·!ēdēⱡē. ᵋnēᵋnak·iⱡē, ᵋnēk·exs
laē gwēgɛmx·ᵋid lāx k!wāⱡaasasa mōsgɛᵋmakwē Kwākŭg·uⱡa. Wä, lä
15   ᵋnēk·a: G·āxᵋmɛn, g·āxdzēᵋmɛn g·āxᵋaʟɛlaxg·ĩn ᵋnɛmōgwisēk·xg·ĩn
Aᵋmāxŭlaⱡēk· g·āx qautēx·āʟō lāʟ, g·Ĩgāmēᵋ ʟ!āsotiwalis. G·āxᵋɛm-
g·ĩn g·Ĩgāmēk· qāstōdxwa t!ɛx·Ĩlaᵋyasēs gagɛmpᵋwŭⱡa qa nɛgɛⱡtɛᵋwē-
sōsek·. G·āxᵋmɛn qautēx·aʟɛla lāxwa k·!ēsēx āⱡɛm āxōᵋ qɛns gwayi-
ᵋlǎlasaxwa āxaᵋyēꭓ qaɛns g·ĩlg·alisaxg·ĩns hamaⱡɛlēk· lēlqwālaʟaᵋya.
20   Wä, g·āxᵋmēsɛn qāstɛwēxg·a t!ɛx·Ĩlēg·asɛn gagɛmpēda ʟ̣ēgadᵋwŭⱡa nɛnō-
lē g·Ĩgāmaᵋyē Wāxɛwĩdᵋwŭⱡa, ǒg·ɛlwatᵋwŭⱡa lāx qautēx·a. Wä, hēᵋmisē
t!ɛx·Ĩlaᵋyasɛn ōmpē Aᵋmawayōsᵋwŭⱡa. Wä, hēᵋmis la t!ɛx·ɛⱡtɛᵋwēsōs-
g·ada g·Ĩgāmēk·, yĩxa ᵋnɛmōgwisɛk·xg·ada ᵋwālasɛk· gwɛᵋyĩmaxg·ĩn
ᵋwālasēk· gwɛᵋyĩma, ᵋnēk·ᵛē.

25   Wä, la ʟ̣āxᵋûlsē Lālak·ots!a yĩx yāq!ɛndēⱡas ʟ!āsotiwalisē. Wä,
lä yāq!ɛg·aᵋⱡ gwēsgɛmāⱡa lāxa mōsgɛᵋmakwē Kwākŭg·uⱡa. Wä, lä ᵋnēk·a:
ᵋya nōs g·Ĩg·ɛgāmēᵋ ādzāᵋmaɛn ʟēsʟɛgwatōx wāⱡdɛmasa g·Ĩgāmaᵋyē yĩxa
ᵋnēk·aē qautēx·ʟaʟɛx ʟ!āsotiwalisa yĩxa g·Ĩg·ɛgāmaᵋyaē ᵋnɛmōgwisa ʟ̣ōᵋ
Aᵋmāxŭlaⱡa. ᵋnēᵋnak·iⱡxg·ĩn laᵋmēk· wŭⱡāʟɛx g·āg·axᵋāsōx ᵋnēk·ēxs
30   laē gwēgɛmx·ᵋĩt ỉāxa k!ŭts!ɛdzāsasa mōsgɛᵋmakwē lēⱡqwālaʟaᵋya. Wä,

to come and sit down. Then (1) the young men went once to call the
Kwāg·uł tribes to sit down./ Then the four tribes sang the songs
of their ancestors for the repayment of the marriage debt./ Then the
four Kwāg·uł tribes sat down some distance/ in front of the place
where the repayment of the marriage debt was going on. Then the
Kwāg·uł tribes sang the (5) songs of their ancestors for the repayment of the marriage debt, singing all at the same time./

When they had finished singing one of the song leaders of the/
ᵋnɛmgis said, "Hū ū ū!" and all said at the same time, "Hū ū!"/ Four
times they shouted in this way like a whale. Then/arose the speaker
of the ᵋnɛmōgwis and Aᵋmāx̣ūlał and spoke (10) turning his face to the
four assembled tribes./ Then he said, "Now we are going to do this.
Now we are going to do this, chiefs of the tribes, this/that is not,
this that is not often shown, even by a high chief,/this great payment of the marriage debt for his princess. I mean this," he said/
and he turned his face to where were seated the four Kwāg·uł tribes
and (15) he said, "I came, I really came. He arrived, my ᵋnɛmōgwis,
and my/Aᵋmāx̣ūlał. We came to pay the marraige debt to you, chief
ʟ!āsotiwalis./ My chief here has come and walks the road made by
his grandfather for him to follow./ I came to pay the marriage debt
in this way, which is not new which/we were made to go by by our ancestors, all the tribes.(20) Now I come, and we go the road made by
my grandfather,the one who had the name,the extravagant/chief, Wāxɛ-
wīd, who was an expert at paying marriage debts. This is the/road
made by my father, Aᵋmawayōs, and this is the road which/this chief,
ᵋnɛmōgwis walks, and this great chief,/this great whale," said he./

(25) Then arose Lālak·ots!a, the speaker of the house of ʟ!āso-
tiwalis/and he spoke turning his face to the four Kwāg·uł tribes and
said,/"Oh my chiefs,do I misunderstand the words of this ,chief,that
he said he would pay the marriage debt to ʟ!āsotiwalis, these chiefs
ᵋnɛmōgwis and/Aᵋmāx̣ūlał? I mean this,I want to ask them if they came
for this," said he (30) and turned his face to the four tribes who

lä ᵋnēk·a hāsᴇla łāwits!ᴇxsdāła: Wŭłaᴌᴇnᴌōʟ g·ɪ̂g·ᴇgāmēs lēlqwā́łaʟēᵋ,
ăngwadzēs qautēx·asōʟaōs qaᴇn wŭʟᴇlēxa ᵋnēk·!ālä qautēx·aʟ, ᵋnēk·ē.

Wä, lä ᵋnāᵋnaxmaᵋya yāq!ᴇndēłas ᵋnᴇmōgwis ʟō̆ᵋ Aᵋmāx̣ŭłałē. Wä,
lä ᵋnēk·a ᷉ G·āxg·ɪ̂n g·ɪ̂g·ᴇgāmēk· yɪ̂xg·a ᵋnᴇmōgwisk· ʟō̆gwa Aᵋmāx̣-
ŭłałk· qautēx·axwa g·ɪ̂gāmaᵋyax ʟ!āsotiwalisax, ᵋnēk·ē.

Wä, hᵉx·ᵋidaᵋmisē Lālak·ots!a hāsᴇla ᵋłāqŭla, ᵋnēk·a gwēsgᴇ-
māła läx g·ōkwas ʟ!āsotiwalisē. Wä, lä ᵋnēk·a: Gwāłlas hᵉ̆ gwaēłē g·ɪ̂gāmaᵋyaa. Gēlag·a dōxᵋwidᴇxg·ada ᵋwālasᴇk· gwēᵋyɪ̂mxg·ada
g·ɪ̂g·ᴇgāmēk· ᵋnᴇmōgwisᴇk· ʟō̆gwa Aᵋmāx̣ŭłałk·. Sōᴇmᵋᴇl qautēx·asō̆ł-
tsᴇk·, ᵋnēk·ē. Wä, g·ɪ̂lᵋmisē q!ŭlbē wäłdᴇmas laasa ᵋnēk·a läx
g·ōkwas ʟ!āsotiwalisē: Waaahai, Wä, hᵉx·ᵋidaᵋmisa ᵋnāx̣wa Kwākŭ-
g·uł ʟēxᴇdzōdxēs k!wädzᴇwēsᴇᵋwē wā̂kᵘ saŏkwē. Wä, g·āxē g·āxᵋwᴇlsa
gᴇlpstâ̆yaxa łᴇk!wisēxa ʟēgadäs Qwax·ila, hᵉ̆ gwēx·s ālᴇ̈xēs gwēᵋyâ̆
qaᵋs hänłᵋɪ̂tsᴇᵋwa. Hᵉ̆ᵋᴇm g·ayuł läx ᵋnᴇᵋmēmutasa Hāānaʟᴇnâ̆. Wä,
g·āxē māk·ɪ̂lēda bᴇgwānᴇmxa ʟēgadäs Nōlis dālaxa sōbayu. Wä, laᴇm
nâ̆łas qaᵋs sōp!ēdēłxēs āläsᴇᵋwa. Wä, laᴇm g·ayuł läx ᵋnᴇᵋmēmutasa
Kŭkwāk!ŭmasa Q!ōmoyâ̆ᵋyē. Wä, g·āxē ᴇlxʟaᵋyē ʟ!āsotiwalis q!wälᴇnkwa.
Wä, lä dᴇxᵘsēᵋsāłaxs g·āxaē g·āxᵋaʟᴇla läx k!ŭts!ᴇdzāsasa mōsgᴇᵋmakwē Kwākŭg·uła. Wä, lāʟa hᵉ̆ᵋnākŭlaᵋmē Qwāx·ila ʟō̆ᵋ Nōlis läx mᴇxē-
dzasasa xwāx̣wak!ŭna. Wä, g·ɪ̂lᵋmisē lāg·aa läx haᵋnēdzasasa xwā-
k!ŭna laē ᵋnēk·ē Lālak·ots!a: Wai, hᵉ̆łamōst!ᴇqalaaixs tsōgŭnsaēx
läxwa ᵋwālasē hawānaqaᵋya, ᵋnēk·ē.

Wä, hᵉ̆ᵋmis la sōp!ēdaats Nōlisaxa xwāk!ŭma. Wä, g·ɪ̂lᵋmisē
gwāł tsōkwa Nōlisaxa ᵋnᴇmts!aqē xwāk!ŭna laē yāq!ᴇg·aᵋła. Wä, lä
ᵋnēk·a: Laᵋmē läx·sᵋᴇʟaᵋya ᵋwālasa hawānaqaᵋya, lēlqwāłaʟē. Hā-
yɪ̂nsᴇlaᵋmē g·ɪ̂g·ᴇgāmēᵋ, ᵋnēk·ᵋēxs g·āxaē qaᵋs g·āxē g·āxᴇqaxa k!ŭ-
sāłaasasa Kwākŭg·uł. Wä, lä ēdzaqwa yāq!ᴇg·aᵋłē Lālak·ots!a. Wä,
lä ᵋnēk·a: Laᵋmē g·ɪ̂g·ᴇgāmēᵋ lᴇnsa. (Hᵉ̆ᴇm ʟēgadᴇs tsōgŭnsa xa qau-
tēx·a.) Qäʟ ā̆łᵋmᴇwēsō ăxāᵋya k·!ēsaaxs āłᴇm ăxāᵋyaxᴇns ᵋnāx̣wax
gwayiᵋłälasaxwa xŭłʟaᵋyē qaᴇns wiwōmpᵋwŭła qa gwāyiᵋłälats. Wä,

who were seated there. Then he (1) spoke loud with an angry voice.
"I want to ask you, chiefs of the tribes,/ to whom will the marriage
debt be paid, for I hear the words 'paying the marriage debt," said
he./

Then the speaker of the house of ᵋnᴇmōgwis and Aᵋmāxŭlał
answered/and said, "My chiefs here, ᵋnᴇmōgwis and Aᵋmāxŭlał, have
come (5) to pay the marriage debt to chief ʟ!āsotiwalis," he said.

Immediately Lālak·ots!a called out loud turning his face/ to the
house of ʟ!āsotiwalis and said, "Do not stay in the house,/ chief.
Come and look at this great whale,/ the chiefs ᵋnᴇmōgwis and Aᵋmāxŭlał! They want to pay the marriage debt to you,"(10) said he. As
soon as his words were finished, then they said in/the house of ʟ!ā-
sotiwalis, "Waaahai!" and immediately all the Kwāg·uł tribes/
beat fast time on the thick boards where they were sitting. Then
came out of the house/ with spanned bow one whose name is Qwax·ila,
as though he was looking/ for something to be shot by him. He belonged to the numaym Haānaṭino. (15) And next came a man whose name
was Nōlis, carrying an axe and/he came with it to search for something to chop. He belonged to the numaym/ Kŭkwāk!ŭm of the Q!ōmo-
yaᵋyē. And last came ʟ!āsotiwalis dressed up./ They came jumping to
the place where were seated the four/ Kwāg·uł tribes and Qwax·ila and
Nōlis went right to the place where the (20) canoes were hauled up
and when they came to the place where a canoe was lying/ then Lālak·o-
ts!a said, "Wai, strike whatever you like and break up these big
canoes that are tied together," said he./

Then the canoe was chopped by Nōlis and when/ Nōlis had broken
one canoe he spoke and (25) said, "Now are broken the great canoes
that are tied together,tribes !/ This chief has been sunk," said he
as he came back among the/Kwāg·uł who were sitting down. Then Lālak-
·ots!a spoke again/and said, "Now the chief has been sunk!" (This
has the name, breaking and sinking the payment of the marriage debt.)/
"Yes, this is not a new way which we are doing, all this (30) marked

yuᵋmēsɛns ᾶɛm la nɛgɛⱡtᴇᵋwēsᴇᵋwōx t!ɛx·Ila̯ᵋyēx qaɛns. ᵋnēᵋnak·iⱡ,
wӓg·iⱡla g·Ig·ɛgӓmēᵋ ᵋnɛmōgwis ʟōᵋs Aᵋmāxͧlaⱡ lāxs ᵋwālasʟɛx wāⱡ- -
dɛmʟōsaxg·In g·Igӓmēk· lāxg·a ʟ!āsotiwalisɛk·, ᵋnēk·ē.

Wӓ,ʼhӗx·ᵋida̯ᵋmisē xwānaⱡᵋidēda hӓᵋyāⱡᵋa qaᵋs lē ʟ̯āxͧmg·aɛlas
5   lāx ᵋmōdzasasa q!ɛng·ӓxtᾶla qaᵋs g·āxē ts!ᾶs lāxa hōsɛlg·Is. Wӓ, lä
ᵋnēk·a: Laɛm ᵋnɛxᵋūnēsēs gɛnɛmōs, yūduxͧp!ɛnyag·i q!ɛng·ӓxtᾶla.
Laɛm lᾶxͧsɛmk·!ɛnēsēs gɛnɛmōs, sɛk·!ax·sōkͧ lᾶxͧsɛma. Laɛm kͧskwᾶ-
ᵋlasēs gɛnɛmōs, maᵋⱡtsɛmg·ustᾶk!wēma kͧskwᾶᵋla. Laɛm kwēkwᾶᵋlēg·a
k·!ōkͧlasēs gɛnɛmōs, maᵋⱡtsɛmg·ustᾶ kwēkwᾶᵋlēg·a. Laɛm dāsdalaasēs
10 gɛnɛmōs, sɛk·!agᾶlok!wēma dāsdalaa. Laɛm dāᵋlēg·a k·!ōkͧlasēs gɛnɛmōs, sɛk·!āsgɛmg·ustᾶ dāᵋlēg·a k·!ōkͧla. Laɛm ēsɛlasēs gɛnɛmōs,
sɛk·!āsgɛmg·ustᾶk!wēma ӗx·ts!ɛma. Laɛm sɛlk·!ɛxawēsēs gɛnɛmōs sɛ-
k·!āx·sōgͧxsa sɛlk· lalax̯wiwaᵋya. Laɛm dɛnxts!ɛwaxͧsēs gɛnɛmōs
nɛqasgɛm dɛnxts!ɛwakwa. Laɛm mɛsInsēs gɛnɛmōs, mamōsgɛmg·ustᾶlasa
15 sɛk·!asgɛm mɛsIna. Laɛm g·Ildatsēs gɛnɛmōs, sɛk·!ax·sōk·ᾶla g·Il-
g·Ildasa. Laɛm hᾶnxasiwālasēs gɛnɛmōs, mōsgɛmg·ustᾶ hᾶnxasiwāla.
Laɛm yIxwIwēsēs gɛnɛmōs, sɛk·!āsgɛmgᾶla yIxwIwaᵋya. Laɛm yIxͧxs-
dēg·ēsēs gɛnɛmōs, sɛk·!āxsagᾶla yIxͧxsdēg·aᵋya. Laɛm k!waxsaᵋlats!e-
sēs gɛnɛmōs, sɛk·!ats!aqᾶla xwāx̯wak!ūna. Laɛm k!waxsaᵋlats!esēs gɛ-
20 nɛmōs, sɛk·!āts!agɛg·ɛya sēsak·Ilisa. Wӓ, laᵋmē ɛlxʟaᵋya k·!ēsᵋowa-
ts!e g·Ildasa.

Wӓ, laᵋmē ʟēᵋlālasɛᵋwē ʟ!āsotiwalisē qa lēs xamāx·ᵋid āxᵋēdɛq.
Wӓ, laᵋmisē qāsᵋidē ʟ!āsotiwalisē āxᵋēdxa k·!ēsᵋowats!e g·Ildas qaᵋs
lē laēʟas lāxēs g·ōkwē. Wӓ, lä hᾶng·aliⱡas lāxa ōgwiᵋwaliⱡasēs g·ō-
25 kwaxs g·āxaē xwēlaqɛwɛlsa. Wӓ, laᵋmē dɛnxᵋēdēda mōsgɛᵋmakwē Kwākͧ-
g·uⱡtsa molx·ᵋIdɛk·!āla q!ɛmdɛma. Wӓ, g·Ilᵋmisē q!ͧlbaxs laē xā-
ʟ!ɛx·ᵋId yāq!ɛg·aᵋⱡē Lālak·ots!a mōlasa qautēnayo. Wӓ, lē nēⱡaxa
ᵋnāx̯wa g·Ig·ɛgӓmēsa lēlqwālaʟaᵋyaxs laᵋmē ᵋyāqomaʟɛsa ᵋnāx̯wa ᵋyā-
k·!ɛlᵋwasax gāalaʟa, ᵋnēk·ē. Wӓ, laɛm gwāⱡ lāxēq.

down by our forefathers to go by. Now (1) we are just following the
road made for us. I mean this,/ go ahead, chiefs, ᵋnɛmōgwis and
Ă⁶māxŭlaⱡ, according to your great speech/addressed to my chief here,
ᴌ!āsotiwalis," said he./

At once the young men made themselves ready and stood at the
sides of the (5) pile of button blankets and they came and gave them
to the counter and/ said, "This is the blankets of your wife, three
hundred button blankets./ These are the shawls of your wife, fifty
shawls. These are the gold ear ornaments/of your wife, twenty pairs
of gold ear ornaments. These are the gold/ bracelets of your wife,
twenty gold bracelets. These are the silver ear ornaments of your
(10) wife, twenty-five silver ear ornaments. These are the silver
bracelets of your wife/ twenty-five silver bracelets. These are the
abalone shells of your wife,/ fifty pairs of abalone shells. These
are ths silk kerchiefs of your wife,/ fifty pairs öf silk kerchiefs.
These are the phonographs of your wife/ ten phonographs. These are
the sewing machines of your wife thirty-five (15) sewing machines.
These are the boxes of your wife, two hundred and fifty/ boxes. These
are the dressers of your wife, forty dressers./ These are the dancing
masks of your wife, fifty dancing masks. These are the dancing/ aprons
of your wife, two hundred and fifty dancing aprons. These are the
canoe seats/ of your wife, twenty five canoes./ These are the boat
seats of your wife (20) fifteen boats. And now last the crest/box."/

Now ᴌ!āsotiwalis was called to go himself and take it/ and ᴌ!ā-
sotiwalis went and took the crest box, and/ he went into his house
and put it down in the rear of his house. (25) Then he came out again.
Now the four Kwāg·uⱡ tribes sang/ thanksgiving songs, and when they
were at an end/ Lālak·ots!a spoke a few words thanking for the payment
of the marriage debt and he told/ all the chiefs of the tribes that
he was going to distribute all of the/ trifles in the morning. Then
this was finished./

Wä, la^εmē ^εmε^εwēʟεla^εyâ ^εnā̱xwa qa^εs gwēx·sdɛmxa gwē^εyō ^εyäk·!ɛl-
^εwas lāx g·ōkwas ʟ!āsotiwalis. Wä, la^εmē ^εnā̱xwaɛm la q!apq!ap!aēła
^εnā̱ł^εnɛmx·^εidała laxēs gwēgwax·sdɛm lax a^εwīstāliłasa g·ōkwē. Wä,
g·il^εmisē ^εnā̱x·^εIdxa gaāläxs laē ʟ!āsotiwalis ʟēεlāla ^εwI^εlaxa ^εnā̱ł-
5 ^εnɛmōkwē q!āq!astōsa nɛqasgε^εmakwē lēlqwālaʟa^εya. Wä, la^εmē k!ūs^εā-
liła nɛqâkwē bēbɛgwānɛm q!āq!astowa. Wä, lä hālamaxsta hā̱mx·^εIda.
Wä, g·il^εmisē gwāł ha^εmāpaxs laē ʟ!āsotiwalisē ʟēεlā̱laxa ^εnā̱xwa Kwā-
kūg·uł qa g·āxēs ^εyä̱qumasa ^εyäk·!ɛl^εwasē lāxa ^εnā̱xwa lēlqwālaʟa^εya.
Wä, la^εmē hē g·il ^εyä̱qumasōsēda Mamalēleqā̱la. Wä, la^εmē q!āq!astōsa
10 Mā̱malēleqā̱la ʟēgēg·ēx ʟēʟεgɛmasa Mamalēleqā̱la lāxēs k!wēk!wa^εyē. Wä,
lanaxwēda hā̱^εyā̱ł^εa ä̱x^εēdxa ^εyaq!wēmaʟē qa^εs lē ä̱x^εāliłas. Wä, lä
dɛnwiłē ^εyaq!wēmäsa kwēkwekwē. Wä, lä mākfI̱lēda ^εnɛ^εmēmutasa Tɛmłtɛmł-
tɛls. Wä, lä māk·fI̱lēda ^εnɛ^εmēmutasa WI̱womasgɛm. Wä, lēda ^εnɛ^εmē-
mutasa ^εwālas, wä la ɛlxʟa^εyō ^εnɛ^εmēmutasa Mamalēleq!ām, hē gwē^εnā-
15 kūlē ^εyä̱qūmaē. Wä, hē̱ɛmxaāwisē gwaēłē ^εyä̱qūma^εyē qaēda ^εnɛmgēsē
ʟε^εwa Ławits!ēsē ʟε^εwa Mādiłba^εyē. Wä, lä ^εnā̱ł^εnɛmp!ɛna ma^εłp!ɛn-
xwasē ^εnā̱läs ^εyä̱qūmasa ^εyäk·!ɛl^εwasē qaxs hē̱ε̱maē ʟēgɛmsē. Wä, g·il-
^εmisē gwāłxa la dzā̱qwaxs laē ^εwI^εla hōqūwɛlsa bēbɛgwānɛmē lāxa g·ō-
kwas ʟ!āsotiwalis qa^εs lē ^εwI^εla nä̱^εnaku lāxēs g·ig·ōkwē.
20 Wä, g·il^εmisē ^εnā̱x^εidxa gaālaxs laē ʟ!āsotiwalisē ^εyālaqasa hā̱-
^εyā̱ł^εa qa lēs qā̱saxa Gwētɛla ʟε^εwa ^εwālas Kwāg·uł ʟε^εwa Q!ōmk·!ū-
t!εsē qa g·āxēs lāx g·ōkwas. Wä, lä hēx·^εidaɛm ^εwI^εla g·āxa yūdux-
^εsε^εmakwē Kwākūg·uła. Wä, g·il^εmisē g·ə̄x ^εwI^εlaēʟɛxs laē hēx·^εidaɛm
hēyasɛlax·^εida. Wä, g·il^εmisē gwāła laē ^εwI^εla q!wālax·^εida. Wä,
25 lēda waōkwē gūms^εida. Wä, g·il^εmisē gwāła laē ^εyālagɛma ma^εlōkwē
q!ülsq!ül^εyaku bēbɛgwānɛm qa lēs q!wāg·aɛls lax ʟ!āsanâ^εyasa ^εyāg·f-
ʟɛlaxōdaats!ē g·ōkwa. Wä, lax·da^εxwē nōqūwɛls lāxa g·ōkwē qa^εs q!wā-
g·aɛlsē. Wä, lēda ^εnɛmōku ^εnēk·a hāsɛla: Laɛms x·Its!ax·fl̄aʟōʟai
Mamalēleqā̱lai laxg·ada ^εyā̱g·ɛʟɛlaxōtg·ai lāxg·a ʟā̱ʟɛliʟ!ag·ai xunōkwas
30 ʟ!āsotiwalisai. Wä, hēx·sä̱^εmisē gwēk·!āla laxtōdalaxa nɛqasgε^εmakwē
lēlqwālaʟa^εya. Wä, lä ^εnēx·naxwēda ^εnɛmōkwē q!ül^εyakua: Halaxsʟɛsai,

(1) Now they took all the different kinds of trifles referred
to into the house of ᴸ!āsotiwalis and they gathered up/each kind by
itself all around the house./ As soon as day came in the morning
ᴸ!āsotiwalis called all the (5) tally keepers of the ten tribes
and the/ ten tally keepers sat down. They ate breakfast quickly
and after/ they had eaten ᴸ!āsotiwalis called all the Kwāg·uᴸ tribes/
to come and distribute the trifles among all the tribes./ They were
first given to the Mamalēleqāla. Then the tally keeper of the (10)
Mamaḷeleqāla gave out the names of the Mamalelēqāla according to
their seats,/ and the young men went and took what was given to
each and put it down, and now/ what was given to the eagles was
standing in a row. Next the numaym Tᴇmᴸtᴇmᴸels/ and next the numaym Wīwomasgᴇm and then the numaym/ ᵋwālas and last the numaym of
the Mamalēleq!ām. In this way they (15) distributed them and that
is also the way in which they were distributed among the ᵋnᴇmgis,/
ᴸāwits!ēs, and Mādiᴸbēᵋ. Sometimes it takes two/days to distribute
the trifles, for that is the way they are called. When/they finish
in the evening then all the men went out of the house/ of ᴸ!āsotiwa-
lis and they went home to their houses./

(20) When day came in the morning ᴸ!āsotiwalis sent the young
men/ to go to invite the Gwētᴇla and ᵋwālas Kwāg·uᴸ and Q!ōmk·!ū-
t!ᴇs/ to come into his house, and immediately the three/ Kwāg·uᴸ
tribes came in and when they were all inside/ they ate before starting their work. After they had done so they all dressed and (25)
others painted themselves with ochre and when this was done two/
old men then were sent to stand in front of the house in which the
trifles were being given away./ They went out of the house and stood
outside./ Then one of them ŝaid aloud, "Now you will witness,/Mama-
lēleqāla, this giving away of trifles for ᴸāᴸēHᴸ!a, the child of
(30) ᴸ!āsotiwalis," and he continued saying this going through the
ten/ tribes, and then the other old man said, "Come quickly," (1)

ᵉnēk·ē. Wä, g·îlᵉmisē ᵉwîlxtōdxa nɛqasgɛᵉmakwē lēlqwǎlaʟaᵉya g·āx-
daᵉxwaē hōgwiʟa lāxa g·ōkwᵽ qaᵉs nēx̣ēxa ᵉnāx̣wa g·îg·ɛgāmēxs lɛᵉmaē
ᵉwîᵉla ᵉlāg̣ǔlaxa lēlqwǎlaʟaᵉyē. Wä, hëx·ᵉidaᵉmisē nenâgadē dɛnxᵉitsa g·îldzɛᵉyāla qǃɛmqǃɛmdɛmsa g·ālä ᵉnɛᵉmēmutsa Yaēx·agɛmaᵉyasa
5 Qǃōmoyâᵉyē. Wä, g·āxᵉmē ᵉwîᵉla hōgwiʟɛlēda ᵉnāx̣wa lēlqwǎlaʟaᵉya.
Wä, g·îlᵉmisē g·āx ᵉwîᵉlaᵉʟa laasē ʟāxᵉwǎlix̣ē Lālak·otsǃa qaᵉs yā-
qǃɛg·aᵉx̣ē. Wä, lä ᵉnēk·aꜱ G̣ēlag·a lēlqwǎlaʟē, g̣ēlag·a hēx̣ᵉālix̣
lāxwa g·ōkwaxsg·în g·îgāmēk· lāxg·a ʟǃāsotiwalisɛk·. Laᵉmō hēx̣i-
ᵉlälakwa qaᵉs g·îg·ɛgāmēs hamax̣ɛl lēlqwǎlaʟēᵉ, ᵉnēk·ēxs laē wäxaxa
10 nenâgadē qa gagasōdēs dɛnxᵉîda.

Wä, laᵉmēda nâgadē dɛnxᵉitsa g·îldzɛᵉyāla qǃɛmdɛmsa g·ālä
ᵉyāg·îʟɛlaxōtsa ᵉnɛᵉmēmotasa Yaēx·agɛmaᵉyē. Wä, g·āxᵉmē wǔqǃᵂäs
ʟǃāsotiwalisē yîx ʟaʟɛliʟǃa yîxwa. Wä, g·îlᵉmisē gwäx̣a laas ᵉyāx-
ᵉwidayowa ᵉyäk·ǃɛᶠwas lāxa ᵉnāx̣wa lēlqwǎlaʟaᵉya. Wä, g·îlᵉmisē ᵉwî-
15 ᵉla ᵉyāxᵉwidayoxs laē ᵉwîᵉla hōg̣ǔwɛlsa bēbɛgwānɛm lāxa g·ōkwas ʟǃāsotiwalisē. Wä, laɛm gwäx̣ lāxēq. Wä, hᵉᵉɛm ʟ̣ēgadɛꜱ lēxēla ᵉyāg·î-
ʟɛlaxōdē. Wä, laᵉmē ᵉwîᵉla nǟᵉndkwa lēlqwǎlaʟaᵉyē lāxēs g·āyîmōlasē.

Wä, läxɛntē mōxᵉûnxē tsǃɛᵉwûnxas laē ʟǃāsotiwalisē ᵉnēx· qaᵉs
qautēx·ēxēs qǃǔlēsē ᵉwālasxa g·ayox̣ē lāx ᵉnɛmēmotasa Haänaʟēᵉnâ.
20 Wä, laᵉmēs qautēx·aq yîsa hēᵉmaxatǃ waxē qautēx·ᵉidayâs ᵉnɛmōgwisaq
ʟ̣ōᵉ Āᵉmāx̣ǔlax̣ē.

Wä, laᵉmē ʟǃāsotiwalisē ʟ̣ēgadɛꜱ ᵉwîᵉlōx̣ᵉalis g·îgāmēᵉ lāx qǃwā-
qǃwaxix̣asa g·ēxsēᵉstala g·îgāmaᵉya. Wä, hēᵉmis ᵉnɛm ʟ̣ēgɛmsē tsǃɛn-
dɛg·ɛm ᵉwîᵉlōx̣ᵉalis g·îgāmaᵉya. Wä, laɛm lāba lāxēq.

said he. As soon as they had called the ten tribes, they came/ into
the house and they told all the chiefs/ that they had called all the
tribes and immediately the song leaders sang the/ ancestral songs
of the first numaym Yaēx·agɛmēᵋ of the (5) Q!ōmoyâᵋyō, and all the
tribes came in./ As soon as they had all come in Lālak·ots!a arose
and spoke/ and said, "Now come, tribes, come tribes, come and take
a good seat/ in this house of my chief ʟ!āsotiwalis here. Now/ it
is well prepared for you, chiefs of all the different tribes," said
he, and he told the (10) song leaders to go ahead and sing the grandfathers' song./

Then the song leaders sang the ancestral song of the first/
giving away of trifles of the numaym Yaēx·agɛmēᵋ. Then came the
sister of/ ʟ!āsotiwalis, ʟāʟelİʟ!a, and danced, and after she had
finished they gave away the/ trifles to all the tribes and when all
(15) had been given away, the men went out of the house of ʟ!āsotiwa-
lis./ Now it was finished after this, and this is called the "big
(round) giving away of trifles." Then all the tribes went home to
the places to which they belong./

I think it was four years that ʟ!āsotiwalis wished to/ pay the
marriage debt to his brother-in-law ᵋwālas, who belonged to the numaym Haānaʟeno. (20) Then he paid his marriage debt to him with the
same amount that was paid by ᵋnɛmōgwis/ and Aᵋmāxŭlaʟ./

Now ʟ!āsotiwalis had the name "chief who obtained everything"
after/ he had grown up to be a chief in every way. There is another
name, "feared,"/for the chief who has obtained everything. Now this
is the end.